THE FALL
OF THE PLANTER CLASS
IN THE BRITISH CARIBBEAN,
1763-1833

THE FALL
OF THE PLANTER CLASS
IN THE BRITISH CARIBBEAN,
1763-1833

A STUDY IN SOCIAL AND ECONOMIC HISTORY

BY

LOWELL JOSEPH RAGATZ, Ph.D.

1971

OCTAGON BOOKS
New York

This volume was originally published from a fund contributed to
The American Historical Association by
The Carnegie Corporation of New York

Reprinted 1963

*by special arrangement with Appleton-Century-Crofts,
Division of Meredith Publishing Company*

Second Octagon printing 1971

OCTAGON BOOKS
A DIVISION OF FARRAR, STRAUS & GIROUX, INC.
19 Union Square West
New York, N. Y. 10003

LIBRARY OF CONGRESS CATALOG CARD NUMBER: 63-20894

ISBN 0-374-96707-5

Printed in U.S.A. by
NOBLE OFFSET PRINTERS, INC.
NEW YORK 3, N. Y.

TO MY MOTHER AND FATHER

WHO, IN GIVING THEIR CHILDREN THEIR BEST,
HAVE NEVER EXPECTED LESS OF THEM

PREFACE

The sugar planters were the conspicuously rich men of Great Britain in the middle of the seventeen hundreds. "As wealthy as a West Indian" was proverbial. With material resources at their command, the owners of Caribbean estates sought and gained political preferment; firmly intrenched in parliament, they exercised a preponderant influence on the course of events. Sugar was king, they who produced it constituted the power behind the throne, and the islands on which their opulence and commanding position had been reared were regarded by all as the most valued of overseas possessions.

Three quarters of a century later found the planters fallen from this high state with the dwindling returns from their decayed properties all but completely engrossed by creditors. The sugar colonies themselves, sunk into social and economic stagnation, were viewed with hostile eyes and their value to the home land was commonly questioned. Never in imperial history has there been a more striking contrast between conditions prevailing in an outlying region in two such briefly separated periods.

The decline of the British West Indies has been given but slight attention heretofore. Associated as it was with abolition and emancipation, those events have been seized upon as affording ready explanations. Yet they were mere contributing factors. The American sugar producing areas within the empire had been overtaken by economic vicissitudes decades before the slightest obstruction to the free importation of new field hands was raised or the faintest popular demand for emancipation was voiced. Had abolition never been instituted, had the régime of forced labor never come to an end, the proprietors there must still inevitably have suffered the general ruin which engulfed them.

Deeper, underlying causes must be sought. Among the chief of these were a wasteful agricultural system, the rivalry of newly-exploited tropical territories, adherence to a policy of restricted trade after all real justification for it had ceased to exist, vicious fiscal legislation in the mother country, and forty years of intermittent warfare.

The wealth of the original West India colonies had had no rational basis. It had been an artificial creation, resting upon a monopoly of supplying the home and British-American mainland markets with Caribbean products, enjoyed by the few residents of a small number of islands. These favored individuals had never fully developed their holdings, the quantity of produce grown had failed to keep pace with the demand, and high prices with exorbitant profits had resulted.

These disappeared before the competition of similar sections added to the empire from the 1760's and of foreign plantations which captured continental European marts as well as in consequence of the disruption of natural commercial relations with Atlantic seaboard ports under which the islanders had procured many essential supplies at minimum cost. The glaring evils of a fundamentally unsound order then stood starkly revealed, but outworn doctrines were tenaciously clung to, basic alterations and readjustments made necessary by changed conditions of production and distribution were not effected, and a general slowing down of life, distress, and ultimate disaster relentlessly followed. The truth of the elementary law that monopoly profit is deceiving and transitory and that every system of exclusive control contains the seeds of its own destruction was again demonstrated in spectacular fashion.

There is here presented a study of this fall of the planter class, based for the most part on contemporary evidence embodied in the governors' official correspondence, the Board of Trade papers, the records of organized groups in England with Caribbean interests, the findings of parliamentary committees, observations of travelers, and the writings of proprietors and their opponents. It is an expansion of a University of Wisconsin doctoral dissertation which was awarded the Justin Winsor Prize of the American Historical Association in 1926.

The tragic course of West Indian history impressed itself strongly upon the minds of men themselves associated with the islands during the years of their decay. Thus, Captain Thomas Southey, a naval officer stationed in tropical American waters early in the nineteenth century and well known as author of the encyclopedic *Chronological History of the West Indies,*[1] wrote in a private letter, "Take it all in all, it is perhaps as disgraceful a portion of history as the

[1] 3 vols., London, 1827.

whole course of time can afford; for I know not that there is anything generous, anything ennobling, anything honourable or con-
solatory to human nature to relieve it, except what may relate to
the missionaries." [1]

Similarly, the Rev. James Phillippo, for a score of years a Baptist leader among the Jamaican negroes, declared: "[These colonies']
whole past history . . . presents only a succession of wars, usurpa-
tions, crimes, misery, and vice . . . ; all is one revolting scene of
infamy, bloodshed, and unmitigated woe, of insecure peace and open
disturbance, of the abuse of power, and of the reaction of misery
against oppression." [2]

Yet, to the impersonal student of economic phenomena and human
organizations, living amidst other scenes in another age, such action
on such a stage is but symptomatic of a diseased social organism
and is of interest chiefly as affording means of correctly diagnosing
the deep-rooted maladies sapping its strength. For him there are
few fields more worthy of careful exploration and which yield a
greater number of problems of absorbing interest than does that of
British Caribbean history between the Peace of Paris and passage
of the Emancipation Act.

The Bahamas have been excluded from consideration. Lying outside the Antilles proper, they had but slight relations with them,
underwent other development, and were confronted by their own per-
plexing questions demanding solution. [3] On the other hand, the opening up of Berbice and Demerara has received considerable attention
since their economy was essentially that of the islands and heavy
exportations made from them after the close of the eighteenth century contributed materially to the latter's misfortunes.

In contemporary popular parlance, the term "abolition" was applied to both the anti-slave-trade movement and to that aiming at
negro liberty. For the sake of clarity, it has been used here only in

---

[1] Quoted, John Davy, *The West Indies, Before and Since Slave Emancipation* (London, 1854), p. vi.

[2] In his *Jamaica: Its Past and Present State* (Philadelphia, 1843), p. 19.

[3] The soil was unsuited for sugar culture and none was raised except for
home consumption. See Johann Schöpf, *Reise durch einige der mittlern und
südlichen vereinigten nordamerikanischen Staaten, nach ost-Florida und den
Bahama—Inseln unternommen in den Jahren 1783 und 1784* (2 vols., Erlangen,
1788). Translated as *Travels in the Confederation* . . . (Philadelphia, 1911).
The commodity seldom appears in the list of exports, and then chiefly as
foreign clayed, received in the course of trade. See Customs 4/5–28, Public
Record Office.

its strict sense of ending commerce in Africans while the effort to secure freedom for the blacks is referred to as the emancipation crusade.

The author is under obligations to Professor Frank W. Pitman of Pomona College, author of *The Development of the British West Indies,* and to Frank Cundall, F.S.A., Secretary and Librarian of the Institute of Jamaica and historian of the colony, for many useful suggestions; to Algernon Aspinall, C.M.G., Secretary of the West India Committee, for being given ready access to that organization's invaluable archives and highly specialized library; to Messrs. Joseph Travers and Sons, Ltd., of London for permission to consult files of their eighteenth and early nineteenth century whole-sale grocery price lists; and above all, to Professor Winfred T. Root of the University of Iowa under whose supervision this work has been written and to whose constant kindly interest and helpful criticism is due such merit as it may possess.

L. J. R.

Washington, D. C.

CONTENTS

PART I

THE OLD PLANTATION SYSTEM

PART II

THE DECLINE OF THE SUGAR ISLANDS

STATISTICAL CHARTS

xiii

PART I
THE OLD PLANTATION SYSTEM

CHAPTER I

Caribbean Society in the Eighteenth Century

The British West Indies were developed as exploitation colonies. Tropical heat, the flocking out of adventurers, and easy credit in Great Britain combined to that end. Climatic conditions made an economic system based on free European workers impossible. Hence arose a régime of forced labor, resting first on the native Indian and, following his virtual extinction, upon the more sturdy imported transatlantic black.

No considerable body of persons inspired by motives higher than the desire to extract the greatest possible amount of wealth from them in the shortest possible time ever reached the smiling shores of the Caribbean colonies. Save during the civil wars of the sixteen hundreds, no haven of refuge from persecution was sought there. Few landed to establish homes and to raise their station in a new world. Instead, the islands became the goal of spendthrift bankrupts eager to recoup their wasted fortunes, of penniless younger sons of gentility desirous of amassing means sufficient to become landed proprietors in the homeland, and the dumping-ground for the riffraff of the parent country.

With the growing wealth of England in the seventeenth and eighteenth centuries, there appeared an ever increasing amount of capital seeking profitable placement. Commerce and industry were undergoing rapid development but by no means engrossed it all, and large sums were available for overseas projects promising ample immediate returns. The tropical American possessions above all afforded such prospects and loans on agricultural enterprises in them early became an extensive form of investment. Thus planting in British territory, almost from its origin, tended to be a capitalistic undertaking.

The results were inevitable. Such small holdings with resident owners as had been opened rapidly disappeared and the large plantation came to be the normal unit of production. Huge profits flowed into the great proprietors' coffers, and they retired beyond the Atlantic to enjoy them. The islands became mere places of temporary abode

3

for all whites with the slightest pretension to quality. They could boast of few long-established families;[1] Great Britain was ever "home," in which all interest and all thought of the future centered.

The true significance of social and economic factors in determining the destiny of the British West Indies may be seen by a glance at neighboring French colonies. The manifold disasters suffered by France in the days of the Grand Monarch drained her of resources. No surplus funds were available for extra-European speculation and in consequence the French Caribbean held but slight attraction for others than persons of average means, contemplating actual settlement.

Newcomers arrived without heavy credit backing and became the owners of only moderate-sized properties yielding meager gains, altogether insufficient to make possible the realization of grandiose dreams of luxurious life in Paris on returns from distant estates. Small planters in the British islands, pressed by the competition of large-scale producers there, sought equal opportunity under the Bourbon flag. The only French possession in which great holdings and absenteeism were general was St. Domingo, developed at a later day when capital had again accumulated in the *métropole*.

A sound social organization developed in the French West Indies. Homes were established there, local ties grew strong, insular pride and feeling appeared. The cost of production was lower since it was not called upon to cover the waste and heavy charges attending a system of non-resident ownership. This enabled the French regularly to undersell their British rivals, a cause of both annoyance and concern to the latter.[2] The contrasting atmospheres of the two

[1] A noteworthy exception to this general rule appeared in the case of Barbados. One of the first British colonies in the Caribbean and developed before the middle of the seventeenth century, it escaped to a marked degree the evils of capitalistic exploitation. Thus, in 1765, there were nearly 4,000 proprietors in the island while at the same time St. James parish, Jamaica, of almost the same size, was divided among but 132. William Gardner, *A History of Jamaica* (London, 1873), p. 160. Smaller estates made for smaller profits which in turn made absenteeism less possible. In consequence, many Barbadians can trace their lineage back to earliest colonial days. See Sir B. Burke, ed. *A Genealogical and Heraldic History of the Colonial Gentry* (2 vols., London, 1891–95). The contrast with Jamaica is marked. See W. A. Feurtado, *Official & Other Personages of Jamaica from 1655 to 1790, to Which is Added, a Chapter on the Peerage, &c. in Jamaica* (Kingston, 1896).

[2] The Molasses Act of 1733 and the Sugar Act of 1764, both passed at the British planters' behest, sought to meet French competition in mainland colonial markets through placing restrictions upon the entry of foreign produce there.

groups of colonies could not fail to impress travelers [1] and was a cause of genuine regret to thoughtful Englishmen of the day.[2]

A peculiar type of civilization, built upon the quantity production of tropical commodities by slave labor, arose in the British West Indies. The white man in tropical America was out of his habitat. Constant association with an inferior subject race blunted his moral fibre and he suffered marked demoralization. His transitory residence and the continued importation of Africans debased life. Miscegenation, so contrary to Anglo-Saxon nature, resulted in the rapid rise of a race of human hybrids. Planter society was based upon whites and blacks, removed to unfamiliar scenes, and their unhappy offspring. The saddest pages of imperial history relate the heartrending attempts to effect adjustment between these discordant elements.

The primary constituent of social organization in the British Caribbean was the European, on whose material resources all industry was based and who furnished the directing force for all enterprise. Most important among the members of this group was the great landed proprietor, about whom the entire plantation system developed.

The center of life on a tropical estate was the "great-house," the home of the owner, or, in his absence, that of the overseer. Those first built were crudely constructed dwellings and even in the latter half of the eighteenth century "miserable, thatched hovels, hastily put together with wattles and plaister, damp, unwholesome, and infested with every species of vermin," [3] structures "not superior to English barns," [4] were still in some cases being put to such use.

But improvement had been progressive and by that time the representative planter's residence had come to be an imposing structure. Wherever possible, it stood in a commanding position, frequently facing the sea. Almost invariably it was set some distance back from

[1] See, for example, Henry Coleridge, *Six Months in the West Indies in 1825* (New York, 1826), pp. 130–132. [Frederic Bayley], *Four Years' Residence in the West Indies, During the Years 1826, 7, 8, and 9* (London, 1833), p. 268. J. E. Alexander, *Transatlantic Sketches. . . .* (Philadelphia, 1833), pp. 141, 142.

[2] Edward Long, *The History of Jamaica* (3 vols., London, 1774), I, 433, 434. The author was a resident of the island from 1757 to 1769 as secretary to his brother-in-law, Sir Harry Moore, lieutenant-governor of the island, and later as judge in the local vice-admiralty court.

[3] Long, *Jamaica*, II, 21, 22.

[4] Bryan Edwards, *The History, Civil and Commercial, of the British Colonies in the West Indies* (2 vols., London, 1793), II, 8, 9—note d. Also published in French, German, Dutch and Spanish.

the road and was approached by an avenue of cedars, palmettos, or cocoanut trees. It was built of wood, stood clear of the ground on stone supports, and was one story in height. The entrance led into a central hall, on either side of which were bedrooms. At the farther end was the entry to a wide and spacious piazza running nearly the length of the house. The dining room was found at one of its extremities and ordinarily another sleeping apartment at the other.

Interiors were plain. The rooms were seldom ceiled and beams protruded. The hall was furnished with a sofa or two, colloquially known as "cots," and a few prints and maps adorned the walls. Each chamber contained a bed with a mattress and a pair of sheets, covered by a framework over which mosquito netting was draped, as well as a set of drawers and a number of rockers. The cool veranda was habitually occupied during waking hours. Comfortable lounges, a backgammon board, chessmen, and a spy-glass to turn on passing ships or horsemen could usually be found. The dining room was fitted out with a table, sideboard, and chairs of mahogany.

Windows were equipped with Venetian blinds to permit the free circulation of air, which buried the occupants of a residence in restful semidarkness. Porkers and poultry were wont to seek relief from the sweltering heat in the shady retreat beneath the house. Culinary operations were performed in a detached building. Servants occupied their own quarters or drowsed about on the hall floor so as to be at their master's call. The negro village, sugar plant, and sundry workshops were situated in the rear.[1]

The estate owner's day opened at five in the morning and did not close until eight at night. Guns in the forts protecting the several islands were fired at both hours. Breakfast was served before six and dinner only in the late afternoon, but lunching in between was common. During planting and harvesting, with their rush of seasonal activities, every moment was occupied; at other times the planter's chief occupation was riding out to his various fields and inspecting the slaves' labor. There was little to break the ordinary

[1] Long, Jamaica, II, 21, 22. Edwards, History, II, 8, 9—note d. Bayley, Four Years' Residence, p. 42. [Mrs. Flannigan], Antigua and the Antiguans (2 vols., London, 1844), II, 205. Davy, The West Indies, p. 106. Cynric Williams, A Tour Through the Island of Jamaica from the Western to the Eastern End in the Year 1823 (London, 1826), pp. 239, 314, 315. Mathew Lewis, Journal of a West India Proprietor Kept During a Residence in the Island of Jamaica (London, 1834), pp. 84, 85. The latter work has also been published under the title Journal of a Residence among the Negroes in the West Indies (London, 1845).

routine beyond the arrival of an occasional visitor and the semi-monthly mail from beyond the Atlantic.[1]

The great-house board was one of rude plenty. In violation of all rules of dietetics, huge quantities of heavy food and drink were disposed of. Many articles were imported. Butter, shipped from Ireland or America, was always rancid but the West Indian palate readily adjusted itself to this. Flour was frequently infested with weevils and one old resident counseled exposing it to the sun before use so that they might be persuaded to shift their quarters.[2]

Recent arrivals never failed to express wonder at the prodigality of the plantation table and the gastronomic feats they saw performed. Lady Nugent, wife of the lieutenant-governor of Jamaica from 1801 to 1806, records in her journal

"Such eating and drinking I never saw! Such loads of all sorts of high, rich, seasoned things, and really gallons of wine and mixed liquors as they drink! I observed some of the party to-day eat of late breakfasts as if they had never eaten before—a dish of tea, another of coffee, a bumper of claret, another large one of hock negus; then Madeira, sangaree, hot and cold meat, stews and fries, hot and cold fish, pickled and plain, peppers, ginger sweetmeats, acid fruit, sweet jellies—in short it was all as astounding as it was disgusting." [3]

Mathew Lewis, once celebrated as author of *The Monk* but now best remembered for having attempted to ameliorate the condition of hands on his Jamaican estates during two visits made in 1815–1816 and 1817–1818, noted enthusiastically:

"Even the lord mayor himself need not blush to give his aldermen such a dinner as is placed on my table, even when I dine alone. Land and sea turtle, quails, snipes, plovers, and pigeons and doves of all descriptions . . . —excellent pork, barbicued pigs, pepperpots, with numberless other excellent dishes form the ordinary fare. . . . Then our tarts are made of pine-apples and pine-apples make the best tarts that I ever tasted; there is no end of the variety of fruits. . . . As to fish . . . it is only to be wished that their names equalled their flesh in taste; for it must be owned, that nothing can be less tempting than the sounds of Jew-fish, hog-fish, mud-fish, snappers, god-dammies, groupas, and grunts !" [4]

[1] Bayley, *Four Years' Residence,* p. 466. Williams, *Tour,* p. 316.
[2] Long, *Jamaica,* II, 34, 526–528.
[3] Frank Cundall, ed., *Lady Nugent's Journal. Jamaica One Hundred Years Ago* (London, 1907), p. 78. Originally published as *A Journal of a Voyage to and Residence in the Island of Jamaica from 1801 to 1805* (2 vols., London, 1839).
[4] *Journal,* pp. 103, 104.

The luxurious menu was in sharp contrast to the service. Dishes were placed upon the table higgledy-piggledy; silver flagons and costly salvers kept intimate company with coarse earthenware. The sable butler alone was privileged to wear shoes and stockings. His assistants, generally one for every diner, were barefooted and but half-clothed; while a meal was in progress, they alternately passed food and drove away swarms of hungry flies with slow rhythmic motions of great palm-leaf fans.[1]

The servants were for the most part colored, numerous, and inefficient. An average great-house staff consisted of at least twenty individuals—a butler, two footmen, a coachman, a postillion, an assistant, first and second cooks, a storekeeper, a waiting-maid, three house-cleaners, three washer-women, and four seamstresses. If there were children in the family each was provided with a nurse and a boy or girl helper. When a planter left his broad acres he was accompanied by a handy man who made the trip on foot, holding onto the tail of his master's horse.[2]

So-called "deficiency laws" were generally adopted during the early eighteenth century in an attempt to increase the white element in the islands. These required the maintenance of a number of Caucasians proportionate to the black population on each estate under penalty of an annual fine for each one short. Both racial ratio and payment varied from time to time. Thus, in Antigua, before 1750, all slave owners were obliged to employ one white man for every thirty negroes with a fine of £20 per deficiency. By 1792, the proportion had decreased, it then being one to forty, while the fine had risen to £53.6.8.[3]

But such efforts proved abortive. In consequence of the stigma attached to labor in the tropics, desirable individuals could seldom be induced to emigrate. Those persons seeking employment who did reach the Caribbean were generally the very dregs of England, Scotland, and Ireland. They were rarely qualified for any type of plantation work nor were they welcome additions to society. There were "carpenters" who had never handled a tool, "bricklayers" who scarcely knew a brick from a stone, and "bookkeepers" who were unlettered and without more than the most elementary knowledge of numbers.

---

[1] Edwards, *History*, II, 8, 9—note d. Flannigan, *Antigua*, II, 80. Williams, *Tour*, pp. 255, 316. Coleridge, *Six Months*, p. 249.

[2] Long, *Jamaica*, II, 281, 282. Francis Baily, *Journal of a Tour in Unsettled Parts of North America in 1796 and 1797* (London, 1856), pp. 91, 92.

[3] Flannigan, *Antigua*, I, 109, 122 ff.

If perchance they were engaged to save a deficiency charge they all too often fomented unrest among the negroes. Female servants normally married at an early date and left their employers.

By 1770, the demand for indentured Europeans had practically ceased, the deficiency laws had become essentially revenue acts, and there were few white employees other than managers, overseers, and bookkeepers to be found in the British Caribbean. Artisans were largely mulattoes.[1]

Plantation life presented certain very marked characteristics. Chief among these were a democratic spirit, an openness of life, hospitality, a tendency to view financial obligations lightly, an intense individualism and lack of public spirit, conservatism, and a striking measure of ostentation.

Origin under a common flag, a rude environment in which rank and title could have but little significance, and instinctive fear on the part of a small number of whites encompassed by hordes of black men combined to create a surprising spirit of free and easy-going fellowship. "The poorest white person seems to consider himself nearly on a level with the richest, and, emboldened by this idea, approaches his employer with extended hand. . . ."[2]

There was little privacy. Newcomers were prompt to note this.

"The houses are absolutely transparent; the walls are nothing but windows—and all the doors stand open. No servants are in waiting to announce arrivals: visitors, negroes, dogs, cats, poultry, all walk in and out, and up and down your living-rooms, without the slightest ceremony. . . . Many a time has my delicacy been put to the blush by the ill-timed civility of some old woman or other, who, wandering that way . . . has stopped her course to curtsy very gravely and pay me the passing compliment of 'Ah, massa! Bless you, massa! How day?' "[3]

[1] Long, *Jamaica*, I, 511 and II, 288, 289. Flannigan, *Antigua*, II, 222. Edwards, *History*, II, 4–6. *An Act to Oblige the several Inhabitants of this Island* [*Jamaica*] *to provide themselves with a sufficient Number of white Men, white Women, or white Children, &c.* (Saint Jago de la Vega, 1789). In 1774, only 8 indentured servants and redemptioners sailed from the port of London for Jamaica, as against 1124 for Maryland, 548 for Virginia, 456 for Philadelphia, 35 for Georgia and 23 for Carolina. These numbers were probably "fairly representative of the usual proportions." M. Dorothy George, *London Life in the XVIIIth Century* (London, 1925), p. 145. For the high cost of indentured labour at this period, which served materially to check the system, see page 130.

[2] Edwards, *History*, II, 7. See also Williams, *Tour*, p. 206; Evangeline and Charles M. Andrews, ed., *Journal of a Lady of Quality* (New Haven, 1921), p. 85.

[3] Lewis, *Journal*, pp. 149, 150.

Another writes:

"I own it appears droll to have people come and chat in at the windows, while we are at supper, and not only so, but if they like the party, they just walk in, take a chair, and sit down." [1]

The arrival of a guest offered contact with other scenes, broke the monotonous course of daily existence and was therefore a real event. Hospitality knew no bounds. To be a stranger was in itself sufficient introduction. Hostelries were consequently almost non-existent and such few as could be found led a precarious existence, giving poor accommodations at high rates to offset the charge of keeping open between patrons. [2]

Plantation operations were carried on essentially by credit based upon anticipated income from the next crop. A virtual barter economy prevailed with the result that values came to be regarded from a credit rather than a money point of view. [3] Proprietors who might have considered matters carefully before arranging for a loan of £1,000 in cash felt no hesitancy at opening an account for £5,000. The ease with which advances might be secured resulted in gross extravagance, brushed aside natural caution in financial matters, and engendered a spirit of speculation without due regard for actual risk involved. It was nothing unusual for an estate owner to owe £50,000 and up. "You are not distinguished, or of any note, unless you are in debt." [4]

Although basically unsound, this system was at least workable so long as high prices for colonial products ruled. But when, from the close of the seventeen hundreds, returns permanently declined, obligations could no longer be met, credit ceased, properties passed into the hands of mortgage holders, and the colonials were ruined.

The exaggerated individualism of the British West Indians asserted

[1] Andrews, ed., *Journal of a Lady*, p. 85.

[2] Edwards, *History*, II, 8. Long, *Jamaica*, II, 262. Flannigan, *Antigua*, II, 181, 183. Early in the nineteenth century, room and board in Jamaican inns averaged from $6 to $8 a day; in Barbados, somewhat over £1 sterling. See [John Stewart], *An Account of Jamaica, and its Inhabitants* (London, 1805), p. 15. Williams, *Tour*, p. 187. Bayley, *Four Years' Residence*, p. 27. The West Indian hotel best known to Europeans was the Clarendon, kept by Betsy Austin in Bridgetown, Barbados. The hostess became a veritable celebrity through the writings of her guests. See, for example, Alexander, *Transatlantic Sketches*, pp. 93–94.

[3] See pages 99 ff.

[4] Long, *Jamaica*, I, 557; and II, 266. Edwards, *History*, II, 15. Williams, *Tour*, p. 97. Cundall, ed., *Lady Nugent's Journal*, p. 239.

itself most markedly in their lack of coöperation in carrying out public enterprises. Roads for hauling heavy loads of produce to shipping points were everywhere a primary necessity, yet they were almost invariably in a deplorable state—cut up and impassable after rains. Owners of plantations near the sea saw no reason for aiding those farther inland to get their crops down easily. Proprietors in the interior were possessed by the haunting fear that their carts might not traverse a given stretch of highway as frequently as some neighbor's, although equal contributions or allotments of negro hands to aid in the work of grading were called for.[1] The same spirit showed itself in the matter of constructing bridges. There were few to be found for the reason that such slight sums as could be raised by subscription made possible the erection of only light wooden affairs, carried away by the first freshet.[2]

Local jealousy was especially marked in Jamaica. St. Jago de la Vega, an inland city under planter control, opposed all measures benefiting the coastal mercantile center, Kingston. In 1755 the capital was removed from the former to the latter; then, in 1758, back to its old seat.[3] This stirred up tremendous feeling. When a practical plan for building a reservoir to guard against the fire danger in Kingston was presented, "a want of unanimity prevented its being carried into execution."[4] A custom-house could not be erected in the seaport metropolis because the expense was too great for the residents to bear unaided and the rural element of the island perversely refused its support.[5] Similarly, the St. Jago de la Vega jail, a disgraceful, ramshackly structure, could neither be repaired nor enlarged because no proposal could be agreed upon, "some having indulged a principle of wantonly opposing every scheme and project offered" for the advantage of that community.[6]

At an earlier period of West Indian history, before society had

---

[1] Long, *Jamaica*, I, 466–470 and II, 52, 53. *Votes of the Honourable House of Assembly of Jamaica, in a Session Begun October 22 and ended December 14, 1793* (St. Jago de la Vega, 1794), session of November 5. [Trelawny Wentworth], *The West India Sketch Book* (2 vols., London, 1834), II, 193.

[2] Long, *Jamaica*, II, 25, 26. Stewart, *An Account of Jamaica*, p. 15. Richard Madden, *A Twelvemonth's Residence in the West Indies During the Transition from Slavery to Apprenticeship* (2 vols., Philadelphia, 1835), I, 209.

[3] Kingston was once more made the capital city in 1872 and remains so to this day.

[4] Long, *Jamaica*, II, 105.

[5] *Ibid.*, II, 116.

[6] *Ibid.*, II, 15.

become static, quite a different atmosphere prevailed. Thus, 218 bequests had been made to churches and the poor and for educational purposes in Jamaica alone between 1667 and 1736.[1] Similarly, Christopher Codrington, governor of the Leewards, bequeathed two Barbadian plantations to the newly incorporated Society for the Propagation of the Gospel in order that a college might be established and maintained. He desired "that the plantations should continue entire, and 300 negroes, at least, [be] always kept thereon, and a convenient number of professors and scholars maintained there, who are to be obliged to study and practice physic and chirurgery as well as divinity, that by the apparent usefulness of the former to all mankind, they may both endear themselves to the people, and have the better opportunity of doing good to men's souls, whilst they are taking care of their bodies."

But in true colonial fashion, few of the Jamaican bequests were properly executed and the good intentions of the one great public benefactor the islands have known were frustrated through the misapplication of funds for upwards of a century.[2] Through most of the seventeen hundreds, the interests of all were the interests of none. Only too true was the observation of one for twenty years resident in the Caribbean, that the West Indians threw away thousands on trifles but would spend nothing for the general good.[3]

Planter conservatism evinced itself in the repeated failure of agricultural societies to establish themselves. Founded upon the initiative of enlightened individuals, generally newcomers, they never aroused widespread popular interest and one and all soon languished and passed out of existence. Because of ingrained hostility to the introduction of innovation, antiquated methods of production were stubbornly clung to and science was ignored in cultivation and preparation of crops for market alike. The melancholy story of the

---

[1] *Journals of the Assembly of Jamaica, 1663–1826.* (14 vols., Jamaica, 1811–29), III, 417–420; XI, 479.

[2] William Brown, *History of the Propagation of Christianity Among the Heathen Since the Reformation* (3 vols., Edinburgh, 1854), III, 410–412. James Anderson, *The History of the Church of England in the Colonies and Foreign Dependencies of the British Empire* (3 vols., London, 1856) III, 530–536. [Thomas Parry], *Codrington College, in the Island of Barbados* (London, 1847). T. Herbert Bindley, "Annals of Codrington College, 1710–1910," in *The West India Committee Circular,* Feb. 1 to April 26, 1910 (reprinted in pamphlet form, London, 1910). Bindley, "The Evolution of a Colonial College," in *The National Review,* LV (1910), pp. 847 ff.

[3] Stewart, *An Account of Jamaica,* p. 170.

numerous unsuccessful attempts made to elevate the plane of agrarian economy in British tropical America is recounted elsewhere.[1]

The spirit of ostentation enjoyed full play in dress and entertainment. Love of finery was universal. "Home" styles were closely followed; Paris creations, often imported by way of Martinique, had a strong hold on the hearts of fair residents. "They have the fashions every six weeks from London, and London itself cannot boast of more elegant shops than you meet with at St. Johns, particularly Mrs. Tudhope . . . at whose shop I saw as neat done up things as I ever met with in my life," commented a vivacious visitor to Antigua.[2] French fashions ruled in Trinidad during the 1820's.[3]

Such common adoption of apparel fashioned for temperate climes naturally resulted in considerable discomfort. "One may see men loaded and half melting under a ponderous coat and waistcoat, richly bedaubed with gold lace or embroidery on a hot day, scarcely able to bear them . . ." writes Long.[4] Another enlarges on the picture with fine scorn.

"Our English belles . . . do not scruple to wear the thickest winter silks and sattins; and are sometimes ready to sink under the weight of rich gold or silver brocades. . . . The winter fashions of London arrive here at the setting in of hot weather. . . . Surely nothing can be more preposterous and absurd than for persons residing in the West Indies to adhere rigidly to all the European customs and manners which . . . are certainly improper, ridiculous, and detrimental in a hot climate."

Similarly, military officers were attired in gorgeous, lace-decorated uniforms and Saxon plumes while ordinary soldiers wore the regulation woolen scarlet.[5]

As for social intercourse affording an opportunity for pretentious parade, "The demon of colonial society is the spirit of rivalry in luxurious entertainments and apparel. If Mrs. S— gives a party, it is incumbent upon Mrs. W— to give a larger; if Miss A— should happen to exhibit a tiara of pearls at the King's house, Miss B— would go into hysterics if she could not display one of diamonds at the next ball. . . . Grand entertainments abound. . . . All 'the small

[1] In Chapter II.
[2] Andrews, ed., *Journal of a Lady*, p. 115.
[3] Bayley, *Four Years' Residence*, pp. 211, 580.
[4] *Jamaica*, II, 520–522.
[5] Alexander, *Transatlantic Sketches*, pp. 135–137.

sweet courtesies' and tranquil enjoyments of friendly intercourse in minor circles, and little reunions of neighboring families, are unknown." [1]

With the exception of St. Jago de la Vega and Kingston in Jamaica, and Bridgetown, Barbados, there were no settlements of any size in the British Caribbean. Such as there were existed to meet the planters' needs. Their location was determined by the convenience of a given spot as a shipping center. Consequently nearly all stood on hot stretches of coastal plain. The more wealthy inhabitants established homes in the refreshing uplands and spent only business hours in the lower altitude.

There was little of beauty about these towns. They were generally laid out in squares, residences and stores alike were constructed of wood, and the streets were poorly cared for. The government house, a public building or two, and the churches alone had the slightest air of elegance. A statue of Nelson in Bridgetown and one of Rodney in St. Jago de la Vega, both objects of great local pride, are worthy of mention merely as having furnished the only evidence of civic pride.[2]

St. John's, Antigua, in the latter part of the eighteenth century, was a "miserable-looking place, there being to outward appearance scarcely a decent house in it, though many of them are fitted up tolerably well on the inside." It was "more like a country village running to ruins than the capital of an island." [3] Its streets were "spacious, but unpaved, nor is the least care taken to keep them clean; the prickly pear bush and other shrubs are suffered to grow therein, to the annoyance of the passenger, the secreting of every species of filth and nastiness, and to the great increase of vermin, insects, and reptiles. . . ." [4]

Mathew Lewis had much the same to say in describing the capital and metropolis of Jamaica: "Spanish Town [St. Jago de la Vega] has no recommendations whatever; the houses are mostly built of wood; the streets are very irregular and narrow; every alternate building is in a ruinous state, and the whole place wears an air of

---

[1] Madden, *A Twelvemonth's Residence*, I, 151, 152.

[2] The former appears on the Barbadian centennial series of postage stamps issued in 1905; the latter on the 2s. Jamaican stamp issued in 1919.

[3] Baily, *Journal of a Tour*, p. 88.

[4] [John Luffman], *Brief Account of the Island of Antigua* . . . (London, 1789), Letter V. Published in German translation as "Briefe über die westindische Insel Antigua," in M. C. Sprengel and G. Forster, editors, *Neue Beiträge zur Völker- und Länderkunde* (13 vols., Leipzig, 1791–1793), I, 3 ff.

gloom. . . . There is not that air of melancholy about Kingston which pervades Spanish Town; but it has no pretentions to beauty; and if any person will imagine a large town entirely composed of booths at a race course, and the streets merely roads, without any sort of paving, he will have a perfect idea of Kingston." [1]

Fires were common and widely destructive. Bridgetown suffered from them in 1756, 1758, twice in 1766, 1821, 1826, and 1828.[2] St. George, Grenada, was all but destroyed in 1771 with a loss of £200,-000 sterling and again in 1775 when property valued at nearly £500,-000 was consumed by the flames.[3] Two hundred sixty buildings and the wharves of St. John's, Antigua, were burned in 1769.[4] Such parts of Savannah la Mar, Jamaica, as had not been devastated by hurricane were wiped out in 1780; Kingston's fire loss in 1782 approximated £500,000. Montego Bay, in the same colony, was laid in ruins in 1808.[5] Twenty-one blocks of Port of Spain, Trinidad, covered by 1,500 buildings including the government and custom houses, the city hall, the jail, and a church were ravaged in 1808.[6]

Up to about 1785, no insurance was procurable on West Indian property. The first concern to issue such policies was the Phoenix Company of Lombard Street, London [7] and many years passed before a competitor entered the field. The dead loss long following conflagration was offset to some extent by contributions received from planters and Caribbean traders as well as benevolent persons resident in England and by parliamentary grants. Thus, the London Society of West India Merchants at various times voted sufferers in St. John's, Antigua, £500, those in St. George, Grenada, £300, and others in Basseterre, St. Kitts, £100 [8] ; Liverpool houses subscribed £346

[1] *Journal*, pp. 160–162.

[2] Robert H. Schomburgk, *The History of Barbados* (London, 1848), pp. 241 ff. Bayley, *Four Years' Residence*, pp. 74–76. See also C. O. 28/50.

[3] Southey, *Chronological History*, II, 408, 422. C. O. 101/16.

[4] C. O. 152/49; Flannigan, *Antigua*, I, 117, 214, 215. "Particulars of the Fire at St. John's in Antigua," in *The Gentleman's Magazine*, Nov. 1769, p. 539.

[5] Southey, *Chronological History*, II, 536; III, 408. George W. Bridges, *The Annals of Jamaica* (2 vols., London, 1828), II, 175, 176, 184. C. O. 137/82.

[6] Southey, *Chronological History*, III, 410. Lionel Fraser, *History of Trinidad* (2 vols., Port of Spain, n.d. and 1896), I, 316–320. A plan of the city, showing the portion destroyed, will be found in C. O. 295/19.

[7] Luffman, *Brief Account*, Letter XXXIV.

[8] West India Committee Archives—*Minutes of the Meetings of the Committee of West India Merchants*, Dec. 5, 1769, April 7, 1772 and Jan. 7, 1777. For the relation of this body to the islands see Chapter III.

to the relief of the Antiguans [1] and parliament in 1812 set aside £50,000 sterling towards the rebuilding of Port of Spain. Several volunteer island fire companies appeared and numerous safety regulations requiring kitchens, blacksmith shops, and bakeries to be constructed of brick were adopted as safeguards against similar catastrophe in the future.[2]

The ports were primarily commercial centers and the homes of professional men. Owing to the British policy of discouraging colonial industry, manufacturing was virtually non-existent. Two refineries were operating in Kingston, Jamaica, about 1770, but they barely met local demand. In fact, most white sugar used by the West Indians came from England and was high in price.[3] Refining for the home market could not be undertaken because of the prohibitive duty placed on the finished article. In 1792, this stood at £4.18.8 sterling per hundredweight as against 15 s. on muscovado.[4]

A foundry, specializing in plantation utensils, was established in Kingston about 1770. The owner is reported to have cleared £4,000 annually. After the American Revolution he began the manufacture of copper pans and kettles as well.[5] But this was a unique case.

Regarding industry in the Leewards, Governor William Burt wrote to the Lords Commissioners of Trade and Plantations about 1780, ". . . no Manufacture, except one Sugar House in [Antigua] . . . , exists within this Government and . . . I do not know of any Trades except the absolutely necessary Blacksmiths, Carpenters, Masons, Taylors, Mantue Makers, Miliners, one or two very bad Shoe Makers, to whom necessity alone drives, some Ordinary botching Sadlers and one tolerable good Harness and Chaise Maker in this island." [6]

The predominant occupation in the towns, then, was the buying

---

[1] Flannigan, *Antigua*, I, 215. A typical appeal for general subscriptions appears in "Address to the Publick, in Favour of the Sufferers at Bridgetown," in *The Gent. Mag.*, Sept. 1766, p. 425. For a list of contributions, see Anon., *An Account of the Donations for the Relief of the Sufferers by Fire, at Bridge Town in . . . 1766 . . .* (London, n.d.).

[2] See for example, *Order in Council [for St. Lucia] Forbidding the Construction of any Wooden Buildings . . .* [Castries, 1823]. *An Ordinance [for St. Lucia] Requiring the Occupiers of Certain Houses, in Castries, to Provide Themselves with Portable Stone or Brick Hearths* [Castries, 1826].

[3] Long, *Jamaica*, II, 120. Edwards, *History*, II, 378. Refined sugar received from England never sold for less than three shillings a pound in Jamaica, according to a visitor of the 1770's. Andrews, ed., *Journal of a Lady*, p. 99.

[4] *Great Britain, House of Commons, Sessional Papers*, 1826, XXII (328). Edwards, *History*, II, 438.

[5] Gardner, *Jamaica*, pp. 163, 164.

[6] C. O. 152/34, no. 75.

and selling of plantation stores. Most merchants were either Scotch or Jewish. They were wealthy men and mixed in the best social circles. Their emporiums were crammed with full lines of European and North American goods—hardware, draperies, clothing, shoes, and what not—and much resembled warehouses. Sale in bulk only was the rule. Small purchases were made at the markets or of hucksters, both regular features of Caribbean life. The expected arrival of shipments was announced by advertisement in the local press. Chalked notices such as "Herrings" and "Choice Madeira" before the mercantile establishments called attention to new stocks.

Prices fluctuated violently with the quantity of supplies on hand and conditions of sale. They rose steadily as shelves were cleared but dropped immediately upon the entry of a merchantman into harbor. Heavy charge accounts were regularly carried, but cash prices ranged from 30 to 40 per cent below credit ones. Wares were offered at double cost on time payment sales, but losses on such transactions reduced actual gains to only half or three-fifths as much.[1]

Physicians and members of the legal profession were much in demand and soon amassed fortunes. An important part of the former's duties was the care of estate negroes. Doctors were engaged by the year, their annual compensation about 1790 being six shillings a slave on a basis of weekly visits to a property, with additional payments for unusual services such as inoculation. The medical expense connected with a plantation manned by 500 hands thus averaged somewhat over £150 sterling per twelvemonth at that time.[2] Each practitioner served several proprietors; the customary fee for calls on whites at a somewhat later period was one doubloon and, as our informant whimsically adds, "the inhabitants are all sick in their turn."[3] The prospect of easy wealth attracted many quacks and persons not qualified by education and training to the islands; licensing systems were therefore commonly adopted during the eighteenth century.

[1] Alexander, *Transatlantic Sketches,* p. 163. Andrews, ed., *Journal of a Lady,* p. 130; Bayley, *Four Years' Residence,* pp. 32, 356. Stewart, *An Account of Jamaica,* p. 151. Flannigan, *Antigua,* I, 211, 212. Long, *Jamaica,* I, 575–577 and II, 29, 105, 106. John Stewart, *A View of the Past and Present of the Island of Jamaica* . . . (Edinburgh, 1823), pp. 125, 126. John Poyer, *The History of Barbados, from* . . . *1605 till* . . . *1801* (London, 1808), pp. 400, 401.

[2] Edwards, *History,* II, 136, note k.

[3] Williams, *Tour,* p. 134. The doubloon was a Spanish coin worth about $8, formerly current in the West Indies. Its value was somewhat over £5 currency in Jamaica in the early 1820's when Williams visited the island.

Lawyers also flourished. The almost limitless amount of credit given proprietors led to incessant litigation for the recovery of debts. Defective titles, particularly in the older colonies, likewise were a source of endless dispute. Legal fees in Jamaica alone during the early eighteen hundreds were estimated at the amazing total of some £500,-000 annually by a former resident.[1]

There was little of a refining nature in British Caribbean society. The Christian church, normally the zealous guardian of learning as well as spiritual guide in rude communities, played a rôle of but slight importance up to the 1790's. Anglicanism was officially intrenched; the tropical American possessions were divided into parishes and handsome religious structures were to be found in some of them. Yet the Established Church itself was long an anomaly. Ecclesiastical jurisdiction over the West Indies was claimed by the Bishop of London under customary authority and, from 1745 to 1784, he licensed twenty-nine churchmen for Jamaica, fourteen for Antigua, thirty-five for Barbados, ten for St. Kitts, six for Dominica, four for Grenada, three for Montserrat, two for Nevis, two for Tobago, and one for St. Vincent.[2] Yet his right to control the island clergy was sharply challenged by local laws and no method of actually directing their work had been evolved.

"The Church in the British West Indies . . . was an Episcopal Church without Bishops; it was a professedly Diocesan system without dioceses. . . . There were . . . no supervising Archdeacons or Rural Deans, no Cathedral Chapters, no Colleges of clergy. . . . There were no lay-readers, or catechists, no Sunday-school teachers, no district visitors. . . . [As for the clergy], each held office by appointment of the Governor and at his pleasure; and knew well that he was not likely to be disturbed except in case of sheer refusal to perform his formal duties, or of gross and scandalous conduct. . . . They met in no synod, nor in any regular conferences, nor indeed do we find any trace even of friendly and informal conferences upon their work. . . . The common bond was the license which necessitated the use in the regular offices of the Church of a common Liturgy, and adhesion to the Creeds and Articles. . . ."[3]

---

[1] Stewart, *An Account of Jamaica*, pp. 41, 42. Charles Osborne, clerk to a conveyancer in Philadelphia and a friend of young Franklin, left Pennsylvania and took up the practice of law in the West Indies where "he became an eminent lawyer and made money." Benjamin Franklin, *Autobiography* (New York, 1901), p. 35.

[2] Anderson, *The Church of England in the Colonies*, III, 546, note.

[3] A. Caldecott. *The Church in the West Indies* (London, 1898), pp. 49, 56–58. See also Long, *Jamaica*, II, 235–237. Gardner, *Jamaica*, p. 195.

The results of such lax supervision were irregular services and a tendency to fill livings with mean individuals.

Speaking of those in holy orders in Jamaica, Long says: "There have seldom been wanting some who were equally respectable for their learning, piety, and exemplary good behavior; others have been detestable for their addiction to lewdness, drinking, gambling, and iniquity, having no controul, but their own sense of the dignity of their function, and the censures of the governor. . . ." Some were "much better qualified to be retailers of saltfish or boatswains to privateers, than ministers of the Gospel." [1]

The Anglican rectors were frequently absentees. This both stirred up keen resentment in the islands and disturbed officials administering the colonies. In dealing with the application of an Antiguan churchman, the Reverend John Trew, already in England, for royal permission to continue his stay, the Secretary of State for the American Department wrote on December 12, 1763, "The absence of the clergy from their Cures in the Plantations having of late years become so general and frequent as to give great Cause of Concern and Complaint to the Bishop of London, Lord Halifax [is determined] not to move His Majesty upon any Request of that kind, untill he shall first be satisfied that the Gentleman applying did obtain the Governor's Leave to return to this Kingdom, upon appointing a sufficient and approved Curate." [2]

To curb this evil further, the Jamaican legislature in 1770 reinforced a statute of 1706/7 denying clergymen absent from their parishes for more than two months a year their stipends. [3]

The general low caliber of West Indian wearers of the cloth is revealed in other ways. One Austin, rector of St. George's parish, Grenada, set himself up as a sugar planter in Surinam about 1800 and when the governor demanded that he return to his duties in the colony's principal church, sought to exchange that post for one in the new possession. [4] Soon after, the Reverend John Audain of Dominica abandoned his charge without leave and occasioned great scandal by openly engaging in mercantile pursuits. [5] In 1811, he was

[1] *Jamaica*, II, 238.
[2] C. O. 152/47.
[3] *Acts of Assembly. Passed in the Island of Jamaica; From 1770, to 1783 inclusive* (Kingston, 1786), pp. 12–14.
[4] Governor Maitland to Lord Castlereagh, Nov. 3, 1805, C. O. 101/42. Surinam was then in English hands.
[5] Lieutenant-Governor Barnes to Lord Castlereagh, Dec. 8, 1808, C. O. 71/43.

suspended from a living in Tortola because of an absence of some years without having left a curate to officiate. "He has not only engaged in Commerce, but has actually commanded Privateers." [1]

William Davis held two benefices in St. Kitts and also acted as an estate manager. Criminal charges were preferred against him for alleged cruelty to the slaves, and in 1813 he was indicted for the murder of a female black, Eliza.[2] Five years later, in the same island, the Reverend William Rawlins was found guilty of having slain Congo Jack on a property in his charge, and was given three months imprisonment as well as a fine of £200.[3]

Lady Nugent records that Mr. Stewart, overseer on a Jamaican plantation, was rewarded for faithful service by his employer's purchasing the living of Savannah la Mar for him and securing his ordination.[4] An old resident, describing local churchmen at about the same time, commented on their greed for gain.[5] Similarly, an adventurer acquainted with conditions in St. Kitts urged that the worthless and disorderly ecclesiastics there be replaced by more virtuous and exemplary men.[6]

But if the Caribbean clergy tended to neglect their duties, it is also true that they received scant encouragement in performing them. The whites for whose spiritual guidance they existed were habitual stay-aways from service. One much interested in colonial religious affairs gives us data on church attendance shortly after the Peace of Paris. At that time, less than a score of worshipers ordinarily assembled in a St. Kitts parish well inhabited by gentry. Four Nevis congregations did not include over sixty persons all told. The one in St. John's, capital of Antigua, numbered but 250; twenty-five was a large Sunday morning gathering in Dominica. Conditions in Barbados were, however, somewhat better.[7] A Jamaican writing in the 1780's commented on the prevalence of empty pews save at funerals and added, "The planters seem to have no religion at all." [8]

---

[1] Governor Elliot to the Earl of Liverpool, May 15, 1811, C. O. 152/97.

[2] Elliot to Earl Bathurst, March 27 and June 1, 1813, C. O. 152/101, 102.

[3] Private letter and despatch of Governor Probyn to Earl Bathurst, March 18 and 21, 1818, C. O. 239/4.

[4] Cundall, ed., Lady Nugent's Journal, pp. 123, 124.

[5] Stewart, An Account of Jamaica, pp. 45–47.

[6] Charles Macpherson, Memoirs of . . . Life and Travels in Asia, Africa and America . . . (Edinburgh, 1800).

[7] William Doyle, Some Account of the British Dominions Beyond the Atlantic . . . (London, 1770), pp. 36–41.

[8] [Peter Marsden], An Account of the Island of Jamaica . . . (Newcastle, 1788), p. 41.

Tithes were customarily paid in kind. This practice served to discourage churchmen, as produce of an inferior sort was given them, and with fluctuating values, their incomes varied considerably from year to year.[1]

The Established Church in tropical America, then, failed sadly both as a religious and a cultural force due to the combination of inferior representatives and general indifference on the part of the planter class. The later work of the sectarists, destined to affect so profoundly social development in the West Indies, was conducted primarily among the slaves and, far from uplifting the proprietors, served rather to arouse their hostility.

Schools in the British sugar colonies were conspicuous by their absence and such as were found afforded instruction for boys alone. Mention has already been made of Codrington College. Unfortunately, the roseate hopes of its generous founder were not realized. At the opening of the nineteenth century, there were but twelve students in attendance;[2] in 1825, the number was fifteen.[3] An inquiry conducted in Jamaica during 1764 showed that while considerable sums had, in the aggregate, been given to develop free educational institutions, the money had not been wisely applied and that little public good had resulted therefrom. Eight such foundations then existed, but seven were of a strictly local nature and the eighth, of wider scope, closed its doors shortly after. A projected male academy failed to materialize due to the death of its promoter.[4]

As a rule, the instruction of planter children was carried on by

[1] Coleridge, *Six Months,* pp. 181, 196. *Memorial of the clergy in Nevis to Viscount Goderich,* C. O. 239/29. For various aspects of the early work of the Established Church in the West Indies see Alfred Barry, *The Ecclesiastical Expansion of England in the Growth of the Anglican Communion* (London, 1895). E. Edwards Beardsley, *Life and Correspondence of . . . Samuel Seabury . . .* (Boston, 1881). C. G. Clark-Hunter, *St. John's Parish, Barbados* (Bridgetown, 1907). W. E. Collins, "The Church in Jamaica," in *The East and West,* January, 1903. John B. Ellis, *The Diocese of Jamaica* (London, 1913). Ellis, *A Short Sketch of the History of the Church of England in Jamaica* (Kingston, 1891). Thomas Farrar, "The Church of England in Jamaica," in *The West India Quarterly,* July 1885. S. Purcell Hendrick, *A Sketch of the History of the Cathedral Church of St. Jago de la Vega . . .* (Kingston, 1911). John Roby, *The History of the Parish of St. James, in Jamaica . . .* (Kingston, 1849). William Seabury, *Memoir of Bishop Seabury* (New York, 1908). G. Robert Wynne, *The Church in Greater Britain* (London, 1911).

[2] George Pinckard, *Notes on the West Indies* (3 vols., London, 1806), I, 356–359.

[3] Coleridge, *Six Months,* p. 54.

[4] Long, *Jamaica,* II, 62, 250–252.

tutors from Great Britain or the mainland colonies. These were seldom of a high order—only large salaries or failure at home could induce teachers to go out to the Caribbean. The average pedagogue was a half-educated adventurer commanding neither the respect of the parents nor the obedience of his pupils.[1] Under such uncertain guidance, both the sons and daughters of the most wealthy families were prepared at home during a period of years for entrance into the best educational institutions of the mother land. More frequently, however, the boys alone were sent abroad, while their sisters continued to study privately.

The number of young West Indians receiving English educations was considerable. Long estimated about 1770 that three-fourths of the proprietors' children growing up in Jamaica went overseas for that purpose. Near the middle of the eighteenth century, some 300 a year took passage; two decades later there were many more.[2] Students aboard merchantmen, bound to or from school, often figure in travel accounts of the day.[3] Those whose means permitted neither private instruction nor the expense of a protracted trans-Atlantic stay grew up largely unlettered.

Educating successive generations of West Indian youth abroad was far from salutary. With few restraining influences and commonly provided with too generous allowances, many quickly succumbed to the pleasures and vices of their strange environment. Swearing, drinking, gaming, and wenching were the young gentlemen's first accomplishments; balls and theatrical performances engaged the creole maidens' attention. Neither studies nor the life in any way fitted them for filling places in island society; instead, associations and habits were formed which made return to childhood scenes seem veritable exile. All the real interests of such students centered in England which became home to them as it had to their elders. Therein lies the explanation for that lamentable lack of local pride

---

[1] Stewart, *An Account of Jamaica*, pp. 165, 166. John Collins, a heavy-drinking and shiftless though not unlearned friend of Franklin, was engaged as preceptor for the sons of a Barbadian gentleman by the captain of a West India merchantman who had been commissioned to hire a teacher and who met Collins while his ship was at Philadelphia. Franklin, *Autobiography*, p. 35.

[2] Long, *Jamaica*, I, 510, 511. The library of the Institute of Jamaica contains a manuscript *Catalogue of Men Born in Jamaica Who Matriculated at Oxford 1689–1885 Extracted from "Alumni Oxonienses" by William Cowper, M. A. Cantab*, listing the names of 268 such students.

[3] See, for example, Andrews, ed., *Journal of a Lady*, p. 20. Wentworth, *West India Sketch Book*, I, 44.

and feeling already noted, and also to a great degree for the vicious system of absenteeism which was ultimately to deal a mortal blow at the entire plantation régime.[1]

Few books were read in the colonies and book shops were quite unknown. An indifferent assortment of printed matter could be found in the general stores, and popular British novels reached the Caribbean in the periodic shipments of estate supplies, but the grower of tropical produce was in no sense a patron of literature. Library societies with collections of standard works for the use of their members were formed in a few of the urban centers such as Bridgetown and Kingston[2] and in a limited way filled a great need.

Each island boasted at least two weekly newspapers, though in Barbados and Jamaica they were more numerous and issues appeared with greater frequency.[3] All were small four page affairs, abominably printed on low grade, semiporous paper. Most were short-lived. Half of their columns were filled with advertisements, notably those of merchants listing new goods in stock or shortly due and those of planters, offering rewards for the return of fugitive slaves. Foreign news was copied verbatim from British and American publications with little use of credit lines. The West Indian press abounded with vitriolic attacks on the trend of local politics and equally burning replies, both indulging freely in personalities and bristling with scathing epithets. One sheet served as the administration organ, its rival as that of the opposition.

The governor's ball was everywhere the social event of the season. All persons of the slightest importance—the great and the would be

[1] Long, *Jamaica*, I, 438 and II, 246–249. Williams, *Tour*, p. 261. Andrews, ed., *Journal of a Lady*, pp. 21, 92. Thomas Atwood, *History of Dominica* (London, 1791), p. 215.

[2] Bayley, *Four Years' Residence*, pp. 32, 577, 578. Coleridge, *Six Months*, pp. 46, 130. Schomburgk, *Barbados*, p. 132. Stewart, *A View . . . of Jamaica*, p. 205.

[3] West Indian newspapers founded before 1776 are catalogued in Isaiah Thomas, *The History of Printing in America* (2 vols., Worcester, 1810), II, 382 ff. For a list of Jamaican newspapers see Frank Cundall, "The Press and Printers of Jamaica Prior to 1820," in *Proceedings of the American Antiquarian Society*, N. S. Vol. XXVI (April-Oct. 1916), pp. 290 ff. and Cundall, *Bibliographia Jamaicensis* (Kingston, 1902), pp. 62–64. The former has been reprinted (Worcester, Mass., 1916). See also Cundall, "The First Jamaica Newspaper," in *The W. I. Comm. Circ.*, Aug. 11, 1914, pp. 370, 371. The early press in Barbados is discussed in Schomburgk, *Barbados*, pp. 124–127.

so—attended in gala attire. Political animosities were forgotten for the moment; island society was then seen at its best.[1]

Regular theaters flourished in the larger settlements. One in Kingston enjoyed heavy patronage near the middle of the eighteenth century, a second was built in 1776, and one opened in Bridgetown in 1812. Elsewhere, large halls accommodated wandering bodies of players. Jamaica's commercial metropolis gave refuge to a company fleeing the American Revolution. Actresses now and then were inter-island passengers. Local talent was frequently afforded an opportunity for expression, though due attention to strict decorum occasioned a sorry lack of females in the cast and forced self-conscious, rosy-cheeked boys to fill such rôles as best they might. Performances were usually given on Saturday evening.

Among the offerings on various occasions were *Venice Preserved, The Mayor of Garratt, The Orphan, The Lying Valet, Les Prétendeurs, The Fair Penitent, King Lear, Jane Shore, Macbeth, Hamlet, She Stoops to Conquer, Harlequin Planter, Adelgitha, The West Indian,* and *The Spoiled Child.* Because of divergent racial and religious elements in Trinidad, productions in Port of Spain were supervised by the chief of police who refused licenses to such as were "of an immoral tendency or the language offensive, by want of decency in expression or of action, towards the inhabitants or their respective religions, or otherwise politically objectionable. . . ."[2]

Conjurers, sleight of hand performers, rope-walkers, jugglers, contortionists, dwarfs, small circuses, and wax-work shows from time to time lent variety to life.[3] Race-courses were found in Trinidad and Jamaica.[4] Drinking bouts and cock-fighting appealed to ruder spirits;

---

[1] For a description of such balls in Jamaica, see Long, *Jamaica,* I, 33 and Cundall, ed., *Lady Nugent's Journal,* pp. 52, 53.

[2] Long, *Jamaica,* II, 117. Luffman, *Brief Account,* Letters XXVII, XXXV, XXXVIII. Flannigan, *Antigua,* II, pp. 211, 212. Lewis, *Journal,* pp. 363, 364. Schomburgk, *Barbados,* pp. 250, 251. Alexander, *Transatlantic Sketches,* p. 84. Madden, *A Twelvemonth's Residence,* II, 11, 12. Fraser, *Trinidad,* II, 105, 106. *Votes of the Honourable House of Assembly of Jamaica, in a Session Begun October 22 and ended December 14, 1793* (St. Jago de la Vega, 1794). [Baron de Montlezun], *Souvenirs des Antilles. Voyage en 1815 et 1816 . . .* (2 vols., Paris, 1818), I, 271–275. Andrews, ed., *Journal of a Lady,* p. 122. Wentworth, *West India Sketch Book,* II, 168–177. Stewart, *A View . . . of Jamaica,* p. 205. Stewart, *An Account of Jamaica,* p. 176.

[3] Stewart, *An Account of Jamaica,* p. 177. Flannigan, *Antigua,* II, 213.

[4] Alexander, *Transatlantic Sketches,* pp. 119, 120; Long, *Jamaica,* II, 32.

anti-gambling statutes reveal marked propensities to court the Goddess of Chance.[1]

The negro, on whom the labor system of the sugar islands rested, was the second great element in tropical American society. Slaves were of two kinds, imported and of local origin. So long as the former predominated, any advance in the station of the colonial peoples and the general elevation of West Indian civilization were equally impossible. Various tribal stocks were represented, some superior and some inferior, some suited for one kind of work and some for another,[2] yet under the uniform conditions of bondage in a new world, differences tended to disappear and a single type, the creole black, developed. In contact with whites from his birth and knowing no other life than serving them, speaking, too, a jargon based on English, he was more tractable than the African, could perform his duties more intelligently, and was less discordant socially. The history of the British West Indies would have been radically different had the native negro early come to form the basis of the servile class.

The townsmen's slaves were employed as servants, porters, and artisans. Among the last were carpenters, coopers, blacksmiths, and masons. They and the carriers were, for the most part, hired out by their owners but not infrequently were allowed to seek employment for themselves and paid their masters specified sums per day or week. The more industrious of them could thus accumulate means and some at times even purchased their own freedom.

The more common form of bondsman, however, was the plantation hand. Only about half the negroes on a given sugar estate engaged in field work; the others were craftsmen, herders, domestics, watchmen, nurses, aged individuals, or young children.[3] Agricultural

---

[1] "An Act for the more effectual preventing of excessive and deceitful gaming, by way of Lottery, Tickets, Numbers, or Figures, Cards, Raffle, or Dice" was passed in Jamaica in 1771. See *Acts of Assembly. Passed in the Island of Jamaica; from 1770, to 1783, inclusive* (Kingston, 1786), p. 5. Similar measures had been enacted at an earlier date, both in that colony and in the other islands as well.

[2] See page 85.

[3] The most detailed record of the actual operations on a plantation known to exist, giving intimate glimpses of planter economy, is the general account book for Worthy Park plantation, St. John's parish, Jamaica, the property of Robert Price of Penzance, England, for the years 1792–96. For a study of the same, see Ulrich B. Phillips, "A Jamaica Slave Plantation," in *The American Historical Review*, XIX, pp. 543–558 and his *American Negro Slavery* (New York, 1918), pp. 57 ff.

laborers were divided into three groups, the big, the second, and the small gangs. The first included the most able-bodied men and women. In crop time they cut and ground the canes and boiled down the juice. At other seasons the land was cleared and hoed as well as planted by them.

The second gang was made up of boys and girls, convalescents, and pregnant females; these weeded the canes and performed other light tasks. Piccaninnies hoeing the garden or cutting grass for the stock so as to be kept out of mischief constituted the other one. A colored foreman, the "driver," was placed over each of the adult bodies. In the small gang, the position was held by a discreet and trustworthy old woman.

The classic description of the field hands' day is that given by Bryan Edwards,[1] a wealthy Jamaican proprietor, later a West India merchant and member of parliament, and celebrated historian of the British Caribbean.

"The first [i. e., big] gang is summoned to the labours of the field either by a bell or the blowing of a conch-shell, just before sunrise. They bring with them, besides their hoes or bills, provisions for breakfast; and are attended by a White person, and a Black superintendent called a driver. The list being called over, and the names of all the absentees noted, they proceed with their work until eight or nine o'clock, when they sit down in the shade to breakfast, which is prepared in the mean time by a certain number of women, whose sole employment it is to act as cooks for the rest. This meal commonly consists of boiled yams, eddoes, ocra, calalue, and plantains, or as many of those vegetables as they can procure; seasoned with salt, and cayenne pepper; and, in truth, it is an exceedingly palatable and wholesome mess. By this time most of the absentees make their appearance, and are sometimes punished for their sluggishness by a few stripes of the driver's whip. . . .

"At breakfast they are seldom indulged with more than half or three quarters of an hour; and, having resumed their work, continue in the field until noon, when the bell calls them from labour. They are now allowed two hours of rest and refreshment; one of which is commonly spent in sleep. Their dinner is provided with the addition of salted or pickled fish, of which each Negro receives a weekly allowance. . . . At two o'clock they are again summoned to the field, where, having been refreshed both by rest and food, they now manifest some signs of vigorous and animated application; although I can with truth assert, that one English labourer could perform at least three times the work of any one negro in the same period. At sunset, or very soon after, they are released for the night . . . and if the day has been wet, or their labour harder than usual, they are sometimes indulged with an allowance of rum. . . .

[1] In his *History*, II, 129–131.

They are employed daily about ten hours. . . . In the crop season, however, the system is different; for at that time, such of the negroes as are employed in the mill and boiling houses, often work very late, frequently all night; but they are divided into watches, which relieve each other. . . . "

Work was carried on daily except Sunday and every other Saturday for most of the year. During harvest, it went on uninterruptedly. Holidays were granted at Easter, Whitsuntide, and Christmas. In most of the colonies the slaves were allotted tracts of waste land for raising provisions such as plantains, yams, bananas, and cocoanuts. They were also permitted to keep hogs, rabbits, fowls, and small stock. Allowances of salt, clothing, cutlery, salt fish, meat, rum, and molasses were issued regularly. The free Saturdays were employed in cultivating garden plots; Sunday was market day, with the slaves trooping to the nearest town even though it be twenty miles off, intent on selling their surplus produce, buying such articles as caught their fancy, and gossiping with friends.

The plantation blacks lived in their own quarter, some distance behind the great-house. The family was the social unit though marriage was practically unknown and unfaithfulness the general rule. The ordinary cottage stood alone, surrounded by trees and shrubs. It was constructed of posts interlaced with twigs and was divided into two rooms. The interior was plastered and whitewashed and the roof was thatched with palm leaves, while the bare ground served as a floor. One half formed a combined kitchen and living-room, the other a bedchamber. Both were fairly comfortably furnished.[1]

The West Indian negro had all the characteristics of his race. He stole, he lied, he was simple, suspicious, inefficient, irresponsible, lazy, superstitious, and loose in his sex relations. The food of the slaves was basically vegetable and was generally stewed or roasted. Singing and dancing were favorite pastimes; overdress and aping the manners of their betters were freely indulged in. The blacks' health was guarded by regular visits of physicians; hospitals and lying-in houses were to be found on most properties. Philosophical speculations brushed aside, the average imported worker doubtless enjoyed a better state than he had known in his African home and the estate labourers' material condition might well have aroused envy among the general run of eighteenth century European peasantry, including the British.

[1] Edwards, *History*, II, 133–135. Lewis, *Journal*, pp. 107–112.

Up to the closing seventeen hundreds, the spiritual welfare of the negro received but scant attention. The Established Church did nothing for him; such as it was, Anglicanism ministered solely to the white residents. Their intellectual level was so far above that of the servile beings about them that the most elementary sermon they could have been expected to follow with any degree of interest would have been far beyond the latter's comprehension. The number of clergymen was small and church accommodations were limited. Then, too, the planters were unanimously opposed to any action likely to arouse discontent in the minds of their slaves. Such religious enterprises as might be undertaken among the blacks must needs, therefore, be carried on by separate bodies not dependent upon local support.

A beginning destined to have far-reaching consequences was made in 1754 when Z. G. Caries, a Moravian missionary, and two companions landed in Jamaica and commenced preaching to the slaves. Two years later, a co-religionist, Samuel Isles, established a mission in Antigua. Others were subsequently opened in St. Kitts and Barbados.

The Moravians wasted no time in theological contention or high-flown phraseology but sought rather to reach the negroes through setting forth simple truths in plain language. Great efforts were made to inculcate ideals of morality and Christian living. Marriage and fidelity were stressed; baptism was administered only after candidates had given practical evidence of a changed mode of living. Close watch was kept over the private lives of their adherents. Exclusion from communion was the punishment accorded backsliders. Progress was rather slow in all fields but Antigua; out of a membership of some 5,650 among British Caribbean residents in 1787, 5,465 were to be found in the latter island.[1]

Active Methodism appeared in the West Indies about the same

[1] Brown, *History of the Propagation of Christianity*, I, 257 ff. A. G. Spangenberg, *Account of the Manner in Which the . . . United Brethren Preach the Gospel and Carry on Other Missions* (London, 1789). Adolph Schulze, *Abriss einer Geschichte der Brüder-Mission* (Herrnhut, 1901). J. E. Hutton, *A History of the Moravian Missions* (London, 1923), Bk. I. Hutton, *Fire and Snow. Stories of Early Mission Enterprise* (London, 1908). T. J. Hamilton, *History of the Missions of the Moravian Church During the Eighteenth and Nineteenth Centuries* (London, 1900). J. H. Buchner, *The Moravians in Jamaica* (London, 1854). Anon., *Retrospect of the History of the Mission of the Brethren's Church in Jamaica, for the Past Hundred Years* (London, 1855). Anon., *Breaking of the Dawn, or Moravian Work in Jamaica, 1754–1904* (no imprint, n.d.).

time. Nathaniel Gilbert, a planter and speaker of the Antiguan assembly, had been in England and while there had received baptism with ten of his slaves at the hands of John Wesley. Upon his return in 1760, he established a congregation in his own home. The organization languished after his death, but a new start was made in 1778 upon the arrival of John Baxter, a shipwright by profession and an ardent Wesleyan, from the mother land. A chapel was built in 1783 and within three years the local membership approached the 2,000 mark.[1]

Baptist doctrines were introduced at the close of the Revolution when a considerable body of American loyalists and their blacks became residents of Jamaica. Among the new settlers were George Liele, a manumitted slave formerly pastor of a coloured Baptist church in Georgia, and Moses Baker, a member of his old congregation. In 1784, they began converting their fellows in this new scene and enjoyed a marked degree of success.[2]

Moravian achievements and the rise of these native churches provide ample evidence of the crying need there was for religious activity among the negroes, and the opportunity which awaited any who might initiate it. The large-scale missionary enterprises begun shortly before 1800, for the most part by dissenters and fraught with momentous consequences for master and bondsman alike, will be discussed elsewhere.[3]

The slave régime was marked by certain notable features—a great and growing disproportion between the number of blacks and whites, the rise of a half-breed class, and the failure of the servile stock to keep up its numbers. The following population tables, compiled principally from official returns, illustrate with some degree of accuracy at least the first of these tendencies.

[1] Thomas Coke, *An Account of the Rise, Progress, and Present State of the Methodist Missions* (London, 1804). Coke, *A History of the West Indies, Containing the Natural, Civil, and Ecclesiastical History of Each Island* (3 vols., Liverpool and London, 1808–1811), I, 212–213 and II, 427–436. George Smith, *History of Wesleyan Methodism* (3 vols., London, 1857–61), I, 560, 561. Abel Stevens, *The History of the Religious Movement of the Eighteenth Century Called Methodism* (3 vols., London, 1860–70), I, 267; II, 645–648.

[2] *The Baptist Annual Register, 1790–93* (London, n.d.), pp. 332–344, 540–545. "Letters Showing the Rise and Progress of the Early Negro Churches of Georgia and the West Indies," in *The Journal of Negro History*, I, 69 ff. F. A. Cox, *History of the Baptist Missionary Society, From 1792 to 1842* (2 vols., London, 1842), II, pp. 12 ff. Phillippo, *Jamaica Past and Present*, p. 106. Gardner, *Jamaica*, p. 344. The name is sometimes incorrectly spelled Lisle.

[3] In Chapters VIII, XI, and XII.

BARBADOS		
Year	*Whites*	*Slaves*
1768 [1]	16,139	66,377
1773 [2]	18,532	68,548
1783 [3]	16,167	57,434
1802 [4]	15,857	64,206

JAMAICA		
Year	*Whites*	*Slaves*
1768 [7]	17,949	166,914
1778 [8]	18,420	205,261
1788 [9]	18,347	226,432

DOMINICA		
Year	*Whites*	*Slaves*
1773 [5]	3,850	18,753
1804 [6]	1,594	22,083

MONTSERRAT [10]		
Year	*Whites*	*Slaves*
1772	1,314	9,834
1778	800	8,285
1811	444	6,732

TOBAGO		
Year	*Whites*	*Slaves*
1770 [11]	238	3,164
1775 [12]	391	8,643
1808 [12]	439	17,009

The relative number of pure Caucasians to full-blooded negroes fell steadily; in many cases the decline was actual as well. Such great disparity occasioned serious alarm. The deficiency laws already mentioned were designed to check this growing evil but were of no real avail. The Jamaican assembly further sought to meet the problem by laying additional charges on the entry of Africans. Thus, by act of February 13, 1774, an increase of 40s. per head duty, to be paid by the importer, was voted. This measure was renewed in December of the same year but, on complaint of British mercantile interests, it

[1] C. O. 28/51.
[2] C. O. 28/55.
[3] C. O. 28/42.
[4] C. O. 28/69.
[5] C. O. 71/4.
[6] C. O. 71/38.
[7] Long, *Jamaica*, I, 376 for the number of whites. *Musgrave Papers*, British Museum, Add. Ms. 8,133, folios 95, 96 for slaves.
[8] *Long Papers*, Br. Mus., Add. Ms. 18, 273, folio 93.
[9] C. O. 137/87.
[10] Enclosure in Governor Elliot to the Earl of Liverpool, March 14, 1811, C. O. 152/97.
[11] C. O. 101/14 (in Grenada correspondence).
[12] Sir William Young, *Statistical Report of the Island of Trinidad*, April 22, 1808, C. O. 285/13 (for both 1775 and 1808).

was disallowed, and Governor Sir Basil Keith was summarily ordered to refrain from assenting to any such legislation under penalty of removal from office.[1]

The exploiting British, amidst a teeming multitude of blacks, stood in constant apprehension of servile revolt. Nor was this without cause. Over a dozen outbreaks occurred in Jamaica alone during the eighteenth century. The most wide-spread of these, in 1760, cost the lives of sixty Europeans and 400 coloured inhabitants.

This danger was met by organizing militias under command of the governors. All whites between the ages of sixteen and sixty, clergymen alone excepted, were obliged to serve in them. Forces were assembled once a month for drill, maneuvers extending over several days were held annually and martial law was almost invariably proclaimed for the holiday season during which large bands of negroes congregated for merry-making. Weapons and uniforms were provided by the users themselves.[2]

Such island troops were, on the whole, very poorly trained. In time of peace the periodic mobilizations tended to degenerate into pleasure gatherings. Commissions were valued chiefly for the prestige they gave holders with the creole beauties; favoritism in granting them was common. During uprisings and invasions the bodies seldom distinguished themselves.[3]

Further protection was afforded by companies of regulars stationed in Jamaica from 1730, and in Barbados after 1780. The question of their support was a periodic source of conflict between colonial assemblies and the home government. Additional troops were sent to the Caribbean during times of war. Privates in West India regiments were, however, the lowest grade of men wearing British uniform. Governor Valentine Morris of St. Vincent wrote pointedly in 1777 that those "which have been sent out these last twelve months, are in general the very scum of the Earth. The Streets of London must

---

[1] The Earl of Dartmouth to Sir Basil Keith, March 3, 1775 and Keith to Dartmouth, June 12, 1775, C. O. 137/70.

[2] Militia laws were passed for short periods only, being renewed from time to time. For typical ones, see *An Act, for Establishing & Regulating a Militia, in the Islands of St. Vincent, Bequia, Canouan, and the Union* (St. Vincent, 1799) and *Militia Law of Tobago* (Bridgetown, 1795).

[3] Stewart, *An Account of Jamaica*, pp. 70–72. Anon., *Thoughts on the State of the Militia of Jamaica* . . . (Jamaica, 1783). The latter is the work of a young officer and urges reforms so as to render the island force a disciplined and truly useful organization.

have been swept of their refuse, the Gaols emptied. . . . I should say the very Gibbets had been robbed to furnish such Recruits, literally most of them fit only . . . to fill a pit with." [1]

Relations between the standing-army officers and the proprietors were far from cordial. There was sharp jealousy of them on the part of militia commission holders; and sad experience had taught the colonials to guard their daughters closely against the wiles of dapper braid wearers. The rank and file were left to shift for themselves socially and readily established relations with the negroes. [2]

The mortality rate among forces in the tropics was nothing short of frightful. Of 19,676 men sent to the British West Indies in 1796, no less than 17,173 died within five years. [3] Departure for Caribbean service was viewed almost as a voyage to the grave. [4] Many factors contributed to that end. In the first place, the soldiery was physically inferior. Then too, primary laws of hygiene and diet were ignored. Barracks were generally located on waste land near marshes and yellow fever took its toll. Quarters were neither roomy, airy, nor clean. Bathing was infrequent. The traditional scarlet designed for use in European climes was issued and salt meat was served five times weekly under standardized old-world rationing regulations. And lastly, new rum, a veritable poison, formed the customary drink. [5]

Home government officials were appalled at such shocking death returns and in 1795 sought to solve the problem of West Indian defence by organizing negro companies recruited through purchase from among the best-conditioned slaves in the islands. The experiment was viewed with horror by the colonials. Although in the midst of war

[1] In C. O. 260/4, under date of February 11.
[2] Stewart, _A View . . . of Jamaica_, p. 161. Bayley, _Four Years' Residence_, pp. 53, 54, 236, 331. Coleridge, _Six Months_. p. 255.
[3] Southey, _Chronological History_, III, 227. Schomburgk, _Barbados_, p. 78.
[4] Pinckard, _Notes_, I, 15, 16.
[5] Alexander, _Transatlantic Sketches_, pp. 135, 137, 147, 149, 150. Joseph, _History of Trinidad_, pp. 34, 35. Schomburgk, _Barbados_, pp. 84, 85. See also Anon., _Suggestions Relative to the Preservation of the Health of the Troops in the West Indies_ . . . (London, 1807). Thomas Dancer, _A Brief History of the Late Expedition Against Fort San Juan, So Far as it Relates to the Diseases of the Troops_ . . . (Kingston, 1781). John Hunter, _Observations on the Diseases of the Army in Jamaica_ . . . (London, 1788). S. E. Maunsell, _Contributions to the Medico-Military History of Jamaica_ (Jamaica, 1891). "Mortality in the regiments sent to the West Indies," in _The Scot's Magazine_, September, 1788, p. 448. John Rollo, _Observations on the Diseases Which Appeared in the Army in St. Lucia, in 1778 and 1779_ (London, 1781). J. Bell, _An Inquiry Into the Causes Which Produce, and the Means of Preventing Diseases Among British Officers, Soldiers, and Others in the West Indies_ (London, 1791).

with the neighboring French,[1] they offered violent opposition to it and were keenly resentful when the project was put into operation over all objections. Their fears that this must lower white prestige and threatened ultimate carnage were well-founded, but fortunately they were never realized. A deliberate arming of bondsmen to defend their masters marks the opening of a new epoch in interracial relations in the Caribbean.[2]

The appearance and rapid growth of a mixed blood element offered concrete evidence of the Anglo-Saxon's moral break-down in the torrid zone. This phenomenon arose chiefly from his transitory residence there. Comparatively few wives were brought out and concubinage was universal. The highest aim of a colored girl of tolerable person was to become the mistress of a planter, overseer, bookkeeper, merchant, or soldier. Mothers sought such unions for their daughters. The position assured them lives of ease, marked prestige in their own circle, and qualified them to become the mates of desirable freedmen when, in the course of time, they should have been cast off. The system pervaded all ranks of society. During the administration of Governor Ricketts in Barbados a comely negress reigned at the government house and enjoyed all a wife's privileges; save presiding publicly at his table.[3]

Varying amounts of Caucasian blood resulted in gradations of color on which a semi-caste system was created. The offspring of a white man and a negro woman was known as a mulatto; the cross between a white and a mulatto, a quadroon; that between a white and a quadroon, a mustee; while the union of white and mustee produced musteefinos. These distinctions were jealously guarded; the farther from negro ancestry an individual stood the higher his social rank. Those above three steps removed from the full black in lineal digression were officially deemed to be white; all below it were mulattos, so-called "persons of color," in the eyes of the law.[4]

Children born of slave mothers followed their status. The artisan class was largely recruited from their ranks. They were, however,

[1] See Chapter VII.

[2] J. W. Fortescue, *A History of the British Army* (In progress, London, 1899–), IV, 542, 543. Alfred B. Ellis, *The History of the First West India Regiment* (London, 1885). West India Committee Archives—*Minutes of the meetings of the West India Planters and Merchants*, III (1801–1804), *passim*. James E. Caulfield, *One Hundred Years' History of the 2nd Batt. West India Regiment from Date of Rising, 1795, to 1898* (London, 1899).

[3] Poyer, *Barbados*, pp. 639, 640.

[4] Lewis, *Journal*, pp. 106, 107; Long, *Jamaica*, II, 321.

frequently manumitted by their fathers. The issue of negresses who had been emancipated were themselves free. Such boys and girls were at times educated in England. But, as limits had in many cases been set to the value of property which a person of color might inherit,[1] private acts of the island legislature were required to secure their recognition as full heirs and to insure their enjoying all the rights of British subjects.[2] The steady growth of a hybrid people, but partially free and suffering numerous disabilities, holding itself above the blacks, yet not granted equality by the whites, portended evil.

A fundamental feature of the old plantation system was the failure of a strong creole stock of negroes to develop and to maintain itself. The case of an Antiguan estate, reported in 1775,[3] which had not had a purchased slave added to its working force in twenty years and on which fifty-two wenches were then with child, was the rare exception. Generally speaking, births were notoriously infrequent and deaths among infants were inordinately high. The supply of laborers could be kept up only through buying hands as age and disease came into play.

This resulted from a variety of causes. To begin with, there was an unhappy lack of proportion between the sexes; less than one third of the slaves imported were women. In 1789, there was an excess of 30,000 males in Jamaica alone. Then too, but slight attempt was made to establish a balance on a given property, the ratio at times being as great as five men to one female. Engrossment of the latter by the whites and the practice of polygamy by head negroes, such as the drivers and artificers, further increased the disproportion.

Licentiousness and profligacy naturally resulted. Yaws, a disease akin to syphilis, was widespread and occasioned innumerable still-births. Miscarriages were frequent. Babes, furthermore, were suckled

---

[1] £2,000 currency in the case of Jamaica by a law of 1768.

[2] Typical private acts of such a nature are that "to entitle Francis Clarke [etc. Six, all told], the reputed children of Robert Clarke, of the Parish of Saint Catherine, Gentlemen, by Charlotte Pawlett, a Free Mulatto Woman, to the same Rights and Privileges with English Subjects, under certain Restrictions," and that "to authorize and enable William Wright of the Parish of Portland, in the County of Surry . . . to sell and dispose of his Estate, both real and personal in this island, by Deed of Will, in such Manner as he shall think proper, notwithstading . . . 'An Act to prevent the inconveniences arising from exorbitant Grants and Devices made by white Persons to Negroes . . .'" in *Acts of Assembly, Passed in the Island of Jamaica; From 1770, to 1783, inclusive* (Kingston, 1786), pp. 11, 30, 31.

[3] Andrews, ed., *Journal of a Lady*, p. 104.

for excessively long periods—a year and a half and even more—during which time pregnancies did not, of course, occur.[1] On Worthy Park plantation in Jamaica, with eighty negresses of child-bearing age, the births at the close of the eighteenth century averaged but nine a year;[2] on one of Mathew Lewis's estates in the same island some time later, with upwards of 330 blacks well divided as to sex, but a dozen children per annum were born.[3]

Fully one fourth of the young negroes died within the first two weeks, largely from lockjaw [4] brought on by the primitive treatment attending accouchement. Ailments peculiar to early infancy, too, took a large toll. Among the females belonging to Lewis, one had but a single child out of ten survive, another, one of seven, a third, two out of fifteen.[5] Only 159 of the 345 children whose births are listed in the Worthy Park records were saved.[6]

Various expediments to encourage procreation and the rearing of healthy offspring were resorted to. Long recommended the granting of rewards to mothers,[7] which was subsequently undertaken by divers planters. Thus, Sir William Young, visiting his St. Vincent properties in the last decade of the eighteenth century, presented "five yards of fine cotton, at 2s. 6d. per yard, of the gayest pattern, to make a petticoat" to each of his wenches who had borne children,[8] and Mr. Cuthbert of Jamaica gave two dollars to every woman whose infant survived.[9]

.The Jamaican slave act of 1788 likewise allowed the owner of each estate twenty shillings per negro child born and residing on the property over and above the decrease among the blacks from death annually, this amount to be deducted from his taxes and to be given to the plantation overseer.[10] In 1792, a new law increased the sum to

---

[1] Edwards, *History*, II, 110, 113, 143, 144. Long, *Jamaica*, II, 385, 435, 436. Lewis, *Journal*, p. 332. Stewart, *An Account of Jamaica*, pp. 276, 277.

[2] Phillips, *American Negro Slavery*, p. 61.

[3] Lewis, *Journal*, pp. 320, 321, 380, 381, 388.

[4] Edwards, *History*, II, 136, note k.

[5] Lewis, *Journal*, pp. 97, 111.

[6] Phillips, *American Negro Slavery*, p. 61.

[7] *Jamaica*, II, 439, 440.

[8] See his "History of the West Indies &c. A Tour Through the Several Islands of Barbados, St. Vincent, Antigua, Tobago, and Grenada, in the Years 1791, and 1792," in Bryan Edwards, *An Historical Survey of the Island of St. Domingo* . . . (London, 1801), p. 271.

[9] Cundall, ed., *Lady Nugent's Journal*, p. 37.

[10] *The New Act of Assembly of the Island of Jamaica . . . Commonly Called the New Consolidated Act, Which Was Passed by the Assembly on the 6th*

£3 and further provided that any negress who was the mother of six living children was to be exempted from field labor while her owner was to be relieved of paying the customary poll tax on her.[1]

But so long as mature workers could be purchased as cheaply as they could be reared and with less trouble, little concern was felt over the necessity of constantly resorting to fresh entries of blacks, and, until such supplies were cut off, only scant attention was paid to conditions making impossible the healthy growth of a domesticated creole stock.

of November—by the Council on the 5th Day of December—and by the Lieutenant Governor on the 6th day of December, 1788; Being the Present Code Noir of That Island (London, 1789).

[1] Published in complete form in Edwards, *History*, II, 151 ff. See clauses XXXV and XXXVI.

CHAPTER II

TROPICAL AMERICAN AGRICULTURE

The agrarian system upon which British Caribbean society rested was characterized by large estates, monoculture, absenteeism, and the use of antiquated methods with tenacious adherence to them as well as by the existence of heavy encumbrances upon plantations and the use of black slave labor which have already been discussed.

The cultivation of tropical crops could best be carried on along lines of large-scale production. Small properties could not support the heavy overhead costs entailed by the purchase and maintenance of negroes and elaborate equipment. The scarcity of good land conveniently located with regard to shipping facilities and rapid soil exhaustion under prevailing methods of exploitation made the patenting of more than could be worked a customary safeguard for the future. Reservation of great tracts was encouraged by the disuse into which quit-rent laws had fallen and the natural disinclination of the governing proprietary body to tax idle ground. Easy credit, too, facilitated the monopolizing of extensive unopened areas by a few opulent individuals.

Throughout the seventeen hundreds, small holdings steadily disappeared. The successful capitalistic grower purchased his less favorably placed neighbors' estates. Such aggrandizements were particularly numerous in times of distress and war when increased expense of production made the small owner's position untenable. More and more did the few-acred men give way to the producer with ample resources. Shortly before the American Revolution, but 132 persons held 106,352 acres of land in St. James parish, Jamaica. Of these, only ten possessed less than fifty each.[1] The average sugar cultivator near the turn of the century owned some 900 acres, and it was then commonly felt "that middling planters will go in their turn." [2] The

[1] Long, *Jamaica*, I, 406. Gardner, *Jamaica*, p. 160.
[2] Bryan Edwards, in outlining the cost of setting up a sugar plantation, went on the basis of 600 acres but stated that the larger area was actually more nearly representative. *History*, II, 250, 251. See also Robert C. Dallas, *The History of the Maroons* (2 vols., London, 1803), II, 370.

fact that properties were seldom divided and that inheritance by primogeniture was the general rule served to aggravate the situation.

Manifold evils arose from the formation of big estates. They prevented the growth of a sound body of proprietors with deep-rooted community interests, made impossible any notable increase in the white population, and checked normal economic advance. Two expedients were resorted to in an effort to check the movement. Antigua penalized reservation by laying heavy assessments against arable parcels of land kept out of cultivation. The Jamaican legislature instituted new quit-rent regulations in 1768, providing for the annual collection of such sums with the taxes. They were, unfortunately, soon discontinued. A combination of the two measures in permanent laws throughout the British West Indies would have had most beneficial results, but control of the local councils and assemblies by the very class to whom they would have been applicable made this impossible. The home government was by no means insensible to the faults of such a land system, but was powerless to remedy them. It did, however, as we shall see, consistently seek to prevent the rise of a similar state of affairs in the territories acquired after the second half of the seventeen hundreds by carefully restricting grants there.[1]

Man, not Nature, bound the Caribbean planter to monoculture. Each property yielded but one product, as sugar, cacao, coffee, cotton, pimento, ginger, or indigo and a given possession's exports consisted primarily of some single commodity. While the "sugar colonies" were adapted to any form of torrid zone agriculture, there was little diversity in crops. The primary one gave them their name, for cane growing, which offered the quickest way to wealth, was most commonly followed. Cotton was raised quite generally but on only a relatively small scale. The other articles seldom or never figured conspicuously in the cargoes cleared out from most of them.

Exceptions to the general rule of monoculture were to be found in Jamaica and in the islands ceded by France at the close of the Seven Years' War. Considerable quantities of all the several varieties of tropical produce were regularly shipped from the former, which enjoyed the advantages of size, great diversity in soil, and different climatic conditions arising from variations in altitude. Yet there, too, the tendency toward making sugar the single staple crop was clearly evident. Cacao, cotton, coffee, indigo, pimento, and ginger were raised on small plantations. When these were included in expanding estates,

[1] See page 113.

no further attention was given to such crops and sugar replaced them. Authorities in London were informed in 1774 that "from the loss of our manufacture of Indigo (having little or no vent for Coffee, Cotton and Pimento) we are daily losing our small settlers and rich individuals buy their Lands, and enlarge their sugar plantations." [1]

The average annual exportation of British-grown cacao from Jamaica to England for the five years 1763–1767 was 18,200 pounds; that to Great Britain (substantially the same market, as Scotch participation in the West India trade was small) for 1815–1819 was but 13,440 pounds, notwithstanding noteworthy development which the island had undergone in the interim. Cotton shipments included both the local product and that received from foreign plantations for sale in Liverpool and thus afford uncertain indications as to the actual extent of its cultivation in Jamaica. It is significant, however, that the average annual exportation to England for 1763–1767 was 566,080 pounds and to Great Britain for 1815–1819 only 672,581. On the other hand, the average annual exportation of sugar to England in the first period was 650,360 hundredweight and that to Great Britain in the later one, 1,593,507, or two and a half times as much. [2]

Sugar production had never become the prevailing occupation in France's West India possessions as it had in the British Caribbean. Cacao, coffee, and cotton properties abounded there, and sugar was but one of several soil-products engaging the French planters' attention. In the case of Dominica, indeed, exports of coffee frequently exceeded those of sugar. The explanation for this healthy diversification is to be found in the fact that many of the French colonists' holdings were too small to make cane growing practical. The contrast between the agrarian systems of the British islands and those settled by France but subsequently transferred to Great Britain is strikingly illustrated by the following table:

IMPORTS FROM THE BRITISH WEST INDIES INTO ENGLAND FOR THE YEAR 1770 [3]

Colony	Cacao, lbs.	Coffee, lbs.	Cotton, [4] lbs.	Indigo, lbs.	Muscovado (i.e., raw) sugar, cwt.
Antigua	——	——	15,958	——	226,469
Barbados	——	——	117,555	——	172,706

[1] In "Answers to Queries Relative to the State of the Island," in C. O. 137/70.
[2] Compiled from Customs 3/63–67 and 5/4–8, Public Record Office.
[3] Compiled from Customs 3/70, P. R. O.
[4] In consequence of there being no difference in duty rates, the custom house records at this period do not distinguish between British-grown and foreign-

IMPORTS FROM THE BRITISH WEST INDIES INTO ENGLAND FOR THE YEAR
1770 (*Continued*)

Colony	Cacao, lbs.	Coffee, lbs.	Cotton, lbs.	Indigo, lbs.	Muscovado (*i.e., raw*) sugar, cwt.
Dominica * Created a free port in 1766. Data give no clue to local development.					
Grenada *	305,400	1,592,600	1,026,296	1,700	196,130
Jamaica	24,100	171,100	606,580	68,521	718,865
Montserrat	——	500	59,206	——	55,370
Nevis	——	——	8,227	——	68,268
St. Kitts	——	100	164,632	——	220,164
St. Vincent *	93,500	299,400	64,714	——	38,394
Tobago *	——	——	——	——	1,686
Tortola Data wholly unreliable because of smuggling activities.					

* Ceded to Great Britain in 1763 by the Peace of Paris, Dominica, St. Vincent and Tobago had technically been regarded as neutral islands, reserved for the natives, since 1748. The first two, however, contained a large number of Frenchmen. Tobago had remained undeveloped and its exploitation was begun by the British. Grenada had been a regular French colony.

Once British, land in the ceded islands was rapidly opened, but characteristically enough, the advance in sugar production was wholly disproportionate to the increased output of other commodities. During the five years 1764–1768, immediately following their change in ownership, the average annual exportation of cacao from Grenada and St. Vincent to England was 287,240 pounds. That for 1774–1778 was 378,700 pounds, an increase of 31 per cent. In the first period, the average annual exportation of coffee from the two islands to England was 1,605,419 pounds; that in the second, 2,826,560 pounds, an increase of 76 per cent. But the average annual exportation of muscovado to England rose from 93,268 hundredweight to 201,741 in the same time, a gain of 116 per cent.[1]

The new fields laid out were, almost without exception, planted in cane. Tobago, which was virgin country, became a sugar island from the first. In St. Vincent and Grenada, British immigrants purchased coffee plantations of such Frenchmen as were desirous of removing to islands still under the Bourbon flag, and turned

grown cotton shipped from the British islands. There is no means of ascertaining the amount of each in the totals. But these figures give some indication at least of the extent of local cultivation. Thus, obviously, Grenada was producing cotton on a scale undreamed of in any of the colonies settled by Englishmen.

[1] Customs 3/64–68, 74–78, P. R. O. Dominica is not included as it was created a free port in 1766. As already stated, the development of Tobago was begun by the British.

them into sugar estates.[1] From 1766, a premium was placed on cane cultivation in Dominica by the parliamentary act of that year establishing a free port at Roseau. This sought to protect the national revenue against fraud by declaring all products imported from the colony into Great Britain, excepting muscovado and rum certified to be of local origin, subject to the customary foreign produce duties,[2] and thereby promptly checked all other forms of agricultural enterprise.

The importance of fiscal legislation in the home country as a factor making for monoculture in the British West Indies is likewise admirably illustrated in the cases of indigo and coffee. During the last half of the seventeenth century, the former had become an important Jamaican product. In 1672, the district of Vere in Middlesex County alone had had sixty works producing about 50,000 pounds a year. Seventy gentlemen there had been enabled to keep carriages on the profits from them. However, an unfortunate parliamentary tax of 3s. 6d. per pound put an end to this prosperity.[3] In the five years 1763–1767, the average annual exportation from the island to England was 43,041 pounds; in the period 1815–1819, it was but 12,756 pounds to Great Britain.[4]

In 1770, there were only some twenty planters growing indigo in Jamaica.[5] Bryan Edwards knew as many more well-qualified persons who had attempted it during his residence of two decades in the colony, but they had uniformly abandoned their projects.[6] Cultivation of this crop in Barbados had ceased by the middle of the seventeen hundreds.[7] Similarly, in 1780, Governor William Burt of the Leeward Islands wrote to the Lords Commissioners of Trade and Plantations, "The high Duties . . . together with the greater advantage which was thought would attend Sugar Works, has entirely annihilated the Indico Plantations so that in fact I do not know of any within this Government." [8]

---

[1] Lieutenant-Governor Morris to the Secretary of State, May 24, 1775, and "Answers to Queries Relative to Grenada" (in French), both in C. O. 101/18.

[2] Governor Shirley to the Earl of Dartmouth, March 3, 1775, C. O. 71/5. For the free port act, see pages 138 ff.

[3] Long, *Jamaica*, I, 415 ff.; II, 71 ff.; III, 675, 680, 681. Edwards, *History*, II, 288.

[4] Customs 3/63–67 and 5/4–8, P. R. O.

[5] Long, *Jamaica*, III, 681.

[6] *History*, II, 287.

[7] Schomburgk, *Barbados*, p. 153.

[8] C. O. 152/34, no. 75.

In vain was the commodity placed on the British free list at the turn of the century and subsequently admitted at low rates;[1] the industry had been definitely ruined.

Coffee production was long checked by the excessive charges which it was forced to bear upon entrance into the British market. These were purposely set high lest extensive introduction of the berry reduce tea consumption. The duty and excise at the close of the American Revolution were nearly five times the product's sales value. In 1783, they were lowered a shilling a pound and imports at once doubled.[2] Nine years later, coffee for home consumption was still burdened with a customs charge of £3.18.6 per hundredweight plus 6½d. per pound to the excise.[3] The duty subsequently varied from 1s. 5⅛d. per pound in 1795 to 1s. 7⅞d. in 1806, but it was reduced to 7d. in 1808 and, after rising again to 1s. in 1819, was set at 6d. in 1825.[4]

The stimulation given coffee planting by these successive favorable readjustments was truly remarkable. The average annual exportation from Jamaica to England had been 37,180 pounds in the five years 1763–1767; that to Great Britain for the period 1815–1819 was 15,229,960 pounds—no less than 410 times as much![5] High duties thus wiped out one form of tropical agriculture and long directly checked the growth of another.

The control of Caribbean properties by absentee interests had its origin in a variety of causes. Tropical America never became home to the English-speaking planters. Limited production coupled with monopolization of the British market under the navigation acts brought the West Indians immense profits and made residence in Great Britain possible for most of them. Thus the islands became but temporary places of abode, to be forsaken so soon as holdings should have been sufficiently exploited to yield ample incomes. The education of creole youth abroad halted the growth

---

[1] For a table of indigo duties, 1789–1823, see *Gt. Br., H. C., Sess. Pap.*, 1823, XVII (58), p. 95.

[2] Edwards, *History*, II, 290.

[3] *Ibid.*, II, 438.

[4] For a table of duties on coffee entered into the United Kingdom, 1792–1829, see *Gt. Br., H. C., Sess. Pap.*, 1830, XXV (466). It is interesting to note that the great reduction of 1808 resulted in coffee becoming a favorite breakfast drink with workingmen in place of the old porter or purl or gin, and that it increased sobriety and renewed the popularity of coffee-houses with excellent social results. George, *London Life*, p. 306.

[5] Customs 3/63–67 and 5/4–8, P. R. O.

of staunch colonial sentiment, as has been seen,[1] and was to a considerable extent responsible for the progressive decline in the nummer of landed residents.

Inheritance and the custom of borrowing heavily in the mother-country with trans-Atlantic real-estate as security likewise played important rôles in the creation of an absentee landlord class. Primogeniture prevailed, both from the force of example in England and because of the peculiar nature of plantation properties which formed single, indivisible units. Younger children were provided for through annuities charged against the estates, and, owning nothing in the colonies and bound to them by no intimate ties, they regularly settled down overseas. When, as frequently happened, one of them became proprietor through the death of the elder brother without legitimate offspring, he was wholly unfitted to assume control of his legacy and seldom even engaged passage to take formal possession of it.

Loaning money on Caribbean mortgages constituted an important form of investment for British capitalists. London, Liverpool, and Glasgow merchants in particular made heavy advances to the planters. When the latter became involved, the hypothecated lands passed to their creditors, few of whom had ever seen the new world and none of whom were qualified to manage tropical farming enterprises. From the close of the eighteenth century when prices on West Indian produce steadily declined, such changes of ownership became both general and rapid.

In the early 1790's, Bryan Edwards wrote: "Much of the greatest part of the present inhabitants of the British West Indies came into possession of their plantations by inheritance or accident. Many persons there are, in Great Britain itself, who, amidst the continual fluctuation of human affairs, and the changes incident to property, find themselves possessed of estates in the West Indies which they have never seen." [2]

Edwards was willed his own plantations by an uncle. Both Mathew Lewis, whose charming journal [3] has frequently been referred to in these pages and Cynric Williams, whose travel book [4] has been

---

[1] Pages 22 ff.

[2] Edwards, *History*, II, 35.

[3] *Journal of a West India Proprietor Kept During a Residence in the Island of Jamaica.*

[4] *A Tour Through the Island of Jamaica from the Western to the Eastern End in the Year 1823.*

drawn upon, also fell heir to properties in Jamaica. Unlike many others, they actually visited them.

The British Caribbean suffered from the curse of absenteeism from earliest times, but not until the second half of the seventeen hundreds did the residence of proprietors abroad become common. Raw sugar, which had sold at an average of 16s. 11¼d. per hundredweight in 1733, rose to 42s. 9½d. by 1747.[1] This sharp advance in selling value was followed by a general exodus of planters for England, where their ample incomes enabled them to indulge freely in conspicuous consumption. The movement went on unchecked for half a century. When the permanent decline in revenues from tropical American holdings then set in, overseas owners as a class failed to return, take personal possession and salvage what they might, but instead, after exhausting credit, they transferred their estates to holders of their paper, while planters actually in the West Indies, becoming hopelessly entangled in debt, pursued a similar course and forsook the colonies.

The increase in absentee proprietorship and its general prevalence during this period are best demonstrated by a consideration of one of the most deplorable consequences which followed in its wake. The varied social results—a growing disproportion between whites and blacks, the fear régime, the absence of local pride and feeling as well as the debasement of island society—have been dealt with elsewhere.[2] The effect on government was even more striking. Places of honor and trust came to be held by mediocre men; multiple office-holding became common and was carried to extravagant lengths. The lamentable outcome was that in many cases the legislatures, courts, and administrations failed to function properly and that the machinery of the representative system actually broke down.

The West Indian colonial governments had been designed to meet the needs of communities embracing considerable bodies of landed whites. Members of the appointive councils were to be chosen from among the most respectable great estate owners; election to the assemblies was likewise on the basis of a property qualification. With the growth of absenteeism, it became increasingly difficult to find suitable persons to sit in the upper houses and the popular bodies tended more and more to be composed of the professional men of

[1] Frank W. Pitman, *The Development of the British West Indies, 1700–1763* (New Haven, 1917), pp. 186, 187.

[2] In Chapter I.

low caliber, little education, mean abilities, and small proprietary interest comprising the resident white population of the colonies.

No one reading the despatches for these years can fail to be impressed by the constant departure of council members for Europe and the frequent necessity there was for making new appointments, as well as by the growing perplexity of the governors over finding proper individuals to fill these important positions. Quorums could not, at times, be formed, and law making was halted. As early as 1767, a memorial from the inhabitants of Barbados to the king complained of the great obstruction to public business occasioned by the absence of many of the local councilmen.[1] This situation became common and, to obviate the evil, executives were instructed some two decades later to grant them permission to sail from the islands only when working groups would still be left, the resignations of those long abroad were called for, and the rule that council members absent for more than one year forfeited their offices was adopted.[2]

The old form of government became quite unworkable in Tobago in 1828 from the almost total lack of resident proprietors. There were then but three plantation owners remaining—the chief justice, the speaker of the assembly, and a one-time member of the council, lately dismissed because of his unfitness for the place. It became necessary, therefore, to form an upper house consisting of the judicial officer and five unpropertied individuals—the attorney-general, the collector of customs who was a foreigner, two estate managers of short residence, and a physician.[3]

By 1820, the Barbadian assembly was composed chiefly of persons of little standing.[4] Dominica's white population declined to such an extent (from 3,850 in 1773 to 1,325 in 1811 and to 805 in 1829) [5] that by 1816 there were few respectable land owners still in the island and its elected chamber consisted of five proprietors, eight mer-

[1] Poyer, *Barbados*, p. 345.

[2] These common sense regulations were ill-received by certain of the absentee members who chose to see in them something of a personal affront. Thus, James Stephen, later celebrated for his anti-slave activities and father of the equally famous James Stephen, legal adviser to the Colonial Office, who had been a member of the council of St. Kitts and had returned to England in 1794, considered himself abused when the Duke of Portland called for his resignation in 1796. He engaged in a caustic controversy over the matter but at length yielded, couching his letter of resignation in terms of offended dignity. See C. O. 152/78, under "Miscellaneous."

[3] Governor Blackwell to Sir George Murray, Sept. 25, 1828, C. O. 285/35.

[4] President Skeete to Earl Bathurst, Dec. 17, 1820, in C. O. 28/89.

[5] See page 30.

chants, one medical practitioner, and five plantation attorneys or managers.[1] Sixteen years later, the greater part of the members held only the minimum amount of fifty acres requisite for election and that merely as a formality, the land generally being waste. A total of 153 electors then returned nineteen assemblymen, but sixteen of these were chosen by no more than ninety-nine voters.[2]

In 1772, Governor Leyborne of Grenada wrote to the Earl of Hillsborough:[3] "I am sorry to say the Assembly does not proceed with business as I could wish, tho, from the people that compose it, it is no more than what I expected. There are so many absentees Elected, that it is with great difficulty they can make a House. . . . The only persons of property and experience that are Elected into the Assembly are unfortunately still absent. Their absence is the more to be regretted, as there is but one member now in the island, that was ever in that capacity before, from this circumstance Your Lordship will not be surprised at the irregularity & confusion that must necessarily be the consequence of such inexperience." In 1775[4] and again in 1790,[5] the Grenadan assembly was unable to take up business because of the lack of quorums.

In the early 1770's, Edward Long reported that the inhabitants of Jamaica were flocking to England and North America beyond the example of former times.[6] The governor at the same time informed home authorities that "from the opulence of the Country, great numbers are enabled to live at home."[7] In making a tour of the island in 1803, Lieutenant-Governor Nugent found scarcely a white family among the proprietors, and did not see a single one in going from St. Catherine parish in the south to that of St. Mary in the north.[8] Out of eighty estate owners in one of the upper districts of the colony, not over three were then in actual residence.[9]

The result was inevitable. "The Representative Body is not composed of the principal landed Proprietors of the Island, very few

---

[1] Governor Maxwell to Earl Bathurst, November 7 and 10, 1816, C. O. 71/52.
[2] Governor MacGregor to the Secretary of State, March 26, 1832, C. O. 71/74.
[3] Under date of April 25, C. O. 101/16.
[4] Governor Leyborne to the Earl of Dartmouth, Nov. 5, 1775, C. O. 101/18.
[5] Lieutenant-Governor Mathew to William Windham, Feb. 27, 1790, C. O. 101/30.
[6] Jamaica, I, 386.
[7] "Answers to Queries," in C. O. 137/70.
[8] Lieutenant-Governor Nugent to Mr. Sullivan, Jan. 15, 1803, C. O. 137/110.
[9] Daniel McKinnen, A Tour Through the British West Indies, in the Years 1802 and 1803 (London, 1804), p. 108.

of whom, comparatively speaking, are resident in it. But among the leading Members are the Agents or Attornies merely of those Proprietors, or of British Merchants and Mortagees . . ." wrote the Duke of Manchester from Jamaica in 1810.[1] Thirteen years after, there was scarcely a member of the assembly with whom he could communicate confidentially, as most of the persons of influence and talent had withdrawn to Great Britain.[2]

A similar situation prevailed in the Leewards. "Very few of the Proprietors of Estates reside in this Island, but have retired with their Families to Europe," declared the legislature of St. Kitts in a petition to the crown in 1770.[3] Conducting public affairs was exceedingly difficult, as "all the landed Proprietors are Settled in Great Britain. . . ."[4] "Of the few white inhabitants who remain, Managers, Overseers, self-created lawyers, self-educated Physicians, and adventurous Merchants, with little real capital and scanty credit compose the greatest part. . . . To collect from such a state of Society, men fit to be Legislators, Judges, or Jurymen, is perfectly impracticable. Individual interest, personal influence, animosity of party feuds, weigh down the scale of Justice and divert the course of Legislative Authority into acts of arbitrary and unjustifiable powers, cloaked under the semblance, and dignified with the name of constitutional Acts."[5]

Government could scarcely be carried on in Montserrat, where the population declined from 1,314 whites in 1772 to 880 in 1788 and to 444 in 1811.[6] "The evil . . . must be accounted for by the defects of a constitution little adapted to the present state of the decreased, and decreasing, white population of this Island, which no longer furnishes a sufficient choice of men fit to fill the Legislatures, the Law Offices, Juries, Militia, or any other public department."[7]

By 1827, the population had decreased to such an extent that it became necessary to impose a fine of £5 currency on jurors for nonattendance and the number of peremptory challenges was reduced from twenty-three to twelve, "as the only means whereby it will be

[1] To the Earl of Liverpool, May 27, 1810, C. O. 137/128.

[2] To Earl Bathurst, Dec. 24, 1823, C. O. 137/154.

[3] Petition of the council and assembly of St. Kitts to the king, praying for the protection of royal troops, C. O. 152/50.

[4] Chief Justice George to the Duke of Portland, March 22, 1798, C. O. 152/78.

[5] Governor Elliot to the Earl of Liverpool, Nov. 21, 1810, C. O. 152/96.

[6] Governor Elliot to the Earl of Liverpool, March 14, 1811, C. O. 152/97.

[7] Governor Elliot to the Earl of Liverpool, Sept. 8, 1810, C. O. 152/95.

practicable to carry on the administration of Justice in the colony." [1]
Sir Patrick Ross, governor of Antigua, Montserrat and Barbuda, favoured the legislative and judicial union of Montserrat with Antigua, as, because of the few landed residents, "the Controul of the Island rests only in Certain Individuals, very few in Number." [2] A sufficient number of persons duly qualified as to property holding could scarcely be found to present themselves as candidates for membership in the assembly of Tobago in 1804.[3]

The filling of offices with unworthy and untrained individuals and the engrossing of several posts by a single person were natural corollaries of extensive absenteeism. Men of little or no legal training held judicial posts; truly remarkable concentrations of governmental functions in given local worthies without the slightest regard for incompatibilities were to be found.

Writing from Antigua in 1786, John Luffman said: "Here is a Court of Chancery and a Court of Vice Admiralty, at both of which the Governor, for the time being, presides; a Court of King's Bench and Grand Sessions at which the President presides; and a Court of Common Pleas, and a Court of Exchequer: the Judges of which are not lawyers, but planters, who are frequently dictated to and even directed by the Barristers, particularly when any cause which requires legal knowledge is in question, thereby giving up their honest opinions to the chicanery and artifice of an insolent and overbearing pleader." [4]

The most exaggerated case of the vesting of offices in a few hands occurred in Tortola. A visitor of the late 1820's has left a racy but in no wise overdrawn account of this.[5]

"Justice, long reputed *blind,* had here all her other faculties impaired; and the moral dry-rot which was abroad, had been allowed to reach and to contaminate the very crutches on which she hobbled.—Her guardian, he, in whom all the obligations of her sacred office had been reposed [one Crabb], and from whom all her salutary dispensations were expected to emanate for the safeguard and welfare of the community—was not only stricken in years and bordering on decrepitude, but he had not even the advantage of a legal education to qualify him for the trusteeship. He was nevertheless a legal Proteus—at one time a judge in the Court of King's Bench—at another, a judge in the Court of Common Pleas—

---

[1] Sir Patrick Ross to Earl Bathurst, Jan. 26, 1827, C. O. 7/19.
[2] To R. Wilmot Horton, Feb. 1, 1827, C. O. 7/19.
[3] Pres. James Campbell to Earl Camden, Aug. 27, 1804, C. O. 285/9.
[4] *Brief Account,* Letter IV.
[5] Wentworth, *West India Sketch Book,* II, 199–202.

then Chancellor, and Baron of the Exchequer—sometimes judge in Admiralty—and occasionally, as matter of course, presiding in the Court of *Error*. He was also *master* and *examiner in Chancery,* which gave him great insight to all matters upon which he might have to decide in the *Equity Court,* and the felicitous satisfaction of *confirming his own reports.* All this was so far well, that it were possible the functions of this hydra-headed judgeship were legally and equitably exercised; but he was also a *planter,* and a *merchant,* not *ostensibly* directing his legal mind to agriculture, and to considerations affecting tare and tret, barter, bottomry —bonds, brokerage, and ballast, and all the manifold detals of commercial enterprise, but he pardicated in the 'profit and loss' account of a co-partnership which subsisted between himself and . . . Mr. Rogers Isaacs, a public functionary of no less official weight in the community than himself.

"Mr. Isaacs bore his honours thick upon him. He was a puisne judge in each of the several courts we have enumerated, acting in concert with his legal and mercantile partner, although like him not qualified by education for the office. He was a member of the legislative council, as was also his colleague,—bearing the distinguished and distinguishing title of *honourable!* and an *aid-de-camp* to the governor. He held several attorneyships, so did his colleague—that is to say, he acted as the agent and representative of absent individuals whose estates he controlled, and he also held the important appointment of 'RECEIVER in chancery' for several other properties, to which he had been nominated either by the court in England, or by the equity judge in Tortola. These appointments had procured for him the occasional vocation and cognomen of a planter. That Mr. Isaacs the *merchant,* should supply Mr. Isaacs the *planter,* with all the necessaries he might require for the estates he controlled, was extremely natural; but we must confess that our finite comprehension recognized something repugnant to common sense and common honesty in the fact, that Mr. Isaacs, the *receiver* in chancery, should go before his mercantile partner the *master* in chancery, to audit and pass his, or rather *their* accounts, and that this legal and mercantile adjunct should afterwards sit in the character of *judge,* to decide upon any exceptions or questions which might be taken, or arise out of such a proceeding. We do really think that such a combination could not possibly exist between any two persons, or body of persons, without militating against justice, and compromising those moral obligations which the laws of civilized society have everywhere prescribed; and it goes far to show us to what a state of degradation the society here was reduced, when those whose station in life demanded of them a cautious regard to established principles of conduct, could manifest such singular indifference to public reproach, and to the gratifying convictions of self-respect."

The faithful discharge of official duties could scarcely be expected under such circumstances. Governor Brisbane of St. Vincent wrote in resigned exasperation in 1780: "You can have no Idea of the listless indifference and apathy that prevails in the conduct of public business in these colonies. Men from vanity accept public offices but few among our very limited population find themselves sufficiently interested in the public welfare to cheerfully perform without fee or reward the duties they have undertaken by accepting them. . . ."[1]

That the departure of such large numbers of proprietors threw unduly heavy burdens of a civil and military nature upon those who remained is self-evident. The absentees enjoyed full property protection afforded by the local governments and militias, yet took no part in conducting the former nor performed any onerous service in the latter. Simple fairness, therefore, dictated that they be required to make larger financial contributions to the support of state than those persons residing in the colonies. Indeed, two laws sought to accomplish this, one adopted in Jamaica which doubled the deficiency tax for 1761 and granted resident owners exemption for thirty slaves or 150 head of cattle,[2] and another of a similar nature enacted in Tobago in 1805.[3] But both were disallowed because of opposition registered overseas and these illuminating attempts to more nearly equalize responsibilities came to naught.

Communities of opulent West Indians were to be found in London and coastal cities such as Southampton and Bristol. Their homes were often luxurious—the Beeston Long mansion in Bishopsgate Street, London, and the Robert Hibbert residence just beyond the city, to mention but two, were noted for the refined splendor of their appointments.[4] Thanks to ample incomes, the planters were able to entertain handsomely. Their carriages were so numerous as to lead to complaint on the part of Londoners that, when they gathered, the streets for some distance about their meeting place were blocked.[5]

The story has oft been told of how, while visiting Weymouth, George III and Pitt encountered a wealthy Jamaican with an imposing equipage, including out-riders and livery that bespoke the rank of royalty. His Majesty, much displeased, is reported to have exclaimed, "Sugar, sugar, eh?—all *that* sugar! How are the duties, eh, Pitt, how are the duties?"[6] The dozens of memorial placques still to

[1] Under date of July 23, C. O. 260/37.
[2] Long, *Jamaica*, I, 387 ff.; II, 463, 464.
[3] William Windham to President Mitchell, July 17, 1806, C. O. 285/11.
[4] The Long home later became part of the London Tavern. Following the decline in value of tropical American property, Hibbert was forced to sell his country estate and moved to town.
[5] A curious protest on this score is to be found in the West India Committee archives.
[6] As in Wentworth, *West India Sketch Book*, II, 70, note. William Cobbett,

be seen on the walls of old churches in centers once inhabited by Caribbean-born whites, as those in All Saints' Church, Southampton,[1] give striking evidence of the social position they once held there.[2]

Some degree of organization prevailed among these absentees dwelling in Great Britain. The Planters' Club of London was formed before 1740 and continued in existence for several decades thereafter.[3] Its membership was made up of proprietors only and the body was distinct from merchant groups of the time. But, with the rise of common problems, the engaging of Caribbean families in the sugar trade and the passing of estates into the hands of creditor business men, the agrarian and trading interests in the capital city drew closer together and finally coalesced about 1780 in the formation of the Society of West India Planters and Merchants, of which more will be said presently. On occasion thereafter, the land owners from a given colony met to consider matters peculiar to it following a general meeting of this body, or, if none was being held, in special sessions called for that purpose.[4]

Non-resident proprietors coöperated with the West India merchants of Great Britain in keeping close watch of legislation touching their mutual interests. Together, they formed a powerful lobby

writing in the 1820's, speaks bitingly of the planters to be found at such resorts. "Cheltenham . . . is what they call a 'watering place,' that is to say a place to which East India plunderers, West India floggers, English taxgorgers, together with gluttons, drunkards and debauchees of all descriptions female as well as male, resort. . . ." "Rural Rides," quoted in Arthur Ponsonby, *English Diaries* (London, 1923), pp. 284, 285.

[1] The side and back walls of this church are liberally sprinkled with tablets in memory of Jamaican families. Bryan Edwards was buried in grave number 57 of the All Saints' catacombs following his death in July, 1800, at the age of fifty-seven.

[2] Members of various West Indian families have attained positions of prominence in English life. Thus, Charles R. Ellis, first Lord Seaford, grandson of George Ellis, one time chief justice of Jamaica, became the acknowledged leader of the West Indian group in parliament. George Ellis, the son of a member of the Grenadan assembly and a grandson, on his mother's side, of a member of the Jamaican council, won considerable fame as an author. Cardinal Henry Manning was a son of William Manning, the London West India merchant. The Mannings were Jamaicans. Rear-Admiral George Tobin and the dramatist John Tobin were sons of James Tobin, a merchant of Nevis. Viscount Lascelles, husband of Princess Mary, is descended from an old Barbadian family.

[3] Lillian M. Penson. "The London West India Interest in the Eighteenth Century," in *The English Historical Review*, July, 1921, pp. 380, 386.

[4] See for example, *Minutes of the Meetings of the Committee of Demerara and Berbice Planters and Mortgagees,* in the West Indian Committee archives.

seeking to secure the passage of bills which would be beneficial to them and to block others held to be inimical. As London was the seat of government and the outstanding planter and merchant groups centered in the metropolis, it was but natural that they should assume the leadership in such attempts. Indeed, only in extreme cases were the support and financial assistance of outport Caribbean organizations ever called for.

The tropical American interest's strength was made effective by the membership of both estate-owners and West India traders in parliament. Office was commonly obtained by purchase—"borough-mongering," as it was known. Two West Indians, Sir W. Codrington and Sir W. Stapleton, sat in the House of Commons as early as 1737.[1] The planters, plutocrats of their day, sought seats for the prestige they afforded as did manufacturers at a somewhat later day, and increased rapidly in number at Westminster.

In writing to his son on December 19, 1767, Lord Chesterfield lamented that although he had offered a borough-jobber £2,500 to secure the young man's election, "he laughed at my offer, and said, That there was no such thing as a borough to be had now; for that the rich East and West Indians has secured them all, at the rate of three thousand pounds at least; but many at four thousand; and two or three, that he knew, at five thousand." [2]

Active representatives of the Caribbean element in the lower house between 1785 and 1830 were Edward Lascelles (first Earl of Harewood), Henry Lascelles (the second Earl), Sir Ralph Payne (later Baron Lavington), William Beckford, Bryan Edwards, Charles Ellis (later Baron Seaford), George Hibbert, Joseph Marryat, John Gladstone (father of the later prime minister), William Manning, James Blair, John Mitchell, Sir Alexander Grant, Sir Edward East, Sir Bethel Codrington, Sir Michael Stewart, Joseph Birch, W. R. Keith Douglas, Sir William Young, Henry Bright, Ralph Bernal, W. Dickinson, Sir Rose Price, H. Dawkins Pennant, John Irving, Robert Gordon, John Plummer, and J. J. Ward.

Among the noblemen interested in trans-Atlantic properties were the Marquis of Chandos, the Earl of Balcarres, the Earl of Airlie,

[1] C. DeThierry, "Colonials at Westminster," in *United Empire,* Jan. 1912, pp. 79 ff.
[2] Philip Stanhope, Earl of Chesterfield, *Letters . . . to His Son, Philip Stanhope, Esq., Later Envoy Extraordinary at the Court of Dresden* (2 vols., London, 1774), II, 525.

Lord Hatherton, Lord Rivers, Lord Shelborne, Viscount St. Vincent, and Earl Talbot.[1] The close relations existing between the organized colonials and parliamentarians with West Indian connections is revealed by the fact that ten out of fifteen members of one of the most important committees in the history of the Society of Planters and Merchants held seats in the national legislature.[2]

The tropical colonists' political power was already impressive by the middle of the eighteenth century. A pamphleteer of 1760 stated that "Many Gentlemen of the West Indies have seats in the British House of Commons;" Mauduit, colonial agent for Massachusetts, wrote in 1764 that the Caribbean proprietors had a "very formidable number of votes" and Franklin at the same time declared that "the West Indians vastly outweigh us of the Northern Colonies." [3] Several measures of tremendous moment were adopted under pressure of the sugar lobbyists. The first of these was the Molasses Act of 1733,[4] striking at the American mainland trade with the French islands and subsequently reinforced by the Sugar Act of 1764.[5] Both were passed over the vigorous opposition of Atlantic seaboard residents [6] and did much to estrange them from the mother country. On Caribbean insistence, a notable concession was made in 1739 when permission was accorded the planters to ship muscovado direct to foreign ports of Europe provided British vessels were employed. Three years later, this privilege was extended to include

[1] Lists compiled from the records of the Society of West India Merchants and Society of West India Planters and Merchants, in the W. I. Comm. archives.

[2] W. I. Comm. Arch., *Min. W. I. Plant. and Mer.*, April 26, 1823. The committee in question aided in the formulation of governmental plans for ameliorating the slaves' condition in 1823. See pages 411 ff.

[3] From Anon., *Remarks on the Letter Address'd to Two Great Men* (London, 1760), pp. 46, 47; "Letter from Jasper Mauduit, Esq. to the Speaker of the House of Representatives . . .," in *Massachusetts Historical Society Collections*, Series I, Vol. 6, pp. 194, 195; and Albert H. Smyth, ed., *The Writings of Benjamin Franklin* (10 vols., New York, 1905–07), IV, 243, respectively, quoted by George L. Beer, *British Colonial Policy, 1754–1765* (New York, 1907), notes on pp. 136, 158.

[4] Geo. II c. 13. It laid a duty of 5s. per hundredweight against foreign plantation sugar of all grades entering the continental colonies, 9d. per gallon against foreign rum, and 6d. per gallon against foreign molasses.

[5] 4 Geo. III c. 15. Pitman, *Development*, pp. 243–270.

[6] See, for example, Anon., *Considerations Upon the Act of Parliament, thereby a Duty is laid . . . on Molasses, and . . . on Sugar of foreign Growth . . .* (Boston, 1764) and Anon., *Reasons Against the Renewal of the Sugar Act . . .* (Boston, 1764).

American bottoms despite the British ship-owners' objections.[1] Again in 1763, complying with the West India interest's demands, Canada was annexed to the empire in lieu of Guadeloupe or Martinique, whose enormous crops, entered in British markets, would have materially lowered prices and have brought the era of prosperity to a sudden close.[2]

We have noted how the absentees secured the disallowance of local acts aimed at them. West Indian agitation for free trade relations with the United States after the Revolution, tropical American opposition to the introduction of sugar from the orient, the proprietors' defense of the slave trade and human bondage, as well as their part in the sending of an expedition against the rival Dutch colonies in 1795 will be discussed in connection with those events.

Non-residents' estates were left in the hands of attorneys engaged under salary or, more commonly, at a commission of six per cent of the annual yield. These positions offered a ready way to affluence. An agent was privileged to occupy the great-house, to be served by the owner's blacks, to use his horses and carriage, to live off plantation produce, to pasture livestock on his own account, and, without expense of any kind, received his compensation as the first charge against the season's crop. In truth, to occupy such a post was frequently better than enjoying title to the land.

"The adage which I have often heard applied to masters of vessels and their owners . . . [is] applicable to these men," wrote John Luffman about 1785. " 'Fat managers and lean employers,' for I am very certain, to be . . . attorney to an estate of a non-resident, is better than to be its owner, the first receiving benefits without the least risque, while the latter is subject to every loss without receiving the advantages which ought, consistent with justice, to be his and not his stewart's." [3]

An heir inspecting his legacy at about the same time characterized attorneys as being "the locusts of the West Indies." [4]

The ill consequences of such a system would have been numerous under the best conditions, but, as it actually operated in the sugar

---

[1] 12 Geo. II c. 30 and 15 Geo. II c. 33. Pitman, *Development,* pp. 166–188. In case the destination was a port north of Cape Finisterre the vessel was, however, obliged to touch at some English one en route.

[2] Pitman, *Development,* pp. 334–360. Also see pages 112 ff.

[3] *Brief Account,* Letter XI.

[4] Anon. ("A—B—"), *A Short Journey in the West Indies* (2 vols., London, 1790), II, 6, 7.

colonies, they beggar description. Since all respectable individuals there with a knowledge of planting were engaged in it on their own accounts, non-agriculturists normally held the attorneyships. Island merchants were preferred as being permanent residents and men of some means and standing. With no check on them, they commonly purchased excessive quantities of stores from themselves in the names of the proprietors, met obligations thus incurred out of the produce remaining after having drawn their commissions, and shipped the balance to Great Britain.

But physicians, lawyers, and even clergymen were at times given charge of estates. Neither they nor the traders could reside on properties because of their professional duties, hence the overseers, men of low station and no learning, were in actual control. Where planters held the post, they likewise lived away from the properties entrusted to their care and gave them only such attention as could be spared from their personal holdings. The resident steward was the great exception rather than the rule.

An attorney, even though absent, might have kept the general management of a given plantation in his hands had that been the only one under his supervision. But direction of several was common and, with the growth in absenteeism, the number under the control of a given person steadily increased. Long states that already in 1770, a single Jamaican frequently superintended the exploitation of many properties.[1] In Tobago in 1823, the senior member of the council had charge of thirty-six, while other persons served as managers for ten and fifteen each.[2] Mr. Isaacs of Tortola, already mentioned, had oversight of half of the thirty sugar estates there a few years later.[3] Obviously, in such cases, an agent could maintain only the most superficial control and the real management fell increasingly into the hands of irresponsible overseers.

With no one whose capital was at stake in charge, the operation of an absentee's holdings was marked by gross extravagance. Not the slightest attempt was made to effect economies in buying; the waste in supplies, too, was notorious. No attention was paid to safeguarding the money originally laid out. The present alone was thought of. So long as the owner received a regular and steady income, he was content. Improvements were seldom made because they tempo-

---

[1] *Jamaica,* II, 406, 407.
[2] C. O. 285/28.
[3] Wentworth, *West India Sketch Book,* I, 236.

rarily reduced net returns. Buildings were dilapidated; fields were tilled until exhausted and then left to grow up in weeds; properties bore the ungenteel signs of general neglect. New lands were opened only at rare intervals because of the large initial expenditure and great amount of supervision required. Thus the actual value of Caribbean investments progressively declined.

Attorneys and overseers were primarily interested in the quantity of produce grown, the former because their compensation rested on a percentage basis, the latter because the test of success was ability to win the agents' favor. The tendency in managing absentees' estates, therefore, was to force output. Many of the inhumanities towards the negroes can be traced to a desire on the part of those directing tropical agricultural enterprises to increase production or at least to maintain it in the face of growing soil exhaustion.

Plantation methods were crude in the extreme but general improvement was impossible because of the non-resident owners' objections to expenditures which would in any way decrease their incomes as well as because of indifference on the part of those in charge. The attorneys, burdened with their own duties and the oversight of many holdings, had neither time nor inclination to undertake experiments which they little understood, and the results of which, even if successful, would scarcely compensate them for their additional effort. Nor did the salaried overseers betray the slightest interest in innovations which promised no obvious and immediate advantage to them. In consequence, all change was scoffed at while time-hallowed custom was obdurately followed.

The West Indians accepted Nature as they found her, being "so accustomed to follow a beaten track, that they tremble to leave it, for almost any consideration." [1] Gilbert Mathison, an enlightened Jamaican proprietor who returned to take possession of his estates in 1808 after a long absence, found the greatest obstacle to improvement "in the *bigotry* and *refractory disposition* of the professional planters; by whom I mean the regular-bred overseers, who are employed to conduct the ordinary business of plantations; and in the . . . old established *habits* of professional agents, who . . . are arrived at the highest situations of confidence and responsibility, by becoming the superintendents of a multiplicity of plantations, and the representatives of absentees." [2]

[1] Long, *Jamaica,* I, 455.
[2] In his *Notices Respecting Jamaica in 1808–1809–1810* (London, 1811), pp. 99, 100.

Henry Coleridge, visiting the colonies two decades later, found so much "statu-quoitism" among the islanders "that fire will hardly burn some of their prejudices out of their heads." [1]

The use of antiquated methods was most evident in the primary industry of sugar production. During the early eighteen hundreds this was still being carried on after the fashion of a century and a half before. When the brush had been cleared away with cutlasses and fired, a field was prepared for planting by digging parallel trenches from fifteen inches to two and a half feet wide and six inches deep the whole length with common hoes. "Holing," to give this its technical name, was the most arduous form of labor on a tropical estate and was performed by the great gang or by a group of hands, the "jobbing gang," especially hired for the purpose. In those exceptional cases where manuring was done, negresses carried out trays and baskets of dung or ashes on their heads and dumped them into the trenches. Cane cuttings were laid in them some inches apart, they were then filled, and the planting process was complete. Weeds were subsequently pulled out or were kept down with hoes and the ripe stalks were harvested with machetes.

Fields once cut grew up again and several crops—commonly three, but as many as five in some cases—were raised before reholing took place. Ratoons developed from the roots of the original canes after these had been gathered in and yielded decreasing quantities of liquid with each growth but were allowed to mature for several successive years to obviate the necessity of setting out a tract anew. When soil exhaustion was reached, a field was abandoned and the exploitation of another area, frequently a virgin one long kept in reserve, was begun.

Juice was extracted by "grinding" the stalks between rollers commonly operated by cattle, mules or horses. Such apparatus was clumsy, much of its force was lost in friction and canes were often not squeezed dry.[2] Boiling was carried on in open coppers. The resultant syrupy mass was allowed to granulate and after draining, which removed much of the molasses, the raw, or muscovado, sugar was packed in hogsheads for shipment to overseas refineries. Rum was distilled both from the scum arising during boiling and from molasses and was run into puncheons for transportation to market.[3]

[1] *Six Months,* pp. 176, 177.

[2] An illustration of an improved crushing apparatus will be found in the second edition of Edwards's *History,* II, Bk. 5, ch. 2.

[3] For the various aspects of sugar culture, see John Baker, *An Essay on the*

A better mode of planting as well as improved crushing and manufacturing processes were sorely needed. At home, scientific agriculture was gradually making headway during the latter part of the eighteenth century, yet this advance went all but unnoticed by the West Indians. Edward Long declared in 1774 that, while forward steps had been taken, the sugar industry in Jamaica was then still less than one third efficient;[1] and William Beckford, a resident from 1773 to 1788, held that one seventh of a crop was regularly wasted by neglect and want of foresight.[2]

Several Jamaicans had made use of plows in preparing the bed for cane cuttings before 1774,[3] either turning over the entire field which made subsequent holing by hoe easy or excavating the trenches themselves, but that implement won only scant favor throughout the Caribbean. British officials advocated its general introduction as a means of lightening the negroes' labor and, when queries on the state of slavery were sent to the colonies in 1788, information regarding its use was sought.

The reply from Antigua stated that while the plow had been experimented with on several plantations, repeated experience had shown it to be a very expensive instrument of cultivation and so wearing on man and beast that "as often as it has been tried, so often has it been laid aside. . . . Nothing has been yet found so completely suited to the disposition of the Slaves, and at the same time so efficacious . . . as the Hand Hoe."[4]

Governor Parry of Barbados reported that plows had been introduced on various local properties at different times, that the soil had proved unsuitable for them and that they had consequently been

Art of Making Muscovado Sugar (London, 1775). M. Cazaud, "Account of a New Method of Cultivating the Sugar Cane," in *Philosophical Transactions of the Royal Society of London*, LXIX (1779), pp. 207 ff. Samuel Martin, *An Essay Upon Plantership* (London, 1773). Johsua Peterkin, *A Treatise on Planting* (Basseterre, 1790). Thomas Roughley, *The Jamaica Planter's Guide* (London, 1823). [Gordon Turnbull], "An Old Planter," *Letters to a Young Planter; or, Observations on the Management of a Sugar Plantation* (London, 1785). Robert Hibbert, Jr., *Hints to the Young Jamaica Sugar Planter* (London, 1825). George R. Porter, *The Nature and Properties of the Sugar Cane; with Practical Directions for the Improvement of Its Culture, and the Manufacture of Its Products* (London, 1830).

[1] *Jamaica*, I, 439–441; II, 226, 227.
[2] *A Descriptive Account of the Island of Jamaica* (2 vols., London, 1790), II, 7.
[3] Long, *Jamaica*, I, 452.
[4] In "Answers to Queries," C. O. 152/67.

cast aside.[1] Lands in Dominica were declared to be of such a nature that plowing was an impossibility.[2] It had been tried on several estates in Grenada, but had been discontinued on all save one, "not answering the Expectations of the Planters." [3] No plows were known to have been used in Montserrat at any time; in Nevis, they had been given a trial on certain holdings but had been discarded because the cattle were unequal to the task of drawing them.[4]

Although Gilbert Mathison declared early in the nineteenth century that his cost of planting had sunk from £10 to £2.6.6½ currency per acre following substitution of the plow for the hoe and that its use reduced negro labor by three fourths,[5] few producers showed any inclination to emulate him. "The people of Jamaica make no novel experiments; they find the sugar planted; and where it is they continue to cultivate it," wrote a visitor more than two decades later.[6] "They find the hoe the ancient implement of the husbandman, and they have no desire to change it for the plough."

As late as 1840, the Reverend James Phillippo, for twenty years a Baptist missionary in the island, wrote: "The old methods . . . are the rule—the improvements the exception. The hoe, the cutlass, and the tray, and others of equal antiquity, still usurp the place of the plough and spade, the muck fork, the wheel-barrow, and the tumbril; whilst the practical knowledge of the last century is still regarded by many as superior to the experience and science of the present day." [7]

Differences in soil texture were commonly ignored; canes were planted wherever they would grow. Production on a given estate consequently varied considerably as the several kinds of land found within its boundaries came into use. Irrigation, long practiced by the French of St. Domingo, was almost unheard of in the British colonies. One or two Jamaican planters had adopted it with success before 1770 [8] and many years later three properties in Barbados were being watered by a spring,[9] but these cases were so unusual as to attract marked attention.

[1] "Answers to Queries," C. O. 28/61.
[2] "Answers to Queries," C. O. 71/14.
[3] "Answers to Queries," C. O. 101/28.
[4] "Answers to Queries," C. O. 152/67.
[5] *Notices Respecting Jamaica,* pp. 85–88.
[6] Madden, *Twelve Months' Residence,* I, 87.
[7] *Jamaica, Past and Present,* p. 41.
[8] Long, *Jamaica,* I, 448.
[9] Schomburgk, *Barbados,* p. 10.

Fertilization was adopted only when merciless cropping had brought on a sharp decline in output. Even so, it was imperfectly understood and was carelessly handled. The quantity of dung available was limited as it could not be conveniently collected. Horses and cattle were seldom stabled but were rather turned into pasture at night. The practice of erecting movable pens on various parts of a field soon to be planted was followed by many. Such soil enrichment was haphazard and, while ashes from burned canes and leaf mold supplemented the animal manure, a piece of ground was never restored to its state of the preceding year—the constant growing of canes mined the soil and exhaustion naturally followed.

The ravages of rats, which destroyed as much as one-twentieth of the entire sugar crop annually,[1] were accepted almost as a matter of course. A negro boy filled the post of catcher and dogs, poison and ferrets were to some extent effective in combating these rodents. But when occasional concerted attacks on them were made, an almost unbelievable number were taken, affording ample evidence of their prevalence. Thus, in one case, no less than 39,000 were slain on a single plantation during the space of six months.[2] The payment of a bounty was introduced on Mathew Lewis's Jamaican estates with wholesome results.[3]

A species of noxious growth, variously known as knot, devil's, and Vassal's grass,[4] was likewise calmly allowed to overrun estates and choke up canefields, causing considerable loss. The concern of a newcomer over this nuisance and his earnest attempts to get rid of it were held up to scorn about a great-house board in St. Kitts.[5]

The ruin worked by one pest, however, thoroughly aroused the planters affected. In the 1770's, carnivorous ants suddenly infested Grenada and, to a lesser extent, Antigua. The surface of the ground was covered by veritable armies of them, canes and trees were totally destroyed, the fields were cleared of rats as if by magic and even stock was at times attacked. In January 1776, the Grenadan legislature at length offered a reward for the discovery of a method of exterminating them.[6] Henry Phillips compounded a powder which,

[1] Stewart, *A View . . . of Jamaica*, p. 75.

[2] Beckford, *Descriptive Account of Jamaica*, I, 56.

[3] Lewis, *Journal*, p. 112.

[4] From the name of one Vassal, said to have introduced it into Jamaica.

[5] Wentworth, *West India Sketch Book*, I, 321, 322.

[6] George Smith, ed., *The Laws of Grenada, from the Year 1763 to the Year 1805* (London, 1808), p. xliv, under "cane ant."

while effective when directly applied, did not reach the insects underground and was impractical because of their number. He nevertheless sought a patent for his formula [1] and, when shortly after, Grenada was taken by the French, he applied to the Lords of Trade for a suitable reward. Upon their recommendation to the Treasury he was voted the sum of £3,600 by the House of Commons in 1781. Meanwhile, a hurricane of the year before had rid the two islands of these troublesome visitors. [2]

Natural forces were utilized to some extent in cane grinding, but most of this work was carried on by the laborious use of animal power, as will be seen by the following table.

Colony	Year	Cattle Mills	Water Mills	Wind- Mills
Jamaica [3]	1768	369	235	44
Tobago [4]	1775	52	9	23
Trinidad [5]	1808	257	8	7

It will be noted that in Jamaica, "the island of springs," considerable use was made of streams, but here, too, less than might have been expected. Typically enough, a project to harness the Cobre River fell through for lack of interest. [6] The greater advance of the French planters in this respect is shown by the fact that in 1772, a decade after Grenada had been transferred to Great Britain, while old influences were still strong, the sugar estates there were equipped with ninety-five mills operated by water, twelve by wind, and but eighteen by horned beasts. [7]

The scrub stock found on Caribbean plantations lacked physical strength. Considerable numbers of animals were employed in juice extraction as turning the crushing apparatus soon exhausted them. In an attempt to better the grade of cattle, the Jamaican legislature during its session of 1789–1790 offered shipmasters a bounty of £30 currency for every bull under three years of age weighing at least eighty-six stone which they landed, while colonists breeding any with a weight of over eighty were to be granted £10 per head. [8]

[1] Governor Macartney to Lord George Germain, Aug. 31, 1776, C. O. 101/20.
[2] David Macpherson, *Annals of Commerce* (4 vols., London, 1805), III, 610.
[3] *Musgrave Papers,* Br. Mus., Add. Ms. 8,133, ff. 95, 96.
[4] Economic returns in C. O. 101/18.
[5] Returns made by commandants of quarters, in C. O. 295/21.
[6] Long, *Jamaica,* II, 57.
[7] "State of Grenada in April, 1772," C. O. 101/18.
[8] *Acts of Assembly, Passed in the Island of Jamaica, From the Year 1784 to the Year 1788 inclusive [to which is added with continuous paging] Acts*

Similarly, an act to raise the quality of horses was passed in 1771 but was repealed seven years later as not having answered the purpose for which it was intended.[1] Further laws of 1784 and 1789 forbade the running of stallions under fourteen hands in common pastures lest they cover mares there, and set up purses to be awarded in annual races.[2] But such efforts were isolated and at most achieved only slight results. The work of turning sugar mills continued to use up livestock at a rapid rate and needlessly increased production costs.

Various individuals brought forth improvements in the crushing process seeking chiefly to reduce friction and to squeeze the stalks more nearly dry. In 1767, the assembly of Jamaica passed an act enabling the Honorable Francis Cooke to carry into execution his newly-invented cattle machine. A year later, William Gilchrist, a millwright, was granted a patent on his grinding apparatus in which the side rollers were larger than the central, main one.[3] A measure of 1770 secured to Cooke the advantage of his mill with a novel form of wheel, while another authorized Robert Rainey, also known as John Stewart, to carry out his project of operating a crushing plant with power generated by a fire-engine. Acts of the same nature covering more efficient methods of juice extraction, devised by John Russell, Peter M'Intosh, John Rogers, and Edward Sergeant were passed in 1775, 1776, 1777, and 1782.[4] In 1793, John Ashley prayed for the exclusive right to exploit his new contrivance for raising water without friction and throwing it against the wheel of a sugar mill, but what action was taken on the petition is uncertain.[5]

The Barbadian legislature in 1776 lent encouragement to Benjamin Buck, a windmill carpenter, in his projection of a device for returning trash to be burned after the cane had been squeezed[6] and

of Assembly Passed in the Island of Jamaica, in the Years 1789 and 1790 (Kingston, 1789 and n.d.), pp. 286, 287.

[1] Acts of Assembly, Passed in the Island of Jamaica; From 1770, to 1783, inclusive (Kingston, 1786), pp. 4, 146.

[2] Acts of Assembly . . . 1784 to . . . 1788 [and] 1789 and 1790, pp. 52–55, 282–286.

[3] Acts of Assembly, Passed in the Island of Jamaica . . . (2 vols., St. Jago de la Vega, 1769, 1771), sessions of 1767, 1768.

[4] Acts of Assembly . . . 1770 to 1783, sessions of years indicated. For an account of Stewart's invention, see his booklet listed under note 2, page 63.

[5] Votes of the Honourable House of Assembly of Jamaica, in a Session Begun October 22 and ended December 14, 1793 (St. Jago de la Vega, 1794), pp. 86, 87.

[6] Samuel More, ed., The Public Acts in Force; Passed by the Legislature of Barbados, from May 11th, 1762 to April 8th, 1800 (London, 1801), abridgement, p. 65.

eight years after, the one in St. Kitts granted the Reverend Temple Croker the sole privilege of erecting his new horizontal windmills to operate crushers at the authorized charge of £50 currency each.[1]

The extent to which these new inventions came into use cannot be determined, but most certainly they were never generally adopted and bettered time-honored practice but little. Nor did the introduction of steam power somewhat later, when its employment in the mother country had become common, make much headway. A *machine à feu* was constructed in London and sent to Jamaica for use in a cane mill as early as 1769, but the experiment did not prove successful.[2] About 1793, Josias Robins, a mechanic, erected a steam pump of his own construction, to be used in cane grinding, on the John Cozens estate.[3] But fifteen years later there were at most only three steam plants in the island.[4] A Boulton and Watt pump was imported into Trinidad for service on Sir Stephen Lushington's plantation about 1805 and several others were subsequently set up in the colony but their number was never large.[5] Two steam engines were in operation in Nevis in 1825[6] but none in Barbados as late as 1831.[7]

The change from animal to steam as a motive force was too great for West Indian conservatism; the rude and costly cattle mill with cumbersome and inefficient machinery continued to be the typical crushing device in the British Caribbean. An English newspaper correspondent's observation regarding the Jamaicans is applicable to their fellow-colonials as well. "They object to the introduction of steam-engines for the sugar-mills, that the scarcity of firewood is too great; and yet, if the finest geologist of Europe were to . . . state that indications of coal were evident in the formations of the neighboring mountains . . . no effort would be made to obtain it."[8]

[1] *Laws of the Island of St. Christopher, from the Year 1711, to the Year 1791* . . . (St. Christopher's, 1791), session of 1784.

[2] M. Cazaud, "Connoissances essentielles pour juger de quelque Espèce nouvelle de Moulin à Cannes qu'on puisse proposer," in *Philosophical Transactions of the Royal Society*, LXX (1780), pp. 318 ff. See John Stewart, *A Description of a Machine or Invention to Work Mills, by the Power of a Fire-Engine, but Particularly Useful and Profitable in Grinding Sugar-Canes* . . . [London, 1767].

[3] *Votes of the . . . Assembly of Jamaica . . . 1793*, p. 118.

[4] Mathison, *Notices Respecting Jamaica*, pp. 36, 37.

[5] Jean Dauxion-Lavaysse, *Voyage aux Isles de Trinidad, de Tobago, de la Marguerite et dans Diverses Parties de Vénézuela, dans l'Amérique Méridionale* (2 vols., Paris, 1813), I, 411.

[6] Coleridge, *Six Months*, p. 176.

[7] Alexander, *Transatlantic Sketches*, p. 87.

[8] Madden, *Twelve Months' Residence*, I, 87.

One great improvement in the manufacture of muscavado was, however, generally adopted before the close of the eighteenth century—clarification before evaporation boiling. This removed most impurities from the liquor and saved considerable labor in skimming. Credit for discovering the merits of the clarifier was given by Bryan Edwards to his friend John Baker, whose treatise on sugar making was published in 1775.[1] But it was patented in Jamaica [2] and Barbados [3] by Samuel Sainthill three years after.

Attempts to better the reduction process were numerous. In 1785 and 1786, the Jamaican legislature passed private acts enabling Robert W. Boussie to carry certain new methods into execution [4] and voted him £1,000 for his discoveries.[5] Such action aroused intense hostility among the members' constituents and inhabitants of Kingston parish petitioned Lieutenant-Governor Clarke to dissolve the lower house because of its lavish expenditures, as evinced by this particular grant.[6]

The interests of Isaac Winn, who had found how juice might be boiled down and how rum might be distilled with much smaller quantities of fuel, were safeguarded by a measure adopted in 1788. Of two acts passed in 1790, one granted John Reeder the benefit arising from his discovery of a varnish for copper and a means of joining the seams of copper vats without the use of solder, while the other afforded Daniel Seldon protection for his new method of hanging boilers over the flame.[7]

In 1796, the Society of West India Planters and Merchants engaged Dr. Bryan Higgins, a London chemist, on a three year contract at a salary of 1,000 guineas per annum, directing him to proceed to Jamaica and there continue experiments in sugar and rum making which had been begun in England.[8] He was accorded a hearty welcome. The local legislators respectfully heard his account of processes whereby the former might be made whiter and more nearly

[1] Edwards, *History,* II, note, pp. 236, 237. For Baker's work, see note 3, page 57.

[2] *Acts of Assembly . . . 1770 to 1783,* session of 1778.

[3] More, ed., *Acts . . . Passed by the Legislature of Barbados . . . 1762 to . . . 1800,* abridgement, p. 65.

[4] *Acts of Assembly . . . 1784 to . . . 1788* [and] *1789 and 1790,* pp. vii, ix.

[5] Edwards, *History,* II, 232, note.

[6] Clarke to Lord Sydney, Feb. 17, 1787, C. O. 137/86.

[7] *Acts of Assembly . . . 1784 to . . . 1788* [and] *1789 and 1790,* pp. xv and xx.

[8] *Min. W. I. Plant. and Mer.,* May 5, 16, 17, 26, 1796; "Dr. Higgins and Jamaica," in *The W. I. Comm. Circ.,* Dec. 18, 1906, p. 607. "An Early West Indian Scientist," in *ibid.,* Feb. 25, 1913, pp. 79, 80.

pure and the latter more "grateful and salubrious and valuable," of how molasses loss through drainage might be prevented and of how fuel economies might be achieved. County committees were dutifully named to aid in introducing these superior methods, the sum of £1,400 a year was voted him over and above his stipend from the English group and, upon his departure, an additional £1,000 was granted in appreciation of his services. But as might be expected, his innovations in the sugar industry, which included remodelling coppers so as to prevent fuel waste while at the same time accelerating boiling, and his rum process, easy, simple, and economical as it was said to be, were adopted by few and were actually permanently continued by almost no one.[1]

The vacuum pan, the apparatus destined to revolutionize sugar manufacture by making possible evaporation at a lower temperature, was invented in 1813 by Edward Howard, likewise a chemist at one time employed by the Society of Planters and Merchants,[2] but was utterly ignored by Caribbean proprietors for over two decades. It was not until 1833 that the first one reached the West India colonies and was erected on the Vreeden Hoop estate, Demerara.[3]

Few improvements were made in cultivating and preparing other produce for market. A private act to encourage George Latham, inventor of a coffee pulping and cleaning apparatus, passed the Jamaican legislature in 1772 [4] as did another for the benefit of Ralph Walker, covering a similar machine, sixteen years later.[5] In 1779, the assembly of Barbados protected the interests of Percival Archer who had invented a windmill for ginning cotton and six years after it did the same in behalf of Edward Wilkie who had also devised an outfit for removing seeds.[6] In 1788, the Jamaican assembly granted to James Small the exclusive right of manufactring his new machine for working cotton-gins.[7] But no practical results followed from any

---

[1] The results of these experiments were published. See Bryan Higgins, *Observations and Advices for the Improvement of the Manufacture of Muscovado Sugar and Rum* (3 parts complete, the fourth incomplete, St. Jago de la Vega, 1797, 1800, 1801, 1803). For Higgins's work in the island see Dallas, *History of the Maroons*, II, 340 ff.

[2] *Min. W. I. Plant. and Mer.*, June 26, Oct. 3, Dec. 9, 1811.

[3] Dr. Edmund von Lippmann, in *Chem. Zeit.*, quoted in *W. I. Comm. Circ.*, March 11, 1913, p. 103.

[4] *Acts of Assembly . . . 1770 to 1783*, session of 1772.

[5] *Acts of Assembly . . . 1784 to . . . 1788* [and] *1789 and 1790*, p. xvi.

[6] More, ed., *Acts . . . Passed by the Legislature of Barbados . . . 1762 to 1800*, abridgements, pp. 66, 70.

[7] *Acts of Assembly . . . 1784 to . . . 1788* [and] *1789 and 1790*, p. xvi.

of these projects.[1] Obsolete methods were the legacy of one generation of planters to another; custom all but ruled supreme.

Antigua alone offered a notable exception to this general rule. Real
interest in agricultural advancement was shown there. "All . . .
probable improvements in the Instruments of Husbandry have from
time to time had a fair trial," wrote a committee of islanders to the
home government in 1788.[2] Although the plow had given little satisfaction at that time, it was in "general (indeed almost universal) use"
by 1820.[3] Trelawny Wentworth, visiting the Caribbean a few years
later, was impressed by its commonness in Antigua as compared with
the other possessions.[4]

Colonel Samuel Martin, the topping planter of the colony during
the third quarter of the eighteenth century, recognized the evils of
monoculture and of mining the soil. After having grown sugar in a
given field for a number of seasons, he turned it to pasturage so that
the ground might regain its fertility.[5] The number of West Indian-
born negroes on Antiguan estates was also larger than elsewhere. Not
one black had been added by purchase to the slave population of
Martin's estate in the twenty years preceding 1775.[6] On one plantation known to John Luffman a decade later, less than 10 per cent of
the workers were Africans and on another manned by 500 hands, the
number of imported ones was only 2 per cent.[7]

The higher level of rural life in Antigua was noticeable in many
ways. The great-houses as a whole were the best in the British tropics
and public institutions were conducted in a markedly exemplary
manner.[8] Relations between bondsmen and masters were cordial. The
Antiguan negro code was strikingly superior to those of the other

[1] Compare the methods described in John Ellis, *An Historical Account of
Coffee. With An Enquiry, and Botanical Description of the Tree. To Which
Are Added Sundry Papers Relative to its Culture and Use, as an Article of
Diet and Commerce* (London, 1774) and John Lowndes, *The Coffee-Planter;
or, An Essay on the Cultivation and Manufacturing of That Article of West
India Produce* (London, 1807).

[2] "Answers to Queries," C. O. 152/67.

[3] Governor D'Urban to Earl Bathurst, Nov. 28, 1820, C. O. 7/6.

[4] *West India Sketch Book*, II, p. 196.

[5] Andrews, ed., *Journal of a Lady*, pp. 105, 106. Colonel Martin's advanced
views on West Indian agriculture were given wide publicity in his popular
An Essay Upon Plantership of 1773 which was reprinted in *Annals of Agriculture*, XVIII (1792), pp. 236 ff. Unfortunately few chose to profit by following them.

[6] Andrews, ed., *Journal of a Lady*, p. 104.

[7] *A Brief Account*, Letter XXVIII.

[8] Coleridge, *Six Months*, p. 221.

possessions with respect to privileges accorded, such as trial by jury, and no restraint was placed on manumissions.[1] This tiny island community was, as we shall see, the only one in the Antilles proper to eventually extend freedom to its slaves without an initial apprenticeship period.[2]

An explanation for the fundamental difference between the stagnation with calm indifference toward progress commonly prevalent and conditions in Antigua is to be found in the fact that by far the greater number of land owners there were permanent residents. In communicating with the Earl of Dartmouth in 1773, Governor Ralph Payne of the Leeward group stated "The number of Proprietors of these Colonies, who live in Europe, is . . . infinitely superior to the very few who are left. . . . Antigua has much the Advantage of the other Islands, with Respect to Men of Fortune and Education, and in Point of an independent and respectable Inhabitancy." [3]

"Antigua has more proprietors . . . than any of the other Islands, which gives it a great superiority," commented a spirited visitor two years later.[4] At the turn of the century, Governor Lavington experienced great difficulty in keeping important offices throughout the Leewards, those of Antigua alone excepted, filled, and attributed this to the slight amount of absenteeism there as compared with elsewhere.[5] About 1825, a planter accounted for the creditable footing upon which local society rested in the same manner.[6]

Stark economic necessity forced the generality of Antiguan estate holders to make their residence in the Caribbean a life-long one. The island had been one of England's first new-world colonies. Soil depletion coupled with drought to which it was peculiarly subject brought about a decline while other West Indian sugar-producing regions, developed later, were still enjoying the heydey of their prosperity.[7] Antigua, furthermore, was the scene of the earliest sectarian activities in the British tropics, and this leavening social influence, discussed

[1] Edwards, *History*, I, 448, 449. Southey, *Chronological History*, III, 508; Flannigan, *Antigua*, I, 112, 118, 126. Davy, *West Indies*, p. 389.

[2] See pages 455 and 456.

[3] Under date of Oct. 6, C. O. 152/54.

[4] Andrews, ed., *Journal of a Lady*, pp. 92, 93.

[5] To Lord Hobart, C. O. 152/83.

[6] Wentworth, *West India Sketch Book*, II, 179.

[7] Southey, *Chronological History*, III, 308. Edwards, *History*, I, 447. It should be noted, however, that absenteeism had been a grave problem in the earlier history of the island. See C. S. S. Higham, *The Development of the Leeward Islands Under the Restoration, 1660–1888* (Cambridge, 1921) pp. 165, 182.

elsewhere,[1] played no small part in raising the whole tone of life.

Attempts to foster the spirit of experimentation through forming agricultural clubs were made in the various colonies from time to time. Such bodies were invariably founded by a few individuals with advanced ideas, generally newly-arrived from Great Britain, were accorded half-hearted support for a brief space, met with increasing irregularity, and finally perished before the stolid indifference of the smug agrarians. A recital of these valiant efforts to elevate the plane of planter economy affords a striking commentary on the ingrained opposition of the West Indians to change.

The first organization of the kind appeared in Jamaica in 1767 and was designed to improve the quality of crops, increase commerce, and extend cultivation. It was not ill received, but came to naught because of the moving spirits' departure from the island.[2] The Cornwall Agricultural Society was founded forty years later. Meetings were held at Montego Bay and the awarding of prizes for discoveries and inventions was projected, but it soon died a natural death and "left no memorial of its labours behind for the benefit of the public." [3]

The Jamaica Horticultural Society was formed in 1825 and a few months later expanded into the Society for the Cultivation of Agriculture and other Arts and Sciences. Its life of two decades was unusually long.[4] The Barbadians organized a Society for the Improvement of Plantership in 1804. Meetings were held at members' homes, papers were read and products were exhibited but it soon passed out of existence for lack of interest.[5] An Agricultural Association suffered the same fate a quarter of a century later.[6] A proposal that one be organized in Dominica fell through about 1790.[7]

Sir William Young, governor of Tobago, made a serious attempt during the early 1800's to interest Caribbean proprietors in modern ways. He was himself the owner of extensive estates,[8] had been an

---

[1] In Chapters I and VIII.

[2] Long, *Jamaica*, I, 436, 440. This would seem to be the agricultural society said by Gardner (*Jamaica*, p. 158) to have been organized in 1769.

[3] Stewart, *An Account of Jamaica*, pp. 113, 114 and his *A View . . . of Jamaica*, pp. 115, 116.

[4] Frank C. Cundall, "Jamaica in the Past and Present," in *Journal of the Society of Arts*, Jan. 3, 1896, p. 113.

[5] Davy, *The West Indies*, p. iii. Schomburgk, *Barbados*, p. 132.

[6] Gov. James Lyon to Sir George Murray, Sept. 14, 1829, C. O. 28/103.

[7] Atwood, *History of Dominica*, p. 283.

[8] See his "A Tour Through . . . Barbados, St. Vincent, Antigua, Tobago, and Grenada in . . . 1791 and 1792," in Edwards's *Historical Survey of . . . St. Domingo*, second edition.

intimate associate of Bryan Edwards and had edited a posthumous edition of his writings,[1] was the author of an important statistical work on the sugar colonies [2] and had long been an active member of the West India group at home, both in and out of parliament.[3] It was his conviction that the new conditions attending tropical agriculture after abolition had become effective, required the utmost attention to scientific methods, the abandonment of monoculture and the more common growing of provisions. Shortly after his arrival Sir William issued a pamphlet urging the formation of a body to study domestic problems and circulated it among the landed residents.[4] Copies were also sent to neighboring islands.

The Tobago Agricultural Society was subsequently founded in 1807 with the far-seeing executive as patron.[5] Home authorities approved of the project, but expressed concern lest the association be perverted to schemes of faction and mischief and urged that it be severely restricted to communicating results of experiments with seeds and tillage. Governor Young therefore agreed in a private letter to Lord Castlereagh to "call together no Notables to Discuss one Subject, who, when met, might prefer to discuss another. . . ." [6] Little need was there for this precaution—the body did not thrive and had already passed out of existence before the death of its enthusiastic promoter in 1815.

A club was likewise formed in St. Vincent in 1807 with the Tobagan one as a model. At an early meeting specimens of yam bread, flour made from arrow-root, and sample hardwood staves and shingles of local origin were exhibited while a means of curing pork

[1] *An Historical Survey of the Island of St. Domingo* . . . (London, 1801).

[2] *The West India Common-place Book, Compiled from Parliamentary and Official Documents, Showing the Interest of Great Britain in the Sugar Colonies* (London, 1807). It contains data largely relative to the trade, produce, and distress of the sugar colonies, compiled during twenty-two years membership in the House of Commons. Unfortunately, there are many errors due to very poor proof-reading. Sir William had already entered in upon his governorship in the West Indies before its publication, so should not be held responsible for them.

[3] The record of many of his activities is preserved in the unpublished West India Committee papers.

[4] William Young, *Prospectus, on Proposal for the Institution of an Agricultural Society in Tobago* [Grenada, 1807].

[5] *The Tobago Gazette,* Nov. 13, 1807. A report of the first meeting was published—*Mount William. Friday, Nov. 6, 1807. At a Meeting held at Mount William, His Excellency Sir William Young, Bart. in the Chair* [begin] . . . [Grenada, 1807].

[6] Under date of March 2, 1808, C. O. 285/13.

in the torrid zone was discussed.[1] Following the normal course, however, this promising beginning was not followed up—little more
was heard of the movement.

Three planter associations were organized in 1820, one in St. Kitts
with the support of Governor Maxwell,[2] one in Antigua through the
efforts of Doctor Nugent, speaker of the assembly,[3] and the third
in Grenada, based on the Philadelphia Society for Promoting Agriculture.[4] The last of these proved the most hardy. Certain of its proceedings were published, a library was formed and annual plowing
matches were conducted.[5] But eventually it, too, met the fate of all
the others.

A more ambitious undertaking was that inaugurated by Josiah
Steele, the Irish writer on prosody who moved to Barbados and assumed personal charge of his sugar estates there in 1780. After a
residence of only a year, he founded the Society for the Encouragement of Arts, Manufactures, and Commerce in an attempt to set up
local industries which would provide employment for indigent natives,
such as the manufacture of cotton yarn, dyestuffs, lace and stockings,
and the preparation of plant fiber to be used in making rope and
bagging.[6] As part of its program, this body from time to time offered
prizes, among them one for a method of destroying insects,[7] and
another for the establishment of standards of taste and smell.[8]

While thus seeking to foster new enterprises in the community as
a whole, Steele, who had become a member of the legislative council,
effected spectacular reforms in the labor régime on his lands. Arbitrary punishments were abolished, courts conducted by the negroes

[1] Governor Beckwith to Lord Castlereagh, Oct. 19, 1807, C. O. 260/22.

[2] Referred to in Address of President Wilson to the legislature, June 2,
1820, C. O. 239/6.

[3] Governor D'Urban to Earl Bathurst, Nov. 28, 1820, C. O. 7/6.

[4] *Proceedings of the Grenada Agricultural Society for the Years 1820 and
1821* (London, 1821).

[5] *Proceedings of the Grenada Agricultural Society for 1827* (No imprint, n.d.).

[6] *Institution and First Proceedings of the Society for the Encouragement of
Arts, Manufactures and Commerce* (Barbados, 1781). This Barbadian organization was modeled after the Society Instituted at London for the Encouragement of Arts, Manfactures, and Commerce, which, as will appear,
was interested in the development of West Indian agriculture. Steele was at
one time vice-president of the latter body.

[7] "Method of Destroying Insects . . . ," in *The Scots Mag.*, Aug., 1787, pp.
385 ff.

[8] Samuel Dent, "Premium by the Society of Arts, &c. in Barbados . . . ," in
The Gent. Mag., July, 1787, p. 564.

themselves were established and wages were paid for all work performed. Finally, in 1789, he divided his properties into manors, making the blacks copyholders bound to their tenements and owing rent and services, the latter to be met by tilling the demesne land at specified times each week.[1] These revolutionary changes instantly aroused a storm of antagonism on the part of the Barbadian public and, during the controversy which followed, the society was disrupted. Steele's death in 1791 made its reorganization impossible.

One other memorable attempt to soften the rigors of the slave system upon which West Indian economy rested was that made by Mathew Lewis on his Jamaican plantations in 1816. This popular novelist, inspecting a legacy, took his new position as owner of human beings seriously. He prohibited whipping, accepted negro evidence, sought to lessen toil by making extensive use of machines and agricultural implements, granted additional holidays, and, with a keen insight into the curse of absenteeism, resolved to visit his possessions regularly and required in his will that his heir must spend at least a quarter on them every third year.

As in the case of Steele, these innovations aroused keen hostility and their protagonist was denounced as an enemy of the general welfare. He persisted nevertheless, but, unfortunately, death overtook him in 1818 on his return to England from a second trans-Atlantic visit and the new owner betrayed no such concern.[2] Lewis's fame as a literary man was ephemeral; his radical departures from convention in the Caribbean, on the other hand, will never be forgotten.

The British West Indians profited greatly by the introduction of new economic plants during the closing decades of the seventeen hundreds. This was brought about primarily through awards for agricultural extension in colonial America being made by the Society Instituted at London for the Encouragement of Arts, Manufactures, and Commerce, commonly known as the Society of Arts, and because of the vital interest of its vigorous head, Sir Joseph Banks, in the

[1] Letters by Steele, describing this system, were published in various issues of *The Barbados Gazette* under the signature "Philo Xylon," in 1787 and 1788. See also William Dickinson, *Mitigation of Slavery* (London, 1814), part one of which contains miscellaneous papers by Steele, and part two, his letters to Thomas Clarkson, relating the details of his great experiment. Also Clarkson, *Thoughts on the Necessity of Improving the Condition of the Slaves in the British Colonies* . . . (London, 1823), pp. 31–44.

[2] See his *Journal, passim*. Anon., ed., *The Life and Correspondence of M. G. Lewis* . . . (2 vols., London, 1839). [Frank Cundall], "Jamaica Worthies— Monk Lewis," in *Journal of the Institute of Jamaica*, Feb. 1892, pp. 65 ff.

matter. So far as the overseas territories were concerned, this association confined its activities almost exclusively to the mainland settlements from its origin in 1754 up to the Revolution, but for a quarter of a century thereafter, during the first half of Sir Joseph's presidency, the sugar islands were made objects of particular attention.[1]

A premium of £100 was offered in 1759 for not less than twenty-five pounds of Jamaican-grown cochineal. In 1760, a similar amount was promised to the individual planting the greatest number of cinnamon trees over 200, as were a gold medal to the first person bringing mango seeds for Caribbean planting to London and another to anyone importing more than a ton of vegetable silk from the West India colonies. In 1761, a new prize of £50 was set aside for whoever might be the first to raise not less than 100 *aloe succotrina* plants. In 1776, a gold medal was made available for anyone introducing the breadfruit tree in the British American tropics. Other awards were tendered for West Indian-grown opium, sarsaparilla, cotton equal to fine Brazilian, indigo of the same quality as that grown in Guatemala, camphor, quinquina, sesamum seed with the oil derived from it, and ground nuts.[2]

In 1783, a gold medal or £100 was offered to anyone presenting nutmegs of colonial Caribbean origin, as were two medals the year after, one to the first person who should distill at least thirty gallons of spirit from coffee pulp and the other to the first who might exhibit two hundredweight of senna grown in the sugar colonies.

In 1788, another such medal was set aside for anyone conveying six breadfruit trees in a growing state from the South Sea to the West Indies and still another of thirty guineas for anyone importing half a ton of cashew gum into England from the British American tropics. Two years later, a gold medal or £50 was made available for the first producer of at least twenty pounds of cinnamon bark in any of the Caribbean possessions.[3]

[1] For a survey of its work, see Henry T. Wood, *A History of the Royal Society of Arts* (London, 1913) ; for Sir Joseph, see Joseph H. Maiden, *Sir Joseph Banks* (Sydney, 1909) and Edward Smith, *The Life of Sir Joseph Banks* (London, 1811).

[2] *Premiums by the Society, Established at London, for the Encouragement of Arts, Manufactures, and Commerce* (Published annually, London, issues for 1758, 1759). *Premiums Offered by the Society Instituted at London for the Encouragement of Arts, Manufactures, and Commerce* (Published annually, London, 1760–1781).

[3] *Abstract of the Premiums Offered by the Society Instituted at London for the Encouragement of Arts, Manufactures, and Commerce* (Published annually, London, 1783–1790).

In 1797, a gold medal or fifty guineas was offered the first exhibitor of not less than twenty pounds of West Indian cloves, as were a gold medal or thirty guineas to the owner of any plantation boasting at least 100 breadfruit trees, the same to any cultivator with a minimum of two acres in kali, and a gold medal or fifty guineas to the discoverer of a means by which the cane borer might be destroyed.[1]

The Society sought to encourage the cultivation of exotics and therefore urged that botanical gardens modeled on the one at Kew be set up in the various islands. The first of these was laid out in St. Vincent in 1763 by Governor Robert Melville.[2] It was made a royal establishment, was placed under the Secretary of War's control and was granted £1,200 support annually by the home government. The director, Dr. George Young, was awarded a medal in 1773 for having a considerable number of turmerics and cinnamon, mango, logwood, and nutmeg trees in a thriving state.[3]

The St. Vincent garden lay half a mile from Kingston and comprised some thirty acres. Under the loving care of Mr. Anderson and Mr. Lockhead, each of whom became island botanist in turn, it developed into the finest tropical experimental station in the world. Specimens grown there were widely distributed and West Indian flora was immeasurably enriched thereby.[4]

But following Lockhead's death in 1814, Mr. Caley, the new caretaker, became embroiled in a controversy with Governor Brisbane;[5] the property was neglected, and in 1818 the latter recommended that it be closed and that the greater part of the plants be removed to Trinidad.[6] This was subsequently done and the parliamentary appropriation ceased; and, although the legislature at first voted small sums for the upkeep of such plots as had been left, these grants were soon discontinued and the establishment fell into total decay.[7]

[1] See *The Gent. Mag.*, April, 1797, pp. 319–336.

[2] C. O. 101/12, 17 contain papers relative to this garden.

[3] *A Register of the Premiums and Bounties Given by the Society Instituted at London for the Encouragement of Arts, Manufactures, and Commerce, from the Original Institution in the Year MDCCLIV to the Year MDCCLXXVI Inclusive* (London, 1778).

[4] L. Guilding, *An Account of the Botanic Garden in the Island of St. Vincent, from its First Establishment to the Present Time* (Glasgow, 1825).

[5] C. O. 260/30.

[6] C. O. 260/35.

[7] C. O. 260/39, 46. Charles Shephard, *Historical Account of the Island of Saint Vincent* (London, 1831), pp. 7 ff. Coleridge, *Six Months*, p. 109. Madden, *Twelve Months' Residence*, I, 48. Alexander, *Transatlantic Sketches*, p. 155. Bayley, *Four Years' Residence*, pp. 221–223.

Two Jamaicans, Hinton East and W. Wallen, afforded the Society of Arts noteworthy coöperation in the Caribbean phase of its activities. The first of these was the colony's receiver general and an acquaintance of Sir Joseph Banks. He imported and grew new species of plants as a hobby and his private botanical garden in St. Andrew parish was characterized by Bryan Edwards, who published a catalogue of the specimens it contained, as being "perhaps the most magnificent establishment of its kind in existence." [1] Mr. Wallen assembled a somewhat smaller collection on Cold Spring plantation.[2] Through their influence, a public garden was instituted by the assembly about 1775 and, thanks to generous gifts of seeds and cuttings made by them, it was soon flourishing. The legislature subsequently acquired the East property from its founder's nephew-heir for a small sum and it thus passed under state control.[3]

Mr. Beggorat, a member of the Trinidad council, developed a private garden for acclimatizing foreign varieties of vegetable growth in Diego Martin Valley, six miles from Port of Spain, at the opening of the nineteenth century. Spice trees throve in it and, following a conversation with the owner, Brigadier-General Thomas Hislop, then in charge of the government, urged that a public one be established.[4] Only a small beginning was made but two decades later, when the station at St. Vincent was being overrun by weeds, Governor Woodford of Trinidad requested that the specimens in it be removed there and was supported in this proposal by Sir Joseph Banks. The Secretary of War at first declined to consider the matter but at length, in November 1821, offered the plants to the colony of Trinidad if it would meet the expense of their transfer.

The proposition was accepted and Mr. Lockhart, director of the small existing establishment, was sent north to supervise the removal of over 3,000 of them. He at the same time secured cuttings and seeds for at least as many more.[5] Medicinal plants were introduced from Demerera somewhat later,[6] the garden developed rapidly, and in 1827

---

[1] *History,* I, 197, note. For the catalogue, see the appendix to Vol. I.

[2] William Harris, "History of the Introduction of the Economic Plants of Jamaica," in *Bulletin of the Department of Agriculture* [Kingston, Jamaica], April, 1910, pp. 181 ff., March, 1911, pp. 243 ff.

[3] Southey, *Chronological History,* II, 414. Dallas, *History of the Maroons,* II, 349 ff. Macpherson, *Annals of Commerce,* IV, 263.

[4] Hislop to the Earl of Camden, Aug. 27, 1804, C. O. 295/8.

[5] Governor Woodford to Earl Bathurst, April 22, 1818, C. O. 295/46. Acting Governor Young to Earl Bathurst, July 29, 1822, enclosures and memorandum, C. O. 295/55.

[6] Woodford to Bathurst, July 3, 1824, C. O. 295/62.

samples of locally-grown nutmegs and pepper were sent to colonial authorities in London.[1]

With the formation of these several botanical collections, private and state owned, attention was turned to the extensive introduction of desirable varieties. Sendings were received from the four corners of the world, but above all from the Orient through the Board of Agriculture's assistance.[2] Plants were generally first carried to England on merchantmen and were then, in due course, trans-shipped on others to the West Indies. In consequence of the long double voyage, a heavy percentage died en route. Others were sent out from Kew. John Ellis, the Irish naturalist and agent for Dominica, took a special interest in the matter and published three treaties on proper methods of packing, together with catalogues of species worthy of entry.[3]

Over 500 different exotics were thriving in the East garden as early as 1790. The number had been considerably increased in 1782 by the capture of a French vessel bound from the Ile de France to St. Domingo, with crates of East Indian specimens. With Admiral Rodney's approbation, this booty had been turned over to Mr. East and had been carefully set out. Most notable among the trees thus procured were the cinnamon, the mango, and the nutmeg. Ginger, pepper, bamboo, camphor saplings, and sago palms were also growing there.[4]

The possibilities of spice culture aroused considerable interest among British officials. In 1787 the matter was taken up in correspondence with Lieutenant-Governor Clarke of Jamaica, but, while the step was held to be a highly advantageous one, nothing came of it.[5]

[1] Woodford to Viscount Goderich, Aug. 31, 1827 and enclosure, C. O. 295/75.

[2] "Oriental Plants Cultivated in the West Indies," in *Annals of Agriculture,* XXXVII (1801), pp. 557 ff.

[3] John Ellis, *Directions for Bringing Over Seeds and Plants, From the East-Indies and Other Distant Countries, in a State of Vegetation: Together With a Catalogue of Such Foreign Plants as are Worthy of Being Encouraged in Our American Colonies* . . . (London, 1770). *Some Additional Observations on the Method of Preserving Seeds from Foreign Parts, for the Benefit of Our American Colonies. With an Account of the Garden at St. Vincent* (London, 1773). *A Description of the Mangostan and the Bread-Fruit* . . . *To Which Are Added, Directions to Voyagers, for bringing over these and other Vegetable Productions, which would be extremely beneficial to the Inhabitants of our West India Islands* (London, 1775).

[4] See the catalogue forming the appendix to Vol. I of Edwards's *History.*

[5] Clarke to Nepean, July 15, 1787, C. O. 137/86 and Dec. 16, 1787, C. O. 137/87.

Ten years later the home government published a treatise on clove culture written by Monsieur Buée, a Dominican planter, and distributed copies among the West India colonists.[1] In 1806 the *Fortitude,* carrying the first lot of oriental laborers from Bengal to Trinidad, brought a direct shipment of nutmeg trees as well.[2]

As with other plants, spice trees were freely distributed from the public gardens and in 1807 one resident of St. Vincent was reported to have 1,500 young cinnamons doing nicely on his estate.[3] But, despite these promising beginnings, spice production never attained commercial proportions in the British American tropics. The trees were viewed as little more than curiosities and old, reliable, staple products continued to engage the proprietors' almost exclusive attention.

Of more significance was the bringing of the breadfruit and the Bourbon and Tahitian canes to the Caribbean in the 1790's. This was accomplished through the joint efforts of the London West India merchants and the Society of Arts and is indissolubly associated with one of the most romantic episodes in seafaring history, the *Bounty* crew mutiny.

Breadfruit first came to the attention of Europeans as a result of Captain Cook's circumnavigation of the globe in the ship *Endeavour* between 1768 and 1771. Joseph Banks, then a young man, accompanied this intrepid explorer in the capacity of botanist and became acquainted with it while at Tahiti. On his return he wrote and spoke much of its value as a food, British fancy was struck by the name, and, hearing of it, Valentine Morris, later governor of St. Vincent, in 1772 wrote to Banks suggesting that the tree be introduced in the sugar colonies.[4]

Three years later the West India merchants of London offered £100 to the first person who might bring a specimen to England in thriving condition.[5] About the same time, the colonial agent, John Ellis, published a book describing the plant and outlining methods of

---

[1] Governor Hamilton to the Duke of Portland, April 9, 1796, C. O. 71/28; circular to West Indian governors, Aug. 24, 1797, C. O. 324/103.

[2] See page 279. Governor Hislop to William Windham, Oct. 26, 1806, C. O. 295/14.

[3] Governor Beckwith to Lord Castlereagh and enclosures, Oct. 27, 1807, C. O. 260/22.

[4] Smith, *Life of Banks,* p. 213.

[5] *Min. W. I. Mer.,* Feb. 7, and March 7, 1775 and July 2, 1776. For this body of organized traders, see pages 93 ff.

packing young ones for removal to the new world.[1] In 1776, the Society of Arts offered a gold medal to whoever might enter the first ones in any of the tropical American colonies. The West India traders held this to be an insufficient stimulus and voted to provide a more ample reward by subscription.[2] But nothing definite was accomplished until 1786 when Banks, urged on by Hinton East, laid the matter before George III and aroused his interest with the result that Lieutenant William Bligh, who had been Captain Cook's sailing master, was commissioned to proceed to the South Sea in the *Bounty* and procure an ample supply for transplanting.

This was done, but disaffection appeared among the men on the return trip from Tahiti in 1789. The commander and eighteen sailors faithful to him were set adrift in a small boat, and the balance of the crew made off with the ship. After great hardships, Bligh and his party reached the Portuguese colony of Timor in the East Indies, 3,600 miles away, and took passage to England. The mutineers meanwhile returned to Tahiti. Nine took native women on board and departed but the others elected to remain. Sixteen of the latter were subsequently located there by a force sent to hunt them down. Of these, two were killed, four drowned in attempting to escape, six were condemned to death by court-martial, and four were acquitted.

The fate of the group which had sailed away remained a mystery for a generation. Finally in 1808, an American ship-captain, stopping at Pitcairn Island, which was supposedly uninhabited, found it peopled with English-speaking persons under the patriarchal rule of John Adams, the sole survivor of the nine. Bligh, in the interim, had been promoted to a captaincy and had headed a second, less eventful expedition in 1791, which was completely successful.[3]

[1] See note 3, page 75.

[2] *Min. W. I. Mer.*, Feb. 18, 1777.

[3] An extensive literature has grown up around this celebrated undertaking and the Pitcairn Island folk. See William Bligh, *A Narrative of the Mutiny on Board His Majesty's Ship Bounty* (London, 1790). Bligh, *A Voyage to the South Sea* (London, 1792). Bligh, *An Answer to Certain Assertions Contained in an Appendix to a Pamphlet, Intituled Minutes of the Proceedings on the Court Martial Held at Portsmouth, Aug. 12, 1792* . . . (London, 1794). Bligh, "The Introduction of Bread-Fruit Trees Into the West Indies," in *Transactions of the Society for the Encouragement of Arts, Manufactures, and Commerce*, XII, p. 305. Anon., ed., *Minutes of the Proceedings of the Court Martial Held at Portsmouth, Aug. 12, 1792, on Ten Persons Charged with Mutiny on Board His Majesty's Ship the Bounty. With an Appendix, containing a full Account of the Real Causes and Circumstances of That Unhappy Transaction* . . . (London, 1794). "Account of the Bread-Fruit Tree

In January 1793 the *Providence* arrived in Jamaica from the southern Pacific and some hundreds of young breadfruits were immediately landed by Bligh. He was fêted like a hero and the assembly voted him 1,000 guineas in addition to the 500 already granted after his first voyage, with 500 more to his chief assistant, Lieutenant Portlock.[1] Other specimens were unloaded at St. Vincent. In London, the Society of West India Planters and Merchants extended Bligh a vote of thanks[2] and the Society of Arts bestowed on him its long-offered gold medal.

It was hoped that the use of this new food plant would markedly decrease flour consumption in the Caribbean and thus to a considerable extent relieve the islanders from their dependence on imported supplies. For that reason, it was widely distributed from the botanical gardens and its cultivation was encouraged in every way possible.

Expedition," in *The Scots Mag.*, Feb. and March 1793, pp. 87 ff., 118 ff. Anon., *An Account of the Mutinous Seizure of the Bounty* . . . (London, 1790). Anon., *Voyages and Travels of Fletcher Christian, and a Narrative of the Mutiny on Board H. M. Ship Bounty at Otaheite* (London, 1798). [Mr. Barrow], *The Eventful History of the Mutiny and Piratical Seizure of H. M. S. "Bounty"* . . . (London, 1813). Lady Belcher, *The Mutineers of the Bounty and Their Descendants in Pitcairn and Norfolk Islands* (London, 1870). "Bread-Fruit-Tree Expedition," in *The European Magazine and London Review*, March, April, May, 1792, pp. 187 ff., 280, 344 ff. "The Bread Fruit Tree in the West Indies," in *The W. I. Comm. Circ.*, April 11, 1906. George Hamilton, *A Voyage Round the World in H. M. Frigate Pandora* (Berwick, 1793). Edward Edwards and George Hamilton, *Voyage of the Pandora, Despatched to Arrest the Mutineers of the Bounty in the South Seas, 1790–91* (London, 1915). Edward Harwood, "The Breadfruit Planted in the West Indies," in *The Gent. Mag.*, April, 1793, pp. 325, 326. "His Majesty's Ship Bounty—Descendants of the Mutineers," in *ibid.*, supplement to Part II, 1815, pp. 597 ff. "John Adams of Pitcairn's Island," in *ibid.*, July, 1818, pp. 37, 38. Ida Lee, *Captain Bligh's Second Voyage to the South Sea* (London, 1920). "List of Persons Found on Pitcairn's Island . . .," in *The Eur. Mag. and Lond. Rev.*, May, 1820, p. 408. "The Mutiny of the Bounty," in *Fraser's Magazine for Town and Country*, Jan. 1832, pp. 673–685. "Pitcairn's Island," in *The Edinburgh Literary Magazine and Literary Miscellany (The Scots Mag.)*, Oct., 1820, p. 353. "Porter's Cruise in the Pacific Ocean," in *The Quarterly Review*, July, 1815, pp. 352 ff. Lieutenant J. Shilliber, *A Narrative of the Briton's Voyage to Pitcairn's Island* . . . (London, 1817). "The Pitcairn Bible," in *Bulletin of the New York Public Library*, June, 1924, pp. 443 ff. Rosalind Young, *The Mutiny of the Bounty and the Story of Pitcairn Island, 1790–1894* (Mountain View, Cal., n.d.).

[1] *Votes of the . . . Assembly of Jamaica . . . 1793*, pp. 8–10, 122–125, Appendix xx. Gardner, Jamaica, p. 328. Hortentius, *pseud.*, "The Introduction of Breadfruit, etc. Into Jamaica," in *The Gent. Mag.*, May, 1796, pp. 377, 378. See also "Account of the Bread-Fruit Tree in the West Indies," in *The Eur. Mag. and Lond. Rev.*, Jan. 1796, p. 4.

[2] *Min. W. I. Plant. and Mer.*, March 18, 1794.

Some proprietors showed real interest. In 1799, S. Mure of Jamaica was awarded a Society of Arts medal for his success in propagating the trees, and President Robley of Tobago received similar awards in 1802 and 1803.[1] But the extravagant expectations of enthusiasts in England were not realized, due primarily to the slaves' preference for the indigenous plantain.[2] Nevertheless, large and reliable supplies of a new edible had been provided; breadfruit lent variety to the simple negro fare, and, with the passing of time, it was increasingly drawn on.[3]

The introduction of new canes was of immeasurably greater moment. About 1790, the French in Guadeloupe and Martinique experimented with varieties imported from the Île de Bourbon, Tahiti, and Batavia. Results were tremendously successful; the first two in particular proved ideally suited to West Indian conditions. Their stalks were larger and contained more liquid than did the old creole kind, they stood dry weather better, ripened earlier, syrup made from their juice granulated more rapidly, and their sugar yield was about one-third greater. On the other hand, they had to be replanted more frequently and exhausted the soil sooner.[4] Cuttings found their way to Montserrat in 1793 and soon after, they were being marketed in all the other British islands. The Bourbon and Tahitian canes secured a firm hold immediately, and within a few seasons practically supplanted the other.

The economic consequences of this change on the West India possessions as a whole will be discussed in detail elsewhere.[5] It need only be said here that as early as 1796 the governor of Tobago informed home authorities that any attempt to foster arrowroot cultivation locally would be predestined to fail, as the yield of a piece of land planted in Bourbon cane had just sold at £70 sterling an acre,

---

[1] Wood, *History of the Royal Society of Arts,* pp. 93–101.

[2] Mathison, *Notices Respecting Jamaica,* p. 33, note. Stewart, *A View . . . of Jamaica,* p. 62.

[3] The private attempts to introduce new economic plants were numerous. The following item covers a typical case. "Lord Seaforth has circulated throughout the Caribee islands the seeds of the palm which produces the fibres from which the cordage and cables, called in the East Indies, gomootoo, are manufactured. . . . The tree also produces the best palm wine known in the East. Lord Seaforth is likewise endeavoring to introduce the culture of a species of the canarium, which yields an oil similar to the best olive oil." *The Annual Register for 1802,* p. 463.

[4] Clement Caines, *Letters on the Cultivation of the Otaheite Cane . . .* (London, 1801).

[5] In Chapter VII.

twice the value of the ground itself, and that the colonists were interested in nothing else.[1] Similarly, in 1798, it was reported that the
proprietors of Dominica were all growing rich, owing in no small
measure "to the wonderful Produce from the Otaheite cane." [2]

The average annual exportation of sugar from Jamaica in the five
year period 1793–97, before the new canes had been set out, was
84,700 hogsheads; that for the years 1800–1804, after they had been
generally adopted, no less than 111,976.[3] While this increased production brought temporary prosperity, it was destined to develop into
one of the paramount factors bringing general ruin to the British
Caribbean. In the long run, then, introduction of the new canes
proved catastrophic.

[1] Governor Lindsay to the Duke of Portland, April 27, 1796, C. O. 258/4.
[2] Governor Johnstone to the Duke of Portland, May 10, 1798, C. O. 71/30.
[3] Compiled from *Gt. Br., H. C., Sess. Pap.,* 1840, VIII (in 527), p. 594.

CHAPTER III

West India Commercial Relations

Exploitation of the British Caribbean during the eighteenth century involved three primary forms of commerce—intercourse with Africa, with the mainland colonies of North America, and with Great Britain. The first of these rested on the planters' need for a steady supply of laborers to open new lands and to replace slaves which did not maintain their numbers. The other two were based upon meeting the differing wants of complementary production areas.

These several kinds of inter-empire trade were coördinate and, together, they long formed one of the most nearly perfect commercial systems of modern times. They were open only to British subjects and were governed by numerous regulations mirroring contemporary mercantilistic doctrines. But such limitations served the West Indians well, for they enabled them to procure supplies at lowest figures, to market their products at top prices and to thus build up immense fortunes.

A fourth trade, anomalous in nature—one direct to foreign Europe —stood outside this system. It had been formally authorized to help the British proprietors meet French competition in old world markets but its creators had so hedged it with restrictions in attempting to harmonize its existence with the continuance of a régime of closed interchange of goods that it never attained more than slight proportions, in no way affected the welfare of the colonists, and consequently merits little more than bare mention.

Through the early decades of the seventeen hundreds, trade with the dark continent formed part of a general three-cornered trans-Atlantic commerce. Thus, a vessel left some port of British North America or Great Britain and proceeded to Africa where its cargo was bartered for blacks; it next crossed to the sugar islands to dispose of them and then returned to the home harbor with a shipment of tropical commodities.

New world participation in such triangular intercourse, however, came to a virtual close before 1750 as a result of the lower prices at which cargoes might be procured in the neighboring French islands where production costs were less, and a four-cornered trade replaced it. The Americans now disposed of negroes to their fellow-colonists in the Caribbean for cash, purchased sugar and other plantation produce of the latter's foreign rivals, and pocketed the difference in cost. This new traffic was most pernicious from the point of view of both the West Indians and the imperial government. The Molasses Act had been devised to close it, but in vain, since with the Atlantic seaboard merchants, economic self-interest overshadowed loyalty to a distant home government seemingly little concerned with their welfare.

At the same time, development of the custom of annually sending out merchant fleets from Great Britain to transport the season's crops to the home market increasingly relieved the West Indians of dependence on the irregular freighting service afforded by European-bound slavers. The triangular trade of the British vessels, too, broke down in consequence, and dealers in blacks from the metropole were forced to raise prices as a means of making up losses incurred through being obliged to return to Great Britain in ballast. Again, it was the planters who suffered.

The American trade to Africa centered in Rhode Island. From 1730 to 1764, some eighteen vessels a year left that colony for the Gold Coast,[1] principally from Newport.[2] Bristol and London were early seats of such commerce in England. The former sent out an average of fifty-seven ships per annum from 1701 to 1709. London's participation was at first even more promising, but soon fell off. In 1701 a total of 104 bottoms cleared out from that port for Guinea; in 1704, fifty; in 1707, only thirty. This intercourse virtually ceased in 1720 with the bursting of the South Sea Bubble.

The merchants of Liverpool were meanwhile primarily interested in supplying the West Indies with Manchester goods, many of which

---

[1] George L. Beer, *The Commercial Policy of England Toward the American Colonies* (New York, 1893), p. 114.

[2] "Commerce of Rhode Island, 1726–1800," in *Collections of the Massachusetts Historical Society*, Vols. LXIX and LXX (Boston, 1914, 1915) contains a portion of the papers of a Newport mercantile firm, long engaged in the African and West India trades. This work is of inestimable value, presenting as it does reports on the state of the markets, current prices, credit, commercial charges, the nature of cargoes, and how slaves were procured. The greater part of the papers fall between 1763 and 1788. See also Verner W. Crane, *A Rhode Island Slaver. Trade Book of the Sloop Adventure, 1773–1774* (Providence, 1922), and Charles W. Taussig, *Rum, Romance and Rebellion* (New York, 1928).

were subsequently smuggled into Spanish America. In 1709, one ship left the port for Africa; then no more did so for twenty years. However, when contraband relations with Spain's new world possessions were seriously hampered by the Grenville treaty of 1747, Liverpool commercial houses turned their attention to trafficking in negroes on a large scale.[1] In 1751, fifty-three of their vessels engaged in this new form of commerce; in 1760, seventy-four; in 1770, ninety-six; in 1792, no less than 132.[2]

The Liverpool traders operated at a considerably lower cost than did those from London and Bristol. The latter paid their captains monthly, granted them cabin privileges, primage, and daily port changes, provided full crews of adults at monthly wages and allowed their factors 5 per cent on both sales and returns. Liverpool merchants, on the contrary, engaged many boys as hands, paid officers and seamen only annually, made none of the above allowances and engaged their agents at salaries.

In consequence of these several economies, they undersold all rivals by about 12 per cent [3] and increasingly came to engross their business. In 1764, but thirty-two vessels cleared out for Africa from Bristol, while seventy-four left the harbor of Liverpool. More than half of the negroes transported to the Americas under the British flag were then passing through the hands of merchants from the latter port and one fourth of its bottoms were slayers.[4] The English trade came eventually to be almost wholly concentrated there; in 1798, 160 vessels cleared out from the city for Africa as compared with only three from Bristol and eight from London.[5]

[1] Gomer Williams, *History of the Liverpool Privateers and Letters of Marque With an Account of the Liverpool Slave Trade* (Liverpool, 1897), pp. 467–469.

[2] [John Corry], *The History of Liverpool, from the Earliest Authentic Period Down to the Present Time* . . . (Liverpool, 1810), p. 265.

[3] Anon., *A General and Descriptive History of the Antient and Present State of the Town of Liverpool* . . . (Liverpool, 1795), quoted by Williams, *Liverpool Privateers*, p. 47.

[4] Williams, *Liverpool Privateers*, pp. 494, 495.

[5] Corry, *History of Liverpool*, p. 266. For various aspects of the Bristol and Liverpool trades, see John Corry and John Evans, *History of Bristol* (2 vols., Bristol, 1816). John Latimer, *The Annals of Bristol in the Eighteenth Century* (Bristol, 1893). Latimer, *The Annals of Bristol in the Nineteenth Century* (Bristol, 1887). Ramsay Muir, *A History of Liverpool* (London, 1907). J. A. Picton, *Memorials of Liverpool Historical and Topographical* . . . (2 vols., Liverpool, 1907). Richard Brooke, *Liverpool as it was During the Last Quarter of the Eighteenth Century* (Liverpool, 1853). Also George F. Dow, *Slave Ships and Shipping* (Salem, Mass., 1927).

Colonial ships handling such human cargoes set out laden with rum to barter for the blacks, while those from the home country carried coarse cloth, beads, hardware, pipes, iron bars, guns, ammunition, sundry trinkets and novelties, and presents for chiefs.[1] The typical New England slaver was of about fifty tons burden and was manned by a captain, two mates, and a crew of not more than six. It carried up to 120 hogsheads of rum and on the outward voyage had but one deck. Crossing to the Caribbean, flooring laid three feet below this provided quarters for the slaves. Ships sailing from Great Britain were of about twice that burden, due to the greater bulk of the commodities on board.[2]

The English negro trade had been in the Royal African Company's hands from 1672 to 1697. For a quarter of a century, this concern had enjoyed a national monopoly of handling blacks and had opened numerous factories on the west coast of the continent. However, in the latter year, private traders had been admitted to operations within its sphere of activities upon payment of import and export duties to aid in maintaining the corporation's forts. In 1730 even those charges were abolished and an annual parliamentary subsidy of £10,000 was substituted therefor.

The company continued to maintain its posts for more than half a century after the loss of exclusive privileges but only at a cost becoming increasingly disproportionate to profit. Slaves were brought there for barter and were subsequently despatched to the sugar islands in Royal African vessels. Individual merchants, on the other hand, kept up no such establishments but passed slowly along the coast on the lookout for smoke signals from persons with blacks on hand. Operating at lower expense, they steadily undersold the corporation and completely undermined its trade. After suffering numerous vicissitudes, it dissolved in 1751 and, from then on, private adventurers held the field.[3]

Negroes were procured in various ways. Prisoners of war and criminals sufficed to meet early needs but, with the development of

[1] Long, *Jamaica,* I, 491; Williams, *Liverpool Privateers,* pp. 545–547.

[2] Phillips, *American Negro Slavery,* pp. 34, 35.

[3] *Ibid.,* pp. 24–30. The papers of the Royal African Company are preserved in the Public Record Office, London, under the group series number T. 70. For the early history of the organization, see George F. Zook, "The Company of Royal Adventurers Trading into Africa," in *The Journal of Negro History,* April, 1919. (Reprinted, Lancaster, Pa., 1919). A continuation of this work, by the same author, covers its activities from 1672 to 1752. This, however, has not as yet been published.

the several groups of Caribbean colonies, that supply came to be wholly inadequate. Minor offenders were then sold into bondage and man-hunts came to be freely indulged in. The entire central Atlantic coast of Africa was ravaged. Such civilization as had developed was destroyed, and the native peoples as a whole were debauched by contact with the whites,[1] yet the number of hands on the market was seldom excessive.

Many ethnographic groups were to be found within the slave-supplying area. Members of certain tribes were more desired by the traders than others because of characteristics making them peculiarly adapted to the plantation régime. The Whydahs, Nagoes, and Pawpaws of the Slave Coast were most highly prized. They developed into good field hands, had sunny dispositions and proved very tractable. The Coromantees of the Gold Coast were marked by firmness of mind and body, ferocity, courage, and stubbornness; they made faithful servants. The Senegalese were the brightest of all and were fitted for the trades and domestic service. They became good drivers, were dependable and could be easily disciplined, but were not capable of performing arduous labor. The Mandingoes were gentle but subject to worm disorders, were born thieves, and were constitutionally unfitted for protracted toil. Eboes, from the Bight of Benin, made poor investments since they were chronically despondent, required gentle treatment, and, while the women were industrious enough, the men betrayed an inborn aversion to any form of exertion. The Congos and Angolas were admirably suited for gang labor but were stupid and the former had marked dropsical tendencies.[2]

The value of these several stocks in the eyes of estate owners is re-

---

[1] Anthony Benezet, *A Short Account of That Part of Africa Inhabited by the Negroes* . . . (London, 1768). Lord Muncaster [i. e., John Pennington], *Historical Sketches of the Slave Trade and of its Effects on Africa* (London, 1792). Mungo Park, *Travels in the Interior Districts of Africa* . . . *in the Years 1795, 1796, and 1797* . . . (London, 1799). Park, *The Journal of a Mission to the Interior of Africa, in the Year 1805* . . . (London, 1815). Thomas Winterbottom, *An Account of the Native Africans in the Neighborhood of Sierra Leone* . . . (2 vols., London, 1804). C. B. Wadstrom, *Observations on the Slave Trade, and a Description of Some Part of the Coast of Guinea, During a Voyage, Made in 1787 and 1788* . . . (London, 1789).

[2] Long, *Jamaica*, II, 403, 404. Edwards, *History*, II, 63, 69, 72–74. Anon., "A Professional Planter," *Practical Rules for the Management and Medical Treatment of Negro Slaves in the Sugar Colonies* (London, 1803), pp. 39–48. Phillips, *American Negro Slavery*, pp. 42–44. West Indian travelers at times reported meeting negroes with a knowledge of Arabic and of the Mohammedan faith (see Madden, *A Twelvemonth's Residence*, I, 99 and II, 108; Williams, *Tour*, p. 31). These were Senegalese.

flected in the clearance papers of dealers on the outward journey from England. Of 150 slaving vessels leaving the port of Liverpool from January 1798 to January 1799, sixty-nine sailed for Angola, thirty-four for Bonny, eleven for the Gold Coast, ten for the Windward shore, ten for New Calebar, six for Old Calebar, three for Benin, three for Gabon, two for Cameroon, and one each for Whydah and Lagos.[1]

The conditions under which negroes were transported to the new world and "the horrors of the middle passage" have been frequently described but with much wild exaggeration. Cargoes contained few children and from two to five times as many males as females.[2] Separation of sexes prevailed. The men were brought on board fettered but their chains were removed some distance out at sea, while women were seldom shackled, even at the outset. All blacks were kept between decks at night and during stormy weather. This space was confessedly narrow, but it was ventilated and was washed and disinfected each morning. The slaves were required to bathe on rising, food was supplied in generous quantities, and a surgeon was in attendance to care for the sick.[3] The days were spent in the open air, with music and other diversions being freely indulged in.

That evils did exist cannot be denied. The temptation to overcrowd was great, quarters were never roomy, provisions and water now and then ran short, the loss of life from epidemics was sometimes serious. Yet such events were the exception rather than the rule; the captains and crews of slavers as a whole were not the inhuman monsters pictured by opponents of the trade. Transporting negroes to the Caribbean was merely one form of commerce to them. Many of the captains were high-minded men. One, indeed, John Newton, subsequently rose to fame as the rector of St. Mary Woolnoth church, London, and was a close friend of the poet Cowper.[4] Such inhumanities as there were arose primarily from the home government's failure to regulate

---

[1] Williams, *Liverpool Privateers*, Appendix XIII.

[2] Long, *Jamaica*, II, 385. Edwards, *History*, II, 113.

[3] "Dimensions of the Ships Employed in the Slave Trade," in *Gt. Br., H. C., Sess. Pap.*, 1788, XXII (565). "Circumstances and Propositions relative to the Slave Trade," in *ibid.*, 1789, XXIV (626, 627). "Minutes of Evidence on the Slave Trade," in *ibid.*, 1789, XXV (635–645), 1790, XXIX (698), XXX (699), and 1790–91, XXXIV (745–748). "Papers respecting the Slave Trade," in *ibid.*, 1789, XXVI (646). "Report of the Lords of the Committee of Council for Trade and Plantations," in *ibid.*, 1789 (646a).

[4] Several persons themselves connected with the trade have left accounts of the voyage. See the work of a former factor, James F. Stanfield, *Observations on a Guinea Voyage* (London, 1787) ; that of an ex-slave captain, William Snelgrave, *Account of Some Parts of Guinea and the Slave Trade* (London,

the traffic. If the Africans suffered hardships and the mortality rate among them was high, it must be acknowledged that the same was true with respect to the white seamen removing them to their new homes.[1]

Once arrived in the islands the slaves were sold either through factors or direct by the captains themselves. Prices varied with the tribal stock, age, and health of the individuals concerned. Newly-purchased hands were distributed among such negroes speaking their tongue as might already be on the plantations. It was from them that they learned the daily routine and mode of living. The "seasoning period," that of acclimatization, lasted for three years. One fourth of the recent arrivals normally died or committed suicide during that time, dysentery arising from changed diet being chiefly responsible for the deaths. The survivors soon adopted the ways of their fellows and readily fitted into the prevailing social order.

The slave trade was in reality one of great proportions. In the five years 1760–1764, 150 ships brought 40,624 Africans to Jamaica, of which number 33,161 were purchased locally; from 1765 to 1769, 149 vessels brought 31,932 of which 27,974 were retained; between 1770 and 1774, no less than 44,409 arrived in 172 bottoms and of these only 5,741 were exported to the other islands.[2] From 1788 to 1796 inclusive, arrivals in Barbados totalled 11,739 head and exports 9,811.[3] Between 1788 and 1804, 27,167 negroes entered Dominica and 16,155 were cleared out;[4] Grenada retained but 14,818 of 44,836 landed from 1789 to 1804.[5]

1784); and that of a one-time surgeon, Alexander Falconbridge, *An Account of the Slave Trade on the Coast of Africa* (London, 1788). For the career of Newton, see his so-called autobiography, *An Authentic Narrative of Some Remarkable and Interesting Incidents in the Life of xxxxx. Communicated in a Series of Letters, to the Reverend Mr. Haweis . . . and by him . . . now made public* (London, 1764), also published as *Out of the Depths. Autobiography of the Rev. John Newton* (London, 1916); his *Thoughts Upon the African Slave Trade* (London, 1788); John Callis, *John Newton—Sailor, Preacher, Pastor, and Poet* (London, 1908); and Anon., "The Author of 'The Good Shepherd,'" *The Slave and the Preacher; a History of the Rev. John Newton . . .* (London, 1851).

[1] A letter from Governor Parry of Barbados to Lord Sydney, dated May 13, 1788, in C. O. 28/61, denounces the unfair treatment accorded the seamen in the slave trade. He reports that they were often discharged in the islands to save expenses and were at times even set ashore without being paid their wages.

[2] Memorial of Stephen Fuller, agent for Jamaica, to the Board of Trade, Jan. 30, 1778, C. O. 137/38.

[3] C. O. 28/72.

[4] C. O. 71/38.

[5] C. O. 101/42.

In a report laid before the Privy Council about 1790, Liverpool merchants estimated that 74,000 negroes were then being transported from Africa annually, of which number 38,000 were being carried in British ships.[1] The prosperity of manufacturing cities such as Manchester and of the shipping center, Liverpool, had come to rest directly upon this branch of the national trade and it was giving employment to so many ships as to constitute "the nursery of British seamen."

Estate owners in the British Caribbean depended almost exclusively upon the continental American colonies for supplies of food-stuffs, livestock,[2] and lumber with which to carry on building operations and construct containers for their produce. Grain cultivation and meat production were unprofitable enterprises for them. "It is true economy in the planter, rather to buy provisions from others, than to raise them by his own labour. The product of a single acre of his cane fields will purchase more Indian corn than can be raised in five times that extent of land, and pay besides the freight. . . ."[3]

Extensive deforestation had taken place in the islands and such timber as still stood was found only in the interior. Poor roads made it so difficult of access and the high price of labor made its cost so prohibitive that little was cut.[4]

The mainland trade was carried on almost exclusively with the thirteen colonies, shipments from Canada, Nova Scotia, and Newfoundland being quite negligible. The comparative importance of these several sources of supply may be seen from the following table, based on custom house records, which cover importations into the British West Indies during 1771, 1772 and 1773.[5]

Product	Unit	From the 13 Colonies	Canada and Nova Scotia	Newfoundland
Boards and timber	feet	76,767,695	232,040	2,000
Shingles	number	59,586,194	185,000	——

[1] Quoted, Edwards, *History*, II, 57.
[2] See Deane Phillips, "Horse Raising in Colonial New England," *Cornell University Agricultural Experiment Station Memoir No. 54* (May, 1922) for an account of the demands of the Caribbean market.
[3] Edwards, *History*, II, 378.
[4] Stewart, *A View . . . of Jamaica*, p. 61.
[5] Excerpted from a publication of the West India interest in London, signed James Allen, Secretary, *Considerations on the Present State of the Intercourse between his Majesty's Sugar Colonies and the Dominions of the United States of America* [London, 1784], p. 24. Similar tables covering imports into Jamaica from 1768 to 1774 will be found in *To the King's Most Excellent Majesty in Council. The Humble Memorial and Petition of the Council and Assembly of Jamaica* [St. Jago de la Vega ?, 1784].

Product	Unit	From the 13 Colonies	Canada and Nova Scotia	New-foundland
Staves	number	57,998,661	27,350	——
Corn	bushels	1,204,389	24	——
Bread, flour	barrels	396,329	991	——
Fish	hogsheads	51,344	449	2,307
Beef, pork	barrels	44,782	170	24
Horses	number	7,130	28	——
Oil	barrels	3,189	139	118

West Indian-North American commercial relations were primarily in the hands of colonials, whose vessels of forty to fifty tons each made up to three round trips a year. British bottoms, originally laden with manufactured goods for the seaboard possessions, at times took on cargoes there and sailed for the islands, from whence they then returned to Great Britain bearing shipments of sugar. Similarly, others arriving in the tropics before crop time employed idle months in making a flying trip each to the continent and back. But these were the exceptions, not the rule.

Homeland ships making the between-season voyage, those under colonial registry engaged in the direct trade, and other American-owned craft returning to new world ports from extended slaving ventures took on rum, molasses, sugar, pimento, coffee, cacao, indigo, ginger, and precious woods for the northern markets. However, as with the American slave merchants, so with their fellow-countrymen dealing in plantation stores—both increasingly tended to dispose of their wares to the British West Indians for cash, to sail next for the French islands where tropical products could be purchased at lower cost, and finally to enter these fraudently in home harbors as being of British origin.[1]

The sale, rather than barter, of slaves and American produce eventually drained the Caribbean colonies of specie. There was no local coinage and a strange conglomeration of foreign pieces, chiefly Spanish and Portuguese, had long passed current at relative sterling values with those from Great Britain and British North America. Such foreign coins were normally received through contraband com-

[1] For an excellent study of this subject see Herbert C. Bell, "The West India Trade Before the American Revolution," in *The American Historical Review*, Jan., 1917, pp. 272–287. Reprinted as part of *Studies in the Trade Relations of the British West Indies and North America, 1763–1773; 1783–1793* (Philadelphia, 1917). See also "Commerce of Rhode Island," in *Coll. of Mass. Hist. Soc.*, LXIX, LXX; Robert E. Peabody, *The Derbys of Salem, Massachusetts* (Salem, 1908); and Peabody, *Merchant Venturers of Old Salem* (Boston, 1912).

mercial relations. The large number of Iberian origin afforded ample evidence of the extent of early eighteenth century operations with Spanish America and Brazil.

Counterfeits abounded; doubloons, one-fourth underweight, made in Rhode Island, circulated extensively in Jamaica about 1770.[1] Base British copper and foreign coins were regularly received from England until the turn of the century, when their exportation to the islands was finally forbidden by act of parliament.[2] Clipped coins, too, were commonly encountered. The unmilled Spanish pieces found in Jamaica during the early 1770's were as much as 30 per cent below standard.[3]

The American traders would accept nothing but genuine, unmutilated coins at face; all others were taken only by weight. Sound money was therefore regularly withdrawn from the British West Indies, and local trade came to be increasingly carried on by means of spurious and light weight pieces passing at fictitious values.

To retain good coins in circulation in the islands, two expedients were officially resorted to. In some cases, plugs were cut from them and they were then reissued at their original worth. At other times, they were stamped with legal tender values above face and were made to pass as these.[4] Naturally, mere temporary relief was thus afforded.

Legislative attempts to give clipped pieces their bullion value and to force counterfeits out of use were rendered futile through opposition on the part of the colonists, who would have been heavy losers thereby. However, a compromise was ultimately effected in Jamaica. A lottery held there in 1773 retired underweight coins at face and the loss was in this way spread over a considerable body of the population; thereafter mutilated ones were accepted by weight alone.[5] This example might well have been generally followed.

[1] Governor Trelawny to the Earl of Hillsborough, Nov. 24, 1770, C. O. 137/66.

[2] Circular letter to West Indian governors, Aug. 16, 1798, C. O. 324/103.

[3] Lieutenant-Governor Dalling to the Earl of Dartmouth, Jan. 3, 1774, C. O. 137/69.

[4] Howland Wood, *The Coinage of the West Indies With Special Reference to the Cut and Counterstamped Pieces* (New York, 1915). Reprinted from *The American Journal of Numismatics*, XLVIII. Plugs were also cut from coins at times to meet shortages of change. See for example, *Proclamation. By His Excellency William Monro . . . Administering the Government in the Island of Trinidad, and its Dependencies* [Port of Spain, 1811], dated June 19, authoring the cutting of plugs from dollars, up to 25,000 in number, the plugs to pass at one shilling and the mutilated dollars at nine shillings each.

[5] Governor Trelawny to the Earl of Hillsborough, Jan. 4, April 12, July 3, and Dec. 15, 1771, C. O. 137/66. Lieutenant-Governor Dalling to the Earl of Dartmouth, Jan. 3, 1774, C. O. 137/69.

Edward Long, during whose residence in Jamaica the shortage of coins first became marked, proposed meeting the problem by reducing the adverse trade balance with the mainland colonies. This could be done by increasing imports from the home country whose merchants accepted tropical produce in payment for their stocks and by turning attention to the local production of numerous commodities then being shipped in from the American continent.

Thus, he declared, more soap, candles, hams, fish, bacon, and cheese should be purchased in Great Britain while beef, pork, and butter should be procured from Ireland and Indian corn should be grown on the plantations; the entry of mules, horses, and horned cattle should be restricted; hoops, heading, and shingles should be made from island-grown lumber and lamp oil should be manufactured in the Caribbean itself. Such goods as must necessarily be brought from North America should be transported in vessels en route from Europe to the West Indies in ballast for, if these touched at American ports, loaded up and then marketed their cargoes to the planters, the latter could make payment in bills of exchange on England rather than in cash.[1]

Francis Cooke of the same colony, on the other hand, advocated borrowing £300,000 sterling with which to purchase gold and silver for coining below the British standards—an effective means of keeping coins at home—and calling in all foreign ones.[2] But nothing came of these various suggestions. Traditional trade relations were maintained; the steady drain of money to the French colonies and the near-by continent as well as the continued regular use of a great variety of foreign pieces and ones of dubious value caused such a scarcity of metal, reduced the circulating medium to such a chaotic state and created so much confusion that domestic commerce in the British plantations was seriously hampered.[3]

For decades the complementary trade between Great Britain's

[1] Long, *Jamaica*, I, 540 ff.

[2] *A Proposal for Introducing into Jamaica, a Quantity of Gold and Silver Specie, Sufficient to Carry on the Internal Commerce of the Country, Without the Assistance of any Foreign Coin* [St. Jago de la Vega], 1773.

[3] See for example *The Report of the Joint Committee of the Legislature of Antigua, Appointed to Take into Consideration the State of the Current Coin* . . . (Antigua, 1803). Address of President Thomson to the Council and Assembly of the Leeward Islands, March 2, 1798, with replies to the same, C. O. 152/78. Governor Lavington to Lord Hobart, April 8, 1803, C. O. 152/85. James McQueen, *A Letter to the Right Honourable Lord Glenelg* (London, 1838), pp. 4 ff. Stewart, *An Account of Jamaica*, pp. 59–61, 149, and his *A View* . . . *of Jamaica*, p. 129.

Atlantic seaboard possessions and her sugar islands was a fundamental factor in the prosperity of both. It gave the northern agriculturist an outlet for his primary products—foodstuffs, livestock, and lumber— for which there was but slight demand in Great Britain; it gave the Caribbean estate owner a steady market for his by-products, rum and molasses, the European consumption of which took but a fraction of the available supply, and thus kept up their price. So long as the tropical and temperate portions of the colonial empire developed apace, with one able constantly to absorb the other's surplus, the closed commercial system applied to them was wholly justifiable. However, were this balance once to be destroyed, its economic basis would cease to exist. The continued application of old restrictions under such new circumstances would inevitably work hardships on the more rapidly expanding region and would arouse resentment among its inhabitants. It was to the misfortune and ultimate ruin of the West Indians that their area of cultivation was so limited that, before the middle of the eighteenth century, they could no longer either take up their mainland neighbor's offerings or meet their demands for tropical produce at reasonable prices.

Commercial relations with the mother country provided stores of manufactured goods and some foodstuffs for the planters while constituting the great outlet for their produce. "A full enumeration of the various articles which furnish the ships bound to the West Indies with an outward freight would indeed comprise a considerable proportion of almost all the productions and manufactures of this kingdom, as well as many of the commodities imported into Great Britain from the rest of Europe and the East Indies." [1]

The bulk of the tropical crops grown was regularly sent home for consumption there or reshipment to foreign old world marts. The West India trade centered chiefly in London, but houses engaging in such commerce were also found in Southampton, Bristol, Liverpool, Lancaster, Glasgow, Leith, and, after the admission of Irishmen to it commencing in 1778, in Cork and Dublin as well. But Scotch [2] and Irish participation was relatively small and more shipments entered the harbor of London than all the others combined. The metropolis's predominant position in the English trade will be seen from the following table.

[1] Edwards, *History*, II, 377.
[2] Archibald Ewing's *View of the Merchants' House of Glasgow* . . . (Glasgow, 1866) contains scattering references to the West India trade from that port, as on pp. 256 ff.

Imports of Muscovado Sugar, the Growth of the British Plantations, from the British West India Islands into England.[1]

Year Ending Christmas	Colony	Into London	Into Out Ports
1763	Antigua	119,050 cwt.	8,903 cwt.
	Barbados	115,402	49,868
	Jamaica	530,625	148,994
	St. Kitts	138,747	11,214
1768	Antigua	187,868	20,120
	Barbados	97,863	58,845
	Jamaica	493,644	204,411
	St. Kitts	185,861	13,738
1774	Antigua	200,347	33,093
	Barbados	76,040	63,523
	Jamaica	618,473	291,255
	St. Kitts	184,871	19,872

The West India merchants were frequently of colonial extraction and holders of property there. Thus, the Longs and the Hibberts, leading eighteenth century dealers in sugar island products, had extensive family possessions in Jamaica; Bryan Edwards, after amassing a fortune as planter there, established a Caribbean trading house in Southampton; Mr. Lascelles, a Barbadian proprietor, became a partner in Lascelles and Maxwell of London.[2] Others came into possession of tropical estates through the foreclosing of mortgages held on them. The interests of the planters and the mercantile element consequently tended to become one and inseparable.

The dealers in tropical goods of each port banded together for mutual protection and the furtherance of common interests. The origin of these bodies is obscure, but it is known that some were in existence shortly after the middle of the seventeen hundreds. They were doubtless at first of an informal nature ultimately developing into powerful organizations with officers, elected members, and detailed records.

Most important of them were the Society of West India Merchants and the Society of West India Planters and Merchants, both of

---

[1] Compiled from Customs 3/63, 68, 74, P. R. O.

[2] See "Memoir of Beeston Long [Jr.] Esq.," in The Eur. Mag. and Lond. Rev., Dec. 1817, pp. 483–486. [Mr. Markland], A Sketch of the Life and Character of George Hibbert, Esq., F. R. S., S. A. and L. S. (London, 1837). Jerom Murch, Memoir of Robert Hibbert . . . (Bath, 1874). Sir Robert Rutherford's "A Distinguished West Indian House," in The W. I. Comm. Circ., Jan. 5, 1906, pp. 10, 11 covers the history of the firm Wilkinson and Gaviller, founded as Lascelles and Maxwell.

London,[1] the Bristol West India Club,[2] and the Glasgow West India Association. The known surviving minute books of the London bodies date from 1769 and 1785 respectively,[3] those of the Bristol organization from 1782,[4] and those of the Glasgow group from two decades later.[5]

That all were in existence at earlier times is, however, certain. Letters of Beeston Long, Sr., for many years chairman of the Society of West India Merchants, to the Duke of Newcastle under dates of 1760 and 1766 amply demonstrate that members of the Caribbean interest in London had already then banded together.[6] The Bristol organization replaced an earlier one whose records have been lost but which is known, by references in the Society of West India Merchants' minute books, to have been active as late as 1777. Glimpses into the activities of other outport West India trading bodies are to be had in the same place.

Bristol's commerce with the tropical American colonies suffered a serious decline at the close of the eighteenth century. Out of a fleet of 101 Jamaican merchantmen reaching England in 1796, a mere seven were from that port; out of 144 in 1797, but seventeen; out of 150 in 1798, only sixteen.[7] The local merchant organization, therefore, developed little strength; the London societies, which were strategically located for influencing legislation and whose members imported the larger part of the West Indian produce entering the United Kingdom, came to wield paramount influence in regulating the trade.

The two capital city bodies were constitutionally distinct. Beeston

[1] For an excellent study of the nature and work of these bodies see Lillian M. Penson, "The London West India Interest in the Eighteenth Century," in The Eng. Hist. Rev., July, 1921, pp. 373 ff.; also her The Colonial Agents of the British West Indies (London, 1924), pp. 194 ff., and "Early Years of the West India Committee," in The W. I. Comm. Circ., XXXV, nos. 559, 560, pp. 66, 77, and Algernon Aspinall, The British West Indies (London, 1912), pp. 377 ff.

[2] Lillian M. Penson, "The Bristol West India Club," in The W. I. Comm. Circ., May 13, 1920, pp. 134, 135.

[3] Minutes of the meetings of the Committee of West India Merchants, I (1769–1779), and Minutes of the meetings of the West India Planters and Merchants, I (1785–1792), both in the West India Committee archives.

[4] Minutes of the meetings of the Bristol West India Club, I (1782–1805), in the possession of the Society of Merchant Venturers of the City of Bristol.

[5] Minutes of the Glasgow West India Association, I (1802–1809), in W. I. Comm. archives.

[6] British Museum, Add. Ms. 32, 902, folio 458. Add. Ms. 32, 975, folios 416, 430.

[7] Latimer, Annals of Bristol in the Eighteenth Century, p. 519.

Long, Sr., and after him Beeston Long, Jr., served as chairman of the Society of West India Merchants for the greater part of the period 1769–1820; Lord Penrhyn long held that office in the Society of West India Planters and Merchants. But their membership was largely the same, they employed a common secretary, James Allen, and during many years Samuel Long acted as treasurer for both. A single working fund raised by a charge on trade (from 1d. to 1s. per cask of sugar, puncheon of rum, or per thousand pounds of coffee handled, or per ton on shipping employed, according to the need for money) was drawn upon to defray all expenses. These societies were, in point of fact, composed of one group of men meeting now to discuss problems of one kind, and again others of another.[1]

The West India merchants were frequently ship-owners; especially was this true of those in Bristol. In other cases, formal agreements were entered into between the commercial organizations and shipping interests and rates agreed upon were duly published.[2] Similarly, the scale of pay was settled with wharfingers, convoys were arranged for in time of war, and more speedy mail service was secured for the islands.[3]

The Society of West India Merchants showed great concern over the matter of pilfering. This was easy under existing conditions and was carried on on a large scale. The only quays where produce could long be legally entered in the capital lay between London Bridge and the Tower. They were but twenty in number and proved wholly inadequate. Cargoes were consequently discharged into lighters below the Bridge and were landed at the quays in that fashion. Little

---

[1] They merged in 1843 and are continued to-day as the West India Committee, an association of 2,500 planters, merchants, and others interested in the British Caribbean, incorporated by Royal Charter in 1904. The Committee seeks to promote the general welfare of those colonies by united action. In the nineteenth century, it played an influential part in the founding of the Colonial Bank, the Royal Mail Steam Packet Company, and the West India and Panama Telegraph Company, three institutions closely related with the well-being of these trans-Atlantic colonies. The Committee has published numerous works on West Indian history and agriculture as well as handbooks, has formed the best West Indian reference library in existence and, through the publication of a fortnightly *Circular,* keeps its members in close touch with world market conditions.

[2] *Rates of Freight, from London to the Sugar Colonies in Time of Peace* (London, 1771). *Rates of Freight . . . for the Year 1777* (London, 1777). *Rates of Freight . . .* (London, 1801), etc.

[3] *Min. W. I. Mer., passim,* as February 22, and July 25, 1780, November 4, 1801.

surveillance could be exercised and in the crowding and bustle of unloading huge quantities of goods were stolen by workers. Five temporary "sufferance" wharves, erected near the close of the century, offered even less protection.

Warehouses on the legal quays could accommodate but 32,000 hogsheads of sugar; those at the temporary ones, 60,000. But importations regularly exceeded these quantities. Such consignments as could not be given shelter were piled up along the wharves. Slight protection was given produce there and, in the aggregate, innumerable hogsheads of sugar and puncheons of rum vanished. Estimates of the annual loss at the end of the seventeen hundreds ran as high as £150,000 for the planters and £50,000 for the state in revenue. More than 10,000 individuals are said to have been plundering merchantmen in the port of London alone and 550 receivers of stolen produce are stated to have been operating there.[1]

In 1765, the Society offered a reward of forty shillings per thief captured and £20 for the discovery of any buyer of pilfered products.[2] Barnabas Linton was engaged as special constable and frequently received sums, as £5.12.6 on October 2, 1770 and £7.9.6. on January 2, 1771, for taking culprits and Mr. Bishop, an attorney at law, was retained to prosecute them.[3] Appeals were made to the Commissioners of Customs and the Lord Mayor as a result of alleged laxity on the part of their officials at the quays and the wharfingers' coöperation was sought.[4] Since many offenders who were pardoned at once returned to their nefarious practices, a petition was presented to the Secretaries of State praying that the Caribbean traders be permitted to lay before them the records of convicted persons preceding the freeing of any thereafter.[5] Elaborate regulations governing the discharging of merchantment were likewise devised; these required, among other things, that henceforth ships crews must themselves unload cargoes.[6] Support was also given individuals against whom action had been brought for conduct in seeking to prevent pilfering.[7]

Still, in 1795, it was reported that "plunderings of Suger in the River are carried on to a greater extent than ever" and, upon in-

---

[1] Patrick Colquhoun, *A Treatise on the Commerce and Police of the River Thames* . . . (London, 1800), pp. 108, 197, 198.

[2] *Ibid.*, p. 100, note.

[3] *Min. W. I. Mer.*, November 6, 1770, October 1, 1771.

[4] *Min. W. I. Mer.*, January 7, 1772, February 2, 1773, December 21, 1779.

[5] *Min. W. I. Mer.*, March 3, 1772.

[6] *Min. W. I. Mer.*, April 27, 1790.

[7] *Min. W. I. Mer.*, June 1, 1779, September 23, 1794.

vestigation, customs officers were found to be involved. The reward for apprehending thieves was raised to £50 per head on conviction plus five guineas on commitment and the king's promise of pardon was secured for such transgressors as might be the means of bringing receivers to justice.[1] The new campaign thus inaugurated assumed considerable proportions; more than £2,500 was expended by the Society in carrying on prosecutions alone during 1797 and 1798.[2] The government was prevailed upon to inflict severe punishments with the result that, early in 1797, one buyer of stolen produce was sentenced to transportation for fourteen years while shortly after two individuals, Smith and White, caught making off with rum, received terms half as long each.[3]

Relief from this state of affairs was ultimately secured through organizing the Thames Marine Police in 1798. Such a body had been projected by other interests [4] but the system of safeguarding shipping in port actually adopted was evolved by Patrick Colquhoun, a Scotchman in the employ of the Society of West India Merchants.[5] The declared object in creating it was "to procure a speedy and regular Discharge of West-India Ships by registered and approved Lumpers, . . . and to protect the Property in every Stage of the Discharge, from the Moment the Ship arrives at her Moorings to the final Delivery of Goods at the King's Beam, by Means of a Civil Force attached to the Police Department." Operations were begun with seventy constables, thirty-five foremen and 350 workmen divided into gangs of ten each.[6]

The Society expended £4,518 in executing its plan during the

[1] *Min. W. I. Mer.,* November 24, 1795.

[2] *Min. W. I. Mer.,* May 23, 1797, June 20, 1798.

[3] *Min. W. I. Mer.,* May 23, 1797, July 7, 1797.

[4] James Elmes, *A Scientific, Historical and Commercial Survey of the Harbour and Port of London* . . . (London, 1838), p. 35.

[5] Colquhoun discussed the problem of pilfering in the Port of London in his *A Treatise on the Police of the Metropolis* . . . (London, 1797). Following the publication of this work the Society invited him to study the matter and to offer specific proposals for preventing such losses. His plan was approved and the system was inaugurated on July 2, 1798, with Colquhoun as Superintendent Magistrate and headquarters at 259 Wapping New-Stairs. *Min. W. I. Mer., passim,* January to July, 1798. "Memoir of Patrick Colquhoun," in *The Eur. Mag. and Lond. Rev.,* March, April, May, June, 1818, pp. 188 ff., 305 ff., 409 ff., 497 ff. "The Thames River Police" in *The W. I. Comm. Circ.,* May 23, 1906, pp. 244, 245.

[6] Circular of announcement with the heading, "Marine-Police Institution . . . for the Prevention of Felonies and Misdemeanors on the River Thames" [1798].

course of two years.[1] The new arrangements proved extremely efficacious and, in 1800, the Marine Police passed under governmental control. The West Indians thereafter employed only a small private force of guards.[2] Colquhoun was voted a piece of plate valued at £500 [3] and subsequently received the appointment as agent for certain of the colonies in appreciation of his services. Stringent legislation about the same time [4] served further to reduce the pilfering evil to a minimum.

The crowded condition of the Port of London was intolerable to the West India traders. As early as 1774, the Society of Merchants considered the "Inconveniences to the Sugar Trade, arising from the confined State of the lawful Keys." At their request the Commissioners of Customs authorized the use of the "sufferance" wharves already mentioned for unloading purposes.[5] These afforded temporary relief, but recourse to them in no way solved the fundamental problem arising from the fact that harbor facilities had in no way kept pace with the tremendous growth of British commerce during the eighteenth century. Vessels were forced to anchor along the four miles of river frontage between the Bridge and Deptford awaiting their turn to unload. This stretch of water could accommodate less than 900 vessels and, in the sugar season, as many as 1,400 frequently entered the Thames within a few days.[6] The consequent delays were vexatious and costly; the loss from plundering greatly increased.

Early in 1790, the formation of a corporation to construct docks with adjoining quays and wharves at Wapping was under serious discussion in the British metropolis. The proposal was approved by the Society of West India Planters and Merchants; but, when a want of unanimity on the part of the principals brought the matter to a halt, certain of its members suggested that, since the Caribbean trade was chiefly responsible for crowding the river and obstructing traffic and at the same time suffered most from existing conditions, it be removed to another point.

George Hibbert became the guiding spirit of the new scheme.

[1] *Min. W. I. Mer.*, August 15, 1800.
[2] *Min. W. I. Mer.*, April 22, May 22, June 19, 1801.
[3] *Min. W. I. Mer.*, August 15, 1800.
[4] 39 and 40 Geo. III c. 87.
[5] *Min. W. I. Mer.*, December 6, 1774, February 7, 1775, January 3, 1776.
[6] Colquhoun, *Commerce and Police of the Thames*, insert table opposite p. 22. Also pp. 25-27.

Under his leadership, plans were drawn up to build wet docks, quays and warehouses for the exclusive use of West India shippers at the Isle of Dogs, some miles below the Bridge, by a joint stock concern. An agreement whereby neither group would oppose the other's interests was effected with those behind the Wapping project, the support of the proprietors and lessees of the legal quays was purchased by guaranteeing them compensation for losses incurred, a bill authorizing the formation of the West India Dock Company to carry out the work was drawn up by committees of the Society of Planters and Merchants and of the Corporation of London which shared jurisdiction of the port with the government and this was presented to parliament.

The measure provided for a capitalization of £500,000. The corporation was to be governed by thirteen representatives of the stockholders, four city aldermen, and four members of the London Common Council. All ships entering the Thames from the Caribbean for the first twenty-one years were to be required to unload at its docks where they were to pay the same port charges and duties as were collected at the old legal quays. Furthermore, all vessels bound for the West Indies were to take on cargoes there. Notwithstanding some opposition on the part of refiners and wholesale grocers to the monopoly clause, the bill passed in 1799, most of the stock was taken up by members of the colonial interest in the capital, Hibbert became chairman of the company, and in four years the new arrangements were in force.[1]

Close relations existed between the Caribbean planters and West India merchants of the home country. The latter purchased little produce outright but rather acted as commission men, receiving ship-

[1] *Min. W. I. Plant. and Mer., passim*, November 16, 1797, to May 31, 1799. Joseph Broodbank, *History of the Port of London* (2 vols., London, 1921), I, 97–108. James Elmes, *A Guide to the Port of London* . . . (London, 1842), p. 76. Elmes, *A Scientific . . . Survey of the . . . Port of London*, pp. 34, 35. A chart with the title "A Plan of the Proposed Canal and Wet Docks for the West India Trade in the Isle of Dogs" (London, 1797). "The Port of London," in *The W. I. Comm. Circ.*, April 28, 1908, p. 197; "The West India Docks," in *The Gent. Mag.*, Oct., 1802, p. 897; "Account of the Ceremony of laying the First Stone of the Isle of Dogs Wet Dock Buildings," in *The Eur. Mag. and Lond. Rev.*, July, 1800, pp. 7, 8; "Description of the West India Docks, from Limehouse to Blackwell," in *The Eur. Mag. and Lond Rev.*, Sept. 1802, pp. 113 ff. The West India Dock Act was the first legislation of its kind. In the case of the Liverpool docks, parliament had conferred the right of construction upon a municipality. The measure of 1799 became the basis for subsequent laws authorizing the creation of the Wapping Docks in 1800 and the East India ones in 1802.

ments on consignment and disposing of them as opportunity afforded. At the same time they served as the proprietors' agents. Mutual confidence in each other's integrity was consequently an essential factor in all their transactions.

The crop grown on a given estate was hauled to the nearest legal port of clearance and was there loaded on board a waiting merchantman for delivery to the broker. Hogsheads, casks, puncheons, and parcels bore distinguishing marks to designate their ownership and those in a given lot were numbered consecutively. Vessels from neighboring colonies assembled in two groups, the Jamaican and Leeward Island fleets, for crossing the Atlantic. Sailings ordinarily occurred during April, June, and August; in time of war, convoys were always provided.

When a sending arrived in port, it was claimed by the consignee who met customs duties, freight charges, primage, wharfage, lighterage, warehouse rental, insurance, cooperage, the expense of weighing, and the "trade rate" assessed to form a fund for advancing common interests as these were incurred and charged them to the shipper's account. Samples drawn and submitted to prospective purchasers likewise went out at the owner's expense.

The gross amounts of sales were placed to his credit when made. Each shipment was normally disposed of to several buyers, one part here and another there, over a period of time. Consequently, no uniform price per given unit was received for the entire lot; instead, it varied in accordance with quality and the trend of the market. The produce placed early in the season, when supplies were ample, brought less than did that held over until stocks had been largely cleared, but the latter faced a greater overhead. If a planter's financial standing was good, his consignment was ordinarily warehoused until values had steadied; if his rating was low, his goods were disposed of immediately upon arrival. When an entire shipment had been placed, a commission, ordinarily 2½ per cent, was charged against sales, and a balance was struck.[1]

But the marketing of tropical products was merely one of several business operations normally involving both proprietor and trader. The latter also served as the estate owner's buyer and banker and not infrequently as his personal representative as well. Lists of needed plantation stores were sent him periodically and he was relied upon to purchase cloth, hardware, crockery, furniture, plate, salt and

[1] For a typical sales account, see Appendix II.

cured meat, butter, hats, shoes, trinkets, and what not, even to musical instruments, current best sellers, and the last word in feminine creations, all at the most advantageous prices. The merchant's position was, in truth, not an easy one; it called for an intimate knowledge of both Caribbean economy and individual preferences. As with sales, purchases were made on commission. Goods were delivered to the agent-buyer, were paid for by him and were forwarded to the Caribbean at a set percentage above cost in a general shipment, ordinarily made once a year, on some outward-bound freighter.

The planter's account was regularly overdrawn. Crops consigned to the merchant went principally to pay for goods sent out some months before. Most of the proprietor's obligations were met by bills of exchange drawn on the trader handling his produce; payments due him were made to the dealer and were placed to his credit there. West Indian children sent to England for educations were met and cared for by their fathers' factors who often chose the schools in which to enroll them. The students' allowances were always paid by these important personages on order from the parents. Where vested with power of attorney, they likewise transacted all kinds of legal business for their clients.[1]

Such an order led to several inevitable consequences. Little actual money passed through the planter's hands; he rather operated on a barter economy, which bred wastefulness and extravagance.[2] The personal nature of the relationship between proprietor and merchant gave it a marked degree of permanency. A given West India house served as representative for a given family through many generations. The number of Caribbean traders was therefore relatively small; entry into this form of commerce was all but impossible save through purchase of an interest in an existing firm or ownership of estates, either of which called for a great outlay of capital.

[1] An intimate glimpse of the multifarious activities of a West India merchant can be gained by consulting the letter and account books in the possession of Messrs. Wilkinson and Gaviller, 34 Great Tower St., E. C., London. This house was founded as Lascelles and Maxwell about 1743 and since then has engaged largely in trade with Barbados. The firm's records commence in 1739/40 and are the most complete known to exist. They constitute an invaluable source for a study of British West Indian commerce and are deserving of thorough exploitation.

[2] The oversupply of equipment was striking. "It is disgraceful to see the waste of coppers, stills, of mill-cases, gudgeons, grating-bars, and . . . of many other plantation-utensils that are scattered upon some properties about the works and pastures; and yet perhaps the same list of stores is annually sent, and of consequence the same expense incurred." Beckford, *Descriptive Account of Jamaica,* II, 24, 25.

The West India factors, enjoying a double profit on dealings with the estate owners and facing little competition, became extremely wealthy. Their investments were limited to advances in the form of goods ordered made in anticipation of the next season's shipments. Risk was small so long as prices of tropical produce ruled high; but when, with their fall at the opening of the nineteenth century, returns from consignments regularly failed to meet such short term loans, the planters became increasingly involved and members of the mercantile class ultimately found themselves the unwilling owners of extensive Caribbean properties burdened with tremendous overhead. Their prosperity clearly rested upon that of the islanders.

An interesting aspect of the home country trade was the fraudulent entry of alien produce into British markets by way of the tropical American colonies. This was freely indulged in by French, Dutch, and Danish groups coöperating with unscrupulous local merchants in Great Britain's several possessions. Small craft from near-by foreign holdings, bearing cargoes of muscovado, rum, and coffee, were run into the mouths of creeks under cover of darkness and unloaded. These commodities were subsequently hauled to port and cleared as being of local origin and therefore subject to the lower British duty-rate charged on colonial-grown products. Such clandestine trade was highly profitable to both parties concerned; for it gave the planters engaged in it quicker and greater returns than were possible from ordinary transactions in their own national markets, and at the same time provided the purchasers with readily salable goods at prices materially below current quotations in the British Caribbean. It was therefore extensively indulged in, and legislative enactments seeking to curtail it proved of but slight avail.

In 1764 the Assembly of Antigua, reviving an earlier resolution, declared "That every person who shall import into this Island any Rum, Spirits, Molasses, Sugar, Syrup, or Paniles [paneles], of the Product or Manufacture of any of the Colonies or Plantations in America not in the possession, or under the Dominion, of His Majesty . . . and every Person aiding and assisting in the Importation thereof by housing them when landed, or lending to the Importers Carts, Cattle, Negroes, Boats or any other Assistance whatsoever, is an Enemy to his Country and . . . is unworthy to be a Member of civil society." [1]

Commencing in 1778, by act of parliament,[2] sugar shipped from

[1] C. O. 152/30, no. 36.
[2] 18 Geo. III c. 58.

beyond the Atlantic for entry into Great Britain at the British plantation rate was required to be accompanied by a certificate declaring it to have been grown in the colony from whence it was cleared. Different local governments, too, sought to check illicit traffic in the same manner. Thus, by a law of 1786, the St. Vincent legislature obliged shippers in the island to make a declaration covering every consignment of sugar or rum, specifying under oath whether it was of British plantation or foreign growth.[1]

The year before, the West India Planters and Merchants had estimated the quantity of French sugar reaching home marts under false entry at nearly 20,000 hogsheads per annum.[2] The Society urged that all proprietors be required to make affidavits similar to those subsequently employed in St. Vincent before local justices of the peace, and recommended the naming of commissioners in all ports of clearance to whom ship masters must present such documents before receiving authorization for departure with their cargoes.[3]

Though the formality of certification might be complied with, illegal trade was not halted thereby. In 1791, Governor Orde of Dominica declared that fully half of the 6,000 hogsheads of muscovado being exported from that island each year were of French origin. "Quantities . . . are often reported, as sworn to be made at certain estates, when it is notorious that such estates are not making Sugar at all, or never make one half the quantity certified to be of their produce." Such action was supported by the entire community.[4]

Foreign wares, too, found their way in considerable quantities into the British Caribbean under cover. Tortola, most important of the Virgin Islands, was the smuggling center of Great Britain's West India possessions at the close of the eighteenth century. Manufactured goods and raw products of all descriptions entered freely from the foreign colonies. The former seeped west and south, the latter were sent home. Returns of exports therefore give not the slightest indi-

---

[1] *The Laws of the Island of Saint Vincent . . . to the End of the Year 1809* (Bridgnorth, Shropshire, 1811), pp. 189–195, 207, 208.

[2] A printed paper, issued for circulation among the trade, *Observations on The Heads of the proposed Regulations for more effectually preventing the fraudulent Introduction of foreign Sugars, Spirits, and Melasses, as British Growth, explaining the general Policy and Necessity of the same . . .* [London, 1785], p. 1.

[3] *Extracts from the Minutes of a Meeting of the Standing Committee of West-India Planters and Merchants, on the 21st of June 1785* [London, 1785], pp. 1, 2.

[4] To W. Grenville, Jan. 18 and April 16, 1791, in C. O. 71/18.

cation of the group's development, inasmuch as Danish-grown sugar was regularly shipped as British from this lawless community with official connivance. Even in the early eighteen hundreds, not more than half of the 7,000 hogsheads annually exported seem to have been actually produced in the island.[1]

The trade of Barbados, Antigua, St. Kitts, Nevis, and Montserrat was subject to a peculiar and iniquitous disability—a four and a half per cent duty on exports. This had arisen shortly after 1650 and had been the price agreed upon by inhabitants of those colonies to secure the extinguishing of proprietary claims and government, under which the titles to many holdings had been challenged on the ground of being defective. Money thus raised had been intended to defray the expenses of government and the cost of defense, but it had actually been diverted to the payment of crown pensions and the meeting of other obligations in no way connected with the sugar plantations. As actually administered, this charge was, all in all, quite the most unjustifiable recorded in the troubled annals of colonial taxation.[2]

[1] Anon., *Letters from the Virgin Islands* (London, 1843), pp. 120, 121. Internal evidence shows these letters to have been written in the decade 1820–30. The writer, an English officer stationed in the islands, gives an interesting account of the smuggling then being carried on. "The portion of our imports entered at the douane is trifling:—shingles and deal-ends, the half cargo of some Yankee in distress, part of the estate supplies purchased at St. Thomas', with a few bale and crate goods from home, make the sum of them. The remainder comes here no one knows how, or cares to inquire. Tea, wines, brandy, cigars, with twenty other articles forbidden in the commercial decalogue, are yet seen among us: the smiling virginities of Tortola have their Leghorn bonnets, and are escorted by beaux in the true wefts of Nankin, without a solitary import id genus being found in his Majesty's revenue books. I write to you on foreign stationery, in waistcoat and hose of excellent French silk, shirt of fine German linen, and brogues made here from the villanous leather of Kentucky; and yet we are told that the West Indies consume annually four millions of British manufacture—if all were in such juxtaposition with a free port as the loyal Creoles of the Virgins, parliament might hear another story" (p. 123). The free port referred to was St. Thomas.

[2] A typical charge against this fund appears in the following item from *The Annual Register for 1773.* "August 2d. On Saturday passed the great-seal, a grant of a pension of 500 l. per ann. to —— Cornwall, Esq., out of the revenue duty, or custom of 4 1-half per cent at Barbadoes, and the Leeward islands, to hold the same during his life" (p. 134). For accounts covering the collection of this duty and payments made from it, see "Payments out of 4½% Duties at Barbados," in *Gt. Br., H. C., Sess. Pap.*, 1816, XIII (520, 255), 125, 285; "Produce of 4½% Duties," in *ibid.*, 1820, XI (22, 23), 355, 363; "Pensions granted upon 4½% Duties in Reversion," in *ibid.*, 1820, XI (110), 371; "Gross and Net Proceeds of 4½% Duties," in *ibid.*, 1821, XVI (690), 313; "Net Produce of 4½% Duties," in *ibid.*, 1822, XX (225), 179; "Pensions charged on 4½% Duties, the Annual Amount of each which

Not only did it in no way benefit the islands on which it was laid —it placed them at a distinct disadvantage in production with respect to the others where no such duty was collected. The latter's preferential treatment weighed heavily on the proprietors of the old estates in Barbados and the Leewards since, to them, 4½ per cent frequently represented the difference between affluence and the bare meeting of operating costs. It was indeed peculiarly inequitable that the colonies exempted from this payment were the very ones possessing the greatest tracts of virgin soil.

The tax was paid in kind. Rum thus coming into crown officials' hands was ordinarily sold on the spot, while sugar was shipped to England for marketing there. Returns were, however, far less than what they should have been. The produce used in meeting this charge was always the poorest part of the crop and sold for low prices. Furthermore, in laying the duty against consignments of sugar, hogsheads were regularly entered as containing twelve hundredweight each while in reality they frequently held as much as one fourth more.[1]

Generation after generation, planters subject to the tax complained bitterly against its collection. British officials and the Crown were appealed to;[2] at times attempts were made to force the home government's hands. In 1780, for example, the Barbadian legislature voted the newly-arrived executive, Cunninghame, a salary of £2,000 currency in lieu of the customary £3,000, but accompanied the act with a

exceeds £100," in *ibid.*, 1822, XX (326), 183; "Amount of 4½% Duties in the last year, and Pensions and Charges payable therefrom," in *ibid.*, 1825, XVII (474), 335; "Amount of 4½% Duties in 1825 and Pensions Payable therefrom," in *ibid.*, 1826, XIX (121), 437; "Proceeds of Produce Paying 4½% Duty . . . 1820 to 1830 . . . ," in *ibid.*, 1830, XXVII (273), 325; "Payments made out of the Surplus which accrued on the 4½% Fund, between 25th March, 1828, and 5th January, 1830," in *ibid.*, 1830, XXVII (680), 335; "Amount of 4½% Duty . . . ; Pensions and Charges payable therefrom, 1820 to 1832," in *ibid.*, 1833, XXIII (317), 739; "Sums paid into the Exchequer on account of the 4½% Duties," in *ibid.*, 1836, XXVII (120), 345.

[1] In 1778, a conscientious collector in one of the Leeward Islands refused to clear cargoes until they had been weighed and duty on them had been paid on the basis of the actual amounts shipped. The planters thereupon agreed among themselves to ship no produce until the old system had been restored. Admiral Barrington soon brought out orders that this be done. *The Annual Regiser for 1778*, p. 197.

[2] See "Note addressed by the Legislative Agents for the Colonies to Viscount Goderich, praying for the Abolition of the 4½% Tax," in *Gt. Br., H. C., Sess. Pap.*, 1831–32, XXXI (562), 251 and "Copy of Act, 1834, by Legislature of Barbadoes, Repealing 4½% Duty; also Memorial of the Council and Assembly of Barbadoes, praying His Majesty to give his assent thereto," in *ibid.*, 1837, XXXIX (289), 257.

declaration that the latter sum would be granted if the export duty were removed.[1]

Such efforts proved entirely futile. Not until 1838, after having been borne for no less than 175 years, was this unjust and wholly insupportable charge at length abolished.[2] To it must be attributed in no small measure the ruin of Barbados and the Leeward group before the competition of newly-acquired territories in the Caribbean.

The absence of banking facilities in the islands [3] was met by carrying credits with factors at home, as already related. It is worthy of note that exchange never stood at par and fluctuated violently with the demand for bills. While money values in the colonies were reckoned in pounds, shillings, and pence, these were not on a sterling basis. Local quotations were always in "currency," the relation of which to British standard varied from season to season. Exchange was particularly disadvantageous to the islanders in time of war and during shortages of coin.

It remains to mention a fourth trade involving the British Caribbean which might legally be engaged in—the direct exportation of muscovado to foreign parts of the old world. As we have seen,[4] this was initiated in 1739 as a concession to the planters whose produce was suffering exclusion from continental marts through the French colonists not being required to first enter their cargoes at home and consequently underselling them. Following an extension of the act in 1742, any British subject meeting certain requirements might clear out from the tropical American colonies in a British ship navigated according to law with a cargo of British-grown sugar and proceed immediately to any port south of Cape Finisterre, or to any one of northern Europe after first touching at some home harbor en route.

Persons desiring to engage in such commerce were obliged to secure special licences from the Customs Commissioners in London or Edinburgh, bonds to guarantee compliance with the terms of the law were required, and certificates of origin had to accompany all ship-

[1] Governor Cunninghame to Lord Germain, July 26, 1780, and enclosures, C. O. 28/57.

[2] See Anon., *A Guide to the Electors of Great Britain, Upon the Accession of a New King and the Immediate Prospect of a New Parliament* (London, 1820), calling on voters to return to the House candidates who would oppose the diversion of funds into pensions and attacking the use made of this export tax for that purpose.

[3] The first bank in the West Indies, the Colonial Bank, was incorporated by Royal Charter in 1836.

[4] Page 53.

ments, in addition, captains were forced to return to England before commencing another outward voyage.[1] The measure, as subsequently renewed in 1744, 1751, 1758, 1764, 1772, 1778, 1786, and 1793,[2] was, in reality, an expansion of the principle first finding expression in the act of nine years earlier which permitted the direct exportation of rice from South Carolina to any port below Cape Finisterre,[3] rather than an innovation in the navigation system.

The trade which developed proved to be of very slight importance. Forty-eight licences to export muscavado south of the cape were issued up to 1753 but only five of these, covering 777 hogsheads, 184 tierces, 253 casks, and 126 barrels, were ever used.[4] The exact quantities shipped at later times are uncertain. In 1787 but one vessel, and that unladen, cleared out from the British tropics for southern Europe.[5] Sendings were certainly never great and must have been negligible during the Seven Years' War and the American Revolution.

The regulations governing direct trade were too onerous. Nor, considering the relations normally existing betwen planter and home merchant, was it strange that such commerce never attained great proportions. Entering into engagements with foreign dealers of necessity injected a large element of risk into marketing, and this would in no way be offset by the vague possibility of greater gain. Consigning cargoes to foreign marts required new credit arrangements, whereas stores must still be purchased through old channels. Such sugar as left the colonies under this act was in all probability shipped by local merchants or was carried by ship-masters making independent ventures rather than being sent on the account of planters.

Be that as it may, the estates owners' welfare continued to rest upon the three fundamental trades. "The conditions and regulations on which it [permission to ship sugar direct to European ports] was granted were so strict and numerous, as to defeat in a great measure the intention of the legislature," wrote Bryan Edwards about 1790.[6] Four years later, during the widespread sugar shortage following the ravaging of St. Domingo, the measure was repealed without debate.[7]

[1] 12 Geo. II c. 30. 15 Geo. II c. 33.

[2] By 17 Geo. II c. 40, 24 Geo. II c. 57, 31 Geo. II c. 35, 4 Geo. III c. 12, 12 Geo. III c. 56, 18 Geo. III c. 45, 26 Geo. III. c. 53, and 33 Geo. III c. 40.

[3] 3 Geo. II c. 28. The privilege was later extended to North Carolina and Georgia as well.

[4] William Wood's Account, March 24, 1753, Treas. 64/274, quoted, Pitman, *Development*, pp. 184, 185.

[5] Macpherson, *Annals of Commerce*, IV, 158.

[6] *History*, II, 372, note.

[7] 34 Geo. III c. 42.

PART II
THE DECLINE OF THE SUGAR ISLANDS

CHAPTER IV

DEVELOPMENT OF THE CEDED ISLANDS

The Peace of Paris, ending the Seven Years' War, profoundly affected the course of British West Indian history. The old colonies (Barbados, Antigua, Barbuda, St. Kitts, Nevis, Anguilla, Montserrat, the Virgin group, Jamaica, and the Caymans), comprising a total of 5,000 square miles, had come under English control during the second and third quarters of the seventeenth century. Excepting Jamaica, conquered from Spain, and the Virgins, taken from the Dutch, all had been acquired through settlement. To these were now added as spoils of victory Dominica, St. Vincent, Tobago, Grenada, and the Grenadines.

The combined area of these new Caribbean holdings was under 700 square miles. Ownership of the first three had long been disputed with France but, since the Treaty of Aix la Chapelle, the two powers had regarded them and St. Lucia as neutral islands, to be left in native possession. France's claim to Grenada and the neighboring islets had never been questioned. At the same time that these bits of territory were incorporated within the British empire, Guadeloupe and Martinique were restored to France while St. Lucia, the fourth neutral island, which had been occupied by British forces, was evacuated and turned over to the French. Cuba, conquered from Spain, was returned to that power as the price of Florida. Great Britain's major gains of 1763 were made in Canada and India.

What with complete triumph in the recent conflict and the great value placed upon tropical colonies as compared with those in the temperate zone during the early period of overseas expansion, this readjustment was at the same time surprising and grievously disappointing to the average Englishman. High hopes for commercial development had arisen with the capture of Havana [1] and these were now rudely dashed to the ground. The unexpected restoration of Guadeloupe and Martinique was even more keenly felt.

[1] Adrien Dessalles, *Histoire Générale des Antilles* (5 vols., Paris, 1847–48), V, 353.

These two islands were highly prized by France; it was from them that she drew a large part of the tropical produce required to meet her own needs and to supply foreign continental marts. The districts in the old British Caribbean adapted to sugar cultivation were so limited in extent that by 1750 production there no longer met the rising demands of home and colonial American consumers. Consequently, under the conditions of monopoly surrounding the trade, high prices prevailed and curtailed both consumption within the empire and exports to the European mainland. Were either Guadeloupe or Martinique to become British, the available supply would be materially increased, market values must of necessity fall, and foreign as well as domestic sales would advance.

It had not been an unreasonable assumption that whatever other terms of peace might be arrived at, one or the other at least of these French possessions would be retained. Yet Canada was taken instead. Of indefinite extent, its exploitation barely begun, its population sparse, offering no commodity in general demand, and enjoying no established commercial connections with Great Britain, that region in 1763 afforded wholly inadequate compensation for either of the restored territories. Well might Choiseul, the astute Minister of War and Marine negotiating the exchange, boast of having trapped the British.[1]

This unnatural and peculiarly disadvantageous settlement can be explained only by the London West India interest's opposition to any considerable extension of control over tropical America since this would seriously impair the value of existing monopoly rights. Unfortunately, the surviving records of organized Caribbean groups in the home country date only from some years later,[2] but recent research has placed full responsibility upon the planter lobby. Burke desired the retention of Guadeloupe and Pitt the holding of Martinique. The West Indians exerted pressure on both since returning the two islands and acquiring Canada would preserve their position in the British market and would, at the same time, provide an additional outlet for some of their produce such as rum, which was then largely unsalable.[3] The government bowed before them. The general

[1] Arthur Girault, *Principes de Colonisation et de Législation Coloniale* (4 vols., Paris, 1921–23), I, 119.

[2] See page 94.

[3] Beer, *British Colonial Policy, 1754–65*, Ch. XII. Pitman, *Development*, Chapter XIV. See also William L. Grant, "Canada Versus Guadeloupe, An Episode of the Seven Years' War," in *The Am. Hist. Rev.*, July, 1912, pp. 735–743.

interest was sacrificed in order that a small but powerful body might continue to enrich itself through the enjoyment of unwarranted privilege.[1]

The consequences of this step were momentous. An opportunity had been afforded Great Britain to restore the economic equilibrium of her empire which was becoming sadly overbalanced on the temperate side through rapid opening up of the northern American provinces. This had not been seized, and the failure to substantially enlarge torrid zone holdings and thus divert into legal channels the large illicit trade carried on by inhabitants of the thirteen colonies with French Caribbean planters in an effort to dispose of their surplus, did much to strain relations between them and the home government during the decade which followed. At the same time, by insuring continued large returns for the proprietors, the Peace of Paris bolstered up the unsound economic system prevailing in the British West Indies and made ultimate, complete ruin more certain.

The ceded islands—Grenada, the Grenadines, Dominica, St. Vincent, and Tobago—were promptly organized as the government of Grenada with representative institutions. All land was declared to be crown property, surveys were made, and in the spring of 1764 regulations governing its disposal appeared. These reveal a firm determination to prevent the rise of large estates and the holding of tracts in idleness by speculators.

Commissioners were despatched across the Atlantic with orders to dispose of parcels by public sale to British subjects only. No person might purchase more than 300 acres in Dominica or 500 in any of the other islands. Twenty per cent of the price was payable immediately, 10 per cent one year later, 10 per cent in another twelve months, and the balance in three annual installments of 20 per cent each. One acre in twenty must be cleared each year until half of a given property was in shape for cultivation, under penalty of a £5 fine for every acre short. One white man or two white women must be maintained for each hundred acres cleared under penalty of an annual fine of £20 per woman or £40 per man deficient. A quit-rent of six pence per acre on all fields was payable to the Crown each year.

Eight hundred acres in every parish were reserved for poor settlers. These were to be given from ten to thirty each in fee simple but such grants were to remain inalienable for seven years. The commissioners

---

[1] The Peace of Paris marks the high point of the British West India interest's influence in British politics.

were furthermore authorized to lease to the French inhabitants for terms up to forty years such lands as had been in their possession under the old régime, provided that they swore allegiance to the British king.[1]

The new possessions were in different stages of development. Grenada, which had been regularly colonized by France, was most fully exploited. Eighty-one sugar plantations and 208 raising coffee, cacao, or stock were in operation in 1763, and twenty-one were then lying abandoned.[2] Dominica, St. Vincent, and Tobago had technically become neutral islands in 1748, but a considerable number of French planters had nevertheless taken up residence in the first two before 1763. No attempt had been made to settle Tobago. Some idea of the relative extent to which they had been opened up at the time of their acquisition can be gained from the following table of exports to England during 1765, the first normal year following the war and before lands opened by new-comers under the sale provisions of 1764 had begun to yield.[3]

Colony	Cacao	Coffee	Cotton	Sugar
Dominica	20,100 lbs.	936,900 lbs.	226,095 lbs.	————
Grenada *	179,200 lbs.	1,285,700 lbs.	368,032 lbs.	64,458 lbs.
St. Vincent	30,600 lbs.	46,700 lbs.	13,000 lbs.	————
Tobago	————	————	————	————

* The produce of the Grenadines was commonly shipped from Grenada and the group must be considered as part of that island at this early date. Although a large amount of cotton was annually cleared out from St. George, this was the growth of Carriacou, largest of the Grenadines, rather than of Grenada proper. See "Answers to Queries Relative to Grenada" (in French), C. O. 101/18.

It will be observed that cane cultivation in Dominica and St. Vincent was of such slight importance that no sugar whatever was shipped out. Nor could Grenada be termed characteristically a sugar island. The French, as has been emphasized, were not monoculturists

[1] *Barbados, January 19, 1765. By the King's Authority* . . . [*begin; a proclamation*], [Bridgetown, 1765]. [*Regulations for the Sale of Land in the Ceded Islands*], [a broadside, Barbados, 1765]. *The Annual Register for 1764*, p. 57. Atwood, *Dominica*, pp. 2–5.

[2] Daniel Paterson, *New Plan of the Island of Grenada, from the Original Survey of Mons. Pinel, Taken in 1763 by Order of the Government* . . . (Faden, 1780). Paterson, *A Topographical Description of the Island of Grenada* . . . *With the Addition of* . . . *Improvements to the Present Time* (London, 1780).

[3] Compiled from Customs 3/65, P. R. O.

nor were they primarily interested in the growth and marketing of saccharine products.[1]

Absentee Caribbean proprietors in Great Britain evinced marked hostility toward any development of the ceded islands despite their small size. The conditions of sale made it impossible for them to establish large estates there and at the same time served to drain lesser whites away from the old colonies in the hope of becoming independent small-scale producers in the new ones. Crops grown on the latter's virgin soil would certainly lower existing prices and cut profits. Any change in the status quo could not fail to affect the established plantation owners adversely. They sought, therefore, to discourage settlement by grossly exaggerating attendant risks and difficulties.

Some, for example, argued that the French would soon seek to regain control, that the terms at which property was offered were impossible to meet and that the laying out of estates involved great hardships. Others, with consummate cunning, added that further supplies of sugar and rum would glut the market, that additional consignments would prove unsalable and that ruin would thus confront the new planters operating with small capital. These fallacious arguments were vigorously combated by an anonymous pamphleteer who exposed the self-interest behind them and encouraged ambitious persons of moderate means to seek fortune there.[2]

It had been quite impossible for more than half a century to secure conveniently located fresh lands at a low price in any of the old West India possessions. The opportunity of now doing so was not to be overlooked and the first immigrants from them arrived in Grenada even before formal cession had taken place.[3] By 1772, that island had 166 new British settlers in addition to 139 long-time French residents. Three hundred thirty-four plantations employing 26,211 negroes were then being worked. The sugar properties embraced 32,011 acres, the coffee estates, 12,796, the cacao ones 712 and those in indigo

[1] See page 39.

[2] Anon., *Considerations Which May Tend to Promote the Settlement of Our New West India Colonies* (London, 1764), *passim*. Other pamphlets of a similar nature are [John Campbell], *Description and History of the New Sugar Islands in the West Indies* (London, 1762); "Ignotus," *pseud., Thoughts on Trade in General, and Our West Indian in Particular* (London, 1763); Anon., *Some Observations Which May Contribute to Afford a Just Idea of the Nature, Importance, and Settlement of Our New West-India Colonies* (London, 1764).

[3] Lieut.-Col. George Scott to Lord Egremont, Jan. 19, 1763, C. O. 101/19.

742. More than 10 per cent of the total number had just been opened. Ninety-five water mills, twelve operated by wind power and eighteen turned by cattle, were then in use.[1] Four years later, taxes were paid on 72,141 acres of land, about 50,000 of which were under actual exploitation. One hundred six sugar plantations were then in cultivation.[2]

By 1773, a total of 95,134 acres had been purchased in Dominica and about one-fourth were actually in crops.[3] Sales in Tobago between 1765 and 1771 amounted to 57,408 acres with the selling price ranging from £1.0.1¾ to £5.17.7 each.[4] There were seventy-eight plantations in cultivation there in 1770 and 5,084 acres had then been cleared.[5] By 1773 no less than 103 properties, forty-one of them sugar estates, were being worked. Fifteen wind, six water, and twenty-nine cattle mills were then in operation;[6] two years later their number had risen to twenty-three, nine, and fifty-two respectively.[7]

The opening of St. Vincent was effected less rapidly because of the grant of two large tracts to favoured individuals and the presence of a considerable body of natives. Twenty thousand acres were gratuitously assigned by the Crown to one Swinburne and another four thousand to General Monckton. Thus, over one-fourth of the colony was withdrawn from the market at the outset. Only 20,538 acres were sold at auction and brought but £162,854 sterling.[8] Monckton subsequently disposed of his grant to speculators for £30,000.[9]

The work of surveying was hindered by the black Caribs who were

---

[1] C. O. 101/16, 18.

[2] [List of Freehold and Leased Estates in the Several Parishes of Dominica], (no imprint, n.d.—ca. 1775). John Byers, References to the Plan of the Island of Dominica, as Surveyed from the Year 1765 to 1773 (London, 1777). Edwards, History, I, 381.

[3] "Answers to Queries," C. O. 71/4.

[4] Sales in 1765 were 4,000 acres at an average price of £1.0.1¾d. per acre; sales in 1766, 11,096 acres at an average price of £1.0.2; sales in 1767, 14,975 acres at an average price of £1.9.2; sales in 1768, 4,632 acres at an average price of £1.10.4; sales in 1769, 5,183 acres at an average price of £2.15.0; sales in 1770, 9,362 acres at an average price of £5.17.7; sales in 1771, 8,160 acres at an average price of £4.13.11. John Fowler, A Summary Account of the Present Flourishing State of the Respectable Colony of Tobago in the British West Indies (London, 1774), p. 64.

[5] Statistical table for 1770, C. O. 101/14.

[6] Statistical table for 1773, C. O. 101/18.

[7] Statistical table for 1775, C. O. 101/18.

[8] John Byers, References to the Plan of the Island of St. Vincent, as Surveyed from the Year 1765 to 1773 (London, 1777). Edwards, History, I, 401.

[9] Shephard, Account of St. Vincent, p. 12.

descendants of shipwrecked Guinea slaves and the indigenous yellow Caribs. These mongrel peoples declared themselves to be independent owners of the soil and disputed the British occupation. They committed numerous depredations on the plantations which had been laid out and matters reached such a point that it become necessary to launch an expeditionary force of North American troops against them in 1772. Their resistance was soon broken. By a treaty of the following year, they recognized British control and accepted a block of land in the northern part of the island, set aside for their exclusive use.[1] The affair aroused considerable opposition in England among well-meaning but misinformed individuals who saw in it nothing but wanton aggression against an inoffensive local people.[2] It was actually a necessary preliminary step to the development of the colony.

When a separate administration was organized for St. Vincent in 1776, instructions issued to Governor Valentine Morris authorized him to make grants of unsold land within his government. This power was a conventional one seldom used. But years of official service in the Caribbean[3] had convinced Morris of the need for a substantial body of small resident owners, and he at once gave out a number of holdings under fifty acres each, subject only to an annual quit rent payment of six pence sterling per acre, which was to be quadrupled after the fourth year on all such parts as had not been brought under cultivation.

This wise and liberal action won the unanimous opposition of large proprietors throughout the British American tropics as the prospect of securing free land would inevitably draw off inferior whites from among them to St. Vincent. At their instigation, the governor was

[1] For this interesting body of natives, see William Young, *An Account of the Black Charaibs in the Island of St. Vincent* (London, 1795). For the expedition and treaty of peace, see C. O. 101/17; "Rise and Progress of the St. Vincent Expedition," in *The Scots Mag.*, April, 1773, pp. 174 ff.; and "An Authentic Account . . . of the Late Reduction of the Caribbs to His Majesty's Obedience," in *The Gent. Mag.*, April, 1773, pp. 180–182.

[2] For this controversy, see *Papers Laid before the House of Commons Relative to . . . the Expedition Against the Caribbs in the Isle of St. Vincent, in 1772* (London, 1773); Anon., ed., *Authentic Papers Relative to the Expedition Against the Charibbs, and the Sale of Lands in the Island of St. Vincent* (London, 1773); "Injustice of the Proceedings in St. Vincent," in *The Scots Mag.*, Nov., 1772, p. 588; and "Authentic Papers relative to St. Vincent," in *The Scots Mag.*, Feb. and May, 1773, pp. 62 ff., 337 ff.

[3] Among other things, Morris had for some years acted as Lieutenant Governor of St. Vincent. It was he who had first proposed introducing the bread-fruit tree into the West Indies. See page 76.

severely censured by Lord Germain, Secretary of State for the American Department, and all grants which he had made were invalidated. His defense and championing of few-acred residents' rights against those of absentee owners of vast estates [1] is a noteworthy episode in the history of tropical colonization.

"The small and middling white Settlers (among which the proportion of those formerly French ones is considerable) may be called the yeomanry of the West Indies, and are by far the most useful and giving the greatest strength to infant colonies. Their ideas are confined to the Spot they have fixed themselves on, their wishes circumscribed to attaining only absolute necessarys, with a very few comforts for themselves and family; they never form an idea of quitting the Government to live in Europe on the revenue of their American possessions, & thus may be deemed permanent inhabitants.

"On the contrary the English think only of making a rapid fortune, to enable them to return to Europe to spend it there, leaving only Servants on their Estates. These are ever attempting to buy out the former class, and very, very often succeed by various acts. The persons thus dispossessed would re-settle on the Island with the money for which they sold their old possessions, if they can get Grants of small tracts easily, & at very little expence. If they cannot, they remove to Martinico, St. Lucia, Trinidad &c. giving strength to our Enemys in proportion as they weaken the British Settlement.

"If there's no way to obtain their wishes but by the delay, circuity and interests of an application home to the Lords of his Majesty's Treasury, the delay and difficultys are too great for them to encounter. Not so of the oppulent planter, who solicits for a large tract, & knows well the channells & mode of application. He applies & in time probably with success. Tracts of land are monopolized. The . . . [drones] enjoy the honey, with relatively little or no pains, while the industrious bees are driven from the hive, which remains less than before. . . . In this wild, mountainous, woody, unsettled country, in so bad a neighborhood, it appears to me evidently for his Majesty's honor & interests that A, B, C, D & perhaps many more should be settlers of small, now useless woody tracts & that as speedily as possible, rather than one individual should agrandize large tracts, possibly to be long witheld from cultivation."

Replying to the charge that he had distributed parcels of ground without consent of the island council, Morris showed this to have been in accordance with precedent set by other West Indian executives. He held that approval of grants by the home government was inadvisable because of resultant vexatious delays and the danger of favoritism but was nevertheless specifically forbidden to assign tracts without

[1] Governor Morris to Lord Germain, October 4, 1777, C. O. 260/5.

direct authorization.[1] The dispute dragged on until the capture of the island by the French, shortly after, brought it to a sudden close.

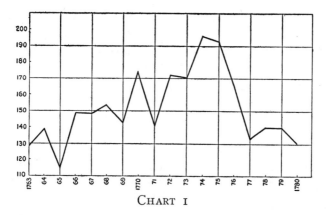

CHART I

Imports of Muscovado Sugar, the Growth of British Plantations, from the British West Indies into England, 1763–1780, in Million Pounds *
* Based on Customs 3/63-80, Public Record Office.

An excellent indication of the extent to which the ceded islands underwent development during the decade following their transfer is to be found in the statistics covering certain exports [2] from Grenada,[3] St. Vincent and Tobago into England [4] during that period.

IMPORTS OF CACAO, THE GROWTH OF BRITISH PLANTATIONS, INTO ENGLAND, 1764–1775 *

Year	Grenada	Saint Vincent	Tobago
1764	108,100 lbs.	— lbs.	— lbs.
1765	179,200	30,600	— No
1766	242,800	113,600	— cacao
1767	216,000	100,000	— shipped
1768	297,800	148,100	— until
1769	234,300	220,100	— 1779
1770	305,400	93,500	
1771	504,800	92,000	

* Customs 3/64–75, P. R. O.

[1] In Lord Germain to Governor Morris, May 15, 1778, C. O. 260/5.
[2] Cotton cannot be included as large quantities of the foreign-grown product were regularly shipped from the British islands without being distinguished from that grown locally.
[3] Including the Grenadines.
[4] Dominica is not included as it became a free port in 1766 (see pages 138 ff.). Since exports would thereafter include much foreign-grown produce,

Year	Grenada	Saint Vincent	Tobago
1772	343,400 lbs.	138,700 lbs.	—
1773	307,400	208,200	—
1774	281,100	178,400	—
1775	266,700	119,100	—

IMPORTS OF COFFEE, THE GROWTH OF BRITISH PLANTATIONS, INTO
ENGLAND, 1764–1775 *

Year	Grenada	Saint Vincent	Tobago
1764	1,416,200 lbs.	— lbs.	— lbs.
1765	1,285,700	46,700	—
1766	1,102,498	350,000	—
1767	1,239,000	273,300	—
1768	1,899,700	414,000	—
1769	1,244,300	481,700	— No
1770	1,592,600	299,400	— coffee
1771	1,374,900	768,700	— shipped
1772	2,475,000	1,050,300	— until
1773	1,739,600	734,700	— 1777.
1774	2,329,900	811,000	—
1775	2,442,300	1,056,700	—

* Customs 3/64–75, P. R. O.

IMPORTS OF MUSCOVADO SUGAR, THE GROWTH OF BRITISH PLANTATIONS,
INTO ENGLAND, 1764–1775 *

Year	Grenada	Saint Vincent	Tobago
1764	65,699 cwt.	— cwt.	— cwt.
1765	64,458	—	—
1766	85,543	700	—
1767	92,776	1,338	—
1768	145,532	10,338	—
1769	125,227	21,173	—
1770	196,130	38,394	1,686
1771	157,762	44,358	4,450
1772	194,451	53,551	13,625
1773	198,159	58,691	14,152
1774	179,375	62,599	30,984
1775	189,939	51,643	50,385

* Customs 3/64–75, P. R. O.

Conditions in the old British West Indies were far from satisfactory on the reëstablishment of peace. The highly profitable "Spanish trade" was virtually at an end. This had been carried on between
Jamaica and Cuba and Porto Rico for upwards of a century with

it was deemed best to protect the revenue against fraud by classifying all
products with the exception of rum and sugar entering Great Britain from
that island as foreign-grown and hence subject to foreign duties.

full approval of authorities at London. It was illegal under Spanish
law and those engaging in it were subject to severe penalties, but all
risks were assumed by the Spanish colonials who employed their own
vessels, came to Jamaican ports for negroes or desired supplies, and,
escaping the vigilance of coast guards at home or bribing them, landed
and distributed goods as best they might. In return for slaves and
British merchandise, the foreigners gave mules and cattle together
with large quantities of bullion and money as the trade balance was
steadily against them. Immense gains had long been made by the
English in a trade unattended by the slightest danger of loss.[1] Now,
after the Peace of Paris, the outlook was anything but bright.

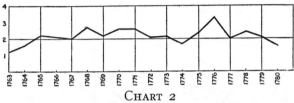

CHART 2

Imports of Rum, the Produce of British Plantations, from the British West Indies into England,
1763–1780, in Million Gallons *

* Based on Customs 3/63–80, Public Record Office.

A Jamaican writing at the time stated: "The commercial concerns
of this part of the world were never known so bad. . . . That part
of trade which was the support of this island and its credit at home
is entirely subsided by orders from home to suppress all commerce
with the Spaniards who were the only people that brought us money
here for our British manufactures, and enabled us to make our remittances to England. Not a Spanish vessel can now come with money
to this island, but what is seized by officers either under the Admiral
or Governor. We have been prevented receiving in this island (since
I arrived) near a million dollars. . . . They now carry their money to
the French and Dutch islands, which would otherwise have centered
with us." [2]

When this prohibition was removed in 1764, the islanders were
jubilant. "We shall now very shortly have the trade with the Spaniards again opened, which has given fresh spirits to the merchants
here," wrote a Kingston resident in July of that year. "The goods

[1] For an account of this trade before 1763, see Pitman, *Development*, pp.
147–153.
[2] *The Gent. Mag.*, July, 1764, p. 337. See, also, *ibid.*, October, 1765, p. 487.

which the Spaniards take most of, are Manchester linens, checks, and handkerchiefs, fine printed linens of all sorts, cambricks, Britannias, Silesias, hats, etc." [1] But hopes for any extensive renewal of this form of commerce were doomed to disappointment; almost none of the old smugglers reappeared.

A committee of the Kingston Society of Merchants, studying the situation in 1766, attributed this to the confiscation of all Spanish vessels in Jamaican harbors at the outbreak of the late hostilities, and held the measure to have been one which had "destroyed all that confiderce and faith under which these unhappy people were encouraged to carry on a trade most lucrative to this nation, at the risque of incurring the utmost severity of their own laws, which they were violating."

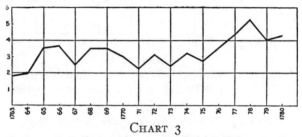

CHART 3

Imports of Cotton from the British West Indies into England, 1763–1780, in Million Pounds *

* Based on Customs 3/63–80, Public Record Office. (Includes both the British and the foreign-grown product shipped from the British island colonies.)

It was also found that the acting naval officer, the harbor master, and the fort commander were all exacting illegal fees from such of them as did renew former relations. "The delays and obstructions which are given to the Spaniards upon their arrival to and departure from this island, together with the above mentioned extortions, are great discouragements . . . and highly detrimental to the commerce of this island." [2]

Distress and poverty arising from an almost complete cessation of intercourse with the Cubans and Porto Ricans was great.[3] By 1770, the commercial decline of Kingston already attracted considerable notice.[4]

[1] *The Annual Register for 1764*, p. 107.

[2] *The Gent. Mag.*, July, 1766, pp. 301, 302.

[3] Lieutenant-Governor Ellotson to the Earl of Shelbourne, Oct. 31, 1767, C. O. 137/63.

[4] Long, *Jamaica*, II, 121.

Jamaica had achieved leadership in the production of tropical commodities throughout the Caribbean during the first half of the eighteenth century. Exploitation had proceeded at a rapid rate.[1] In 1768, 651 sugar plantations were in operation,[2] and a few years later, 110 cotton properties, 100 pimento walks, eight indigo works, thirty estates growing ginger, and 150 coffee.[3] The increased cultivation in the period following the Seven Years' War is reflected in the following table.

IMPORTS OF BRITISH GROWN PRODUCE FROM JAMAICA INTO ENGLAND [4]

Product	1763	1769	1775
Cacao	33,100 lbs.	32,400 lbs.	93,900 lbs.
Coffee	65,700 lbs.	91,400 lbs.	402,800 lbs.
Sugar	679,619 cwt.	725,686 cwt.	953,812 cwt.

But the quantity of virgin soil adapted to torrid zone agriculture was rapidly declining and the older plantations, some of which had been laid out over half a century before, were approaching exhaustion. Then, too, the French colony of St. Domingo was fast outstripping Jamaica in crop yield. In after years the latter's residents held that the height of prosperity had been reached about 1775.[5]

Barbados was already suffering acutely from a general wearing out of the land by 1763. It had been settled for nearly a hundred and fifty years, and no fresh tracts remained to be opened. Sugar and cotton were the principal crops. Production of the first and its by-product, rum, dropped steadily from before the middle of the eighteenth century. The average annual exports in the period 1740–1748 were 209,220 hundredweight of sugar and 1,288,400 gallons of rum;[6] for 1765–1769 they were but 159,760 hundredweight and 349,265 gallons.[7]

Cotton imports from Barbados into England had been exceeded only by those from Jamaica about 1760. However, with the development of the ceded islands, Barbados soon dropped to fifth place. The

[1] Long states that the number of sugar works in the island rose from seventy in 1670 to 429 in 1739 and that the exportation of sugar increased 75 per cent between 1728 and 1764. *Ibid.*, I, 105.

[2] *Ibid.*, I, 379, 494. Another report says 648. *Musgrave Papers,* Br. Mus., Add. Ms. 8,133, folios 95, 96.

[3] Long, *Jamaica*, I, 495, 496.

[4] Customs 3/63, 66, 69, 72, and 75, P. R. O.

[5] Edwards, *History*, I, 247.

[6] *Ibid.*, I, p. 352.

[7] Customs 3/65–69, P. R. O.

average annual shipments from there to the mother country for the years 1763–1767 were 230,678 pounds; for 1771–1775, only 156,519.[1] Indigo culture had virtually ceased before the war;[2] that commodity figures but twice among entries from Barbados into England between 1763 and 1775 and the total quantity then imported was but 7,948 pounds.[3] Further evidence of the colony's decline is to be found in the decrease in population which fell from 18,419 whites and approximately 70,000 negroes in 1762[4] to 16,167 and about 55,000 respectively in 1783.[5]

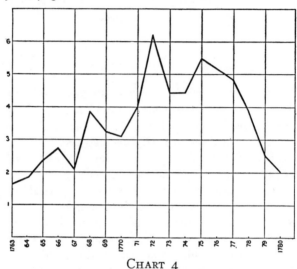

CHART 4

Imports of Coffee, the Growth of British Plantations, from the British West Indies into England, 1763–1780, in Million Pounds *

* Based on Customs 3/63–80, Public Record Office.

Barbados merely illustrated in extreme form the state of affairs existing throughout the old Caribbean colonies. Antigua, St. Kitts, Nevis, Montserrat, and the Virgins, too, had passed the golden age of immense returns from slight effort. Continued ruinous exploitation was fast mining the soil and the situation of the planters as a class had become precarious. With the prevailing high prices, they were outwardly prosperous enough, but this affluence was basically

[1] Customs 3/63–67, 71–75, P. R. O.
[2] Schomburgk, *Barbados*, p. 153.
[3] Customs 3/63–75, P. R. O.
[4] Governor Pinfold to the Board of Trade, June 1, 1762, C. O. 28/32.
[5] C. O. 28/42.

unsound. Production was forced, capital was deteriorating annually
and the point had been reached where any shock to the existing order
would be sharply felt; while a severe one, such as that occasioned by
the competition of any considerable areas of newly-opened sugar lands
either within or outside of the empire, must bring ruin to all. For this
reason, the established proprietors not only shaped the peace settlement
of 1763 to their own ends, but also followed the rapid expansion of
France's West India holdings with growing concern.

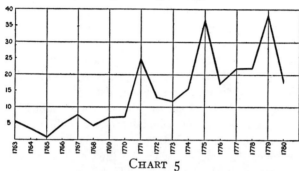

CHART 5

Imports of Indigo, the Growth of British Plantations, from the British West Indies into England,
1763–1780, in Ten Thousand Pounds *

* Based on Customs 3/63–80, Public Record Office.

Fifty thousand acres of canes in Guadeloupe, Grand-terre and
Mariegalante were producing 40,000 hogsheads of clayed sugar and
10,000 of muscavado in 1769. Twenty-two wind, 143 water and 240
cattle mills were then in operation there.[1] Forty-four sugar estates
and about 800 producing cacao, coffee, and cotton had been opened
in St. Lucia by 1776.[2] But the output of all other French possessions
paled beside St. Domingo's. In 1783, the amazing quantities of 716,-
103 hundredweight of clayed sugar, 410,305 of muscovado, 41,271,-
700 pounds of coffee, 4,510,000 of cotton, and 1,730,300 of indigo
were legally cleared from its ports.[3]

[1] Governor Woodley (of the Leeward Islands government) to the Earl of
Hillsborough, Dec. 28, 1769, C. O. 152/31.
[2] Governor Macartney to Lord George Germain, Jan. 10, 1779, C. O. 101/23.
[3] *A Report from the Committee of Warehouses of the United East India
Company, Relative to the Culture of Sugar* [*February 29, 1792*] (London,
1792). Reprinted as part of *East India Sugar. Papers Respecting the Culture
and Manufacture of Sugar in British India. Also Notices of the Cultivation of
Sugar in Other Parts of Asia* . . . (London, 1822). See Appendix I, p. 12.
The figures given in this report have been reduced to the standard English
weights shown above.

In the same year, only 1,584,275 hundredweight of British plantation sugar were imported into Great Britain.[1] St. Domingo was then
producing substantially two-thirds of the French-grown tropical
produce and nearly as much sugar as all of the British Caribbean
colonies combined!

The rivalry between British and French sugar in continental European markets had grown steadily during the eighteenth century and
was keen by 1750. During much of the Seven Years' War period,
France herself had been supplied with enemy products from Hamburg, the foremost distributing center for British goods on the mainland. But in 1765 the French were shipping from 50,000 to 60,000
hogsheads to that port and were driving their great competitors out
of the local trade.[2] This was occurring elsewhere in Germany as well
as in Holland, Scandinavia, and Russia. France's successful invasion
of marts long supplied by Great Britain is to be explained by the more
favorable price at which her colonial produce could be sold because
of lower production and marketing costs.

In communicating officially with the Earl of Dartmouth in 1774,
Governor Hay of Barbados wrote: "The French . . . produce the
same commodities as we do, in greater Abundance and at less Expence. They pay lower Duties, and they can afford to undersell us, in
every foreign Markett in Europe." [3]

When seeking the reasons for their smaller overhead a few years
later, the home government was informed by Lieutenant-Governor
John Nugent of the Leeward Islands that "The English Planter certainly cultivates his Land at double the expence in all the old Islands
as we require double the number of negroes to manure and cultivate
our Lands which . . . are more worn out than the Lands in the
French Islands. The produce of the latter is therefore of course
more certain, greater and made at less Expence." [4]

But the exploitation of fresher regions does not alone afford sufficient explanation. The fundamental cause is to be found in the fact
that the French holdings, save only St. Domingo, were developed by
small resident owners while, with the single exception of Antigua, all
of the long-held British colonies were cultivated under the direction

[1] *East India Sugar.* . . . Appendix I, pp. 10, 11. Also "Report from the Committee on the Commercial State of the West India Colonies," in *Gt. Br., H. C.,
Sess. Pap.,* 1807, III (65), p. 73.

[2] Macpherson, *Annals of Commerce,* III, 430.

[3] Under date of August 31, in C. O. 28/55.

[4] "Answers to Queries," in despatch to Lord Sydney, Jan. 9, 1789, C. O.
152/67.

of large absentee proprietors' representatives, which made operating expenses materially lower in the former.[1] Similarly, the French West Indians' marketing costs were considerably less than were the British planters' due to their enjoying the privilege of exporting crops directly to foreign European markets. In order to more nearly equalize competition on this score, parliament had accorded British colonists the same right in limited form commencing in 1739,[2] but nevertheless the difference in prime costs remained such that French sugars regularly undersold the British by a fourth to a third.

The anticipated adverse effects of opening the ceded colonies were soon experienced in the old Caribbean possessions. In 1770, when petitioning George III for royal troops, the council and assembly of Nevis declared. "The frequent Emigrations from this Island to Your Majesty's late Con-quer'd and Ceded Islands have so reduced the number of White Inhabitants that the Slaves exceed Your Majesty's Liege Subjects about Eight to One." [3] "We are losing our small settlers," stated a report from Jamaica in 1774.[4] Governor Sir Ralph Payne wrote to the Secretary of State for the Southern Department in the same year, "The inhabitants of all and every one of the Leeward Islands are exceedingly decreas'd within the last ten Years. The very considerable Emigration from the Leeward to the ceded Southern Islands . . . has been the principal and indeed the only accountable Cause of this Misfortune." [5]

Not only were many whites drawn off to the recently-acquired colonies by the powerful attraction of virgin soil at low price—a judicial decision placed those territories in a peculiarly privileged position. Before the sale of crown lands opened the king had issued Letters Patent declaring exports from Dominica, St. Vincent, Tobago, Grenada, and the Grenadines subject to the 4½ per cent charge long levied on commodities shipped from the other islands. The duty was duly paid but murmurings against it were heard from the first. Some time later, when representative government was granted Dominica, the governor fostered a bill providing for its regular collection but the assembly refused to entertain the matter and members did not hesitate to express the opinion that collection in the past had been illegal.[6]

[1] See Chapters I and II.
[2] See page 53.
[3] In C. O. 152/50.
[4] In "Answers to Queries Relative to the State of the Island," C. O. 137/70.
[5] Under date of June 26, in C. O. 152/54.
[6] Gov. William Young to the Earl of Hillsborough, Oct. 31, 1771, C. O. 71/3.

Opposition in Grenada was more vigorous. One Campbell, who had purchased an estate there in 1763, brought suit against Mr. Hall, the royal collector, seeking to recover the taxes laid against his shipments on the ground that they had not been imposed by lawful authority. This became the test case and was heard in England. In a celebrated ruling of November 28, 1774, Lord Mansfield held that the Crown made an irrevocable grant of its legislative power when an elected assembly was set up in any colony under instructions from the sovereign, that any attempt to collect the duty was therefore *ultra vires* and found for the plaintiff.[1]

This decision was hailed with great rejoicing in the ceded islands and with dismay by proprietors elsewhere who thus found themselves most unfairly discriminated against. In an address to His Majesty four years after, the council and assembly of Barbados declared that the local planters, cultivating worn-out fields, could not possibly compete with those on the fresh lands of the new islands who enjoyed the further advantage of exemption from this iniquitous tax.[2]

Collection of the 4½ per cent duty by exercise of the royal prerogative ceased with Mansfield's judgment, but attempts were then made to secure it through grants of the several legislatures instead. Thus, Valentine Morris, heading the new government of St. Vincent created in 1776, was instructed to lay such a proposal before the first assembly. The colonists, however, proved keenly resentful. They endeavored to return only candidates opposed to the project, even going so far as to exact specific promises of voting against it if elected, and Morris consequently deemed a delay advisable.[3]

In 1783, when Dominica once more became British, Governor Orde was directed to suggest payment of the tax with the understanding that "a considerable part" of the receipts would be applied to local uses. This became known prematurely through private channels and

---

[1] William Murray, Earl of Mansfield, *The Genuine Speech . . . in Giving the Judgment of the Court of King's-Bench . . . in the Cause of Campbell against Hall . . .* (London, 1774). See also "Judgement in the four and a half per cent cause," in *The Scots Mag.,* Dec. 1774, pp. 641 ff.; Hume Wrong, *Government of the West Indies* (Oxford, 1923), p. 20, note 1; Anon., *Considerations on the Imposition of 4½ Per Cent Collected on Grenada, and the Southern Charibbee Islands, by Virtue of His Majesty's Letters Patent Under Pretence of the Prerogative Royal Without Grant of Parliament* (London, 1774); and John Campbell, *The Lives of the Lord Chancellors and Keepers of the Great Seal of England . . .* (7 vols., London, 1845–1847), V, 513.

[2] The address, dated April 14, 1778, will be found in C. O. 28/57.

[3] Morris to the Secretary of State, Sept. 6, 1776, C. O. 260/4.

such feeling developed among the islanders that the matter was quietly dropped.[1]

The ceded islands remained permanently freed of this disability on their trade. Meanwhile, some months before the decision, a legislature had been set up in the Virgin group on the promise of the residents to enact a law making grant of the duty. This was done as of August 20, 1774 [2] and the charge thus became legally established there as well as in the other old colonies, which would have been quite impossible twelve months later.

The period of readjustment and fluctuating prices after 1763 bore heavily upon planters in the British Caribbean. The opening up of the new colonies coupled with France's development of St. Lucia and the rapid expansion of cultivation in St. Domingo created an unprecedented demand for field hands. Seventy-four Liverpool vessels were engaged in transporting Africans to the new world in 1760 and within a decade their number had risen to ninety-six.[3] Bristol, too, profited by the stimulus thus given the trade.[4] Between 1765 and 1769 a total of 31,932 slaves were landed in Jamaica from 149 slavers;

[1] Lord North to the Governor of Dominica; Governor Orde to Lord North, Feb. 27, 1784 (private); Lord Sydney to Governor Orde, May 6, 1784, all in C. O. 71/8.

[2] Dartmouth to Gov. Sir Ralph Payne, April 6, 1774, in C. O. 152/54. There was great need for orderly administration in the Virgin Islands. They were officially included in the Leeward government but had long been neglected. Land titles were in dispute and there were no courts, so settlers steered clear of them. Society was in a primitive state; no governor had visited the group since early in the eighteenth century. See C. O. 152/53 for correspondence on the subject. The islanders agreed to the payment of the 4½% tax rather reluctantly, specifying at first that the returns must be used for the erection of public buildings and to meet other local expenses and that hogsheads of sugar (weighing from twelve to fourteen cwt. each) must be computed as weighing but six cwt. However, they finally gave in on both points. During the next four decades the correspondence of the governors of the Leeward Islands was filled with constant complaints regarding the political chaos and irregularities in the courts there. Papers were seldom drawn up correctly and returns of all kinds were invariably incomplete and were generally found to be incorrect. For the state of the Virgins in the first decade after having been given separate government, see the account of the chief justice, George Suckling, *An Historical Account of the Virgin Islands in the West Indies, from their being settled by the English . . . to their Obtaining a Legislature of Their Own . . . and the lawless State in which His Majesty's Subjects in these Islands have remained since that time* (London, 1780). The Government was reorganized in 1811 (See Governor Elliot to the Earl of Liverpool, May, 15, 1811, C. O. 152/97) and in 1816 the group was included in the government of St. Kitts.

[3] Corry, *History of Liverpool*, p. 265.

[4] Latimer, *Annals of Bristol in the Eighteenth Century*, p. 343.

in the period 1770 to 1774, no less than 44,409 blacks were disembarked there from 172 ships.[1] Notwithstanding the greater number of arrivals, the cost of negroes soared. A male who might have been purchased for £25 in 1755 cost £60 fifteen years later.[2]

In 1774, Governor Sir Ralph Payne of the Leewards government wrote, "Slaves at present sell for more than double the Sum which was given for them 30 Years ago." The advance had been 33⅓ per cent within the past five years and proprietors were greatly distressed thereby. The local black population was decreasing noticeably because exorbitant prices kept estate owners from replenishing their supplies.[3] A quarter of a century later, Bryan Edwards wrote "It appears to me, that the British slave trade . . . attained . . . its highest pitch of prosperity a short time before the commencement of the late American war."[4]

An agrarian crisis was averted in Jamaica by resorting to the expedient of leasing gangs of slaves. Such groups were formed by monied persons and were hired out under several year contracts at from £8 to £12 a head per annum, losses through death being borne by the lessees. This became a favorite kind of investment, combining as it did a return of about 15 per cent with perfect safety.[5]

The cost of indentured servants likewise mounted steadily as poor whites departed for the ceded islands. In 1770, right to the services of a male immigrant for four years reached the unprecedented figure of £154. Fewer were being engaged each year as the planters chose to pay deficiency taxes rather than such large sums and the system virtually broke down within a decade after the Peace of Paris.[6]

The prices of supplies purchased abroad also advanced materially. This was due in part to the natural increase in values attending a boom period and in part to additional taxes and duties which had been widely laid for revenue purposes because of the war. Nearly every manufactured article required by the colonists went up in cost.[7] Lumber, live-stock, and provisions reached these prices shortly before the American Revolution.

[1] Memorial of Stephen Fuller, agent for Jamaica, to the Board of Trade, Jan. 30, 1778, C. O. 137/38.
[2] Long, *Jamaica*, I, 381, 382.
[3] In "Answers to Queries," June 26, C. O. 152/54.
[4] *History*, II, 55.
[5] Long, *Jamaica*, I, 399, 400.
[6] *Ibid.*, II, 290, 291. The price early in the eighteenth century had been but £14 for the four years.
[7] *Ibid.*, I, 381, 382, 500.

Commodity	Barbados [1]	Jamaica [2]	Leeward Is. [3]
Shingles, per M	—	22s.6d.–45s.	18s.–30s.
White Oak Staves and Heading, per M	—	£10–£18	£7–£10
Red Oak Staves, per M	—	£6–£12	£5–£8
Lumber, per M	—	£6–£12	£5–£8
Rice, per cwt.	—	13s.9d.–20s.	18s.–24s.
Indian Corn, per bu.	2s.6d.–3s.9d.	2s.6d.–6s.3d.	4s.–8s.
Beef, per bbl.	60s.–70s.	—	50s.–80s.
Pork, per bbl.	70s.–100s.	—	66s.–90s.
Flour, per cwt.	15s.–25s.	15s.–27s.6d.	20s.–30s.
Salt Fish, per quintal	12s.6d.–25s.	—	—
Horses, each	£20	—	£16.10–£35
Horned Cattle, each	£5–£7.10	—	£16.10–£19.16

By 1770, thoughtful West Indians were frankly pessimistic as to the future and viewed the position of the planters in the old islands with particular alarm. Edward Long saw the peril in rising production costs and fully realized that extension of sugar cultivation in the British and foreign colonies would make the industry decreasingly profitable. He therefore advocated prompt adoption of economy measures, holding that they alone would enable the proprietors to maintain themselves.[4] But his was a voice crying in the wilderness.

The most striking features of agricultural development in the British Caribbean colonies from 1763 to 1775 were the rise of the cacao industry, the growth of coffee culture in Jamaica, the general ruin of its producers, and the establishment of sugar estates in the ceded islands.

The average annual importation of British-grown cacao from the West Indies into England rose from 325,873 pounds in the period 1763–67 to 630,934 pounds during 1771–1775.[5] Extensive cacao walks were being laid out in St. Vincent, Grenada, and Jamaica. By 1775, 300,000 trees were bearing in Grenada, for the most part twice a year, new lands were being planted in them, and many persons were of the opinion that cacao would one day be the island's chief product.[6] The average annual exportation increased from 188,480 pounds to 340,-

[1] Memorial of George Walker, Agent for Barbados, to Lord Germain, C. O. 28/56.

[2] Report on the prices of supplies, C. O. 137/85.

[3] Enclosure in Governor Shirley to Lord Sydney, Sept. 7, 1785, C. O. 152/64.

[4] Jamaica, I, 382, 536.

[5] Customs 3/63–67, 71–75, P. R. O.

[6] "Answers to Queries Relative to Grenada" (in French), C. O. 101/18.

680 in these two five year periods; Jamaican shipments, from
18,200 pounds to 93,000.[1]

Imports of British-grown coffee from the West Indies into England rose from 2,335,900 pounds in 1765 to 5,483,100 a decade later
due to the demand for reëxportation to foreign markets. Continental
orders, chiefly German, afforded a powerful stimulus to cultivation.
Of the quantity imported in the former year, but 66,600 pounds came
from the old colonies; in the latter, entries included 404,910 pounds
grown there. While coffee production in the ceded islands doubled
during this period, it increased over 500 per cent in the others, largely
through expansion of the industry in Jamaica. The average annual
exportation from that possession to England soared from 37,180
pounds in 1763–67 to 412,980 in 1771–1775.[2]

Cargoes of British-grown sugar from the Caribbean landed in England averaged 1,359,621 hundredweight annually from 1763 to 1767
and 1,746,990 during 1771–1775. In 1765, but 64,458 hundredweight
had been imported from the new colonies; by 1775, this had risen to
332,649, an increase of four per cent in a single decade. Imports of
rum, the produce of British plantations, into England averaged
1,851,481 gallons annually from 1763 to 1767 and 2,169,482 between
1771 and 1775.[3]

To encourage consumption of this sugar by-product, the Society of
West India Merchants in 1769 accepted the proposal of Robert Dossie
to print a pamphlet [4] on its wholesomeness as a drink in comparison
with brandy provided, that the body subscribe for a considerable
number. With the assistance thus given him, the author disposed of
3,000 copies.[5] A new outlet was found in 1775 when the victualling
office was authorized to contract for West Indian rum instead of
French brandy for use in the navy [6] through the efforts of Stephen
Fuller, agent for Jamaica.

A financial crisis arising in the mother country in 1772 promptly

---

[1] Customs 3/63–67, 71–75, P. R. O.

[2] Customs 3/63–67, 71–75, P. R. O.

[3] Customs 3/63–67, 71–75, P. R. O.

[4] Robert Dossie, *An Essay on Spirituous Liquors, With Regard to their
Effects on Health, in which the comparative Wholesomeness of Rum and
Brandy Are particularly considered* (London, n.d.). The author was closely
connected with the Society of Arts and was an early chronicler of its work.
Witt Bowden, *Industrial Society in England Towards the End of the Eight-
eenth Century* (New York, 1925), p. 44.

[5] *Min. W. I. Mer.*, meetings of Aug. 1, Sept. 5, Dec. 9, 1769, and June 12,
1770.

[6] *Min. W. I. Mer.*, March 7, 1775; "French Brandy and British Rum," in
The W. I. Comm. Circ., April 18, 1906, p. 172.

made itself felt beyond the Atlantic. The great acceleration of industry following the war and the resultant general prosperity came to a spectacular close. Money grew scarce, the British merchants serving as factors for the planters faced bankruptcy and credit suddenly ceased. Advances were essential for all the West Indians and an absolute necessity for those opening new estates; consequently great hardships followed.[1] In seeking means to ease the situation, parliament considered proposals that foreign loans on freehold and leasehold estates in the Caribbean be authorized and that the legal interest rate on mortgages against tropical properties negotiated at home be increased.

The first of these relief measures was sponsored in the House of Commons by Mr. Pulteney, a Windward Island proprietor, and won the West India merchants' hearty support. It was argued that the planting interest could be saved from ruin only through extensive borrowing, that this could not be done in Great Britain and that large numbers of estate owners must fail, much land would revert to the Crown and British commerce and industry would be seriously injured if banking resources abroad were not drawn on. It was believed that Dutch financiers in particular would gladly avail themselves of such an opportunity.[2]

Certain individuals with overseas investments offered strenuous objections, however, holding that aliens would in this manner secure control of valuable Caribbean properties, that they would dispose of the produce grown on them in Great Britain and thus enjoy the benefits of the colonial monopoly but would spend the proceeds abroad. Then, too, many cargoes would doubtless be illegally shipped to continental markets, foreign manufactures would be illicitly introduced into the islands and further easy credit would serve to increase absenteeism and profligacy among the islanders.[3]

The bill nevertheless passed in 1773, and under it citizens of other countries were permitted to make loans at 5 per cent interest and were given the same rights in recovering debts during times of war and peace alike as though they were British subjects.[4]

---

[1] Governor Leyborne to the Earl of Dartmouth, July 17, 1773, C. O. 101/16.

[2] Anon., "A West India Planter," *Considerations on the State of the Sugar Islands, and on the Policy of Enabling Foreigners to Lend Money on Real Securities in Those Colonies* (London, 1773).

[3] Anon., *Reasons Against the Encouraging of Aliens to Lend Money Upon Mortgage in the West India Islands* (London, 1772).

[4] 13 Geo. III c. 14; "To encourage Subjects of Foreign States to lend Money upon Securities in the West India Colonies," *Gt. Br., H. C., Sess. Pap.*, 1773,

The second plan was designed to attract capital in Great Britain itself. The legal interest rate there stood at 5 per cent and this was theoretically the figure at which proprietors could borrow on the security of West Indian plantations. But ample outlets for funds available at such terms existed in the home country where extensive industrial development was under way and investors proved increasingly disinclined to take up further West Indian paper. Although the various legislatures established higher rates for local loans, no attempt was made to attract British capital by legalizing a more favorable one on mortgages drawn up in the mother land.

Parliamentary action was therefore resorted to as a means of inducing wealthy Britons to place their money in the colonies. An act of 1774 authorized the lending of any sums against Caribbean real estate at whatever interest charge might prevail where the property lay, provided only that the transaction be duly registered in the possession concerned.[1] Borrowing became markedly easier following adoption of these measures, but unfortunately the early outbreak of hostilities with America once more tightened the money market to such an extent as to render them quite nugatory.

Estate owners in the Leewards meanwhile suffered heavy losses in August, 1772, from the most destructive hurricane in decades. Few plantations escaped. Buildings were razed, provisions beds were torn up, and crops were ruined.[2] The decline in muscovado exports for 1773 as compared with those of the preceding twelve months reveals the extent of the damage done. The raw sugar cleared out from Antigua to England in 1772 totalled 114,220 hundredweight as against but 80,885 for the storm year; shipments leaving Montserrat for there fell from 58,008 hundredweight to 33,375, while those made from Nevis and St. Kitts in 1773 were but 27,429 hundredweight and 106,367 respectively, half the quantities of the year before.[3]

Added to crop losses was the additional expense incurred in restoring properties to their former state. Owners fell into arrears for supplies sent out and became still further involved through the heavy credit purchases made necessary by reconstruction work. Their debts had not been liquidated three years later, and the opening of the

VII (245). See Leland Jenks, *The Migration of British Capital to 1875* (New York, 1927), p. 7.

[1] 14 Geo. III c. 79.

[2] C. O. 152/52. Anon., *An Account of the Late Dreadful Hurricane, Which happened on the 31st of August, 1772* . . . (St. Christopher, 1772).

[3] Customs 3/72, 73, P. R. O.

American Revolution found them in a singularly weakened condition, ill-prepared to withstand the shock which that struggle must inevitably give their economic system.[1]

Events wholly beyond the coffee planters' control plunged them into acute distress in 1773. German mercantile houses had regularly purchased the greater part of their produce; but new duties and restrictions now laid by princes east of the Rhine greatly reduced sales without warning. At the same time, the Dutch in Berbice and Surinam, and French planters in the Caribbean, the Île de Bourbon, and Mauritius opened a vigorous campaign to capture Teutonic marts by offering berries at low rates made possible through lighter overhead.[2]

The danger of dependence upon foreign demand at once became painfully apparent. Warehouses in England filled, the British market was glutted, and selling prices fell by half within a single season.[3] Domestic consumption in Britain had never been great because of the heavy excise tax levied to protect the East India Company's tea trade.[4] Now, faced by ruin, the Jamaican and Grenadan coffee growers petitioned that this be lowered or removed so that the home demand might be substantially increased.[5]

Describing the situation arising in Dominica through the late English bankruptcies and the crash in coffee values, Governor Thomas Shirley wrote in 1775: "A great part of the Adventurers in planting here . . . are now so embarrassed among themselves and so involved with the Merchants at home, that it is expected many of their Estates will fall into the hands of other persons and for these reasons, that the Improvement of the Island, in point of Cultivation, must continue very much at a stand. That this is the present state of this Government no stronger Argument need be offered in proof of it, than that of the decay of the Slave Trade here, which is in so declining a Condition, that since my Arrival, I have observed, that out

[1] Address of the Assembly of St. Kitts to the Crown, Sept. no date, 1778, C. O. 152/58.

[2] Petition to parliament, in Governor Leyborne to the Earl of Dartmouth, Nov. 23, 1774, C. O. 101/18.

[3] Petition of John Ellis, Agent for Dominica, to the House of Commons, C. O. 71/4.

[4] The duty about 1770 was £1.13.6 per cwt., which was the same rate paid on East Indian coffee. Long, *Jamaica*, I, 590.

[5] Memorial of Stephen Fuller, Agent for Jamaica, to the Lords Commissioners of the Treasury, C. O. 137/69. Petition to parliament in Governor Leyborne to the Earl of Dartmouth, Nov. 23, 1774, C. O. 101/18.

of a considerable number of Vessels from the Coast of Guinea, which have been sent to this Market, the Cargoes of only very few of them have been received by the Factors here for disposal." Berry growers on every hand turned their estates into sugar properties in a desperate effort to save themselves.[1]

Soon after, the islanders declared that they could no longer meet installments remaining due on land purchased from the Crown and prayed that their obligations be reduced to £1 per acre of wood land and £5 per acre of cleared ground as a means of affording relief.[2]

In Grenada, great debts had been contracted on coffee plantations in expectation of the market price remaining high.[3] When the sudden slump came, the cultivation of sugar and cacao instead was resorted to. A somewhat exaggerated report from the colony held that coffee production in 1774 was but half of that for 1761.[4] An interesting attempt at debtor legislation was made by the Grenadans in 1774 when a bill providing for the establishment of a two year moratorium passed both the assembly and council. It was, however, disallowed by the home government.[5]

Four years later, Governor Macartney reported that he knew of not a single British subject within his jurisdiction but who was financially involved; that mortgages to the amount of £2,000,000 sterling, for the most part at 15 per cent, were registered on local estates and that the planters were in reality mere stewards for their British and Dutch creditors rather than actual owners of the properties they exploited.[6]

The French coffee producers of St. Vincent became discouraged at their losses. A considerable number sold out to Englishmen interested in cultivating sugar and emigrated to St. Lucia or Martinique.[7] Prices remained low, and before the breaking out of the American war the industry was generally ruined.

Important commercial readjustments were effected in the Caribbean during the post-war decade. An order of August 18, 1763, issued by M. de Bourlamague, governor-general of Guadeloupe, and

---

[1] To the Earl of Dartmouth, March 3, in C. O. 71/5.
[2] Address, Memorial, and Petition of the Assembly of Dominica to His Majesty, in C. O. 71/6. Another was sent to parliament.
[3] Petition to parliament, in Leyborne to Dartmouth, Nov. 23, 1774, C. O. 101/18.
[4] "Answer to Queries Relative to Grenada" (in French), C. O. 101/18.
[5] Madden, *A Twelve Months' Residence*, I, 63, 64.
[6] To Lord Germain, Oct. 25, 1778, C. O. 101/23.
[7] Lieut.-Gov. Valentine Morris to the Sec. of State, May 24, 1775, C. O. 101/18.

M. de Peinier, the island intendant, regulated the French West Indian-British American mainland trade on terms highly advantageous to France's sugar colonies and detrimental to Great Britain's. This authorized the entry of specified foreign goods under written permission from the intendant provided that sugar and rum alone were taken in payment. Among the desired imports were lumber, provisions, and horses, products of New England and the middle colonies.

The new arrangement served to materially reduce the quantities of those supplies reaching the British islands, while at the same time further closing the North American outlet for their produce. In the past, ship-masters from the adjacent continent had been wont to enter stores there, to barter as little as possible but rather to dispose of them for cash, and then to resort to the French possessions where West Indian produce might be purchased at lower prices because of smaller production costs. Such commodities had subsequently been smuggled into home harbors on a large scale to avoid payment of the high duties levied against them. Henceforth this double transaction became unnecessary as cargoes could now be disposed of to the French by barter in the first instance and many traders consequently altogether ceased calling at Great Britain's tropical ports.

British Caribbean proprietors showed immediate apprehension lest such large importations be made into the Atlantic seaboard colonies that they themselves would suffer seriously thereby.[1] The London planting interest took the matter in hand and, playing on the government's need for greater revenue, sought to reduce the menace by securing passage of the celebrated Sugar Act of 1764.[2] This increased the duty on foreign white and clayed sugars entering the British American colonies by £1.2.0 per hundredweight and, while the old foreign molasses duty of sixpence per gallon was halved, its rigorous collection was provided for as a direct means of discouraging commercial intercourse with the French. The further importation of any but colonial rum was at the same time prohibited.

The institution of free ports in the Danish islands of St. Thomas and St. John in 1764 further aided the mainland British colonists in securing cheap tropical produce of foreign origin and gave alien planters in the West Indies a new and easy outlet to old world markets. Under the act throwing these islands open, European

---

[1] Governor Thomas (of the Leeward Islands government) to the Sec. of State for the Southern Department, Sept. 9, 1763, in C. O. 152/47, with copy of the order.

[2] 4 Geo. III c. 15.

merchandise might be transported thither only in Danish ships provided with passports and was subject to a 2 per cent ad valorem duty. On the other hand, all American products were admitted in the ships of any nation at reduced duty rates and such bottoms were permitted to clear out with any goods in the ports duty free, excepting only that produce intended for European markets must be shipped out under the Danish flag. Sugar which had not been grown in the Danish islands could be entered into the home country only for reëxportation, at which time it was subject to a 1 per cent duty.[1]

Americans quickly flocked to the two colonies and bartered lumber and provisions for sugar and rum. The French colonials secured manufactured goods there in return for sugar, large quantities of which were eventually sold in Germany and Russia, helping to force the British article out of those countries.

Most important of the new commercial arrangements, however, was the creation of free ports in the British West Indies. The London ministry had had frequent occasion to meet bodies of transatlantic merchants during the debates on raising revenue in the American colonies after the Seven Years' War and had thus gained an intimate knowledge of the mainland and Caribbean trades. With the opening of Danish colonial harbors, parliament received numerous petitions from business centers praying that similar action be taken for certain of the Caribbean possessions to increase the consumption of British manufactures, above all in Spanish America.[2] These led to the act of 1766, establishing free ports in Dominica and Jamaica from the first of November.[3]

Under it, cattle and all goods and commodities except tobacco, which were the growth or produce of non-British territories in the new world, received the right of entry into Prince Rupert's Bay and Roseau, Dominica, in foreign vessels with no more than one deck arriving from any part of America not within the empire. Live stock and all foreign products except sugar, coffee, pimento, ginger, molasses, and tobacco might likewise be landed from such bottoms at Kingston, Savannah la Mar, Montego Bay or Santa Lucea, Jamaica.

---

[1] *The Annual Register for 1764*, pp. 89, 90.

[2] *The Annual Register for 1766*, p. 47.

[3] 6 Geo. III c. 49. See "[Bill] for opening and establishing certain Ports in Jamaica and Dominica," in *Gt. Br., H. C., Sess. Pap.*, 1766, V (150); *Act for Opening and establishing certain Ports of the Islands of Jamaica and Dominica, for the more free Importation and Exportation of certain goods and merchandise* (London, 1766); *Regulations for Opening the Island of Dominica as a Free Port . . .* (London, 1766).

The importation into these two islands of foreign manufactures and of copper ore, cotton, ginger, dye woods, hemp, indigo, molasses, furs, sugar, cacao, coffee, pimento, hides, pot and pearl ashes, silk, and whale fins from the British colonies was at the same time prohibited.

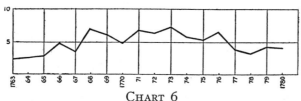

CHART 6

Imports of Cocoa Nuts, the Growth of British Plantations, from the British West Indies into England, 1763–1780, in Hundred Thousand Pounds *
* Based on Customs 3/63–80, Public Record Office.

The reëxportation in single-decked foreign vessels of negroes entered under the British flag was authorized, as was the clearing out of all articles of British origin legally entered save for naval stores, tobacco, and American iron. The shipping of goods from Dominica to continental European ports north of Cape Finisterre was not permitted, but foreign sugar arriving in the colony might be marketed directly in old world ports south of that point. The reëxportation of European and East India goods from Dominica to the British American colonies was, however, forbidden.

A duty of 30s. sterling was levied on each African brought to Dominica and on every slave leaving Jamaica in foreign vessels, as were charges of sixpence per barrel of beef and pork, firkin of butter, and hundredweight of sugar, cacao, and coffee entering Dominica.

To prevent frauds against the revenue, all American goods, excepting certified rum and sugar, imported into Great Britain from Dominica after January 1, 1767, were classified as being of foreign origin. Sugar and rum produced on local estates might be entered there or in any part of the empire in British bottoms upon payment of the regular British produce duty provided that shipments were accompanied by certificates showing them to be bona-fide.

No sugar or rum other than certified might be imported from Dominica into any British possession. Non-British sugar, rum, and other products might be entered into Great Britain from Dominica under regulations different from those governing ordinary foreign importations—muscovado was subject to a tax of only three pence per hundredweight and other goods were charged but half the customary tonnage and poundage rates; they must be warehoused immediately upon landing and could normally be released only for reëxportation abroad. In case, however, that it should subsequently be desired to enter them for domestic consumption, the balance of the regular foreign produce charges must then be paid on them, and they became bound by all restrictions laid upon commodities of such a nature.

Most striking of the results following the adoption of this comprehensive measure, for our purpose, were those arising from the disability it placed upon the planting of any crop but sugar in Dominica. The levying of foreign produce rates against the cacao and coffee grown there and entered into Great Britain for domestic consumption led to a serious setback in their cultivation, their illicit sale to foreigners, and a marked stimulation of cane culture.

When the German markets closed in 1773, the coffee planters of Dominica were most severely hit as it was utterly impossible for their shipments to compete with those from the other colonies in the British Isles and their entire crop had been sold abroad. Under the circumstances, they presented a memorial to the home government praying that Dominican cacao and coffee be admitted under certificate as were sugar and rum.[1]

The hoped-for revival of the Spanish trade with Jamaica did not materialize. Authorities at Madrid were alive to British intentions and changed the coast-guards in Porto Rico and Cuba, sending over new ones from Spain, unconnected with the colonies, to replace those who had been bought by the traders and who winked at the landing of goods.

The requirement that foreign traders resorting to Jamaica answer certain questions and make declarations which were sent to the commissioners of customs in London in order that the effects of the free port act might be ascertained, proved a further hindrance to the reëstablishment of old relations. The information called for included the names of the merchants and their vessels, their home ports, their destinations, and detailed accounts of purchases made. The Cubans and Porto Ricans feared, not without reason, that the Spanish ambassador in England would gain access to such reports through

[1] Memorial of the Commander in Chief and the Council and Assembly of Dominica to Lord North and the Earl of Dartmouth, in C. O. 71/4.

bribery and use the information contained therein against them, and hence stayed away.[1]

Nor did the act work altogether smoothly in other respects. The coffee growers of Jamaica complained in 1773 that large quantities of foreign berries were being smuggled into the island on board vessels arriving under the free port act and that they were being fraudulently shipped to Great Britain as being of British origin. They therefore petitioned that all local ports be again closed.[2] In general, it was felt by the West India planters that, however beneficial such centers of commerce might be to the merchants, they were detrimental to the landed interest because of the additional quantities of tropical produce thus brought to market.[3] The fact that British manufacturers found it possible to purchase French colonial cotton in the free ports thirty per cent cheaper than through France [4] and that this naturally cut the price of the British Caribbean article would seem to lend some force to their argument.

Nevertheless, in 1773, the Barbadian assembly petitioned parliament to open some harbor in that island,[5] and the legislature of Antigua prayed that St. John's and Parham be placed on an equal footing with Prince Rupert's Bay and Roseau.[6] Neither request was granted, and a new free port act of that year affected only Dominica and Jamaica.[7]

Existing arrangements were continued in the former island until 1780 and in the latter until November, 1774. The Dominican proprietors' plea was heeded; cacao and coffee grown there were thenceforth given the right of entry into Great Britain at British produce rates upon certification that they were actually of local origin. The duty on slaves entered into Dominica or cleared out from Jamaica after November 1773 was at the same time cut from 30s. to 2s. 6d. per head.

[1] Enclosure in Lieutenant Governor Dalling to the Earl of Dartmouth, April 11, 1773, C. O. 137/68.
[2] Memorial of Coffee Planters in the Island of Jamaica to the Earl of Dartmouth, C. O. 137/68.
[3] Gov. Ralph Payne to the Earl of Dartmouth, Aug. 20, 1773, C. O. 152/33.
[4] Bowden, *Industrial Society,* pp. 38 ff., *passim.*
[5] Poyer, *Barbados,* p. 366.
[6] Petition from the Council and Assembly of Antigua, C. O. 152/33, enclosed with No. 7.
[7] 13 Geo. III c. 73.

CHAPTER V

The Sugar Colonies During the American Revolution

The planter and merchant interests in England and residents of the British West Indies followed the ominous course of the controversies between the home government and the mainland transatlantic possessions after 1763 with growing apprehension. The threat of the latter to cut off commercial relations with Great Britain and her Caribbean holdings unless grievances were promptly adjusted changed their fear to open alarm. "Without frequent Supplies of Biscuits, Wheat Flour, Rice and Indian Corn from the Continent of America," wrote Sir Ralph Payne, governor of the Leeward Islands in June 1774, "the Inhabitants could not subsist." [1] It was believed, however, that even if a policy of non-intercourse were officially adopted, enforcement would be impossible because of the number of Americans interested in the West India trade. [2]

The decision of the first Continental Congress to close the ports of the thirteen colonies to British Caribbean produce from December 1, 1774, and to stop exportation to the islands after September 10, 1775, if its demands had not been met, adopted in September of the former year, roused both the West Indians and groups in the home country to action.

The Jamaican assembly took the remarkable step of championing colonial rights in general and of approaching the Crown as suitor in behalf of the North Americans. A petition voted at the close of its session in December, 1774, professed profound loyalty to the king and denied the slightest intention of offering resistance to the British government, but held it to be an established principle of the constitution that no part of His Majesty's subjects could legislate for any other part and that no law could bind Englishmen unless it had received the assent of their representatives. Parliament's claim of the right to legislate for the colonies was denied. The assembly lamented

[1] To the Secretary of State for the Southern Department, "Answer to Queries," in C. O. 152/54, no. 17.

[2] Gov. Ralph Payne to the Earl of Dartmouth, July 3, 1774, C .O. 152/54, no. 18.

the exercise of such power in the past and, while accepting laws regulating the external commerce of the island, demanded that none injurious to its constituents' interests be enacted and forced upon them in the future. It furthermore stoutly declared that depriving colonials of equal rights with Englishmen at home dissolved their dependence upon the parent state and appealed to the sovereign to mediate between his British and his American subjects.[1]

This celebrated memorial was the work of the radical mercantile element from Kingston and was kept secret until the business of the session had been largely completed and conservative rural members from outlying parts of the island had left St. Jago de la Vega, the capital, in order to reach their estates before the opening of the holiday season during which negro insurrections were always feared. It was presented when but twenty-six of the forty-three assemblymen were present, was passed despite the opposition of the speaker, and was sent to the governor for transmission but a few hours before prorogation.[2]

Its arrival in Great Britain occasioned a storm. The Earl of Dartmouth, Secretary of State for the American Department, fulminated against the "so indecent, not to say criminal conduct of the Assembly" and held that dire consequences would follow.[3] The house of representatives of Connecticut[4] and the Continental Congress[5] on the other hand extended votes of thanks to the Jamaicans for their efforts in the cause of peace.

A general meeting open to all persons having relations with the Caribbean colonies was held in the London Tavern, Bishopsgate Street, on January 18, 1775, to consider what measures should be taken for the preservation of common interests in the existing crisis.[6] A petition to parliament was determined upon, subscriptions to meet the expense attending it were called for, and copies were presented to the two houses early in February. These set forth the alarm felt over

[1] Peter Force, ed., *American Archives* (9 vols., Washington, 1837–53), 4th series, I, cols. 1072–1074. "Memorial from the General Assembly of Jamaica Relative to the Present State of American Affairs," in *The Gent. Mag.*, Supplement for 1775, pp. 617, 618. See also the summary of a thesis by J. W. Herbert, "Constitutional Struggles in Jamaica, 1748–1776," in *Bulletin of the Institute of Historical Research,* June, 1928, 36–39.

[2] Sir Basil Keith to the Earl of Dartmouth, January 4 and June 12, 1775, C. O. 137/70.

[3] Dartmouth to Keith, March 3, 1775, C. O. 137/70.

[4] Force, *Archives,* 4th series, II, col. 108.

[5] *Ibid.,* 4th series, II, col. 1891.

[6] *Min. W. I. Mer.,* Jan. 3, 1775.

the late step taken by congress, declared that British property in the West Indies valued at £30,000,000 sterling and shipping worth many millions more employed in trading with them would be endangered if free access to North American supplies were ended, predicted acute distress in the Caribbean coupled with a heavy falling off in the national revenue if the American agreement stood, and prayed for the adoption of such measures as would avert the threatened evil and restore the old harmony.[1]

In the House of Commons, the matter was referred to a committee and, some weeks later, the West Indians were called upon to submit evidence in support of their contention that the sugar colonies were altogether dependent upon the thirteen mainland ones for supplies.[2] Their memorial to the Lords fared worse. The Marquis of Rockingham sought to lay it and others from North American traders before the upper chamber but was interrupted by the Earl of Dartmouth who desired the floor. Then followed a long and acrimonious debate on a point of order which became involved with the question of whether or not the Lords should support the Commons in an address to the throne on affairs in America declaring rebellion to exist there. At length the Marquis moved that the grievances be considered and, when a division was taken in the early hours of the morning, the motion was lost, 104 to 29. Immediately after, by an affirmative vote almost as large, it was decided to join in the address. Eighteen members protested against the refusal to hear the petitioners but to no avail.[3] The commencement of hostilities shortly after brought to an end all hope of a settlement through West Indian intervention.

The military and naval events in the Caribbean during the period of the Revolution are in themselves of less consequence for our purpose than are the results which flowed from them. Throughout the war, considerable difficulty was experienced in getting the Jamaican assembly to meet the expense of quartering troops. That body steadily refused to provide new barracks and showed great resentment over

---

[1] Min. W. I. Mer., Feb. 7, 1775.

[2] The Evidence Delivered on the Petition Presented by the West-India Planters and Merchants to the Hon. House of Commons, as it was introduc'd at the Bar, and summ'd up by Mr. Glover [London, 1775]. The Substance of the Evidence on the Petition Presented by the West India Planters and Merchants to the House of Commons, as . . . Introduced at the Bar, and summ'd up by Mr. Glover on . . . the 16th of March, 1775 (London, n.d.).

[3] The Annual Register for 1775, pp. 71 ff.

the frequency with which the militia was called out.[1] Barbados possessed a turbulent lower house which was constantly challenging the governor's authority in an effort to get power into its own hands and numerous untoward incidents occurred.[2] But all of the British islands remained loyal to the mother country.

During the first phase of the struggle, the sugar colonies were in no actual danger from aggression. A negro insurrection in Jamaica was nipped in the bud and thirty blacks were executed as an example.[3] The foolhardy proposal of Silas Deane, to further incite the slaves of the island to rebellion and to stir up the Caribs of St. Vincent,[4] was fortunately barren of results. But the war was felt from the first; heavy loss and expense attended the depredations of privateers swarming in the Caribbean; and hardships and even suffering arose from the shortage of supplies.

The decline in shipping arriving in the port of London from the West Indies and in the quantity of sugar entered from there is shown by the following table.[5]

Year	Number of Vessels	Casks of Sugar
March 1774 to March 1775	354	131,778
March 1775 to March 1776	329	115,511
March 1776 to March 1777	299	100,302
March 1777 to March 1778	243	76,700

To reduce captures under letters of marque, the Society of West India Merchants arranged with the Lords of the Admiralty for the convoying of both outward-bound and incoming merchantmen. Notice was given traders and ship owners of the appointed places and dates of departure, protection was afforded from the Downs to Caribbean waters and return and losses were thus reduced to a minimum.[6] Insurance on produce-laden vessels en route to Great Britain nevertheless rose to 23 per cent[7] and freight rates soared. In August 1776, those on goods bound from England to the islands were set at one-fourth over the schedule adopted by agreement be-

---

[1] The record of these controversies is preserved in C. O. 137/71–84.
[2] For these conflicts see C. O. 28/56–60.
[3] Papers covering the affair will be found in C. O. 137/71.
[4] Deane to John Jay from Paris, Dec. 3, 1776, in Force, *Archives,* 5th series, III, col. 1051.
[5] Record of annual entries, in the archives of the West India Committee.
[6] *Min. W. I. Mer.,* Vols. I (1769–1779) and II (1779–1788), *passim.*
[7] Macpherson, *Annals of Commerce,* III, 594.

tween the ship owners and West India merchants in 1771 [1] and they rose to double the peace-time ones a year later.[2] Rates in 1777 stood as follows—boards, £4.10.0 per 1160 feet; hoops, £4.4.0 per thousand; staves, £5 per thousand; puncheon packs, 5s. each; and white oak staves and headings £5.10.0 per thousand.[3] In 1781 they were increased to £6, £5, £7, 7s., and £7.10.0 respectively on these several items when shipped to the Leeward Islands.[4] A year later the Society of West India Merchants was obliged to resort to law to force ship masters to accept freight at even these high figures.[5] Homeward-bound rates meanwhile had been set at freight and a half in 1776.[6]

The quantity of mainland supplies in the sugar colonies at the outbreak of the war was large and prices were low. "Provisions of all kinds from the continent of America are cheaper and more plentiful than they have been in the memory of man," declared Governor Payne of the Leewards.[7] Governor Hay of Barbados reported them never so cheap as in May 1775 [8] and wrote a year later "It is wished to talk of Famine, in the most plentiful Island of all the West Indies, and where I, who have no plantation and must buy all the provisions for my Table, can assure your Lordship that scarcely One Article of provisions and live Stock of the Island has varied in price for near these three Years that I have been here." [9] Barbadian warehouses were "crammed full" a short time after.[10] Grenada, too, was well supplied with beef and flour. Several vessels arriving there in the fall of 1776 soon departed in search of better markets.[11] Dominica, on the contrary, suffered from scarcity as early as the beginning of that year.[12] However, highly favorable as conditions in general were, the entire cutting-off of shipments from the principal source of supply made an ultimate widespread shortage of plantation stores inevitable.

That it was not more immediate was due to several causes. An act

---

[1] *Min. W. I. Mer.*, Aug. 6, 1776. *Rates of Freight, from London to the Sugar Colonies in Time of Peace* (London, 1771).

[2] *Min. W. I. Mer.*, Sept. 2, 1777.

[3] *Rates of Freight, from London to the Sugar-Colonies, for the Year 1777* (London, 1777).

[4] *Min. W. I. Mer.*, Oct. 30, 1781. The rates to Jamaica were not increased at that time.

[5] *Ibid.*, Dec. 17, 1782.

[6] *Ibid.*, Nov. 27, 1776.

[7] In a despatch to Lord Dartmouth, quoted in Andrews, ed., *Journal of a Lady*, p. 85, note.

[8] Despatch to the Earl of Dartmouth, Aug. 29, 1775, C. O. 28/56.

[9] Despatch to the Earl of Dartmouth, April 13, 1776, C. O. 28/56.

[10] Desptach to the Earl of Dartmouth, July 25, 1776, C. O. 28/56.

[11] Governor Macartney to Lord Germain, Sept. 3, 1776, C. O. 101/18.

[12] Governor Shirley to the Earl of Dartmouth, Feb. 17, 1776, C. O. 71/6.

of parliament prohibiting intercourse with the rebellious colonies and formally closing the mainland-West Indian trade was accompanied by elaborate regulations governing the condemnation and sale of captured ships in Caribbean vice-admiralty courts.[1] These provided a fairly regular means of supply for some time, especially after the opening of commercial relations between the United States and the foreign tropical American possessions by resolution of congress in October 1775 in an attempt to secure ammunition and guns.[2]

But only holders of commissions from the Crown and seamen and soldiers serving under them were legally permitted to share in the disposition of prizes. Islanders engaged in capturing American bottoms on their own account were soon in difficulties with royal judges and considerable hard feeling resulted. After a ruling of the Attorney and Solicitor General of England, that governors had not been empowered to grant commissions, they were, in 1777, specifically authorized to issue letters of marque. Individuals whose applications for them met approval were thereafter by law entitled to the entire value of enemy vessels they seized. If, however, captors were unprovided with them, such ships were forfeited to the king.[3]

Distress was also to some extent averted by the local cultivation of ground crops, by increased importations from Great Britain and Ireland, and by the development of commercial relations with the French and Spanish Caribbean. From the first, considerable tracts normally employed in cane growing were turned to the production of foodstuffs. The act providing for the sale of prize cargoes in the sugar colonies was followed by another authorizing the sending out of 100,000 quarters of wheat and its products from London, Bristol, Liverpool, and Glasgow to them during 1776.[4] This was subsequently renewed annually.[5]

But the relief thus afforded did not meet expectations. The assembly of Barbados declared with its customary querulousness in the fall of 1776, "Whatever may have been the provident care of his Majesty and both Houses of Parliament, in the prohibitory act in our

---

[1] 16 Geo. III c. 5.

[2] Force, *Archives,* 4th series, III, col. 1901. Gov. William Burt to Lord Germain, May 4th and Sept. 17, 1777, C. O. 152/56 and Dec. 1 and 14, 1777, C. O. 152/57.

[3] Petition of the Owners of the Sloop "Reprizal" to the King. Address of the Council and Assembly of Antigua to the King. Lord Germain to Governor Burt, June 8 and 26, 1777. All are in C. O. 152/56.

[4] 16 Geo. III c. 37.

[5] As for example by 18 Geo. III c. 45, 22 Geo. III c. 13, 23 Geo. III c. 6.

favour, yet we are not sensible that the inhabitants of this Island have actually received the least benefit from such indulgence; and from the other act, to allow the exportation of wheat from England to the East and West Indies, the benefit is yet to be received." [1]

Singularly enough, in the face of threatened scarcity, stocks in the islands were actually exported beyond the Atlantic. In 1775, Barbadian traders attempted to ship 2,000 barrels of flour to their English correspondents.[2] The fleet sailing from the Leewards a year later carried home considerable quantities of rice. "Such is the Avidity for gain," wrote Governor Burt, "that I am confident that Merchs. will again export from hence to England if the Prices shou'd be kept high there." He consequently urged that parliament lay an embargo on shipments of lumber, rice, and provisions from the sugar colonies into England during the period of the American war.[3]

The neighboring foreign West Indies were drawn on to an even greater extent. In response to appeals made in 1777 [4] by the legislatures of Antigua, St. Kitts, Montserrat, and Nevis, which islands were still suffering from the hurricane of five years before, Governor Burt authorized the importation of provisions [5] and lumber [6] from the French and Spanish colonies into the Leewards in British bottoms. Foodstuffs illegally brought from Spain's possessions in Spanish vessels were later admitted [7] and, before the close of 1778, ports in the Leewards were opened to any but enemy ships for the entry of edibles.[8] Burt likewise advocated granting lumber and fish from the Baltic countries and Russia direct entry, payment for them to be made in rum,[9] but his suggestion bore no fruit.

Representations of Barbadian planters to the British government, made late in 1777, that famine loomed, accompanied by loud calls for aid, resulted in the sending out of a provision fleet to the island by the Lords of the Treasury with directions that the supplies be dis-

---

[1] Force, *Archives,* 5th series, II, cols. 812–814.
[2] Governor Hay to the Earl of Dartmouth, Aug. 29, 1775, C. O. 28/56.
[3] Burt to Lord Germain, Dec. 1, 1777, C. O. 152/57.
[4] Contained in C. O. 152/56.
[5] Burt to Lord Germain, Sept. 17, 1777, C. O. 152/56 and Nov. 30, 1777, C. O. 152/57.
[6] Burt to Lord Germain, March (no date) 1778, C. O. 152/57.
[7] Burt to Lord Germain, July 30, 1778, C. O. 152/59.
[8] Burt to Lord Germain, Nov. 2, and Dec. 17, 1778, C. O. 152/59.
[9] Burt to Lord Germain, Sept. 17, 1777, C. O. 152/56 and Dec. 1, 1777, C. O. 152/57.

posed of by the governor and council at prime cost with no freight charge. Six vessels with cargoes of flour, beans, and peas, accompanied by two laden with fish, arrived early in 1778.[1] The stores were gratefully enough received, but, in characteristic fashion, the suggestion of the Secretary of State accompanying them, that the assembly make provision for supporting such rebel prisoners as might be brought to the colony, was not adopted and Governor Hay was obliged to care for them at his own expense.[2]

Governor Burt's urgent request that four shiploads of coarse bread, flour, barley, beans, and peas be sent to the Leewards on the same terms[3] was refused by Treasury officials on the grounds that no call for aid had been received from local proprietors or traders and that doing so would prevent private persons from placing orders and merchants from sending out the usual quantities of goods.[4]

The removal of restrictions on the trade of Ireland with the West Indies[5] in 1778,[6] whereby the direct exportation of Irish produce and of most kinds of manufactures was authorized and Irish woolens were placed on a footing with British ones, tended to increase the supply of provisions in the sugar islands. The first year that the new regulations were in force they depended solely on Ireland for salted meats.[7] The freeing of the Spanish trade in 1778[8] likewise, for a short time, gave the British planters further access to stores. Unfortunately for them, the declaration of war between Great Britain and Spain almost immediately thereafter once more closed the ports of Cuba, Porto Rico, and the Main to them.

But the opening of such new sources of supply in no way compen-

---

[1] Governor Hay to Lord Germain, Feb. 7, 1778, C. O. 28/57.

[2] Poyer, *Barbados,* pp. 385, 386.

[3] Burt to Lord Germain, March (no date) 1778, C. O. 152/57 and June 17, 1778, C. O. 152/58.

[4] Lord Germain to Governor Burt, Sept. 2, 1778, C. O. 152/58.

[5] For the nature of the Irish-West Indian trade see [James Caldwell], "An Enquiry How Far the Restrictions Laid Upon the Trade of Ireland, by British Acts of Parliament, Are a Benefit, or Disadvantage, to the British Dominions in General, and to England in Particular . . . ," in *Debates Relative to the Affairs of Ireland, in the Years 1763 and 1764* (2 vols., London, 1766), II, p. 769 ff.

[6] 18 Geo. III c. 55. From 1780, by 20 Geo. III c. 10, the Irish-American trade was carried on in like manner as that from Great Britain to America.

[7] *Min. W. I. Mer.,* June 4, 1778.

[8] *Ricardo Levene, "Comercio de Indias, Antecedentes Legales (1713–1778),"* in *Documentos Para la Historia Argentina,* V (Buenos Aires, 1915), pp. xxvi-xxxv.

sated for the cutting off of the American trade, and a shortage of provisions and lumber was evident by the close of 1776. A temporary embargo on exports of mainland produce was laid in St. Kitts in December, 1775;[1] this was made permanent five months later,[2] and the exportation of negro clothing and woolen goods was soon similarly prohibited.[3] A fire which consumed Basseterre in 1776 destroyed most of the stores in the island and, because no relief could be secured from the near-by colonies, an appeal for assistance was sent to the Crown.[4]

The situation throughout the Leewards became critical; actual famine set in. In a private letter to Lord Germain, Governor Burt wrote from Antigua at the close of 1777, "At Montserrat they were reduced to such distress that not a Morsel of Bread was to be had in the Island for a Day or two. luckily a Sloop went from hence with Flower, since that they have scarcely had from hand to mouth. Many Negroes have Starved, the same has happn'd in Nevis. here & at St. Christophers we have not been so Bad but in great Want. . . ."[5] In another letter, written from St. Kitts in the following spring, "From the best information I have been able to collect, The Island of Antigua has lost above a thousand Negroes, Montserat near twelve Hundred, & some Whites—Nevis three or four Hundred, & This Island as many from the Want of Provisions. . . . during our Distress I received from Montserrat Intelligence they had not a Morsel of Bread in that Island and that for three Successive Days Hundreds of People came to Town in Search of it & returned Empty."[6]

Prosecutions for the recovery of debt became so numerous in St. Kitts that upwards of three hundred men—nearly half the militia —fled from the island between March and September 1778 to escape court action.[7] In the same year, the local assembly declared the suffering to be so general that the colony was incapable of bearing a tax sufficient to meet the expense of repairing the fortifications[8] and the legislatures of Montserrat and Nevis held that the state of those

---

[1] Proclamation by Pres. Craister Greatheed, Dec. 23, 1775, C. O. 152/55.

[2] President Greatheed to Lord Germain, June 5, 1776, C. O. 152/55.

[3] Proclamation by President Greatheed, Nov. 26, 1776, C. O. 152/56.

[4] Address of the Council and Assembly of St. Kitts to the Crown, in C. O. 152/55.

[5] Under date of December 1, in C. O. 152/57.

[6] Burt to Germain, March 17, 1778, C. O. 152/57.

[7] Burt to Germain, Sept. 30, 1778, C. O. 152/58.

[8] Address of the Assembly to Governor Burt, enclosed in the latter's despatch of March (no date) 1778, C. O. 152/57.

islands was so low as to make it impossible for them to provide for their own defense.[1]

The scarcity of supplies in Barbados brought to a head differences which had been brewing between Governor Edward Hay and the assembly since soon after his arrival. The lower house of the legislature contained a number of assertive individuals; the governor was a wilful and self-centered official with little knowledge of colonial affairs and with but slight understanding of the Caribbean viewpoint. His optimistic reports at the outbreak of the Revolution have been quoted. When Captain Payne, a British officer, arrived soon after to purchase provisions and livestock for the consumption of royal forces at Boston, he was allowed to draw on stocks as he saw fit. This occasioned great resentment among the Barbadians, and, through the activity of Mr. Duke, solicitor-general of the colony, the assembly adopted an address to the Crown on the threatened shortage of foodstuffs. Duke had, from the first, been on bad terms with Hay; the latter seized this opportunity, suspended him for thus "disturbing the King's peace of mind" and would have dissolved the body had the speaker not opposed such a measure.[2]

The document was in due course presented to Lord Germain by George Walker, the island agent, who accompanied it with a memorial setting forth a melancholy state of affairs—the negroes and poor whites even then on the point of starvation and compelled to plunder and pillage for the means of subsistence while all were facing the immediate future with alarm. Lord Germain replied that since, by evidence in the governor's despatches, the distress could not possibly be as great as was claimed, nothing would be done.

When Walker's report relating this reached the assembly, an uproar ensued. Resolutions were passed affirming that body's right to address the throne, maintaining that there had been good and sufficient ground for the late petition and declaring that "His Excellency The Honourable Edward Hay has by application to His Majesty's Secretary of State for the Colonies done what lay in his power to intercept His Majesty's Relief towards his loyal and distressed Subjects of this Colony." A second address to the king was voted following a violent speech by Mr. Duke. This declared that the governor had made an unjust attempt to frustrate the sovereign's favorable in-

---

[1] Petitions of the Councils and Assemblies of Montserrat and Nevis, in C. O. 152/59.
[2] Governor Hay to Lord Germain, Feb. 15, 1776, and enclosures, C. O. 28/56.

clinations towards the faithful islanders and prayed for interposition in their favor so that they might secure much-needed stores.[1]

In replying to the governor's speech at the opening of the new session in September, 1776, the assembly minced no words in assailing the exportation to Boston and in upholding its contention that supplies were so low that the island was in danger.[2] Some months later Hay, with ill-concealed glee, refused his assent to a bill continuing Walker as agent, at the same time declaring his readiness to concur in the appointment of anyone else.[3]

Meanwhile, although urging the presence of plenty in Barbados, the governor complained about the high prices at which commodities were being held and requested Admiral Young, commander of the British fleet in the local station, to grant passports to such vessels as might come to the colony with North American produce procured in the foreign Leewards. The latter consented, but, to prevent an abuse of that indulgence at the hands of private adventurers, recommended the formation of a colonial company which would be given the exclusive right to carry on such a trade. The council approved the project and proposed the issuing of 200 shares at £20 currency each to secure the requisite capital. Lack of subscriptions, however, caused the plan to fall through.[4]

The increased cost of supplies and of marketing bore heavily on the Barbadians. In 1778, the colony was "decayed and impoverished," credit had ceased and trade was very low.[5] "The inhabitants . . ." wrote Governor Hay, "seem to be much in a desponding way. . . . Their Credit lessens dayly; Creditors become Sollicitous to recover their Debts. Two Planters have lately run away and have left their Estates to be broken up by their Creditors. Many others are much involved."[6] During all this time, the conflict between governor and assembly grew more bitter; it was ultimately carried to such lengths that the popular body steadfastly refused to reform the militia and to provide fortifications and ended only with Hay's death in 1779.[7]

In Jamaica, the situation was less critical though there, too, the scarcity was severely felt. An embargo on the exportation of pro-

[1] Governor Hay to Lord Germain, July 25, 1776, C. O. 28/56.

[2] Force, *Archives,* 5th series, II, cols. 812–814.

[3] Hay to Germain, Feb. 26, 1777, C. O. 28/56.

[4] Hay to Germain, May 10, and July 25, 1776, C. O. 28/56.

[5] Address of the Council and Assembly of Barbados to the Crown, April 14, 1778, C. O. 28/57.

[6] To Lord Germain, June 4, 1778, C. O. 28/57.

[7] Poyer, *Barbados,* pp. 372 ff.

visions was already in force in January, 1776,[1] and the request of the Count d'Ennery, governor of St. Domingo, to be permitted to purchase stores in the island was courteously but firmly refused.[2] But two years later provisions were more plentiful. The mercantile class then petitioned the governor to remove the embargo and this was subsequently done.[3]

On the whole, the experience of the first period of the war demonstrated the truth of the planters' claims regarding their dependence upon free access to American supplies,[4] and facts were against those few individuals who still professed to see no ground for serious alarm in a derangement of the old relations with the mainland.[5]

The increase in the cost of essential plantation goods at about this time is shown by the following comparative tables.

MARKET QUOTATIONS IN BARBADOS [6]

Commodity	Price in 1774–1775	Price in 1776
Flour, per cwt.	15s. to 25s.	30s. to 37s. 6d.
Indian corn, per bu.	2s. 6d. to 3s. 9d.	10s. to 13s.
Salt fish, per quintal	12s. 6d. to 25s.	30s. to 40s.
Salt beef, per bbl.	60s. to 70s.	90s. to 130s.
Salt pork, per bbl.	70s. to 100s.	100s. to 150s.
Herring, per bbl.	25s. to 32s. 6d.	45s. to 55s.

PRICES IN JAMAICA [7]

Commodity	Before the War	During the War
Rice, per cwt.	13s. 9d. to 20s.	40s. to 80s.
Indian corn, per bu.	2s. 6d. to 6s. 3d.	6s. 8d. to 17s. 6d.
Common flour, per cwt.	15s. to 20s.	20s. to 50s.
Pitch pine lumber, per M	£8 to £12	£15 to £40
Shingles, per M	£1.2.6 to £2.5.0	£4 to £7
White oak staves, per M	£10 to £18	£20 to £50

[1] Sir Basil Keith to the Earl of Dartmouth, Jan. 18, 1776, C. O. 137/71.

[2] Keith to Dartmouth, June 6, 1776 and enclosures, C. O. 137/71.

[3] Gov. John Dalling to Lord Germain, April 25 and Oct. 8, 1778, C. O. 137/73.

[4] Anon., *The West India Merchant. Being a Series of Papers Originally Under That Signature in the London Evening Post* . . . (London, 1778).

[5] Anon., "A West-India Planter," *Remarks on the Evidence delivered in the Petition Presented by the West India Planters and Merchants to the Hon. the House of Commons, on the 16th of March 1775* . . . (London, 1777).

[6] Memorial of George Walker, Agent for Barbados, to Lord Germain, C. O. 28/56.

[7] Report made in March 1785, C. O. 137/85.

COST OF SUPPLIES IN THE LEEWARD ISLANDS [1]

Commodity	Before the War	During the War
Rice, per cwt.	18s. to 24s.	50s. to 55s.
Indian corn, per bu.	4s. to 8s.	12s. to 16s. 6d.
Beef, per bbl.	50s. to 80s.	100s. to 160s.
Pork, per bbl.	66s. to 90s.	132s. to 198s.
Flour, per cwt.	20s. to 30s.	50s. to 66s.
Lumber, per M	£5 to £8	£20 to £40
Shingles, per M	18s. to 30s.	£3.6.0 to £8
White oak staves, per M	£7 to £10	£20 to £40
Red oak staves, per M	£5 to £8	£16.10.0 to £33

The entry of the French into the war in 1778 as allies of the Americans and the outbreak of hostilities between Spain and England a year later greatly changed the British planters' position for the worse. Hitherto in safety in a military sense, they were now directly attacked; and food and lumber from the French and Spanish possessions, which had alleviated their distress in the past, were at the same time cut off.

It was a foregone conclusion that the conflict would be carried to the Caribbean. The Continental Congress had authorized its commissioners seeking an alliance with France to promise that power any British sugar colonies which might be captured by Franco-American action.[2] A proposal made to the West India merchants of London, that they interest themselves in a separate neutrality for the islands, was met with the declaration that this was impracticable.[3] Early in 1778 confidential information that war seemed unavoidable was sent to the British governors, and they were directed to prepare in every way possible for the defence of their territories.[4]

Relations between the British and French colonists in the Antilles had been badly strained because American privateers had been permitted to fit out in Guadeloupe and Martinique and to dispose of their prizes there. But through refusing to return runaway slaves from Guadeloupe unless this were brought to a halt, Governor Burt

[1] In Governor Shirley to Lord Sydney, Sept. 7, 1785, C. O. 152/64.
[2] Force, *Archives*, 5th series, III, col. 1617.
[3] *Min. W. I. Mer.*, March 3, 1778. The matter of keeping war out of the two groups of West India colonies had been under frequent consideration since earliest days. See index to Higham, *Leeward Islands*, under "Neutrality."
[4] For example, see Lord Germain to Governor Burt, May 15, 1778, C. O. 152/57, referring to earlier despatches on that subject.

of the Leeward group had received a promise from the Count d'Arbaud shortly before the declaration of war to close that island's ports to them. Indeed, as a sign of his good will, the French executive had even extended a cordial invitation to Burt and his daughter to pay him a visit. But no success had attended numerous efforts to secure a similar engagement from the Marquis de Bouillé in Martinique.[1]

In order that they might be spared the horrors attendant upon indiscriminate pillaging at each others' hands, de Bouillé, immediately upon the outbreak of the Anglo-French struggle, suggested to neighboring English governors that privateers from their respective colonies be prohibited from committing acts of hostility, violence, or depredation on the shores or within the roads or ports of any island belonging to the other, and that vessels sailing under letters of marque be permitted to operate only upon the high seas.[2] His proposal was gladly acceded to and the agreement was scrupulously observed on both sides.[3]

Few of the West India islands were in any position to resist attack. On September 7, 1778, Dominica, lying between Guadeloupe and Martinique, protected by only forty-six regulars including officers and 150 militia men with almost worthless weapons, and weakened by the presence of a considerable number of French planters, capitulated to an expeditionary force from the latter island.[4] A few months later, St. Lucia [5] fell before the British whom it served as a naval base throughout the war.

[1] Governor Burt to Lord Germain, Jan. 6, 1778, C. O. 152/57.

[2] Marquis de Bouillé to the Lieutenant-Governor of Dominica, Aug. 19, 1778.

[3] For example, in 1778 de Bouillé expressed his willingness to return 37 slaves taken from the island of Mistique, belonging to Grenada, by a French vessel (Lieutenant-Governor of Dominica to Lord Germain, Sept. 5, 1778, C. O. 71/7) and in 1782, Governor Shirley of the Leeward Islands government ordered the release of the *Nimrod* of Philadelphia, the *Susanna* of Newburn, N. C., and of the *Jane* of New London, captured by British privateers while at anchor in the road of Basseterre, St. Kitts, then under French control (Shirley to the Earl of Shelburne, June 11, 1782, C. O. 152/62).

[4] The Lieutenant-Governor of Dominica to Lord Germain, Sept. 9, 1778, C. O. 71/7. For a contemporary French account, see Anon., *Relation de la Prise Faite par les François sur les Anglois, de l'isle de la Dominique* . . . (Laon, 1778).

[5] For the importance of this colony from the French point of view, see [Daniel Chardon], *Essai sur la Colonie de Saint-Lucie* . . . (Neuchatel, 1779), Chapter IV.

The spirit animating the two forces of European soldiery, each faithful to orders from a distant home country covering an enterprise in which there was little personal interest, is revealed by episodes recorded in the narrative of Colin Lindsay, a British officer participating in the descent on St. Lucia. Before the surrender of the island the French commander restored to General Meadows of the invading army his strayed horse, loaned him the services of the French chief surgeon, and returned a silver-hilted sword dropped by one of his captains. French sentries likewise did not fire at enemy soldiers passing near their posts and the two groups of officers agreed heartily that the climate was "most villainous" and the island "not worth fighting for." [1]

The conquest of St. Lucia was one of the few British successes in the war. In 1779 both Grenada and St. Vincent [2] were lost. Their capture was facilitated through aid being given the French by their resident countrymen. A dispute between Governor Valentine Morris and the legislature of St. Vincent, originating in his having made grants of free land to small settlers as described elsewhere,[3] and the criminal conduct of Lieutenant-Colonel Etherington, commander of the royal troops stationed there, in employing his men to open up a recently-acquired plantation instead of in throwing up fortifications,[4] had furthermore made that colony singularly vulnerable.

Without access to stores in the French and Spanish Caribbean, the Leeward Islander's distress became acute. "Previous to the arrival of the Cork Fleet on Wednesday last . . . , there was not one Barrel

---

[1] Colin Lindsay, "Narrative of Events in the Island of St. Lucie," in *A Military Miscellany* (2 vols., London, 1793), II, 441–483. Also published under the title "Narrative of the Occupation and Defence of the Island of St. Lucie, 1779," in Alexander Lindsay's *Lives of the Lindsays, or a Memoir of the Houses of Crawford and Balcarres* (4 vols., Wigan, 1840), III, 195–235.

[2] Papers on the surrender of these colonies will be found in C. O. 101/23.

[3] Pages 117 ff. The dissension between them was carried to such extremes that Morris received little of the salary due him and was obliged to meet public expenses with money raised on personal security. Bills drawn on the Treasury by him were dishonored and, after his return to England following the loss of the island, he was imprisoned by holders of them who ruined him by forcing the sale of his property. Some of the bills were met in 1789, after his death. This was one of the most disgraceful episodes in West Indian history. (See C. O. 260/5, 6 for papers on it). For a spirited work written in self-justification, see Morris's *A Narrative of the Official Conduct of Valentine Morris, Esq., Late Captain General, Governor in Chief, &c. &c. of the Island of St. Vincent* (London, 1788).

[4] Shepherd, *Account of St. Vincent*, pp. 37, 38.

of any kind of Salted Meat for sale," declared the legislature of Antigua to Governor Burt in April 1779.[1] Long-continued lack of rain rendered the situation of the Antiguans even more deplorable than the mere scarcity of supplies would have. Reporting the state of affairs home in the spring of 1779, Governor Burt wrote: "Their present Crops are Distroyed by a long very long severe Drought: nor have they now any Prospect of a Succeeding Crop; they have not had a thorough Season of Rain since October was a Twelvemonth. Their Cysterns are and have been some time Emptied: Their large Ponds are in the same state; they are Compelled to carry Water for their familys use many Miles, for which they pay Eighteen Pence a Gallon. Heaven has denied them not only Seasons but even refreshing Showers from whence they might raise Pulse and Vegetables or some Provisions for their Negroes. . . . That Island which has I am well assured made Thirty Six thousand Hogsheads often 32 and on an average Twenty thousand will this year scarcely Turn four thousand. If this Produce belonged to one Proprietor of the whole Island it would not pay the Taxes, Servants Wages and defray the necessary repairs and Contingent Expenses much less Add the Great Expence of feeding their Slaves, which in tolerable Years are generally supported one third of the year by Country Produce." Neither local nor British merchants would extend further credit.[2]

In this crisis the legislature called on the British government to send out 3,000 barrels of flour, fifty thousand of ship-bread and as many bushels of peas and beans, agreeing to pass an act securing payment for them if the request were granted.[3] The governor, too, was urgently requested to lend his approval to a proposed bill without a suspending clause, providing for the issuing of £30,000 worth of paper money to circulate for two years at 6 per cent. Although this was contrary to his instructions, Burt was inclined to view the measure favorably as being essential to the salvation of the island.[4]

But it was at length decided that both steps would bear too heavily on local business interests and, instead, bills of exchange to the amount of £20,000 were drawn on the Lords of the Treasury for the purchase of provisions to be deposited in public granaries, from whence they were to be distributed among slave owners. A capitation tax was at

[1] Under date of the thirtieth, C. O. 152/59.
[2] May 3, 1779, C. O. 152/59.
[3] Resolutions of April 8 and 13, 1779, C. O. 152/59.
[4] Burt to Lord Germain, May 24, 1779, and the enclosed address of the legislature, C. O. 152/59.

the same time levied on servile blacks for the creation of a fund with which to meet the obligation thus incurred.[1] "It is with real sorrow I assure your Lordships," wrote the governor, "had not this measure been adopted Famine must have been our lot. . . . Many hundreds of Negroes have starved. This woeful state will, by this Act be closed. The Credit thus given to Individuals by the Public will, I am convinced, save the Lives of Hundreds." [2] In the opinion of law officers in England, this extraordinary act was highly expedient upon grounds of public policy and justice; it was consequently not disallowed and the bills were duly accepted by the Treasury.[3]

A disheartening series of natural disasters in 1780 and 1781 brought widespread ruin in its wake. In the autumn of the former year two terrific hurricanes, an earthquake, and a tidal wave ravaged the West Indies; another tropical storm in 1781 was almost as destructive. Jamaica and Barbados were especially hard hit. Losses ran into the millions sterling. In Barbados alone deaths exceeded 3,000; Bridgetown was all but totally destroyed.[4] Starvation was averted in that island and in St. Lucia only by the timely arrival from the Leewards of 1,300 barrels of the flour sent by the Crown to relieve Antigua.[5]

Subscriptions were promptly raised in Great Britain and Ireland, while parliament appropriated £80,000 for relief work in Barbados. By ill chance the assembly and Governor Cunninghame, successor to the hapless Hay, fell at outs over its disposition and their inopportune struggle, carried on until the executive's recall some time later,[6] largely defeated the good intentions of the home government. In Jamaica, surplus military stores were placed at the planters' disposal and rice and corn were imported from Georgia and South

---

[1] C. O. 152/34, no. 52.

[2] To the Lords Commissioners for Trade and Plantations, Sept. 26, 1779, C. O. 152/34.

[3] Lord Germain to Governor Burt, Oct. 8, 1779, C. O. 152/59.

[4] C. O. 28/57, 58; C. O. 137/79, 81. Anon., *Dreadful Effects of a Hurricane Which Happened at Barbadoes in 1780* . . . (London, n.d.). "Brief Account of the Desolation Made in Several of the West India Islands by the Late Hurricanes," in *The Gent. Mag.*, Supplement for 1780, pp. 620–623. Anon., *An History of Jamaica and Barbados, with an Authentic Account of the Lives Lost, and the Damage Sustained in Each Island, by the late Hurricanes* (London, 1781). Mr. Fowler, *A General Account of the Calamities occasioned by the Late Tremendous Hurricanes and Earthquakes in the West-India Islands* . . . (London, 1781).

[5] Gov. William Burt to Lord Germain, November (no date) 1780, C. O. 152/60.

[6] C. O. 28/58, 59.

Carolina,[1] but, to add to the misery of the residents, fire destroyed much of Kingston and a good share of the supplies there, causing a further loss of £400,000 sterling.[2] Famine soon made its appearance and some thousands of negroes perished of starvation.[3]

Operations in the Caribbean in 1780 brought the British one notable success—the capture of San Juan, Nicaragua, from the Spanish by a Jamaican expeditionary force. But the breaking out of yellow fever soon after turned victory into defeat and survivors were speedily withdrawn.[4] The following year was more propitious. While Great Britain suffered the loss of Tobago to France [5] and Roseau, Dominica, then under French occupation, was burned, a heavy attack on St. Lucia was repulsed and the Dutch colonies of Demerara, Essequibo, and Berbice on the Main, and St. Eustatius, off St. Lucia, were taken.

The latter had long been the scene of extensive international commercial activity to the immense profit of the Hollanders. A feminine visitor about 1775 declared, "Never did I meet with such variety. Here was a mercht. vending his goods in Dutch, another in French, a third in Spanish, etc. etc. . . . From one end of the town of Eustatia to the other is a continued mart, where goods of the most different uses and qualities are displayed before the shop doors. Here hang rich embroideries, painted silks, flowered Muslins, with all the Manufactures of the Indies. Just by hang Sailors' Jackets, trousers, shoes, hats, etc. Next stall contains most exquisite silver plate, the most beautiful indeed I ever saw, and close by these iron-pots, kettles, and shovels. Perhaps the next presents you with French and English Millinary-wares. But it were endless to enumerate the variety of merchandize in such a place, for in every store you find everything, be their qualities ever so opposite." [6]

Early in the war, St. Eustatius had become an entrepôt for supplying the Americans with manufactured goods and military supplies while the British planters received from there at greatly enhanced

[1] Gov. John Dalling to Lord Germain, Aug. 19, 1781, C. O. 137/81.

[2] For accounts of the fire and the damage done, see C. O. 137/82.

[3] Report of a committee of the assembly of Jamaica, quoted in Edwards, *History*, II, 413.

[4] The papers relative to the attack on San Juan will be found in C. O. 137/77–81. A contemporary account is that of the physician Thomas Dancer, who accompanied the troops, *A Brief History of the Late Expedition Against Fort San Juan, So Far as it Relates to the Diseases of the Troops . . .* (Kingston, 1781).

[5] C. O. 101/24.

[6] Andrews, ed., *Journal of a Lady*, pp. 136–138.

prices a considerable part of the mainland provisions and lumber which reached them. The trade carried on in the Danish Virgins was insignificant by comparison, yet the Danish West India Company, trading to them, declared repeated 100 per cent dividends in the period of the Revolution.[1]

As the principal neutral port in the Caribbean after 1778, St. Eustatius become one vast warehouse and its merchants rolled in gold. The fitting out there of American privateers under protection of the Dutch flag was particularly exasperating to the British, who came to regard it as "a nest of heterogeneous beings" and likened these to vultures.[2] By their unceasing pursuit of gain in meeting the rebel seaboard colonists' wants, the Dutch laid up a terrible store of hatred against themselves.

So high did the feeling against them run that Great Britain opened war with Holland in 1780 largely over the question of St. Eustatius. Like action might have been taken against the Danes had the danger from further flouting the League of Armed Neutrality not been too great to be risked for the purpose of closing their relatively small trade. Full vengeance was therefore wreaked upon the Dutch; their possessions on the South American mainland were captured by British privateers and forces under Admiral Rodney and General Vaughan made a descent upon St. Eustatius.

The depot island was wholly undefended and when, on February 3, 1781, the British appeared before it, an unconditional surrender was made. More than £3,000,000 sterling worth of supplies and tropical produce were found on shore and aboard richly-laden ships in the harbor. Included in the goods seized were consignments from British and West Indian merchants which had been entered under free port regulations in the expectation of immense profits, as well as stocks of resident Englishmen, become Dutch citizens for purposes of commerce.

All inhabitants were held as prisoners of war and all property, both public and private, was indiscriminately confiscated to the king. British, American, Dutch, and French merchants were soon expelled, carrying only their personal effects. Many sought refuge in St. Kitts, where the legislature voted them relief. The Jews were most harshly treated; all were banished without their families on a day's

---

[1] Southey, *Chronological History*, III, 6.
[2] President Johnson of St. Kitts to Lord Germain, Feb. 13, 1781, C. O. 152/61.

notice, and were so closely searched for concealed wealth upon their departure that the lining of their garments was ripped out.

The seizure of St. Eustatius was followed by one of the greatest auction sales in history. Naval stores were sent to Antigua, provisions to Jamaica, and West Indian and American produce to the home country, but all goods of European origin were put on the block. Under the promise of protection and clear title to purchasers of all nations, British Caribbean merchants and agents representing French and American buyers flocked to the island. So great was the quantity of commodities offered that there was little competition between bidders and lots on the average sold at one fourth of their value. Supplies became more plentiful throughout all the British colonies than they had been at any time since the outbreak of the war.[1]

Rodney sought to justify his taking over of the British traders' property on the ground that they had engaged in supplying the enemy.[2] The merchants of St. Kitts were the heaviest colonial losers and the island assembly challenged the admiral to prove his charges by offering a reward for the discovery of the alleged traitors.[3] That most of the British goods sold in St. Eustatius had found their way to the revolting mainland or to the French islands, even though by devious channels, is certain; that some few at least of the West Indian traders had been in commercial correspondence with the Americans and Frenchmen is probable. But it was not then by law treasonable for British subjects in neutral territory to trade with the enemy during time of war, provided that they dealt in no warlike stores,[4] and there was scarcely sufficient cause for the drastic action taken.

The outcry raised against Rodney and Vaughan in the British Caribbean was tremendous. A resolution before the assembly of St. Kitts sought to bring their action to the king's attention.[5] The West

[1] J. Franklin Jameson, "St. Eustatius and the American Revolution," in *The Am. Hist. Rev.*, July 1903, pp. 702–705.

[2] Sir George Bridges [Lord Rodney], *Letters . . . to His Majesty's Ministers, &c. &c. Relative to the Capture of St. Eustatius . . .* (London, 1790).

[3] *The Annual Register for 1781*, pp. 104 ff.

[4] Opinion of Attorney-General Northey, March 22, 1703/4, in George Chalmers, *Opinions of Eminent Lawyers, on Various Points of English Jurisprudence, Chiefly Concerning the Colonies, Fisheries, and Commerce of Great Britain* (London, 1858), p. 645.

[5] Anon., *A Speech, Which Was Spoken in the House of Assembly of St. Christopher, Upon a motion made on Tuesday the 6th of November, 1781, for Presenting an Address to His Majesty, Relative to the Proceedings of Admiral Rodney and General Vaughan at St. Eustatius . . .* (London, 1782).

India merchants in London likewise took a hand in the matter and presented a remonstrance to the Crown.[1] In May and again in December, 1781, Burke moved the opening of a parliamentary inquiry into the confiscations made, declaring them to have been contrary to the law of nations and holding that, in consequence of the sale, the enemy had been provided with much-needed supplies at low cost. Making use of the loss of the island to the French in November, 1781, he accused the commanders of having wasted their time in commercial operations instead of having followed up their military success and charged them with having profited personally thereby.

The pair, present as members of the House of Commons at the time of the second attack, denied all charges *in toto* and, through the machinations of Lord North, both attempts to investigate the affair were defeated by two to one votes.[2] But a series of civil suits arising from it harassed Rodney in the years which followed; out of sixty-four claims presented, only thirteen were settled by 1788 and in nine of these restitution of appropriated property was ordered.[3]

The position of the French by the close of 1781 thoroughly alarmed the West Indians in Great Britain. The government was repeatedly called upon to provide naval and military reinforcements sufficient to defend properly the colonies and a similar address was made to the Crown.[4] Nor were these fears without foundation. The first quarter of 1782 saw a continuation of French successes. The inhabitants of St. Kitts capitulated in February after a spectacular defence of their fortress-citadel, Brimstone Hill;[5] Montserrat and Nevis fell shortly after.[6] All of the Leeward Islands, excepting Antigua alone were then in the hands of the enemy, as were St. Vincent, Grenada, and Tobago. Demerara, Essequibo, and Berbice were lost. Attacks on

[1] "Petition of the West India Merchants to the King," in *The Scots Mag.*, June 1781, pp. 283 ff.

[2] *Parliamentary History of England*, XXII, cols. 218–262, 770–785.

[3] Jameson, "St. Eustatius," *Am. Hist. Rev.*, July 1903, p. 707. See also Anon., *An Explanation of the Case Relating to the Capture of St. Eustatius* . . . (London, 1786).

[4] *Min. W. I. Mer.*, Nov. 28 and Dec. 18, 1781, Jan. 29, 1782. *To the King's Most Excellent Majesty. The Humble Address and Petition of the Planters and Merchants . . . on Behalf of Themselves and Others Interested in the British West-India Islands* [London, 1782].

[5] A journal and report of the siege will be found in C. O. 152/62. The story is well told in Algernon Aspinall's *West Indian Tales of Old* (London, 1912), Ch. III.

[6] C. O. 152/62.

Antigua, Barbados, and Jamaica by the united Franco-Spanish sea forces were momentarily expected; the outlook for the British planters was dark indeed when, on April 12th, a victory by Rodney over the French fleet commanded by de Grasse suddenly turned the tables.

This celebrated marine battle, fought between Martinique and Guadeloupe, introduced a new maneuvre made possible by a sudden shift of wind, "breaking the enemy's line" instead of engaging the foe in the traditional mere artillery duel. It at the same time reestablished British naval supremacy and saved her sugar colonies to Great Britain.[1] Largely in consequence of Rodney's memorable success, his country secured the restoration of all her captured colonies but Tobago, while she returned St. Lucia to France upon the reestablishment of a peace a year later.

At the same time that they were being plunged into acute distress

---

[1] Contemporary accounts are given in Sir Gilbert Blane, *Account of the Battle Between the British and French Fleets in the West Indies, on the Twelfth of April 1782* . . . [London, 1782]; Comte de Grasse, *Mémoire . . . sur le Combat Naval, du 12 Avril, 1782, Avec les Plans des Positions Principales des Armées Respectives* [Paris, 1782]; Joachim du Perron, *Journal Particular d'Une Campagne aux Indes Occidentales (1781–1782),* (Paris, n.d.); J. Mathews, *Twenty-one Plans, With Explanations, of Different Actions in the West Indies, During the Late War* (Chester, England, 1784). See also Alexandre de Grasse, *Notice Biographique sur l'Amiral Cte. de Grasse d'après les Documents Inédits* (Paris, 1840); Commander Nankivell, "Rodney's Victory Over De Grasse," in *Journ. of the Inst. of Jam.,* April 1895, pp. 114 ff.; N. D. Davis, *The Battle off Dominica in 1782* (Demerara, 1882). The maneuvre of breaking the line gave rise to a discussion which was the occasion for an acrimonious pamphlet war half a century later. Such tactics were suggested in the work of a civilian, John Clerk, *Essay on Naval Tactics* (2nd edition, London, 1804) which probably never came to Rodney's attention. Clerk himself claimed public credit in the second edition while others gave it to Rodney and still others to Sir Charles Douglas, captain under the admiral. In a third edition of Clerk's work, London, 1827, an anonymous naval officer expanded the latter's claim to the honor. The challenge was taken up by Sir Howard Douglas, son of Sir Charles. Others entered the lists on the several sides and the controversy was carried to ridiculous lengths without a conclusion being reached. See Howard Douglas, *A Statement of Some Important Facts . . . Relating to the Operation of Breaking the Enemy's Line . . .* (London, 1829) and his *Additional Statement of Facts . . .* (London, 1830) and *Naval Evolutions . . .* (London, 1832); Anon., "An Old Naval Officer," *Breaking the Line. Statement of Facts . . . Connected with the Great Battle 12th April, 1782* (Cheltenham, 1830); Sir Charles Knowles, *Observations on Naval Tactics; and on the Claims of Mr. Clerk of Eldin, &c.* (London, 1830); "Naval Tactics—Breaking the Enemy's Line," in *The Edinburgh Review,* April 1830, pp. 1–38; Thomas White, *Naval Researches* (London, 1830); [John Barrow], "Rodney's Battle of 12th April," in *The Quarterly Review,* Jan. 1830, pp. 50–79; and "Naval Evolutions," in *Fraser's Magazine,* March 1833, pp. 359–364.

by the lack of supplies, by increased costs of marketing, by natural disasters, and by enemy successes, the British planters suffered yet further misfortunes through increased customs charges being laid against produce entering the mother country and from their increasing inability to dispose of crops there for lack of carriers. An act of 1778, declaring that no taxes or duties would thereafter be laid in the North American or West Indian colonies with the exception of such as were necessary for the regulation of commerce and whose net proceeds would be at the disposal of the assemblies of those colonies in which they might be levied,[1] gave great satisfaction to the West Indians, some of whom, as we have seen, had not hesitated to challenge parliament's right to tax Englishmen overseas. But when that body, urged by the necessity of augmenting the national revenue to meet war expenses, made successive advances in the duty collected upon incoming colonial products, resentment was great.

The new rates were assailed as being contrary to the spirit of the act of 1778, since all sums assessed were paid by planters' agents and were charged to the proprietors' accounts and the latter were not represented in parliament. They were likewise held to be unjust because they fell only upon the colonial cultivators and not upon home retailers and consumers, and impolitic because they discouraged cultivation.[2] Considerable bitterness arose over the question and matters reached the point where serious opposition to coöperation with the home country in its prosecution of the war developed.

The increases in the duty on sugar, the principal crop, were especially felt. The charge per hundredweight of muscovado entered for home consumption at the outbreak of the Revolution was 6s. 3$\frac{9}{10}$d. A tax of 5 per cent on customs and excise, effective April 5, 1779, increased this to 6s. 7$\frac{13}{20}$d.; two years later, the rate was set at 11s. 8$\frac{7}{10}$d., and on July 25, 1782, at 12s. 3$\frac{2}{5}$d.[3]

The legislature of Jamaica took the lead in protesting at these several advances. Complaint against the new charge of 1779 was made in an address to the King in Council. "Whatever may be the Conveniences arising to Government from such a measure . . . , the consequences must be fatal to the good People of this Island. Their Produce is already heavily taxed, and subject to so great and many Charges, from the unavoidable circumstances of the times, that it

[1] 18 Geo. III c. 12.
[2] John Kemeys, *Free and Candid Reflections Occasioned by the late Additional Duties on Sugar and on Rum* . . . (London, 1783).
[3] *Gt. Br., H. C., Sess. Pap.*, 1826, XXII (328).

hardly remains of value sufficient for the Planters to induce them to carry on their Plantations, therefore such tax will in a short time render such Properties not worth the Cultivating." [1]

The practical doubling of the duty in 1781, the year marked by the second of the disastrous hurricanes, aroused a storm. The king was again memorialized, this time without a mincing of words. "Permit us to speak with freedom. You have visited us, under all our calamities of war and tempest, with an additional burden of taxes which will drive your faithful subjects from their land. You must relieve us, or we must abandon the colony." [2] When this urgent plea was disregarded, the assembly refused to grant further sums for fortifying the island and maintained its position until French victories in the Leewards and the threatened invasion of Jamaica itself caused better judgment to prevail. [3]

The closing of American markets and the departure of a smaller number of freighters for Great Britain each year made it impossible for the planters to place all of their produce and worked great hardships. A large share of the annual production of rum and molasses had been regularly sold in the thirteen colonies but from the outbreak of revolution their exportation was authorized only under license and then merely to the few ports in British hands. As Lord Howe soon complained that the rebels were being supplied through improper use of such papers, no further permits were issued except to contractors supplying the king's forces and sales fell off sharply. Even though the clearing out of rum for the use of civilians in occupied territory was later authorized, following representations on the subject by the West India traders in London, [4] only a fraction of what had once been shipped was sent to the mainland after 1776.

Furthermore, in consequence of the scarcity of shipping, rum and molasses, articles of lesser value, increasingly gave way to sugar for shipment home while new war-time duties, raising the prices, cut down the effective demand for them there. [5] Rum, indeed, became such a drug on the colonists' hands [6] that the planter-merchant interest in

[1] Under date of July 3, C. O. 137/75.

[2] *Journals of the Assembly of Jamaica,* VII, p. 381.

[3] Governor Dalling to Lord Germain, Nov. 24, 1781 and Lieutenant-Governor Campbell to Germain, March 25, 1782, C. O. 137/82.

[4] *Min. W. I. Mer.,* March 3 and 9, 1778.

[5] Address of the Legislature of Jamaica to the King in Council, July 3, 1779, C. O. 137/75.

[6] Governor Macartney of Grenada to Lord Howe, Dec. 5, 1777, C. O. 101/21.

the British capital sought to have it substituted for French brandy in navy rations, but without success.[1]

As a means of aiding the West Indians to meet losses occasioned through the difficulties attending marketing, while at the same time enabling them to better bear the war charges on their produce, it was suggested that the selling price of sugar in Great Britain be raised through prohibiting the distillation of grain and requiring use of the Caribbean product instead. This proposition was never seriously considered,[2] but higher returns per unit for such shipments as did reach British ports followed from the natural course of events.

The allies' capture of homeward-bound merchantmen coupled with the French victories, which followed one another in alarming succession, steadily reduced the quantities of West Indian commodities landed in Great Britain. While possession of their estates and crops in the occupied islands was guaranteed British owners, produce could be exported from them only to French or neutral harbors and then only in non-British vessels.[3] In 1776, the imports of British-grown cacao from tropical America into England were 653,300 pounds; from 1777 to 1780 inclusive, the average annual importation was but 395,475 pounds. Imports of coffee, the growth of British plantations, from the West Indies into England, dropped from 5,179,114 pounds in 1776 to 2,075,600 in 1780. Similarly, imports of British muscovado sugar from the Caribbean into England declined from 1,656,624 hundredweight in 1776 to 1,300,056 in 1780;[4] imports by way of London sank from 80,867 casks in the twelve months beginning March, 1780, to 72,866 and 74,976 casks respectively in the two succeeding years.[5] Imports of rum, the produce of British plantations, from the West India colonies into England fell from 3,341,020 gallons in 1776 to 1,617,808 in 1780;[6] entries in the port of London dwindled as follows—15,308 casks from March, 1779 to March, 1780; 12,123 the year after; 10,305 in 1781–82; and but 9,554 in the next annual period.[7]

[1] Min. W. I. Mer., Sept. 24, Dec. 17, 1782.

[2] The Annual Register for 1776, p. 123.

[3] The Petition of His Majesty's Subjects . . . Interested in Dominica, to Lord Germain, C. O. 71/7. Arrets of His Most Christian Majesty Relating to the Island of Granada, And its Dependencies, &c. &c. [London, 1780]. Tobago. Case and Opinions, November 1781. [London, 1781].

[4] Cacao imports in 1777 were 398,200 lbs.; in 1778, 338,600 lbs.; in 1779, 433,700 lbs.; in 1780, 411,400 lbs. Coffee imports in 1777 were 4,831,500 lbs.; in 1778, 3,879, 700 lbs.; in 1779, 2,527,700 lbs. Customs 3/76–80, P. R. O.

[5] Record of annual entries, in the West India Committee archives.

[6] Customs 3/76, 80, P. R. O.

[7] Record of annual entries, in the West India Committee archives.

The result of such a marked falling off of supplies was a large increase in selling prices in Great Britain. The fluctuation in the value of sugar, the commodity affecting the majority of planters, was most marked. In 1775, the London market for muscovado ranged from 25 to 39s. per hundredweight, in 1776 from 29 to 47s. and in 1777 from 39 to 65s.[1] The wholesale quotations of Smiths, Nash, and Kemble, a leading London sugar house, rose from 56–74s. per hundredweight according to quality for muscovado in April 1778 to 50–106s. per hundredweight in 1782.[2] The fortunes of war are closely reflected in the figures on offerings. Following the loss of Grenada, raw sugar at once rose 4s. per hundredweight;[3] after the French successes

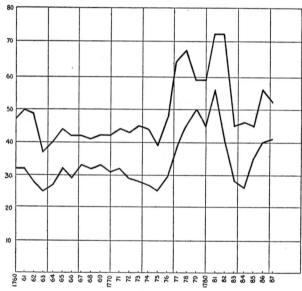

CHART 7

Range in the Price of British West Indian Muscovado Sugar Sold in London, 1760–1787, in Shillings per Hundredweight *

* Based on data in the West India Committee Archives. Upper line = top price for the year. Lower line = bottom price for the year.

[1] Edwards, *History*, II, p. 267, note.

[2] During 1779, prices ranged from 48s. to 84s., during 1780, from 46s. to 84s. during 1781, from 58s. to 100s. From the quarterly circulars issued by Smiths, Nash and Kemble of London and successors in the archives of Joseph Travers and Sons, Ltd. in the British capital.

[3] Price list of Smiths, Nash, Kemble, and Travers, Sept. 9, 1779.

early in 1782, the advance was 6s. per hundredweight.[1] The wholesale price of molasses similarly rose from 18s. 6d. per hundredweight
in 1779 to 24s. 6d. in 1782.[2]

Increased selling prices afforded those planters so fortunate as
to get their products into the hands of dealers some measure of compensation at least for greater costs of production and marketing, but
they checked sales and, in the cases of sugar and molasses, proved
ruinous to the refining and brewing industries. Testifying before a
parliamentary committee in 1781, Francis Kemble of the house
Smiths, Nash, Kemble, and Travers declared that the country grocery
trade in sugar had declined a third within the past four years as a result of the prevailing high prices even though it was being retailed at
little over cost to keep up the sale of tea.[3] Home consumption in 1780
was 36,000 hogsheads of muscovado below the annual average of
the six preceding years; in 1781, it was 30,000 less than that of the
year before.[4]

A decade before the opening of war with America there had been
159 sugar refineries in operation in or about the capital city; in 1781
there were but 125. The refining business of London fell off a third
in the four years after 1777; a similar state of affairs prevailed in
Liverpool, Hull, and Bristol. Auxiliary trades likewise suffered. In
1776, eight potters were specializing in the manufacture of dishes
employed in the refining process; in 1781 there were but half that
number—the rest had gone into bankruptcy or were in debtors'
prison. One plant which had formerly employed fifty hands then had
work for but twenty.[5] Thomas Slade, the largest producer of earthenware utensils in England, who had devoted his entire attention to
the needs of the refiners for more than ten years, was obliged to
close his works in June of that year. Coopers, wharfingers, lightermen,
copper-smiths, and iron-founders, too, were all adversely affected
by the decline of the sugar trade. Brewers who had formerly taken
from fifty to a hundred hogsheads of molasses in a single order for
use as a malt substitute in making cheap beer no longer called for that

---

[1] Price list of Smiths, Nash, Kemble, and Travers, March 30, 1782.

[2] *Ibid.*, Sept. 9, 1779, and Oct. 31, 1782.

[3] "Report from the Committee to Whom the Petition of the Sugar-
Refiners of London was Referred," *Gt. Br., H. C., Sess. Pap.,* 1781, V (44),
pp. 28, 29.

[4] "Reports from the Committee to Whom the Petition of the Sugar-
Refiners of London was Referred," *Gt. Br., H. C., Sess. Pap.,* 1782, V (47),
p. 5.

[5] "Report," *Gt. Br., H. C., Sess. Pap.,* 1781, V (44), pp. 27, 28, 32, 40, 42.

much in the course of a whole year because of the cost and their business suffered markedly.[1]

In this situation a vigorous attempt was made by the sugar refiners to break the West Indian monopoly of supplying the home market and thus to increase supplies and lower prices. Foreign sugars taken in prize ships were, by law, given entry into Great Britain for domestic consumption only upon payment of the regular foreign duty charges, set prohibitively high in the interest of British planters. Early in 1780 the London refiners proposed to the Commissioners of Customs that such sugars be admitted at reduced rates in the future. When consulted by the Commissioners, the Society of West India Merchants entered vigorous protest. If foreign produce of any kind were entered more freely than at present, "the most fatal consequences must ensue to the Sugar Colonies, and to the Navigation, Commerce, Revenue & Manufacture of Great Britain thereon dependent."[2]

The Board of Trade and Plantations, on the other hand, held it to be a highly expedient measure and thought that no reasonable objection could be made by the Caribbeans if the importation of prize consignments at low duties were authorized only when British sugar should have exceeded a certain price.[3] Representatives of both the colonial and refiner interests were invited to appear before the Lords of the Treasury in February, 1781, in the hope that common ground might be found, but this attempt to reach an understanding proved abortive because of the former's intransigent stand that "the refining of foreign sugar in England under whatever specious Pretence, will prove ruinous to the Sugar Plantations."[4]

Despite West Indian opposition, a petition of the London refiners, setting forth the sorry state of the trade arising from a shortage in the market and praying that captured enemy shipments be entered for home consumption at the colonial Caribbean rate for a limited time in order to increase available supplies, was presented to parliament on May 3, 1781.[5] On the ninth, a similar plea was laid before it on behalf of the refiners of Bristol,[6] as was another, two days later, by the London grocers.[7] All were referred to a committee directed

[1] "Report," *Gt. Br., H. C., Sess. Pap.,* 1781, V (44), 4, 10, 12.
[2] *Min. W. I. Mer.,* March 1, 1780.
[3] *Journals of the House of Commons, 1780–1782,* p. 440.
[4] *Min. W. I. Mer.,* Feb. 3 and 27, 1781.
[5] *Journals of the House of Commons, 1780–1782,* p. 440.
[6] *Ibid.,* p. 451.
[7] *Ibid.,* pp. 457, 458.

to examine the true state of the refining industry. That body's report, rendered at the close of the month, revealed most deplorable conditions amply justifying relief measures.[1]

The prospect of suffering an invasion of their monopoly gave the West Indians serious concern. They marshalled their forces and employed their influence in parliament to defeat the refiners' proposal. Statistics prepared by the latter, demonstrating a shortage,[2] were met by others designed to show the planters' ability amply to supply British needs.[3] A general counter-petition,[4] and another by Stephen Fuller, agent for Jamaica,[5] both protesting against any change, were presented. The strength of the planter and merchant interest was sufficient to secure a vote of 142 to 62 against a motion for taking the report on the refiners' petitions into consideration.[6] As a demonstration of their interest in the public welfare, the West Indians then expressed their willingness to allow the entry of sugar from Demerara and Essequibo, lately taken from the Dutch, at the British plantation rate although technically it was subject to foreign duties.[7]

With relief thus denied them, the majority of the London refiners entered into an agreement to operate their plants but three days a week for a year commencing June 30, 1781, as the only possible means of maintaining themselves.[8] Prize sugars were nevertheless not forgotten and pamphleteering was resorted to to gain public support against the colonials.[9]

French gains early in 1782 meanwhile threatened to create a fur-

[1] This document will be found listed under note 3, page 168.

[2] *Epitome of the Sugar Trade* (London, n.d.), printed for distribution among members of parliament.

[3] *Account of British Plantation-Sugar, refined or consumed raw in England, in the . . . Years [1731–1780]* (London, n.d.).

[4] *To the Honourable the Commons of Great Britain, in Parliament Assembled. The Petition of the Planters and Merchants Interested in, and Trading to the British Sugar Colonies* (London, n.d.).

[5] *To the Honourable the Commons of Great Britain. . . . The Petition of Stephen Fuller, Esq., Agent for Jamaica* (London, n.d.).

[6] *Journals of the House of Commons, 1780–1782,* p. 495.

[7] *Min. W. I. Mer.,* May 29, 1781. By 6 Geo. III c. 52 all sugar imported from any British colony on the mainland was to be regarded as foreign. These colonies had not, of course, been within the original meaning of the act but a literal interpretation of the same would have placed this disability upon their produce. To remove all uncertainty on that score, 21 Geo. III c. 62 gave special authorization for its entry at the regular British West Indian rate.

[8] John M. Hutcheson, *Notes on the Sugar Industry of the United Kingdom* (Greenock, 1901), pp. 13–15.

[9] Anon., *Prize Sugar Not Foreign. An Essay intended to vindicate the Rights of the Public to the Use of the Prize Sugars; and to shew the Im-*

ther and most serious sugar shortage. In an attempt to avert it, parliament, with the approval of the planter-merchant group,[1] enacted a measure permitting the produce of St. Kitts, Nevis, and Montserrat to enter Great Britain at British plantation duties when brought there in neutral vessels even though the islands were then in foreign hands.[2] The refiners promptly made capital of the new situation and presented another petition to the lower house, stressing the totally decayed state of their trade due to a lack of the raw product, questioning the efficacy of a measure which rested their securing of supplies upon the pleasure of enemy governors, and praying for the rights to import muscovado from neutral ports in neutral vessels and to enter captured foreign-grown sugar for preparation for domestic consumption at the colonial West Indian rate.[3]

This bold attack upon their position, bringing forward as it did the further question of the admission of neutral sugar, threw consternation into Caribbean circles. Vigorous counter-petitions were presented by the planters and merchants of London and by Stephen Fuller, agent for Jamaica. These held that shipments from St. Kitts, Nevis, and Montserrat would most certainly keep stocks on the market up to the average of recent times. However, even if such hopes were not realized, that would scarcely afford sufficient justification for the proposed total overturning of the preferential system upon which West Indian agriculture was based. Employing an argument based on mercantilistic philosophy, they further maintained that, while the price of sugar might be high, the nation suffered no injury because of it since the whole amount centered in Great Britain whereas, if neutral produce were admitted, money would be sent out of the kingdom, making it poorer thereby.[4]

A solicitor, Mr. Potts, was engaged to support colonial claims against the refiners' proposals;[5] and at a general meeting held in the London Tavern on June 5th, the West Indians reaffirmed the stand taken a year before, not to consent to a change in the privileged position accorded them in the home market under any limitation or

policy, as well as Injustice, of forcing the Prize Cargoes out of the Kingdom, at a Time when the Manufactory is languishing through the Want of due Employment, and the People are aggrieved by the excessive Price of the Commodity . . . (London, 1782).

[1] Min. W. I. Mer., June 5, 1782.
[2] 22 Geo. III c. 30.
[3] Journals of the House of Commons, 1780–1782, p. 987.
[4] Ibid., pp. 1012, 1013.
[5] Min. W. I. Mer., May 28, 1782.

modification whatsoever. It was held that only a substantial price on such part of their produce as could be gotten to market would afford any degree of compensation for the heavy war losses being suffered. They agreed, however, not to oppose the entry of the products of the territories recently lost at British plantation duties.[1]

The refiners' second petition, like the first, was referred to a parliamentary committee and a further report on the state of their industry, showing a sharp decline over but eleven months before, was presented to the House on June 11th.[2] The West India interest once more brought its forces into play and a few days later, by a vote of 114 to 31, secured the adjournment of a proposed debate on these latest findings.[3]

Importation of sugar from St. Kitts into the port of London under the act of 1782 totalled 13,243 casks from March 25, 1782 to March 25, 1783; those from Montserrat, 2,946; and those from Nevis, 2,628.[4] The indulgence thus afforded British planters under alien rule caused complaint on the part of the Jamaicans who charged that, through laxity in carrying out the law, French-grown muscovado was being poured into home ports to their own great detriment.[5] This allegation was doubtless well-founded, but no preventive measures could be devised and the importations made, even if of enemy origin in part, averted a general sugar famine in Great Britain.

Upon the suspension of hostilities early in 1783, a measure enacted at the solicitation of the West India merchants [6] granted neutral vessels clearing out from foreign ports in Europe for St. Kitts, Nevis, Montserrat, Dominica, St. Vincent, Grenada, and the Grenadines before April 1, 1783, the right to land their cargoes there and to enter the produce of those islands and of Tobago and St. Lucia as well into Great Britain upon payment of the regular British plantation duties. At the same time, products imported from those islands while still under French occupation and then in warehouses were allowed to be released upon payment of the ordinary charges.[7] This law afforded prompt relief to the refiners, and with the reëstablishment of peace a few months later all pressure on the sugar industry was removed.

---

[1] Min. W. I. Mer., June 5, 1782.

[2] "Report," Gt. Br., H. C., Sess. Pap., 1782, V (47).

[3] Journals of the House of Commons, 1780–1782, p. 1059.

[4] Record of annual entries, in the West India Committee archives.

[5] The Humble Memorial and Petition of the Council and Assembly of Jamaica, Feb. 27, 1783, C. O. 137/83.

[6] Min. W. I. Mer., Jan. 28, 1783.

[7] 23 Geo. III c. 14.

CHAPTER VI

THE NEW ERA OF RESTRICTED MAINLAND TRADE

Recognition of the United States as a sovereign nation raised a question of momentous import for the planters in the British Caribbean. With the old political relationship between the late mainland colonies and the one-time common mother country dissolved, would they be suffered to enjoy free access to their natural source of supply for essential stores as in ante bellum days or would imperial commercial policy demand the erection of barriers to check the normal flow of trade between them and the Americans?

There was no question regarding the attitude of the West India interest in England, the residents of the sugar islands and statesmen of the new republic. At a meeting of a committee of the Society of Planters and Merchants, held in April, 1783, a straightforward representation was made to the ministry.

"Under a just and reasonable attention to mutual Interests, the Committee entertain no doubt but such a share of the American Trade may be preserved to the Sugar Colonies as will greatly tend to their support, and, upon every principle of true Policy and proper regard to the views and purposes of rival Nations, be highly deserving of the utmost countenance and assistance from the Mother Country. To this Intercourse, the Committee apprehend, the permission of American Ships, as heretofore, freely to bring the Produce of the Dominions of the United States to the Sugar Colonies, and take back our Produce in return, is so obviously essential, that they need not adduce any farther arguments in support of that proposition." [1]

The council of Jamaica in the same month unanimously urged that commercial relations with the United States be placed upon a liberal footing,[2] and, on its recommendation to the governor, American vessels were provisionally allowed to enter local ports with supplies and to clear out with cargoes of tropical produce exempt from the payment of any duty.[3]

[1] *Min. W. I. Plant. and Mer.,* April 29, 1783.
[2] Governor Campbell to Lord Sydney, April 26, 1783, C. O. 137/83.
[3] Campbell to Lord North, June 28, 1783, C. O. 137/83.

173

"Without a free admission of all kinds of provisions into the Islands," wrote Robert R. Livingston, first American Secretary of State for Foreign Affairs to Benjamin Franklin in 1782, "our agriculture will suffer extremely." [1] John Adams, in correspondence with Livingston from Paris under date of June 23, 1783, held similar views:

"The commerce of the West India Islands is a part of the American system of commerce. They can neither do without us, nor we without them. The Creator has placed us upon the globe in such a situation that we have occasion for each other. We have the means of assisting each other, and politicians and artful Contrivances cannot separate us. Wise statesmen, like able artists of every kind, study nature, and their works are perfect in proportion as they conform to her laws. Obstinate attempts to prevent the islands and the Continent, by force or policy, from deriving from each other those blessings which nature has enabled them to afford, will only put both to thinking of means to come together. And an injudicious regulation at this time may lay a foundation for intimate combinations between the islands and the continent, which otherwise would not be wished for or thought of by either." [2]

But ship owners in Great Britain, the large body of loyalists who had taken refuge in the remaining North American colonies, a notable part of the British public which sympathized with them, and exponents of mercantilism united in opposition to the slightest relaxation of commercial laws in favor of citizens of the United States. John Baker Holroyd, Lord Sheffield, a recognized authority on trade and agriculture and a rigid doctrinaire, became spokesman for these groups and in a forceful work, *Observations on the Commerce of the American States*,[3] piled argument upon argument for maintaining the navigation system inviolate.

The American nation, declared he, was foreign and must be treated as such. The admission of its nationals to West Indian ports under any conditions whatsoever would lead to their gaining complete control of the island carrying trade, would place the planters in dangerous dependence upon a rival power, and would encourage the

[1] Jared Sparks, ed., *The Diplomatic Correspondence of the American Revolution* . . . (12 vols., Boston, 1829–1830), IV, p. 13.
[2] Charles F. Adams, ed., *The Works of John Adams* . . . (10 vols., Boston, 1853–1856), VIII, 74, 75.
[3] First issued in 1783 and elaborated in subsequent editions which appeared at short intervals. The sixth (London, 1784) contains his arguments in fully developed form. The references here given are to pages of that edition.

late enemy's shipping while at the same time ruining the British merchant marine and menacing Great Britain's command of the seas. The mother country bore the heavy expense of protecting her Caribbean colonies in order that she alone might engross the gains from transporting their freight and could enjoy the exclusive right of purchasing their produce. If the Americans were allowed to participate in the trade with them in any way, it would be unprofitable for Great Britain to longer retain them.[1]

Congress, he continued, might well close the ports of the United States to British ships if its citizens were not granted the right of direct intercourse with the West India possessions, but such a measure could only deprive that country of the best market for a large portion of its produce and would not prevent British ship-masters from securing cargoes of American products. The mainland traders' self-interest would lead them to engage in extensive smuggling operations in defiance of any prohibitory law. Furthermore, it would be difficult for the thirteen states to present a united front on such a question.

Unlimited quantities of lumber could be procured from Nova Scotia and Canada, stated Sheffield, if encouragement were but given their residents; the loyalists who had recently established themselves in those colonies had every right to such consideration. The latter region could likewise supply the wheat needs of the islanders; Bermuda, fresh provisions, Indian corn, and rice. Enforcement of the navigation laws against the Americans would subject the planters to no further inconvenience than paying somewhat more for their essential stores—there would be no shortage.[2]

The monopoly of supplying the home market, enjoyed by the Caribbean proprietors, increased the prices of tropical produce sold in Great Britain from 15 to 30 per cent above those which would prevail if free importations from the foreign West Indies were permitted. The estate owners of the sugar islands owed their prosperity to the British connection and could not justly feel aggrieved at increased costs arising from the adoption of a new policy dictated by imperial interests. If they should proclaim their independence they could not defend themselves, nor could they find protection in the small American army. If the British possessions fell under French control, the planters would be ruined by the lower selling prices pre-

[1] Sheffield, *Observations*, pp. 157–164.
[2] *Ibid.*, pp. 169–176, 245–247.

vailing in the markets of France. The excessively high prices received for their produce by the British planters was a matter which should be taken under serious consideration.[1]

"The Navigation Act, the basis of our great power at sea, gave us the trade of the world. If we alter that Act, by permitting any state to trade with our islands . . . we desert the Navigation Act, and sacrifice the marine of England. But if the principle of the Navigation Act be properly understood and well followed, this country may still be safe and great." [2]

Publication of this exceedingly able work gave the sign for the spilling of huge quantities of printer's ink. The foremost attacks on Sheffield's representations were made by members of the London West India group. Bryan Edwards, recently returned from his properties in Jamaica, made his début as author through penning a pamphlet designed to demonstrate that Caribbean estate owners could not prosper without supplies at the cheapest rate from the United States.[3] His friend Edward Long, historian of the colony, adopted the same argument in a well reasoned statement of the island point of view.[4] More important, however, was a work of several hands issued under the signature of James Allen, secretary of the Society of Planters and Merchants, *Considerations on the Present State of the Intercourse Between His Majesty's Sugar Colonies and the Dominions of the United States of America,*[5] given over largely to a refutation of the claim that British North America could supply the planters' needs.

Employing custom house records, it was shown that in the years 1771–1773 the British West Indies had imported 76,767,695 feet of lumber from the thirteen colonies; 232,040 feet from Canada and Nova Scotia; and but 2,000 feet from New Foundland. Shingles to the number of 59,586,194 had been imported from the thirteen colonies in that time, as against only 185,000 from Canada and Nova Scotia, and none whatever from Newfoundland. Imports of corn from the three regions had been 1,204,389 bushels, 24 bushels, and

---

[1] Sheffield, *Observations,* pp. 187–197.

[2] *Ibid.,* pp. 264, 265.

[3] *Thoughts on the Late Proceedings of Government, Respecting the Trade of the West India Islands with the United States of America* (London, 1784). His *History* of some years later also makes a plea for the establishment of free trade relations between the two. Vol. II, 392–425.

[4] *A Free and Candid Review of a Tract Entitled "Observations on the Commerce of the American States . . ."* (London, 1784).

[5] London, 1784.

none respectively; imports of bread and flour, 396,329 barrels, 991 barrels, and none; imports of fish 51,344 hogsheads, 449 hogsheads, and 2,307 hogsheads; imports of beef and pork, 44,782 barrels, 170 barrels, and 24 barrels. In general, Newfoundland had supplied little, and Canada and Nova Scotia but an insignificant fraction of the stores imported.[1] Of 1,208 cargoes of American supplies entering the British West Indies in 1772, all but thirteen had cleared out from the late colonies.[2]

The first shipment of flour—154,807 bushels—had been made from Canada in 1772. The highest amount exported at any time had been 463,494 bushels in 1774, a mere trifle compared to the demands of the sugar islands. But all sales of Canadian grain products outside the colony had been prohibited from 1779 to 1782, and cargoes of flour were actually being sent there from England by the close of the Revolution. No peas were grown for exportation in Canada and the price of labor was so high as to make the cost of even the lower grades of Canadian lumber prohibitive.[3] Nova Scotia had never grown enough grain to feed its own inhabitants and, instead of exporting lumber, had been importing it from New England. Cattle had never been shipped from there. Nor was the situation in Newfoundland better; except for fish, its exports were negligible.[4]

"To suppose those colonies *at all* productive for the purposes of a substantial exportation, is to anticipate the slow effect of many years of that steady and expensive system of encouragement from the Mother-country, which raised the other North American Colonies to independence; and to suppose that at any time their produce can be rendered adequate to the West Indian demand, appears vastly beyond what the climate and other natural disadvantages can ever admit, under any encouragement whatsoever.

"The truth is, that the Sugar Colonies can alone be supplied with lumber from the Dominions of the United States, and that they cannot either well or cheaply be supplied with many essential articles of provisions from any other country. Flour in particular will not keep in the West Indies, and requires a constant supply by as short a voyage as possible. Even in the voyage from England it frequently grows sour; and livestock of all kinds obviously require a short voyage at a favourable season of the year. Without these supplies, *the cultivation of the Sugar Colonies cannot be carried on . . .*"[5]

[1] See Appendix I.
[2] *Considerations*, p. 25.
[3] *Ibid.*, pp. 26–30.
[4] *Ibid.*, pp. 31–33.
[5] *Ibid.*, p. 34.

Lord Sheffield, however, had many and capable defenders. Replying to the declaration of Bryan Edwards, that restrictions would result in an inequitable increase in the cost of supplies, John Stevenson argued that planter products should then be sold for more so that the consumer, not the producer, would bear the additional cost. If it was true, as stated, that American ships could operate more economically than British ones in supplying the West Indies, then those of the remaining mainland colonies could most certainly do likewise. If citizens of the new republic were allowed to enter the Caribbean trade, they would soon be competing with Great Britain in supplying European markets. The planters and Americans would doubtless be mutually benefited by free intercourse, but this would work such injuries to British trade as to make it altogether impermissible.[1]

Arthur Young, representing the agrarian interest in England, fully supported Sheffield's stand.[2] George Chalmers, formerly a Baltimore lawyer and from 1786 chief clerk of the committee of the privy council for trade and foreign plantations, accused the planters of wallowing in wealth and declared that although the erection of trade barriers would result in a higher cost of production for them, this price was a small one to pay for holding the exclusive right of supplying the British market.[3]

Americans with one accord naturally opposed any modification of the old relation. Indeed, it was one of them, William Bingham, commercial agent for the Continental Congress, writing anonymously, who first answered Sheffield.[4] Residing in England, he shrewdly enough stressed the advantages which that country would derive from uninterrupted intercourse between the late colonies and the British Caribbean. If the planters were obliged to pay more for their supplies, the prices of tropical produce must be increased and the public would suffer. With cheap stores from the United States at their command, a greater portion of the proprietors' incomes would be available for spending at home and manufacturing there would be

---

[1] *An Address to Brian* [sic] *Edwards, Esq., Containing Remarks on His Pamphlet Entitled "Thoughts on the Late Proceedings of Government . . ."* (London, 1784), pp. 23, 25, 53, 72.

[2] "Considerations on the Connection Between the Agriculture of England and the Commercial Policy of Her Sugar-Islands, Particularly Respecting a Free Trade With North America," in *Annals of Ag.*, I (1784), pp. 437 ff.

[3] *Opinions on Interesting Subjects of Public Law and Commercial Policy; Arising from American Independence* (London, 1785), pp. 88, 89.

[4] Sheffield, *Observations*, p. ii.

stimulated. If direct trade were not permitted, Great Britain would be put to heavy expense to curb smuggling. Common opposition to British policy would draw all the American states together. Retaliative measures on the part of Congress would inevitably follow any attempt to close the West India trade. British industry and commerce would suffer heavy losses; a powerful merchant marine would be established beyond the Atlantic and this would take over the carrying trade between Europe and the new world until then so largely in British hands.[1]

A somewhat belated anonymous response to Sheffield, originally appearing in a Philadelphia periodical[2] and containing the stock arguments of the planters viewed from an American angle, was subsequently republished in part in the London *Morning Chronicle* by members of the capital city Caribbean interest at a cost of four guineas.[3]

Self-interest was obviously the motivating force behind these various lines of argument. But logic lay wholly on the side of the Sheffield group. There was no reasonable basis for the islanders' clamor to be given access to supplies from a foreign source while continuing to enjoy their peculiar century and a quarter old marketing rights. Yielding to them on this score would be striking a death blow at the old colonial system; in the light of eighteenth century economic teachings, it would mean the surrender by Great Britain of a primary advantage attached to the possession of colonies while allowing the West Indians the continued full enjoyment of the benefits derived from the "colonial contract." Yet, with a fine disregard for the inconsistency of their demand, the planters continued agitating for free intercourse for upwards of a decade until, under the exigencies of war with France, that right was, as we shall see,[4] finally accorded them in qualified form.

While the controversy regarding the policy to be adopted towards the late transatlantic possessions was at its height, action of some sort was necessary. The ports of the United States were opened to British shipping without discrimination and William Pitt, then Chan-

---

[1] *A Letter from an American, Now Resident in London, to a Member of Parliament . . . Containing Strictures on Lord Sheffield's Pamphlet on the Commerce of the American States* (Philadelphia, 1784) pp. 6–13.

[2] "A Brief Examination of Lord Sheffield's Observations on the Commerce of the United States," in *The American Museum or Universal Magazine,* March to July, 1791. Also reprinted in pamphlet form, Philadelphia, 1791.

[3] Clipping in the West India Committee archives, with notation.

[4] See pages 230 ff.

cellor of the Exchequer, proposed the temporary institution of a liberal system of commercial relations giving vessels under American registry the right to import stores freely from the new country into the West Indies and to depart from there laden with tropical produce.

There was, however, a practical problem—the powers claimed by the legislatures of the thirteen states were so extensive that the competency of Congress to conclude a general commercial treaty was seriously doubted.[1] Furthermore, with a change in ministry, Pitt went out of office in April, 1783, and was no longer in a position to carry through his project. Arrangements of a different nature were therefore made. An act of parliament passed the following month gave American vessels the right to enter British ports and to clear from them without manifest, certificate, or other document, and vested the king in council with power to regulate the American-West Indian trade for the time being.[2]

Three orders of July 2, September 5, and December 26, 1783, issued in accordance with this measure, set forth the conditions under which American supplies might enter British Caribbean ports. His Majesty's subjects were permitted to import all kinds of lumber, live stock, grain, flour, and bread from the United States into the islands in British bottoms. They were likewise allowed to export rum, sugar, molasses, coffee, cacao, ginger, and pimento from them to the United States upon payment of the same duties and conforming to the same regulations as if those products were cleared out for a British colony. American vessels, on the contrary, were wholly excluded from any share in the trade, and American meat and fish were forbidden entry in the interests of pork and beef producers in Ireland and the Newfoundland fisheries.[3]

These orders, intended merely to meet the needs of the moment, were subsequently continued in force under the authority of various

[1] *A Report of the Lords of the Committee of Privy Council, appointed for all Matters relating to Trade and Foreign Plantations, on the Commerce and Navigation between His Majesty's Dominions, and the Territories belonging to the United States of America. 28th January 1791* [London, 1791], p. 6. A summary of this document appears in W. C. Ford, ed., *Report of a Committee of the Lords of the Privy Council on the Trade of Great Britain with the United States, January, 1791* (Washington 1888). See also Chalmers, *Opinions on Interesting Subjects*, pp. 167, 168.

[2] 23 Geo. III c. 39.

[3] *American State Papers, Class IV, Commerce and Navigation* (2 vols., Washington, 1832, 1834), II, 251. For a detailed discussion of the orders, see John Reeves, *A History of the Law of Shipping and Navigation* (Dublin, 1792), pt. III, ch. 1.

enabling acts [1] until 1788 despite attempts at retaliative commercial legislation on the part of Congress and the several state legislatures [2] and loud West Indian remonstrance. The regulations were then made permanent by statute.[3]

The government's policy, evinced by these orders in council, was subjected to attack by both the London West India group and the islanders. In the spring of 1784, the Society of Planters and Merchants secured a privy council hearing and there brought forth evidence designed to demonstrate the dependence of the islands on the United States, and the inability of British North America to supply their needs. But the committee named to consider their representations was in no way convinced and supported the new arrangement.[4] The Jamaican legislature about the same time expressed astonishment that the Americans should be denied entry into British Caribbean ports, while they were being freely admitted to those of Great Britain, Ireland, and the North American colonies, and denounced such distinction between Englishmen as being invidious. Prediction was

[1] As for example 24 Geo. III session 1, c. 15; session 2, cc. 1 and 23; 25 Geo. III c. 5; 27 Geo. III c. 7.

[2] For an exhaustive and scholarly study of such measures, see Albert A. Giesecke, *American Commercial Legislation Before 1789* (New York, 1910). Two examples, chosen from a large number, may be mentioned here. Meeting the challenge of the July 2 order in council, Congress in April, 1784, asked the states for the right to prohibit all importations or exportations in vessels owned or navigated by subjects of foreign powers not having commercial treaties with the United States, for a period of fifteen years. The proposal fell through for lack of unanimity. In New York, after 1785, all goods imported in British vessels were subject to double duties.

[3] 28 Geo. III c. 6. For a good discussion of American-West Indian trade relations after the Revolution see Herbert C. Bell's "British Commercial Policy in the West Indies, 1783–93," in *The Eng. Hist. Rev.*, July 1916, pp. 429–441. Reprinted as part of *Studies in the Trade Relations of the British West Indies and North America, 1763–1773; 1783–1793* (Philadelphia, 1917). See also William Hill, "The First Stages of the Tariff Policy of the United States," in *Publications of the American Economic Association*, VIII, no. 6 (Nov. 1893), pts. II and III; J. Franklin Jameson, ed., "Letters of Phineas Bond . . . ," in *Reports of the American Historical Association*, 1896, I, 513 ff. and 1897, pp. 454 ff.; A. C. McLaughlin, *The Confederation and Constitution, 1783–1789* (New York, 1905); and Anna L. Lingelbach, "The Inception of the British Board of Trade," in *The Am. Hist. Rev.*, July, 1925, pp. 701 ff.

[4] "A State of the Allegations and Evidence produced, and Opinions of Merchants and other Persons . . . upon the Representation of the West-India Planters and Merchants, purporting to shew the distressed State of His Majesty's Sugar Colonies by the Operation of His Majesty's Order in Council of the 2d of July, 1783," in *Gt. Br., H. C., Sess. Pap.*, 1784, V (59).

made that, if the direct trade remained closed, large numbers of planters not too heavily involved would depart for neighboring foreign possessions, while those finding emigration impossible because of debts must suffer total ruin of their property and sink into indigence.[1]

In a memorial to the ministry, Stephen Fuller, agent for Jamaica, urged that American citizens be allowed to enter at least lumber, cattle, and such provisions as could not be supplied by Great Britain, Ireland, or British North America in small vessels which should be permitted to load up only with clayed or refined sugar.[2] The government was, however, entirely unmoved by such pleas. Failure to secure a reopening of free commercial relations between the United States and the British West Indies at the close of the Revolution was the first great defeat suffered by members of the planter interest.

Large-scale smuggling was an inevitable result of placing restraints on trade with the mainland. Such activities were especially common in the Leeward Islands and Jamaica due to their proximity to the continent. "A great deal of American produce is introduced into these Islands, by methods which are contrived to evade the restrictions of the late order in Council," wrote Governor Shirley of the Leeward group to Lord Sydney in the summer of 1784.[3] A report from Jamaica, made a year and a half after the new regulations had gone into effect, stated "There is every reason to believe that the fraudulent importation from the United States of America is very considerable . . . ; the Amount . . . is probably equal to that which is imported legally."[4]

The experiences of Captain Horatio Nelson, assigned in November, 1784, to service on the ship *Boreas,* off St. Kitts-Nevis, are illuminating. Under orders issued by Rear-Admiral Sir Richard Hughes,

---

[1] *To the King's Most Excellent Majesty in Council. The Humble Memorial and Petition of the Council and Assembly of Jamaica* [St. Jago de la Vega, 1784]; in manuscript form in C. O. 137/85. See also Stephen Fuller, [*The communication of the substance of eleven petitions from as many different parishes of Jamaica to the island House of Assembly, recommending the taking of such measures as would bring about a renewal of free intercourse with the United States, and the Memorial of the Council and Assembly of Jamaica to the Crown on that subject, December 1784, to both houses of parliament* . . .] (no imprint, 1785).

[2] Stephen Fuller, *The Representation of . . .* [*the*] *Agent for Jamaica, to His Majesty's Ministers* [London, 1785].

[3] Under date of July 30, C. O. 152/63.

[4] Answers to the several heads of inquiry referred to in the Secretary of State's letter to the Lieutenant-Governor of Jamaica dated November 11, 1784, in C. O. 137/85.

commander of the fleet in those waters, all foreign vessels appearing in the vicinity of the British colonies were being detained and reports as to the nature of their cargoes were being sent in each case to the nearest governor. If the latter favored admitting a given bottom, it was not hindered from entering port.[1] A large-scale irregular traffic with the Americans was thus connived at.

The future victor of Trafalgar found the harbors filled with their vessels and promptly forced them to depart. In consequence, he was not shown the respect due his rank and was denounced as one injuring the colonists. Despite his ordering away such American ships as approached the islands, they frequently got into port a short time after while he was procuring wood, water, or provisions elsewhere. Ten were unloaded in Basseterre road during one such absence alone.

The officers of American merchantmen furthermore enjoyed the support of Caribbean customs authorities. When they entered harbor claiming to be in need of repairs, the latter readily granted them permits to unload their cargoes to meet alleged expenses entailed and refused to provide Nelson with information on the subject. The same officials held that they were not answerable to him for their conduct [2] and at times knowingly admitted mainland bottoms provided with fraudulent papers purporting to show British registry.

When Nelson seized four American vessels flying the Union Jack in the road of Nevis in the spring of 1785 and secured their condemnation, the local merchants prompted the several ship masters, one of whom the captain had never even seen, to procure writs for his arrest, claiming damages of £4,000 for assault and imprisonment although they had suffered no ill-usage whatever.

Feeling in the island was so against Nelson that the attorney-general advised him not to appear for trial and he was obliged to remain on board ship for two months to keep beyond the reach of colonial law officers.[3] The defence of this suit was subsequently conducted at public expense upon orders from the home government.[4] After vexatious delays, Nelson was at length cleared of the charges

---

[1] Enclosure in Governor Shirley to Lord Sydney, June 10, 1785, C. O. 152/64.

[2] Captain Nelson to Lord Sydney, March 20, 1785, C. O. 152/64.

[3] Nelson to Lord Sydney, June 23, 1785; To the King's most Excellent Majesty. The Humble Memorial and Representation of Horatio Nelson Esquire . . . ; Certification of Judge John Ward of the vice-admiralty court of Nevis, all in C. O. 152/64.

[4] Lord Sydney to Governor Shirley and Sydney to Captain Nelson, both under date of August 4, 1785, in C. O. 152/64.

brought against him.[1] Sir Richard, meanwhile, had wished to court-martial him for his independent conduct but refrained upon hearing that the captain enjoyed his fellow-officers' full support. Some time later he coolly accepted for himself the thanks of Treasury officials for his zeal in protecting British commerce![2]

Returns covering all ships entering British Caribbean ports, required by the home government after July, 1783, prove conclusively that the lumbering and fishing industries in British North America were greatly stimulated by the new commercial policy towards the United States. No small part of the wood and sea-food products thenceforth marketed in the islands were of British origin. The increase in imports from Canada, Nova Scotia, and Newfoundland over those preceding the Revolution was marked from the first, and, from the imperial point of view, afforded ample justification for the prohibition placed on American participation in the West India trade. But it is also evident that the loyalists' ability to provide plantation needs had been overestimated, especially as regarded grain. The thirteen states still remained the principal, though no longer the almost exclusive, source of supply they had been in the colonial period.

From the promulgation of the July order in council to early February, 1785, a total of 253 vessels provided with British registers legally entered Jamaican harbors from the United States laden with these cargoes—50,686 barrels of bread and flour; 2,241 barrels of rice; 20,-832 bushels of corn and peas; 1,575,589 thousand feet of lumber, and 2,521,000 staves, headings, and shingles. In the same period, thirty bottoms arrived from Nova Scotia and Canada with 10 barrels of bread and flour; 2,681½ hogsheads and barrels of fish; 381 tierces and barrels of rice; and 99,237 thousand feet of lumber as well as a considerable number of staves and hoops.[3]

In the year commencing October 1, 1784, eighty-nine ships under British registry legally entered Barbadian ports from the United States as did thirty-six from British North America. The former brought 9,103 barrels of flour; 2,317 barrels of bread; 421 barrels of rice; 22,187 bushels of corn and peas; 595 horses; 1,974,000 feet of

[1] Letters of Captain Nelson, Nov. 17, 1785 and Feb. 4, 1786, C. O. 152/64.
[2] *Dictionary of National Biography*, XXVIII, 187; XL, 191. For Nelson's years in the Caribbean, see Robert Johnstone "Nelson in the West Indies," in *Journal of the Inst. of Jam.*, Dec. 1897, pp. 380 ff., and March, 1899, pp. 521 ff. See also Thomas Liburd, "Lord Nelson and the Island of Nevis," in *The W. I. Comm. Circ.*, Oct. 13, 1905, pp. 412, 413.
[3] Report in C. O. 137/85.

lumber; and 3,854,000 staves and shingles. Imports from the mainland colonies were 541 barrels of flour; 10 barrels of bread; no rice; 598 barrels of fish; 1,458 hogsheads of fish; 400 bushels of corn and peas; no horses; 571,000 feet of lumber; and 892,000 staves and shingles.[1]

Not only did the remaining continental possessions increasingly supply the planters with fish and lumber; they afforded a growing market for the latter's produce as well. The number of vessels leaving the sugar islands for British North America was, by 1787, more than half as large as the number of those legally clearing out for the United States, as shown by this table.

From	To the U.S.A.	To Br. N.A.	From	To the U.S.A.	To Br. N.A.
Antigua [2]	71	34	Totals cd. fwd.	321	185
Barbados [3]	54	41	Montserrat and		
Dominica [4]	16	14	Nevis [2]	20	7
Grenada [5]	47	30	St. Kitts [2]	21	19
Jamaica [6]	133	66	St. Vincent [7]	21	0
			Virgin Is. [2]	3	4
Totals	321	185			
			Grand totals	386	215

The Society of Planters and Merchants actively interested itself in the securing of additional outlets for tropical products in Canada, Nova Scotia and Newfoundland.[8] In 1787, exports of sugar from the British Caribbean to British North America were 9,891 hundredweight as compared with 19,921 hundredweight legally sent to the United States. Similarly, legal exports of rum in that year were 874,580 gallons and 1,620,205 respectively.[9]

Unfortunately, at the same time, to offset these gains, shipments made to the United States in accordance with law steadily declined. Thus, legal exports of sugar from the British islands there fell from 47,595 hundredweight in 1784 to 46,142 hundredweight in 1785, and 35,801 in 1786. In the same years, legal exports of rum to the United States sank from 2,742,277 gallons to 2,188,000 and 1,-

[1] Report in C. O. 28/60.
[2] From customs records, in Edwards, *History,* I, 463.
[3] *Ibid.,* I, 355.
[4] *Ibid.,* I, 420.
[5] *Ibid.,* I, 389.
[6] *Ibid.,* I, 231.
[7] *Ibid.,* I, 406.
[8] *Min. W. I. Plant. and Mer.,* March 3, 1786, April 5, 1787.
[9] From customs records, in Edwards, *History,* II, 418, 419.

399,040 respectively.[1] Consignments cleared out in 1787 are noted above.

Nevertheless, from the point of view of the empire as a whole, the new régime early and fully justified itself—British North America and the Caribbean colonies rapidly drew closer together and the latter's dependence upon the United States became markedly less.

But, however warrantable in imperial interests American exclusion from the West India trade may have been, it bore heavily upon the planters. Their fellow-colonials on the mainland were unable to provide supplies as cheaply, and British carriers could not deliver them from either the continental possessions or the United States at as low rates as the Americans. These differences in costs are to be explained in several ways. The distance from British North America was greater than that from the United States, resulting in fewer trips and greater charges. Whereas the Americans employed small coasting vessels in their commercial operations in the Caribbean, the British used transatlantic sailers, operated at more expense, almost exclusively. Ships built in Great Britain cost more than those constructed in the United States and higher freights were necessary to afford adequate returns on investments.

Furthermore, the price of labor in sparsely-settled Canada, Nova Scotia, and Newfoundland was higher than in the more fully developed states to the south. Largely due to this factor, stores could be procured in the United States for a third less than in British North America.[2] The increased cost of supplies to the planters after the Revolution, arising in part from the institution of new trading regulations and in part from a natural rise in values following the conflict, is shown below. Peace brought an end to scarcity and wartime quotations, but the prices of essential commodities failed to return to ante bellum figures and the proprietors were not afforded the much-needed relief they had anticipated.

Prices in Barbados [3]

Article	Cost before the War	Cost in 1784
Lumber, per M	£4	£8
Horses, each	£20	£30
Horned Cattle, each	£5 to £7.10.0	£10

[1] From customs records, in Macpherson, *Annals of Commerce*, IV, 161.

[2] Report on the effects of the closing of the American trade, made in March, 1785, C. O. 137/85.

[3] In Governor Parry to Lord Sydney, Dec. 26, 1784, C. O. 28/60.

Article	Cost before the War	Cost in 1784
Rice, per cwt.	12s. 6d.	30s.
Indian Corn, per bu.	2s. 6d.	3s. 9d.
Beef, per bbl.	50s.	60s.

PRICES IN JAMAICA [1]

Article	Cost before the War	Cost in 1785
Rice, per cwt.	13s. 9d. to £1	£2.2.6 to £3.10.0
Indian Corn, per bu.	2s. 6d. to 6s. 3d.	7s. 6d.
Common Flour, per cwt.	15s. to £1	£1 to £2.10.0
Superfine Flour, per cwt.	£1 to £1.7.6	£1.7.6 to £3
Common Boards, per M	£6 to £10	£10 to £30
Pitch Pine Lumber, per M	£8 to £12	£12 to £30
Shingles, per M	£1.26. to £2.5.0	£2.15.0 to £5.10.0
White Oak Staves, per M	£10 to £18	£12 to £20
Red Oak Staves, per M	£6 to £12	£10 to £18

PRICES IN THE LEEWARD GROUP [2]

Article	Cost Before the War	Cost in 1785
Boards, per M	£5 to £8	£12 to £16.10.0
Shingles, per M	18s. to 30s.	£2 to £3
White Oak Staves, per M	£7 to £10	£15
Red Oak Staves, per M	£5 to £8	£12 to £15
Horses, each·	£16.10.0 to £35	£30 to £70
Cattle, each	£16.10.0 to £19.16.0	£20 to £40
Rice, per cwt.	18s. to 24s.	38s. to 41s. 3d.
Indian Corn, per bu.	4s. to 8s.	8s. 3d. to 10s.
Beef, per bbl.	£2.10.0 to £4	£4 to £6.12.0
Pork, per bbl.	£3.6.0 to £4.10.0	£6.12.0 to £7.10.0
Flour, per cwt.	£1 to £1.10.0	£1.10.0 to £2.5.0
Ship Bread, per cwt.	£1 to £1.10.0	£1.18.0 to £2.5.0

Considerable quantities of goods originating in the United States reached the British West Indies indirectly by way of the foreign islands after 1783. "The old intercourse with The Dutch Island St. Eustatius is again opened, and through that medium we get many American Commodities, but [at] an advanced price," reported Governor Shirley of the Leeward Islands government early in 1785.[3] Such large amounts of produce were received in this manner in Dominica that somewhat over a year later vessels arriving from

[1] Report in C. O. 137/85.
[2] Enclosure in Governor Shirley to Lord Sydney, Sept. 7, 1785, C. O. 152/64.
[3] To Lord Sydney, January (no date), C. O. 152/64.

Nova Scotia were unable to dispose of their cargoes.[1] Governor Lincoln wrote to Lord Sydney from St. Vincent: "The Commerce among the Islands is carried on by Sloops and Schooners navigated according to Law. These vessels trade to Martinico, Guadeloupe, but in particular to St. Eustatia where they are laden with Lumber, Provisions &c., from the Americans purchased at nearly the same price as before the War & retailed to the Planters at 50 to 100% profit. The result of which is, that whilst the Planter is compelled to give an exorbitant price for these necessary articles, the Americans find nearly the same demand as formerly, and consequently are only irritated, not injured by the restrictions contained in the Proclamation, their trade is thrown into a new Channel, not destroyed by their separation from the Mother Country, while our natural Enemies derive advantage by their Islands becoming Deposits for all American Goods, and their Ports are crowded with their Vessels. From all the Information I have been able to collect, & my enquiries have been as extensive as my situation would permit, I have not learned that a single vessel has returned with the Cargo she brought out." [2]

So extensive became this roundabout intercourse with the United States that an act of 1787 forbade the entry of any flour, bread, rice, wheat, other grains, and lumber from the foreign West Indies into the British islands except in cases of emergency when the governor and council might permit their importation for a limited time only.[3] This provision was continued by the statute of the following year, definitely establishing the existing restrictions on the American trade, with the further proviso that entries in such cases must be made in British bottoms.[4]

Due advantage was taken of the privilege of making emergency importations. Thus, the port of Roseau, Dominica, was opened in December, 1787 and again in the following July to relieve distress occasioned by a hurricane,[5] as were the ports of St. Kitts and Nevis in 1789 in consequence of a shortage of provisions.[6]

The close of the Revolution naturally once more gave the British Caribbean planters ready access to the markets of Great Britain

[1] Governor Orde to Lord Sydney, Sept. 29, 1786, C. O. 71/11.
[2] Under date of Dec. 1, 1785, C. O. 260/7.
[3] 27 Geo. III c. 7.
[4] 28 Geo. III c. 6.
[5] Proclamations of Governor Orde, Dec. 17, 1787 and July 12, 1788, C. O. 71/14.
[6] Lieut.-Gov. John Nugent to Lord Sydney, July 13, 1789, C. O. 152/67.

and brought to an end the piling up of produce in the islands, unsalable for the lack of carriers. Imports of muscovado sugar, the growth of British plantations, into Great Britain, averaged 1,865,742 hundredweight per annum in the decade commencing 1783.[1] Imports of British West Indian rum into Great Britain averaged 2,523,275 gallons per annum from 1783 to 1785 and 3,068,144 gallons annually from 1791 to 1793.[2] Imports of colonial Caribbean cacao averaged 4,985 hundredweight and 3,676 hundredweight annually in these two periods; coffee imports rose from 17,272 hundredweight in 1783 to 40,736 hundredweight in 1791.[3]

The vastly increased quantities of tropical produce reaching Great Britain after the reëstablishment of peace caused a sharp drop in market prices. Wholesale quotations for muscovado in London, which had ranged from 50s. to 106s. per hundredweight in 1782, stood at from 38s. to 80s. per hundredweight in 1783, and at from 54s. to 84s. in 1790. Molasses, which had sold as high as 30s. per hundredweight in 1782, fell to 17s. 6d. in the year following, and from 1786–1790 quotations averaged about 20s.[4] In 1782, the price of West Indian cotton in Liverpool ranged from 20d. to 42d. per pound; in 1783 from 13d. to 36d.; and in 1790 but from 12d. to 22d.[5]

A crying evil attending the collection of British customs duties was the levying of a specific rather than of an ad valorem charge on sugar. Although the selling price suffered such a great drop after 1783, the high war rate, set at 12s. 3⅖d. per hundredweight in 1782, was continued. In February, 1783, both the Society of West

---

[1] Imports in 1783 were 1,584,275 cwt.; in 1784, 1,782,386 cwt.; in 1785, 2,075,909 cwt.; in 1786, 1,613,965 cwt.; in 1787, 1,926,621 cwt.; in 1788, 2,065,-817 cwt.; in 1789, 1,936,440 cwt.; in 1790, 1,882,106 cwt.; in 1791, 1,808,950 cwt.; in 1792, 1,980,973 cwt. *East India Sugar. Papers Respecting the Culture and Manufacture of Sugar . . .*, Appendix I, pp. 10, 11; "Report . . . on the Commercial State of the West India Colonies," in *Gt. Br., H. C., Sess. Pap.*, 1807, III (65), p. 73.

[2] "Report . . . on the Commercial State of the West India Colonies," in *Gt. Br., H. C., Sess. Pap.*, 1807, III (65), p. 74.

[3] *Ibid.*, p. 75.

[4] Offerings were made at from 34s. to 70s. per cwt. in 1784; from 40s. to 74s. in 1785; from 42s. to 76s. in 1786; from 40s. to 76s. in 1787; from 42s. to 74s. in 1788; and from 45s. to 74s. in 1789. Quarterly circulars issued by Smiths, Nash, and Kemble and successors, in the archives of Joseph Travers and Sons, Ltd., London.

[5] The price ranged from 12d. to 25d. in 1784; from 14d. to 28d. in 1785; from 22d. to 42d. in 1786; from 19d. to 34d. in 1787; from 14d. to 33d. in 1788; from 12d. to 22d. in 1789; from 13d. to 30d. in 1791 and from 20d. to 30d. in 1792. *Gt. Br., H. C., Sess. Pap.*, 1847-48, IX (in 511), p. 393.

India Merchants [1] and the legislature of Jamaica [2] prayed for a reduction, the latter urging a return to the pre-Revolution figure of 6s. 3$\frac{9}{10}$d. But any lowering whatever was declared to be impossible, as the sugar tax was one of the most productive sources of national income and the public welfare demanded its continuance. Lord North held that since the planters had profited in an extraordinary manner from the increased selling values prevailing during the recent struggle and that since the petitions of the sugar refiners had been rejected in their interest, they had no just cause for complaint if the duty now bore heavily upon them.[3] Indeed, instead of being cut, it was subsequently increased to 12s. 4d. per hundredweight in 1787 and to 15s. in 1791.[4]

The greater cost of supplies after 1783, the drop in the market prices of tropical produce and the continued levying of high duties in Great Britain had a withering effect on West Indian agriculture. Hopes that peace would be followed by quick recovery were rudely shattered. The decade 1783–1793 brought no relief to the planters; large numbers fell beneath the weight of accumulated distress.

Great dissatisfaction and apprehension were felt in Jamaica at the closing of the American trade and the refusal of the home government to reduce the war rate on sugar. To obviate the hardships arising from a doubling in the cost of mainland supplies upon publication of the July order in council,[5] the assembly applied to Governor Campbell for a nine month suspension of its operation so that sufficient stocks might be secured, but this request was denied.

An address to the executive, then drawn up by a committee of the assembly, declared that, unless another policy was adopted, the smaller proprietors would certainly be ruined. Resentment was so great that it was even proposed to make no provision for royal troops stationed in the island or for the maintenance of fortifications under the circumstances.[6]

A memorial and petition of the island legislature to the home government in December, 1784, portrayed a melancholy state of affairs

---

[1] *Min. W. I. Mer.*, Feb. 25, 1783.

[2] The Humble Memorial and Petition of the Council and Assembly of Jamaica, Feb. 27, 1783, C. O. 137/83.

[3] North to Governor Campbell, May 10, 1783, C. O. 137/83.

[4] *Gt. Br., H. C., Sess. Pap.*, 1826, XXII (328).

[5] "A State of the Allegations and Evidence produced, etc.," *Gt. Br., H. C., Sess. Pap.*, 1784, V (59), p. 7.

[6] Governor Campbell to Lord North, Nov. 26, 1783, C. O. 137/84.

—property saddled with debts incurred in defending the colony during the late war and the owners of estates facing ruin. Freeing the American trade, reducing the duties on West Indian produce, encouraging sugar refining in the colonies by removing the prohibitive duty then levied on the finished product entering Great Britain, and permitting sugar to be bonded in warehouses where it might be held for a rise in price rather than requiring the immediate payment of duty upon unloading, were recommended as measures which would relieve their desperate situation.[1]

A year later, taxes were heavily in arrears and the public debt remained unpaid. Much of the rum produced in the island could not be sold because of the high duty then in force and a generous reduction in this or the opening of the American trade were again petitioned for, to afford relief.[2]

Further hurricanes in 1784, 1785, and 1786, making an unprecedented total of six in seven years, created a tense situation in the colony. Faced with the danger of famine and rebellion on the part of the negroes, Lieutenant-Governor Clarke, on advice of the council, in August, 1784, opened local ports for the free importation of provisions and lumber and they were not again closed until the end of January, 1785. Under the circumstances, this action was approved by the home government,[3] but it failed to avert a serious food shortage. A committee of the lower house estimated the number of slave deaths from actual starvation or from diseases occasioned by scanty and unwholesome diet following these several natural disasters at no less than 15,000.[4]

An assembly report made in 1792 revealed a deplorable situation. Comparison was made between conditions in the island during two periods, from 1772 to 1775 and from 1788 to 1791, both free from war and wind storms. In the first of these, the price of slaves had averaged £34.10.3 sterling per head as against £47.2.6 in the second. The price of labor had likewise risen from 14d. to 21d. per day; American lumber had gone up 37 per cent, salt beef from Ireland 22½ per cent; and herring, for the negroes, 66 per cent.

---

[1] Memorial and petition of the council and assembly of Jamaica, December, 1784, C. O. 137/85.

[2] Memorial of the assembly of Jamaica to the King, Dec. 24, 1785, C. O. 137/86.

[3] Lieut.-Gov. Clarke to Lord Sydney, Aug. 15, 1784 and enclosure; Sydney to Clarke, Nov. 18, 1784, and July 6, 1785, C. O. 137/84.

[4] Report of the committee, quoted in Edwards, *History*, II, 415.

In the first period the taxes raised annually averaged £27,855 sterling; in the second, £102,328. In 1772, there had been 775 sugar estates in operation; in 1791, there were but 767 including forty-seven lately opened. Of the total number, only 451 were in the hands of their old proprietors; 177 had been sold for debt since 1772; and ninety-two were held by mortgagees. The amazing number of 80,021 executions, totalling £22,563,786 sterling, had been lodged in the office of the provost marshal of Jamaica, serving as sheriff, between 1772 and 1791, on judgments obtained in the supreme court of judicature and the assize court.[1]

Matters in the other Caribbean colonies stood no better. The closing of ports to the Americans threw the Leeward Island planters into greater distress than they had known at any stage of the war. Prices at once rose 50 per cent. A petition of the assembly of Antigua to the governor, requesting a temporary suspension of the July order, was barren of results.[2] Such quantities of rum remained unsold that by February, 1784, the price had fallen as low as from 2s. 6d. to 3s. per gallon.[3]

The raking of salt for sale to the Americans had been an important industry in Anguilla. The inhabitants now found that product wholly unsalable and suffered indescribable hardships in consequence.[4]

Despite the illegal importations which have been noted, an acute shortage of supplies arose after the hurricane of August, 1785. Appeal was made to Governor Shirley to open the ports of Antigua and St. Kitts to American vessels, but he refused.[5] In May, 1787, there was but a month's supply of provisions in Nevis;[6] in July, 1789, both St. Kitts and Nevis were left with less than a week's stock each. Importations were therefore quickly made from Antigua and the harbors of both possessions were opened to cargoes imported from the foreign West Indies in British bottoms.[7]

[1] *Proceedings of the Hon. House of Assembly of Jamaica, on the Sugar and Slave-Trade, in a Session Which Began the 23d of October, 1792* (London, 1793).

[2] Address of the assembly of Antigua to Governor Shirley, Oct. 9, 1783, C. O. 152/63.

[3] "A State of the Allegations and Evidence produced, etc.," in *Gt. Br., H. C., Sess. Pap.*, 1784, V (59), p. 26.

[4] Governor Shirley to Lord Sydney, July 23, 1785, C. O. 152/64.

[5] Shirley to Lord Sydney, Oct. 1, 1785, C. O. 123/64.

[6] Communication of the assembly of Nevis to Governor Shirley, May 31, C. O. 152/65.

[7] Lieut.-Gov. Nugent to Lord Sydney, July 13, 1789, C. O. 152/67.

By 1787, the greater part of the plantations in Antigua were under mortgage to merchants in London, Liverpool, and Bristol.[1] A succession of droughts and ravages of the cane-borer brought the island to the verge of ruin. Describing St. John's in 1792, Sir William Young wrote, "The town . . . has the appearance of ruined trade and habitancy." The distress of the planters was such that they could make but scant allowances of provisions for their negroes.[2]

Members of the legislature, in an address to the king, declared:

"The Towns of the Island exhibit a melancholy picture of poverty and decay. Streets once crowded with industrious Inhabitants now untrodden and solitary; Shops and Warehouses formerly filled with Manufactures of Great Britain and Ireland now empty and shut up, Dwelling houses untenanted, Harbours without Shipping, Mechanics without work, and men of every profession in want of employment. . . . Many Inhabitants sinking under the pressure of such accumulated distress and unable by the utmost efforts of their industry to acquire a sufficiency to support their families are daily emigrating to Trinidad and other foreign Countries, where the earth is more regularly productive, and Commerce, being less restrained, more flourishing." [3]

In Barbados, rum became all but unmarketable following the institution of the new commercial policy toward America. In consequence, the planters engaged in extensive illicit relations with the Dutch from the Main to the South. One smuggler even went so far as to slip cable and carry off a customs officer who had boarded his vessel. A small ship was subsequently provided by the home government to break up such enterprises, but great difficulty was experienced in keeping the situation in hand.[4] The high price of lumber prevented much-needed repairs from being made on the many buildings destroyed by hurricane.[5]

Dominica had suffered most severely of all the British islands during the war. The long-continued French occupation, during which trade had ceased and Roseau had been burned, had blasted the hopes of those engaged in developing the colony. The decade after the Revolution found them deeply involved, unable to secure further credit, and with payments due the Crown for land purchased far in arrears. A negro revolt further complicated the situation. In despair,

[1] Luffman, *Brief Account*, Letter XII.
[2] "A Tour," in Edwards, *Historical Survey of St. Domingo*, pp. 282–283.
[3] In C. O. 152/72.
[4] Governor Parry to the Secretary of State, Nov. 11, 1783, and March 4, 1784; Secy. of State to Parry, July 7, 1784, C. O. 28/60.
[5] Governor Parry to the Secretary of State, Sept. 7, 1784, C. O. 28/60.

the planters petitioned for a remission of the balances still due on their estates and for such other relief as would seem meet.[1] About 1790, but fifty sugar plantations were in operation; some thirty had then been abandoned.[2]

A grant of all the waste lands in St. Vincent, made by the king of France to one Madame Swinburne, a lady-in-waiting at the royal court, during the period of the war, checked the opening of new estates in that colony until 1786, when the British government regained possession of such tracts through the payment of £6,500 in compensation for her claims.[3]

American independence resulted in the addition of a valuable element to the population of the British Caribbean, through which Jamaica and Dominica in particular profited. On August 15, 1782, following the evacuation of Savannah, Georgia, transports landed a body of loyalists, their goods, and 1,400 slaves in the former island. All whites were temporarily provided for by the government and the negroes were set to work in behalf of their masters.[4] The home ministry interested itself in the fate of these refugees to the extent of authorizing the assigning of blocks of crown land to proper persons among them.[5] The surrender of Charleston some months later likewise led to the departure of 3,891 persons for Jamaica. Nine hundred of these were adult whites, 378 white children, and 2,613 negroes.[6] They disembarked at Port Royal on January 13, 1783.[7]

The arrival of these groups of uprooted fellow-colonists awakened lively sympathy among the Jamaicans. The legislature met the situation in liberal fashion. An act passed early in 1783 provided that any resident of North America who, by reason of his loyalty to the British government, had been deprived of or forced to abandon his property and who had taken refuge in Jamaica with the intention of becoming a permanent resident, should be exempted from the payment of duties on such of his slaves as he had entered and from the

[1] In C. O. 71/9. See also The Humble Address and Petition of the Council and Assembly to the Crown, C. O. 71/10.

[2] Atwood, *Dominica*, p. 72.

[3] C. P. Lucas, *A Historical Geography of the British Colonies—the West Indies* (2nd edition, revised by C. Atchley, Oxford, 1905), p. 214, note 2.

[4] Major-General Campbell to the Earl of Shelburne, Sept. 20, 1782, C. O. 137/82.

[5] Despatch to Campbell, Nov. 26, 1782, C. O. 137/82.

[6] Joseph W. Barnwell, "The Evacuation of Charleston by the British in 1782," in *The South Carolina Historical and Genealogical Register,* Jan. 1910, p. 26.

[7] Governor Campbell to Thomas Townshend, Jan. 25, 1783, C. O. 137/83.

payment of public and parochial taxes, excepting only quit-rents, and from all public service, with the exception of that in the militia, for a period of seven years.

The expense of patenting crown lands which might be taken up by them was to be met from public funds. Such holdings must be settled and planted at least in part within two years after having been granted. Claims for the right to enjoy these privileges were to be made before the magistrates of the parishes or precincts in which the refugees proposed to settle. Those officials would issue certificates to qualified persons authorizing them to participate in the benefits of the act. The latter was subsequently extended to cover persons fleeing from the Mosquito Shore on the Bay of Honduras as well.[1]

Various classes were represented among the loyalists landing in Jamaica—planters, gentlemen, surgeons, tradesmen, Quakers from Philadelphia, widows, and former soldiers in the royal forces.[2] Some applied for allotments and received estates, chiefly in the interior of the island.[3] Among such new proprietors were several indigo growers, desirous of resuming their occupation in the Caribbean. They requested, therefore, that the bounty of four pence per pound which had been paid upon British-grown indigo landed in Great Britain until 1782 be renewed.[4]

The professional men soon established themselves and offered their services to the public. One of this number was Dr. William Johnston, son of a former president of the council of Georgia. In addition to building up a substantial general practice, he was nominally attached to a local regiment and was allowed to draw £1 a week for himself, 10s. a week for his wife, and 5s. a week for each child.[5] Others engaged in commerce. Mechanics had no difficulty in securing work. The slaves, including some 200 who were the property of Sir James Wright, late governor of Georgia, and half as many owned by the Honorable William Bull, formerly lieutenant-governor of

---

[1] *An Act to Exempt from Taxes, for a Limited Time, Such of His Majesty's Subjects of North-America, as from Motives of Loyalty have been, or shall be, obliged to relinquish or abandon their Possessions in that Country, and take Refuge in this Island, with Intent to settle here* (Saint Jago de la Vega, 1783). See also *Acts of Assembly . . . 1770–1783*, p. 337–339.

[2] Wilbur H. Siebert, *The Legacy of the American Revolution to the British West Indies and Bahamas* (Columbus, Ohio, 1913), p. 38.

[3] A list of persons receiving such grants appears in *Journals of the Assembly of Jamaica, 1663–1826*, VIII, 36.

[4] Governor Campbell to Lord North, Aug. 1, 1783, C. O. 137/83.

[5] Elizabeth L. Johnston, *Recollections of a Georgia Loyalist* (New York, 1900), p. 83.

South Carolina, were employed on public works and in jobbing gangs.[1]

The burden of caring for the refugees fell almost exclusively upon the inhabitants of Kingston parish. Of 174 certificates issued in the island under the act of 1783, 145 were to persons taking up residence in or near the bustling south coast port. By the end of November, 1784, £3,173 had been expended in providing for them.[2]

The undue proportion of the total expense incurred through the coming of the loyalists, borne by the parish, was represented in a petition of the justices and vestrymen of Kingston, to the assembly. Seventy householders were to be found among the newcomers there. Although many were persons of means engaged in extensive commercial enterprises or well-paid tradesmen or mechanics, occupying some of the choicest dwellings in the community, they were not subject to taxation. The parish house was crowded with their poor fellow-sufferers and, despite a grievous addition to parochial rates and generous private acts of charity, many of the latter were not being properly provided for. It was desired that the wealthy loyalists be subjected to taxation and that general colonial rather than parish funds be drawn upon for the care of all needy ones in the future. But no action seems to have been taken on this common sense proposal.[3]

Certain of the late arrivals from the mainland had no desire to remain in Jamaica but wished to be transported to the Mosquito Shore and to be provided with tools as well as a nine months' store of provisions in order that they might set up as planters there. Their request was not approved by Governor Campbell,[4] but when a further band of 243 loyalists touched at the island in 1784, en route from Florida to Honduras Bay, he issued them rations sufficient for a third of a year.[5] Unhappily, misfortune stalked at the heels of those going to the Shore—hardly had they established themselves when British territorial claims there were relinquished and they were obliged to abandon their holdings on short notice without indemnification. The Jamaicans were therefore once more turned to for assistance.[6]

---

[1] Siebert, *Legacy*, p. 38.

[2] *Ibid.*, pp. 37, 38.

[3] *Journals of the Assembly of Jamaica, 1663–1826*, VIII, 32, 33.

[4] Campbell to Lord North, July 14, 1783, C. O. 137/83.

[5] Governor Campbell to Lord Sydney, July 3, 1784 and enclosure, C. O. 137/84.

[6] Memorial to the Superintendent of the Mosquito Shore, in C. O. 137/86.

Early in 1783, the Society of West India Merchants urged that inducements be offered loyalists in general to settle in the islands.[1] A more definite step on the part of the London colonial interest was taken in November, when a group of Dominican proprietors, meeting in the British metropolis, urged the home government to grant crown lands in that island to such British residents of East Florida as might desire to take them up. It was further recommended that they and their effects be transported free of all cost, that they be provisioned for at least nine months, and that the colonial legislature exempt them from taxation for fifteen years.[2]

All of these proposals were promptly adopted. Governor Tonyn of Florida was officially notified that emigrants to Dominica would be provided with a year's supply of foodstuffs and crown lands gratis, made the same known in a proclamation and, in the summer of 1784, he despatched a transport laden with loyalists and their possessions southward from St. Augustine. For some inexplicable reason, Governor Orde had received no word of the British ministry's intentions and his first knowledge of the matter came with the arrival of the party at Roseau and their presenting him with a petition calling for the promised supplies and land. Much perplexed as to the line of conduct he should follow, Orde issued provisions sufficient for thirty days, allowed the Floridans to erect temporary homes, recommended generous action on the part of the residents, and wrote home for instructions.

The legislature promptly voted indigent persons in the body tools and building material to the value of £1,650 currency, granted all exemption from taxes for fifteen years, and urged the establishment of a relief fund by private subscription.[3] Allotments of land were subsequently made [4] and the distribution of rations at the colony's expense was continued [5] until the spring of 1785, when the Lords of the Treasury sent out supplies [6] of pork and flour large enough to last the 110 persons entitled to draw them for three and four years respectively.[7]

A second body of loyalists, 150 in number, arrived from Florida in June, 1785, the beginning of the rainy season. The colony was in

---

[1] *Min. W. I. Mer.*, meeting of April 29.
[2] Minutes of a meeting held on Nov. 25, 1783, in C. O. 71/8.
[3] Governor Orde to Lord Sydney, July 6, 1784 and enclosures, C. O. 71/8.
[4] Sydney to Orde, Sept. 2, 1784, C. O. 71/8.
[5] Orde to Sydney, Nov. 25, 1784, C. O. 71/9.
[6] Sydney to Orde, Feb. 6, 1785, C. O. 71/9.
[7] Orde to Sydney, June 20, 1785, C. O. 71/9.

no condition to receive them. Governor Orde was much disturbed. He wrote to home authorities: "How those poor unfortunate people are to be disposed of I really am at a loss to know. There is not a House or Shed to be got here to cover them, every place is full. I will however do all in my power either by detaining the Transport for a short Time or otherwise to protect and cover them. . . . They shall be furnished with rations and provided for as lies with me, with spots to put Houses upon. Your Lordships' instructions how far they may be accommodated with such Lands as remain ungranted, I hope soon to receive. . . ."[1]

In August, between two and three hundred more arrived. All were provisioned and were given plots on which to build cabins, while those who would plant them were granted holdings up to thirty acres each in addition. But such land was almost worthless, which accounts for its not having already been taken up; Orde had no authority to dispose of the stretches of good soil formerly leased by the French or forfeited to the Crown.[2]

Further shipments of tools and food for the loyalists were sent out from England.[3] Unfortunately, the latter had been so poorly packed that the fish were entirely spoiled and other articles were in a poor state. Twelve months' supply was therefore issued at once and the recipients were authorized to use or dispose of their respective shares as they saw fit, while the balance was sold.

Nearly a year after the latest group's appearance, no instructions governing land grants had yet been received and deep discouragement as well as keen resentment at their shameful neglect were rife among the refugees.[4] The situation of these miserable people was made even more wretched by a destructive hurricane in 1787.[5] They were, however, ultimately provided for. It may be added that the cultivation of rice was introduced into Dominica by certain of them.[6]

Loyalists filled various public positions in other of the West India islands after the Revolution. Thus, Samuel Quincy of Massachusetts served as attorney to the Crown in Antigua until his death in 1789; Nathaniel Coffin of Boston became collector of customs at St. Kitts and held that position for thirty-four years; while James Robertson,

[1] Orde to Sydney, June 20, 1785, C. O. 71/9.
[2] Orde to Sydney, Aug. 24, 1785, C. O. 71/9.
[3] Sydney to Orde, Dec. 12, 1785, C. O. 71/9.
[4] Orde to Sydney, June 13, 1786, C. O. 71/9.
[5] Orde to Sydney, Sept. 23, 1787, C. O. 71/13.
[6] Southey, *Chronological History*, II, 542.

former attorney-general of Georgia, became chief justice of the Virgin Islands.[1] Though nowhere so numerous as in Jamaica and Dominica, the healthy, leavening influence of this new element in planter society was felt throughout the British Caribbean.

Two noteworthy developments along agricultural lines marked the post-revolutionary decade—the growth of coffee culture and the attempt made to stimulate cotton cultivation. Production of the former increased at an astonishing rate after 1783, due largely to the home government's lowering the excise duty from 1s. 6d. per pound, which rate had been set about 1730 as a protection for the tea trade, to 6d. Before this drastic reduction was made, the charges laid against coffee entering Great Britain had been no less than 480 per cent of its market value.[2]

Imports rose rapidly following the encouragement thus given the industry. In 1783, but 17,272 hundredweight were landed in the mother country from the West India possessions; in 1784, the total mounted to 41,147 hundredweight; in 1785, it was 37,036 hundredweight.[3] The ten years following the cutting of the excise duty by two-thirds saw a greater advance in colonial coffee culture than had taken place in the quarter of a century preceding.[4] The total production of Jamaica from 1772 to 1775 inclusive had been but 2,114,842 pounds and was steadily declining. In 1791 alone 2,299,874 pounds were raised in the island and in the following year 607 coffee estates employing 21,011 negroes were being worked.[5]

To encourage use of this beverage, which had remained practically unknown to a large portion of the population because of its high price before 1783, the Society of Planters and Merchants purchased 2,000 copies of a pamphlet by Benjamin Moseley, *A Treatise Concerning the Properties and Effects of Coffee*,[6] for £250 and secured their general distribution.[7]

---

[1] Siebert, *Legacy*, p. 48.

[2] Edwards, *History*, II, 290.

[3] "Report . . . on the Commercial State of the West India Colonies," in *Gt. Br., H. C., Sess. Pap.*, 1807, III (65), p. 75.

[4] Edwards, *History*, II, 299.

[5] *Proceedings of the Hon. House of Assembly of Jamaica . . . in a Session Which Began the 23d of October, 1792.*

[6] London, 1785.

[7] *Min. Sub-Committee W. I. Plant. and Mer.*, March 1, 1792. The work was given wide publicity in popular periodicals of the day. See "Dr. Moseley on the Medicinal Virtues etc. of Coffee," in *The Eur. Mag. and Lond. Rev.*, Sept. 1785, pp. 215 ff., and "Dr. Moseley's Elucidation on the Virtues of Coffee," in *The Gent. Mag.*, Dec. 1785, pp. 944 ff.

Efforts to further cotton planting were not so successful. Its cultivation in the tropical American colonies had gradually declined from the middle of the eighteenth century on, due to the competition of growers on the fresh soil of the foreign West Indies whose product was given free access to the markets of Great Britain by way of her Caribbean island ports.

Peculiar circumstances, too, discouraged producers in certain of the British islands. Thus, the output to the Virgin group dropped from 1,000 bales annually around 1770 to half as many less than fifteen years later, largely because the sugar planters had accorded their slaves permission to grow the commodity. As they could sell cotton freely, the blacks committed such extensive depredations against the properties of small proprietors seeking to raise it on a commercial scale that these quite generally abandoned the attempt. In 1783, the legislature sought to abolish the evil by passing an act forbidding blacks to engage in cotton cultivation, but the mischief could not be undone. Then too, "it is here as it is elsewhere, the larger fish swallow up the small. The estates of the poor cotton planters which were contiguous to Sugar estates have been swallowed up by them." [1]

Although importations of cotton from the tropical American possessions into Great Britain in 1783, 1784, and 1785 were 6,100,191 pounds, 6,874,961 pounds, and 8,230,716 pounds respectively,[2] considerably less than half of those quantities were actually the growth of British plantations.[3]

The arrival of the loyalists, some of whom had been cotton growers on the mainland, raised hopes that its cultivation might be revived in the Caribbean colonies. Upon the textile manufacturers of Manchester representing to the Lords of Trade and Plantations the necessity for promoting the industry there as a means of lessening their dependence upon foreign supplies, a circular despatch was sent to the several governors in March 1786, instructing them to recommend the planting of the crop to the colonials in strong terms and to afford all who might be interested due encouragement. The use of only the best seeds, to insure a high-quality crop, was urged.[4]

---

[1] Excerpt from the letter of President Fahie of Tortola, enclosed in the despatch from Governor Shirley to Lord Sydney, May (no date), 1784, C. O. 152/63.

[2] "Report . . . on the Commercial State of the West India Colonies," *Gt. Br., H. C., Sess. Pap.*, 1807, III (65) p. 78.

[3] See the tables in Edwards, *History*, II, 278, 279.

[4] President Lucas to Lord Sydney, June 9, 1786, C. O. 101/26. Governor Orde to Sydney, June 13, 1786, C. O. 71/10. Governor Shirley to Sydney, June 13, 1786, C. O. 152/64.

Governor Parry of Barbados, where considerable quantities had always been grown, adopted a sanguine tone in his reply. "I dare venture to say that His Majesty's wishes respecting the cultivation of cotton in general, to answer the expectations of the Manufacturers, will be met by the success already attending its rise here."

He submitted samples of thread,[1] and, some time later, specimens of locally woven cotton cloth as well, not failing, however, to forestall inquiries regarding Barbadian manufactories by adding that such weaving was allowed only to give employment to a few indigent whites who would otherwise emigrate to the foreign colonies and that it could never injure home industry.[2]

Governor Orde of Dominica took the instructions to give every possible assistance to persons interested in cotton planting at face value. A proclamation issued by him in September 1786 offered free grants of from thirty to sixty acres of unappropriated land each to all who might petition for them and would agree to use them for this purpose.[3] Numerous applications were received and approved by the governor and council;[4] but, through lack of coördination between the several branches of the home government, authority covering such proposed grants had not been received by the summer of 1788 and the executives' good intentions were frustrated. Lord Sydney then once more applied to the Privy Concil for its approval of Orde's plan[5] but apparently without result, for no more was heard of the project.

Reliable statistics are lacking—the 12,330,109 pounds of cotton imported from the British West Indies into Great Britain in 1791 and the 12,576,874 pounds imported in 1792[6] included large quantities of the French-grown product entered under free port of regulations. Exports from Barbados show no increased production there.[7] Cotton was seldom mentioned in despatches and it is certain that this

---

[1] To Lord Sydney, May 31, 1786, C. O. 28/60.

[2] Parry to Sydney, Oct. 4, 1786, C. O. 28/60.

[3] Proclamation in *The Dominica Gazette or, General Intelligencer,* Sept. 23, 1786.

[4] Governor Orde to Lord Sydney, Sept. 1, 1787, C. O. 71/13.

[5] Orde to Sydney, March 30, 1788 and Sydney to Orde, July 12, 1788, C. O. 71/14.

[6] "Report . . . on the Commercial State of the West India Colonies," in *Gt. Br., H. C., Sess. Pap.,* 1807, III (65), p. 78.

[7] See report in C. O. 28/63. A total of 8,156 bales and 2,400 bags was exported between April 1788 and April 1789. Exports for the three following years were 7,549 bales and 455 bags; 4,939 bales and 2,421 bags; and 10,897 bales and 35 bags respectively.

interesting attempt to stimulate cultivation of the crop in the Caribbean colonies was almost barren of results.

The reopening of free ports in certain of the British West India possessions after the Revolution was an event of capital importance to the commercial interests, both local and in Great Britain. Attempts to secure such action were made immediately upon the conclusion of the war in 1783, at which time representations on behalf of their respective islands were sent to the home government by the legislatures of Barbados,[1] Antigua,[2] and St. Kitts.[3] Large numbers of persons, including former leading merchants of St. Eustatius, took up their residence in Dominica in the expectation that Roseau would again be opened.[4]

But Lord Sheffield was unalterably opposed to the granting of such concessions. He declared free ports to be quite unnecessary, since the planters could secure all needed supplies upon reasonable terms without them. Their reëstablishment, according to him, would be equivalent to giving the West India trade to the Americans.[5] A Dominican free port bill, under consideration by the government in 1785, was objected to by members of the London Caribbean interest on the ground that it did not sufficiently guard against foreign produce being admitted into Great Britain [6] and was subsequently dropped. Fear of losing advantages accruing to the empire from the new régime of restricted trade if free ports were again opened long delayed such action.

A bill finally passed in 1787 sought to meet the West Indians' demands while at the same time obviating this danger.[7] Under the terms of this act cotton, indigo, cacao, drugs of all sorts, dyestuffs and dye woods, hides, skins, furs, tallow, turtle-shell, hardwood or mill timber, cabinet woods, horses, mules, and cattle, the produce of any foreign European colony in America, were admitted into Kingston, Savanna-la-Mar, Montego Bay, and St. Lucea in Jamaica, St. George in Grenada, Roseau in Dominica, and Nassau in the Bahamas in single-decked vessels of not over seventy tons

[1] In C. O. 28/60.
[2] Governor Shirley to Thomas Townshend, April 15, 1783, C. O. 152/63.
[3] Petition and representation of the council and assembly of St. Kitts (2 documents), in C. O. 152/63.
[4] Governor Orde to Lord Sydney, March 19, 1784, C. O. 71/4.
[5] Sheffield, *Observations*, pp. 256–258.
[6] *Min. W. I. Plant. and Mer.*, May 18, 1785.
[7] 27 Geo. III c. 27.

burden each, owned by residents of those colonies in which the goods originated.

Such bottoms were permitted to export British plantation rum, negroes, and all goods legally imported excepting naval stores, tobacco, and iron from the British colonies in America. Foreign produce thus entering the ports specified might be shipped to Great Britain or Ireland under the terms of existing shipping laws. The exportation of European or East India goods from Grenada, Dominica, and the Bahamas to any other British colony was at the same time forbidden.

Three years later this act was amended so as to remove the limitation on the burden of the vessels while still requiring them to be single-decked [1] and, in 1792, the freedom of importation into the several ports was made perpetual.[2] The policy thus inaugurated in 1787 was subsequently applied unchanged to other ports and colonies until the close of the century.[3]

[1] 30 Geo. III c. 29.

[2] 32 Geo. III c. 37.

[3] By 33 Geo. III c. 50, Port Antonio, Jamaica and St. John's, Antigua, were made free ports on the same terms as the harbors already opened, in the latter case only to July 10, 1797, however. By 36 Geo. III c. 55, Scarborough in Tobago was opened for the admission of foreign single-decked vessels under the usual regulations and restrictions. By 37 Geo. III c. 77, San Josef, Trinidad, was also made a free port. Under 38 Geo. III c. 39, the carrying of European goods and manufactures from Grenada, Dominica, Antigua, Trinidad and the Bahamas to any British colony in America was permitted and British vessels were allowed to export from them and from Jamaica all kinds of merchandise lawfully imported into them from any colony in America belonging to any foreign European power.

CHAPTER VII

THE INSULAR POSSESSIONS IN THE FRENCH WAR

Most productive of all Caribbean holdings during the closing decades of the eighteenth century was St. Domingo, the jewel of
France's colonial empire, occupying the western third of the island
of Hispaniola. It had been settled by a nondescript assortment of
buccaneers who had successfully defied Spanish attempts to dislodge
them and had found protection under the Bourbon flag in the late
1600's. St. Domingo's agricultural development began to receive
serious attention only about 1725, but proceeded with such marvelous
rapidity that, within fifty years, it was the foremost tropical colony
in the world and boasted the proud name "Queen of the Antilles."
Seven hundred ninety-two sugar estates, 2,810 coffee plantations,
705 cotton properties, and 3,097 growing indigo were being worked
about 1790. The negro population was then some 455,000[1] and production approximately equalled that of all the British tropical American possessions combined.[2]

[1] From an account drawn up by order of the legislative assembly of
France, in Macpherson, *Annals of Commerce,* IV, 224 and Lionel M. Fraser,
History of Trinidad (2 vols., Port of Spain, n.d. and 1896), 1, 21.

[2] Legal exports from St. Domingo in 1784 included 602,343 cwt. of clayed
sugar; 716,152 cwt. of muscovado; 48,967,700 lbs. of coffee; 4,404,500 lbs.
of cotton; and 1,439,900 lbs. of indigo. (*East India Sugar. Papers Respecting
the Culture and Manufacture of Sugar . . . ,* Appendix I, p. 12. The weights
as given above have been reduced to English standards). In the same year,
the importation of sugar from all of the British West India colonies into
Great Britain—the greater part of their total production—was 1,782,386
cwt. (*Ibid.,* Appendix I, pp. 10, 11; "Report . . . on the Commercial State
of the West India Colonies," in *Gt. Br., H. C., Sess. Pap.,* 1807, III [65],
p. 73); the importation of coffee, 4,114,700 lbs.; and of cotton, including
foreign grown, 6,874,961 lbs. ("Report . . . on the Commercial State of the
West India Colonies," in *Gt. Br., H. C., Sess. Pap.,* 1807, III [65], pp. 75,
78.)
In 1788, the legal exports of St. Domingo included 650,256 cwt. of clayed
sugar; 862,754 cwt. of muscovado; 63,102,900 lbs. of coffee; 5,820,500 lbs.
of cotton; and 861,100 lbs. of indigo. Sugar imports from the British West
Indies into Great Britain in that year were 2,065,817 cwt. Exports from St.
Domingo in 1789 included 439,968 cwt. of clayed sugar; 850,925 cwt. of muscovado; 70,635,600 lbs. of coffee; 6,362,200 lbs. of cotton; and 887,600 lbs. of

Distant rumbles of revolution in the mother land early caught the ear of the large mulatto element resident there. The triple doctrine of liberty, fraternity, and equality fell among members of that unfortunate class like the proverbial spark in a powder chest. They rose against the whites, claiming political equality; the slaves in turn revolted and demanded personal freedom. Thereupon followed the most ferocious race war in history and the almost total ruin of a fair and prosperous colony in the attendant anarchy.[1]

Momentous consequences for the planters in the neighboring British islands followed this ravaging of St. Domingo. The sudden withdrawal of its immense supplies of tropical produce from the general European market occasioned widespread scarcity; continental buyers hastily turned across the English Channel to fill their needs. Importations of muscovado sugar from the West India colonies into Great Britain, which had averaged 1,814,190 hundredweight per annum from 1783 to 1785, rose to 2,330,026 hundredweight in 1794 in consequence of this unusual demand.[2] But the British planters could scarcely begin to meet the shortage arising from the deflection of the Santa Domingan crop and a similar situation existed in regard to other torrid zone products, especially coffee.

A rapid and marked rise in quotations followed. This afforded relief to the Caribbean proprietors after nearly twenty years of depression and brought a return of the old-time prosperity which was to last until the turn of the century. In 1792, the average price of muscovado sold in London by agents of the West India planters ranged from 54s. 3d. to 56s. 6d. per hundredweight, exclusive of duty, at quarterly intervals of January, April, July, and October; in 1796, from 62s. 2d. to 69s. 2d.[3] Wholesale offerings of molasses there varied

indigo. Sugar imports from the British West Indies into Great Britain in the same year were 1,936,440 cwt. (*East India Sugar. Papers Respecting the Culture and Manufacture of Sugar* . . . , Appendix I, pp. 10–12. The weights covering shipments from St. Domingo have been reduced to English standards).

[1] For a very satisfactory treatment of the subject see Theodore Lothrop Stoddard, *The French Revolution in San Domingo* (Boston, 1914).

[2] Importations of muscovado from the British West Indies into Great Britain were 1,808,950 cwt. in 1791; 1,980,973 cwt. in 1792; 2,115,308 cwt. in 1793; and 1,871,368 cwt. in 1795. "Report . . . on the Commercial State of the West India Colonies," in *Gt. Br., H. C., Sess. Pap.*, 1807, III (65), p. 73.

[3] The average price of muscovado ranged from 51s. 8d. to 59s. 7d. in 1793; from 38s. 1d. to 50s. 4d. in 1794; from 58s. 6d. to 64s. 7d. in 1795; from 65s. 8d. to 68s. 8d. in 1797; from 68s. 1d. to 73s. 1d. in 1798; and from 61s. 6d. to 68s. 5d. in 1799. Reports on the average price of muscovado published weekly in *The London Gazette* from June 1792 by authority of parliament.

from 18s. 6d. to 21s. 9d. per hundredweight in 1790; eight years later, the price had doubled.[1] Jamaican coffee sold in Great Britain at from 77s. to 95s. per hundredweight in 1793–1794 and at from 185s. to 196s. per hundredweight early in 1799.[2]

In 1790 that grand edifice, the old plantation system in the British West Indies, was tottering from structural weakness. The decade of high returns following the St. Domingan disaster propped it up and delayed its total collapse for a quarter of a century. A statement of the Jamaican assembly in an address to the king, "tho' we lament the principal cause of such high prices, we declare to your Majesty that only such accidental and temporary increase in the value of our Staples could have saved this Island from absolute Bankruptcy," [3] was applicable to Great Britain's Caribbean colonies as a whole.

The increased cost of sugar commencing in 1791 caused general dissatisfaction in the mother land. The grocers of London called upon the planters to augment production.[4] The refiners, as usual during times of shortage, attacked the West Indian monopoly and urged that the duty on foreign muscovado entered in British bottoms be lowered from the prohibitive rate of 29s. 10d. per hundredweight as against 15s. charged the colonial transatlantic product,[5] to 17s. or 18s. They recommended, likewise, that East Indian sugar be admitted on exactly the same basis as that from the new world and advocated a lowering of the bounty [6] paid upon exportation of the refined article.[7]

So serious was the shortage that exports were, of necessity, regu-

[1] Molasses ranged from 23s. to 28s. 6d. in 1791; from 25s. to 25s. 3d. in 1792; from 24s. to 30s. in 1793; from 23s. to 28s. 3d. in 1794; from 25s. 3d. to 38s. in 1795; from 32s. 6d. to 37s. in 1796; from 33s. to 37s. 3d. in 1797 and from 29s. to 39s. 6d. in 1799. Quarterly circulars issued by Smiths, Nash, and Kemble and successors, in the archives of Joseph Travers and Sons, Ltd., London.

[2] Thomas Tooke, *A History of Prices* (6 vols., London, 1838–1857), I, 190.

[3] Dated May 8, 1792, C. O. 137/90.

[4] *Resolutions of the Grocers and Consumers of Sugar* (London, 1792).

[5] "Rates of Duty on Muscovado Sugar Imported Into the United Kingdom, 1791–1836," in *Gt. Br., H. C., Sess. Pap.*, 1847–48, LVIII (400).

[6] The duty paid on the entry of raw sugar into Great Britain was repaid in whole or in part upon such quantities as were reëxported. The refund thus made was known as a "drawback." The drawback was allowed and a premium or "bounty" as well was paid on refined sugar exported.

[7] *A Report of the Proceedings of the Committee of Sugar-Refiners, for the Purpose of Effecting a Reduction in the High Prices of Sugar, by Lowering the Bounty on Refined Sugar Exported, and Correcting the Evils of the West India Monopoly* (London, 1792), pp. 9–14, 41, 42.

lated. A suggested measure which would prohibit shipments of British-grown sugar out of the country whenever the price of muscovado should exceed 65s. per hundredweight including the duty of 15s., was presented to the sugar refiners and the Society of West India Planters and Merchants by the Board of the Privy Council for Trade. This was opposed by the former on the grounds that it would destroy them and not benefit the public. The colonial group, on the other hand, held the limiting price to be altogether too low, and urged that it be set at 60s. per hundredweight, exclusive of duty.[1]

An act for the prevention of excessive exportation to the detriment of British consumers, drawn along the lines proposed to the refiners and West Indians, was subsequently passed by parliament in June 1792. Under it, the clerk of the Company of Grocers in London was authorized to obtain weekly accounts of the quantities and prices of sugar sold in the capital from local importers who were required to give such information under oath. The average price for the week was to be computed from this data and was to be officially published in *The London Gazette*. The average prices for the six week periods preceding the middle of February, June, and October were likewise to be determined and made known.

If the average price of muscovado at the close of July, 1792, should exceed 60s. exclusive of duty or, at the end of October of the same year, should be above 55s., or, in the six weeks preceding the third Wednesday of any February, June, or October thereafter, should be in excess of 50s., the drawback and bounties allowed upon exportation of the raw and refined product respectively should cease in such case for a period of four months. During this suspension of normal custom house regulations, no sugar might be exported from the West India colonies direct to European ports as authorized under the act of 1739.[2]

At the same time, arrangements were made enabling British merchants to supply continental markets with foreign tropical produce. Sugar and coffee grown in the colonies of other nations were admitted into the ports of London, Bristol, Liverpool, Lancaster, Glasgow, and Leith in British vessels, might be warehoused there at the importer's expense without payment of duty, and might subsequently be freely reëxported whenever desired. If such goods were removed

[1] *Report . . . for the Purpose of . . . Correcting the Evils of the West India Monopoly*, pp. 23, 24, 28, 29, 34, 35.
[2] See page 53.

from storage and were entered for home consumption, they of course became subject to the customary foreign rates.[1]

The remuneration of the clerk of the Grocers' Company for his services as outlined was set at £200 per annum.[2] Quotations covering sales of colonial Caribbean sugar in London became a regular feature of the *Gazette* from June 1792. Excepting in 1794,[3] when overspeculation brought a temporary decline,[4] the average price never fell below 50s. per hundredweight exclusive of duty until the close of the century. But the regulating act of 1792, through discouraging exportation of the British-grown product, kept sugar on the home market at a considerably lower level than it would normally have reached.

This was a great grievance to the West Indians. They considered fifty shillings altogether too low a maximum price at which the drawback and bounties were allowed. A pamphleteer, writing in their behalf, predicted that the measure would discourage cultivation and would decrease production.[5] Bryan Edwards declared that it operated wholly against the planters' interest.[6] News of parliament's action caused intense dissatisfaction among the proprietors of the Leeward group;[7] merchants and estate owners in Barbados raised their voices against any attempt on the part of the home government to regulate prices on colonial produce.[8] Copies of their protest were circulated in neighboring islands with the proposal that a meeting of deputies be held to concert and frame a general remonstrance.[9] But nothing came of this.

Exportation was further checked by decreasing the drawback and

---

[1] 32 Geo. III c. 43. The regulation of exports through publication of the weekly average. prices was no innovation; this had been done with respect to grain for many years. The right to export sugar from the British West Indies direct to foreign ports in British vessels, long since fallen into disuse, was subsequently rescinded by 34 Geo. III c. 42.

[2] J. Aubrey Rees, *The Grocery Trade. Its History and Romance* (2 vols., London, 1910), II, 83.

[3] See the weekly reports in *The London Gazette.*

[4] William Reed, *The History of Sugar and Sugar Yielding Plants . . .* (London, 1886), p. 146.

[5] Anon., *Remarks on the New Sugar Bill, and on the Compacts Respecting the Sugar Trade and Slave Trade* (London, 1792).

[6] *History*, II, 453, note.

[7] Governor Woodley to Henry Dundas, Sept. 17, 1792, C. O. 152/72.

[8] *The Humble Petition, of the Planters and Merchants of the Island of Barbados, to the Honourable the House of Commons, of Great Britain, in Parliament Assembled* (no imprint, 1792).

[9] Governor Orde to Henry Dundas, June 21, 1792, C. O. 71/23.

bounties from time to time. The former, which had been set at 15s. per hundredweight, the whole amount of the duty, in 1791, was lowered to 13s. 6d. per hundredweight in 1796, while the duty was increased to 17s. 6d. When this was raised to 19s. 4d. in 1798, the drawback remained at the figure set two years before, and, when the duty was further increased to 20s. per hundredweight in 1799, the drawback was once more actually reduced, this time to 11s.[1]

From 1791, bounties stood at 15s. per hundredweight on bastards, broken loaves, and powdered sugar and at 26s. on single refined, complete loaves, and the doubly refined article. Those sums were reduced to 13s. 6d. and 23s. respectively in 1796 and to 11s. and 19s. in 1799.[2] The London West India interest opposed all such action because it cut sales abroad and lowered selling prices,[3] but to no avail.

Exports of British plantation sugar from Great Britain sank from 250,086 hundredweight in 1796 to 183,307 hundredweight in 1797 following the first of these readjustments. The reëxportation of foreign muscovado warehoused in England under the act of 1792 averaged 151,073 hundredweight a year from 1796 to 1802 inclusive.[4] Demand on the Caribbean colonists was lessened by this amount; such trade, then, also served to prevent British West Indian sugar reaching prices it would have attained without parliamentary intervention.

The question of admitting oriental sugar, brought up by the refiners, was an interesting one. Small quantities had been entered into England by the East India Company early in the seventeenth century, but the venture had not proved successful in consequence of the much lower marketing costs enjoyed by proprietors of the rapidly developing plantations in the American tropics.[5]

[1] "Rates of Duty . . . and Drawbacks . . . 1776–1826," in *Gt. Br., H. C., Sess. Pap.,* 1826, XXII (328).

[2] "Bounty per Cwt. Paid on Various Grades of Clayed Sugar . . . 1776–1826," in *Gt. Br., H. C., Sess. Pap.,* 1826, XXII (328).

[3] See for example, *Resolutions of the West India Planters and Merchants, against a Bill for reducing the Draw-back and Bounty on Sugar Exported* (London, 1795).

[4] 92,278 cwt. were reëxported in 1796; 139,844 cwt. in 1797; 130,593 cwt. in 1798; 152,865 cwt. in 1799; 112,032 cwt. in 1800; 271,825 cwt. in 1801; and 158,074 cwt. in 1802. *East India Sugar. Papers Respecting the Culture and Manufacture of Sugar . . . ,* Appendix IV, p. 5.

[5] W. Foster, ed., *The English Factories in India, 1618–54: A Calendar of Documents in the India Office, British Museum, and Public Record Office* (9 vols., Oxford, 1906–15). See the volume covering 1630–33, p. 19.

None had been commercially imported from the Far East for more than a century and a half when, in 1789, a committee of the East India Company recommended that its introduction be again undertaken. The prevailing low selling prices coupled with high freight charges afforded small possibilities for profit, but the General Court nevertheless directed the Government of Bengal to make a trial sending. The Company also engaged itself in 1791 to purchase all the sugar that might be grown by Lieutenant John Paterson, residing in north-eastern India, during a period of twelve years. Early in 1791, a shipment of five tons arrived at the London warehouse under the order placed two years previous.

East India officials had taken it as a matter of course that they would be permitted to enter any sugar imported from the orient at the Caribbean plantation rate, then 15s. per hundredweight, and had acted on this assumption in approaching prospective buyers. But, since it was not enumerated in the tariff covering regular Company importations, revenue officers levied an ad valorem duty of £37.16.3 per cent on the gross sales price against this initial consignment, as on any manufactured article. Application made to the Treasury, seeking entry for it at the specific West Indian rate, was unavailing and, as market prices were then high because of events in St. Domingo, the sending was eventually accepted under the custom house classification. The sugar was profitably disposed of at from 88s. 6d. to 105s. per hundredweight,[1] but a disastrous precedent had been set.

At the close of 1791, a gathering of British consumers called upon the Company to lend its assistance in effecting a price reduction by making periodic importations from the territories under its control. Early the next year, one of the organization's committees urged such action since the cost to retail buyers had then become so great as to threaten a serious falling off in the consumption of tea. No attempt should be made to compete with the West India merchants in any of the centers which they habitually supplied; the Company should seek primarily to dispose of shipments in continental markets which British traders had long since lost to their French rivals and which the colonial group was seeking to regain following the deflection of the St. Domingan crop.[2]

Sugar, declared that body, could be produced more cheaply in the East than in the West Indies, for slaves doing hand labor manned

[1] *East India Sugar. Papers Respecting the Culture and Manufacture of Sugar* . . . , Appendix I, pp. 3-7.
[2] *Ibid.*, Appendix I, pp. 22, 23.

estates in the latter while work in the orient was performed by free men employing proper tools and implements. Furthermore, the overhead was greater on the expensively equipped properties in the Caribbean.

Great Britain would benefit in numerous ways through encouraging cane cultivation in Bengal. The West Indians alone had been unable to meet the needs of the home country—the deficiency might thus be made up. India offered a limitless market for manufactured goods while the tropical American demand was stationary. The transatlantic colonies were insecurely held and were defended at great expense while native troops garrisoned the East and maintained firm control at no cost to the British Treasury. The West Indies were developed to their full extent and were in no state to supply the wants of European sugar buyers while Bengal could readily do so. If Great Britain failed to provide the continent with the oriental product, the foreign Caribbean colonies would be resorted to. Since the distance from Bengal to British ports was much greater than that from them to the West Indies, a sugar trade with the East would be a more effective nursery of seamen than was that with the holdings in the new world.[1]

Pitt and Dundas, then in power, strongly favored attempting the capture of continental marts with East Indian sugar.[2] But the planter-merchant group in England was emphatically opposed to this, and drew up a lengthy protest to the ministry declaring that any favor shown traders to Asia would be in violation of the unwritten compact between the colonies and the home country establishing mutual monopolies in each other's markets.[3] Bryan Edwards denounced the hypocrisy of Company officials in professing to seek the less restricted admission of Bengal sugar on grounds involving the public welfare, and charged them with attempting to ruin the West Indians in order that their organization might itself secure the latter's monopoly.[4] The project, held a nameless pamphleteer, would inevitably ruin

[1] *East India Sugar* . . . , Appendix I, pp. 52–59.

[2] *Min. W. I. Plant. and Mer.*, Feb. 24, and March 17, 1792.

[3] "Reasons general and particular, on the subject of certain innovations projected in the long established laws of Great Britain respecting Sugars . . . ," in the archives of the West India Committee. See also *The Legal Claim of the British Sugar-Colonies to enjoy an Exclusive Right of supplying this Kingdom with Sugars, in Return for sundry restrictions laid upon these Colonies* . . . [London, 1792], adopted at a meeting of the West India Planters and Merchants, March 23, 1792.

[4] Edwards, *History*, II, 469–471. This work was written at the height of the controversy.

both the planters and the traders associated with them, if carried out.[1]

When an attempt was made by the East India Company in the spring of 1792 to secure more equitable treatment in the matter of the sugar duty, the Caribbean lobby was able to defeat the effort. The high rate charged on importations from the orient, accidentally set in 1791, became definitely established [2] and the protection accorded the West Indian product was steadily maintained in subsequent readjustments of the custom house schedule.[3]

This serious disability did not prevent the East India Company from entering increasing quantities into Great Britain. Sales there rose from 3,839 hundredweight in 1792 to 107,154 hundredweight in 1796 and 220,836 hundredweight four years later. The total value of oriental sugar thus marketed in the decade 1791–1800 was £2,-886,777.[4] The benefit derived by the public through the lowering of prices following the opening of this new source of supply is evident from wholesale offerings of the day. The East Indian article was first quoted by Smiths, Kemble, Travers, and Kemble of London in December 1794 at 72s. to 84s. per hundredweight as against 52s. to 80s. for West Indian muscovado. In June of the following year, it was noted as being "much cheaper" than the latter.

A report on trade conditions in March 1796 contained the significant statement, "There are few Raw Sugars in the Market, and the Prices [are] very high. A small Fleet from Jamaica is daily expected, and there will be a Sale of East-India Sugar about the middle of April, which, we hope, will prevent any further Advance. . . ." A year later, the crops were "said to be short, but we shall have a toler-

---

[1] Anon., *The Case of the Sugar Colonies* (London, 1792).

[2] *East India Sugar. Papers Respecting the Culture and Manufacture of Sugar* . . . , Appendix I, pp. 1, 2.

[3] Thus, when the duty on West Indian muscovado was increased from 15s. to 17s. 6d. per cwt. in 1796, that on sugar from the orient was raised from 2s. 8d. per cwt. plus the ad valorem rate of £37.16.3 per cent to 5s. 2d. plus £37.16.3 per cent. In 1789 the rates were set at 19s. 4d. and 5s. 2d. plus £40.16.3 per cent respectively; in 1799, at 20s. and 3s. 2d. plus £42.16.3 per cent. "Rates of Duty on Muscovado Sugar Imported into the United Kingdom, 1791–1836," in *Gt. Br., H. C., Sess. Pap.*, 1847–48, LVIII (400). "Rates of Duty on Muscovado Sugar Imported into Great Britain from the East Indies, 1792–1829," in *Gt. Br., H. C., Sess. Pap.*, 1830, XXV (466).

[4] Sales in 1793 were 43,205 cwt.; in 1794, 62,225 cwt.; in 1795, 161,829 cwt.; in 1797, 105,216 cwt.; in 1798, 203,631 cwt.; and in 1799, 102,767 cwt. *East India Sugar. Papers Respecting the Culture and Manufacture of Sugar* . . . , Appendix I, p. 13.

able Supply of India Sugars, which we hope will prevent the Prices being more Extravagent than they now are." From 1796 on, the Company's importations in jobbers' hands were generally quoted at prices below those on shipments from the Caribbean.[1]

Such successful competition of East Indian sugar with that from the West Indies in the home market despite fiscal advantages enjoyed by the latter, and its effect in preventing a rise to exorbitant price levels, were disconcerting to the plantation owners. A vigorous attack on the West Indian monopoly by persons interested in trading to the orient inevitably followed.[2] In the face of indisputable evidence of the East India Company's ability to place large quantities on the market at low prices, the planter-merchant interest in Great Britain could only fall back upon the time-worn plea that abolition of their preferential rate would be a contravention of the ancient, existing compact and would spell ruin for the tropical American colonies—an argument given new currency in a propaganda booklet written and issued under the auspices of the Society of West India Planters and Merchants.[3]

This had sufficient weight with the government to render assaults on the colonials' position unavailing. Pitt's proposal to supply European consumers with East Indian sugar largely came to naught in consequence of the high ad valorem charge imposed upon its initial entry into home markets. In 1796, but 23,369 hundredweight of the unrefined East Indian article were exported from Great Britain as against 250,086 hundredweight of muscovado grown in the British West Indies. In 1798, exports were 71,636 hundredweight and 359,-

[1] In December of that year, offerings were made at from 80s. to 84s. for East India sugar and at from 72s. to 94s. for West Indian; in June, 1797, at from 72s. to 78s. and 80s. to 94s. respectively; in September, 1799, at from 52s. to 64s. and 62s. to 98s.; and in June, 1800, at from 48s. to 66s. and 60s. to 86s. Quarterly circulars in the archives of Joseph Travers and Sons, Ltd., London.

[2] See "Cultivation of Sugar, &c. in Bengal," in *Annals of Ag.*, XVII (1792), pp. 504, 505. Anon., *The Right of the West India Merchants to a Double Monopoly of the Sugar-Market of Great Britain, and the Expedience of all Monopolies, Examined* (London, 1793). Anon., "A Planter and Distiller in Bengal," *Bengal Sugar. An Account of the Method and Expence of Cultivating the Sugar Cane in Bengal, with Calculations of the First Cost to the Manufacturer and Exporter, and Suggestions for Attracting that Article of Eastern Produce Exclusively to Great Britain* (London, 1794). [Henry T. Colebrooke], *Remarks on the Present State of the Husbandry and Commerce of Bengal* (Calcutta, 1795), pp. 105 ff.

[3] Gilbert Francklyn, *Remarks on a Pamphlet, Entitled "Bengal Sugar"* . . . (London, 1795).

050 hundredweight respectively, and in 1800 a total of 59,446 hundredweight as against 238,574.[1]

The general shortage of tropical products following revolution in St. Domingo stimulated agriculture in the British Caribbean to a marked degree. While the public in Great Britain was resorting to the use of treacle and other saccharous substitutes because of the high cost of sugar,[2] estate owners and their factors were seeking to increase output in every way possible. Only small quantities of land suitable for exploitation remained to be opened; primary attention was therefore paid to the introduction of new species of cane yielding greater quantities of juice and to the adoption of less wasteful methods.

Cultivation of the enormously productive Bourbon and Tahitian varieties was begun at this time and within a few years they had largely replaced the old creole plant. In 1796, Dr. Bryan Higgins was sent to Jamaica by the Society of Planters and Merchants to conduct experiments in improving the process of manufacture, as related elsewhere.[3] The striking development of sugar culture in that colony during the 1790's and immediately after is reflected in the following table.

EXPORTS OF MUSCOVADO FROM JAMAICA [4]

Year	Hogsheads	Tierces	Barrels
1793	77,575	6,722	642
1794	89,532	11,158	1,224
1795	88,851	9,537	1,225
1799	101,457	13,538	1,321
1800	96,347	13,549	1,631
1801	123,251	18,704	2,692

Imports from the West India colonies into Great Britain rose from an annual average of 2,105,567 hundredweight in 1793–1795 to an annual average of 3,591,508 hundredweight in 1801–1803.[5]

Coffee growing, too, expanded at an unprecedented rate during

[1] *East India Sugar. Papers Respecting the Culture and Manufacture of Sugar . . .* , Appendix IV, p. 5.
[2] "Cheap Substitute for Sugar," in *The Scots Mag.*, May, 1795, pp. 303 ff. "Useful Hints. Sugar from Potatoes," in *Ibid.*, March, 1801, p. 179.
[3] Pages 64, 65.
[4] "Exports of Sugar from Jamaica, 1772–1836," in *Gt. Br., H. C., Sess. Pap.,* 1840, VIII (in 527), p. 594.
[5] "Report . . . on the Commercial State of the West India Colonies," in *Gt. Br., H. C., Sess. Pap.,* 1807, III (65), p. 73.

the last decade of the century, especially in Jamaica. We have noted the stimulation afforded by a reduction of duty in 1783.[1] Continental demand encouraged the setting out of new trees to such an extent that imports from the Caribbean colonies into Great Britain soared from 40,736 hundredweight in 1791 to 525,964 hundredweight ten years later,[2] Jamaican exports rose from 2,299,874 to 13,401,468 pounds during the same decade. Production in the island reached its peak in 1814 when 34,045,585 pounds—nearly fifteen times as much as before the ruin of the St. Domingan plantations—were shipped to the mother country.[3]

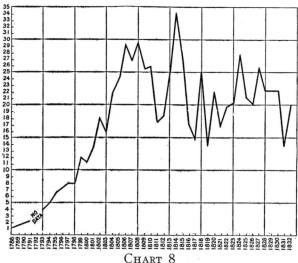

CHART 8

Exports of Coffee from Jamaica, 1788–1832, in Million Pounds *

* Based on *Great Britain, House of Commons, Sessional Papers*, 1840, VIII (in 527), 594.

Like their fellow-colonials, the sugar planters, coffee cultivators in the British West Indies enjoyed a preferential rate against the East India Company. The duty on berries entering the home market

[1] See page 199.

[2] Coffee imports from the British West Indies into Great Britain totalled 90,547 cwt. in 1793 and 181,744 cwt. in 1795. "Report . . . on the Commercial State of the West India Colonies," in *Gt. Br., H. C., Sess. Pap.*, 1807, III (65), p. 75.

[3] Coffee exports from Jamaica were 3,983,576 lbs. in 1793; 6,318,812 lbs. in 1795; and 11,745,425 lbs. in 1799. "Exports of Ginger, Pimento, and Coffee from Jamaica, 1772–1836," in *Gt. Br., H. C., Sess. Pap.*, 1840, VIII (in 527), p. 594. Also reprinted in R. Montgomery Martin, *The British Colonies* (6 vols., London, n.d.), IV, 107.

from the tropical American colonies stood at 10⅝d. per pound in 1792, and that on shipments from the orient at 2s. ⅛d. This disability of 1s. 1½d. against the East Indian product was regularly maintained to 1799 through several advances. West Indian preference was then actually increased through addition of a £2 per cent ad valorem tax on importations made by the East India Company. In 1802, rates were 1s. 6d. as against 2s. 7½d. plus £2 per cent.[1] The more than doubling of the selling price of West Indian coffee between 1793 and 1799 [2] and their favored position in Great Britain brought undreamed of wealth to the British coffee growers beyond the Atlantic.

Revolutionary excesses in France meanwhile brought about strained relations between that country and her traditional foe across the Channel. The execution of Louis XVI in January 1793 was the signal for the outbreak of hostilities which were promptly carried to the West Indies. Disturbances had arisen in most of the French Caribbean possessions since 1789. Now, torn by dissension and without assistance from the métropole, the French islanders were in no position to meet the foreign danger and success was for the most part on the side of the British. Tobago, which had come into the possession of Great Britain in 1763 and had been opened up by British planters and British capital, but which had again passed under French control at the close of the American Revolution,[3] was captured in April 1793 after feeble resistance on the part of a handful of soldiers and officials. The residents were predominantly Eng-

---

[1] In 1795, the rates were increased to 1s. 5⅛d. and 2s. 6⅝d. respectively; in 1796, to 1s. 5¼d. and 2s. 6¾d.; in 1797, to 1s. 5½d. and 2s. 7d.; in 1798, to 1s. 5⅞d. and 2s. 7⅜d.; in 1799, to 1s. 5⅞d. and 2s.7⅜d. plus £2 per cent ad valorem. "Rates of Duty on Coffee . . . 1792–1829," in Gt. Br., H. C., Sess. Pap., 1830, XXV (466).

[2] See page 206.

[3] Large debts remained due British merchants at the time of the transfer. An arrêt of 1786 resulted in numerous judgments of confiscation against them on the ground of alleged usury. The creditors thereupon appealed to the national assembly of France for a repeal of the measure in question. See Anon., Representation by the Creditors of the Island of Tobago . . . praying for a Repeal of the Arrêt of 29th July, 1786 . . . (no imprint, 1791) and the French edition of the same. Representations faites par les Créanciers des Colons de Tabago . . . par lequel ils demandent la révocation de l'Arrêt du 29 Juillet 1786 . . . (no imprint, 1791). Their statement of the case was replied to by M. Roume de Saint-Laurent, author of the well-known scheme to colonize Trinidad with Frenchmen, who was then commissioner and ordonnateur of Tobago. See M. Roume, Mémoire . . . Qui réfute des représentations faites par les Créanciers Anglais des Colons de Tobago . . . (Paris, 1791). Upon the capture of the island in 1793, English law once more went into effect.

lish. They had established no close relations with France, had experienced many hardships under alien rule, and welcomed the re-establishment of British control.[1] Scarborough was subsequently made a free port.[2]

Certain of the foremost St. Domingan planters, chief among whom was Venault de Charmilly, a member of the assembly, had sought refuge in England following the outbreak of disorders in their midst. From the first, they had urged British intervention, claiming that resident whites would most willingly place themselves under the protection of Great Britain. The opportunity of acquiring the richest colony in the Caribbean had been tempting, but no step was taken until after the Anglo-French rupture. In September 1793, an expeditionary force including de Charmilly as an officer, was finally sent eastward from Jamaica. Jeremie, Cap Nicola, Tilburon, and Port au Prince were occupied within the next few months, but losses from yellow fever became so great that further progress was impossible.[3] An exceedingly favourable impression was created by the invaders when they permitted inhabitants of such regions as accepted their rule to export produce to Great Britain at the preferential colonial rates.[4]

In the spring of 1794, a British fleet under Sir John Jervis,[5] transporting military forces headed by Sir Charles Grey, appeared in the Antilles and reduced Martinique, Guadeloupe, and St. Lucia.[6] The

[1] For papers relative to the taking of Tobago, see C. O. 28/64.

[2] 36 Geo. III c. 55.

[3] Papers concerning the St. Domingan expedition will be found in C. O. 137/91–101.

[4] Lieutenant-Governor Williamson to Henry Dundas, Oct. 6, 1793, C. O. 137/91.

[5] Later the Earl of St. Vincent. Capt. E. P. Brenton's *The Life of the Earl of St. Vincent* (2 vols., London, 1838) is unreliable. More accurate but strongly biased is the work of his one-time secretary, Jedediah S. Tucker, *The Memoirs of the Earl of St. Vincent* (2 vols., London, 1844). By far the best book on Jervis is Capt. W. V. Anson's *The Life of John Jervis, Admiral Lord St. Vincent* (London, 1913).

[6] Papers relative to this expedition will be found in C. O. 28/64. A personal narrative is given by Cooper Willyams, a naval chaplain, in his *An Account of the Campaign in the West Indies in the Year 1794* . . . (London, 1796). See also W. M. Gilpin, *Memoirs of Josias Rogers, Esq., Commander of His Majesty's Ship Quebec* (London, 1808). Rogers took part in the attacks on these islands. Secondary accounts are Captain E. O'Callaghan, "Seven British Captures of St. Lucia," in *Colburn's United Service Magazine*, Jan. 1888, pp. 29 ff. and Algernon Aspinall, "Faulknor the Undaunted," in *The W. I. Comm. Circ.*, Feb. 8 and 22, and March 8, 1917, pp. 47–49, 71–74, and 89–92 respectively.

first two were highly developed along agricultural lines; St. Lucia
was valued primarily for its harbor facilities. Sugar cultivation there
had begun only in 1765.[1] Because of the disturbance of normal relations during the American Revolution and hurricane losses, 123
estates of one sort or another had been abandoned by 1787, and fifty-
three others then lay untilled.[2] A few years after the British conquest, forty-one sugar estates, 318 cotton plantations, 118 coffee
properties, and sixty-seven growing cocoa were in operation.[3]

The three colonies formed so rich a prize in every way that their
capture raised the cupidity of Jervis and Grey. Taking Rodney's action at St. Eustatius as a precedent,[4] the commanders declared all
property in them subject to confiscation and levied heavy charges
against the owners for relinquishing alleged rights over the same.

Their action aroused intense indignation among members of the
West India interest in London. The Society of Planters and Merchants declared in a memorial to the Duke of Portland, "The Man
who in the moment of Danger exerts himself for the protection of
his country does not thereby become subject to military Execution,
wherever situated within the range of the Conqueror's Sword."
They denounced "the late deviation from the general Rules of public
Warfare hitherto observed by civilised Nations," called attention to
the magnanimous attitude of the French government toward British
planters following the capture of Grenada in the last war and
declared that, unless these officers' action was promptly disavowed,
British Caribbean colonists must inevitably suffer from retaliations
following future French successes.[5] A further communication, early
in 1795, called for an inquiry into the affair and for official disap-
probation of the principle on which the two had acted.[6]

Neither public opinion nor the government supported Jervis and
Grey; they were, in due course, ordered to refund all sums they
had collected.[7] But this by no means satisfied the West Indians. These
then called upon parliament for a formal denial of the power of a

---

[1] Henry H. Breen, *St. Lucia: Historical, Statistical, and Descriptive* (London, 1844), p. 277.

[2] M. De Latour, *Map of St. Lucia, 1787 . . . Together With a General
Description of the Island* (London, 1883), pp. 3 ff.

[3] In Brigadier-General Provost to the Duke of Portland, Nov. 12, 1799,
C. O. 253/3.

[4] See pages 161 and 162.

[5] *Min. W. I. Plant. and Mer.,* Aug., 28, 1794.

[6] *Ibid.,* Feb. 6, 1795.

[7] *Ibid.,* May 1, 1795.

commander to demand commutation payments in lieu of his exercising any "right" of confiscation [1] and, despite the request of Henry Dundas that they discontinue "a discussion which can have no other tendency than to injure the feelings of meritorious officers, to whose great exertions their country is much indebted, and in particular that part of the British Empire, in which the West India Planters and Merchants are so deeply interested," a committee was named to establish facts.[2]

When the Duke of Portland declared that parliament could not, with any degree of propriety, take such action considering that both men were still in active service,[3] counsel was retained. Grey and Jervis were kept informed of the course of events, accused the colonial group of wilful misrepresentation, and demanded a hearing before the House of Commons.[4] This was accorded. The popular body cleared them of charges of misconduct and confirmed a vote of thanks for services to the nation tendered in the preceding session.[5] In view of the officers' position, no other verdict could have been expected, but, by securing publicity for the episode, the West Indians made certain that no similar attempt on the part of commanders to enrich themselves would be made in the future.

Guadeloupe was again lost after having been in British hands for but a few months; other reverses were suffered during the course of 1795. Victor Hugues, a disciple of Robespierre who had arrived in the Caribbean from France the previous year and who had proclaimed the emancipation of the blacks as well as raised an army of former slaves, recaptured St. Lucia.[6] At the same time, insurrection was stirred up among discontented elements in Dominica, Grenada, and St. Vincent.

These three colonies, although British for more than a quarter of a century, contained large bodies of unassimilated Frenchmen who

[1] *Min. W. I. Plant. and Mer.,* May 4, 1795.
[2] *Ibid.,* May 9, 1795.
[3] *Ibid.,* May 16, 1795.
[4] *Ibid.,* May 25, 1795.
[5] *The Annual Register for 1795,* p. 216.
[6] An excellent account by a participant, one time staff officer to Hugues, is Alexandre M. de Jonnes's *Aventures des Guerres* (2 vols., Paris 1858), translated as *Adventures in Wars of the Republic and Consulate, 1791–1805* (London, 1920). See also Anon., *Facts Relating to the Cruel Treatment of the English Prisoners of War at Point à Pitre and St. Martins* (Antigua, 1796) and Lieut.-Col. H. de Poyen, *Les Guerres des Antilles de 1793 à 1815* (Paris, 1896). The latter is based upon a study of documents in French archives.

clung tenaciously to their speech, religion, and customs, remaining almost wholly apart from their English speaking neighbors. Old ties had been renewed during the years of French occupation in the period of the American Revolution and hopes which might have been entertained for a gradual amalgamation of the two nationalities were dashed to the ground in consequence of the new animosities thus engendered. The situation was particularly critical in Grenada where the French inhabitants were denied the right of election to the assembly, of appointment to the council, and of holding commissions in the militia.[1] Furthermore, the Catholic church lands on the island had recently been confiscated by crown agents and sold.[2]

An attack on Dominica from Guadeloupe was successfully repulsed by a small company of soldiers stationed in the island, aided by the British planters. French residents who had taken up arms in aid of the invaders were defeated and some 600 were deported to England.[3] In Grenada, the French and free people of color rose in civil war during March, imprisoned the lieutenant-governor and the topping British proprietors, and seized control of the government. A struggle, marked by ferocity and wanton destructiveness unlike any hitherto known in the British islands and in many ways paralleling that in St. Domingo, followed. Long dormant hostility having its origin in race hatred was given full play; no quarter was given by either party.[4]

Immediately upon receiving news of the rebellion in Grenada, the Caribs and French of St. Vincent likewise gathered forces against the British. The latter were unable to suppress the movement and only with the utmost difficulty succeeded in maintaining themselves.

[1] Anon., *A Brief Enquiry Into the Causes of, and Conduct Pursued by, the Colonial Government, for Quelling the Insurrection in Grenada . . .* (London, 1796). See also the papers in C. O. 101/30.

[2] Papers relative to this matter will be found in C. O. 101/26, 33.

[3] C. O. 71/27.

[4] For papers connected with the war, see C. O. 101/34, 35. Contemporary accounts are Anon., *A Brief Enquiry;* Anon., *Recit des Troubles Survenus à la Grenade* (no imprint, no date); [Gordon Turnbull], *A Narrative of the Revolt and Insurrection of the French Inhabitants in the Island of Grenada* (Edinburgh, 1795); and Thomas Wise, *A Review of the Events, Which Have Happened in Grenada, from the Commencement of the Insurrection to the 1st of May* (St. George's, Grenada, 1795). John Hay, *A Narrative of the Insurrection in the Island of Grenada, Which took place in 1795* (London, 1823), is the account of an English resident of the island, made a prisoner by the French in March, 1795. This work and that of Turnbull have been used almost exclusively by D. G. Garraway in his *A Short Account of the Insurrection of 1795-96* (Grenada, 1877).

So precarious did their situation become that the dangerous expedient of arming slaves was resorted to.[1]

Civil war ruined the crops of Grenada and St. Vincent and blighted their trade. British merchants, serving as factors for the planters in those colonies, suddenly found themselves called upon to bear advances made in anticipation of consignments for 1795 and stood upon the verge of bankruptcy. In that critical situation, they turned to parliament for assistance. A petition in their behalf was presented by Lord Sheffield, their case was promptly heard,[2] and, with the support of Pitt and Dundas, a measure designed to afford ample relief was adopted. This act authorized the issuing of exchequer bills to an amount not exceeding £1,500,000 at any one time to such persons in Great Britain connected with the two islands who might be in straits occasioned by the late disasters and who were in a position to provide proper security. Loans were to be made through commissioners, were to bear interest at the rate of 5 per cent, and were to be repaid in three equal installments on January 5 and October 10, 1797, and July 5, 1798.[3]

This somewhat unusual piece of emergency legislation had the salutary effect of saving the business interests it was designed to aid. Certain planters, too, subsequently sought loans to cover the cost of reconstruction. But the ravaging of the islands proved to be so extensive that it was found politic on several occasions to advance the date for repayment. Thus, in 1797, an extension of two years was granted.[4] Various borrowers were still in difficulties in 1800. Alexander Houston and Company of Glasgow, who had been advanced £240,000, then owed £265,008 with interest; the estate of Charles Ashwell, which had received £16,000, owed £17,177; and the indebtedness of William Johnstone, a London merchant who had been loaned £10,000, totalled £11,209.[5] Further acts extended the final

---

[1] Shephard, *St. Vincent,* pp. 61–174.

[2] "Report from the Committee, to whom the Petition of the Merchants connected with, and trading to, the Islands of Grenada and Saint Vincent, was referred," in *Gt. Br., H. C., Sess. Pap.,* 1794–95, XV (119).

[3] 35 Geo. III c. 127. A precedent for such procedure had been set in 1793 when, by 33 Geo. III c. 29, the loan of exchequer bills to the amount of £5,000,000 to merchants and bankers of Great Britain was authorized in order that they might be tided over a financial crisis which began at the close of the previous year.

[4] 37 Geo. III c. 27.

[5] "Reports of the Committee to whom the Petition of William McDowall, Esquire, and also the Petition of the Executors of Charles Ashwell, deceased, and William Johnstone, late of the Island of Grenada, Esquire, were severally referred," in *Gt. Br., H. C., Sess. Pap.,* 1799–1800, XXVIII (171).

date for repayment to March 5, 1804.[1] By 1802, a total of £1,179,300 had been placed at the disposal of persons with interests in Grenada and £188,300 had been made available to others connected with St. Vincent. No less than £734,270 of the former and £104,633 of the latter then still remained unpaid.[2]

The need for soldiers on the continent of Europe was so pressing and the mortality among whites in tropical American service was so high that the home government in 1795 requested the colonial legislatures to form black corps for purposes of local defence. This proposal left the islanders aghast; they declared that placing weapons in the hands of negroes, slaves or free, would mark the end of white supremacy and would precipitate a reign of terror like that in St. Domingo.[3] Despite such opposition, the plan was inaugurated on a small scale, as we have seen.[4] French gains in the Caribbean meanwhile occasioned sharp criticism of the ministry, and it became necessary for Dundas to make a public defense before the House of Commons on April 28, 1796, in which he maintained that reverses were in no way attributable to governmental negligence.[5]

Although confronted by much greater problems arising from operations in the old world, the repulsing of the enemy in the West Indies became a matter of great concern to Pitt. Generals Ralph Abercromby and John Moore effected the reduction of St. Lucia in May, 1796. Such Frenchmen and free blacks as surrendered were transported to England as prisoners of war. Moore assumed the governorship of the island and began the slow task of wearing out bands of guerillas in the interior while Abercromby went to the relief of St. Vincent and Grenada.

Necessity dictated a strong show of force which would make a repetition of the late horrors impossible. Immediately following the suppression of insurrection in the latter island, therefore, the rebels were rounded up. They were given summary trials and were hanged in wholesale fashion; the least culpable were banished and their property was confiscated.[6] The Frenchmen in St. Vincent were similarly

[1] 39 Geo. III c. 11. 39/40 Geo. III c. 13. 41 Geo. III c. 27.
[2] "Loans to Planters and Merchants Interested in the Islands of Grenada and St. Vincent," in *Gt. Br., H. C., Sess. Pap.*, 1801–02, IV (43), p. 159.
[3] See for example the view of the assembly of Barbados, in C. O. 28/65.
[4] Pages 32 and 33.
[5] *Facts Relative to the Conduct of the War in the West Indies: Collected from the Speech of the Right Hon. Henry Dundas . . . and from the Documents Laid Before the House Upon That Subject* (London, 1796).
[6] Papers covering the punishments meted out will be found in C. O. 101/34–37.

dealt with.[1] The Caribs, to the number of 5,000, were deported to the islet of Balliceaux in the Grenadines as they were captured and were subsequently removed to the island of Ruatan in Honduras Bay.[2]

The expulsion of the Caribs raised the question of what disposition should be made of the region set aside for them following the native war of 1772.[3] Sound policy demanded that the formation of great estates be prevented, that the land be sold rather than distributed in the form of free grants, and that there be no sales to speculators. Writing to the Duke of Portland, Governor Bentinck declared "Great caution should be used in the disposal of the Lands to prevent a Monopoly of Estates, which if sold in large quantities must be the Case, for the purpose of retailing the Land at high prices. Such a disposal of the Charaib country would decidedly prevent its settlement for some Years, and destroy the very object in View. I should therefore recommend that Purchasers should enter into a Contract to lay out adequate Sums or cultivate a certain proportion upon every Grant in a given time, in default of which the Grant should become Void, and the Land revert to the Crown."[4]

President Ottley recommended that tracts suitable for the cultivation of sugar be disposed of to the higher bidders. When certain colonists proposed that the Carib country be distributed among sufferers in the late struggle to indemnify them for losses, Ottley declared that this would be impolitic, since any division which might be made would most certainly lead to dissatisfaction and quarrels.[5] Somewhat later, when considering ways in which the white population of the island might be increased, this executive suggested that grants of from forty to fifty acres each be made to families of poor whites coming out from England. He urged, however, that mere seven year leasehold rights be given immigrants and then only upon the express condition that cultivation be immediately undertaken. Parcels of land thus received should be inalienable and title in fee simple should be given to no settlers, except those who had shown themselves industrious and in every way worthy during the seven year period.[6]

No action was taken until the opening of the nineteenth century. At length, in 1802, under pressure from the estate owners, Governor

[1] See C. O. 260/14.
[2] Papers relative to the removal of these unhappy natives will be found in C. O. 260/15.
[3] See page 117.
[4] December 22, 1798, C. O. 260/16.
[5] Despatch to the Duke of Portland, June 6, 1799, C. O. 260/16.
[6] President Ottley to Lord Hobart, May 7, 1802, C. O. 260–17.

Bentinck granted the use of 5,262 acres to veterans of the war, the same to be held during the pleasure of the Crown. The leading colonists shared in this provisional disposition of a portion of the old reserve and new fields were immediately opened in the expectation that the land would eventually be placed upon the market and might then be purchased by the holders. As a step in that direction, a local act of 1804 declared the natives to have forfeited their rights by rebellion and revested the Carib country in the king.[1]

But all calculations were upset when word reached the colony that a grant of 6,000 acres suitable for cultivation had been made by the home government to Colonel Thomas Browne, an American loyalist. This individual, a Georgia planter, had commanded forces of irregulars and had served as superintendent of the Indian tribes attached to the British army during the Revolution. He had removed to the Bahamas after 1783; but, as the soil there proved infertile and as a French attack from St. Domingo was feared, he wished to locate elsewhere and was successful in his application for a share of the rich, newly-available land of St. Vincent.[2]

News of the Browne grant created a tense situation in the island. Andrew Ross, a member of the council, Alexander Cruikshank, speaker of the assembly, and John Cruikshank and John Keane, both magistrates, were among the occupants of the territory given over to the former Georgian. They refused to vacate and were consequently suspended from office by the new governor, Beckwith. Ross was a colonel in the militia, John Cruikshank a lieutenant-colonel, and Keane a captain. All were dismissed from their commands. The commissions of Lieutenant-Colonel Sebastian French, Captain Thomas Patterson, Lieutenant Robert Sutherland, and Lieutenant Alexander Cumming, who were also cultivating land included in the Browne grant and would not surrender it, were likewise revoked.[3] Ross and Keane died while under suspension, and Browne was slated for the former's office.[4]

Brought face to face with such violent opposition on the part of the colonials, the Lords Commissioners of the Treasury ordered a temporary suspension of the entire grant.[5] Occupants attempted to purchase their portions from the Colonel at £20 an acre or to cultivate

[1] Shephard, *St. Vincent*, p. 178.
[2] *Ibid.*, pp. 180, 181.
[3] Governor Beckwith to William Windham, May 20, 1806, C. O. 260/20.
[4] Beckwith to Windham, Oct. 7, 1806, C. O. 260/20.
[5] Windham to Beckwith, Oct. 3, 1806, C. O. 260/20.

them under leave from him, but he would entertain neither proposition.[1] Meanwhile, a group of his negroes arriving from the Bahamas was put to work laying out a plantation within the limits of the territory assigned him.[2]

A settlement was ultimately effected whereby each holder of Carib land was given the opportunity of securing title to his portion by making a payment of its original unimproved value to the Crown. Those refusing to do so would forfeit all claims that might have arisen from their occupancy. Properties reverting to the king in this manner were to be transferred to the Colonel upon his paying the Crown the value of such improvements as had been made thereon.[3] Under this arrangement, the loyalist leader received but 1,700 acres. The remaining 4,300 were disposed of to the occupants at £22.10.0 each and Browne was given £25,000 of the sum thus realized as compensation for failing to receive the entire acreage originally set aside for him. His celebrated grant was thus divided into eight large estates.[4]

While Grenada and St. Vincent were undergoing the devastation of civil war, Jamaica was suddenly confronted with a formidable rebellion of the Maroons, descendants of Spanish plantation hands, who had fled into the interior of the island at the time of the English conquest, and bodies of British slaves who had successfully resisted capture in the early part of the eighteenth century. Since about 1740, these bands of blacks had been recognized as free, had occupied reserves assigned to them, and had been left undisturbed under the rule of their own chieftains assisted by white superintendents. A series of grievances arising from the actions of such a white resident culminated in revolt in 1795, following the administration of floggings to two Maroons found guilty of theft by a much-despised slave.

Military leaders found it impossible to make headway in the wild mountain retreats of these negro tribesmen and, with events in St. Domingo striking terror into the hearts of all West Indian whites, desperate measures were adopted to crush the uprising before disaffection had spread among the slaves. A hundred man-hunting bloodhounds in charge of forty keepers were secured from Cuba through

[1] Shephard, *St. Vincent*, pp. 181, 182.
[2] Beckwith to Windham, Nov. 24, 1806, C. O. 260/21.
[3] *St. Vincent. By His Excellency George Beckwith . . . a Proclamation* [Kingston, 1807], in C. O. 260/22.
[4] Shephard, *St. Vincent*, pp. 182, 183. For a map showing the limits of the Browne grant (1829), see T 62, Public Record Office.

courtesy of the Spanish governor. So savage were these beasts that a negress striking one was torn to bits and a soldier teasing one suffered severe laceration of his arm and was saved from death only with great difficulty, while four of them caught a steer and tore it asunder in a moment.[1]

Use of these ferocious animals had most salutary effects; they proved more efficacious than regiments of soldiery, for they frightened the blacks. At the close of the year, a treaty was concluded between the Maroon leaders and General Walpole, whereby the former agreed to make immediate submission in return for being permitted to remain in the island. But, as their followers were widely scattered, the chiefs had difficulty in getting them together, and the day set for a formal surrender passed without the several bands putting in an appearance. The lieutenant-governor, the Earl of Balcarres, an imperious individualist, thereupon declared the treaty to have been broken and, despite the vigorous protests of Walpole, who felt his honor to be at stake, imprisoned the Maroons upon their eventual arrival and, in the spring of 1796, deported 600 to Nova Scotia. Those who survived the rigors of the climate were removed to Sierra Leone four years later through the efforts of English humanitarians.[2]

[1] The Earl of Balcarres to the Duke of Portland, Dec. 29, 1795, C. O. 137/96.

[2] Papers covering the war, the surrender, the dispute between Walpole and Lord Balcarres, and the deportation will be found in C. O. 137/95–97. See also "Letters Respecting the Settlement of the Maroons of Jamaica in Nova Scotia," in *Gt. Br., H. C., Sess. Pap.,* 1796–97, XLIV (889, 890); "Papers Relative to the Settling of the Maroons in Nova Scotia," in *Gt. Br., H. C., Sess. Pap.,* 1797–98, XLV (925a); [Bryan Edwards], "Observations on the . . . Maroons and a Detail of the Origin, Progress, and Termination of the Late War Between Those People and the White Inhabitants," prefaced to *The Proceedings of the Governor and Assembly of Jamaica, in Regard to the Maroon Negroes* (London, 1796), also published as *An Account of the Maroon Negroes in Jamaica and a History of the War in the West Indies* (London, 1807); *Proceeding of the Honourable House of Assembly relative to the Maroons: including the correspondence between the Right Honourable Earl Balcarres and the Honourable Major General Walpole, during the Maroon rebellion; with the Report of the joint Special Secret Committee, to whom those papers were referred* (St. Jago de la Vega, 1796); "The Rise, Progress, and Termination of the Maroon War, Illustrated by a Selection from the Public Despatches and Private Correspondence of Alex. Earl of Balcarres . . . ," in Alexander Lindsay, *Lives of the Lindsays,* III, ix–xlviii and 7–192. Dallas, *History of the Maroons,* has slight historical value. Other secondary works are Anon., "The Maroons of Jamaica," in *Once a Week,* Dec. 16, 1865; Lady Blake, "The Maroons of Jamaica," in *The North American Review,* Nov. 1898, pp. 558 ff.; [Col. T. W. Higginson], "The Maroons of Jamaica," in *The Atlantic Monthly,* V, 213 ff. For their subsequent removal to Sierra Leone, see page 272.

This unfortunate affair aroused intense feeling in Great Britain. King George III himself expressed his abhorrence at the use of dogs and Lord Balcarres was ordered "to remove forthwith and to extirpate from the Island, the whole Race of those tremendous Animals. . . ."[1] So severe were denunciations of this native war that the assembly felt called upon to publish a complete set of official papers relative to it both in the colony and in England.[2] At the same time Mr. Sewell, the island agent, was requested to secure legal advice as to whether or not the printer of *The New Annual Register* could be sued for libel because of having published an account of happenings, denominated "the greatest compilation of Falsehoods and wilful Misrepresentations."[3] He advised, however, that it be ignored and left to oblivion.[4] A knowledge of the true situation in the American tropics, with insurrection running its bloody course in near-by St. Domingo and with French revolutionists seeking to ferment disorder in Great Britain's colonies, does much to exculpate the Jamaicans in their handling of the Maroons.

Success continued with the British in the south Caribbean during 1796 and 1797. Since Holland and Spain had been drawn into the European conflict as allies of France, their possessions were now lawful prizes. An expedition sent from Barbados to the South American mainland upon the solicitation of British merchants trading to Demerara[5] captured that colony and Essequibo without resistance.

[1] The Duke of Portland to the Earl of Balcarres, March 3, 1796, C. O. 137/96.

[2] Listed under note 2, page 226.

[3] The Earl of Balcarres to the Duke of Portland, Dec. 12, 1796, C. O. 137/98. For the account in question, see *The New Annual Register for 1795*, p. 255. It denounced the "war of extermination" proclaimed against the Maroons and waxed eloquent against the use of bloodhounds "to hunt down these wretched Indians."

[4] Portland to Balcarres, April 7, 1797, C. O. 137/98.

[5] Fortescue, *British Army*, IV, 431, 432. The author is severe in his denunciation of the self-interest which brought about this expedition. He declares that it was undertaken "almost avowedly, not for the furtherance of any object in the war, but to secure the profits of a clique of merchants who had ventured their capital, from motives the reverse of patriotic, in the Dutch colonies. It was nothing that a British General, worn down with anxiety and overwork, was striving with a handful of sickly exhausted troops to stem the overwhelming flood of negro insurrection; nothing, that six hundred men in British pay should be shipped off together with their British officers at huge expense to their death; nothing, that other merchants and planters in the British West Indies should have their property exposed to devastation and themselves and their families to unspeakable outrage and murder. Such considerations were not to be weighed in the balance against the sacred property of the West India Committee, that blind, selfish, and rapacious body which—I write

Their produce was at once admitted to the British market, shipments being made for the most part by way of Bridgetown, with the Barbadains levying a 4½ per cent import tax on all consignments as a means of counter-balancing the duty payable upon exportation of their own produce.[1] In February 1797, the Spaniards surrendered Trinidad to Abercromby, commanding a force sent from Martinique. San Josef was thereupon made a free port.[2]

The foothold gained in St. Domingo in 1793 was meanwhile gradually being lost. Not only was no further progress made after 1794— the British could not even maintain their position. The death toll from yellow fever was appalling. Of 18,000 soldiers sent to the island in 1795 and 1796, no less than 7,300 had perished of that disease by September of the former year, and by the end of 1796 another 5,000 were dead.[3]

Members of the London West India interest had no desire to see the colony under British control. Its enormous production, poured into the home market, would lower prices, destroy their privileged position, and ruin them. Bryan Edwards, able spokesman for the group, consequently turned his pen to a history of the island in which he stressed the frightful human cost of the occupation, denounced the conduct of the French planters toward those who had come to their rescue, and sought to show the impolicy of continued interference in affairs there.[4] This brought forth a reply by Colonel de Charmilly who had sought to secure a transfer of St. Domingo to British sovereignty, in which the self-interest of the planters in opposing its acquisition was berated.[5]

In 1798, the government abandoned all attempts at conquest and occupation. General Maitland, representing Great Britain, entered

not in haste nor without investigation and experience—has for two centuries and a half been the curse of the West Indies" (p. 432). It is interesting to note that the latter statement was retracted in 1923 and will not appear in future editions.

[1] See C. O. 28/65. On the Barbadian export tax, see pages 104 ff.

[2] 37 Geo. III c. 77.

[3] See Hector M'Lean, *An Enquiry Into the Nature and Causes of the Great Mortality Among the Troops at St. Domingo* . . . (London, 1797).

[4] *An Historical Survey of the French Colony in the Island of St. Domingo* . . . (London, 1797).

[5] *Lettre à Monsieur Bryan Edwards, . . . en Refutation de son Ouvrage Intitulé Vues Historiques sur la Colonie Française de Saint-Dominique* (Londres, 1797) ; in English translation, *Answer by Way of a Letter to Bryan Edwards, Esq., M.P., F.R.S., Planter of Jamaica, etc. Containing a Refutation of His "Historical Survey on the French Colony of St. Domingo, etc.,"* (London, 1797).

into a treaty with the negro leader, Toussaint L'Ouverture, whereby the British forces were to be withdrawn. Such French proprietors as had accepted foreign protection went with them. The St. Domingo fiasco was ended.[1]

When France undertook to regain control three years later, no obstacle was thrown in her way as L'Ouverture's continuance in power threatened the West Indians more than did restoration of the colony to the old mother land.[2] French officers who had served in St. Domingo under the British, including de Charmilly, took refuge in Jamaica, where they were frequently entertained at the government house.[3] Most cordial relations existed between the French seeking to reduce St. Domingo and British officials. Madame Leclerc,[4] whose husband, Captain-General Victor Leclerc, commanded the army from France, sent Lady Nugent, wife of the lieutenant-governor of Jamaica, "a pink and silver dress," "a second cargo of Parisian fashions," and "a beautiful muslin handkerchief, embroidered in gold," which was used as a mantle in the christening of George Edward, the Nugent heir. The Jamaican executive and his wife reciprocated with some English cut glass and a "hobby-horse with silver appointments," the latter intended for little Astyanax Leclerc.[5]

The menace to the West Indian proprietors' position, which the free admission of produce from newly acquired territories into the home market entailed, came to an end in 1802 with the restoration of all conquests in the Caribbean country, excepting Trinidad under the Treaty of Amiens—a settlement winning the planters' and merchants' unanimous support.

The nine year war with France resulted in a complete breakdown of the system of restricted American trade inaugurated at the close of the Revolution. Captures by French privateers, the removal of carriers from West Indian waters, and heavy losses accompanying attacks and civil war brought on a severe shortage of stores. Lumber sold in Jamaica rose from £11–£12.10.0 per thousand feet to as high as £16–£18 by November 1793.[6] In the same year, mess beef was quoted in Dominica at £7.8.6, mess pork at £8.5.0, and flour at £5.15.6

---

[1] See Colonel Chalmers, *Remarks on the Late War in St. Domingo* (London, 1803).

[2] Private and confidential despatch from Lord Hobart to Lieutenant-Governor Nugent, Nov. 18, 1801, C. O. 137/106.

[3] Cundall, ed., *Lady Nugent's Journal*, pp. 45, 48–50, 62, 63.

[4] Formerly Pauline Bonaparte, sister of Napoleon.

[5] Cundall, ed., *Lady Nugent's Journal*, pp. 142, 149, 156, 157, 167.

[6] *Votes of the . . . Assembly of Jamaica . . . 1793*, p. 96.

per barrel.[1] In 1795, after the French had been repulsed, these commodities were priced at £9.18.0, £10.14.0, and £7.8.6 respectively while rice sold at £4.4.6 per hundredweight and peas at £3.6.0 per barrel.[2] At the close of the Carib war in 1796, pitch-pine boards and planks were offered in St. Vincent at £26.8.0 per thousand feet, white-pine boards and planks at £16.10.0, shingles at £5.15.6 per thousand, beef and pork at £16.10.0 per barrel, flour at £7.8.6, herrings at £4.19.0 per barrel, and Indian corn at £1 per bushel.[3]

A visitor to Antigua in 1796 found prices very high;[4] Lord Lavington, governor of the Leewards, wrote in 1801: "Such is the enormous & frightful Price of all the Necessaries of Life, at this Time, in the West Indies [that] with all the Management & Frugality that the best Occonomist can practice, £3,000 a Year, in Addition to the Profits of my Government, will not by any Means defray the Expenses of my Domestic Establishment in it."[5]

Relief from scarcity and mounting prices was sought by authorizing importations in British bottoms from the foreign islands, by granting vessels of friendly nations access to British Caribbean ports and allowing them to barter their cargoes for rum and molasses, and, as a last resort, by permitting them to take sugar in payment.

The neutrals profiting most by the situation in the Antilles were the Americans. Under two decrees of February 19, and March 26, 1793,[6] they were admitted to trade with the French colonies upon mere payment of the duties charged French citizens.[7] Members of the London West India interest, in conference with Dundas during the summer of 1794, urged that ships from the United States be given similar privileges in British colonial ports.[8]

The necessity of suffering them to engage in the West India trade was so patent that the Jay treaty,[9] negotiated in the same year,

---

[1] "Current Prices," in C. O. 71/24.
[2] "Current Prices," in C. O. 71/28.
[3] In Governor Seton to the Duke of Portland, May 22, 1797, C. O. 260/14.
[4] Baily, Journal of a Tour, pp. 94, 95.
[5] To the Duke of Portland, April 22, C. O. 152/80.
[6] Girault, Principes de Colonisation, I, 239.
[7] Lieut-Gov., Stanley to Henry Dundas, June 27, 1793, C. O. 152/74.
[8] Min. W. I. Plant. and Mer., June 13 and 20, July 3, 1794.
[9] See Samuel F. Bemis, Jay's Treaty. A Study in Commerce and Diplomacy (New York, 1823); Bemis, "The London Mission of Thomas Pinckney, 1792–1796," in The Am. Hist. Rev., January, 1923, pp. 228 ff.; William Jay, The Life of John Jay (2 vols., New York, 1833); Henry Johnston, The Correspondence and Public Papers of John Jay (4 vols., New York, n.d.); George Pellew, John Jay (Boston, 1890); William Whitelock, Life and Times of John Jay (New York, 1887).

temporarily accorded them the privilege. American vessels of not over seventy tons burden were to be allowed to enter American produce and manufactures into the British Caribbean possessions for the period of the war and two years thereafter, without discriminating duties being levied against them. They might export the products of the islands to the United States but that country must engage to prohibit the carrying of molasses, sugar, coffee, cacao, and cotton in its bottoms from either its own harbors or those in the British West Indies to other parts of the world.[1]

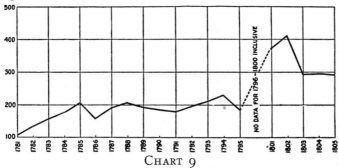

CHART 9

Imports of Muscovado Sugar, the Growth of British Plantations, from the British West Indies into Great Britain, 1781–1795 and 1801–1805, in Million Pounds *

* Based on Custom House Statistics in "Report from the Committee on the Commercial State of the West India Colonies," in *Great Britain, House of Commons, Sessional Papers, 1807,* III (65), 73 and Benjamin Moseley, *A Treatise on Sugar* (London, 1799), p. 193. (The original Custom House records for this period have been destroyed.)

Unhappily, the Senate considered the conditions surrounding this concession on the part of Great Britain too onerous and rejected that article of the treaty embracing it. In consequence, American trade with the British sugar colonies officially continued to rest on the footing established by the regulating act of 1788;[2] but through its repeated temporary suspension by the governors of the several West India islands, traders from the United States enjoyed free entry for practically the whole period of the war, and that measure was virtually abrogated. Frequent acts of indemnification were passed by

[1] *Treaty of Amity, Commerce, and Navigation, Between His Britannic Majesty and the United States of America . . . Nov. 19, 1794* (London, 1795). The treaty is briefed in Macpherson, *Annals of Commerce,* IV, 313 ff.

[2] See page 188.

parliament to protect the colonial executives from legal process in consequence of their having authorized such suspensions.[1]

The ports of Grenada were opened early in 1793 for the importation in British bottoms of corn, staves, heading, shingles, and boards from foreign settlements.[2] In the summer, when not over a month's stock of lumber and provisions remained in the island, the Americans were permitted to enter [3] and continued to come freely throughout the civil war and after.[4] Writing in 1805, Governor Maitland reported, "This indulgence has been, I am informed, extended without Intermission in this Colony, since the period of the Insurrection." [5]

Vessels of all nations in amity with Great Britain were admitted into Barbados in the first summer of the war.[6] Following a representation of the Jamaican assembly that the local supply of lumber was low, the governor in the late fall of 1793 opened the colony's ports to neutral vessels laden with such cargoes.[7] Proclamations authorizing the importation of supplies into Dominica in neutral bottoms were renewed quarterly for the greater part of the decade 1793–1803.[8] Neutral vessels were first admitted into Tobago in the spring of 1794; the privilege then accorded them was frequently renewed.[9] The ports of St. Vincent, too, were opened to neutral vessels in 1793.[10] All such suspensions of the act of 1788 were "not disapproved" by the home government.[11]

The temporary embargo laid on shipping by the American government in March, 1794, threatened general scarcity in Great Britain's Caribbean possessions and led to actual shortage in Grenada.[12] The

[1] 36 Geo. III c. 32. 37 Geo. III c. 64. 38 Geo. III c. 72. 39 Geo. III c. 57. 39/40 Geo. III c. 76.

[2] Lieutenant-Governor Home to Henry Dundas, Feb. 15, 1793, C. O. 101/33.

[3] Home to Dundas, Aug. 31, and Dec. 31, 1793, May 2, and Aug. 1, 1794, C. O. 101/33.

[4] See sundry proclamations in C. O. 101/34, 35.

[5] To Earl Camden, August 13, C. O. 101/42.

[6] Governor Parry to Henry Dundas, Aug. 3, 1793, C. O. 28/64.

[7] Votes of the . . . Assembly of Jamaica . . . 1793, pp. 26, 27, 136.

[8] Lord Hobart to Governor Prevost, Sept. 23, 1803, C. O. 71/36.

[9] Governor Ricketts to Henry Dundas, April 28, 1794; President Robley to Dundas, Sept. 11, 1794 and Feb. 21, 1795; Governor Lindsay to the Duke of Portland, Feb. 1, 1796, in C. O. 285/3 and President Robley to the Duke of Portland, Dec. 22, 1800, C. O. 285/7.

[10] Governor Seton to Henry Dundas, July 1 and Nov. 10, 1793, C. O. 260/12.

[11] See for example the Duke of Portland to President Robley of Tobago, May 6, 1795, C. O. 285/3.

[12] Lieutenant-Governor Home to Henry Dundas, Aug. 1, 1794, C. O. 101/33.

planter-merchant body in London urged the home government to meet the situation by permitting supply ships to leave British waters without waiting for convoys and by offering bounties on stores of all kinds from British North America and on lumber from the Baltic, shipped to the West Indies. Vessels laden with provisions were promptly authorized to sail unattended whenever specific request was made to the Privy Council.[1] The embargo was, however, lifted at about the same time and this resulted in the West Indian market again being well supplied from the Atlantic seaboard states. Such permission was consequently little sought.

In the Leewards alone were the Americans long denied right of entry. The importation of stores from neutral colonies in British bottoms was sanctioned by Governor Woodley in the summer of 1793; but, although scarcity continued, John Stanley, temporarily in charge of affairs following that executive's death, resolutely refused to admit vessels from the United States.[2] To meet shortages in Antigua and Montserrat, he despatched convoyed merchantmen to St. Eustatius and St. Bartholomew[3] for supplies.[4] Authorization to admit lumber and foodstuffs in neutral bottoms when absolutely necessary was subsequently received,[5] but only after the assembly of Antigua had made a fourth application for such action did Stanley give his consent early in 1794. Even then, no salt provisions could be entered by neutrals.[6] Fearful lest the privilege thus reluctantly accorded be again withdrawn, the Antiguans directed W. Hutchinson, the island agent, to petition the home government for a formal opening of the trade with the mainland during the continuance of the war.[7]

Stanley's attitude was not capricious. He viewed the duties of his office seriously, the more so since he might have gained some thousands of pounds sterling through privateering had the government not devolved upon him. His conduct attracted marked attention and high praise was accorded him by his superiors in England. He was furthermore slated for the governorship of Guadeloupe and

[1] *Min. W. I. Plant. and Mer.*, June 20, 1794; *Min. W. I. Mer.*, June 27, 1794.

[2] John Stanley to Henry Dundas, July 27, 1793, C. O. 152/74.

[3] Under Swedish sovereignty since July 1, 1784, when it had been traded to that power by France in exchange for the right to establish an entrepôt in Gothenburg.

[4] Stanley to Dundas, Aug. 15, and Sept. 7, 1793, C. O. 152/74.

[5] Dundas to Stanley, Oct. 31, 1793, C. O. 152/74.

[6] Stanley to Dundas, Dec. 31, 1793 and Jan. 11, 1794, C. O. 152/74.

[7] The petitions, dated July 2, 1794, will be found in C. O. 152/75.

would have assumed charge of the island government, had not the turn in the fortunes of war already noted brought about its recapture by the French.[1]

The home government, then, in the exigencies of war, raised no objections to the mainlanders' entering colonial Caribbean ports and their clearing out with cargoes of rum and molasses. But sugar was so scarce in Great Britain that its exportation from the West India colonies to the United States was steadfastly opposed. Nevertheless, when the Americans refused payment for their supplies in any form but sugar or cash, Governor Ricketts of Barbados suffered them to take the former in amounts not exceeding a third the value of their cargoes.[2] After the outbreak of civil war in St. Vincent, its shipment from there to America was authorized by Governor Seton; a total of 559 hogsheads, eighty-six tierces, and 351 barrels was cleared out for the United States up to February 1797.[3] Free exportation by the Americans was also permitted in the Leewards soon after Stanley's departure.[4] In Grenada, customs officers connived at such action and refused to answer Lieutenant-Governor Houston's queries in regard to it.[5] Orders were consequently sent to the West India governors in a circular despatch of December 9, 1796, forbidding the practice.[6]

But the need for supplies was so great in Barbados that, when the Americans persisted in their refusal to accept plantation by-products, they were illegally permitted to take sugar in partial payment for their stocks as in the past.[7] In 1799, upon urgent request of the legislatures of Antigua and Nevis, following a shortage of shipping, President Robert Thomson granted Americans the privilege of bartering sugar to a third the value of supplies they landed there for a period of six months.[8] This violation of instructions occasioned a protest on the part of the Society of West India Merchants [9] and resulted in the acting executive being severely reprimanded. Thomson's conduct was held to be "inaccountable and unjustifiable," he

[1] The Duke of Portland to Stanley, Jan. 9, 1795, C. O. 152/76.
[2] Ricketts to the Duke of Portland, Feb. 16, 1797, C. O. 28/65.
[3] Seton to the Duke of Portland, Feb. 16, 1797, C. O. 260/14.
[4] Archibald Esdaile to the Duke of Portland, Sept. 20, 1796, C. O. 152/78.
[5] Houston to the Duke of Portland, Feb. 21, 1797, C. O. 101/35.
[6] See acknowledgment in President Thomas to the Duke of Portland, Feb. 12, 1797, C. O. 152/78 and reference in circular of July 1, 1799, C. O. 324/103.
[7] Governor Ricketts to the Duke of Portland, Aug. 19, 1799, C. O. 28/65.
[8] Thomson to the Duke of Portland, April 10, 1799 and enclosures, C. O. 152/79.
[9] *Min. W. I. Mer.*, July 4, 1799.

was reminded that any breach of the navigation laws was highly penal, and was threatened with the most signal marks of the royal displeasure if he allowed further exportations to take place.[1] A new circular letter declared it to be absolutely necessary for governors to put an end to such practices.[2]

Despite such positive orders, Governor Ricketts of Barbados continued to disregard the wishes of the ministry on the ground that making full payment in money would be ruinous to the circulation. He however reduced exportation in American vessels from one-third to one-fourth the value of the supplies entered.[3] As he died soon after, the Duke of Portland vented his wrath in a despatch to President Bishop in which he fulminated against Ricketts and threatened his temporary successor with removal and a fine of £1,000 if such exportation were not forthwith and entirely stopped.[4]

Bishop, needless to say, lost no time in obeying such a peremptory command.[5] Prices rose sharply at once[6] and the Americans' disinclination to barter for rum and molasses resulted in such a shortage of stores that by October all bakeries had closed for want of flour and the few barrels remaining in dealers' hands sold for £30 each at auction. But illegal exportation of sugar formally ceased.[7]

In 1800, in consequence of a glutting of the British market, a scarcity of carriers, and a lack of specie, the Earl of Balcarres authorized the exportation of any island products from Jamaica by the Americans to the value of the stores they entered.[8] Heavy shipments of sugar were immediately made whereupon he, too, was strongly called to account and threatened with removal and a fine.[9] Thereafter, none was openly cleared out from any of the British West India colonies in American bottoms so long as the act of 1788 remained operative.

The part played by vessels from the United States in supplying Great Britain's Caribbean possessions during the French war is

[1] Portland to Thomson, July 1, 1799, C. O. 152/79.

[2] Dated July 1, 1799. In C. O. 324/103.

[3] Ricketts to the Duke of Portland, Feb. 4, 1800, C. O. 28/66.

[4] Portland to Bishop, May 29, 1800, C. O. 28/66.

[5] Bishop to Portland, July 1, 1800, C. O. 28/66.

[6] John Ince, Secretary of the Committee of Correspondence, to John Brathwaite, agent for Barbados, July 7, 1800, C. O. 28/66.

[7] President Bishop to the Duke of Portland, Oct. 15, 1800 and Bishop to Mr. Brathwaite, same date (under "miscellaneous"), C. O. 28/66.

[8] Balcarres to the Duke of Portland, Feb. 24, 1800 and enclosures, C. O. 137/103.

[9] Portland to Balcarres, May 29, 1800, C. O. 137/104.

shown by statistics covering St. Vincent's trade from 1794 to 1805, compiled from local custom house records and submitted to the home government in 1806, reproduced in the following table.

Commodity	Imported from the United Kingdom	From British North America	From the U. S. A. in British Bottoms	From the U. S. A. in American Bottoms
Staves, number	23,960	129,500	1,122,300	7,025,000
Hoops, number	3,830,100	141,950	17,000	384,900
Lumber, feet	—	940,500	466,000	34,237,000
Bread and Flour bbls.	16,307	3,384	15,136	67,036
Beef and Pork, bbls.	23,588	1,216	443	15,393
Dry Fish, quintals	2,485	110,768	464	28,169
Pickled Fish, bbls.	19,949	5,788	1,168	6.406

The admission of American bottoms likewise provided an important outlet for West Indian rum and molasses. Exports from St. Vincent to British North America in the above period included 140 hogsheads, 22 tierces, and 175 barrels of sugar; 7,080 puncheons of rum; and 2,852 puncheons of molasses. Exports to the United States in British vessels in the same period were 708 hogsheads, 125 tierces, and 435 barrels of sugar; 1,403 puncheons of rum; and 681 puncheons of molasses. Exports to the United States in American bottoms were 32,159 puncheons of rum and 5,613 puncheons of molasses.[1]

Revolutionary disorders in the Caribbean possessions of France led to the introduction of a new population element, French royalists, into Great Britain's neighboring colonies. Their coming was an event of considerable economic consequence, especially to Jamaica and Trinidad. The first influx of those wretched individuals occurred at the close of 1792, when large numbers from Martinique and Guadeloupe, among them Governor D'Arrot of the latter colony, sought safety in the Leewards. All but the negroes were admitted; the latter were excluded lest they spread pernicious doctrines amongst the British blacks.[2]

Between five and six thousand refugees landed in Dominica from Martinique during the summer of 1793 with little but their clothing. They were housed on porches and in sheds, three tons of flour and 3,500 pounds of salt fish a week were issued them as rations, and a

[1] Compiled from the report in C. O. 260/21.
[2] Governor Woodley to Henry Dundas, Dec. 28, 1792 and Jan. 7, 1793, C. O. 152/73.

public subscription to provide for their care was opened.[1] Other Martiniquans, including Governor Behague, found security in St. Vincent.[2] The presence of such large groups of destitute aliens was in part responsible for suspensions of the navigation act which took place in those colonies.[3]

The revolutionary French government's recapture of Guadeloupe in 1794 resulted in a precipitate flight of royalist planters to neighboring British colonies. A total of 257 whites and 271 slaves arrived in Montserrat within three days, many in ordinary rowboats. No able-bodied males were, however, allowed to remain, as it was feared that they would ferment disturbance.[4] Early in 1795, the number of Frenchmen in Antigua alone was 1,300, of whom some 900 were slaves.[5] Following the French succession of that year, the legislature of St. Kitts removed 500 refugees to Martinique, providing them with passage and provisions at public expense, lest their presence endanger the island's safety.[6]

Under authority from the home government,[7] 250 French subjects in Antigua, not including slaves, were being fed at an expense of £130 sterling a week in June 1795. Over £1,600 sterling had already then been expended in providing for them.[8] Many of the refugees subsequently returned to their old homes or emigrated to Trinidad, but others began life anew in these foreign havens.

Fifty-one French families with their domestics were licensed to reside in Jamaica in 1793.[9] The British evacuation of St. Domingo five years later was accompanied by the flight of the greater part of those planters who had placed themselves under the invaders' protection following their early triumphs. A chilling welcome attended them in Jamaica. Their loyalty to Great Britain was questioned and Jacobin songs sung by their slaves furnished convincing argument that they should not be harbored. Consequently, but 200 were allowed to

[1] Lieutenant-Governor Bruce to Henry Dundas, July 13, 1793, C. O. 71/25.
[2] Governor Seton to Henry Dundas, July 1, 1793, C. O. 260/12. Governor Woodley to Dundas, Feb. 27, 1793, C. O. 152/73.
[3] Governor Woodley to Henry Dundas, Jan. 7, 1793, C. O. 152/73; Lieutenant-Governor Bruce to Henry Dundas, July 13, 1793, C. O. 71/25; and Governor Seton to Dundas, July 1, 1793, C. O. 260/12.
[4] John Stanley to Henry Dundas, June 23, 1794, C. O. 152/75.
[5] Stanley to the Duke of Portland, Feb. 7, 1795, C. O. 152/75.
[6] Stanley to Portland, May 2, 1795. C. O. 152/77.
[7] Portland to Stanley, April 10, 1795, C. O. 152/76.
[8] Stanley to Portland, June 18, C. O. 152/77.
[9] *Votes of the . . . Assembly of Jamaica . . . 1793*, p. 89.

remain; most of the others established themselves in Trinidad.

Those settling in Jamaica were largely coffee growers. The remarkable development of that industry in the island during the early nineteenth century is attributable in no small degree to their presence.[1] Others became residents of Kingston, where some of them gave occasional concerts to gain a livelihood.[2] The more trim appearance of that city about 1810, with tracts of ground, formerly in weeds, then laid out in gardens or walks, with better built houses, and with more taste shown in fence building, was attributed to the presence of these St. Domingan refugees by a former resident.[3] A quarter of a century later, the truck gardens about the city were almost exclusively owned by them and their descendants; they were a respectable and industrious class of people. Like the coffee cultivators, they had proved to be a valuable addition to the white population of the colony.[4]

[1] Gardener, *Jamaica*, p. 239. Madden, *A Twelvemonth's Residence*, I, 125.
[2] Stewart, *An Account of Jamaica*, p. 176.
[3] Mathison, *Notices Respecting Jamaica*, p. 6.
[4] Madden, *A Twelvemonth's Residence*, I, 82.

CHAPTER VIII

The Abolition Movement

A striking social phenomenon, the growth of altruism, evinced itself in the western world from the closing decades of the eighteenth century. The traditional stolid indifference, the callous self-sufficiency of middle and upper class folk then gave way to serious interest in persons of lower station and a sincere desire to ameliorate their lot. The effects of this movement were far-reaching and led to such diverse results as restricting the labor of women and children, factory legislation, poor relief, prison reform, missionary enterprise, and a popularization of education.

But, in many respects, the most signal triumphs of the new humanitarianism were the abolition of the immensely lucrative traffic in human beings needed to man overseas plantations and the ultimate overthrow of the slave system prevailing there. The fact that the latter was proving ruinous as a form of labor and must inevitably have come to an end through the operation of simple economic laws, even had there been no general clamor against it, in no way lessens the force of the victory. The slave trade and African bondage were anachronisms in a world animated by the new spirit of egalitarianism and brotherhood. Their extirpation constituted a defeat of deeply-rooted vested interests with their "sacred rights" of property by an abstract ethical principle. Nowhere was this more evident than in the British empire.

In the middle of the seventeen hundreds, the great majority of Englishmen accepted the servile régime unquestioningly and as a matter of course. For decades, custom had sanctioned the transportation of negroes from Africa and the exploitation of the plantation colonies by their forced toil. A considerable body of parliamentary legislation assuming both the trade and slavery to be legal had, moreover, placed them under the protection of the law. But they were not wholly unchallenged. The Friends as an organization and scattered enlightened individuals occasionally raised their voices, now against one, now against the other, and sought to rouse the slumbering consciences of their fellows. Thus, with estate owners at the height of prosperity, the undermining of the old plantation system in the British West Indies was begun.

George Fox, the founder of Quakerism, in speaking of his Barbadian converts in 1671, had stated that he wished them to treat their slaves mildly, to give the latter religious instruction, and to grant them freedom after some years of servitude.[1] A quarter of a century later, the Yearly Meeting of Friends in the colony of Pennsylvania had urged that members of the society "be careful not to encourage the bringing of any more negroes." Now, in 1755, a rule adopted by the same body declared that all persons importing Africans in the future should be debarred from the religious communion of the Society.[2]

The London Yearly Meeting had already in 1727 adopted a resolution condemning the traffic and censuring Friends participating in it. In 1758, it warned members of the organization to avoid being in any way concerned with "reaping the unrighteous profits arising from the iniquitous practice of dealing in slaves," and soon after excluded all persons engaged in the business. Fourteen years later, the hope was expressed that it might be abolished.[3]

Adam Smith, writing about 1760, opposed the trade, declaring that the negroes transported to the colonies were often above "the refuse of the gaols" who carried them into bondage.[4] In 1766, while preaching before the Society for the Propagation of the Gospel, William Warburton, Bishop of Gloucester, branded the buying and selling of Africans an infringement of divine as well as human law.[5] Anthony Benezet, a Pennsylvania Quaker, devoted himself to international anti-slave propaganda from about 1760, and sought in three widely-

[1] John K. Ingram, *A History of Slavery and Serfdom* (London, 1895), p. 156, note.

[2] Edward Channing, *A History of the United States* (in progress, New York, 1905 to —), II, 396.

[3] Anon., *A Brief Statement of the Rise and Progress of the Testimony of the Religious Society of Friends against Slavery and the Slave Trade, 1671–1787* (Philadelphia, 1843). Rufus M. Jones, *The Later Periods of Quakerism* (2 vols., London, 1921), I, 320. Thomas Clarkson, *History of the Rise, Progress and Accomplishment of the Abolition of the African Slave Trade by the British Parliament* (2 vols., Philadelphia, 1808), I, 112–116.

[4] "The Theory of Moral Sentiments," in *Essays* (London, 1867).

[5] *A Sermon Preached before the Incorporated Society for the Propagation of the Gospel in Foreign Parts; At Their Meeting in the Parish Church of St. Mary-Le-Bow, on Friday February 21, 1766* (London, 1766). Reprinted in Anon., ed., *Twelve Anniversary Sermons Preached Before the Society for the Propagation of the Gospel in Foreign Parts* (London, 1845).

read works to demonstrate how negro hunters ravaged the western portion of the dark continent, as well as to portray the horrors attending the shipment of slaves to the new world.[1]

An anonymous pamphleteer proposed in 1772 that Florida be settled by emancipated, educated blacks and that a system of free labor be gradually introduced into the continental colonies farther north and into the Caribbean, until slavery should have been entirely exterminated.[2] In the same year, James Beattie, professor of moral philosophy and logic in Marischal College and the University of Aberdeen, condemned forced labor as being inconsistent with the free spirit of the British nation.[3] Thomas Day, eccentric author of the celebrated children's story *Sanford and Merton,* sang the sorrows of a sable servant who had committed suicide while aboard a ship on which he was being returned to tropical America from England against his will.[4] Somewhat later he sought to convince a correspondent in America of the sinfulness of human bondage.[5]

The question of whether or not slavery was agreeable to the law of nature was argued at the Harvard graduation exercises of 1773.[6] A colonist in Massachusetts, writing about the same time, declared it to be contrary to Scripture and natural law and held that the trade in negroes depopulated Africa, kept it in a constant state of conflict, and hindered the development of a profitable trade in precious metals, ivory, and spices.[7]

In Pennsylvania, Dr. Benjamin Rush accompanied a petition to the assembly, praying for an increase in the duty levied on blacks im-

[1] *A Short Account of That Part of Africa Inhabited by the Negroes . . . and the Manner by Which the Slave Trade is Carried on;* also his *A Caution and Warning to Great Britain and her Colonies on the calamitous State of the enslaved Negroes* (Philadelphia, 1767) and *Historical Account of Guinea* (Philadelphia 1771). See Carter G. Woodson, "Anthony Benezet," in *The Journal of Negro History,* II, 37 ff.

[2] *A Plan for the Abolition of Slavery in the West Indies* (London, 1772). "A Plan for the Abolition of Slavery . . . ," in *The Gent. Mag.,* July, 1772, pp. 325, 326.

[3] *An Essay on the Nature and Immutability of Truth, in Opposition to Sophistry and Scepticism* (London, 1772).

[4] *The Dying Negro* (London, 1773).

[5] *Fragment of an Original Letter on the Slavery of the Negroes, Written in the Year 1776* (London, 1784).

[6] Anon., *A Forensic Dispute on the Legality of enslaving the Africans, Held at the public Commencement in Cambridge, New-England, July 21st, 1773, By Two Candidates for the Bachelor's Degree* (Boston, 1773). The names of the disputants are not given. There was apparently no decision.

[7] James Swan, *A Dissuasion to Great-Britain and the Colonies, from the Slave Trade to Africa. Shewing the Injustice thereof, &c.* (Boston, 1773).

ported into the colony, with an address to the inhabitants of the British settlements as a whole in which he declared slavery to be unjust. and inhumane and urged abolishing the trade as well as educating and eventually freeing the young Africans.[1] When a member of the planter interest showed that Moses had not forbidden the institution and held that emancipation would ruin the West Indians and seriously affect England's prosperity,[2] Rush retorted that it was repugnant to religion, the true interests of the home country, and the economy of nature.[3]

A Jamaican debating society in 1774 considered whether the negro trade was consistent with sound policy, the laws of nature and of morality, a question which had been proposed by Thomas Hibbert, for nearly half a century a local Guinea factor. It is interesting to note that the decision was in favor of the negative.[4] The island assembly, alarmed at the rapidly increasing disproportion between blacks and whites in the colony, in that year imposed an additional tax of £2 per head upon all slaves imported, in an attempt to discourage the trade. As we have seen elsewhere, such action was subsequently disallowed by the home government.[5]

John Wesley, the father of Methodism, described the evil conditions attending the commerce in Africans and the Caribbean labor régime to his followers, rigorously opposing both. He declared: "I absolutely deny all slave-holding to be consistent with any degree of natural justice. . . . It were better that all those islands should remain uncultivated forever; yea, it were more desirable that they were altogether sunk in the depth of the sea, than that they should be cultivated at so high a price as the violation of justice, mercy, and truth; and it would be better that none should labour there, that the work should be left undone, than that myriads of innocent men should be murdered, and myriads more dragged into the basest slavery."[6]

The first actual step toward effecting reform was taken in 1775, with the organization of the Pennsylvania Society for Promoting the Abolition of Slavery, for the Relief of Free Negroes Unlawfully

[1] [Rush], "A Pennsylvanian," *An Address to the Inhabitants of the British Settlements, on the Slavery of the Negroes in America* (Philadelphia, 1773).

[2] [Richard Nisbet], "A West Indian," *Slavery Not Forbidden by Scripture . . .* (Philadelphia, 1773).

[3] [Rush], "A Pennsylvanian," *A Vindication of the Address, To the Inhabitants of the British Settlements . . . in Answer to a Pamphlet entitled, "Slavery not Forbidden by Scripture . . ."* (Philadelphia, 1773).

[4] Southey, *Chronological History*, II, 420, 421.

[5] Pages 30 and 31.

[6] *Thoughts on Slavery* (London, 1774).

Held in Bondage, and for Improving the Conditions of the African Race, an undenominational body founded in Philadelphia through the instrumentality of Doctor Rush and James Pemberton.[1] At about the same time, an unnamed religious writer declared slavery to be inconsistent with Christianity.[2] Adam Smith expanded his earlier views by now speaking unfavorably of slavery itself in his monumental *Wealth of Nations;*[3] a visitor to Jamaica condemned the planters' cruelty and painted the miserable lot of the negroes in a poetic effusion of slight merit;[4] a white man was hung in the West Indies for the murder of a slave despite his plea that the victim's station precluded punishment;[5] Samuel Johnson showed himself bitterly hostile to forced labor of the negroes and thus at hopeless variance with the faithful Boswell;[6] and John Millar, professor of law in the University of Glasgow, denounced it because of its evil effects on industry, population, and morals.[7]

A series of communications in the widely-circulated *Gentleman's Magazine* during 1780 and 1781 attacked both the trade and slavery.[8] Thomas Day[9] and an anonymous author[10] denounced the inconsistency of Americans who retained blacks in bondage while fighting, as they said, for liberty. Benevolent patrons published the stilted

[1] Jones, *Quakerism*, I, 319.

[2] "Philalethes," *pseud.*, *Christian Piety. With Extracts from Different Authors, and Some Notes on the Slave Trade* (no imprint, 1775?).

[3] (2 vols., London, 1776), Bk. I, ch. 8; Bk. III, ch. 2; Bk. IV, ch. 7. See also "Remarks on Slavery by Dr. Adam Smith," in *The Eur. Mag. and Lond. Rev.*, Nov. 1792, pp. 323 ff.

[4] Anon., *Jamaica, a Poem, in Three Parts. Written in that Island, in the Year MDCCLXXVI. To Which is Annexed, a Poetic Epistle from the Author in that Island to a Friend in England* (London, 1777).

[5] Southey, *Chronological History*, II, 425.

[6] James Boswell, *The Life of Samuel Johnson, LL.D.*, Everyman's Library edition, II, 146 ff.

[7] *The Origin of the Distinction of Ranks; or, An Inquiry Into the Circumstances Which Give Rise to Influence and Authority, in the Different Members of Society* (London, 1779).

[8] Anon., "A West Indian," "Cruelty Attending the Slave Trade as at Present Practiced, With a Project for Abolishing It," issue for October, 1780, pp. 458, 459. "Publicus," *pseud.*, "On Negro Slavery," issue for Dec. 1780, p. 564. Anon., "Negro Slavery, its Cruelty, Injustice, etc." issue for March, 1781, pp. 122, 123. Anon., "An Englishman," "On the Condition and Treatment of Negroes," issue for Sept., 1781, pp. 417, 418.

[9] *Reflections on the Present State of England and the Independence of America* (London, 1782).

[10] *A Serious Address to the Rulers of America, on the Inconsistency of their Conduct respecting Slavery: Forming a Contrast Between the Encroachments of England on American Liberty, and American Injustice in Tolerating Slavery* (London, 1783).

correspondence of a deceased colored grocer in Westminster, given some education by three spinster sisters whose servant he had been for many years, as concrete evidence of what a negro could actually accomplish when given an opportunity.[1] In 1783, upon addressing the Society for the Propagation of the Gospel in Foreign Parts, Beilby Porteus, then Bishop of Chester, urged that the slaves on the organization's two Barbadian estates, which had been left it for the support of Codrington College,[2] be given religious instruction.[3] George Gregory, a divine of the established church and a man of letters,[4] and William Paley, arch-deacon of Carlisle,[5] spoke strongly against the trade and proposed that the slaves be freed. William Cowper, the poet, sought to awaken sympathy for the transported Africans in his *The Task*.[6]

While this desultory opposition was evincing itself, a momentous change in the status of the negro in England was brought about through the efforts of Granville Sharp, a poor but indefatigable philanthropist.[7]

Early in the eighteenth century Chief Justice Holt had ruled that "one may be a villeyn in England, but not a slave." This decision had soon fallen into abeyance and the opinion of Attorney-General Philip York and Solicitor-General Charles Talbot, given in 1729, that "a slave by coming from the West Indies to Great Britain, or Ireland, either with or without his master, doth not become free; and that his master's property or right in him is not thereby determined or varied; and that baptism doth not bestow freedom on him, nor make any alteration in his temporal condition in these kingdoms . . . [and] that the master may legally compel him to return to the plantations," had come to be regularly accepted.

---

[1] Ignatius Sancho, *Letters of . . . an African. To Which Are Prefixed, Memoirs of His Life* (2 vols., London, 1782).

[2] Page 12.

[3] *A Sermon Preached before the Incorporated Society for the Propagation of the Gospel in Foreign Parts, at Their Anniversary Meeting in the Parish Church of St. Mary-Le-Bow, on Friday, February 21, 1783* (London, 1783). Reprinted in Anon., ed., *Twelve Anniversary Sermons* . . .

[4] *Essays, Historical and Moral* (London, 1783), published anonymously.

[5] *The Principles of Moral and Political Philosophy* (London, 1785).

[6] "*The Task*," to Which Are Added the "*Epistle to Joseph Hill*," "*Tirocinium*," and "*John Gilpin*" (London, 1785).

[7] See Prince Hoare, *Memoirs of Granville Sharp, Esq., Composed From His Own Manuscripts* (London, 1820). "Memoir of Granville Sharp, Esq.," in *The Eur. Mag. and Lond. Rev.*, Dec., 1816, pp. 483 ff. C. D. Michael, *The Slave and His Champions.* . . . (London, 1891). E. C. P. Lascelles, *Granville Sharp* (Oxford, 1928).

Blackstone, the eminent jurist, wavered on the subject. He first held that a slave fell under the protection of English law upon his landing in the country and so "becomes a freeman, though the master's right to his service may probably still continue." Subsequently became uncertain on this point, and, in the fourth edition of his *Commentaries on the Laws of England*,[1] altered this sentence to read "though the master's right to his service may possibly still continue." Estimates of the number of bond-servants in England between 1764 and 1770 range from 15,000 to upwards of a third again as many. Blacks were advertised and freely sold at auction in various parts of the country, but particularly in London and Liverpool.[3]

The wretched state of runaways and of slaves abandoned by their masters because of illness attracted Sharp's attention, and in 1765 a peculiarly distressing case came to his notice. David Lisle, a planter of Barbados, had brought a servant, Jonathan Strong, to London with him, had abused him and had turned him out to die. Sharp's brother, a physician in Wapping, took pity on the negro and placed him in a hospital where he was cured, after which a position was found for him. Two years later Lisle chanced to meet Strong, claimed him as his property and sold him to John Kerr for £30. The negro sent word to Granville Sharp who interviewed the Lord Mayor of London and secured a hearing of the case which resulted in the negro's release on the ground of his having been taken without a warrant.[4]

In 1768, Sharp aided a black, Hylas, in the prosecution of one Newton for having kidnapped his wife and having sent her to the Caribbean; the court ordered the defendant to immediately return the woman to England. When, shortly after, Thomas Lewis, an African, was seized by three Englishmen, one of whom represented himself as his owner, and was put aboard a vessel bound for Jamaica, Sharp effected his removal through a writ of habeas corpus. A jury subsequently denied the alleged master's claim. Other negroes threatened with transportation to the new world against their wills were freed in the same way—one was even removed from a ship already in the Downs, under way to the colonies.[5]

---

[1] 4 vols., Oxford, 1770.

[2] Channing, *History of the United States,* III, 554, 555.

[3] Williams, *Liverpool Privateers,* pp. 474–477. Clarkson, *History of the Abolition of the Slave Trade,* I, 65, 66.

[4] Clarkson, *History of the Abolition of the Slave Trade,* I, 66–70.

[5] *Ibid.,* I, 72–75.

Sharp was greatly hampered in these efforts by the uncertainty of law officers and legal experts as to the exact status of blacks in the country. He therefore turned to a study of English law. In a pamphlet published two years after Strong's release, he declared that, according to precedent established by the Holt decision, slavery there was illegal.[1] In 1772, he forced a test case to at length determine the matter.

Charles Stewart had come to England from Virginia bringing with him a slave, James Somerset, as servant. The latter had absconded, had been captured, and had been placed in the hands of a ship-master for conveyance to Jamaica where he was to be sold. News of the affair reached Sharp, he had Somerset freed under writ of habeas corpus and secured a trial before Chief Justice Mansfield.

The case covered the first half of the year, being argued in three sittings of the court, and created a tremendous sensation. Members of the planter interest were eager to secure the passage of a bill forbidding the entry of slaves into the home country while not interfering with the ownership of negroes in the British colonies, thus obviating the necessity for a ruling.[2] Lord Mansfield himself was by no means averse to such action, but, when the requisite legislation was not forthcoming, he handed down a memorable decision on June 22, declaring that any slave became free immediately upon setting foot on English soil.[3] At a single stroke, through the efforts of one man, all unfree negroes in the country were liberated. The first victory leading to emancipation had been won.

[1] *A Representation of the Injustice and Dangerous Tendency of Tolerating Slavery; or of Admitting the Least Claim of Private Property in the Persons of Men, in England* (London, 1769). Published in condensed form under the title *Extract from "A Representation of the Injustice and Dangerous Tendency of Tolerating Slavery . . ."* (London, 1769). Later added to by *An Appendix to the "Representation (Printed in the Year 1769) of the Injustice and Dangerous Tendency of Tolerating Slavery . . ."* (London, 1772).

[2] [Samuel Estwick], "A West Indian," *Considerations on the Negro Cause Commonly So Called, Addressed to the Right Honourable Lord Mansfield . . .* (London, 1772). The author was at this time assistant agent for Barbados.

[3] *State Trials,* XI, 339. Clarkson, *History of the Abolition of the Slave Trade,* I, 76–79. See also the work of Francis Hargrave, one of the attorneys engaged by Sharp, *An Argument in the Case of James Sommersett A Negro, Lately Determined by the Court of King's Bench . . .* (London, 1772); "An Argument Against Property in Slaves," in *The Gent. Mag.,* July, 1772, pp. 309, 310; and Henry G. Tuke, *The Fugitive Slave Circulars. A Short Account of the Case of Sommersett the Negro, and of Lord Mansfield's Celebrated Judgment . . .* (London, 1876). A similar test case, that of the slave Joseph Knight, was heard in Scotland some time later and resulted in the negro's being declared free (1777). See Boswell, *Johnson,* II, 154, 156.

Such action naturally proved disconcerting to the West Indians. Edward Long, then engaged in writing his *History of Jamaica,* paused to denounce the decision in an unsigned pamphlet, declaring it to be incompatible with the spirit of British commerce.[1] It was also assailed as injuring property protected by divers acts of parliament.[2] Sharp, on the other hand, now urged the government to put an end to both the trade and slavery, holding them to be utterly irreconcilable with the principles of the British constitution of religion.[3]

Four years after this epoch-making decision, David Hartley, a member of the House of Commons from Hull, moved the adoption of a resolution declaring traffic in Africans to be contrary to the laws of God and the rights of man. The motion was seconded by Sir George Savile, but this premature attempt to sound out the lower chamber was side-tracked and nothing further came of it.[4]

With the status of negroes in England thus favorably determined, Sharp devoted himself to arousing sympathy for the slaves in the colonies, to attacking involuntary servitude as such,[5] and to replying[6] to apologies in its behalf.[7] Some years later, he gave wide publicity to revolting testimony presented in a suit arising from the underwriters unsuccessfully disputing a claim of the owners of the *Zong* to Liverpool for insurance on 132 sick slaves thrown overboard en route from Africa to the West Indies.[8]

American independence restricted the negro question in the British new world colonies to the Caribbean. The decade following the restoration of peace brought together the several individuals who had independently opposed the slave trade and witnessed the launching of an organized movement to educate the public and to bring

[1] "A Planter," *Candid Reflections Upon the Judgement lately awarded by The Court of King's Bench in Westminster Hall, on what is commonly called the Negroe-cause* (London, 1772).

[2] "West Indian," "Considerations on a Late Determination in the Court of King's Bench on the Negro Cause," in *The Gent. Mag.*, July, 1772, pp. 308, 309.

[3] Clarkson, *History of the Abolition of the Slave Trade*, I, 79.

[4] *Ibid.*, I, 84, 85.

[5] *An Essay on Slavery* (London, 1776). *The Law of Retribution, or a Serious Warning to Great Britain and her Colonies . . . of God's Temporal Vengeance Against Tyrants, Slaveholders, and Oppressors* (London, 1776).

[6] *The Just Limitation of Slavery in the Laws of God; Compared With the Unbounded Claims of the African Traders and British-American Slave-holders* (London, 1776).

[7] Thomas Thompson, *The African Trade for Negro Slaves Shown to be Consistent With the Principles of Humanity and With the Laws of Revealed Religion* (Canterbury, 1772).

[8] Clarkson, *History of the Abolition of the Slave Trade*, I, 95–97.

about its abolition. In 1783 the Friends petitioned parliament to put an end to such commerce and to consider the general state of the negroes in the overseas possessions.[1] They likewise authorized the publication of a booklet setting forth the Society's views against the traffic in human beings.[2] The distribution of a new edition of Benezet's *A Caution . . . to Great Britain and Her Colonies . . .* was undertaken soon after.[3]

A group of six Quakers, William Dillwyn, George Harrison, Samuel Hoare, Thomas Knowles, John Lloyd, and Joseph Woods, meeting in private during July, 1783, "to consider what steps should be taken for the relief and liberation of the Negro Slaves in the West Indies, and for the discouragement of the slave-trade on the coast of Africa," determined to instruct the inhabitants of Great Britain as to the true state of affairs. They promptly secured the insertion of various articles setting forth the slaves' sad lot in London and provincial newspapers, and financed the publication of a work of propaganda [4] by one of their number.[5]

At about the same time, the Rev. James Ramsay, vicar of Teston in Kent, for twenty years a resident of the West Indies as naval chaplain and clergyman in St. Kitts where he had become embroiled with the colonists in consequence of his having given plantation hands religious instruction, opened an attack on the trade and slavery as he knew them from first-hand information and personal experiences.[6] He soon became involved in an acrimonious controversy, particularly with James Tobin, a merchant of Nevis [7] then in England, during which personalities were freely indulged in.[8] This had the salutary result of attracting considerable attention.

[1] Clarkson, *History of the Abolition of the Slave Trade,* I, 118, 119.

[2] Signed by John Ady, *The Case of Our Fellow-Creatures, the Oppressed Africans. Respectfully Recommended to the Serious Consideration of the Legislature of Great-Britain, by the People Called Quakers* (London, 1783).

[3] Clarkson, *History of the Abolition of the Slave Trade,* I, 122.

[4] Joseph Woods, *Thoughts on the Slavery of the Negroes* (London, 1784).

[5] Clarkson, *History of the Abolition of the Slave Trade,* I, 124, 125.

[6] *An Inquiry Into the Effects of Putting a Stop to the African Slave Trade, and of Granting Liberty to the Slaves in the British Sugar Colonies* (London, 1784). *An Essay on the Treatment and Conversion of African Slaves in the British Sugar Colonies* (London, 1784). Ramsay also edited *A Letter from Capt. J. S. Smith to the Rev. Mr. Hill, on the State of the Negroe Slaves . . .* (London, 1786).

[7] Father of Rear-Admiral George Tobin and of John Tobin, the dramatist.

[8] [James Tobin], "A Friend of the West India Colonies and Their Inhabitants," *Cursory Remarks Upon Mr. Ramsay's Essay on the Treatment and Conversion of African Slaves in the Sugar Colonies* (London, 1785).

In 1785, the borough of Bridgewater transmitted a petition against the trade of parliament, but it was tabled.[1] In the same year, Doctor Peckard, vice-chancellor of Cambridge and himself a foe of slavery, proposed the question *Anne liceat invitos in servitutem dare?*[2] to the senior bachelors of art at the university as the subject for a Latin prize dissertation. A young student, Thomas Clarkson,[3] who had been awarded two earlier prizes, began to study the question, read Benezet's *Historical Account of Guinea,* and wrote the winning essay. The information he had gathered preyed on his mind and he continued his investigation. This brought him into touch with Sharp and Ramsay and, while a guest at the latter's home, Clarkson pledged his life to the cause of the slaves. With the encouragement of the two older men, an expansion of his original essay was published in English [4] shortly after.[5]

Thus far, abolition had lacked a champion in parliament. William Wilberforce, member of the House of Commons for Yorkshire,[6]

Anon., "Some Gentleman of St. Christopher," *An Answer to the Reverend James Ramsay's Essay on the Treatment and Conversion of Slaves in the British Sugar Colonies* (Basseterre, 1785). James Ramsay, *A Reply to the Personal Invectives and Objections Contained in Two Answers . . . to An Essay on the Treatment and Conversion of the African Slaves, in the British Colonies* (London, 1785). Tobin, *A Short Rejoinder to the Rev. Mr. Ramsay's Reply . . .* (London, 1787). Ramsay, *A Letter to James Tobin, Esq. Late Member of His Majesty's Council in the Island of Nevis* (London, 1787). Tobin, *A Farwel* [sic] *Address to the Rev. Mr. James Ramsay . . .* (London, 1788).

[1] Clarkson, *History of the Abolition of the Slave Trade,* I, 105–107.

[2] Is it right to make slaves of others against their will?

[3] James Elmes, *Thomas Clarkson* (London, 1854). Anon., *A Sketch of the Life of Thomas Clarkson* (London, 1876). Michael, *The Slave and His Champions.* Thomas Taylor, *A Biographical Sketch of Thomas Clarkson . . .* (London, 1839).

[4] *An Essay on the Slavery and Commerce of the Human Species, particularly the African* (London, 1786).

[5] Clarkson, *History of the Abolition of the Slave Trade,* I, 205–230.

[6] Robert and Samuel Wilberforce, *The Life of William Wilberforce* (5 vols., London, 1838), also published in abridged form in one volume, London, 1843. R. and S. Wilberforce, ed., *The Correspondence of William Wilberforce* (2 vols., London, 1840). A. M. Wilberforce, *Private Papers of William Wilberforce* (London, 1897). Archibald Primrose, *Pitt and Wilberforce* (Edinburgh, 1897). "Memoir of William Wilberforce, Esq. M.P.," in *The Eur. Mag. and Lond. Rev.,* October, 1814, pp. 287, 288. Joseph Gurney, *Familiar Sketches of the Late William Wilberforce* (Norwich, 1838). [Sir James Stephen], "Life of William Wilberforce," in *The Ed. Rev.,* April, 1838, pp. 142 ff. Stephen, *Essays in Ecclesiastical Biography* (2 vols., London, 1849), II, 203 ff. J. S. Harford, *Recollections of William Wilberforce* (London, 1864). John Colquhoun, *William Wilberforce: His Friends and Times* (London, 1866). John Stoughton, *William Wilberforce* (London, 1880). Michael, *The Slave and His*

had been interested in the subject for some time. The publication of Clarkson's effort resulted in his meeting the enthusiastic author and other opponents of the trade. After due deliberation, he expressed willingness to sponsor and defend a measure seeking to end it.[1]

A preliminary campaign of public instruction was determined on and, in accordance with this plan, the Society for Effecting the Abolition of the Slave Trade was founded in May, 1787, with Granville Sharp as chairman. Among the eleven other charter members were five of the six men who had constituted the group formed in 1783, and Thomas Clarkson. All but Sharp, Clarkson, and one other were Friends.[2] An office was opened at Number 18 in the Old Jewery and correspondence was entered into with the anti-slavery society in Philadelphia, just reorganized with Benjamin Franklin as president,[3] and with *La Société des Amis des Noirs,* founded in Paris in the same year by Brissot, Sieyès, and Robespierre.[4]

Within a year, £2,760 was received in subscriptions and 15,050 copies of a pamphlet by Clarkson, *A Summary View of the Slave-trade, and of the Probable Consequences of its Abolition;* [5] 2,000 of his *An Essay on the Impolicy of the African Slave Trade;* [6] 6,025 copies of a work by a former surgeon in the African trade, Alexander Falconbridge's *An Account of the Slave Trade on the Coast of Africa;* [7] 1,500 of Benezet's *Historical Account of Guinea;* 4,000 of a booklet by James Ramsay, *Objections to the Abolition of the*

Champions. Travers Buxton, *William Wilberforce* (London, 1903). R. Coupland, *Wilberforce: A Narrative* (Oxford, 1923). James A. Williamson, *Builders of the Empire* (Oxford, 1926), section on Wilberforce.

[1] Clarkson, *History of the Abolition of the Slave Trade,* I, 241, 253, 254. The question of the importance of Wilberforce's meeting these opponents of the trade as a factor in his forming the decision to assume the parliamentary leadership for abolition became the subject of an unfortunate dispute half a century later. The sons of Wilberforce took the point of view in their joint five volume biography (see preceding note) that their father was the original and principal leader in the movement and held that Clarkson's *History* was an attempt on its author's part to claim for himself honors which were due their parent alone. This false assumption and especially the ungenerous and wholly unfounded charges cut the aged Clarkson to the quick and he made a dignified reply in *Strictures on the Life of William Wilberforce, by the Rev. W. Wilberforce and the Rev. S. Wilberforce . . .* (London, 1838).

[2] Clarkson, *History of the Abolition of the Slave Trade,* I, 255–257.

[3] *Ibid.,* I, 191.

[4] *Ibid.,* I, 444–446. Girault, *Principes de Colonisation,* I, 234.

[5] London, 1787.

[6] London, 1788.

[7] London, 1788.

Slave Trade, with Answers; [1] and 14,000 of *A Letter to the Treas-urer of the Society Instituted for the Purpose of Effecting the Abolition of the Slave Trade,* [2] written by Robert Nickolls, Dean of Middleham and himself a native of the sugar islands, in support of the anti-slave trade movement, were published and distributed.[3] Branches were established in various parts of the country and nu-merous public meetings were held.[4]

Legislative action against the shipping of negroes from Africa to beyond the Atlantic was begun in the session of parliament which opened in November, 1787. More than a hundred petitions praying for its abolition, including ones from the corporation of London, groups of clergymen, and the universities of Oxford and Cambridge, were presented.[5] Three months later, King George III directed a com-mittee of the privy council to make an inquiry into that branch of national commerce. Wilberforce was ill; hence in May, Pitt person-ally brought forward a motion to take the circumstances of the trade complained of in the petitions into consideration during the following session. This was carried.

A measure provisionally regulating the traffic in blacks was adopted in the summer of 1788. Vessels were thenceforth permitted to carry no more than five slaves for every three tons of their regis-tered burden up to 201 tons and but one for every ton in excess of that capacity. Furthermore, they were required to have at least one trained surgeon each on board; and, to place a premium upon proper care for the Africans, £100 and £50 respectively were offered by the government to all commanders and medical men who should make the transatlantic passage with a mortality rate of not more than 2 per cent, or half those sums if losses in the human cargo did not exceed three in a hundred.[6]

This act was renewed in 1789, with additional clauses to safeguard the lives and interests of seamen on board the slavers [7] and was thereafter regularly continued for ten years, with the additional pro-

---

[1] London, 1788.

[2] London, 1788.

[3] *List of the Society Instituted in 1787 for the Purpose of effecting the. Abolition of the Slave Trade* (London, 1788).

[4] See for example, the report of a meeting held in Manchester on December 27, 1787 in *Society [Instituted in 1787] for the Purpose of Effecting the Abo-lition of the Slave Trade* (Manchester, 1788).

[5] *List of the Society . . .*

[6] 28 Geo. III c. 54.

[7] 29 Geo. III c. 66.

vision from 1794 that underwriters were not in the future to be held liable for natural deaths, for those arising from ill-treatment of the negroes, or for damages suffered in conflict with African princes or peoples when such injuries had been occasioned by the traders' aggressions.[1] A special act of 1797 required a minimum perpendicular space of four feet one inch between decks so as to afford the slaves at least some degree of comfort and ventilation.[2]

The report of the council committee, containing a large body of evidence secured from colonial governors, island legislatures and persons engaged in supplying the West Indians with laborers, was presented in the spring of 1789.[3] The question of abolition came before the lower chamber on May 12th when Wilberforce moved the adoption of twelve propositions condemning the trade, accompanying them with a three and a half hour speech, one of the most brilliant of his career. He was supported by Pitt, Fox, and Burke. Lord Penrhyn and Mr. Gascoyne, members for Liverpool, home port of the African merchants, were his leading opponents. The propositions were carried without a division, but the planter and commercial interests were given leave to present their side of the case more fully and action on the main matter was postponed to the following session.[4]

The hearing thus granted closed in April, 1791. Wilberforce promptly presented a motion to end the trade, but even with Pitt, Burke, and Fox as active champions of the measure, it was lost by a vote of 163–88 after a two day debate.[5] A year later, with more than five hundred petitions praying for abolition before parliament,

[1] As by 29 Geo. III c. 66; 30 Geo. III c. 33; 31 Geo. III c. 54; 32 Geo. III c. 52; 33 Geo. III c. 73; 34 Geo. III c. 80; 35 Geo. III c. 90.

[2] 37 Geo. III c. 118.

[3] "Report of the Lords of the Committee of Council for Trade and Plantations," in *Gt. Br., H. C., Sess. Pap.*, 1789 XXVI (646a).

[4] *Parliamentary History of England*, XXVIII, cols. 42–102. *The Speeches of Mr. Wilberforce, Lord Penrhyn, Mr. Burke, Sir W. Young, Alderman Newham, Mr. Dempster, Mr. Martin, Mr. Pitt, Mr. Grenville, Mr. Fox, Mr. Gascoyne, Alderman Sawbridge, Mr. Smith, &c. &c. on a Motion for the Abolition of the Slave Trade, in the House of Commons, May the 12th, 1789. To which Are Added, Mr. Wilberforce's Twelve Propositions* (London, 1789). William Wilberforce, *The Speech . . . on Wednesday the 13th of May, 1789, on the Question of the Abolition of the Slave Trade* (London 1789). [*Report of the Debate on the*] *Slave Trade, House of Commons, May 13, 1789* [London, 1789].

[5] *Parliamentary History of England*, XXIX, cols. 250–359. *Debate on a Motion for the Abolition of the Slave-Trade, in the House of Commons, on Monday and Tuesday, April 18 and 19, 1791* (London, 1791). William Pitt, *The Debate on a Motion for the Abolition of the Slave Trade in the House of Commons, on the 18th and 19th April, 1791* (London, 1791).

Wilberforce presented a second such measure to the House of Commons. It carried 238–85, but supporters of the trade scored a victory by pledging that body to the principle of gradual rather than immediate action.[1] Although the date for closing the traffic was subsequently set at January 1, 1796,[2] the bill was lost in the House of Lords.

Abolition measures were thereafter regularly introduced at each session by Wilberforce until 1799, but were repeatedly rejected by one body or the other.[3] The rising tide of liberalism in Great Britain was checked by the French Revolution. After 1792, events in St. Domingo constituted a potent argument against any change in the status quo of the slave régime.

Agitation carried on by the Society for Effecting the Abolition of the Slave Trade and attacks on such commerce at Westminster awakened tremendous interest throughout the country. Pamphlets on the subject found ready readers. The number appearing fluctuated with parliamentary action on the question. Those assailing the trade and slavery itself averaged twice as many as those written in their defense. Forty-three of the former and nineteen of the latter published in 1788 have been located, as have been twenty-one and nine respectively issued in 1789, nine and three dated 1790, twelve and four, 1791, and twenty-four and twelve, 1792. To examine these works here in detail would be as unprofitable as wearisome; more fruitful will be a consideration of the outstanding arguments pro and con, contained in representative ones.

Supporters of the Liverpool and West India interests declared that negroes sold into bondage were criminals and prisoners of war who would be slaughtered were there no market for them and that

---

[1] *Parliamentary History of England*, XXIX, cols. 1055–1158. *The Debate on a Motion for the Abolition of the Slave-Trade in the House of Commons, on Monday the Second of April, 1792, Reported in Detail* (London, 1792). William Pitt, *The Speech . . . on a Motion for the Abolition of the Slave Trade in the House of Commons, on Monday the Second of April, 1792* (London, 1792).

[2] *Parliamentary History of England*, XXIX, cols. 1203–1293.

[3] The best account of these efforts is contained in Clarkson, *History of the Abolition of the Slave Trade*, already referred to. See also, F. W. Newman, *Anglo-Saxon Abolition of Negro Slavery* (London, 1889); John R. Spears, *The American Slave Trade* (New York, 1900); and Frank J. Klingberg, *The Parliamentary History of the Abolition of the Slave Trade in the British Colonies*, a doctoral dissertation in the Yale University library. Robert Bisset's *History of the Negro Slave Trade in connection with the commerce and prosperity of the West Indies, etc.* (2 vols., London, 1805) sketches these attempts; it is an uncritical tirade against and vilification of the abolitionists.

intercourse with Europeans resulting from the trade made the Africans less barbarous.[1] Abolitionists maintained that the slaves purchased included large numbers of kidnapped individuals and that the possibility of selling captives fomented wars among the native tribes. Relations with the whites debauched the blacks, demoralized them, and ruined native industries.[2]

The former found proof for their contentions in the works of Robert Norris, a Guinea trader,[3] and Archibald Dalzel, former governor of Wydah;[4] the latter, in Mungo Park's classic account of his first explorations in the hinterland of the little-known continent.[5]

Opponents of abolition declared that the Africans were beings of a lower order, without morals or any just notion of religious duty and in a wretched material situation. Removal to the West Indies conferred a benefit upon them, for on the Caribbean estates their physical well-being was assured and they could there taste the comforts of protection, the fruits of humanity, and the blessings of religion.[6]

Such charges of negro inferiority were met by sponsoring a mediocre enough attack on the trade, from the pen of one Ottobah Cugoano, a negro,[7] and the autobiography of Olaudah Equiano, another

---

[1] [Gordon Turnbull], *An Apology for Negro Slavery* . . . (London, 1786). Anon., "A Clergyman," *A Proposal for the Consideration of Those, Who Interest Themselves in the Abolition of the Slave Trade* (Wolverhampton, 1788).

[2] Anon., *A Summary View of the Slave Trade, and of the Probable Consequences of its Abolition* (London, 1787). Muncaster, *Historical Sketches of the Slave Trade.*

[3] *Memoirs of the Reign of Boffa Ahadee, King of Dahomey. To Which Are Added, The Author's Journey to Abomey, the Capital, and a Short Account of the African Slave Trade* (London, 1789).

[4] *The History of Dahomy, an Inland Kingdom of Africa; Compiled from Authentic Memoirs* (London, 1795).

[5] *Travels in the Interior Districts of Africa, passim.* It is interesting to note, however, that, probably due to Bryan Edwards's influence, Park, who had his assistance in bringing out the work, does not advocate immediate abolition (p. 298).

[6] William Beckford, Jr., *Remarks Upon the Situation of Negroes in Jamaica* . . . (London, 1788). Veritas, *pseud., Thoughts on the Slavery of the Negroes as it affects the British Colonies, in the West Indies* . . . [London, 1788]. Anon., *A Country Gentleman's Reasons for Voting Against Mr. Wilberforce's Motion for a Bill to Prohibit the Importation of African Negroes into the Colonies* (London, 1792).

[7] *Thoughts and Sentiments on the Evil and Wicked Traffic of the Slavery and Commerce of the Human Species, Humbly Submitted to the Inhabitants of Great Britain* (London, 1787).

black,[1] and by recounting the achievements of other Africans [2] as proof of what those given an education could accomplish. Plantation hands in bondage, held the humanitarians, could scarcely be expected to consider the benefits alleged to accrue to them from involuntary residence in the American tropics, sufficient compensation for their removal from the freedom of happy homes across the sea. The forcing of such dubious advantages upon unwilling people on the theory that they would be benefited thereby could not be justified. To support slavery because transporting negroes to the new world gave them the opportunity to become Christians was like vindicating a highway robber because he gave a portion of his receipts to the church.[3]

In reply to the defense of slavery on the ground that it had always existed,[4] the abolitionists declared negroes to be white men's brethren and argued that the brotherhood of man forbade the institution.[5] Claims that the status of blacks in the Caribbean colonies compared favorably with that of British soldiers, sailors, the peasantry, and paupers [6] brought forth the retort that the mere state of freedom elevated an individual, no matter what his material condition might be, accompanied by accounts of exaggerated forms of cruelty attending the forced labor system of the sugar islands.[7]

Members of the shipping interest lent their support to the trade

[1] *Interesting Narrative of the Life of Olaudah Equiano, or Gustavus Vassa, the African, Written by Himself* (London, 1793).

[2] William Dickson, *Letters on Slavery . . . To Which Are Added Addresses to the Whites and to the Free Negroes of Barbadoes, and Accounts of some Negroes Eminent for their Virtues and Abilities* (London, 1789). See also "An Argument used by some Writers in Defence of the Legality of the Slave Trade, viz. the Mixture of an Owran-Outang with a Female African, by which they think a Race of Animals may be produced, partaking of the Nature of each, refuted," in *The Eur. Mag. and Lond. Rev.*, Feb. 1788, pp. 75 ff.

[3] Rush, *An Address to the Inhabitants of the British Settlements.*

[4] Gilbert Francklyn, *An Answer to the Rev. Mr. Clarkson's Essay on the Slavery and Commerce of the Human Species . . .* (London, 1789).

[5] [Dr. P. Peckard], *Am I Not a Man, and a Brother? With all Humility Addressed to the British Legislature* (Cambridge, 1788). Anon., *The Negro Boy* (London, n.d.), the latter a booklet issued by the Religious Tract Society of London.

[6] Gilbert Francklyn, *Observations, Occasioned by the Attempts Made in England to Effect the Abolition of the Slave Trade . . .* (London, 1789). Anon., *Remarks on the Advertisement of the Committee for the Abolition of the Slave Trade, Inserted in the Public Press* (London, 1791).

[7] Anon., *The Contrast; Or, the African Slave, and the English Labourer* (Woodbridge, n.d.).

as being a nursery for British seamen. They maintained that a large
share of the nation's commerce and manufacturing rested upon the
investment of over £7,000,000 sterling in the West Indies, which had
been encouraged by parliament. To impair this capital in any way
would react most unfavorably upon economic conditions in the home
country.[1] Such claims resulted in the charge that the transportation
of Africans beyond the Atlantic was directly responsible for the
deaths of from 1,500 to 2,000 seamen annually and did not train
fifty. It was likewise held that abolition would not ruin the Caribbean trade and that this reform would be followed by the rise
of an extensive and profitable commerce in the raw products of
Africa.[2]

No phase of the controversy occasioned greater dispute than did
the question of whether the slave trade and slavery were supported
or condemned by Scripture. The point was one appealing to the
eighteenth century mind and the most was made of it; both parties
quoted Holy Writ extensively as positive proof of their particular
contentions. The slavery group enjoyed the advantage here. Hebraic
bondage was well delineated in the Old Testament and such New
Testament excerpts as "Servants, be obedient to them that are your
masters according to the flesh," [3] "Servants, obey in all things your
masters according to the flesh," [4] "Exhort servants to be obedient
unto their own masters, and to please them well in all things" [5] were
directly applicable to a state of slavery. Human beings were even
specifically named as objects of sale.[6] The institutions' opponents,
on the contrary, were obliged to go to such tortuous lengths of inter-

---

[1] Anon., "A Planter and Merchant, of Many Years Residence in the
West Indies," *West India Trade and Islands. Commercial Reasons for the
Non-Abolition of the Slave Trade in the West India Islands* (London,
1789). Beckford, *Descriptive Account of Jamaica,* II, 317 ff. Lord Sheffield,
*Observations on the Project for Abolishing the Slave Trade, and on the
Reasonableness of Attempting Some Practical Mode of Relieving the Ne-
groes* (London, 1791). [William Innes], "A West India Merchant," *The
Slave Trade Indispensable. In Answer to the Speeches of William Wilber-
force, Esq.* (London, 1792).

[2] S. Hollingsworth, *A Dissertation on the Manners, Governments, and
Spirit of Africa. To Which is Added, Observations on the Present Applications to Parliament for Abolishing Negro Slavery in the West Indies* (Edinburgh, 1788).

[3] *Ephesians* VI, 5.

[4] *Colossians* III, 22.

[5] *Titus* II, 9.

[6] *Revelations* XVIII, 13.

pretation as to quote "Thou shalt not oppress an hired servant that is poor and needy, whether he be of thy brethren or of thy strangers that are in thy land within thy gates" [1] as an argument for free labor.[2]

Particularly disconcerting to the abolitionists was an exceedingly clever and well-written work of the Rev. Raymond Harris, a Spanish-born Jesuit of English extraction in the employ of a Liverpool trading house,[3] *Scriptural Researches on the Licitness of the Slave-Trade*.[4] This renegade churchman undertook to prove the trade in conformity with the laws of nature and of Moses and with Christian dispensation as set forth in the Bible. He summed up his arguments as follows: "Since no abuses or malepractices whatever, though of the greatest magnitude, committed in former times in the prosecution of the Slave-Trade (*Gen.* 35:22; *Exod.* 21:8, 16, 20, 26, 27; *Levit.* 19:20; *Jerem.* 34:8–18) ever induced the Almighty to prohibit or abolish that Trade, but only to check by wholesome and coercive Laws the violence of unnatural masters (*Exod.* 21:7, 12, 16, 20, 21, 26, 27; *Levit.* 19:20, 21, 22; *Ibid.*, 25:39–43) and to punish the transgressors with the greatest severity (*Jeremiah* 34:17–22), there appears no reason whatever, why the abuses and malepractices said to be perpetrated in our days in the prosecution of the same Trade, evidently subject to the control of the Legislature, should be deemed a powerful inducement to proceed to the abolition of it." [5]

His pamphlet attracted national attention; five replies appeared

---

[1] *Deuteronomy* XXIV, 14.

[2] Other quotations in support of slavery were *Genesis* XII, 16; XVI, 6 and 9; XX, 14; XXIV, 35; XXVI, 14; XXXII, 5; XXXVII, 27 and 28; *Exodus* XII, 44; *Leviticus* XXV, 44 to 46; *I Corinthians* VII, 20; *I Timothy* VI, 1; *I Peter* II, 18. Anon., *A Letter to Philo Africanus, Upon Slavery . . .* (London, 1788). Other quotations against it were *Genesis* IX, 6; *Deuteronomy* XIX, 10, 13, and 32; *Psalms* XII, 5; *Isaiah* III, 13 and 15; *Jeremiah* V, 26 to 29; *Ezekiel* XXII, 13, 14, and 29. *The Gent. Mag.* April, 1789, pp. 319, 320. See also "Slave Trade Prohibited in Scripture," in *ibid.*, May, 1792, p. 416; Anon., *Arguments from Scripture For and Against the Slave Trade, as Stated in a Series of Letters, Lately Published in The Glasgow Courier* (Glasgow, 1792); William Agutter, *Abolition of the Slave Trade from a Religious Point of View* (London, 1788); and Anon., *Scripture the Friend of Freedom* (London, 1789).

[3] Picton, *Memorials of Liverpool,* I, 225.

[4] London, 1788.

[5] *Scriptural Researches,* p. 77.

within a few months [1] and the common council of Liverpool voted the author a gratuity for his efforts.[2]

When friends of the trade held up the revolt in St. Domingo as an example of what must follow in the British colonies if agitation in behalf of the slaves did not cease, abolition leaders declared the real cause of the disasters there to have been the pouring of thousands of greatly wronged and mistreated blacks into the island annually, which had not permitted civilizing influences to work among them. They in turn predicted similar uprisings in Great Britain's possessions if this practice were not promptly ended.[3]

The trade was fought with mordant satire,[4] lurid accounts of atrocities,[5] and a considerable quantity of abominable verse,[6] as well as by appeals to religion, humanitarianism and reason. Its opponents themselves were assailed in puerile poetry dedicated to the Caribbean planters and merchants.[7]

[1] [William Roscoe], *A Scriptural Refutation of a Pamphlet Lately Published, by the Rev. Raymond Harris* . . . (London, 1788). Henry Dannett, *A Particular Examination of Mr. Harris's "Scriptural Researches . . ."* (London, 1788). Rev. W. Hughes, *An Answer to the Rev. Mr. Harris's "Scriptural Researches . . ."* (London, 1788), James Ramsay, *An Examination of Mr. Harris's Scriptural Researches* (London, 1788). [Thomas Burgess], *Considerations on the Abolition of Slavery and the Slave Trade, Upon Grounds of Natural, Religious, and Political Duty* (Oxford, 1789).

[2] Picton, *Memorials of Liverpool*, I, 225.

[3] [Thomas Clarkson], *The True State of the Case, Respecting the Insurrection at St. Domingo* (Ipswich, 1792). [William Roscoe], *An Inquiry into the Causes of the Insurrection of the Negroes in the Island of St. Domingo* (no imprint, n.d.).

[4] *To the Honourable House of Commons of Great Britain, in Parliament assembled. The humble Petition of Persons concerned in the Manufacturing of Neckyokes, Collars, Chains, Hand-cuffs, Leg-bolts, Drags, Thumb-Screws, Iron Coffins, Cats, Scourges, and other necessary Instruments of Torture, for the Use of the African Slave Trade* [Manchester, 1788].

[5] *Description of a Slave Ship* (London, 1789). Anon., *The Trial of Capt. John Kimber, for the Murder of Two Female Negro Slaves, on Board the Recovery* . . . (London, 1792). *Remarks on the Methods of Procuring Slaves, With a Short Account of Their Treatment in the West Indies, &c.*, a broadside (London, 1794). Anon., *Slave Trade! An Account of the Murder of a Female Negro, Who was Flogged to Death by order of an Unmerciful Captain* . . . (London, n.d.).

[6] [Edward Rushton], *West Indian Eclogues* (London, 1787). [William Roscoe and James Currie], *The African* (London, 1788). Hannah More, *Slavery: a Poem* (London, 1788). Anon., *Humanity, or the Rights of Nature: A Poem. In Two Books* (London, 1788). "The Slaves—an Elegy," in *The Scots Mag.*, April 1788, pp. 199, 200. James Stanfield, *The Guinea Voyage, A Poem in Three Books* (London, 1789). Anon., *An Elegy, Occasioned by the Rejection of Mr. Wilberforce's Motion for the Abolition of the African Slave Trade* (London, 1791).

[7] Anon., *No Abolition of Slavery; or, The Universal Empire of Love* (London, 1791).

Among the influential supporters of abolition were Joseph Priestly, the eminent theologian and scientist [1] and the Rev. John Newton, himself once the captain of a slaver and more recently become celebrated as a London pastor and writer of church hymns.[2] Such popular periodicals as *The Gentleman's Magazine, The Monthly Review,* and *The Scots Magazine,* through reviews of pamphlets and miscellaneous notices, were generally favorable to the movement.

The discussion centering around the negro problem aroused widespread interest in the tropical American colonies, their history, the state of planter society, and tropical agriculture. An unprecedented number of works on the British West Indies appeared in the two decades 1787–1807,[3] were snatched from the press, and were read with great avidity.

The vogue of Edwards's *History,* splendid though its literary quality may be, is to be explained primarily by its appearance at the height of the abolitionist controversy. Indeed, but for the latter, it would probably never have been written. This classic is fundamentally an attractively disguised defense of the planter interest against the several attacks to which it was being subjected about 1790 and its chief value to-day lies in the fact that it presents West Indian views on contemporary questions at their best.

Authors of the various descriptive accounts and histories of the sugar islands appearing from 1787 on were regularly subjected to praise and censure by supporters of the trade [4] and its opponents,[5] according to their point of view, and were frequently assailed on grounds of truth and prejudice.

[1] *A Sermon on the Subject of the Slave Trade* . . . (Birmingham, 1788).
[2] See page 86. His views on the subject are given in *Thoughts Upon the African Slave Trade* (London, 1788).
[3] Marsden, *An Account of the Island of Jamaica,* Luffman, *Brief Account.* Beckford, *Descriptive Account of Jamaica.* Anon., "A–B–," *Short Journey to the West Indies.* J. B. Moreton, *Manners and Customs of the West India Islands* (London, 1790). Atwood, *History of Dominica.* Maria R[iddell], *Voyages to the Madeira and Leeward Caribbean Isles.* (Edinburgh, 1792). Edwards, *History;* Young, *Account of the Black Charaibs.* Macpherson, *Memoirs of . . . Life and Travels in Asia, Africa, and America.* Young, "A Tour," in Edwards's *Historical Survey of St. Domingo.* Dallas, *History of the Maroons.* F. Mallet, *Descriptive Account of the Island of Trinidad* (London, 1802). McKinnen, *A Tour Through the British West Indies.* Pinckard, *Notes on the West Indies.* Robert Renny, *A History of Jamaica* (London, 1807).
[4] Samuel Mathews, *The Lying Hero, or an Answer to J. B. Moreton's "Manners and Customs in the West Indies"* (St. Eustatius, 1793).
[5] William Preston, *A Letter to Bryan Edwards, Esquire, Containing Observations on Some Passages of his History of the West Indies* (London, 1795).

The defeat of abolition measures in 1791 and 1792 occasioned an interesting attempt to effect social reform through economic pressure. The opposition of the powerful Liverpool and Caribbean interests had rendered all attempts to end the trade fruitless; parliament had shown itself hopelessly subservient to the planters and merchants. It was believed, however, that both the colonists and the government could be coerced through the institution of a systematic boycott of West Indian sugar and rum as the former were dependent upon ready sale of those products for their incomes and a large part of the national revenue was derived from duties collected upon their entry for home consumption. The efficacy of such a measure had been discussed by Thomas Cooper in a booklet issued as early as 1787 [1] and now, four years later, the abolitionists began a concerted attempt to thus force their opponents' hands.

Advocates of the boycott declared that power to end the negro trade and even slavery itself lay in the individual.

"The CONSUMER of West India produce may be considered as the *Master-spring* that gives motion and effect to the whole Machine of Cruelties . . . [The selling of human beings constitutes] a *chain* of WRETCHEDNESS every link of which is stained with blood! and it involves in *equal criminality* the AFRICAN TRADER—the WEST INDIA SLAVE HOLDER—and the BRITISH CONSUMER! Nothing can be more evident . . . than that the CONSUMER of *West India Produce* is the principal cause, both of the continuance of the SLAVE TRADE and of the prevalence of SLAVERY. For . . . *why* is the Slave Trade pursued at all? Is it not to supply the Planters with *men* to cultivate their lands? And why are the *lands* cultivated if not to furnish the people of Europe with their produce? It must be clear then, that if that produce were not *consumed,* it would not be imported—if it were not imported, it would not be raised—and if it were not raised, there must be an end to the whole system of slavery . . . The SLAVE TRADE can receive from no man *greater encouragement,* than by his *Consumption of the* PRODUCE . . . If then we are *sincere* in wishing the ABOLITION of the SLAVE TRADE—if we indeed *compassionate* the *poor* SLAVES! we are bound, from every consideration, *to* ABSTAIN *from the* CONSUMPTION *of the* PRODUCE *which* THEY *cultivate!*" [2]

[1] *Letters on the Slave Trade,* published in Manchester.
[2] Anon., *The Duty of Abstaining from the Use of West India Produce, A Speech, Delivered at Coach-Maker's Hall,* Jan. 12, 1792 (London, 1792), pp. 8, 11, 12.

Each user of Caribbean products was directly and personally responsible for the existing state of affairs. "Every person who habitually consumes one article of West Indian produce, raised by Slaves, *is guilty of the crime of murder*—every one who does it, when convinced that what has been said is true is *deliberately guilty,* and rendered more criminal by it being preceded by every species of cruelty and torture, which inventive barbarity can devise."

The fact that a given consumer was but one of many in no way exculpated him. "Shall it be said that the abstinence of an individual can produce no effect? When a thousand musquets are levelled at an innocent bosom, is it no crime in me to direct another bullet at the victim?" [1]

Each household could appreciably aid the abolition cause and prevent mistreatment of the blacks by participating in the boycott. If a family consuming five pounds of sugar and a proportionate amount of rum refused to purchase either commodity for twenty-one months, that family would "prevent the slavery or murder of one fellow-creature; eight such families in 19 years and a half would prevent the slavery or murder of 100, and 38,000 would totally prevent the Slave Trade to supply our islands. Nay, so necessarily connected are our consumption of the commodity, and the misery resulting from it, that in every pound of sugar used (the product of the slaves imported from Africa) we may be considered as consuming two ounces of human blood, besides destroying an alarming number of seamen by the slave-trade, and spreading inconceivable anguish, terror, and dismay, through an immense continent, by the burning of their villages, tearing parents from their families, and children from their parents; breaking every bond of society, and destroying every source of human happiness. . . . Our refraining from the consumption of the sugar-cane for a few years would destroy the Slave Trade to the West India Islands, bring fresh land into culture, and place the slaves in such a position, that they must rapidly increase." [2]

A special plea to join in the movement was made to "the LADIES *of* ENGLAND . . ., the Models of every just and virtuous sentiment. . . . Their EXAMPLE . . . must silence every murmur—

[1] Thomas Cooper, *Considerations on the Slave Trade; and the Consumption of West Indian Produce* (London, 1791), p. 14.

[2] [William Fox], *An Address to the People of Great-Britain, on the Propriety of Abstaining from West-India Sugar and Rum* (London, 1791), pp. 3–5. The authorship is revealed in later editions, as the fourteenth.

must refute every objection—and render the *performance* of the Duty as UNIVERSAL as their INFLUENCE!" [1]

All Christians were called upon to give a practical demonstration of the principles of their faith by refusing to use products defiled with blood; [2] children were asked to forgo accustomed sweets and thus prevent the selling of their little black brothers into bondage; [3] royalty was urged to set an example of abstinence which must needs be followed by all persons of importance in the country. [4]

Lest mere appeals to Christian charity and humanitarian sentiment prove inefficacious, William Fox, the philanthropist friend of Wilberforce and Sharp and an ardent advocate of popular action, sought to arouse feelings of disgust and nausea in his readers by presenting a revolting account of how West Indian sugar and rum were prepared for market, drawn with a fervid imagination and nicely calculated to achieve the desired end. Muscovado, he declared, "is brought out of the Sugar house on a Negro's shoulders, and emptied from the Pots into the Hogshead; into which two or three stout fellows, nearly, or altogether naked, are immediately placed, to tread it down with their feet, as it is thrown in; constantly laboring with all their might, till the Cask is full. . . . I will leave it wholly to my Readers to determine the quantity of the fluid that may reasonably be supposed to flow from the Bodies of these three men, almost in contact with each other, toiling hard under a sultry Sun, till relieved by others. . . . Every Hogshead of sugar, imported into England from the West Indies, is more or less impregnated with this liquid from the human body.

"There are also many other disagreeable ingredients, which with great propriety, we may suppose to be mixed with it. For instance, it is well known that the wooly head of the Negro is as fertile in the propagation of a certain domestic insect, as the flaxen locks of the European. Is it then, any way strange to conceive, that while the labouring Slave, perspiring at every pore, with his head as wet as

---

[1] *The Duty of Abstaining from the Use of West India Produce*, pp. 22, 23.

[2] Anon., *Considerations Addressed to Professors of Christianity of Every Denomination on the Impropriety of Consuming West-India Sugar and Rum, as Produced by the Oppressive Labour of Slaves* (Dublin, 1792).

[3] See "Letter Written by a Boy in Defence of the Use of Sugar," in *The Eur. Mag. and Lond. Rev.*, March 1792, pp. 185, 186, an ingenious defense of the planter interest indicative of the nature of the appeals then being made to the juvenile mind.

[4] Anon., *An Address to Her Royal Highness, the Dutchess [sic] of York Against the Use of Sugar* (London, 1792).

Gideon's first fleece, jumping in the Cask with all his might, some of this numerous race, who inhabit the Capital, may inadvertently lose their hold, and fall in among the Sugar; or be carried there with the large drops as they fall from his reeking locks?"

Other ingredients of sugar, according to this self-confessed authority, were pus from sores on the bodies of blacks suffering from the yaws and jiggers from their feet. As for rum, in a puncheon of the Jamaican product lately ordered by a merchant there had been found "The whole Body of a roasted Negro . . . stretched out, and fastened down in the bilge of the Cask, opposite the bung hole. . . . Now far be it from me, to insinuate from hence, that any such methods are used to meliorate West India Rum; I will only take upon me to affirm, as a certain fact, that the Carcase of a Dog, Cat, Sheep, Goat, Man or Woman, thoroughly burnt, and put in the bottom of a large vessel, full of Spirits of any kind, will greatly tend to meliorate and soften them. But whether there exist such indelicate wretches, who from avaricious motives, are capable of doing this, I leave to my Readers to determine, and to ruminate in what they have read." [1]

Various other bids for public support were made both in prose [2] and in verse. [3]

The undertaking attained sufficient proportions to cause the London West India interest serious concern. Early in 1792, the Society of Planters and Merchants commissioned Mr. Clutterbuck, author of *Vindication of the Use of Sugar, the Produce of the West-India Islands*, [4] to prepare a second, enlarged edition of his work [5] in which it was argued that the consumption of Caribbean products was not criminal because of their being slave-grown and that their disuse could never seriously injure the slave trade, would make the plantation workers' position less supportable, would distress seamen em-

[1] [William Fox], "An Eye Witness to the Facts Related," *A Second Address to the People of Great Britain: Containing a New, and Most Powerful Argument to Abstain from the Use of West India Sugar* (Rochester, 1792), pp. 6–11. For the earlier work, see note 2, p. 261. The author had already become celebrated as the founder of the Sunday School Society.

[2] Anon., *Remarkable Extracts and Observations on the Slave Trade: with Some Considerations on the Consumption of West India Produce* (London, 1791). Anon., *An Address to the People of Great Britain, on the Consumption of West India Produce* [London, n.d.]. Anon., *No Rum . . . No Sugar! or, The Voice of Blood, Being Half an Hour's Conversation, Between a Negro and an English Gentleman . . .* (London, 1792).

[3] Timothy Touchstone, *pseud., Tea and Sugar; or, The Nabob and the Creole; A Poem, in Two Cantos* (London, 1792).

[4] London, 1791.

[5] *Min. Sub-Comm. W. I. Plant. and Mer.,* Feb. 9, and March 1, 1792.

ployed in the negro traffic, would cause heavy losses to British merchants, and would lower the health of residents of the home country.[1]

A writer of a generation after [2] tells us that his aunt "imbibed an unaccountable prejudice" against tropical American produce at this time, that she refused to use sugar in her tea, and did not taste "pie, pudding, tartlet, or any other eatable of which this ingredient composed a part" for twenty years. The increase in sale of East Indian sugar from 4,047 hundredweight in 1791 to 43,205 hundredweight in 1793 [3] was due in part to numerous buyers calling upon their grocers to supply them with the free-labor product from the orient.[4]

The idea of forcing action through popular pressure was less hare-brained than might appear at first glance. We have already noted the weak economic position of the colonial agrarian group about 1790.[5] But the movement never won the open support of abolition leaders and did not attain the hoped-for momentum. Moreover, the sudden rise in the prices of Caribbean produce at the very time it was launched, resulting from the wars in St. Domingo,[6] removed all force from the undertaking.[7]

The concerted attack on the planters' method of recruiting their labor supply, involving adverse criticism of the plantation system itself, which opened in 1787, aroused great resentment among the inhabitants of the tropical American colonies and among the West Indians at home. They sought to explain the motives activating the humanitarians in terms of desire to secure revenge or of economic self-interest rather than of genuinely altruistic feeling. It was charged that the Quakers played such a leading rôle because of wrath on their part at not having been exempted from service in the colonial

[1] *Vindication*, edition of 1792, pp. 17–21.

[2] Frederic Bayley, author of *Four Years' Residence in the West Indies.* See p. 4.

[3] *East India Sugar. Papers Respecting the Culture and Manufacture of Sugar . . .* , Appendix IV, p. 5.

[4] Macpherson, *Annals of Commerce,* IV, 232. It is interesting to note that an anti-saccharist campaign was being waged against the West India planters in the northern American states at this same time. Persons opposed to the use of slave-grown sugar purchased maple-sugar instead. One mathematically inclined individual estimated that 263,000 acres of land planted in maple trees beyond the Appalachians could provide the 42,000,000 lbs. of sugar then being used annually in the United States. *Ibid.,* IV, 209–211.

[5] Pages 191 and 192.

[6] Pages 205 ff.

[7] For cursory notes on the movement, see "The Anti-Saccharists, A Curious Sect of 1792–1820," in *The W. I. Comm. Circ.,* April 27, 1922, p. 191.

militias [1] and that the underlying cause of the abolition movement as a whole was dissatisfaction over the increased cost of West Indian produce resulting from restrictions laid on the American trade. "Discontent at the high price of sugar is called sympathy for the wretched," declared Bryan Edwards, "and the murmurs of avarice become the dictates of humanity." [2]

Uncertainty as to the outcome of the parliamentary attack on the trade resulted in a depreciation of Caribbean land values and tended to discourage the opening of new estates.[3] The colonials readily enough approved of governmental control in the hope that the adoption of such measures would calm the clamor which had been raised against the traffic in general. Thus, in 1788, a committee of the Jamaican assembly, speaking of the regulating act of that year, held it to be "founded in justice, humanity, and necessity" and recommended that the purchase of kidnapped blacks be prohibited, that ship captains be obliged to transport an equal number of both sexes, and that a law be passed requiring slavers to be equipped with ventilators and well-stocked with provisions and water.[4]

The cutting off of their supply of negroes was, however, quite another matter. At a joint meeting of the council and assembly of the same colony, held in November 1789 to determine what steps should be taken to oppose abolition, Bryan Edwards ably handled the subject in what proved to be the outstanding speech of his distinguished career. He frankly recognized the evils involved in commerce in human beings, but held that no good could come from its being discontinued by one power alone, and presented a series of propositions

[1] This charge was brought against them even four decades later. See Williams, *A Tour Through the Island of Jamaica*, pp. 214, 215.

[2] *History*, II, 421, 422. It may be noted that one supporter of that trade held the high price of sugar commencing in 1791 to be due to alarm occasioned by abolitionist agitation. See Anon., "An Old Trader," *Thoughts on the present High Price of Sugar, proving it to have arisen from the Rumour of the Slave Bill, and from that cause only* . . . (London, 1792).

[3] Letter of John Rae, a member of the Grenadan assembly, Oct. 7, 1789, C. O. 101/30.

[4] *Two Reports (one presented the 16th of October, the other on the 12th of November, 1788) from the Committee of the Honourable House of Assembly of Jamaica, Appointed to examine into, and report to the House, the Allegations and Charges contained in the several Petitions which have been presented to the British House of Commons, on the Subject of the Slave-Trade, and the Treatment of the Negroes, &c. &c. &c.* (London, 1789). Replied to by an anonymous abolitionist, *Notes on the Two Reports from the Committee of the Honourable House of Assembly of Jamaica* . . . (London, 1789).

meeting those placed before parliament by Mr. Wilberforce a few months earlier.[1] A formal remonstrance of the island legislature against any closing of the trade, embodying Edwards's propositions and calling for compensation if such a measure were adopted, was soon after prepared by a committee of the two houses for transmission to England.[2]

Three years later, a committee of the Jamaican assembly denied parliament's right to enact legislation applicable to the colonies or to lay a proposed tax against slaves imported into them, declaring that the islanders "have the indefeasible right of giving and granting their own money, and of legislating for themselves; . . . it is the indispensable duty of the assembly of Jamaica to maintain . . . the just privileges of the colonials; and . . . they will oppose, in every constitutional manner, any attempt to deprive them of such rights and privileges. . . ."[3]

No uniform negro code, such as existed in those French possessions where slavery prevailed, was found in the British West Indies. Viewing the adjustment of labor questions as a purely local matter and with characteristic confidence in the ability of the colonists to settle their own problems better than could parliament, in the far-off mother country and with but little first-hand information, the home government permitted each island legislature to draw up its own slave law and to provide for its enforcement. There was consequently great variation in detail, but such bodies of regulations uniformly protected the masters' interests and denied rights to the blacks. In the latter part of the eighteenth century, these codes generally consisted of a considerable number of individual acts adopted from time to time in the past, many of them decades before, couched in phrases and embodying concepts of the ruder age in which they had been drawn.

Their study gave a wholly false picture of the slaves' actual position at that time. Constant contact between the two races and long-continued intimate association had considerably tempered the

---

[1] Bryan Edwards, *A Speech Delivered at a Free Conference Between the Honourable the Council and Assembly of Jamaica, Held the 19th Nov. 1789, on the Subject of Mr. Wilberforce's Propositions in the House of Commons, Concerning the Slave Trade* (Kingston, 1789).

[2] *Report, Resolutions, and Remonstrance, of the Honourable the Council and Assembly of Jamaica, at a Joint Committee, on the Subject of the Slave-Trade, in a Session which Began the 20th of October, 1789* (London, 1790).

[3] *Proceedings of the Hon. House of Assembly of Jamaica . . . in a Session Which Began the 23d of October, 1792.* p. 15.

letter of the law and custom had progressively improved the negroes' status from that of earlier times. Since the abolitionists and opponents of slavery drew many of their leading arguments from these antiquated codes, no time was lost in effecting revisions so as to make them correspond more nearly with reality.

The Jamaicans had already taken a great step in that direction in 1784, but all existing legislation governing slaves in the colony was repealed three years later and a milder worded, consolidated measure which actually did not alter the Africans' standing in the slightest degree from what it already was, replaced the earlier heterogeneous mass of laws with which the British were familiar.[1] A further redrawing occurred a year later [2] and this new act in turn gave way to a third instituted in 1792, designed to meet criticism in England.[3]

The adoption of these several codes was given wide publicity; they were published and distributed at home by Stephen Fuller, the island agent, to controvert charges of the planters' adversaries. A new slave law was similarly adopted in the Leeward Islands a few years later.[4]

The Society of West India Planters and Merchants combated the abolition movement both in and out of parliament. A subcommittee was named in February 1788 to watch the progress of the House of Commons' inquiry into the trade. In June of the same year, a petition was sent to the upper chamber praying that the regulating measure then before it [5] be rejected.[6] When Mr. Wilberforce moved his propositions ten months later, protests against ending the trade were presented.

[1] *The Act of Assembly of the Island of Jamaica. To Repeal Several Acts, and Clauses of Acts, respecting Slaves, and for the better Order and Government of Slaves, and for other Purposes; Commonly Called the Consolidated Act, as Exhibiting at One View Most of the Essential Regulations of the Jamaica Code Noir, Which was passed by the Assembly on the 19th Day of December 1787, and by the Lieutenant Governor and the Council on the 22d of the said Month* (London, 1788).

[2] *The New Act of Assembly of the Island of Jamaica . . . Commonly Called the New Consolidated Act, Which Was Passed by the Assembly on the 6th of November—by the Council on the 5th Day of December—and by the Lieutenant Governor on the 6th Day of December, 1788; Being the Present Code Noir of That Island* (London, 1789).

[3] Printed in Edwards, *History*, II, 151 ff.

[4] This is most readily accessible in briefed form in Flannigan, *Antigua*, II, 126–129.

[5] See page 251. Subsequently passed as 28 Geo. III c. 54.

[6] *Min. W. I. Plant. and Mer.*, June 30, 1788.

Expenses incurred in opposing abolitionist efforts were met from a fighting fund raised by increasing the trade tax on each hogshead of sugar, puncheon of rum, and bag of cotton handled by members of the organization from 1d. to 6d. in April, 1789 [1] and to 1s. from March, 1792.[2] The rate was varied thereafter as occasion demanded.[3] Mortagees, annuitants, and general creditors of the Caribbean colonists were appealed to for contributions and the West India merchants of Liverpool, Glasgow, and Bristol were urged to levy a charge on their commerce equalling that paid in London and to remit sums thus raised to the Society of Planters and Merchants.[4] The Glasgow traders declined to lend aid; and, while those of Liverpool complied with the request, this was not done without objection on the part of certain individuals there.[5] No response seems to have been received from elsewhere.

In January, 1792, the subcommittee named four years earlier was enlarged and was given a new duty, "to circulate such publications in the Newspapers and otherwise, as shall seem to them useful not only for obtaining the objects then and since referred to them, but for the purpose of defending the Cause of the Colonies, so far as respects the Colony system in general, and the protection of its Articles of produce and the extension of their Consumption." £300 was voted for such work;[6] further appropriations totalling £1,300 were made within the next quarter.[7]

A series of propaganda pamphlets was promptly issued under auspices of this body. The cost of publishing a collection of speeches made to the National Assembly of France by deputies from St. Domingo on disorders there [8] was met, and a second edition of 3,000

[1] *Min. W. I. Plant. and Mer.*, April 24, 1789.

[2] *Ibid.*, May 16, 1792.

[3] It was lowered to 6d. a year later (*Ibid.*, June 1, 1793); in 1794 it was again doubled (*Ibid.*, May 20, 1794); and twelve months after, when opposition had declined, it was reduced to 2d. (*Ibid.*, May 20, 1795.) In 1799, the rate was once more raised to 1s. (*Ibid.*, June 24, of that year.) This was cut to 6d. from March 1803 (*Ibid.*, June 9, 1804. A retrogressive measure); in 1805, it was set at 3d. (*Ibid.*, June 6, 1805).

[4] *Ibid.*, Feb. 11, 1790; June 1, 1793.

[5] *Ibid.*, May 5, 1796.

[6] *Ibid.*, Jan. 19, 1792.

[7] *Ibid.*, Feb. 20, and April 13, 1792.

[8] Anon., *A Particular Account of the Commencement and Progress of the Insurrection of the Negroes in St. Domingo, which Began in August Last: Being a Translation of the Speech Made to the National Assembly . . . by the Deputies . . . from St. Domingo* (London, 1792).

copies, to be edited by George Hibbert and to be sold at a moderate price, was ordered.[1] Evidence favorable to the trade and slavery, given before committees of the privy council and of the House of Commons, was printed [2] at its direction.[3] One hundred twenty copies of Gilbert Francklyn's "work on the slave trade" [4] were purchased at £9.7.6 for distribution "in the Country, particularly at Cambridge." [5]

Eight thousand copies of an ingenious work setting forth the comfortable position of the negroes, each with "a snug little house and garden, and plenty of pigs and poultry," [6] were issued,[7] and copies, together with summaries of the evidence on the trade, were sent to the aldermen and members of the common council of London.[8] Five hundred copies of a booklet by a former West Indian physician, holding the slaves' lot to compare favorably with that of the lower classes in England,[9] were distributed among members of the House of Commons.[10] A thousand copies of a speech prepared for delivery in that body by a member of the Caribbean interest, maintaining that popular opinion was not demanding abolition and that petitions calling for it were secured by artifice,[11] were printed and circulated.[12] The copyright on a report of the parliamentary debate of April 2, 1792, at which time the lower chamber declared itself in favor of ·

[1] Min. Sub-Comm. W. I. Plant. and Mer., Jan. 23, 1792.

[2] [Mr. Vaughan, editor], A Summary of the Evidence Produced Before the Committee of the Privy Council, and Before a Committee of the House of Commons; Relating to the Slave Trade (London, 1792).

[3] Min. Sub-Comm. W. I. Plant. and Mer., Feb. 9, 1792.

[4] Either his An Answer to the Rev. Mr. Clarkson's Essay or Observations, Occasioned by the Attempts Made . . . to Effect the Abolition of the Slave-Trade.

[5] Min. Sub-Comm. W. I. Plant. and Mer., March 1, 1792. Cambridge was an important abolitionist center; one of the leaders in the movement there was Dr. Peckard of the university.

[6] Anon., "A Plain Man," The True State of the Question, Addressed to the Petitioners for the Abolition of the Slave Trade (London, 1792).

[7] Min. Sub-Comm. W. I. Plant. and Mer., March 22, 1792.

[8] Ibid., March 30, 1792.

[9] Jesse Foote, A Defence of the Planters in the West Indies (London, 1792).

[10] Min. Sub-Comm. W. I. Plant. and Mer., March 28, 1792.

[11] Anon., Substance of a Speech Intended to Have Been Made on Mr. Wilberforce's Motion for the Abolition of the Slave Trade, April 3, 1792; But the Unwillingness of the Committee to Hear Any Thing Further on the Subject after Mr. Pitt Had Spoken Prevented the Member from Being Heard (London, 1792).

[12] Min. Sub-Comm. W. I. Plant. and Mer., April 17, 1792.

gradual rather than of immediate abolition,[1] was purchased for £100.[2]

Great use was made of newspapers in carrying on this work. *The Morning Chronicle, The Public Ledger, The Oracle, The Star, The Whitehall Evening Post,* and *The Argus* in particular were frequently employed. In February, 1792, a letter by George Hibbert centering about a pamphlet, the work of Lord Sheffield, opposed to immediate abolition,[3] was published in the first of these journals under the signature "Candour" at a cost of four guineas.[4] The same sheet later carried two letters by G. Francklyn, signed "Detector," in which it was charged that the St. Domingan insurrection was brought about through the activities of the French abolitionist society, *Les Amis des Noirs,* as well as speeches of the island deputies before the National Assembly on the causes of the war,[5] the latter at a cost of £21.0.6.[6] In March 1792, members of the group agreed to meet daily between twelve and three for the purpose of perusing current papers and "of replying to what may be therein inserted by the Favourers of the Abolition of the Slave trade, against the Interest of the Sugar Colonies, though the medium of the . . . Papers, which are open to the directions of this Committee. . . ."[7]

A Mr. Bell was hired at £5 a week to communicate with country papers, particularly those published in parts of England which had sent petitions praying for abolition to parliament, "to find out which will, and which will not, insert paragraphs from this Committee," and to supply friendly ones with "such paragraphs or Essays that come from the sub-committee." He was in the employ of the Society for a year.[8] Joseph Gerald, a hack writer, was likewise engaged at £100 per annum "for the purpose of drawing up Paragraphs etc. to be inserted in different Newspapers under the direction of the Sub-committee." He was instructed to be attentive to items against the colonial interest appearing in the general press and to furnish timely answers to well-disposed journals. His salary was continued to

---

[1] [Mr. McCarthy, ed.], *An Appeal to the Condour and Justice of the People of England, in Behalf of the West India Merchants and Planters, Founded on Plain Facts and Incontrovertible Arguments* (London, 1792).

[2] *Min. Sub-Comm. W. I. Plant. and Mer.,* April 19, 1792.

[3] *Observations on the Project for Abolishing the Slave Trade. . . .*

[4] *Min. Sub-Comm. W. I. Plant. and Mer.,* April 19, 1792.

[5] Already published in pamphlet form by the Society. See note 8, p. 268.

[6] *Min. Sub-Comm. W. I. Plant. and Mer.,* Feb. 20, and March 1, 1792.

[7] *Ibid.,* March 22, 1792.

[8] *Ibid.,* March 22 and 27, 1792; March 25, 1793.

October, 1792, from which time he was paid for accepted work.[1]

An order for 600 copies of *The Argus* was placed with McCarty, the editor, early in April, 1792, following the pledging of the House of Commons to the principle of gradual rather than immediate abolition "in order to give encouragement . . . for a favourable Report to the Interests of the Sugar Colonies" of the debate which preceded the vote on the question.[2] In June, £66.1.0 was paid for the insertion of letters in *The Oracle* and *The Morning Chronicle;*[3] in July, £50 was similarly appropriated in order that the West Indians might continue to receive favorable treatment in *The Whitehall Evening Post*. At the same time, works opposing abolition were ordered bound into convenient volumes for transmission to circulating libraries in the different watering places, where, presumably, it was hoped that they would fall into the hands of vacationing legislators.[4]

The subcommittee purchased and circulated numerous copies of Dr. Moseley's pamphlet on coffee and engaged Mr. Clutterbuck to bring out a new edition of his booklet defending the use of slave-grown sugar, as already noted,[5] in fulfillment of its duty of seeking to increase the consumption of island produce. With the defeat of the abolition measure of 1792, the body's activities virtually ceased and the Society of Planters and Merchants as a whole once more directed the opposition. Richard Shawe, a solicitor, was voted £4,400 in 1795 for his services in having directed the anti-abolition fight in parliament during the three past years.[6]

An interesting experiment in colonization—the settling of Sierra Leone on the west coast of Africa with free blacks—occurred in the midst of all this agitation. The project was formulated by Henry Smeathman, formerly resident in that portion of the world, and Granville Sharp, who was ever concerned with the welfare of the negroes in England. Wilberforce, too, soon became one of its promoters. Land was purchased and the first group was sent out in 1787. Deaths from fever and an attack by a hostile chieftain nearly annihilated the colony.

To place the enterprise on a more substantial footing, the Sierra

---

[1] *Min. Sub-Comm. W. I. Plant. and Mer.,* March 22, May 11, Aug. 13, and Oct. 9, 1792.

[2] *Ibid.,* April 2 and 4, 1792.

[3] *Ibid.,* June 9, 1792.

[4] *Ibid.,* July 16, 1792.

[5] See pages 199 and 263.

[6] *Min. W. I. Plant. and Mer.,* May 20, 1794, May 20, 1795.

Leone Company was organized by opponents of the slave trade and English merchants. A charter of incorporation was secured from parliament in 1791,[1] despite the opposition of members of the West India interest who feared the competition of the new colony's produce in home markets,[2] and Zachary Macaulay,[3] father of Thomas Babington Macaulay and later one of the leading spirits of the emancipation movement, assumed the duties of governor.

In 1792, more than a thousand former slaves, who had joined the British forces during the American Revolution under promise of freedom, arrived in charge of John Clarkson, brother of Thomas Clarkson, from Nova Scotia where they had been settled but which they found too cold. Some 550 of the survivors of the Maroon war who had been deported from Jamaica to Nova Scotia [4] were similarly removed to Sierra Leone eight years later. After numerous disasters, which afforded supporters of slavery ample opportunity for deriding the "quixotic philanthropy" of the humanitarians, the colony took root and eventually justified the benevolent intentions of its founders.[5]

We have noted Wilberforce's fruitless attempts to secure the adoption of abolition at each session of parliament up to 1799. There was a marked decline in public interest in the negro cause after 1792— the French war turned attention to other matters. The use of bloodhounds against the Jamaican Maroons occasioned a short-lived outburst of feeling,[6] but this soon died down. Bryan Edwards, now member of parliament for Southampton, secured the repeal of that portion of an act of more than half a century's standing,[7] permitting slaves to be seized and sold for their masters' debts,[8] a reform he had strongly advocated in his writings some years earlier.[9] A general measure regulating the slave trade along the lines drawn in the

---

[1] Under 31 Geo. III c. 55.

[2] *Min. W. I. Plant. and Mer.*, May 13, 17, 18, and 19, 1791.

[3] See Anon., *A Brief Sketch of the Life of the Late Zachary Macaulay, Esq. F. R. S. As Connected With the Subjects of the Abolition of the Slave Trade and Slavery* (London, 1830); M. de Saint-Anthoine, *Notice Nécrologique sur M. Zacharie Macaulay* (Paris, 1838); and George Trevelyan, *The Life and Letters of Lord Macaulay* (London, 1881), the early chapters of which give much information on the subject's father.

[4] See page 226.

[5] The company was dissolved in 1807 and Sierra Leone thereupon passed under the immediate authority of the crown.

[6] See pages 225, 226.

[7] 5 Geo. II c. 7.

[8] 37 Geo. III c. 119.

[9] *History*, II, 148, 149.

provisional acts dating from 1788 was adopted in 1799.[1] The traffic
in blacks, now placed on a humane basis, seemed intrenched as a
permanent feature of the British commercial system. For half a decade no attempt was made in parliament to end it. But interest in the
matter was by no means dead. It is significant that Lady Nugent,
wife of the lieutenant-governor of Jamaica, was earnestly reading
abolition literature at the opening of the century.[2]

A noteworthy incident of the last years of the crusade against the
African trade, which served to hold public attention, was the accusation brought against Sir Thomas Picton,[3] former governor of Trinidad, of having permitted the torture of accused slaves as a means
of securing confessions from them. Picton had been named executive
following the capture of the island in 1797 [4] and had ruled the rest-
less population with the firm hand the situation demanded.

Upon its formal annexation five years later,[5] a commission form
of government was instituted. Colonel William Fullarton was named
First Commissioner and Sir Samuel Hood and Picton were associated
with him. Thus the latter, by a stupid, short-sighted disregard for
means of insuring administrative harmony, was superseded without
being recalled. Fullarton was a vain and overbearing self-seeker, soon
at outs with his fellow-officials. The former governor almost immediately found his position intolerable, left the colony in the
summer of 1803, and returned to England,[6] only to be followed
shortly after by his superior.

Casting about for means of justifying his attitude toward Picton,
Fullarton opened a general assault upon the latter's administration,
capitalizing the fact that certain steps taken by his predecessor had
been at variance with English law. As a matter of fact, because of
the diverse racial elements found in the island, which would make

---

[1] 39 Geo. III c. 80.

[2] Cundall, ed., *Lady Nugent's Journal,* Nov. 23, 1801—"I have lately devoted
much of my time to Mr. Wilberforce's works" (p. 57). Dec. 31, 1801—
"Read Wilberforce" (p. 69). Jan. 13, 1802—"Study Wilberforce till breakfast time" (p. 72).

[3] "Memoir of Lieutenant-General Sir Thomas Picton, K. G. C. B. M. P.,"
in *The Eur. Mag. and Lond. Rev.,* Sept. 1815, pp. 195 ff. H. B. Robinson,
*Memoirs of Lieutenant-General Sir Thomas Picton . . . Including His Cor-
respondence, from Originals in Possession of His Family* (London, 1835).

[4] See page 228.

[5] See page 292.

[6] See the papers in C. O. 295/4-7. *Trinidad. A Proclamation. By Their Ex-
cellencies Brigadier General Thomas Picton and Commodore Samuel Hood . . .*
[Port of Spain, 1803]. *Trinidad. A Proclamation By William Fullarton, His
Majesty's First Commissioner . . . in Trinidad* [Port of Spain, 1803].

the introduction of representative government a hazardous undertaking, Spanish law had been maintained by order of the home government and Trinidad was ruled as a crown colony.[1] This was viewed
as a great grievance by British settlers who held that they were thus
being deprived of their cherished rights as Englishmen,[2] but the
foreign code only gradually gave way to the more familiar home
one during the nineteenth century [3] and all acts carried out by Governor Picton under the Spanish system were in every sense legal.

To secure substantial support for his case, Fullarton played upon
public feeling at home by charging the late executive with having
ordered the torture of prisoners as a means of wringing confessions
from them. The affair of Louisa Calderon, fifteen year old mulatto
mistress of a Spanish resident whom she and a paramour had been
accused of robbing, was seized upon as one apt to appeal to British
susceptibilities and was duly exploited. This negress had denied her
guilt in the face of clear evidence to the contrary and had consequently, with Picton's consent, been treated in accordance with Spanish law covering such situations.

In the presence of a physician, a belt had been tied around her
body, she had been lifted off the ground by a pulley attached to the
ceiling, her feet had been allowed to rest upon two pieces of wood
with square tops, and she had been informed that she would remain
thus suspended until she admitted her crime. A confession was forthcoming at once and she was lowered to the ground none the worse
for her experience.

A wildly exaggerated account of the episode given by the First
Commissioner found willing believers among well-intentioned but
misguided friends of abolition. Lurid wood-cuts portraying a comely
wench dangling by one arm, with her feet vainly seeking support on a
sharp spike,[4] were widely circulated. Louisa's arrival in London with

[1] See pages 389 and 390.
[2] Anon., "A Gentleman of the Island," *A Political Account of the Island of
Trinidad . . . in a Letter to His Grace the Duke of Portland* (London,
1807). John Sanderson, *An Appeal to the Imperial Parliament. Upon the
Claims of the Ceded Colony of Trinidad, to be Governed by a Legislature
and Judicature, Founded in Principles Sanctioned by Colonial Precedents and
Long Usage* . . . (London, 1812).
[3] For the slow substitution of English for Spanish law, see Charles Reis, *The
Government of Trinidad* (London, n.d.).
[4] For example, see the illustrations in Anon., *The Trial of Thomas Picton
. . . for Torturing Louisa Calderon, in the Island of Trinidad* (London,
1806) ; John Fairburn, ed., *Inhuman Torture!! The Trial of Thomas Picton
. . . for Torturing Louisa Calderon* . . . (London, n.d.).

Colonel and Mrs. Fullarton and her daily drives about the city with her patroness created a furor. By his appeal to blind prejudice and passion, Fullarton succeeded in converting his despicable personal attack on Picton into the worst case of persecution in West Indian history.

The whole matter was thoroughly aired in a series of pamphlets by the accuser [1] and the accused [2] from 1804 to 1806 and both found staunch champions in other writers.[3] In the latter year, Picton was at length brought to trial before the court of king's bench on the specific charge of having ordered the woman to be tortured and was found guilty.[4] A hearing before the privy council in 1807 resulted in a report in his favor.[5] The case was retried in 1808, and, when it was proved that the former governor's action had been in accordance with the law of Castile, he was released from bail without judgment being given.[6] Colonel Fullarton's death occurred at about the same time and, although his widow sought to press his charges,

---

[1] Fullarton, A Statement, Letters, and Documents Respecting the Affairs of Trinidad . . . (London, 1804). Also Refutation of the Pamphlet Which Colonel Picton Lately Addressed to Lord Hobart (London, 1805) and his Letter to . . . Lord —— . . . on the Subject of Torture Introduced Into the British Colonies, as Connected with the Laws of Old Spain (London, 1806).

[2] Picton, A Letter, Addressed to the Right Honourable Lord Hobart . . . (London, 1804). Colonel Picton's Preface [to "A Letter Addressed to the Rt. Hon. Lord Hobart . . ."]—Colonel Fullarton's Answer [London, 1805].

[3] Thus, the ex-governor's conduct is supported in "The Pictonian Prosecution," in The Anti-Jacobin Review and Magazine, May, 1806, pp. 47-72 and in Edward A. Draper, An Address to the British Public, on the Case of Brigadier-General Picton . . . with Observations on the Conduct of William Fullarton, Esq. . . . and the Right Honourable John Sullivan (London, 1806). He is attacked in Pierre F. M'Callum, Travels in Trinidad During the Months of February, March, and April, 1803 (Liverpool, 1805) and in Decius, pseud., Letters . . . in Answer to the Criticism Upon the Political Account of Trinidad . . . (London, 1808).

[4] Anon., Sir Thomas Picton's Evidence, Taken at the Port of Spain, in the Island of Trinidad, in the Case of Louisa Calderon (London, 1806). Anon., The Trial of Governor T. Picton for Inflicting the Torture on Louisa Calderon . . . , on the 24th of February, 1806 (London, n.d.). Colonel Thomas Picton, Evidence Taken at Port of Spain . . . in the Case of Louisa Calderon . . . (London, 1806).

[5] For attacks on the report see Fullarton's A Letter to Field Marshal His Royal Highness the Duke of York (Brentford, 1807) and his Substance of the Evidence Delivered Before the . . . Privy Council, in the Case of Governor Picton . . . Submitted . . . to the Consideration of the Imperial Parliament . . . (no imprint, 1807).

[6] For a succinct account of the whole affair see J. N. Brierley, Trinidad: Then and Now (Trinidad, 1912).

her attempt was unsuccessful.[1] Picton's heroic death at Waterloo subsequently resulted in a great change in public opinion in his favor.

The question of abolition was meanwhile again brought before parliament in 1804. A bill providing for it then passed the House of Commons, but was thrown out by the Lords. A year after, the measure was lost in the lower chamber, but it was adopted there in 1806 and, in 1807, despite vigorous opposition on the part of the West India interest which enjoyed the Duke of Clarence's support,[2] it passed the House of Lords, received the royal assent on the twenty-fifth of March, and became effective for vessels clearing out of the United Kingdom as of May 1, 1807 and for those arriving in the colonies as of March 1, 1808.[3] Engaging in the trade was subsequently made a felony [4] and later, piracy.[5] The victory of the reformers was a crushing defeat for the planter-merchant group and constituted a triumph of moral principle over the power of vested interest and property.

Intense excitement prevailed in the Caribbean possessions when news of the humanitarian triumph crossed the Atlantic. To give but one example, a committee of the Jamaican assembly recommended that the subsistence of 3,000 troops stationed in the islands be discontinued in retaliation. A heated dispute arose, Mr. Stewart opposing all further appropriations of such a nature while Mr. Shand

[1] One of Picton's supporters was made defendant in a libel suit brought by Fullarton and continued by the latter's widow. See Mrs. H. Fullarton, *Proceedings on the Several Motions for Judgment in the Case The King versus Draper . . . for a Libel Against the Late Colonel Fullarton . . .* (Brentford, n.d.). Another became involved in a dispute with John Sullivan of the colonial department over statements of great importance alleged to have been made by the latter, but denied by him. See F. T. Lynch, *A Letter Addressed to the Rt. Hon. John Sullivan . . .* (London, 1808).

[2] The Duke, later William IV, saw service in the West Indian naval station commencing in 1786 (see Charles P. Bowen and E. G. Sinckler, *Royal Visits to Barbados*, Barbados, 1887; Frank Cundall, "Royal Visits to the West Indies," in *The W. I. Comm. Circ.*, Aug. 19, Sept. 2, 16, and 30, and Oct. 14, 1920 and Cundall, "The Visits of Prince William Henry to Jamaica," in *Journal of the Institute of Jamaica*, Jan. 1893, pp. 189 ff.) and developed colonial sympathies sufficiently strong to lead him to ardently oppose ending the slave trade. He attended a meeting of the Society of West India Planters and Merchants held early in 1805, at which time it was resolved to oppose the progress of any bill looking towards abolition by all legal means. *Min. W. I. Plant. and Mer.*, Feb. 14, 1805.

[3] 47 Geo. III, sess. 1, c. 36. See Franz Hochstetter, *Die wirtschaftlichen und politischen Motive für die Abschaffung des britischen Sklavenhandels im Jahre 1806, 1807* (Leipzig, 1905).

[4] 51 Geo. III c. 23.

[5] 5 Geo. IV c. 17.

advocated granting the customary sum. After an unparalleled scene of disorder, the latter's view prevailed, but so great was the animosity engendered between the two leaders thereby that they promptly fought a duel in which both were wounded.[1] A series of resolutions was subsequently passed, denying parliament's authority to enact legislation regulating local affairs,[2] but no overt action occurred and opposition to the home government's policy gradually declined, not, however, without leaving deep-seated resentment in the hearts of the colonials.

An aftermath of the success of 1807 was the contesting of Wilberforce's seat for Yorkshire by a member of the West India body in the same year. Parliament was suddenly dissolved shortly after having instituted abolition, and in the ensuing election the great humanitarian's political position was challenged for the first time in a quarter of a century. Two opponents appeared, Lord Milton of the house of Fitzwilliam and Henry Lascelles of the house of Harewood, the latter the holder of extensive estates in Barbados.

Each spent upwards of £100,000; Lascelles declared himself ready to part with all his tropical properties if need be to gain the office. A fund of £65,000 was collected by Wilberforce's supporters to enable him to meet such formidable rivals. The polls at Yorktown were open for fifteen days and so great was the demand for vehicles to transport electors, that it became impossible to hire carriages since all were already in use. When ballots were counted early in June, it was found that Wilberforce had received 11,806 votes, Milton 11,177, and Lascelles 10,989. The West Indian attack on the champion of abolition had failed.[3]

The closing of the slave trade was an event fraught with momentous consequences for the British sugar islands. With the supply of labor cut off, the price of negroes rose sharply and materially increased production costs. Of far greater consequence, however, were the social results. Self-interest thereafter compelled the proprietors to pay more attention to the physical well-being of their hands and

[1] Lieut.-Gov. Sir Eyre Coote to Viscount Castlereagh, June 14, and Oct. 29, 1807, C. O. 137/119.

[2] The Secretary of State to the Duke of Manchester, Sept. 8, 1808, C. O. 137/122.

[3] [Sir Robert Rutherford], "North Countryman," "An Old Time Election," in *The W. I. Comm. Circ.*, Jan. 19, 1906, pp. 32, 33. Papers connected with Mr. Lascelles' candidacy are in the possession of Messrs. Wilkinson and Gaviller, 34 Great Tower Street, E. C. 3, London, successors to Lascelles and Maxwell as traders to Barbados.

thus reduced losses by death. The supply of workers after 1808 was recruited by birth rather than by purchase, hence more attention was given the condition of pregnant females and to a reduction of the shocking infant mortality rate noted elsewhere.[1]

With the steady introduction of large bodies of ignorant Africans into the British Caribbean brought to a close, the rise of a creole stock of blacks, less savage and more contented than the imported ones because of their birth in the colonies and their having associated with whites from earliest childhood, followed. Such native negroes were milder mannered, spoke an English patois rather than some African dialect, and were in a better mental state to receive instruction of any sort than were those transported across the Atlantic and sold into slavery at a mature age. No general rise of the lower strata of colonial society was possible so long as the slave trade continued. Unfortunately, the manumission of meritorious individuals was checked at the same time, for after 1808 it became increasingly difficult to purchase help of any kind.[2]

Abolition proved disastrous for the development of the American colonies conquered from the Spanish, French, and Dutch during the Napoleonic wars. The humanitarians had been insistent that Trinidad should be opened by free rather than by slave labor[3] and the colonial office had been led to inquire whether, if this policy were adopted, it would be possible to exploit the island through such natives of the neighboring mainland as might be induced to take up residence there.[4] To prevent, so far as possible, the investing of British capital in Berbice, Demerara, St. Lucia, Surinam, and Tobago until their ownership should have been definitely determined at a peace settlement, an order in council of August, 1805[5] and an act of parliament a year later[6] had prohibited the importation of negroes into them for the purpose of opening new estates and had limited annual entries to 3 per cent of the existing number of slaves. Planters there had consequently been unable to lay in stocks of hands in anticipation of the general abolition act going into effect as was done in the neighboring British possessions.

[1] See pages 34 ff.
[2] See Lewis, *Journal,* pp. 76, 200 on this score.
[3] See [James Stephen], *The Crisis of the Sugar Colonies* . . . (London, 1802) ; for a reply to this demand, "The Crisis of the Sugar Colonies," in *The Ed. Rev.,* Oct., 1802, pp. 216–237.
[4] The Secretary of State to Governor Picton, Feb. 18, 1802, C. O. 295/2.
[5] Circular despatch of Aug. 21, 1805, C. O. 324/103.
[6] 46 Geo. III c. 52.

The scarcity of blacks in the rich soil colony of Trinidad led to an interesting experiment destined to be undertaken on a large scale some generations later—the use of indentured oriental labor. This had been advocated in the last decade of the eighteenth century [1] and was under discussion early in the 1800's.[2]

One hundred ninety-two Chinamen, engaged by Kenneth Macqueen of the East India Company to proceed to Trinidad in the hope that they might introduce rice cultivation, arrived from Bengal on board the *Fortitude* [3] in October, 1806.[4] They soon found employment under contracts carefully drawn by the local government [5] but became dissatisfied because of the lack of women with whom they might associate [6] and in less than a year signified a desire to return home.[7] The few who remained in the island ultimately abandoned agriculture and became fishermen and pork butchers.[8]

A considerable number of former American slaves, who had aided the British during the war of 1812, were established in Trinidad as free settlers in 1815 and 1816,[9] and demobilized West Indian colored troops were granted holdings there commencing in 1818.[10] The labor question, however, continued to be a pressing one, and in 1829 the price of plantation workers averaged $800 per head as against $300 in Grenada, while wages were double those in Barbados.[11]

Another phase of the new altruism animating the British mind

[1] Anon., *Remarks on the New Sugar Bill.*

[2] William Laymen, *Outline of a Plan for the Better Cultivation, Security, and Defence of the British West Indies* . . . (London, 1807).

[3] The vessel was seized by the local naval officer as it had a consignment of East India goods on board. See the papers in C. O. 295/18. Before directions to admit the ship and its cargo had been received from the Lords of the Committee of Council for Trade and Foreign Plantations, they had been sold at auction. The *Fortitude* was bought in by the island council for the East India Company at £4,150 sterling and the cargo brought £15,000 sterling, netting Macqueen some £2,500 profit. Governor Hislop to William Windham, Feb. 8, 1807, C. O. 295/16. The *Fortitude* also brought oriental plants for propagation in Trinidad. See page 76.

[4] William Windham to Governor Hislop, Aug. 22, 1806; Hislop to Windham, Oct. 26, 1806, C. O. 295/14.

[5] Proclamation of Governor Hislop, Oct. 18, 1806, C. O. 295/14.

[6] Hislop to Windham, March 8, 1807, C. O. 295/16.

[7] Hislop to Windham, July 23, 1807, C. O. 295/16.

[8] Andrew Halliday, *The West Indies* (London, 1837), pp. 293, 294. E. L. Joseph, *History of Trinidad* (Trinidad, n.d.), p. 233.

[9] Governor Woodford to Earl Bathurst, June 6, Aug. 5, Nov. 30, 1815, C. O. 295/37; Aug. 28, and Nov. 10, 1816, C. O. 295/40.

[10] Woodford to Bathurst, Jan. 29, 1818, C. O. 295/46; Dec. 12, 1819, C. O. 295/48; Dec. 6, 1824, C. O. 295/63.

[11] Major General Grant to the Secretary of State, April 14, 1829, C. O. 295/80.

toward the turn of the century was the concern felt for the Caribbean negroes' spiritual welfare. This resulted in noble, large-scale efforts to Christianize them through missionary activities. The movement had its origins in the period preceding the opening of the great anti-slave trade drive, but soon became closely allied to it. Accounts of the blacks' debased state, broadcast by the abolitionists, led the generality of Englishmen to commiserate them and to actively support enterprises seeking to improve their situation. Church workers in the islands, on the other hand, sent home full reports on conditions as they found them and thus provided opponents of the trade and slavery with ammunition.[1] The work of converting the Africans was carried on both by agents of the Church of England and by nonconformists, but more particularly and with greater success by the latter.[2]

The indifference to religion among the planters, the Established churchmen's utter neglect of the negroes, the magnificent work of the Moravians among them, and the rise of native Methodist and Baptist religious establishments have been discussed elsewhere.[3] True it is that the frigidity of formal Anglicanism would have made but slight appeal to the emotional Africans; their mental plane, furthermore, was at such a low level that they could have profited but little from attendance at the white man's centers of worship. This, however, in no way excuses the parish clergy's entire disregard for their spiritual welfare.

The success of the Moravian workers and of the native dissenting preachers is to be explained by the free manner in which they mingled with their charges and by the fact that all instruction was carefully adapted to negro capacity. The new missionary movement begun at the close of the 1700's was carried on by organizations in no way connected with local white congregations and deriving no financial support from the colonials. Their representatives devoted themselves exclusively to the blacks and employed those methods which experience had proved to be productive of most beneficial results.

---

[1] See for example the large number of accounts in *The Arminian Magazine,* continued as *The Methodist Magazine* after 1797, and in *The Evangelical Magazine* (founded in 1793).

[2] See Brown, *History of the Propagation of Christianity,* I, 257–259, 441–504; II, 78–97, 436–449, 504–509; III, 410–412, 448, 449. Also John Horsford, *A Voice from the West Indies: Being a Review of the Character and Results of Missionary Efforts in the British and Other Colonies in the Charibbean Sea* (London, 1856) and George Smith, *Short History of Christian Missions* . . . (Edinburgh, 1884), Part III, chs. 14 and 15.

[3] In Chapter I.

The initiative was taken by the Methodists. Their activities began with the fortuitous landing of Thomas Coke, "the father of Wesleyan missions," [1] in the Caribbean on Christmas day, 1786. This dynamic churchman had sailed for Nova Scotia from Gravesend with three assistants twelve weeks before. Long-continued storms had at length led their ship captain to abandon hope of reaching his port and he had turned south instead, entering harbor in Antigua.

Coke found the native Methodist church in a flourishing condition, then visited St. Vincent, St. Kitts, Nevis, and Dominica and, being struck by the opportunity for effective work in the sugar islands, he assigned his helpers to service there. The condition of the Caribs in St. Vincent also aroused his sympathy, and he secured a grant of 150 acres of land from the island legislature for the purpose of erecting a school for them which was to be provided with two teachers.[2] In 1788, he returned to the colonies with three additional missionaries, stopping at Barbados, Jamaica, and subsequently Grenada and the Virgin Islands as well.[3]

Thereafter, the West India islands constituted one of the chief seats of Wesleyan endeavor overseas and representatives were regularly sent out. The management of affairs lay in the hands of

[1] Samuel Drew, *The Life of the Rev. Thomas Coke* . . . (London, 1817). Robert Southey, *The Life of Wesley, and the Rise and Progress of Methodism* (2 vols., London, 1820), II, chs. 26 and 27. J. W. Etheridge, *The Life of the Rev. Thomas Coke, D. C. L.* (London, 1860). Stevens, *History of the Movement Called Methodism*, II, 510 ff., 646–653. William Moister, *Stories, Sketches, Facts and Incidents, Illustrative of the Providence and Grace of God in Connexion With the Missionary Enterprise* (London, 1868). Moister, *The Father of Our Missions: Being the Story of the Life and Labours of the Rev. Thomas Coke* . . . (London, 1871). Moister, *Heralds of Salvation* (London, 1878). Warren Candler, *Life of Thomas Coke* (Nashville, Tenn., 1923). G. G. Findlay and W. W. Holdsworth, *The History of the Wesleyan Methodist Missionary Society*, 5 vols. (London, n.d.), II, ch. 2.
[2] [Thomas Coke], *The Case of the Caribbs in St. Vincent's* [London, 1787].
[3] Personal accounts are given in Thomas Coke, *An Extract of . . . Dr. Coke's Journal from Gravesend to Antigua* . . . (London, 1787); Coke, *A Farther Continuation of Dr. Coke's Journal* . . . (London, 1787); Coke, *Some Account of the Late Missionaries to the West Indies* (London, 1789); Coke, *A Farther Account of the Late Missionaries to the West Indies* (London, 1789); Coke, *A Journal of . . .* [a] *Visit to Jamaica* (London, 1789); Coke, *A Journal of the Rev. Dr. Coke's Third Tour Through the West Indies* (London, 1791); Coke, *Extracts of the Journals of . . . Five Visits to America* (London, 1793), also found in Anon., ed., *Extracts of the Journals of the Late Rev. Thomas Coke* . . . (Dublin, 1816); Coke, *An Account of the Methodist Missions;* Coke, *History of the West Indies*, I, 412, 413; II, 65 ff., 134 ff., 253, 351, 437; III, 12 ff., 56 ff., 111; Coke and Mr. More, *The Life of the Rev. John Wesley, A.M.* . . . (London, 1792), pp. 472–477.

Coke and the Methodist pastors in London, who formed an advisory committee.[1] Funds were secured through appeals made to the British public, generally following addresses by the great leader, and a total of £6,016 was collected in this manner from 1787 to 1793. Reports and financial statements were issued from time to time for the information of contributors.[2]

The Methodists at first enjoyed Quaker support, but this was soon withdrawn as the Friends did not approve teaching the negroes to observe forms or to go through "inefficacious ceremonies." [3] By the close of the century, Wesleyan agents were to be found in most of the tropical American possessions, numerous chapels had been built, religious instruction was being regularly given, and thousands of blacks, particularly creoles, had become nominal Christians.[4]

One other sectarian body, the Scottish Missionary Society, undertook work among the West Indian slaves before abolition became effective. Three workers arrived in Jamaica in 1800, but two died shortly after landing and the third, losing heart, became a teacher instead. A quarter of a century later, the organization had not yet reopened its activities in the island.[5]

Missionary effort in the Caribbean colonies under auspices of the Church of England opened in 1794, with the founding of the Society

[1] Brown, *History of the Propagation of Christianity,* I, 441.

[2] See for example, Thomas Coke, *To the Benevolent Subscribers for the Support of the Missions Carried on by Voluntary Contributions in the British West Indies, for the Benefit of the Negroes and Caribbs* (London, 1789) and Coke, *A Statement of the Receipts and Disbursements for the Support of the Missions Established by the Methodist Society for the Instruction and Conversion of the Negroes in the West Indies* (London, 1794).

[3] Catherine Phillips, *Reasons Why the People Called Quakers Cannot so Fully Unite with the Methodists in Their Missions to the Negroes in the West India Islands and Africa, as Freely to Contribute Thereto* . . . (London, 1792).

[4] Thomas Jackson, *The Centenary of Wesleyan Methodism. A Brief Sketch of the Rise, Progress, and Present State of the Wesleyan-Methodist Societies Throughout the World* (London, 1839), pp. 154 ff. Peter Duncan, *A Narrative of the Wesleyan Mission to Jamaica* (London, 1849). Smith, *History of Wesleyan Methodism,* II, 620 ff. Henry Foster, *Rise and Progress of Wesleyan-Methodism in Jamaica* (London, 1881). William Moister, *Conversations on the Rise, Progress, and Present State of Wesleyan Missions* (London, 1869). Moister, *A History of Wesleyan Missions in All Parts of the World* . . . (London, 1871), ch. III. Henry Adams, *Methodism in the West Indies* (London, 1908).

[5] Brown, *History of the Propagation of Christianity,* II, 436 ff. See page 405.

for the Conversion and Religious Instruction and Education of the Negro Slaves in the British West India Islands.

A century before, the sum of £5,400 had been placed in the hands of a body of trustees, one of them the Bishop of London, by a Mr. Boyle, with the stipulation that the income be used to advance Christianity among heathen peoples. This had long been paid to the College of William and Mary in Virginia for the education of Indian children, but remittances had ceased upon the outbreak of the Revolution. Action subsequently brought by the authorities of that institution to recover arrearages had been lost. It became necessary, therefore, to devise some new plan for employing the charity.

The then Bishop of London, Beilby Porteus, for many years actively interested in the welfare of the negroes,[1] accordingly proposed that it be used in carrying on Christian work among them. The project was approved, about £1,000 a year was set aside for this purpose, the society to carry on the enterprise was organized under royal charter, and Porteus was named president.[2] A number of churchmen were then assigned to the Caribbean with directions to secure the consent of masters before undertaking operations and to exercise no compulsion.[3] The former proved hard to obtain and the venture, while not a failure, fell far short of its guiding spirit's hopes.

Missionary activities among the negroes, irrespective of the workers' sect, aroused colonial fear and distrust. Teaching the doctrine of brotherly love was held to be pernicious and reports on the state of the slaves, sent to organization headquarters by all these agents, raised opposition against them to white heat. The clergy of the Established Church, too, looked askance at nonconformist efforts and almost solidly opposed them. The islanders' virulence was directed chiefly against the Methodists because of their being the most numerous and most active of the sectarists as well as because of the peculiar disfavor in which they stood in the mother land. Large numbers of estate owners prohibited the instruction of slaves on their properties and also forbade their hands to attend services in the various chapels.

---

[1] See page 244.

[2] Robert Hodgson, *The Life of the Right Reverend Beilby Porteus D.D. Late Bishop of London* (London, 1811), pp. 110 ff. Brown, *History of the Propagation of Christianity*, III, 448. *Some Account of the Incorporated Society for the Conversion and Religious Instruction and Education of the Negroe Slaves in the British West Indies, Incorporated by Royal Charter, 1794* (London, 1823).

[3] Anon., *Instructions for Missionaries to the West Indies* (London, 1795).

More direct attempts, too, were made to check the activities of dissenting groups. In 1793, the assembly of St. Vincent forbade the holding of services by unlicensed, itinerant preachers, but this act was disallowed by the home government.[1] Fire was set to the Wesleyan church in Nevis three years later. About the same time, one of Coke's representatives in Dominica was ordered to perform militia service on Sunday and subsequently was ordered to depart.[2] Widespread opposition showed itself when, in 1799, Methodist workers in Tortola were accused of having incited a revolt,[3] and when, some months after, President Ottley of St. Vincent charged local Wesleyan representatives with stirring up insubordination and discontent among the blacks.[4]

In 1800, the Barbadian legislature forbade individuals, not invested with holy orders according to the rites and ceremonies of the Church of England, from engaging in religious enterprises in the island, and fined and jailed a Methodist missionary who refused to discontinue his efforts. This law stood for three years.[5]

In 1802, similar hostile legislation was enacted in Jamaica. This resulted in the sole surviving agent of the Scottish Missionary Society abandoning his career, as already noted, and in the imprisoning of numerous Wesleyans. The act was disallowed in 1804. When the home government submitted the draft of a bill which would be acceptable, the assembly declared that it would never submit to British interference in internal legislation. Later, as a means of circumventing the home government, an ordinance of the same tenor was passed by the common council of Kingston, where non-Anglican activity centered. Slavery regulations of 1807 forbidding the nonconformists to instruct negroes were likewise disallowed;[6] and in consequence of these various attempts to hamper missionary labors, the home government in 1809 instructed West Indian governors to withhold their consent to all religious acts until approved by the Crown, unless they contained suspending clauses.[7]

Those few clergymen of the Church of England who took an interest in the blacks fared no better than did the dissenters. When the Rev. Charles Peters, a Dominican rector in correspondence with

---

[1] Southey, *Chronological History,* III, 73.
[2] *Ibid.,* III, 110.
[3] *Ibid.,* III, 165.
[4] In a despatch to the Duke of Portland, June 5, 1800, C. O. 260/16.
[5] Southey, *Chronological History,* III, 182.
[6] *Ibid.,* III, 223, 242, 291, 389–391, 406.
[7] Circular despatch of June 8, 1809, C. O. 324/103.

Wilberforce, preached two sermons on Good Friday and Easter, 1800, urging masters to adopt equitable and judicious measures for the welfare of their hands and denouncing the practice of overworking them,[1] a storm broke. He was summoned before the local council, and found it advisable to resign his charge and hastily leave the island. A local paper, in announcing his departure, described him as a "diminutive wolf in sheep's clothing" and recommended that he "exchange his gown for the party-coloured trappings of the French Republicans." [2]

[1] These sermons were subsequently published. See Charles Peters, *Two Sermons, Preached at Dominica, on the 11th and 13th of April, 1800, and Officially Noticed by His Majesty's Privy Council in That Island* . . . (London, 1802).

[2] *The Dominica Journal, or Weekly Intelligencer,* April 26, 1800.

CHAPTER IX

AGRARIAN DISTRESS IN THE OLD CARIBBEAN HOLDINGS

"If ever . . . it could happen, that Great Britain should become the sole consumer of sugars imported from our islands, by her inability to find a vent for the superfluity at foreign markets, this event cannot happen without the desolation of some of our islands; and it is evident, those will suffer most immediately, whose only dependence for support is rested on this staple."

—Edward Long, *History of Jamaica,* I, 526, 527.

British planter prosperity following revolutionary outbreaks in France's American colonies reached its peak early in 1799. The high prices marking the last decade of the eighteenth century had arisen, as we have seen,[1] from the demand of continental merchants formerly supplied with St. Domingan produce. These foreign buyers operated for the most part from Hamburg, well removed from the theater of the war then sweeping Europe. Overtrading and speculation in the great German mart brought on a financial panic during the summer of 1799. Between August and November, eighty-two firms, with engagements totaling some £2,500,000, failed. Most were in close relations with leading West India houses in England and the latter rushed £140,000 across the North Sea to tide over their clients. Unfortunately, the warship transporting it was wrecked en route, and this heroic effort to avert general ruin proved unavailing.[2]

The commercial crash abroad led to a general stagnation of British trade in tropical goods. Shipments of muscovado leaving the United Kingdom dropped from 920,170 hundredweight in 1798 to 360,975 the following year,[3] while exports of refined sugar from Great Britain fell off by half in the same time.[4]

A committee of the organized West India Merchants in London,

[1] Pages 205 ff.

[2] Tooke, *History of Prices,* I, 233. Macpherson, *Annals of Commerce,* IV, 484, 485.

[3] "Quantities of Muscovado Sugar Imported Into the United Kingdom, Quantities Retained for Consumption There, etc. . . . , 1793–1834," in *Gt. Br., H. C., Sess. Pap.,* 1847–48, LVIII (400).

[4] From 248,534 cwt. to 122,638. *East India Sugar. Papers Respecting the Culture and Manufacture of Sugar . . . ,* Appendix IV, p. 5.

named to study the causes of such an alarming decline in overseas sales, reported an exceedingly disquieting state of affairs. The protracted conflict with the French had checked trade on the mainland and had greatly lessened consumption of plantation produce there. As a direct consequence of it, exports to Holland had ceased entirely.

But the fundamental cause for the prevailing depression lay deeper. The huge profits attending tropical agriculture in late years had led to a tremendous extension of cultivation in the foreign plantations, particularly in Brazil, but also to a marked extent in the enemy colonies and neutral West Indies. Increasing quantities of produce from those sources were regularly being offered in continental markets in competition with shipments from the British possessions. Such foreign commodities were, of course, free from the tax imposed on reëxportations from Great Britain by setting drawbacks at lower rates than the duties. Furthermore, they were carried direct to Europe. In consequence, they could be sold for less than those of British origin received by way of England.

The Americans in particular were engaged in an extensive carrying trade, transporting cargoes from both the British and enemy West Indies to the United States and from thence to Europe. Between March 8, and September 10, 1799, no less than 146 of their vessels, laden chiefly with sugar and coffee, entered the port of Hamburg alone. Three ships of other foreign registry also arrived from Havana, likewise seven from the East Indies, eighteen from neutral Caribbean colonies, and fifty-six from Lisbon and Oporto, making a total of 230 non-British bottoms laden with tropical products, for the most part the growth of foreign plantations, entering the principal European mart for British West Indian goods in the space of six months.

During the same period but 211 craft, of smaller average tonnage and carrying but partial cargoes of British tropical produce, were entered from Great Britain. Clearly, "far from exclusively possessing the Supply of Foreign Markets with Sugar and Coffee," that country had "already lost the pre-eminence she formerly enjoyed over her Rivals . . ." there.[1]

At the very time that British sugar exports suffered this severe decline, imports reached an unprecedented height. A bumper crop was shipped home from the Caribbean in 1799. Consignments of muscovado to the United Kingdom totalled 3,458,945 hundredweight

[1] *Min. W. I. Mer.*, Sept. 18, 1799.

in 1799 as against 2,168,511 in 1797 and 2,745,209 in 1798.[1] Exports from Jamaica rose from 87,896 hogsheads, 11,725 tierces, and 1,163 barrels in 1798 to 101,457 hogsheads, 13,538 tierces, and 1,321 barrels a year later.[2] So great was the production that although 829 British vessels arrived in colonial West Indian ports during 1799 as against only 655 the preceding season,[3] a deficiency in shipping occurred and, as has been noted,[4] the Americans were permitted to export produce from the Leeward Islands under their own flag.

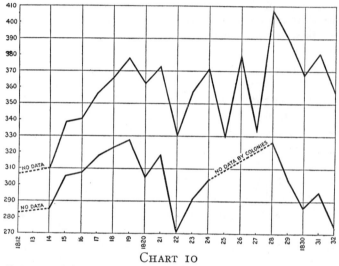

CHART 10

Imports of Muscavado Sugar, the Growth of British Plantations, from the British West Indies, Demerara, and Berbice into Great Britain, 1812–1832, in Million Pounds *

* Based on Customs 5/2–21, Public Record Office. Upper line = from all the colonies. Lower line = from the insular possessions only (not including Demerara and Berbice).

Decreased sales coupled with increased output glutted the British market. The East India Company could dispose of but 102,767 hundredweight of sugar in 1799 as against 203,631 a twelvemonth

---

[1] "Quantities of Muscovado Sugar Imported Into the United Kingdom, Quantities Retained for Consumption There, etc. . . . , 1793–1834," in *Gt. Br., H. C., Sess. Pap.,* 1847–1848, LVIII (400).

[2] "Exports of Sugar from Jamaica, 1772–1836," in *Gt. Br., H. C., Sess. Pap.,* 1840, VIII (527), p. 594.

[3] Report on West Indian Shipping, B. T. 6/141.

[4] Page 234.

before.[1] English dealers in Caribbean goods suddenly found themselves greatly involved. So critical was the situation of those in Liverpool and Lancaster that parliament authorized a loan of £500,000 in exchequer bills to them on much the same terms as had been accorded the merchants trading to St. Vincent and Grenada in 1795.[2] Property valued at over £2,000,000 was given as security.[3]

The Society of West India Merchants of London sought relief for such of its members as were pressed through a loan from the Bank of England. This was easily arranged as several of the more prominent traders, including Beeston Long, Jr., were directors of that institution. The sum of £1,500,000 was quickly placed at their disposal, but proved to be far more than was needed. The possibility of securing funds eased credit and only eleven six month advances ranging from £1,150, to £47,000 and totalling £176,720, were made to firms in the capital city. Five renewals to the amount of £59,520 were subsequently arranged, but all borrowings had been repaid by July 1, 1800.[4]

A sharp drop in selling prices followed the cramming of warehouses. The average cost of British-grown muscovado purchased of factors in London sank from 68s. 5¼d. per hundredweight in April, 1799, to 47s. 1½d. a year later, to 43s. 10¾d. in December, 1801, and 35s. 6d. at the close of 1802.[5] In the spring of 1799, the grocery trade was offered British muscovado at from 84s. to 110s. per hundredweight; the year following, at from 60s. to 78s., with one exception the lowest quotation since the early summer of 1791.[6] By February, 1800, sugar had declined so greatly that the specific duty charged on the entry of the West Indian product exceeded the ad valorem tax levied against that from the Orient—the protection afforded the former had ceased to exist.[7] The value of other tropical American produce slumped in similar fashion. Between the early months of 1799 and the first quarter of 1801, Jamaican coffee sold in

[1] *East India Sugar. Papers Respecting the Culture and Manufacture of Sugar* . . . , Appendix IV, p. 13.

[2] 39 and 40 Geo. III c. 5. For the relief generously extended in 1795, see page 221.

[3] Tooke, *History of Prices,* I, 235.

[4] *Min. W. I. Mer.,* Oct., 2, 1799, August 15, 1800. Records covering such loans are preserved in a special book in the archives of the West India Committee.

[5] Weekly returns in *The London Gazette.*

[6] Quarterly circulars issued by Smiths, Nash, and Kemble and successors, in the archives of Joseph Travers and Sons, London.

[7] *Min. W. I. Mer.,* Feb. 12, 1800.

the home country fell from 185s.–196s. to 116s.–130s. per hundred-weight and rum from 7s. 2d.–8s. to 3s.–5s. per gallon.[1]

The turn of the century found Great Britain confronted by a serious grain shortage arising from the cutting off of imports from across the Channel. As a means of conserving the food supply and at the same time easing the situation of the West Indians by affording them a new outlet for sugar, parliament in October, 1799, forbade the distillation of spirits from wheat or wheat flour in England to June 1, 1800, and reduced the duties on liquor manufactured from molasses or sugar.[2] These lower rates were maintained by several acts to January 1, 1802.[3] The use of grain of any sort in Scotch distilleries was prohibited at the same time [4] and this regulation was continued in force to 1802.[5] Fiscal encouragement was likewise given the production of spirits from sugar or molasses in Scotland [6] and the use of grain for beverage purposes in Ireland was temporarily declared illegal.[7]

The Society of West India Merchants sought to encourage the use of sugar by English distillers when corn was again made available to them by securing a drawback of 10s. per hundredweight on all quantities purchased for such purposes but were unable to effect this as the Chancellor of the Exchequer feared it would lead to fraud.[8] Upon representation of the traders,[9] however, brewers too were permitted to employ sugar in the manufacture of beer from July, 1800; this additional vent for surplus produce was kept open for eighteen months.[10]

While consumption within the British Isles was being thus increased, members of the colonial interest sought to revive the export business in tropical produce through securing a readjustment of drawbacks and bounties. A subcommittee of the Society of Merchants, in

---

[1] Tooke, *History of Prices*, I, 190, 235.

[2] 39 and 40 Geo. III c. 8. The use of grain, meal, flour, or bran in distilleries had been previously forbidden from July, 1795 to February, 1796 by 35 Geo. III c. 119. This measure was, however, designed to conserve the grain supply and not to increase the consumption of sugar and molasses. When it was continued their use in distillation was likewise forbidden. 36 Geo. III c. 20.

[3] By 39 and 40 Geo. III c. 61, 41 Geo. III c. 5, and 42 Geo. III c. 5.

[4] 39 and 40 Geo. III c. 7.

[5] By 39 and 40 Geo. III c. 21, 41 Geo. III c. 5, and 42 Geo. III c. 5.

[6] 41 Geo. III c. 29, 42 Geo. III c. 5.

[7] 41 Geo. III c. 16.

[8] *Min. W. I. Mer.*, Feb. 12, and March 15, 1800.

[9] *Ibid.*, Jan. 7, Feb. 12, March 15, 1800.

[10] 39 and 40 Geo. III c. 62, continued by 41 Geo. III c. 5.

conference with the Chancellor of the Exchequer, recommended that
both be raised;[1] the Society of Planters and Merchants urged that
the entire duty levied against Caribbean products upon their entry
into England be refunded upon subsequent reshipment abroad and
that the maximum price at which drawbacks and bounties were
payable be increased from the low figure of 50s. per hundredweight
exclusive of duty, set in 1792.[2]

Legislation to encourage sales overseas followed. An act of May,
1800,[3] repealed duties of 2s. 6d. per hundredweight on foreign sugar,
6s. 6d. per hundredweight on the East Indian article, and 4s. per
hundredweight on coffee, charged upon their exportation from Great
Britain under a measure of the preceding summer.[4] It further provided that 6s. 6d. of the drawback on British sugar, withheld under
two laws of 1796[5] and 1799,[6] be again allowed until November and
freed that of East Indian origin, purchased by foreigners, from an
additional import tax laid in 1799.[7] Then too, if the average price of
muscovado sold in London during the six weeks before November
10, 1800, should not have exceeded 75s. per hundredweight inclusive
of duty, the increased drawback and the exemption of East Indian
sugar were to continue in force until May, 1801.

Shortly after, the maximum price at which the drawback and
bounties on British-grown sugar were payable was set at 70s. per
hundredweight exclusive of duties,[8] an increase of 20s. over that
adapted in 1792,[9] and both were placed on a sliding scale in accordance with selling values, as follows.

If the average price of British muscovado did not exceed	This drawback was to be allowed on British muscovado and this bounty was to be paid on bastards, ground and powdered sugar and broken loaves exported	This bounty was to be paid on whole loaves and refined lump sugar exported
58s. per cwt.	20s. per cwt.	34s. per cwt.
60s.	18s.	31s.
62s.	16s.	27s.

[1] *Min. W. I. Mer.*, Oct. 2, 1799.
[2] *Min. W. I. Plant. and Mer.*, March 19, 1800.
[3] 39 and 40 Geo. III c. 48.
[4] By 39 Geo. III c. 63.
[5] 36 Geo. III c. 18.
[6] 39 Geo. III c. 63.
[7] By 39 Geo. III c. 63.
[8] 41 Geo. III c. 44.
[9] See page 207.

Average Price	Drawback	Bounty
64s.	14s.	24s.
66s.	12s.	20s.
68s.	10s.	17s.
70s.	8s.	13s.
Over 70s.	Nothing	Nothing

This arrangement was continued in later years with still further increase in drawbacks and bounties when the average London selling price fell below 58s. per hundredweight.[1] Under such stimulus, shipments of raw sugar from Great Britain rose from 410,052 hundredweight in 1799 to 981,730 hundredweight in 1800 and to 635,068 hundredweight in 1801 while exports of the refined article advanced from 122,638 hundredweight in 1799 to 397,542 hundredweight and 333,942 hundredweight in the two years which followed.[2]

The organized West Indians in the national capital[3] and the legislature of Jamaica[4] also attempted to secure a lowering of the duties paid on British plantation produce entered into Great Britain for home consumption, and, as further means of affording the planters direct relief, urged placing the sugar tax on an ad valorem basis and freeing the American trade, but to no avail.

No group within the British empire welcomed the peace of Amiens more than did those persons with plantation connections. The restoration of all conquests in the Caribbean excepting Trinidad was immensely pleasing to them, for the produce of such territories was thus withdrawn from home markets and no longer competed there with their own output.

The immediate consequent decline in imports was marked. Shipments of British West Indian cacao to Great Britain sank from 7,828 hundredweight in 1801 to 3,075 hundredweight in 1803;[5] imports of coffee from 525,964 hundredweight to 157,453;[6] of cotton, from 19,-957,307 pounds to 7,036,104;[7] and of pimento, from 1,676,542

---

[1] 42 Geo. III c. 47, 42 Geo. III c. 59, 43 Geo. III c. 11, 44 Geo. III c. 5, 45 Geo. III c. 24, 45 Geo. III c. 93, and 46 Geo. III c. 10.

[2] *East India Sugar. Papers Respecting the Culture and Manufacture of Sugar . . .* , Appendix IV, p. 5.

[3] *Min. W. I. Mer.*, Feb. 12, 1800. *Min. W. I. Plant. and Mer.*, March 19, 1800, March 26, and April 5, 1802.

[4] *Report from the Committee of the Honourable House of Assembly, Appointed to Inquire into the State of the Colony, as to Trade, Navigation, and Culture, &c. &c. &c. . . .* (St. Jago de la Vega, 1800).

[5] "Report . . . on the Commercial State of the West India Colonies," in *Gt. Br., H. C., Sess. Pap.*, 1807, III (65), 76.

[6] *Ibid.*, p. 75.

[7] *Ibid.*, p. 78.

pounds to 1,133,477.[1] Sugar imports in the two periods were 3,729,-264 and 2,925,400 hundredweight respectively.[2] But 3,954,770 gallons of colonial Caribbean rum were entered in 1803 as compared with 4,417,765 two years before.[3]

The cessation of hostilities led to a prompt and sharp revival of continental demand. Exports of muscovado from Great Britain in 1802 totalled 1,142,729 hundredweight as against an annual average of 588,755 from 1795 to 1801; sales of refined sugar abroad in the same year were 531,787 hundredweight as against an average of but 247,759 a year earlier.[4]

The arrival of smaller supplies and the general briskness of foreign trade soon reduced warehoused stocks and raised values. Thus, in 1802, the average price of British-grown muscovado sold in London varied from 35s. 1¼d. per hundredweight exclusive of duty to 39s. 7d.; by 1803, when the market had been cleared, it had risen to from 40s. 3d. to 48s. 6½.[5] Renewal of the war with France after a short interval of peace proved catastrophic for the West Indians. British victories in the Caribbean led to the prompt recapture of St. Lucia and Tobago from the French and Essequibo, Demerara, and Berbice from the Dutch. An enemy force under La Grange descended on Dominica in February 1805; Roseau was lost and Sir George Prevost, the governor, commanding the local forces, retreated to the north end of the island. But the task of reducing the colony proved too arduous, and less than a week later, the French departed after levying a contribution upon the inhabitants.[6] Some months after, the arrival of Villeneuve's fleet menaced the British plantations and Barbados in particular. Nelson's prompt appearance happily prevented an attack, and the subsequent destruction of the French navy at Trafalgar removed all danger on that score.[7]

[1] "Report . . . on the Commercial State of the West India Colonies," in *Gt. Br., H. C., Sess. Pap.*, 1807, III (65), 77.

[2] *Ibid.*, p. 73.

[3] *Ibid.*, p. 74.

[4] *East India Sugar. Papers Respecting the Culture and Manufacture of Sugar . . .* , Appendix IV, p. 5.

[5] Weekly returns in *The London Gazette.*

[6] An account of the attack on Dominica is given in Aspinall, *West Indian Tales of Old.* Sir George was presented with a piece of plate valued at 300 guineas by the Society of West India Planters and Merchants, and was accorded a vote of thanks by that body for his "distinguished gallantry" in the defense of the colony. *Minutes*, May 22, 1805. This silverware was in the possession of his great-grandson, Sir Charles Prevost, in 1908.

[7] For Nelson's chase after Villeneuve see Alfred Mahan, *The Influence of Sea Power Upon the French Revolution and Empire, 1793–1812* (2 vols., Cam-

Following the success of British arms, agricultural products of the reconquered regions once more poured into home harbors as colonial-grown. Imports of cacao from the West Indies into Great Britain rose to 3,483 hundredweight in 1804 and 7,562 in 1806.[1] Shipments of coffee were increased to 328,013 and 497,739 hundredweight respectively in the same periods;[2] those of cotton, to 20,535,574 and 17,-712,344 pounds;[3] and of pimento, to 2,239,032 and 2,109,678 pounds.[4] Rum imports were 2,756,329 gallons in 1804 and 3,570,774 gallons two years later;[5] sugar imports, 2,968,590 and 3,673,037 respectively.[6]

Exports at the same time naturally fell off and, after the institution of the continental system in 1806, markedly so. Raw sugar sent abroad from Great Britain in 1803 totalled 762,919 hundredweight; 307,799 hundredweight in 1806; and but 354,359 in 1808. Sales of refined sugar overseas in the same years were 547,274 hundredweight and 415,080 and 327,243 respectively.[7]

With increased imports and decreased exports, warehouses once more became crowded and market values again declined. The average price of muscovado sold in London, which varied from 51s. 10d. to 57s. 5¼d. per hundredweight exclusive of duty in 1804, had fallen to from 32s. 9d. to 36s. 4d. by 1807.[8] Cotton, selling at from 12d. to 38d. per pound in Liverpool during 1802, dropped to from 8d. to 15d. in 1803 and, although it rallied somewhat subsequently, the top quotation in 1807 was only 19d.[9]

bridge, 1892); N. Darnell Davis, *Westward Ho! With Nelson in 1805* (Demerara, 1896) and Sir Nevile Lubbock, "Nelson-1805-Trafalgar," in *The W. I. Comm. Circ.*, Oct. 13, 1905, pp. 407–410. The West India interest passed resolutions in appreciation of Nelson's services in securing the safety of the islands. See "Resolutions of the West India Merchants Concerning Lord Nelson," in *The Eur. Mag. and Lond. Rev.*, Nov. 1805, p. 392. The grateful residents of Barbados subsequently erected his statue, already mentioned (page 14), in Bridgetown.

[1] "Report . . . on the Commercial State of the West India Colonies," in *Gt. Br., H. C., Sess. Pap.*, 1807, III (65), p. 76.

[2] *Ibid.*, p. 75.

[3] *Ibid.*, p. 78.

[4] *Ibid.*, p. 77.

[5] *Ibid.*, p. 74.

[6] *Ibid.*, p. 73.

[7] *East India Sugar. Papers Respecting the Culture and Manufacture of Sugar . . .* , Appendix IV, p. 5.

[8] The average price varied from 47s. 9½d. to 51s. 2¾d. in 1805 and from 38s. ½d. to 49s. 6½d. in 1806. Weekly returns in *The London Gazette*.

[9] Cotton ranged from 10d. to 18d. in 1804, from 14d. to 19d. in 1805, and from 15d. to 21½d. in 1806. "Prices on Cotton Other than East Indian [i. e. West Indian and American] at Liverpool, 1793–1833," in *Gt. Br., H. C., Sess. Pap.*, 1847–48, IX (in 511), p. 393.

Prosecution of the Napoleonic war called for a substantial increase in the national revenue. As a means of partially meeting this, the British government felt constrained to augment the domestic duties on West Indian products precisely at the time when their prices were falling sharply. Thus, the charge on coffee was advanced from 1s. 6d. per pound in 1802 to 1s. 6¾d. in 1803 and by successive stages to 1s. 7⅞d. in 1806.[1] That on cotton was increased from 10s. 6d. per hundredweight to 16s. 8d. in 1803 and 16s. 10½d. in 1805.[2] Also, the customs and excise payable on rum consumed in Great Britain was raised from 9s. ¾d. per gallon to 13s. 4¼d. in 1803 and eventually reached 13s. 6½d. in 1806, while payments due on rum sold in Ireland rose from 6s. 11¼d. to 8s. 6¼d. in 1803 and to 9s. 2¾d. in 1804.

Following the adoption of this new schedule, shipments of colonial Caribbean rum to Great Britain sank from 3,212,611 imperial proof gallons in 1803 to 1,813,736 in the next twelve months and dealers in the Clyde River ports reported a decrease in imports from 206,348 gallons during the last half of 1802 to 82,534 gallons between July and the close of December, 1803.[3]

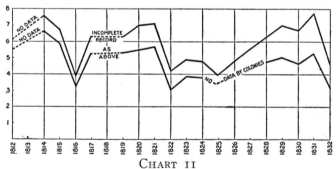

CHART II

Imports of Rum, the Produce of British Plantations, from the British West Indies, Demerara, and Berbice into Great Britain 1812–1832, in Million Gallons *

* Based on Customs 5/2-21, Public Record Office. Upper line = from all the colonies. Lower line = from the insular possessions only (not including Demerara and Berbice).

[1] The duty was set at 1s. 7¼d. in 1804 and at 1s. 7½d. in 1805. "Rates of Duty on Coffee Entered Into the United Kingdom, 1792–1829," in *Gt. Br., H. C., Sess. Pap.*, 1830, XXV (466).

[2] "Duties on Cotton, 1792–1829," in *Gt. Br., H. C., Sess. Pap.*, 1830, XX (466).

[3] "Rum Admitted Into the United Kingdom for Home Consumption, 1800–1828, With Rates of Duty Payable Thereon," in *Gt. Br., H. C., Sess. Pap.,*

The duty on muscovado sugar, the growth of British plantations, entered for use in Great Britain, was likewise increased from 20 to 24s. per hundredweight in 1803, to 26s. 6d. in 1804, and to 27s. in 1805.[1] The following year, it was set at 30s. with the provision that if the average price fell below 49s. but not below 48s. in any of the four month periods preceding January 5, May 5, and September 5, one shilling would be remitted by customs officials; if the value of the raw article stood between 48 and 47s., the rate would be lowered by two shillings and if selling prices fell below 47s., by three shillings, but no more, irrespective of what low point might be reached.[2] Market conditions were such that the charge actually remained 27s. until May, 1810, by which time muscovado had risen sufficiently to advance it 2s.[3]

The East Indian sugar duty was regularly advanced with the West Indian. Furthermore, upon representation of the planters that the levying of an ad valorem tax against imports from the Orient, while their own crop paid a specific one, afforded them no protection whatever during the existing depression,[4] an arrangement was adopted whereby the former bore a specific duty higher than did colonial Caribbean sugar, plus a low ad valorem rate as well. The government refused, however, to accord the colonists a much-desired 25 per cent preference.[5] The East Indian impost was thus changed from 3s. 2d. per hundredweight plus £42.16.3 ad valorem to 26s. 4⅘d. plus £1.4.0 in 1803 and was raised to 29s. 1⅘d. plus £1.6.6 in 1804 and to 29s. 8⅖d. plus £1.7.0 the year after.[6]

These new rates, instituted in face of a falling market, bore heavily on colonial produce from the American tropics. The defects of a revenue system which laid charges against commodities without regard to their shifting value became glaringly evident through the increasing proportion between the duty on sugar and the latter's market price.

The average cost of muscovado purchased in London in 1793, dur-

---

1830, XXII (375). "Memorial of the importers, and others interested in the sale of rum, at the ports of the Clyde, to the Lords Commissioners of H. M. Treasury," B. T. 6/141.

[1] "Rates of Duty . . . on British Plantation Muscovado Sugar . . . , 1776–1826," in *Gt. Br., H. C., Sess. Pap.*, 1826, XXII (328).

[2] 46 Geo. III c. 42.

[3] *East India Sugar. Papers Respecting the Culture and Manufacture of Sugar* . . . , Appendix IV, p. 12.

[4] See page 289.

[5] *Min. W. I. Plant. and Mer.*, Feb. 15, 1803.

[6] "Rates of Duty on Muscovado Sugar Imported Into Great Britain from the East Indies, 1792–1829," in *Gt. Br., H. C., Sess. Pap.*, 1830, XXV (466).

ing the wave of prosperity following the deflection of St. Domingo's crop, was 55s. 9d. per hundredweight and the duty 15s., or 26.9 per cent. In 1797, with the average price at 65s. 8d. and the duty 17s. 6d., the situation was approximately the same. However, by 1803, when the former had sunk to 43s. 1d., the latter had risen to 24s.—55.7 per cent of the current quotation, and in 1806, with the average purchase cost 43s. 9d., the duty was 27s., no less than 61.7 per cent of the wholesale price.[1] The sliding schedule then inaugurated was a feeble concession to the sugar growers, who were pressing for the adoption of an ad valorem system, but established no equitable relation between the worth of their product and the sum levied upon its entry for home consumption.

New regulations governing trade with the United States occasioned a scarcity of supplies and increased the cost of lumber and provisions in the British West Indies, while the proprietors' incomes were dwindling. We have seen how, under the exigencies of war, the navigation acts were virtually suspended in 1793 so far as they concerned American participation in island commerce, and that the mainlanders thereafter had free access to their old pre-Revolutionary markets.[2] The Treaty of Amiens in no way changed the situation; vessels under American registry continued to enjoy direct trade relations with the British sugar colonies under proclamations issued by the several governors. During the brief period of peace, the United States government sought to place this intercourse upon a firm basis through negotiating a commercial treaty, but no solution of the numerous problems involved had been arrived at when war between England and France again broke out.[3]

The dominant position which the foreigners along the Atlantic seaboard had come to occupy in the Caribbean by the opening of the century, occasioned great concern among British ship-owners. It had long been their wont to meet informally as occasion demanded to consider matters of mutual interest, but they now determined at a general gathering held in the London Tavern on May 6, 1802, to organize "in order more effectually . . . to promote and protect the

---

[1] "Quantities of Muscovado Sugar Imported into the United Kingdom, . . . [and] Average Prices . . . , 1793–1834," in *Gt. Br., H. C., Sess., Pap.*, 1847–48, LVIII (400). "Rates of Duty Per Cwt. on British Plantation Muscovado Sugar on Entry for Home Consumption, . . . 1776–1826," in *Gt. Br., H. C., Sess. Pap.*, 1826, XXII (328).

[2] Pages 230 ff.

[3] *American State Papers*, Class I, Foreign Relations, (6 vols., Washington, 1832–1859), II, 497–499, 501–503.

shipping interest of Great Britain, and to endeavor to prevent any further infringement of the navigation laws." [1]

A pamphlet issued shortly after protested at the Americans' being permitted to engage in the West India trade; [2] and, in 1804, Lord Sheffield, spokesman for the shippers and arch-exponent of enforcing the closed commercial system against the citizens of the United States, attacked the policy of granting them the right of entry to colonial ports under any conditions, demanding that suspensions of the law in their favor cease forthwith.

The sugar island trade, he declared, was the most productive branch of British commerce, and the most essential for maintaining naval supremacy. The only advantages the mother country derived from possessing the Caribbean colonies were those accruing to her navigation, manufactories, and agriculture from meeting the planters' needs. The latter's monopoly of supplying the home market resulted in tropical products sold there costing a full 20 per cent more than if they had been procured through foreigners and consequently the colonials had no claim for special consideration. "If the admittance of American shipping into the West-India ports is to be allowed, those islands will become dependent on the American states; and . . . rather than surrender the carrying trade of the Islands, it would be incomparably better to renounce the Islands themselves." [3]

Mr. Jordan, agent for Barbados, on the other hand, defended open intercourse as being essential for the welfare of the estate owners.[4] Lieutenant-Governor Nugent of Jamaica informed the government that if the renewal of the Jay treaty, then under discussion, granted proprietors the right of bartering produce for stores of lumber, the local legislature would meet the expense of maintaining 3,000 soldiers stationed there.[5] But, after careful consideration of the question, the committee of the privy council for trade and foreign plantations supported the stand of the Society of Shipowners and recommended that existing restrictions be enforced.

Governors were therefore directed in September, 1804, not to open

[1] Anon., ed., *Collection of Interesting and Important Reports and Papers on the Navigation and Trade of Great Britain, Ireland, and the British Colonies in the West Indies and America* . . . (London, 1807), pp. lvii, lviii.

[2] Anon., *The Case of the Owners of British Ships* (London, 1803).

[3] *Strictures on the Necessity of Inviolably Maintaining the Navigation and Colonial System of Great Britain* (London, 1804), pp. 46, 49, 50.

[4] G. W. Jordan, *The Claims of the West India Colonists to the Right of Obtaining Necessary Supplies from America and of Employing the Necessary Means of Effectually Obtaining Those Supplies Under a Limited and Duly Regulated Intercourse, Stated and Vindicated* (London, 1804).

[5] Nugent to Lord Hobart, April 14, 1804, C. O. 137/111.

the ports of their respective colonies for the admittance of articles from the American states which were denied entry by law except under stress of very great necessity, and to report fully the circumstances attending all such cases.[1] Some time later they were instructed to admit nothing but lumber and provisions in American bottoms under any circumstances, and then only what could not be supplied by the mother country or British North America, and to seize any other goods which might be entered, together with the ships which had brought them to the islands.[2]

These regulations caused great consternation in the Caribbean. A mass meeting of Jamaicans urged that the several ports there be kept open under the discretionary clause; and, although the merchants of Kingston stated that ample supplies could be secured from British sources,[3] American vessels were admitted by both Lieutenant-Governor Nugent and his successor, Lieutenant-Governor Sir Eyre Coote.[4] In consequence of a shortage of flour, the harbor of Castries, St. Lucia, was opened in the spring of 1805 [5] and, following the city's destruction by fire a few months later, citizens of the United States were allowed to take sugar as well as rum and molasses in payment for their cargoes of lumber and foodstuffs.[6] The great extent to which the trade of that island remained in American hands is shown by the following tables.[7]

IMPORTS BETWEEN JUNE, 1803, AND JULY, 1806

Commodity	From the United States in American Bottoms	From the United States in British Bottoms	From the United Kingdom	From British North America
Flour	13,096 bbls.	150 bbls.	None	None
Bread	1,115 bbls.	120 bbls.	None	None
Corn	5,269 bu.	None	None	500 bu.
Cod-fish	20,322 quintals	None	None	2,713 quintals
Pickled fish	1,765 bbls.	None	15 bbls.	230 bbls.
Beef	2,944 bbls.	None	595 bbls.	None
Pork	771 bbls.	None	1,689 bbls.	None
Boards	5,305 M	None	None	58 M
Shingles	7,550 M	30 M	None	49 M

[1] Circular of Sept. 5, 1804, C. O. 324/103.
[2] Circular of Jan. 16, 1805, C. O. 324/103.
[3] Gardner, *Jamaica,* p. 242.
[4] See their several proclamations in C. O. 137/114, 116.
[5] Brig. Gen. Robert Brereton to the Earl of Camden, April 10, 1805, C. O. 253/3.
[6] Brereton to Lord Castlereagh, Oct. 27, 1805, C. O. 253/3.
[7] In Brereton to William Windham, Nov. 16, 1806, C. O. 253/3.

EXPORTS TO NORTH AMERICA BETWEEN JUNE, 1803, AND JULY, 1806

Com- modity	To the United States in American Bottoms	To the United States in British Bottoms	To British North America
Rum	120,261 gals.	1,100 gals.	9,060 gals.
Molasses	232,091 gals.	850 gals.	73,797 gals.
Sugar	2,325,231 lbs.	335,424 lbs.	163,972 lbs.

The ports of Dominica were promptly closed upon receipt of the September order but were reopened shortly after at the request of resident traders.[1] Following the departure of the French expeditionary force in February, 1805, the Americans were granted permission to export coffee and sugar to one-sixth of the value of their cargoes, or sugar alone to a third of such amounts.[2] Their right to clear out with produce of any sort was revoked at the close of the year, but Dominican harbors remained open to them.[3]

Ship captains from the United States were likewise allowed to land a variety of lumber products and eatables, with the exception of salted provisions, in the Leeward Islands [4] and, late in 1805, when no beef or pork remained on sale, they too were admitted in American bottoms for a limited time. The shortage of candles and soap was so great that domestic comfort was seriously affected; even persons of means were obliged to burn oil. Special permission was therefore given for the entry of those goods.[5] The ports of Tobago, too, were kept open,[6] but such small shipments were received that no European or American beef, butter, or fish, Indian corn, peas, or American flour were on the market in April, 1805.[7]

High hopes for relief were entertained by the planters in consequence of pourparlers between the British and American governments in 1806 to abolish existing discriminations against one another's commerce. These, however, came to naught through the former's unwillingness to throw open the West India trade.[8]

[1] Governor Prevost to Lord Camden, Nov. 15, 1804, C. O. 71/36.
[2] Lord Castlereagh to President Metcalfe, Nov. 21, 1805; Metcalfe's proclamation of June 18, 1805, and Metcalfe to Castlereagh, Sept. 3, 1805, C. O. 71/38.
[3] Metcalfe to Castlereagh, Jan. 4, 1806, C. O. 71/40.
[4] Proclamation of Governor Lavington, Nov. 29, 1804, C. O. 152/86.
[5] Lavington to Viscount Castlereagh, March 10, 1806, C. O. 152/88.
[6] Despatch of Pres. James Campbell, March 15, 1805, C. O. 285/10.
[7] Report on current prices, C. O. 285/10.
[8] A convention removing discriminations of tonnage and impost on trade between the United States and British territories in Europe was actually signed by the plenipotentiaries of the two powers but was rejected by the

But it was becoming increasingly evident in London that the regular admission of Americans into Caribbean harbors was a sheer necessity under existing circumstances. Despite shipper opposition,[1] this was consequently authorized by an act of July 21, 1806, empowering the king in council to allow the importation of any goods which might seem proper into the West India or South American colonies in vessels belonging to states in amity with Great Britain for the period of

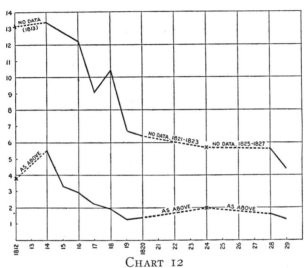

CHART 12

Imports of Cotton from the British West Indies, Demerara, and Berbice into Great Britain, 1812–1820, 1824, 1828, 1829, in Million Pounds *

 * Based on Customs 5/2–9, 13, 17, 18, Public Record Office. (Includes both the British-grown product and that foreign-grown but shipped to the British market by way of the Caribbean Colonies.) Upper line = from all the colonies. Lower line = from the insular possessions only (not including Demerara and Berbice).

American government due to its not being extended to include the West India trade. W. S. Culbertson, *International Economic Policies*. (New York, 1925), pp. 435, 436.

   [1] Anon., ed., *Collection of Interesting and Important Reports and Papers*, pp. cxxi, cxxii, clviii–clxi. See also I. Alley, *A Vindication of the Principles and Statements Advanced in the Strictures of Lord Sheffield* . . . (London, 1806) and Anon., ed., *A Collection of Debates in Parliament, on the Act of Navigation, on the Trade Between Great Britain and the United States of America, and the Intercourse between the latter and the British West-India Islands* . . . *&c. from 1783–1807* (London, 1807), both issued in the interest of strict enforcement of the traditional commercial laws against the Americans.

the war and six months after the ratification of peace, with the provision, however, that such commodities, with the exception of staves and lumber, must be of the growth or produce of the country to which the ship entering them belonged, and that no sugar, indigo, cotton, coffee, or cacao might be exported in such foreign bottoms.[1] The entry of staves and lumber and of provisions, excepting beef, pork, and butter, in the vessels of friendly nations, as well as the exportation of rum and molasses in the same, was permitted shortly after,[2] as was the landing of a cargo of ice and snow from an American freighter into Antigua by one William Tudor, who had earlier successfully transported them to Martinique.[3]

The restrictions thus imposed upon traffic with the foreign mainland unfortunately worked numerous hardships on the planters. The American traders, provoked at the exclusion of their salted meats and at being denied the privilege of bartering for sugar, refused to dispose of their wares except for bills of exchange or money, both of which were scarce, and a general shortage of supplies resulted.

In February, 1807, there was less than a ten day stock of flour on hand for the free population of St. Kitts, the bins of the island bakers stood nearly empty, there was not sufficient negro food to feed the blacks for a single day then on sale, while half the estate store-rooms were bare and the remainder nearly so. Hence the legislature prayed that the prohibition against the exportation of sugar by the Americans be removed.[4]

About the same time, inhabitants of the Leeward Islands were "experiencing a State of Calamity which can scarcely be conceiv'd but by Eye-witnesses of it."[5] In Trinidad, the planters and merchants who had been accustomed to exchange sugar for foodstuffs and lumber received word of the new regulations with consternation and expressed a strong belief that the colony's development would be checked thereby. The royal order in council was actually not made effective locally until April, 1807, so that engagements entered into under the old conditions might be fulfilled.[6]

Proprietors in St. Lucia soon felt the scarcity of provisions and were unable to market all of their sugar under the altered conditions

[1] 46 Geo. III c. 111.

[2] Circulars of Sept. 21 and Oct. 3, 1806, C. O. 324/103.

[3] Governor Lavington to William Windham, Feb. 20, 1807, C. O. 152/89.

[4] Resolutions of the Council and Assembly of St. Kitts, Feb. 17, 1807, C. O. 152/89.

[5] Governor Lavington to William Windham, Feb. 28, 1807, C. O. 152/89.

[6] Governor Hislop to William Windham, Dec. 4, 1806, C. O. 295/15.

of trade with the United States. They therefore petitioned for permission to barter that commodity for needed stores.[1]

With foreign beef and pork denied admission, the prices on Irish meats soared to such heights that the planters of St. Vincent could no longer afford to purchase them. Fewer Americans came to the island than for many years past and, during nineteen weeks in the spring of 1807, only a two months' supply of negro food was received. The port of Kingston was consequently opened to salt provisions from the mainland for three months and the prompt arrival of ten ships somewhat relieved the situation.[2]

In the summer of 1807, Governor Hislop of Barbados and the customs officials at Bridgetown authorized the unloading of twenty-five hogsheads of tobacco from the *Adams,* under American registry. Lieutenant Briarly, a meddlesome naval officer, promptly seized her as having entered goods contrary to the order of a year before,[3] but lost his case when it was heard in the vice-admiralty court.[4]

While these readjustments in West Indian commerce were being effected, Great Britain and the United States became embroiled in a bitter dispute over the rights of neutral carriers, closely related to the welfare of the British planters in the Caribbean. During the Anglo-French war of 1793–1802, the government at London had permitted American citizens to trade freely with France's tropical possessions, both supplying them and purchasing their crops. Vessels registered in the United States had furthermore been allowed to re-export French colonial produce from home ports to any in the world not under blockade, even in France. The arrival of American merchantmen in Hamburg with cargoes of enemy origin has already been noted.[5]

The legality of such action had been sharply challenged by British shippers and merchants, but all doubt on the matter had been dispelled through an opinion rendered by His Majesty's Advocate General in 1801, that the neutrals were acting wholly within their rights, although direct trade between the enemy mother country and her colonies on their part was not tolerated.[6] This view had been offi-

[1] Brig. Gen. Robert Brereton to William Windham, April 27, 1807, C. O. 253/3.

[2] Governor Beckwith to William Windham, May 15, 1807 and enclosures; Beckwith to Lord Castlereagh, June 20, July 3, and Aug. 19, 1807, C. O. 260/22.

[3] Governor Hislop to Viscount Castlereagh, Aug. 15, 1807, C. O. 295/16.

[4] Governor Hislop to Viscount Castlereagh, July 26, 1808, C. O. 295/19.

[5] See page 287.

[6] *American State Papers, Foreign Relations,* II, 491.

cially transmitted to Washington and to the several British admiralty courts, and it was therefore commonly held that the landing of French Caribbean produce in America and paying duties on the same legalized its subsequently being cleared out for Europe. In practice, however, the customs charges had not actually been paid. Importers had given bonds for the proper amounts and, upon entering the goods for reëxportation, often immediately after, they had received debentures for the total sums minus 3½ per cent, payable the same day as the duties. The entire transaction had thus become a mere technical compliance with the conditions which made the trip from the French colonies to France a broken one.

Upon the renewal of war in 1803, the Americans had once more engaged extensively in this profitable trade until two judicial decisions of 1805 and 1806 [1] had ruled that the mere payment of duty in the United States was not proof of a bona fide importation having taken place, and British ships had begun to capture laden American merchantmen en route to France in large numbers.[2]

Economic self-interest underlay this change in point of view. The first period of hostilities had been one of unparalleled prosperity for the British planters in consequence of the existing world shortage of tropical products. In the second, scarcity was being overcome by a rapid extension of cultivation in foreign colonies throughout the equatorial belt and British West Indian produce was being increasingly shut out from European markets. This exclusion was due for the most part to the fact that, while British Caribbean crops were saddled with war duties and were obliged to bear war-time shipping charges, the Americans were transporting enemy produce to continental marts at normal rates under the protection of their neutral flag and could therefore easily undersell the British. By 1806, the planters' position had altered materially; their traditional sympathy for the Americans in the latter's commercial disputes with Great Britain had vanished, and they raised a loud cry against them.

The attack on this neutral trade, so injurious to the interests of the West Indians, was led by James Stephen, formerly a lawyer in St. Kitts where he had handled numerous cases involving illegal trad-

[1] In the *Essex* and *William* cases.

[2] W. Shaw Lindsay, *History of Merchant Shipping and Ancient Commerce* (4 vols., London, 1874–76), II, 383–388. See also Herbert W. Briggs, "The Doctrine of Continuous Voyage," in *Johns Hopkins Studies*, XLIV, no. 2 (Baltimore, 1926). Papers relative to a considerable number of such prizes will be found in the New York Public Library, the Library of Congress, and that at Brown University.

ing on the part of the mainlanders, and, singularly enough, a decade later, an arch-foe of the Caribbean estate owners because of his leadership in the emancipation movement. In ringing phrases, he denominated the American carrying trade war in disguise, a prop supporting Napoleon, and demanded that it be brought to an end.[1] The seizure of American vessels engaged in the traffic, commencing at about the same time, created a delicate situation and brought the two countries to the very brink of war.[2] The flow of French colonial crops to European markets thus came to a sudden and spectacular close.

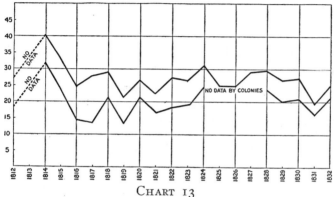

CHART 13

Imports of Coffee, the Growth of British Plantations, from the British West Indies, Demerara, and Berbice into Great Britain, 1812–1832, in Million Pounds *

*Based on Customs 5/2-21, Public Record Office. Upper line = from all the Colonies. Lower line = from the insular possessions only (not including Demerara and Berbice).

[1] *War in Disguise, or the Frauds of Neutral Flags* (London, 1805). See also "The Frauds of the Neutral Flags," in *The Ed. Rev.*, April, 1806, pp. 1–33.

[2] A considerable number of pamphlets on the rights of neutrals appeared during the controversy. The following are representative of those opposed to the claims of the American shipping interest—[James Stephen]. "Author of War in Disguise," *Observations on the Speech of the Hon. John Randolph, Representative for the State of Virginia, in the General Congress of America: on a Motion for the Non-Importation of British Merchandize . . .* (New York, 1806); [William Smith], "Phocion," *pseud., American Arguments for British Rights; Being a Republication of the Celebrated Letters of Phocion on the Subject of Neutral Trade* (London, 1806); [Smith], *The Numbers of Phocion, Which Were Originally Published in the Charleston Courier, in 1806, on the Subject of Neutral Rights* (Charleston, 1806); "Vindex," *pseud., On the Maritime Rights of Great Britain* (London, 1807). John Randolph, in his *The Speech . . . in the General Congress of America; on a Mo-*

The second French war was a time of acute distress and stark discouragement for the planting interest in the British Caribbean possessions. "Bankruptcy is universal," wrote Governor Lavington from Antigua in the summer of 1805, "and is not confin'd to the Public Treasury, but extends to the Generality of Individuals resident in the Colony." The fall in the price of sugar and long-continued drought, which reduced the crop of that year to a third the average amount, involved the Antiguans to such an extent that taxes could not be paid, the government became insolvent, and, following a precedent established in a similar crisis in 1779,[1] bills for £10,000 sterling were drawn on the home Treasury to tide it over the emergency.[2]

By 1807, the situation of the proprietary class as a whole had become critical. A total of 1,464,102 hundredweight of sugar was warehoused or on board ship in English ports in December, 1806. This was 284,098 hundredweight more than had been on hand a year previous. The increase was due to greater imports and a falling off of sales abroad. The average cost of sugar production in Jamaica, making no allowance for interest on investments or depreciation, was then 21s. 6d. per hundredweight and that in the other islands 20s.; the cost of marketing was 16s. and 15s. 6d. respectively; the duty, 27s. The entire charge against Jamaican sugar then being sold in Great Britain was consequently £3.4.6 per hundredweight and that on consignments from the other islands, £3.2.6. Yet the average price of muscovado sold in London in the quarter preceding January 5, 1807, was only £3.7.7¼ per hundredweight inclusive of duty. Hence Jamaican growers were making a profit of but 3s. 1¼d. per hundredweight on sales and those in the other colonies, 5s. ¼d., from which returns on their capital outlay were to be derived.[3]

But worse was still to come. The average price of raw sugar continued to fall during the course of 1807. On April 1, it was 36s. 4d.

<hr />

tion for the Non-Importation of British Merchandize . . . (London, 1806), urged that the French carrying trade was but a mushroom commerce and should not lead to a rupture between Great Britain and America. Anon., An Examination of the British Doctrine Which Subjects to Capture a Neutral Trade Not Open in Time of Peace (London, 1806) held the British claim of the right to intercept this carrying trade to be both preposterous and pernicious. See also [Gouverneur Morris], An Answer to War in Disguise (New York, 1806).

[1] See pages 157 and 158.

[2] Lavington to the Earl of Camden, July 30, C. O. 152/87.

[3] "Report from the Select Committee Appointed to consider the expediency of permitting the distillation from sugar and on the Distress of the Sugar Colonies," in Gt. Br., H. C., Sess. Pap., 1806–7, II (83), pp. 73, 74.

per hundredweight exclusive of duty; on July 1, 34s. 4½d.; on September 30, 32s. 9d.; on December 30, 33s. 5¾d.[1] As the cost of producing and transporting it to the British market ranged from 35s. 6d. to 37s. 6d. per hundredweight, that commodity was then actually being sold at a loss even without considering interest on capital invested.

Whereas sugar estates had yielded returns of about 10 per cent net toward the close of the eighteenth century, profits had progressively declined until they had disappeared on the great majority of properties by 1807. Hyde Hall plantation in Jamaica, an exceptionally well located one, had paid 12 per cent from 1795 to 1798, 6 per cent from 1801 to 1804, and 3 per cent in 1805; in 1807, it was barely meeting operating costs.[2]

Toward the close of 1807, a committee of the Jamaican assembly reported that sugar grown locally was being sold in England at 2s. 3d. sterling per hundredweight below the cost of production, and estimated the loss for the average individual grower at £236 sterling on the season's crop. At the same time it was maintained that the planters would not derive adequate returns unless they received at least thirty shillings per hundredweight clear profit on sales. Considering the danger from hurricane and insurrection and the rapidity of soil exhaustion, 10 per cent was a fair rate of interest on money invested in sugar production. Yet this would not be received until muscovado sold at an average price of 93s. 8d. per hundredweight instead of 34s. 7d. as was then the case.[3]

"This colony is in a most deplorable situation," declared Brigadier-General Wood in a despatch from St. Lucia at the same time. There was no market for the island's produce and supplies were scarce. "The planters have no Money to purchase nor can they get credit from the Merchants who cannot afford to give any thing for the Sugars made here as the Duties, Freights & Insurance would absorb the whole at the British market." [4]

The proprietors of St. Vincent and Grenada had not shared in the

---

[1] Weekly returns in *The London Gazette.*

[2] "Report . . . on the Commercial State of the West India Colonies," in *Gt. Br., H. C., Sess. Pap.,* 1807, III (65), pp. 3 ff.

[3] "Report of a Committee of the House of Assembly of Jamaica, November, 1807," Appendix 42 to "Report from the Select Committee on the expediency of confining the distilleries to the use of sugar and molasses only, and on the relief to the Growers of Sugar in the West India Colonies," in *Gt. Br., H. C., Sess. Pap.,* 1808, IV (178), pp. 215 ff.

[4] To Lord Castlereagh, October 24, C. O. 253/3.

general prosperity of a decade earlier, since the civil disturbances in those islands had ravaged their properties and had plunged them into debt.[1] Decreased returns now made it impossible for them to meet their obligations and many estates were sold to meet the demands of creditors, often for less than the debts against them.[2] But 30,537 acres of land were being cultivated in Tobago during 1807,[3] half the amount which had been sold by the Crown from 1765 to 1771 alone.[4]

In Jamaica, where there had been "only three subjects of conversation . . . —debt, disease, and death" four years before,[5] a committee of the assembly reported that sixty-five plantations had been abandoned between 1799 and 1807, that thirty-two had been sold under decrees of the court of chancery in the past five years to meet claims against them, and that suits were then pending against 115 more.[6] The abolition of the slave trade, coming at this singularly unfavorable time, wholly disheartened the Caribbean colonists. Clearly the long-favored children of fortune had fallen upon evil times.

The West India interest in London attributed the perilous position of the proprietors largely to the progressive abandonment of colonial preference in the home market since the beginning of the late era of prosperity. The encouragement given sugar cultivation in oriental territories not on the footing of colonies and hence not subject to the restrictions of the colonial system was a primary grievance. The average annual sale of East Indian sugar had risen from 17,030 hundredweight in 1791–1793 to 90,941 in 1804–1806,[7] and reduced demand for the Caribbean article to that extent.

The opening of free ports in the islands resulted in foreign tropical produce being transported to European marts in British bottoms via the United Kingdom. The average annual amount of such non-British sugar entered there for reëxportation from 1801–1803 was 133,927 hundredweight and 130,263 hundredweight between 1804 and 1806.[8]

[1] See pages 219 ff.
[2] Governor Beckwith to Lord Castlereagh, Dec. 5, 1807, C. O. 260/23.
[3] Young, *Prospectus . . . for the Institution of an Agricultural Society in Tobago.*
[4] See page 116.
[5] Cundall, ed., *Lady Nugent's Journal*, p. 239.
[6] "Report of a Committee of the House of Assembly of Jamaica, November, 1807," Appendix 42 to "Report . . . ," in *Gt. Br., H. C., Sess. Pap.*, 1808, IV (178).
[7] *East India Sugar. Papers Respecting the Culture and Manufacture of Sugar . . .* , Appendix IV, p. 13.
[8] "Quantities of Muscovado Sugar Imported Into the United Kingdom, Quantities Retained for Consumption There, etc. . . . , 1793–1834," in *Gt. Br., H. C., Sess. Pap.*, 1847–48, LVIII (400).

Demand for the British-grown product from the continent declined in proportion as the foreign article was handled.

The reduction in bounties and drawbacks on West Indian sugar shipped from the homeland increased its cost to the continental buyer, encouraged production in foreign equatorial holdings including those of the enemy, and resulted in the rise of the American carrying trade and the exclusion of British sugar from markets formerly wholly supplied by it. Thus, the average annual exportation of sugar from Havana rose from 85,251 cases in 1790–1792 to 175,-336 in 1804–1806.[1]

Members of the planter-merchant group in the capital had other grievances. It was declared that admission of the conquered colonies' crops into the United Kingdom under the classification "the growth of British plantations" gave their inhabitants, mostly Frenchmen and Dutchmen cultivating virgin soil, an unfair advantage over loyal native-born subjects whose estates were suffering from soil-exhaustion and who could therefore not meet such unjust competition. Higher duties on sugar had impeded the natural increase in home consumption and had thus prevented the rise of a market for the greater production of the genuinely British properties.

War with France had furthermore doubled the cost of imports from Great Britain, while the renewal of restrictions on the American trade cut off the principal outlet for rum and made supplies of lumber and foodstuffs both uncertain and high in price.[2]

Members of the Jamaican legislature attributed the low English selling prices on British West Indian products in part to their exclusion from European markets through the operation of the continental system and in part to their being undersold in such centers by foreign colonial goods entered from the United States.[3]

Planter distress at this time became a matter of sufficient concern to be made the subject of parliamentary inquiry. Three committees studied the question during 1807 and 1808, considered measures of relief, and issued six voluminous reports on the situation.[4]

---

[1] "Exports of Sugar from Havana," in *Gt. Br., H. C., Sess. Pap.,* 1831-32, XX (in 381).

[2] *Min. W. I. Plant. and Mer.,* April 14, 1806, Feb. 26, 1807.

[3] "Report of a Committee of the House of Assembly of Jamaica, November, 1807," Appendix 42 to "Report . . . ," in *Gt. Br., H. C., Sess. Pap.,* 1808, IV (178).

[4] "Report from the Select Committee appointed to consider the expediency of permitting the distillation from Sugar and on the Distress of the Sugar Colonies," in *Gt. Br., H. C., Sess. Pap.,* 1806-07, II (83). "Report from the

The causes for the deplorable state of the West Indians were, in general, found to be the same as those which they themselves had adduced.

The first investigating body found that decreased demand for British sugar had resulted in lower selling prices, while the cost of production and marketing had remained stationary or had risen.[1] The second declared that the Caribbean proprietors constituted the only group in the country which was not being indemnified for increased costs by an equivalent rise in selling values.

This arose from the home market being glutted through the falling off in foreign demand, brought about by the facility of intercourse between the colonies of enemy countries and continental Europe under the American flag. The freight and insurance charges on sugar from such territories to the United States and from there to the ports of Holland and Flanders were 8s. 11d. per hundredweight less than were those on British sugar carried to the same distribution points in British ships operated at war time rates; in the case of shipments to the Mediterranean, the difference was 12s. 6d. Under such conditions, British produce could not compete with that of French origin and the British planters suffered while those in enemy colonies prospered.

During the year commencing October 1, 1805, the Americans had exported 106,249,397 pounds of muscovado, 39,378,637 pounds of clayed sugar, 47,001,662 pounds of coffee, 6,846,758 pounds of cacao, 1,833,187 pounds of cotton, and a considerable quantity of molasses, all for the most part the produce of France's plantations, and serving materially to exclude the same British products from the continent.[2]

The third committee, reporting in 1808, stressed the competition of the conquered French and Dutch colonies' produce in Great Britain with that from the West India possessions of long standing as a factor in having brought the planters whose holdings lay in the latter to a low state. "The cultivation of the old British Colonies has done

Select Committee on the Commercial State of the West India Colonies," in *Gt. Br., H. C., Sess. Pap.*, 1807, III, (65). "Four Reports from the Select Committee on the expediency of confining the Distilleries to the use of Sugar and Molasses only, and on the relief to the Growers of Sugar in the West India Colonies," in *Gt. Br., H. C., Sess. Pap.*, 1808, IV (178, 278, 300, 318).

[1] "Report from the Select Committee . . . on the Distress of the Sugar Colonies," in *Gt. Br., H. C., Sess. Pap.*, 1806–07, II (83).

[2] "Report . . . on the Commercial State of the West India Colonies," in *Gt. Br., H. C., Sess. Pap.*, 1807, III, (65).

little more than to keep pace with the extension of British Consumption, and the excessive glut of the Market is imputable chiefly to the admission of the Produce of the conquered Colonies into the privileges of our own, at a time too, when access to the Foreign Market was subjected to unusual difficulties."

While tropical estate owners had remained subject to a monopoly in favor of British goods and shipping, their exclusive right of supplying the home market had thus been extensively invaded. Supplies, too, cost them much more at a time when their returns were decreasing.[1]

The manifold vicissitudes befalling the West Indians occasioned widespread popular comment and many and varied were the explanations and suggestions offered. Thus, one nameless inquirer found the cause in overproduction, brought about by a too rapid extension of cultivation during the previous decade under the stimulus of high prices and by the general introduction of Bourbon cane.[2] Another pamphleteer held that the world-market was overstocked following the opening up of vast acres of cane land in tropical regions under European control;[3] a third, that the abolition controversy had discouraged Caribbean agriculture and was therefore responsible for the proprietors having been reduced to such severe straits.[4]

Proposed relief measures were legion. One group interested in the problem urged the planters to decrease sugar production as the only means of alleviating their distress; another advocated increasing consumption of Caribbean produce in the United Kingdom; some persons, raising exports to the continent; still others, removing restraints placed upon the islanders under the old colonial system.

A member of the West India interest declared that the situation could be improved only by restricting sugar cultivation to meet the needs of the British and Irish markets;[5] other well-informed and

---

[1] "Four Reports . . . ," in *Gt. Br., H. C. Sess. Pap.*, 1808, IV (178, 278, 300, 318). See especially the fourth report (318), p. 396. Joseph Lowe, *An Inquiry Into the State of the British West Indies* (London, 1807) also attributes the planters' difficulties to the free entry given the produce of the conquered colonies.

[2] *Emancipation in Disguise, or the True Crisis of the Colonies* (London, 1807) pp. 5, 6.

[3] Archibald Bell, *An Inquiry Into the Policy and Justice of the Prohibition of the Use of Grain in the Distilleries . . .* (Edinburgh, 1808), pp. 2, 3.

[4] [John Robley], "A West India Merchant," *A Permanent and Effectual Remedy Suggested for the Evils Under Which the British West Indies Now Labour* (London, 1808), p. 5.

[5] *Ibid.*, pp. 5–8.

forceful writers declared that the difficulties would never be ended until production had been severely and deliberately limited.[1] A change to another staple was also advocated.[2]

As for enlarging consumption, it was declared that if sugar, rum, and coffee duties were lowered, selling prices would fall, increasing the demand, and that the West Indians would thus be relieved of their existing surplus while the revenue would not be injured because of the greater quantities which would be handled.[3] In the case of rum, the rate should be reduced so as to equalize it with that laid on British spirits.[4] The sugar tax should be made ad valorem instead of specific,[5] or should, in some other way, be more closely regulated by the average selling price.[6] Preference on the West Indian article entered in the home market should at the same time be increased [7] and sugar should be admitted for use in distilleries and breweries.[8]

New uses for plantation products were sought. In 1807, William Orson of the Isle of Man satisfied officers of the Society of West India Planters and Merchants that muscovado could be employed as a cattle food and received a gift of £200 from that body for having made the discovery.[9] Raw sugar was then highly recommended to

[1] William Spence, *The Radical Cause of the Present Distresses of the West India Planters Pointed Out* (London, 1808). "Pamphlets on West Indian Affairs," in *The Ed. Rev.*, Jan. 1809, pp. 382–413.

[2] See the reference to this in "Fourth Report from the Committee on the Distillation of Sugar and Molasses . . . ," *Gt. Br., H. C., Sess. Pap.*, 1808. IV (318).

[3] *Min. W. I. Plant. and Mer.*, April 14, 1806, Feb. 26, 1807, Feb. 10, 1808. "Report . . . on the Commercial State of the West India Colonies," in *Gt. Br., H. C., Sess. Pap.*, 1807, III (65). Edgar Corrie, *Letters on the Subject of the Duties on Coffee* (London, 1808).

[4] *Min. W. I. Plant. and Mer.*, Feb. 26, 1808.

[5] *Ibid.*, April 14, 1806; "Report of a Committee of the House of Assembly of Jamaica, November, 1807," Appendix 42 to "Report . . . ," in *Gt. Br., H. C., Sess. Pap.*, 1808, IV (178). Charles Bosanquet, *A Letter to W. Manning, Esq. M. P. on the Proposition submitted to the Consideration of Government, for Taking the Duties on Muscovado Sugar ad Valorem* [London, 1806]. Anon., *Thoughts on the Justice, Practicability, and Expediency of Levying the Duties on Sugar by a Rate According to Value* (Liverpool, 1807).

[6] "Report . . . on the Commercial State of the West India Colonies," in *Gt. Br., H. C., Sess. Pap.*, 1807, III (65). "Fourth Report from the Committee on the Distillation of Sugar and Molasses . . . ," in *Gt. Br., H. C., Sess. Pap.*, 1808, IV (318), p. 396.

[7] *Min. W. I. Plant. and Mer.*, April 14, 1806.

[8] *Ibid.*, Feb. 26, and Oct. 15, 1807. Charles Bosanquet, *A Letter to W. Manning, Esq. M. P. on the Causes of the Rapid and Progressive Depreciation of West India Property* (London, 1807), pp. 30–34.

[9] *Min. W. I. Plant. and Mer.*, June 2, 1807, and June 8, 1809. See also Anon., *On the Uses of Sugar for fattening Cattle* [London, 1808]; Anon., *Facts and Experiments on the Use of Sugar in Feeding Cattle* . . . (London, 1809).

dairymen and stock raisers and the government was urged to grant a drawback upon all consumed in this fashion, with the recommendation, however, that it be first contaminated so as to prevent its illicitly entering ordinary trade channels.[1] The issuing of colonial rum for the army and navy liquor ration [2] and discontinuing the importation of foreign spirits, especially French brandy, under license of the privy council,[3] were advocated as means of providing large additional outlets.

Two methods of increasing British West Indian exports to the European mainland were suggested. First, that the sugar drawback and bounties be raised and readjusted from time to time in accordance with market conditions.[4] The planters desired both set sufficiently high to place them on an equal footing in the chief distribution points with inhabitants of the French and Spanish possessions.[5]

But a far more efficacious way of raising sales abroad was to create a demand for British produce, above all in Holland, Germany, and the Baltic countries, through preventing supplies from enemy colonies crossing the Atlantic. The adoption of this policy was vigorously called for by island legislators [6] and members of the West India interest in London [7] and was recommended by two of the parliamentary investigating committees.

French colonial crops, it was held, should be kept from continental consumers by blockading France's Caribbean ports and by restricting commerce between neutrals and the enemy countries. It was realized that this would lead to difficulties with the United States, the nation chiefly engaged in the carrying trade, and would, in all probability, result in the cutting off of supplies of lumber and provisions from

[1] "Fourth Report from the Committee on the Distillation of Sugar and Molasses . . . ," in *Gt. Br., H. C., Sess. Pap.,* 1808, IV (318). "Pamphlets on West India Affairs," in *The Quar. Rev.* Aug., 1809, pp. 1 ff.

[2] *Min. W. I. Plant. and Mer.,* Oct. 15, 1807. "Report . . . on the Commercial State of the West India Colonies," in *Gt. Br., H. C., Sess. Pap.,* 1807, III (65).

[3] "Second Report from the Committee on the Distillation of Sugar and Molasses," in *Gt. Br., H. C., Sess. Pap.,* 1808, IV (278).

[4] *Min. W. I. Plant. and Mer.,* April 14, 1806. "Report . . . on the Commercial State of the West India Colonies," in *Gt. Br., H. C., Sess. Pap.,* 1807, III (65).

[5] "Report of a Committee of the House of Assembly of Jamaica, November, 1807," Appendix 42 to "Report . . . ," in *Gt. Br., H. C., Sess. Pap.,* 1808, IV (178).

[6] "Report of a Committee of the House of Assembly of Jamaica, November, 1807," Appendix 42 to "Report . . . ," in *Gt. Br., H. C., Sess. Pap.,* 1808, IV (178).

[7] *Min. W. I. Plant. and Mer.,* Oct. 15, 1807.

there to the British West Indies; but it was argued that, while the direct American trade was advantageous to the colonials, it was not necessary to their existence and was less important for their welfare than was the securing of an outlet for their produce in foreign Europe.[1]

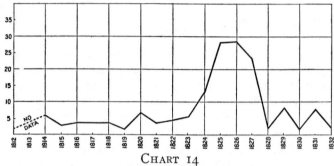

CHART 14

Imports of Indigo from the British West Indies, Demerara, and Berbice into Great Britain, 1812–1832, in Ten Thousand Pounds *

* Based on Customs 5/2–21. (Imports from Demerara and Berbice were usually quite insignificant, never being in excess of 800 pounds save in 1833 when they totaled 12,937 pounds.)

The freeing of the planters from restrictions imposed upon them by virtue of the colonial compact had many champions. A common proposal was that neutrals, meaning the Americans, be given free entry into Caribbean harbors and that residents there be permitted to barter sugar and coffee as well as rum and molasses for stores of food and lumber.[2] One writer went so far as to urge opening even the British West Indian-European carrying trade to citizens of the United States.[3]

The parliamentary committee of 1808 recommended encouraging the colonists to refine sugar in the plantations themselves by repeal-

---

[1] "Report . . . on the Commercial State of the West India Colonies," in *Gt. Br., H. C., Sess Pap.,* 1807, III (65). "Third Report from the Committee on the Distillation of Sugar and Molasses," in *Gt. Br., H. C., Sess. Pap.,* 1808, IV (300).

[2] *Min. W. I. Plant. and Mer.,* Feb. 26, 1807, Feb. 26, 1808. "Report of a Committee of the House of Assembly of Jamaica, November, 1807," Appendix 42 to "Report . . . ," in *Gt. Br., H. C., Sess. Pap.,* 1808, IV (178). "Third Report from the Committee on the Distillation of Sugar and Molasses," in *Gt. Br., H. C., Sess. Pap.,* 1808, IV (300). Anon., *Emancipation in Disguise,* p. 129.

[3] Bosanquet, *Letter on the Depreciation of West India Property,* p. 41.

ing the existing prohibitive duty of £8.8.0 per hundredweight on the manufactured article entering the home country. This would save them an annual loss of £600,000 from the drainage of muscovado en route to the United Kingdom plus £300,000 freight paid on quantities thus lost, would provide them with additional waste material for the distillation of rum, and would introduce a considerable body of Europeans to carry on the industry into the islands.

Preparing sugar for market on the western side of the Atlantic would lower selling prices to consumers and would encourage sales; hence there would be no falling off in the demand for shipping and no decline in the revenue. The actual loss involved in closing down refineries in the British Isles would be but £819,000—less than what the estate proprietors lost each year through their being obliged to send the raw commodity to the mother country.[1] Adoption of this striking relief measure was supported by both liberal[2] and conservative[3] party organs.

One of the best informed pamphleteers of the day, on the other hand, advocated removing the 4½ per cent export duty levied on the produce of the Leeward Islands[4] and the introduction of free oriental laborers as the best means of improving the planters' position.[5]

Members of the Caribbean group, however, did not enjoy the sympathy of all their countrymen. There was no need for extending them aid in any form, declared the wielder of a peculiarly acrid pen— it was ridiculous to believe that sugar was being sold for less than the cost of production. "We see West India Merchants still living like princes; but when they come before Parliament they have . . . the whining cant of beggars."[6] This caustic critic, unfortunately for his case, failed to distinguish between proprietors and factors.

The first step taken by the British government to improve the situation was an attempt to close the American carrying trade. The seizure of vessels registered in the United States, laden with enemy produce, began in 1805 and became increasingly frequent in the next

[1] "Fourth Report from the Committee on the Distillation of Sugar and Molasses . . .," in *Gt. Br., H. C., Sess. Pap.*, 1808, IV (318).

[2] "Pamphlets . . . ," *The Ed Rev.*, Jan. 1809, pp. 382 ff.

[3] "Pamphlets . . . ," *The Quar. Rev.*, Aug. 1809, pp. 1 ff.

[4] See pages 104 ff., 127 ff.

[5] Anon., *Emancipation in Disguise*, pp. 130, 132.

[6] Macall Medford, *Oil Without Vinegar, and Dignity Without Pride: or, British, American, and West Indian Interests Considered* (London, 1810), p. 30. This elicited a reply by Francis Ilsley, a late resident of Jamaica, *A Statement of Facts, Relating to the Prime Cost of Sugar; With Observations in Behalf of West India Planters* (London, 1810).

two years. The orders in council issued in reply to Napoleon's Berlin Decree were designed to put an end effectually to such objectionable commerce. The West India interest, as was natural, warmly supported the new policy. Alexander Baring, a contemporary publicist, charged its members with primary responsibility for the rapid progress of the movement looking to war with America.[1]

At the same time that this overt measure was adopted, exportation was encouraged by the annual renewal of laws continuing the regulation of drawbacks and bounties by the selling price under the system inaugurated some years before [2] and extending it.[3] Thus, the drawback on muscovado leaving Great Britain was increased from 26s. 6d. per hundredweight to 28s. 6d. in 1810 and to 29s. 6d. in 1813,[4] and the bounty on single refined sugar in complete lumps rose from 45s. ⅗d. per hundredweight to 48s. 5⅖d. in 1810 and to 50s. 4⅕d. in 1811.[5]

The American embargo and non-intercourse act served further to exclude shipments other than British from continental Europe and wholesalers there increasingly turned across the Channel for stocks, as had been anticipated. Between 1805 and 1807, the average annual exportation of raw sugar from Great Britain was 469,124 hundredweight; during 1808 and 1809, it was 533,903 hundredweight. The increase was not as much as had been hoped for, nor, unfortunately, did it in any way benefit the British planters. Whereas an annual average of 369,443 hundredweight of colonial muscovado had been cleared out from Great Britain between 1805 and 1807, the average for 1808 and 1809 was but 260,324 hundredweight—the British Caribbean produce was being undersold by that from the foreign West Indies warehoused in Great Britain for exportation.

Then, with the spread of the continental system, sales to the mainland again dropped. The average annual exportation in 1809 and

[1] *An Inquiry Into the Causes and Consequences of the Orders in Council; and an Examination of the Conduct of Great Britain Towards the Neutral Commerce of America* (London, 1808).

[2] See pages 291 and 292.

[3] 47 Geo. III sess. 1 c. 22, 48 Geo. III c. 16, 49 Geo. III c. 11 and c. 98, 50 Geo. III c. 18, 51 Geo. III c. 13, 52 Geo. III c. 15, 53 Geo. III c. 31 and 54 Geo. III c. 24.

[4] "Rates of Duty Per Cwt. on British Plantation Muscovado Sugar . . . and Drawbacks Allowed on the Same . . ., 1776–1826," in *Gt. Br., H. C., Sess. Pap.*, 1826, XXII (328).

[5] "Bounty per Cwt. Paid on Various Grades of Clayed Sugar Exported from Great Britain . . . , 1776–1836," in *Gt. Br., H. C., Sess. Pap.*, 1826, XXII (328).

1810 was 506,651 hundredweight as against 327,072 hundredweight during the two years which followed.[1] So tight a commercial cordon did Napoleon draw about Europe that at one time the sugar reaching the German states came by way of Salonica and sold at from 5s. to 6s. per pound.[2]

Attempts were made, too, to free continental consumers from their dependence on Great Britain for supplies of this essential foodstuff and, in so far as they were successful, they decreased demand. A scientific search for cane substitutes was made in France and, under the stimulus of prizes offered by the emperor, experimenters sought to obtain saccharous material from grapes, apples, pears, plums, quinces, mulberries, chestnuts, figs, sorghum, and corn-stalks. In 1811, a total of 2,000,000 kilograms of syrup and 500 kilograms of sugar was produced from grapes in France. Sugar had been derived from beets in Germany as early as 1747; and in 1801 a factory to produce it on a commercial scale had been established in Breslau.[3] The beet sugar industry was now fostered west of the Rhine, and, in 1812, some 7,000,000 pounds were produced.[4]

Another relief measure adopted was the admission of muscovado into distilleries and later into breweries as well. This expedient, as we have seen,[5] had been resorted to during the previous glutting of the market at the close of the century, when supplies of grain were low. Two of the three parliamentary committees, considering the state of the Caribbean plantations, gave their chief attention to the question of whether or not such permission should be renewed.

The first of these investigating bodies, after weighing the proposal, reported adversely, declaring that raw sugar must sell under 47s. per hundredweight, duty included, instead of at 67s. 7¼d., the average price in the last quarter of 1806, before it could meet malt in the manufacture of beer, and at 32s. or 33s. before it could replace barley and malt in spirits production, the existing prices of grain and comparative saccharous yields considered. Lack of a uniform distillery law for the United Kingdom, which would lead to complications, and the decreasing of national revenue which would follow the

[1] *East India Sugar. Papers Respecting the Culture and Manufacture of Sugar* . . . , Appendix IV, p. 5; Customs 11/1-4, P. R. O.

[2] Reed, *History of Sugar*, p. 149.

[3] See "Sugar from the Beet Root," in *The Scots Mag.*, Jan. 1801, p. 30.

[4] H. C. Prinsen Geerlings, *The World's Cane Sugar Industry Past and Present* (Manchester, 1912), pp. 13, 15, 16.

[5] Page 290.

entry of sugar for this special purpose were further adduced as arguments against its use in place of grain.[1]

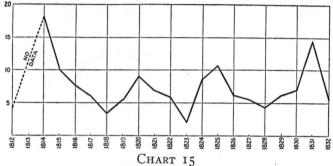

CHART 15

Imports of Cocoa Nuts, the Growth of British Plantations, from the British West Indies, Demerara, and Berbice into Great Britain, 1812–1832, in Hundred Thousand Pounds *

* Based on Customs 5/2–21, Public Record Office. (Shipments from Demerara and Berbice were at most but 10 per cent of the total; they were often negligible and in 1831 none at all were made from there.)

However, the select committee of 1808, making four elaborate studies of the situation, declared that Great Britain had become dependent upon foreign countries for supplies of corn to the extent of 770,000 quarters per annum; that, in the then serious state of foreign affairs which threatened to cut off shipments from abroad, it was advisable to conserve for food the 470,000 quarters consumed each year in the British distilleries alone, and recommended that the use of grain in liquor production there be temporarily forbidden as a precautionary measure.[2]

A memorable parliamentary struggle ensued.[3] There was actually then no shortage of corn, and English agrarians, fearing a drop in price, naturally opposed the adoption of a measure which would lower demand for their crops.[4] The West Indians defended the proposed

[1] "Report from the Select Committee appointed to consider the expediency of permitting the distillation from Sugar . . . ," in *Gt. Br., H. C., Sess. Pap.,* 1806–07, II (83), pp. 74–78.

[2] "Four Reports from the Select Committee on the expediency of confining the distilleries to the use of Sugar and Molasses only . . .," in *Gt. Br., H. C., Sess. Pap.,* 1808, IV (178, 278, 300, 318).

[3] For a good summary of the conflict between the grain growers and the planters see William F. Galpin, *The Grain Supply of England During the Napoleonic Period* (New York, 1925), Ch. 4.

[4] "Grand Distillery Question: Will stopping the Malt Distillery be injurious to the Agriculture of the Kingdom?" in *Annals of Ag.,* XLV (1808),

exclusion of grain as being a means of easing their situation while relieving the country from the necessity of importing food materials of prime importance,[1] and these two powerfully intrenched groups battled royally over the issue. George Hibbert, William Manning, Charles Ellis, Henry Lascelles,[2] W. Lushington, Joseph Marryat, and J. F. Barham,[3] prominent members of the Caribbean interest in the House of Commons, led the fight for debarment, while representatives for the corn counties, Norfolk, Suffolk, and Essex, under the leadership of Mr. Coke, formed the opposition.[4]

The planters proved the stronger and achieved a signal triumph. In June, 1808, the distillation of grain in the United Kingdom [5] was forbidden,[6] and, shortly after, the use of sugar was encouraged by a lowering of duties on spirits made from it.[7] The act of 1808 was continued for the United Kingdom the following year,[8] for Great Britain in 1810,[9] and, after a temporary lapse, was again renewed for the several parts of the United Kingdom to the close of 1813.[10] In 1812, sugar was also admitted to the breweries of Great Britain,[11] a privilege which was continued to October, 1813.[12] Some idea of the extent of the relief afforded may be had from the fact that the distilleries alone consumed about 50,000 hogsheads of 13 hundredweight each annually.[13]

pp. 513 ff. Bell, *Inquiry Into the Policy and Justice of the Prohibition of the Use of Grain in the Distilleries.*

[1] W. Lushington, *The Interest of Agriculture and Commerce Inseparable* (London, 1808). The author was agent for Grenada.

[2] Wiberforce's unsuccessful opponent in the 1807 Yorkshire election (see page 277). He had been returned from Westbury shortly after.

[3] See his *Substance of a Speech, Delivered in the House of Commons . . . on Monday, May 23, 1808, on the Motion for Prohibiting Corn, and the Substitution of Sugar, in the Distilleries* (London, 1808).

[4] *Cobbett's Parliamentary Debates,* XI, columns 55 ff., 428 ff., 493 ff., 702 ff., 816 ff., 867 ff.

[5] The distillery committee of 1808 had recommended the measure for Great Britain alone.

[6] 48 Geo. III c. 118.

[7] 48 Geo. III c. 152 and 51 Geo. III c. 42 applied to Great Britain; 49 Geo. III c. 33 and 53 Geo. III c. 52 to Ireland.

[8] 49 Geo. III c. 7.

[9] 50 Geo. III c. 5.

[10] 52 Geo. III c. 3 renewed it for Great Britain, 52 Geo. III c. 47 for Ireland and 53 Geo. III c. 7 for the United Kingdom.

[11] 52 Geo. III c. 65.

[12] 53 Geo. III c. 1.

[13] *Min. W. I. Plant. and Mer.,* June 13, 1811. "Copy of the Representation and Petition of the Assembly of Jamaica, to His Royal Highness the Prince Regent, 10 Dec. 1811," in *Gt. Br., H. C., Sess. Pap.,* 1812, X (279).

The West Indians scored another striking success in 1809 when, following the taking of Martinique, they secured the passage of a bill subjecting coffee and sugar grown in that island to foreign duties upon their entry into the British market.[1] Not all members of the planter-merchant body were agreed as to the wisdom of such discriminatory legislation. Joseph Marryat, subsequently agent for Grenada, opposed it on the grounds that it would bring no advantage to British estate owners, would injure the refiners, and would be a violation of faith toward the inhabitants of the colony who had capitulated in expectation of being accorded the same privileges as residents of the other conquered enemy territories.[2] But there is no question that enactment of the measure prevented a new cramming of warehouses which would have offset all that had been accomplished toward alleviating the colonials' plight. On the other hand, shipments of sugar reaching Great Britain from Mauritius after its capture (the first, in 1812, amounting to 9,692 hundredweight, and those of the two following years to 5,494 hundredweight and 10,342 hundredweight respectively[3]) entered at the East Indian rate, gave the Caribbean body no concern.

Adoption of these various regulations had a most salutary effect upon the muscovado market. The average price, which had ranged from 32s. 9d. to 36s. 4d. in 1807, rose to from 34s. 11¼d. to 52s. 3d. the following year and had increased to from 44s. 2¾d. to 53s. 9¾d. by 1810.[4]

Although interruption of the American carrying trade from the foreign plantations to Europe did temporarily provide an increased outlet for British tropical produce, the retaliative embargo and nonintercourse act bore so heavily upon the British West Indians as to render this heroic attempt to aid them nugatory. Traders in the United States were encouraged to violate the Jeffersonian law by being given free entry to and clearance from Great Britain's Caribbean ports without presenting the regulation shipping papers,[5] but few

---

[1] 49 Geo. III c. 61.

[2] See *The Substance of a Speech Delivered . . . in the House of Commons, on Monday the Fifteenth of May, 1809. Upon the Second Reading of the Martinique Trade Bill* (London, 1809).

[3] "Sugar Exported from Mauritius Commencing With the English Conquest," in *Gt. Br., H. C., Sess. Pap.*, 1826–27, XVIII (283).

[4] Weekly returns in *The London Gazette.*

[5] Circular instructions to West Indian governors, April 11, 1808, C. O. 324/103.

seem to have done so [1] and a serious shortage was soon experienced. This was by no means unexpected; an anonymous patriot had, in fervid terms, fully represented the situation which would arise if relations with the mainland were once more interrupted and had advocated settling the Cape of Good Hope as a means of relieving the planters of their dangerous reliance upon the good will of a foreign power for their own welfare.[2]

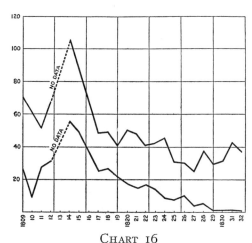

CHART 16

Exports of Muscovado Sugar from Great Britain, 1809–1832, in Million Pounds *

* Based on Customs 11/1–23, Public Record Office. Upper line = total exports, from all sources of origin. Lower line = exports of the British West Indian product alone (excluding that from foreign plantations, the East Indies, and Mauritius).

Under stress of the Napoleonic wars, all exportation of grain from the United Kingdom was forbidden and shipments of supplies reaching the sugar islands from the British North American colonies were wholly inadequate, as the following statistics will show.

[1] Only occasional references are found to the arrival of American vessels in the British colonies at this time, as in 1809 when four unloaded cargoes of fish, flour, corn, tobacco, and lumber in St. Vincent. See Governor Brisbane to Lord Castlereagh, March 1 and May 16, 1809, C. O. 260/25.

[2] Anon., *Softly, Brave Yankees!!!* or the *West Indies Rendered Independent of America; and Africa Civilized* (London, 1807).

AVERAGE ANNUAL IMPORTATIONS INTO TOBAGO
1805, 1806 AND 1807 [1]

Commodity	From British North America	From the United States
Flour, bbls.	73	3,336
Biscuits, bbls.	——	224
Cornmeal, bu.	——	3,544
Beef and pork, bbls.	101	1,412
Dried fish, quintals	796	1,486
Pickled fish, cwt.	2,751	3,373
Lumber, feet	9,027	1,983,170
Staves and heads, no.	1,567	926,439
Hoops, no.	833	30,093
Shingles, no.	7,000	1,631,798
Value, sterling	£7,600	£96,786

IMPORTS FROM BRITISH NORTH AMERICA, 1807 AND 1808

Commodity	Into Trinidad [2]	Into Barbados [3]	Into St. Vincent [4]
Flour and Bread	2,339 bbls.	8,239 bbls.	793 bbls.
Beef and Pork	389 bbls.	692 bbls.	365 bbls.
Rice	73 casks	——	——
Peas and Beans	13 bbls.	——	——
Dried Fish	{ 2,901 hhd. 95 tierces 2,033 boxes	52,767 quintals	24,661 quintals
Pickled Fish	3,389 bbls.	{ 419 hhd. 5,852 bbls.	2,212 hhd.
Smoked Fish	1,013 boxes	——	——
Shingles	38,000	40,000	——
Staves	47,990	49,969	66,910
Hoops	56,490	32,450	43,780
Lumber	253,523 ft.	25,768 ft.	129,500 ft.
Puncheon Packs	285	——	——

Exports of fish from Newfoundland, Lower Canada, and the adjoining possessions to the British West Indies were relatively high in 1806 and 1807 because of a bounty system having been instituted during the former year. In 1804, the merchants and certain residents of New Brunswick and Nova Scotia had sought protection against the

[1] Sir William Young's statistical report on the state of Tobago, April 22, 1808, C. O. 285/13.
[2] Returns of imports, C. O. 295/21.
[3] In President Spooner to Viscount Castlereagh, April 26, 1809, C. O. 28/78.
[4] Governor Brisbane to Lord Castlereagh, May 1, 1809, C. O. 260/25.

Americans through being granted the exclusive privilege of supplying the Caribbean plantations with fish caught in new world waters, declaring that, if given proper encouragement, they could regularly provide all that might be needed.[1] The committee of the privy council for trade and foreign plantations had given the matter due consideration and, in the spring of 1806, announcement was made that the Treasury would pay a bounty of 2s. sterling per quintal on all salt fish imported from British North America into the sugar colonies in British bottoms for one year commencing June 1, together with bounties of 1s. 6d. per barrel of pickled shad, 2s. 6d. per barrel of pickled herring, 3s. per barrel of pickled mackerel, and 4s. per barrel of pickled salmon. Governors were directed to secure the enactment of measures by their respective legislatures reimbursing the home government for sums thus expended. At the same time, the several bodies themselves were to arrange for the granting of a shilling sterling per quintal bounty on colonial American fish so imported and for the imposition of a duty on all received from the United States, both to become effective on June 1, 1807.[2]

With such encouragement, shipments to the Caribbean increased; but the entire scheme was viewed with ill favor in the West India colonies and considerable difficulty was experienced in recovering the amounts laid out in London. For example, the Jamaican legislature agreed to meet bounty payments as of November 14, 1806, but refused pointblank to appropriate £2,000, the sum paid by British Treasury officials on imports there from the first of June.[3] Similarly, the revenue of Trinidad proved insufficient to meet the bounties after June, 1807.[4] The system was consequently abandoned. Payments were continued in Great Britain from June to August, 1807, but only on imports into those islands which had made provision for reimbursement,[5] and then ceased altogether.

[1] These petitions appear in Hugh Gray, *Letters from Canada, Written During a Residence There in the Years 1806, 1807, and 1808; Shewing the Present State of Canada. . . . Exhibiting Also the Commercial Importance of Nova Scotia, New Brunswick, & Cape Breton; and Their Increasing Ability, in Conjunction with Canada, to furnish the necessary Supplies of Lumber and Provisions to our West-India Islands* (London, 1809), pp. 385–400.

[2] Circular letters of March 21, and April 2, 1806, in C. O. 324/103.

[3] Lieut.-Gov. Sir Eyre Coote to Viscount Castlereagh, June 29, 1807, C. O. 137/119.

[4] Governor Hislop to Viscount Castlereagh, Sept. 7, 1807, C. O. 295/16. In 1813, £1031.0.6 sterling still remained due the British government from that colony (Major General Monro to Earl Bathurst, April 10, 1813, C. O. 295/29).

[5] The Secretary of State to Lieutenant-Governor Coote, May 7, 1807, C. O. 137/119.

This attempt to bolster up the North American fisheries through fiscal assistance having proved unsuccessful, the home government considered the proposal of John Tobin Cross, residing in Nevis, to supply the Leeward Islands with fish from Nova Scotia under a monopoly right, and consulted the West Indians in regard to it.[1] They proved solidly opposed to granting any individual the exclusive right of providing the plantations with such an essential foodstuff under any conditions [2] and the matter was consequently dropped.

With bounties no longer being paid, importations of fish from the colonial mainland promptly declined; in June, 1808, their free entry in vessels of friendly nations into those colonies which had made provision for repaying the mother country was authorized. Excluding such as had not done so from enjoyment of this privilege was a strong-arm method of forcing reimbursement. But the American embargo cut off expected shipments from the United States at precisely the time they were being relied on to augment the dwindling supplies of the one article which, in the past, had been received from the North American colonies in considerable quantity.

In March, 1808, the assembly of St. Kitts expressed apprehension lest the scarcity of provisions there lead to a famine and called upon the home government to purchase and send out 2,500 hogsheads of beans, suggesting that they be sold through customs officials.[3] By late summer, the prices on planter stores in the Caribbean reached war-time figures. Pitch-pine lumber cost £30 per thousand feet in Jamaica; white-pine only £2.10.0 less; cypress shingles stood at £7.10.0 per thousand; white-oak staves, £40 per thousand; red-oak ones, £32.10.0; British pork, £9.6.8 per barrel and British beef £8.10.0; flour £9 per barrel; and corn 15s. per bushel.[4]

Relief was sought through making importations from the foreign West Indies.[5] In 1809, goods were admitted into St. Vincent from St. Bartholomew [6] and cargoes from neighboring non-British islands were allowed to enter the Leewards.[7] A year later, the entry of lum-

---

[1] Circular to West Indian governors, Sept. 17, 1807, C. O. 324/103.

[2] See for example the papers setting forth the objections of the Jamaicans to any such monopoly scheme in C. O. 137/120.

[3] Resolutions passed on March 25, C. O. 152/92.

[4] Report on current prices in Kingston, Jamaica, Sept. 1, 1808, C. O. 137/22.

[5] Under 28 Geo. III c. 6. See page 188.

[6] Governor Brisbane to Lord Castlereagh, March 1, May 16, June 22, 1809, C. O. 260/25.

[7] President Julius to Viscount Castlereagh, Oct. 23, 1809, C. O. 152/94.

ber, flour, bread, rice, corn, and cornmeal into Jamaica was authorized.[1]

Increased local cultivation of food crops was likewise resorted to. Already in 1807, the president of the Barbadian council had urged proprietors under his jurisdiction to free themselves from dependence upon outside sources in this manner.[2] Similar action was subsequently recommended by the British government in calling the attention of the Duke of Manchester, governor of Jamaica, to the agricultural societies recently founded in Tobago and St. Vincent[3] and urging him to institute one.[4] The area given over to provision growing in Tobago was increased several fold at this time largely through the efforts of Governor Sir William Young, founder and chief patron of the colony's agricultural body.[5]

Writing in 1809, Lord Sheffield, ancient opponent of the planters on the question of the American trade, declared that the embargo had brought little disadvantage to Great Britain's tropical possessions and reiterated his old claim that British North America could amply supply the Caribbean proprietors with all needed stores of provisions and lumber if citizens of the United States were permanently excluded from commercial relations with them.[6] Speculation as to the part the mainland colonials might possibly play in the economic system of the British West Indies at some future time was easy, but certain it is that stern facts were against this ardent protagonist of rigid navigation law enforcement. The simple truth was that Congress's interrupting the flow of goods from America by adopting the non-intercourse policy resulted in a deficiency which could not be met by increased importations from the St. Lawrence region and the foreign West Indies, coupled with greater local production of foodstuffs. Widespread want prevailed—one observer some time later declared the Leewards in particular to have stood continually on the verge of starvation after 1807[7]—and the high prices on such com-

[1] The Duke of Manchester to the Earl of Liverpool, Feb. 11, 1810, C. O. 137/128.
[2] Schomburgk, *Barbados*, p. 370.
[3] See page 69.
[4] The Secretary of State to the Duke of Manchester, Jan. 19, 1808, C. O. 137/121.
[5] Governor Young to Viscount Castlereagh, Oct. 10, 1807, C. O. 285/12, and to the Earl of Liverpool, August 28, 1811, C. O. 285/16.
[6] *The Orders in Council and the American Embargo Beneficial to the Political and Commercial Interests of Great Britain* (London, 1809), pp. 28–38.
[7] See the letter from St. Bartholomew dated Sept. 30, 1820, in *American State Papers, Foreign Relations*, V, 88.

modities as were offered for sale at a time when returns on their crops were the lowest in years only increased the estate owners' hardships.

Despite governmental attempts to afford the planter-merchant interest relief, the home mart for colonial goods remained depressed. "There is at present little demand for sugar for British consumption, and no demand for export," declared a report of the organized West Indians in October, 1810. "Excepting the market which still remains for sugar for home consumption, the chief Articles of . . . produce (and coffee more especially) are now unsalable." [1]

New outlets for these surplus products were therefore sought in Great Britain. The Society of Planters and Merchants made available £500 to encourage the use of sugar in the manufacture of wine.[2] One James Smith of the capital city who declared that he had discovered a method of "producing by fermentation, from West India Commodities, pure and genuine Wines, of qualities equal to any which the World can produce . . . with more ease and less attention than what is necessary to make a cup of good coffee," was voted £100 and 14 hundredweight of muscovado to carry out his experiments.[3]

Edward Howard, a chemist,[4] was engaged at a salary of £200 to discover some method of contaminating sugar so as to make it unfit for human consumption while remaining suitable for feeding cattle.[5] The invitation of F. A. Windsor of London to give confidential information regarding a new use he had found for raw sugar, provided that he be paid £1,000 and 1s. per hundredweight on all muscovado thus employed, was accepted, but his proposal, whatever it may have been, was found impractical.[6] The sum of £5,000 was appropriated to set up an establishment for the sale of British rum together with £4,000 to operate another for selling Caribbean coffee.[7] But, by the end of 1814, the first showed a loss of £1,498.3.6 and was closed,

---

[1] Min. W. I. Plant. and Mer., October 24.

[2] Ibid., March 26, 1811.

[3] Ibid., Dec. 9, 1811. It was interesting to note that a Frenchman, writing over three decades previously, had similarly proposed to use sugar in manufacturing all grades of wine. See M. Beaumé, Mémoire sur la meilleure Manier de Construire les Alembics et Fourneaux propres à la Distillation des Vins, pour en Tirer les Eaux-de-Vie (Paris, 1778).

[4] He subsequently invented the famous vacuum pan. See page 65.

[5] Min. W. I. Plant. and Mer., June 26, Oct. 3, Dec. 9, 1811.

[6] Ibid., June 26, and Dec. 9, 1811.

[7] Ibid., July 8, 1812.

while the latter, then already run with a deficit of £222.8.9, continued in business only a short time longer.[1]

This prolonged stagnation of the tropical trade profoundly affected conditions in the West Indies. Plantation values suffered a sharp decline.[2] In 1811, a body of Barbadians set forth the critical local situation, with all residents deeply involved financially, in a petition praying for permission to barter their produce against American supplies, for the institution of an ad valorem system of duties, and for removal of the prohibition on grain exportation from Great Britain.[3]

The legislatures of St. Vincent and Jamaica both addressed the Prince Regent on the situation. The former declared that the planters' crops were unsalable, that their incomes had consequently ceased, and that they were unable to secure stores as dealers, finding it impossible to collect debts, refused to carry further charge accounts;[4] the latter, that sugar properties were being cultivated at a loss and that mercantile houses were seizing many to recover money due them. "Estate after estate has passed into the hands of mortgagees and creditors absent from the island until there are large tracts, whole parishes, in which there is not a single proprietor of a sugar plantation resident."[5]

Inhabitants of Tobago likewise affirmed in a communication to Prince George that the selling price of sugar in 1811 did not equal the cost of production, that credit was practically at an end, and that, while the government received £20 sterling duty on each hogshead of muscovado and the shipping-trading interest £10 in charges, the growers themselves gained not a sixpence.[6] As for the proprietors of St. Lucia, they were "so much in debt that they with the greatest difficulty & disadvantage obtain further Credit. Hence some of them possessing great Estates & living with the greatest frugality can hardly procure the means of existence for their Slaves."[7]

---

[1] *Min. W. I. Plant. and Mer.*, Feb. 8, 1815.

[2] Mathison, *Notices Respecting Jamaica*, p. 56.

[3] *The Barbados Mercury, and Bridge-Town Gazette*, Nov. 2, 1811.

[4] In President Paul to the Earl of Liverpool, Dec. 21, 1811.

[5] "Copy of the Representation and Petition of the Assembly of Jamaica, to His Royal Highness the Prince Regent, 10 Dec. 1811," in *Gt. Br., H. C., Sess. Pap.*, 1812, X (279).

[6] Address of planters, merchants, and others interested in the Island of Tobago, C. O. 285/16.

[7] Brigadier-General Wood to the Earl of Liverpool, Sept. 1, 1811, C. O. 253/6.

The sugar cultivators were by no means alone in their straitened circumstances; the position of the coffee growers was even more precarious. Their crop was intended primarily for exportation to the continent and, under the stimulus of foreign demand, production in the British Caribbean had increased enormously during the first decade of the nineteenth century. Shipments out of Jamaica alone had risen from 11,116,474 pounds to 29,528,273 between 1800 and 1808. But, with the continental system steadily closing markets, coffee could soon no longer be sold across the Channel and became unmarketable in the colonies. Jamaica's exports in 1811 were but 17,-460,068 pounds, three-fifths the quantity of three years before.[1]

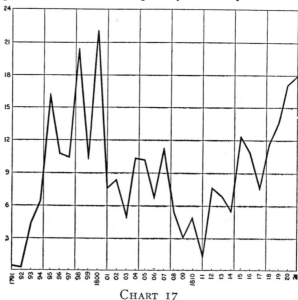

CHART 17

Quantities of East Indian Sugar Sold by the East India Company at Its Sales in London from the Date of the First Importation in 1791, through 1821, in Million Pounds *

* Based on Appendix IV to *East India Sugar. Papers Respecting the Culture and Manufacture of Sugar in British India* . . . (London, 1822), the celebrated so-called "East India Company Sugar Report" of that year.

In August of that year, a total of 1,114,820 hundredweight—sufficient to supply the home demand for twenty years at the existing

[1] "Exports of Ginger, Pimento, and Coffee from Jamaica, 1772–1836," in *Gt. Br., H. C., Sess. Pap.*, 1840, VIII (in 527), p. 594.

rate of consumption—were stored in British warehouses, much of the last crop remained in the producers' hands, and a new one was coming on. Thus, facing ruin, the coffee planters of Dominica [1] and Jamaica [2] addressed the Regent, praying that use of the beverage be encouraged by a lowering of the duty and excise and that they be allowed to barter with the Americans. The cotton growers, too, found themselves in serious difficulties because of the closing of European ports and the competition of virgin soil plantations in the United States and Brazil.[3]

The War of 1812 served to complicate the situation still further. American privateers regularly captured western-bound supply ships as well as produce-laden merchantmen returning to Great Britain. The exportation of sugar and coffee to Bermuda, where they might be exchanged for grain, meat, fish, and lumber, was authorized,[4] but an acute shortage was nevertheless experienced from the first. So extensive was it in the Leewards that the several islands each prohibited the clearing out of foodstuffs to the others.[5] Only the occasional capture of an American bottom, scanty importations from the foreign West Indies, and the admission of neutral vessels prevented actual famine there.[6]

"A very great and general scarcity of provisions prevails here," wrote the Duke of Manchester from Jamaica in 1813.[7] The island legislature offered prizes such as £200 for curing and salting not under ten barrels of beef and £200 for a twenty acre patch of yams,[8] to stimulate local food production.

Prices on stores reached new heights. In 1813, pitch-pine lumber was quoted at £40 per thousand feet in Grenada, the white-pine article at £35, cypress shingles at £8.2.0 per thousand, Irish beef at £16.10.0 per barrel, and salt fish at £4.10.0 per hundredweight.[9]

To add to the general misery, the Dominicans suffered such severe

[1] Petition in C. O. 71/46.

[2] "Copy of the Representation and Petition of the Assembly of Jamaica, to His Royal Highness the Prince Regent, 10 Dec. 1811," in *Gt. Br., H. C., Sess. Pap.*, 1812, X (279).

[3] Anon., *Facts, Relative to the Present State of the British Cotton Colonies, and to the Connection of Their Interests With Those of the Mother Country* (Edinburgh, 1811).

[4] Under 52 Geo. III c. 79. See circular letter of Sept. 14, 1812. C. O. 324/103.

[5] Governor Elliot to Earl Bathurst, Oct. 12, 1812, C. O. 152/100.

[6] Governor Elliot to Earl Bathurst, Nov. 19, 1812, C. O. 152/100; April 27, 1813, C. O. 152/101.

[7] To Earl Bathurst, July 13, C. O. 137/136.

[8] Gardner, *Jamaica*, p. 325.

[9] Report on current prices, C. O. 101/53.

depredations at the hands of Maroon negroes at this juncture that it became necessary to send out an expeditionary force against them;[1] and the island was devastated by two hurricanes in 1813, one in 1814 and another in 1816.[2]

By the last years of the Napoleonic era, the planters in the British sugar islands had all but sunk beneath their load of accumulated distress and discouragement. Only a sudden rise in the price of their staple could save them from immediate ruin; the prompt reopening and firm retention of the continental trade alone afforded prospects of recovery. Should the proprietors lose their privileged position in the home market or should their produce meet keen competition in Europe after the restoration of peace, general bankruptcy and the permanent decline of the tropical American colonies were inevitable.

---

[1] For papers relative to the affair, see C. O. 71/49–51. The hunting down of these bands of destructive runaways was misinterpreted in England and misguided philanthropists led by Sir Samuel Romilly succeeded in having Governor Ainslie summoned home to explain his having used troops against them. See *An Address of the Inhabitants of the Island of Dominica, to His Excellency Governor Ainslie* [Roseau, 1814]; Anon., ed., *A Collection of Plain Authentic Documents, in Justification of the Conduct of Governor Ainslie; in the Reduction of a Most Formidable Rebellion Among the Negro Slaves in the Island of Dominica* (London, 1815).

[2] C. O. 71/48, 49, 52.

CHAPTER X

THE WEST INDIA QUESTION

The collapse of the continental system during the last days of Napoleon's power tremendously increased shipments of tropical produce from Great Britain to adjacent mainland markets. Thus, exports of muscovado leaped from 231,009 hundredweight in 1811 to 920,121 in 1814 and 757,303 during the following twelve months. Whereas sales of British plantation sugar abroad had totalled but 8,175 hundredweight in the first of these years, they were 419,809 and 379,097 hundredweight respectively in the latter two.[1]

Renewed demand served to stabilize the West India trade as a whole. Under the stimulus of heavy buying from Germany, Holland, and the Baltic, coupled with considerable local speculation, the average price of raw sugar sold in the English capital, which had ranged from 34s. ¾d. to 43s. 9¼d. per hundredweight exclusive of duty in 1811, rose steadily thereafter until it reached 57s. 7¼d. to 75s. 1½d. in 1815.[2]

Heavy inroads on warehoused stocks likewise increased the selling prices of other Caribbean products. Exports of British West Indian coffee from the United Kingdom were 672,700 hundredweight in 1814 as compared with imports of 515,645 hundredweight; in 1815, they stood at 478,836 hundredweight as against 392,816.[3] Consequently, early in 1814 Jamaican berries were being quoted at from 118s.–142s. per hundredweight, more than double their value during 1810–1811.[4] Cotton also advanced from 12¼d.–16d. per pound in 1812 to from 18d.–25½d. three years after [5] because of the American

---

[1] Customs 11/3, 5, 6, P. R. O.

[2] Prices varied from 42s. 1½d.–51s. 2½d. in 1812, from 52s. 6¼d.–76s. 11d. in 1813, and from 54s. 3½d.–97s. 2½d. in 1814. Weekly returns in *The London Gazette*.

[3] "Imports Into, Exports From and Home Consumption of British West Indian Coffee in the United Kingdom, 1814–1834," in *Gt. Br., H. C., Sess. Pap.*, 1831–32, XX (in 381).

[4] Tooke, *History of Prices*, I, 302, 344–347. The rate in the earlier period hovered around 54s. per cwt.

[5] The price varied from 13d.–23½d. in 1812, from 21d.–30d. in 1813, and from 23d.–37d. in 1814. "Prices on Cotton . . . at Liverpool, 1793–1833," in *Gt. Br., H. C., Sess. Pap.*, 1847–48, IX (in 511), p. 393.

War. Great was the rejoicing among the planters who saw in these events an end to their decade and a half of depression.

But such fond hopes were altogether illusory. The treaties of Paris and London definitely added the conquered French islands, St. Lucia and Tobago and Holland's South American possessions, Demerara, Essequibo, and Berbice to the British empire in 1814. Members of the London colonial interest who had suffered from the competition of those regions' produce at home for more than ten years had urged in vain that the Dutch territories be restored and that disabilities be placed for a considerable period upon the crops of St. Lucia and Tobago entering the United Kingdom.[1] Their fear that the bringing of further tropical areas under national control would adversely affect the old sugar colonies was promptly realized. Development of the newly-ceded territories and of Trinidad, which had been yielded by Spain in 1802[2] but whose exploitation had been checked by the wearing contest with France, proceeded apace after the restoration of peace and the rising stream of agricultural wealth pouring eastward soon flooded the British market.

Demerara, Essequibo, Berbice, and Trinidad were sparsely settled, frontier regions. Large numbers of persons were drawn to them from the long-exploited Caribbean possessions, where society was static and soil exhaustion prevailed, by the opportunity they afforded of procuring extensive, virgin tracts at low cost. Landless whites left the old colonies to become proprietors in the new ones and discouraged planters moved to them in the hope of retrieving their fortunes under more favorable conditions.

From the grower's point of view, conditions there were truly well nigh ideal—the ground was rich and required no manuring, only occasional replanting of the canes was necessary, and returns were immense.[3] Thus, one estate owner in Trinidad produced 100 hogsheads of sugar with the aid of seventeen slaves and four hired hands; another, 600 hogsheads with less than 200 blacks. The yield in islands to the north, on the contrary, averaged but one hogshead per worker and fell below this on many plantations.[4]

Emigration was particularly heavy from Grenada,[5] which had suf-

---

[1] *Min. W. I. Plant. and Mer.,* June 30, 1814.

[2] Page 292.

[3] Acting Governor Farquharson to the Secretary of State, Oct. 12, 1825, C. O. 295/78.

[4] Major-General Young to the Secretary of State, May 26, 1829, C. O. 295/80.

[5] Governor Shipley to Earl Bathurst, Nov. 7, 1813, C. O. 101/53.

fered so grievously from civil disorders,[1] from Dominica [2] where recovery from the shock of French attack during the late war had been
checked by negro disturbances and a series of hurricanes,[3] and from
the Leewards, where the wearing out of the land had been general.
Following the arrival of considerable bodies of new settlers, the production of Trinidad increased from 216,040 hundredweight of sugar,
487,142 gallons of rum, and 1,158,163 pounds of cacao in 1814 [4] to
311,278 hundredweight, 496,817 gallons, and 1,648,114 pounds respectively seven years later.[5]

Custom House records graphically reveal the exact extent to which
the empire's Caribbean acquisitions of 1802 and 1814 entered into
competition with the old West Indian islands in the home market. Of
the total sugar shipments entering Great Britain from the tropical
American possessions in 1815, 20 per cent and 24 per cent in 1820
came from the late enemy territories. The same was true of rum and
coffee; after the institution of peace, from a fifth to three-tenths of
the total imports of those commodities from British holdings in the
West India region were regularly the produce of the new colonies.
The figures for cacao and cotton are even more striking. About 80
per cent of the former came from them in 1820; [6] of cotton, 82 per
cent in 1821.[7]

[1] See pages 220 and 221.
[2] Governor Maxwell to Earl Bathurst, Aug. 23, 1817, C. O. 71/54, and the
petition of the Dominican proprietors to Bathurst in C. O. 71/57.
[3] See pages 329 and 330.
[4] Returns of commandants of quarters, Dec. 31, 1814, C. O. 295/33.
[5] Returns of commandants of quarters for 1821, C. O. 295/53.
[6] The following statistics were compiled from Customs 5/4, 9, P. R. O.

Commodity	Imports of British-Grown Produce from all of the Caribbean Colonies into Great Britain, 1815	Imports from the New Colonies, 1815	Percentage of Total Imports
Sugar	3,381,790 cwt.	678,279 cwt.	20
Rum	6,741,668 gals.	1,323,456 gals.	20
Coffee	33,186,700 lbs.	10,000,400 lbs.	31
Cacao	1,015,800 lbs.	847,600 lbs.	83
Commodity	Imports of British-Grown Produce from all of the Caribbean Colonies into Great Britain, 1820	Imports from the New Colonies, 1820	Percentage of Total Imports
Sugar	3,622,461 cwt.	889,712 cwt.	24
Rum	7,002,772 gals.	2,112,119 gals.	30
Coffee	26,573,245 lbs.	5,808,350 lbs.	22
Cacao	943,200 lbs.	760,490 lbs.	80

[7] Imports of cotton, the growth of British plantations, from the Caribbean
colonies into Great Britain were 5,495,471 lbs. in 1821. Of this amount, no
less than 4,530,680 lbs., or 82 per cent, was received from the new colonies.
(Compiled from Customs 5/10, P. R. O.) No statistics are available for the pe-

The planters of the old West Indies were confronted by another danger as well, which served to make their position still more uncertain. This was a vastly increased importation of oriental sugar, particularly marked in the decade following Napoleon's downfall. Shipments from the East to the United Kingdom advanced from the relatively slight amount of 49,849 hundredweight in 1814 to 269,162 seven years later,[1] due for the most part to the transfer of Mauritius from France to Great Britain under the terms of the peace settlement. That island's exports alone rose from 25,049 hundredweight in 1815 to no less than 274,008 in 1823.[2]

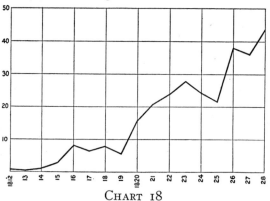

CHART 18
Sugar Exported from Mauritius, 1812–1828,
in Million Pounds *
* Based on *Great Britain, House of Commons, Sessional Papers*, 1826–1827, XVIII (283).

Although the East India Company had lost its monopoly of Asiatic commerce upon securing a charter renewal in 1813,[3] most of the eastern muscovado entering the British market thereafter continued to pass through its warehouses. From 1815 to 1821 inclusive, the

riod before 1821 as customs records at earlier dates did not distinguish between British-grown cotton and that which was foreign-grown but was received by way of British West Indian ports.

[1] Imports were 127,203 cwt. in 1816 and 205,527 cwt. in 1819. East India *Sugar. Papers Respecting the Culture and Manufacture of Sugar . . .* , Appendix IV, p. 4. "Quantities of Muscovado Sugar Imported Into the United Kingdom . . . , 1793–1834," in *Gt. Br., H. C., Sess. Pap.*, 1847–48, LVIII (400).

[2] Exports were 65,834 cwt. in 1817 and 155,247 cwt. in 1820. "Sugar Exported from Mauritius Commencing With the English Conquest," in *Gt. Br., H. C., Sess. Pap.*, 1826–1827, XVIII (283).

[3] However, all monopoly features of the Company's trade did not disappear until the next renewal of the charter, in 1833.

corporation disposed of 916,882 hundredweight valued at £1,819,158.[1]
The Barbadians and Jamaicans had opposed throwing the India
trade open on the ground that they could never compete with the
cheap labor and teeming soil of the Orient, and must inevitably be
ruined if independent merchants were permitted to freely enter tropical goods from there.[2] This plea had been ignored, but the planter interest was, at its request,[3] later granted a preferential duty of 10s.
per hundredweight on sugar which continued in force from 1816 to
1830.[4]

The proprietors whose produce was thus being met more and more
at home by that of the new Caribbean and Indian ocean colonies were,
by one of life's little ironies, called upon to aid materially in paying
the war debt incurred in defeating the French and Dutch and securing
those very possessions. Despite their vehement protests,[5] war duties
were not removed and rates after the laying down of arms were
actually higher than they had been at any time during the late conflict.

Thus, the import tax on British-grown unrefined sugar, which had
stood at 15s. per hundredweight in 1791, was set at 27s. in 1816, at
30s. in 1818, at 28s. in 1819, and permanently at 27s. in 1826.[6] The
customs and excise charge payable on colonial rum entering Great
Britain continued at 13s. 10½d. per gallon from 1813 to 1819 when
a penny was added. In 1824, a reduction to 12s. 7⅕d. was effected; it
remained at that figure until 1826.[7] After having been in force for
six years, the duty on West Indian coffee was increased from 7¾d.
to 1s. per pound in 1819; that rate then prevailed until 1825.[8]

[1] *East India Sugar. Papers Respecting the Culture and Manufacture of
Sugar . . .* , Appendix IV, p. 13.
[2] Governor Beckwith to Earl Bathurst, Oct. 13, 1812 and enclosures, C. O.
28/81. *Report From a Committee of the Honourable House of Assembly [of
Jamaica] on the commerce and agriculture of the Island; the probably effects
thereon of opening the trade to the East Indies, and the operation of the
present maximum on the exportation of sugar* (Jamaica, 1813).
[3] *Min. W. I. Plant. and Mer.*, March 8, 1813.
[4] "Rates of Duty Per Cwt. on British Plantation Muscovado . . . , 1776–
1826," in *Gt. Br., H. C., Sess. Pap.*, 1826, XXII (328). "Rates of Duty on
Muscovado Sugar Imported Into Great Britain from the East Indies, 1792–
1829," in *Gt. Br., H. C., Sess. Pap.*, 1830, XXV (466).
[5] *Min. W. I. Plant. and Mer.*, Feb. 28, and March 13, 1815.
[6] "Rates of Duty Per Cwt. on British Plantation Muscovada . . . , 1776–
1826," in *Gt. Br., H. C., Sess. Pap.*, 1826, XXII (328).
[7] "Rum Admitted Into the United Kingdom for Home Consumption,
1800–1829, With Rates of Duty Payable Thereon," in *Gt. Br., H. C., Sess.
Pap.*, 1830, XXII (375).
[8] "Rates of Duty on Coffee Entered Into the United Kingdom, 1792–1829,"
in *Gt. Br., H. C., Sess. Pap.*, 1830, XXV (466).

While the field of imperial production was widening and war-time duties on the planters' crops were being continued and even raised, outlets abroad were contracting. Total exports of muscovado from England and Scotland to the mainland of Europe declined steadily from 920,121 hundredweight in 1814 to 289,847 nine years later. Shipments of the British Caribbean article to the continent by way of Great Britain sank from 419,809 hundredweight to 9,668 in the same period, a startling decrease.[1] Cargoes of British West Indian coffee clearing out from the United Kingdom similarly fell off from 41,-446,360 pounds in 1816 to 17,908,962 in 1823.[2]

The slump in sugar exportation was in part attributable to fiscal legislation. In 1816, the bounty on bastards and broken loaves was reduced from 33s. 1½d. per hundredweight to 30s., that on other single refined sugar in complete loaves from 47s. 8⅖d. to 46s., and that on the double refined product from 57s. 8⅖d. to 54s.[3] These rates were set without regard for shifting values and remained in force for upwards of a decade notwithstanding considerable variation in price.[4]

In May, 1819, the drawback on raw colonial Caribbean sugar leaving the home country was 27s. 6d., but half a shilling less than the duty,[5] and materially stimulated sales through enabling British merchants to meet more nearly the quotations of their foreign rivals. Two months later, as an early expression of the new commercial doctrines securing a foothold in British law, it was wholly discontinued,[6] and was not subsequently renewed. Adoption of this measure was, from the West Indian point of view, equivalent to imposing a tax of that amount on all British plantation muscovado sold overseas.[7]

[1] Exports were 360,325 cwt. in 1817, 240,821 cwt. in 1819, and 333,718 cwt. in 1821 (muscovado from Great Britain to foreign Europe) and 133,264 cwt. in 1817, 52,988 cwt. in 1819, and 7,500 cwt. in 1821 (West Indian muscovado to foreign Europe) respectively. Compiled from Customs 11/5, 8, 10, 12, 14, P.R.O.

[2] Exports were 22,076,642 lbs. in 1819. "Imports Into, Exports From and Home Consumption of British West Indian Coffee in the United Kingdom, 1814–1834," in *Gt. Br., H. C., Sess. Pap.,* 1831–32, XX (in 381).

[3] "Bounty per Cwt. Paid on Various Grades of Clayed Sugar Exported from Great Britain . . . , 1776–1826," in *Gt. Br., H. C., Sess. Pap.,* 1826, XXII, (328).

[4] 58 Geo. III c. 34, 1 Geo. IV c. 64, 5 Geo. IV c. 35, etc.

[5] "Rates of Duty Per Cwt. on British Plantation Muscovado . . . and Drawbacks Allowed on the Same . . . , 1776–1826," in *Gt. Br., H. C., Sess. Pap.,* 1826, XXII (328).

[6] 59 Geo. III c. 52.

[7] The West India Committee archives contain numerous complaints on this score.

Of far greater moment, however, was the fact that continental consumers were increasingly turning to new tropical areas where produce might be obtained more cheaply. The development of Cuba and Brazil, begun during the period of high prices ushered in by the French Revolution, was carried on at an astonishing rate. It has been estimated that 320,000 slaves were imported into the first of these regions alone between 1791 and 1825 as against but 93,000 during all the decades preceding.[1]

The ease with which their labor supply could be recruited and its relatively low price gave the Spanish and Portuguese colonists a signal advantage over the British. Since 1807, the latter had been obliged to raise rather than purchase their estate hands. This was a slow and costly process—the expense of rearing a negro child which survived to the age of fourteen, when it could be put to profitable work, was at least £120 sterling in Jamaica and £135 for the Caribbean possessions as a whole. The entering of adult Africans was clearly more expedient as well as more advantageous from the financial point of view.

Cuba's and Brazil's deep, rich soil, the decayed vegetation of millenniums, required no fertilization and yielded enormous returns from slight effort as the old West Indian islands had in their virgin state a century before and earlier, but not in recent times.[2] Furthermore, settlers in them were not obliged to market products through the home countries as were inhabitants of the British colonies.

These several favoring circumstances so lowered production and marketing costs that the Brazilians' and Cubans' factors were regularly in a position to undersell English dealers throughout the European mainland. Whereas British-grown sugar could not be profitably disposed of on the continent under 53s. per hundredweight following discontinuance of the drawback, Cuban cultivators grew opulent with theirs bringing a mere 30s.[3]

Shipments leaving Havana rose from an average of 206,487 cases in the period 1811–1814 to 300,211 in 1823.[4] Nearly 20,000 chests and boxes of sugar were entered from the Cuban metropolis into Ant-

[1] A. G. Keller, *Colonization* (New York, 1908), pp. 333, 334.

[2] "Statements, Calculations, and Explanations Submitted to the Board of Trade, Relating to the Commercial, Financial, and Political State of the British West India Colonies, Since the 19th of May 1830," in *Gt. Br., H. C., Sess. Pap.*, 1830–31, IX (120), pp. 518–521.

[3] *Ibid.*, p. 560.

[4] Exports were 217,076 cases in 1817 and 236,669 cases in 1821. "Exports of Sugar from Havana," in *Gt. Br., H. C., Sess. Pap.*, 1831–32, XX (in 381).

werp in 1820 and 52,276 three years after. Hamburg imported 63,886
chests and boxes from Brazil and Cuba in 1822 and Prussia about
120,000 hundredweight.[1]

What with entries into the United Kingdom vastly exceeding national consumption and foreign sales dwindling daily, the price of
raw sugar—that index of Caribbean prosperity—reached the lowest
point in history. The average price of muscovado sold in London,
ranging from 43s. 3¼d.–56s. 8¾d. per hundredweight exclusive of
duty in 1816, fell to from 27s. 7¼d.–34s. by 1822.[2]

Each hundredweight of Jamaican sugar offered in the home country during this period represented an investment of 29s. 4d. on the
part of the grower-shipper; that from the other colonies, 28s.[3] Profits
fell off progressively from 1816 and, during 1821 and 1822, West
Indian muscovado was frequently sold at an actual loss to the planter.

Coffee, too, declined from 118s.–142s. per hundredweight in 1814
to 77s.–104s. in 1816,[4] while the price of cotton sank from 18d.–
25½d. per pound in 1815 to 5¾d.–11d. seven years after in consequence of the restoration of peace with the United States and the
great influx of accumulated stores from there.[5]

In the period of general reorganization following the dramatic
close of the Napoleonic wars, the British government renewed its
policy of excluding Americans from direct commercial intercourse
with the Caribbean colonies and rigorously adhered to it,[6] thus continuing the scarcity and high prices of stores dating from the receipt
of the September 1804 order.[7]

Mainland shippers were greatly incensed at this and, employing
their influence, in 1817 secured the adoption of two successive meas-

[1] "Imports of Cuban and Brazilian Sugar into Continental Ports," in *Gt. Br.,
H. C., Sess. Pap.,* 1830–31, IX (120), p. 540.

[2] Prices ranged from 44s. 9¼d.–60s. 6¾d. in 1817, from 47s. 9½d.–52s.
3¼d. in 1818, from 35s. 3¾d.–50s. 2d. in 1819, from 34s. 7d.–38s. ½d. in
1820, from 29s. 9d.–36s. 4¼d. in 1821, and from 31s. 7¾d.–37s. in 1823. Weekly
returns in *The London Gazette.*

[3] *Min. W. I. Mer.,* July 10, 1822.

[4] Tooke, *History of Prices,* I, 344–347; II, 11.

[5] The price varied from 16½d.–22d. in 1818 and from 8d.–13¾d. in 1820.
"Prices on Cotton . . . at Liverpool, 1793–1833," in *Gt. Br., H. C., Sess. Pap.,*
1847–48, IX (in 511), p. 393.

[6] A commercial convention providing for reciprocal national treatment for
American and British vessels in the direct trade between the United States
and British territories in Europe was signed in July 1815. The American request for an equal footing for the vessels of the two countries in the colonial
trade was denied. Culbertson, *International Economic Policies,* pp. 436, 437.

[7] See pages 299 ff.

ures of reprisal by Congress, the first imposing a discriminating duty of $2 per ton upon foreign ships coming into American ports from any abroad, where the regular entry for trading purposes of bottoms registered in the United States was not allowed, and the second permitting the importation of British Caribbean produce only in American vessels or in those owned by the colonists themselves, while not forbidding the exportation of American goods to the West India colonies in bottoms which were the property of citizens of Great Britain itself.[1] By subsequent legislation of a year later, however, the country's harbors were closed after September, 1818, to British vessels arriving from colonies where Americans were denied admittance and British ship masters clearing out from the United States with cargoes of American goods were thereafter required to give bond that these would not be landed in ports closed to its citizens.[2]

Bermuda had enjoyed free trade with the adjacent continent since the outbreak of the war of 1812.[3] St. John, New Brunswick and Halifax, Nova Scotia were now opened to merchantmen of all nations [4] as a means of weakening the force of the last of these shipping laws shortly before it became effective. Furthermore, the importation of tobacco, rice, grain, peas, beans, and flour from the foreign West Indies into the Caribbean colonies in British bottoms was authorized [5] and the purchase of other American supplies there was permitted, as always, in cases of real necessity.[6]

Hence, the action taken by the United States in retaliation for the shutting out of its nationals from the lucrative Caribbean trade proved far less efficacious than had been hoped as a means of wringing concessions from the statesmen in London. To bolster up its exceedingly unsatisfactory position, Congress from 1820 on refused the right of entry to British vessels arriving from the Bermudas, the Bahamas, or Great Britain's West Indian and scattered continental American possessions. Only goods the growth, production, or manufacture of any of those territories might thereafter be imported from them and then only directly in American bottoms.[7]

---

[1] 3 Stat. at Large 344 and 351 respectively.
[2] 3 Stat. at Large 432.
[3] See page 329.
[4] Under 58 Geo. III c. 19 and an order in council of May 27, 1818.
[5] Under 58 Geo. III c. 27.
[6] Emergency importations were made under 28 Geo. III c. 6. See page 188.
[7] 3 Stat. at Large 602. An excellent study of the subject is F. Lee Benn's "The American Struggle for the West India Carrying-Trade, 1815–1830," in

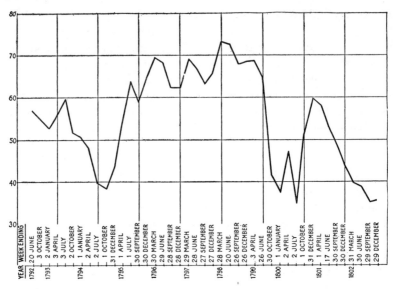

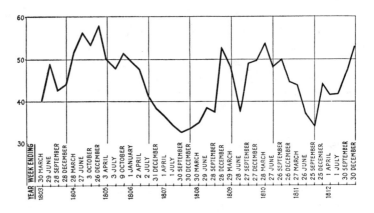

CHART 19

The Average Prices, Exclusive of Duty, Paid for British West Indian Muscovado Sugar by London Importers, 1792–1833, in Shillings per Hundredweight *

* Based on Computations by the Clerk of the Grocers Company, published in *The London Gazette* under authority of 32 George III c. 43.

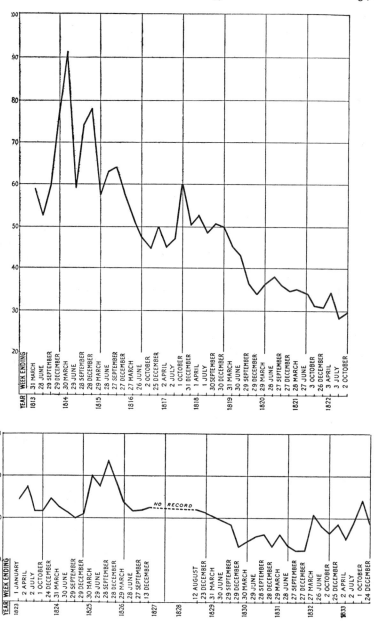

CHART 19 *(Cont.)*

Thenceforth, under joint operation of the two contending countries' laws, the British plantations could be legally supplied with provisions and lumber from the United States only through foreign West India ports and none of their produce normally reached that long-established mainland market.

British North America again proved altogether unable to meet the needs of the Caribbean colonists. The indirect shipment of American supplies by way of Bermuda, St. John, Halifax and the foreign West Indies between 1818 and 1820, and by way of the latter alone from then on, augmented their price to such an extent that this new enforcement of the navigation laws proved extremely injurious to the proprietors.

Soon after debarment of the Americans had become effective, Governor Probyn of the Leeward group reported "A great and serious scarcity of Provisions . . . prevails among these Islands, there being no vessel in the British American Trade, and a want of Capital to establish such. . . ."[1]

Writing from Antigua in 1821, Governor D'Urban declared: "Whether our North American Colonies can, or cannot, afford the requisite supply of such wood as they produce, for those in the West Indies, I will not presume to determine. His Majesty's Ministers, I believe, are impressed with a conviction that they can; Some of the best Informed people in the West Indies think they cannot. However this may be, certainly the actual Supply is very insufficient and precarious and when it is procured it is at great disadvantage to the Planters, who can no longer pay for it in Rum as formerly, because Rum is no longer of any use (excepting so far as the trifling quantity goes which they want for their own consumption) to our North American Colonies, who cannot now, as heretofore, pay it away, in their turn, to the United States."[2]

Early in 1817 but 263 barrels of flour, twenty-five and a half tierces of rice, and four puncheons of corn-meal remained on sale in St. Kitts and none could be procured in neighboring British colonies.

Indiana University Studies, X, March 1923 (Study no. 56). See Chapters II and III of that work for the period 1815–1822. A summary of the controversy from 1815–30 will be found in Culbertson, _International Economic Policies_, Appendix V.

[1] To Earl Bathurst, Aug. 8, 1816, C. O. 239/2.

[2] Private communication to Earl Bathurst, July 2, C. O. 7/7.

Importations from the French, Spanish and Danish islands were therefore resorted to.[1]

Following a hurricane in August, 1819, the need for stores became so great that the ports of St. Kitts and Nevis and Tortola in the Virgin Islands were opened to foreign vessels, including those from America, for six months, and the exportation of sugar to one third the value of the goods landed was authorized.[2] The harbor of Tortola was not closed at the expiration of that time[3] and remained open until 1821 when the home government ordered this long suspension of imperial commercial regulations to cease forthwith.[4]

The Leewards were in the grip of a severe lumber shortage during the latter year. Not a shingle or a board could be bought in Montserrat; the dead there were even being buried in old boxes and trunks.[5] Another tropical storm aggravated the situation and the importation of lumber in British bottoms from the foreign West Indies into St. Kitts, Nevis, and the Virgins was permitted,[6] as was the entry of any vessels of foreign registry laden with provisions and lumber, into Aguilla.[7]

As houses were being torn down in St. Vincent in 1815 to provide headings for sugar casks, several cargoes of American lumber were admitted in order that the planters might ship their crops properly.[8] Local harbors were opened to importations from the foreign West Indies in British bottoms two years later because of continued scarcity.[9]

President Balfour of Tobago permitted one American trader to land produce in the island early in 1815[10] and was sharply reprimanded for his violation of instructions.[11] There was, however, full justification for such action. In May of that year there was "not a

[1] Governor Probyn to Bathurst, Jan. 17, Feb. 20, March 20, July 9, 1817, C. O. 239/3.

[2] Governor Maxwell to Earl Bathurst, October 3 and 14, 1819, C. O. 239/5.

[3] Proclamation in C. O. 239/6.

[4] Pres. John Wilson to Earl Bathurst, March 10, 1821, C. O. 239/7.

[5] Pres. Joseph Herbert to Governor D'Urban, July 18, C. O. 7/7.

[6] Pres. John Wilson to Earl Bathurst, Feb. 26, March 26, and Oct. 1 and 26, 1821, C. O. 239/7.

[7] Wilson to Bathurst, Dec. 18, 1821, C. O. 239/7; Aug. 4, 1822, C. O. 239/8; March 11, 1823, C. O. 239/9.

[8] Governor Brisbane to Earl Bathurst, July 18, C. O. 260/32.

[9] President Paul to Earl Bathurst, May 31, 1817, C. O. 260/34.

[10] Balfour to Earl Bathurst, March 30, 1815, C. O. 285/20.

[11] Balfour to Earl Bathurst, June 24, 1815, C. O. 285/20.

Stave either Red or White, a foot of Lumber, or a Shingle for Sale in the Island;"[1] by summer, "not a Barrel of Beef or Pork, or a Firkin of Butter" could be purchased.[2] Entries from the foreign islands were therefore authorized, but supplies could not be secured at less than twice the usual cost and one lot of lumber sold to the Tobagans by French merchants in Martinique gave the latter 800 per cent profit.[3] None was received in the colony from British North America for more than a year.[4]

Purchases made in the French and Spanish possessions drained Trinidad of coin; its inhabitants sought to secure the right of bartering produce for needed commodities, but in vain.[5]

The destruction of Castries, capital of St. Lucia, by fire in 1813 resulted in a keen demand for lumber there. Supplies from New Brunswick, Nova Scotia, and Canada were insignificant, hence extensive importations were made from the French colonies during 1815–1816, and, despite prohibitions to the contrary, two American merchantmen were admitted under the specious plea of being in need of repairs.[6] Stores were likewise smuggled in on a large scale; one sloop, the *Sophia,* alone made seventeen trips to Martinique and back from July to October, 1816. About that time, the local deputy naval officer, charged with enforcing British commercial law, was himself caught on board the *Panther* which had entered the port of Castries laden to the gunwale with prohibited articles by the acting governor, Major-General Douglass. Customs officials refused to seize trading vessels engaged in such illicit traffic, hence this was done by military officers with the former as highly interested spectators.[7]

Castries harbor was opened for the importation of food and lumber from the foreign islands in January, 1817, because of a shortage amounting almost to famine. The exportation of rum and molasses to them was authorized at the same time.[8] Following a hurricane in October, foreign bottoms, irrespective of their registry, were admitted and after January, 1818, they were permitted to clear out laden with

---

[1] Balfour to Earl Bathurst, May 16, C. O. 285/20.
[2] Balfour to Earl Bathurst, July 19, C. O. 285/20.
[3] Balfour to Earl Bathurst, June 3, Aug. 24, and Oct. 11, 1815, C. O. 285/20.
[4] Balfour to Earl Bathurst, Nov. 25, 1815, C. O. 285/20; Feb. 4, 1816, C. O. 285/21.
[5] Governor Woodford to Earl Bathurst, Dec. 17, 1820, C. O. 295/51.
[6] Major-General Stehelin to Earl Bathurst, Feb. 28, 1816, C. O. 253/10.
[7] Major-General Douglass to Earl Bathurst, Nov. 8, 1816, C. O. 253/10.
[8] Major-General Seymour to Earl Bathurst, Jan. 4, 1817, C. O. 253/11.

sugar to the value of the cargoes of provisions which they entered.[1] But these later measures did not find favor with the Board of Trade, and foreign shipping was again excluded from the colony in April. Flour at once rose from $20 a barrel to $30, and other goods in proportion.[2]

Importations from neighboring, foreign West India possessions in British bottoms were allowed as before but few were made;[3] and, following several negro deaths from starvation, American merchants were again given access to local markets in May, but were permitted to load up with only rum and molasses.[4] Under the circumstances, such action was not disapproved.[5]

Once more in October, 1819, St. Lucia was laid waste by storm. The unlimited entry of provisions and the exportation of all kinds of tropical produce under alien flags was then instituted for a year.[6] Twenty-nine American ship masters availed themselves of the opportunity. They were again shut out from October, 1820, but the bringing in of needed supplies from the foreign Caribbean colonies in British bottoms was permitted thereafter.[7]

Laying restrictions on American-West Indian commerce not only occasioned an acute shortage of badly-needed plantation wares and greatly enhanced their price—it also closed a primary outlet for the estate owners' rum and molasses, neither of which was in great demand in the United Kingdom. Exports of the former from British insular territories in tropical America to the United States dropped precipitately from nearly two million gallons in 1818 to less than 54,000 in 1821, while molasses shipments slumped from over a million gallons in 1817 to but some 12,000 four years later.[8]

[1] Colonel O'Hara to Earl Bathurst, Feb. 20, 1818, C. O. 253/12.
[2] Colonel O'Hara to Earl Bathurst, April 18, 1818, C. O. 253/12.
[3] Colonel O'Hara to Earl Bathurst, May 15, 1818, C. O. 253/12.
[4] Colonel O'Hara to Earl Bathurst, May 25, 1818 and Governor Keane to Earl Bathurst, July 24, 1818, both in C. O. 253/12.
[5] A memorandum appended to O'Hara's despatch of May 25 reads "Send to the Board of Trade for their consideration expressing Lord B[athurst]'s opinion that however objectionable the measures of opening the port to American ships may be under ordinary circumstances, Lord B[athurst] cannot but feel that the urgent distress of the island authorized the acting governor in thus departing from the strict enforcement of the law."
[6] Gov. John Keane to Earl Bathurst, Oct. 27, 1819, C. O. 253/13.
[7] Keane to Bathurst, Nov. 21, 1820, C. O. 253/14.
[8] The following table was compiled from "Rum and Molasses Exported from the British West Indies to the United States and to British North America, 1814–1829," in *Gt. Br., H. C., Sess. Pap.,* 1830, XXI (648).

The sudden and complete cessation of the importation of negroes, following the adoption of abolition, resulted in a scarcity of laborers throughout the islands, increasingly felt as the older blacks died off without being replaced by new, adult workers. This was already causing grave concern by the close of the war period and further added to the difficulties of members of the agrarian-merchant group by forcing considerable numbers of properties out of cultivation.

Mathew Lewis, visiting Jamaica in 1816, noted in his journal: "Throughout the island many estates, formerly very flourishing and productive, have been thrown up for want of hands to cultivate them, and are now suffered to lie waste: four are in this situation in my own immediate neighborhood. Finding their complement of negroes decrease, and having no means of recruiting them, proprietors of two estates have in numerous instances found themselves obliged to give up one of them, and draw off the negroes for the purpose of properly cultivating the other." [1]

A committee of the assembly reported shortly after that no further extension of agriculture could be looked for locally with shipments of slaves at an end and plantations already in operation generally undermanned. [2]

The labor problem was peculiarly aggravated in St. Lucia where almost no Africans had been landed since the outbreak of revolutionary disorders at the close of the past century. Uncertainty as to what disposition would eventually be made of the colony had, as we

EXPORTS OF RUM AND MOLASSES FROM THE BRITISH WEST INDIES TO THE
UNITED STATES

	Rum	Molasses
1815	1,017,793 gals.	—
1816	1,387,582	544,443 gals.
1817	1,335,182	1,127,307
1818	1,925,315	763,549
1819	576,568	278,884
1820	476,139	241,187
1821	53,941	11,959

[1] Pp. 95, 96.
[2] *A Report of a Committee of the Honourable House of Assembly of Jamaica, Presented to the House, December 10, 1817, Relative to the Present State of the Island, With Respect to its Population, Agriculture, and Commerce, and Other Matters Referred to That Committee, by Order of the Honourable House* (London, 1818), p. 2.

have seen,[1] prevented their wholesale introduction on the eve of the great reform measure.

The island afforded a vivid illustration of the well-known failure of slaves to maintain their own stock. The surviving offspring of blacks born during the three years commencing July 1, 1816 were 947 fewer in number than were deaths among the negroes in the same period.[2]

The result was inevitable. Writing in 1816, acting governor Major-General Douglass stated, "Some very fine Plantations have recently been forsaken, the proprietors having concentrated their Slaves on other Estates which had also too few negroes to cultivate them." [3] Upwards of 200 were thus abandoned between 1799 and 1817.[4]

Decreasing returns coupled with higher prices for stores and a labor shortage soon put an end to the common expectation that the new era of peace would bring a return of prosperity to the British West Indies; by the early 1820's the position of the planter class as a whole was desperate.

The forts of Barbados were in "a sad delapidated State and . . . very rapidly falling into decay," yet so general was the poverty that little could be done about putting them into a respectable state.[5] Few estates in Tobago were more than meeting operating expenses; the incomes from many were so low as to make the payment of interest on mortgages impossible.[6] Even proprietors in the highly productive colony of Trinidad found themselves unable to meet their obligations.[7]

Drought in St. Kitts increased the already sore straits of the residents to such an extent that Governor Maxwell volutarily relinquished a portion of his colonial salary.[8] By 1823 taxes in Nevis were so far in arrears that the island legislature found it necessary to arrange for a British treasury loan of £4,000 to meet public bills.[9]

In the Virgin group, returns from the very best situated estates

[1] See page 278.

[2] Governor Keane to Earl Bathurst, Nov. 1, 1820, C. O. 253/14.

[3] Despatch to Earl Bathurst, October 16, C. O. 253/10.

[4] Major-General Seymour to Earl Bathurst, Jan. 20, 1817, C. O. 253/11.

[5] Governor Warde to Earl Bathurst, Jan. 17, 1822, C. O. 28/91.

[6] Petition of the legislature of Tobago to the House of Commons, C. O. 285/28.

[7] Governor Woodford to Earl Bathurst, April 11, 1821, C. O. 295/53.

[8] Maxwell to Earl Bathurst, Sept. 10, 1822, C. O. 239/8.

[9] Maxwell to Bathurst, May 6, July 4, Nov. 12, 1823, C. O. 239/9.

failed to meet operating costs and their proprietors, once persons of opulence, experienced great difficulty in obtaining sufficient credit to carry on cultivation. Means were totally lacking to pay off governmental obligations of some £10,000 and an advance from the mother country to cover them was sought.[1]

Long-continued dry weather in Antigua reduced crops to a fraction of their usual size and most proprietors' accounts were soon heavily overdrawn. Their factors one and all declined in 1822 to honor further bills of exchange on them, including those for customary yearly shipments of food and supplies. When these failed to arrive, a crisis rapidly developed. All slaves were put on rations and more than 1,500 were fed at public expense during the fall of the year. Following a precedent set earlier in the colony's history,[2] a draft for £10,000 sterling was drawn on the Lords of the Treasury,[3] but this was not paid and the position of the Antiguans was thus further complicated.[4]

If an English gentleman touring Jamaica at this juncture may be believed, he was twice greeted by armed men upon his arrival at plantations where he was mistaken for a deputy marshal seeking to make a levy for the recovery of debts.[5]

The situation in Dominica, St. Vincent, and St. Lucia was particularly bad. In addition to receiving low prices for their produce, the planters of the former island had, as we have noted, experienced grievous losses through invasion by the French, a series of hurricanes, and negro troubles.[6] Discouragement resulted in such heavy emigration to the new Caribbean possessions that production sank rapidly. The average annual exportation of British-grown cacao to Great Britain in the five years 1816–1820 was but 4,300 pounds, as compared with an annual average of 48,445 pounds exported to England alone from 1771–1775. Despite the tremendous development of Dominican coffee culture at the close of the seventeen hundreds, the average annual exportation of that commodity to Great Britain from the reëstablishment of peace to 1820 stood at only 1,399,500 pounds as compared with an average of 1,527,510 shipped to England in the

---

[1] Memorial of the legislature to the Crown, in Governor Maxwell to Earl Bathurst, March 11, 1823, C. O. 239/9.

[2] See pages 157 and 158.

[3] Governor D'Urban to Earl Bathurst, July 2, 1822, C. O. 7/8.

[4] D'Urban to Bathurst, Jan. 13, 1823, C. O. 7/8.

[5] Williams, *Tour*, pp. 275, 276, 320, 321.

[6] See pages 293, 329, and 330.

earlier period. Similarly, the average annual exportation of muscovado sugar, which had become a primary product of the colony after :ts acquisition in the Seven Years' War, to Great Britain between 1816 and 1820 was less than 41,000 hundredweight, in contrast with 28,295 entered annually on the average in England only from 1771–1775.[1]

The decline of Dominica, beginning with the opening of the century, was progressive and proceeded at such a rate that within two decades total output had been cut in half. Local proprietors were convinced that there was small likelihood of the colony's remaining valuable as an agricultural one and pinned their hopes for a return of prosperity on commerce instead.[2] Indeed, James Colquhoun, one of the island agents, reported from London that Dominica was to be abandoned and that the ministry contemplated removing its residents to Demerara.[3]

In 1815, public creditors could be paid only in treasury acceptances receivable for taxes; the salaries of all officers were eight months in arrears a year later. The planters who had not emigrated at that time declared themselves quite unable to bear the expense of maintaining white soldiers and of meeting an allowance to the local chief justice which was withdrawn by the home government.[4]

Estate owners of St. Vincent, who had failed to recover from the shock of civil war in 1795,[5] suffered one of the greatest natural disasters in West Indian history in May, 1812, when Mount Soufrière, a long-dormant volcano, erupted with such force as to blow away its summit and devastate the greater part of the island.[6] Most of the cacao and coffee trees were destroyed through a heavy ash fall and the sugar crop was ruined.

[1] Customs 3/71–75; 5/5–9, P. R. O.

[2] Governor Maxwell to Earl Bathurst, Oct. 5, 1816, C. O. 71/52. Petition of the proprietors of plantations in Dominica, resident in or near London, to Earl Bathurst, C. O. 71/57.

[3] Governor Maxwell to Henry Goulburn, private letter of Feb. 22, 1818, C. O. 71/55.

[4] Governor Maxwell to Earl Bathurst, Oct. 30, 1816, C. O. 71/52.

[5] See pages 220 ff. and 307 ff.

[6] Contemporary reports on the events will be found in C. O. 260/29, C. O. 28/81 and C. O. 285/17. The explosion, heard in Barbados and Tobago, was there mistaken for cannonading on the sea. In both cases, troops were called out to ward off attacks it was feared the French would make. C. O. 28/81, C. O. 285/17. See also "On the Fall of Volcanic Dust in Barbados," in *Blackwood's Edinburgh Magazine*, May, 1817, pp. 134, 135.

Following this catastrophe, the average annual exportation of British-grown cacao from the colony to Great Britain between 1814 and 1822 fell to but 4,800 pounds and that of British plantation coffee to 7,032 pounds.[1] Assistance was sought from parliament [2] and £25,000 was voted the sufferers.[3] The grant, generous enough considering the home country's financial difficulties, covered a mere fraction of the losses and such a setback received in a dark hour could only thoroughly dishearten the residents and hasten decay and general bankruptcy throughout St. Vincent.

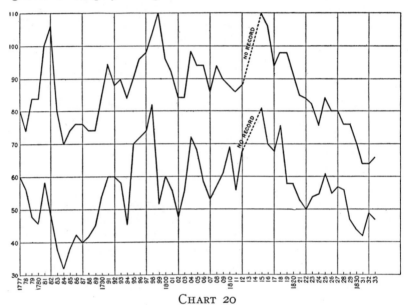

CHART 20

Range in the Wholesale Price of British West Indian Muscovado Sugar Offered English Grocers, 1777–1833, in Shillings per Hundred-weight *

* Based on quotations made by Smiths, Nash, and Kemble and successors of London, in the archives of Joseph Travers and Sons, Ltd. Upper line = top price for the year. Lower line = bottom price for the year.

[1] Customs 5/3–11, P. R. O. From 1771 to 1775 the average annual exportations to England alone had been 147,280 lbs. and 884,280 lbs. respectively. Customs 3/71–75. P. R. O.

[2] Anon., *Case of the Proprietors of Estates in the Island of St. Vincent, Who suffered by the Eruption of the Volcano on the Morning of the 1st of May, 1812* [London, 1812]. "Report from the Select Committee of Persons interested in Estates in St. Vincent," in *Gt. Br., H. C., Sess. Pap.,* 1812–13, III (182), p. 375.

[3] 53 Geo. III c. 136.

French commercial law governed relations between the planters of St. Lucia and the merchant class.[1] Mortgages were not registered. The sole method of forcing the payment of monies due there was by seizing the debtors' crops or movable property—real estate could not be levied upon. As implements and personal effects were seldom worth taking over, credit was, in effect, extended against the security of growing crops alone. Whenever the market value of tropical products declined, the proprietors at once experienced marked difficulty in arranging advances. Consequently their situation in the post-bellum period was desperate.

The produce grown on the six cacao, sixteen cotton, eighty-one coffee, and 102 sugar estates in the island, representing an investment of approximately £2,500,000 sterling, was valued at but £117,136 in 1819. British factors were then refusing to longer carry accounts over from one season to another and local commercial houses would not transact business except on a cash basis. Since crop seizures to recover long outstanding obligations were being freely made and many planters thus found themselves deprived of their one means of procuring stores, they commonly resorted to concealing a portion of their output and secretly shipped it to Martinique where sales for money were readily made.

There was no incentive to better methods or to increase production. Cultivation was carried on in half-hearted fashion, and resident traders, finding it ever less possible to collect back accounts, sought to recoup losses by raising prices on their wares to such exorbitant figures that few could afford to buy them.[2]

Caribbean properties declined materially in value as returns from them dwindled. A Jamaican plantation producing 200 hogsheads of sugar per annum was normally worth £43,000 currency; about 1820 several such sold for as low as £30,000.[3] Two estates in St. Kitts, for which £45,000 had been paid in 1817, brought less than half that sum at auction in London five years after.[4] Even a smaller fraction of their former value was secured for those in the Virgin Islands sold at about the same time.[5]

[1] See pages 389 and 390.

[2] Governor Keane to Earl Bathurst, Nov. 1, 1820, C. O. 253/14. *An Ordinance for the More Effectual Repression of the Illicit Exportation of the Produce of the Colony* [Castries, 1822].

[3] Stewart, *A View . . . of Jamaica*, pp. 112, 113.

[4] Benns, "American Struggle," in *Indiana University Studies*, no. 56, p. 74.

[5] Memorial of the legislature to the Crown, in Governor Maxwell to Earl Bathurst, March 11, C. O. 239/9.

This falling off in tropical American real estate values made it constantly more difficult for the West Indians to raise loans on mortgages. Nor could British dealers in colonial produce come to their assistance where they were so minded because of being too deeply involved themselves. "There is an end of any use of Colonial Property in the way of Sale or of Security. . . .," declared the Society of Merchants in a memorial to Earl Bathurst in 1823. "The calamities impending over the Colonies must be aggravated by the inability of the Mercantile Body to supply those funds which will be necessary for their relief." [1]

Their precarious position and means of improving it were subjects of great discussion among the islanders. A petition of the Jamaican assembly to the Crown in 1821 set forth the colonists' plight—their produce being met at home by importations from the new transatlantic possessions and India and abroad by the crops of territories not under British jurisdiction still enjoying the slave trade, their profits from sugar culture negligible, rum being sold at a loss, supplies from America both scarce and dear—and prayed that the discriminatory rate against East Indian sugar be increased, that duties on Caribbean products entering the United Kingdom be lowered, that a drawback on exports be allowed, that direct intercourse with the United States be reëstablished, and that the right of bartering for supplies be granted.[2] An address of the following year called for a parliamentary inquiry into the causes of distress;[3] another of 1823 prayed for the removal of war-time duties in the mother country.[4]

The legislature of Grenada urged the opening of free trade relations with America, increased preference over oriental sugar, the placing of West Indian duties on the ad valorem basis, and the granting of permission to export rum directly to continental old world ports in British vessels.[5] The council and lower house of the Virgins advocated the same measures and in addition called for the payment of bounties on refined sugar exported from Great Britain to boost sales abroad.[6]

[1] *Min. W. I. Mer.,* October 21.

[2] *Addresses and Memorials to His Majesty, from the House of Assembly at Jamaica, Voted in the Years 1821 to 1862 Inclusive; and Which Have Been Presented to His Majesty by the Island Agent* [London, 1828], pp. 7–14.

[3] *Ibid.,* pp. 15–18.

[4] In C. O. 137/154.

[5] In C. O. 101/61.

[6] Memorial to parliament in Governor Maxwell to Earl Bathurst, March 11, 1823, C. O. 239/9.

President Wilson of St. Kitts attributed the colonists' embarrassments primarily to the high charge laid against their sugar at home;[1] Governor Keane proposed solving St. Lucia's individual problem by introducing the English commercial code and curbing fraudulent exportations of produce by debtors.[2]

West India factors and planters resident in the British capital joined forces to meet the situation. They strove hard to obtain a more advantageous tariff. It was argued that coffee and sugar could be sold at lower prices if duties were reduced, that consumption would then be increased, and that the revenue would consequently not be injured. An effort was also made to bring about the removal of a preferential rate of 1s. 1½d. per gallon on British spirits over rum from the colonies.

But the greatest concessions offered by the ministry were an equalization of raw and clayed sugar charges and a general reduction of the impost on molasses from 10s. to 1s. per hundredweight. One proved as unacceptable to members of the Caribbean interest as the other because, as they declared, the former would merely operate as an encouragement to East Indian sugar which was frequently classified as clayed and the other would apply to oriental molasses as well as to that from the British-American tropics.[3]

Through efforts of the Society of West India Merchants,[4] colonial cacao was now given preference over that from abroad for consumption in the navy and home demand was thereby somewhat increased. Whereas the Victualling Board purchased 239,680 pounds of the British-grown product in 1821 and 1822 and 112,000 pounds from foreign sources in 1821, it placed no orders for any of the latter the next year.[5]

Renewed allowance of a drawback on muscovado and of bounties on refined sugar exported were also sought, but the government was deaf to all pleas on this score, its spokesmen declaring the artificial encouragement of trade to be so objectionable and so opposed to new economic doctrines that such measures would meet with serious and probably successful opposition in parliament.[6]

[1] Despatch to Earl Bathurst, Sept 13, 1821, C. O. 239/7.

[2] Despatch to Earl Bathurst, Nov. 1, 1820, C. O. 253/14.

[3] *Min. W. I. Plant. and Mer.,* July 12, 18 and 22, 1822; Nov. 27, 1823; June 23, 1824.

[4] *Min. W. I. Mer.,* Sept. 5, and Oct. 3, 1821.

[5] "Cocoa Consumed in the British Navy," in *Gt. Br., H. C., Sess. Pap.,* 1830-31, X (380), p. 341.

[6] *Min. W. I. Plant. and Mer.,* July 4, 10, and 19, 1822.

Following a suggestion of the London Caribbean group, Sir Charles Bagot, the ambassador at St. Petersburg, was instructed by the Foreign Office at about the same time to press for a reclassification of British plantation sugar in a proposed new Russian tariff schedule so as to encourage exports there.[1]

The colonists were advised to reduce production costs and to retrench public expenditures wherever possible.[2] The Society of Merchants endeavored to secure authorization for the loan of £5,000,-000 in exchequer bills to West India houses upon personal security and plantation mortgages. This would have made possible the carrying over of the hard-pressed planters' obligations, but the ministry proved adamant and nothing came of the project.[3]

The need for adopting relief measures was generally acknowledged —the question was, which course of action would prove most efficacious? To statesmen of the day, imbued with free trade principles, the obvious solution was a general relaxation of the navigation system against which the islanders railed so bitterly. This, it was believed, would provide them with outlets for their surplus produce as well as with ample stocks of supplies at first hand. Legislation removing checks on the normal flow of trade would, it was urged, increase the proprietors' returns, lower their operating expenses, and thus end their difficulties.

The West India body in England welcomed the proposal and, despite the stout opposition of British shippers who saw personal ruin in any general invasion of their privileged position and of the British North Americans who were keenly aware of the impossibility of their meeting competition from the United States on an equal footing, this view prevailed—a series of laws enacted in 1822 and 1825 completely reversed the historic policy of a closed new world tropical trade and removed the restrictions hampering the Caribbean possessions' commerce.

The twenty-fourth of June, 1822, stands a memorable date in imperial economic history. Two measures then adopted gave the British planters direct access to foreign markets and threw open the trade of Great Britain's sugar colonies to American citizens.

The former, the colonial trade act, revived the right of direct sugar exportation to continental European markets, initiated in 1739 and

[1] *Min. W. I. Plant. and Mer.,* March 18, 1820; Feb. 14, 1821.
[2] Meeting of July 22, 1822.
[3] Meetings of June 9 and 27, 1823.

continued in force, as has been noted, until the 1790's,[1] and extended it so as to allow the shipping of any articles grown, produced, or manufactured in the Caribbean colonies to all foreign ports of Europe and Africa and to Gibraltar, Malta, and the Channel Islands, in British-built ships which might also enter enumerated goods from thence upon the payment of specified duties.[2]

The latter authorized the importation of grain, live stock, provisions, lumber, naval stores, cotton, wool and tobacco from any non-British territory in North or South America or foreign West India island into specified ports of British North America and the Caribbean colonies in British ships or those of the nations in which the goods so entered originated when brought direct from there.

Import duties averaging 10 per cent ad valorem were levied against foodstuffs and lumber arriving from foreign regions in bottoms under either national or alien registry. The exportation of any articles or commodities excepting only warlike stores was permitted in foreign vessels clearing out directly for home as well as in British ones. These privileges were, however, extended only to the ships of those countries giving similar rights to the British in their own ports.

Foreign fish and salted meats were excluded in the interest of the mainland American colonists, and, to further protect them, no import duties were laid against their produce entering the sugar colonies.

This measure was drawn so as to foster commercial relations with the new South American republics and the rights it accorded were not restricted to the plantation settlements, but it was commonly understood that only the trade between the latter and the United States would be materially affected by it and it had been presented under the significant name "West Indian and American trade bill." Thus the planters' four decade long struggle to secure the enjoyment of permanent direct intercourse with their natural source of supply ended in triumph.[3]

[1] See page 207.

[2] 3 Geo. IV c. 45. For a local measure based on the same, see *An ordinance imposing certain colonial Duties upon Articles imported . . . under authority of an Act of Parliament . . . Intitled "An Act to regulate the Trade between His Majesty's Possessions in America and the West Indies, and other Parts of the World"* [Castries, St. Lucia, 1822].

[3] 3 Geo. IV c. 44. The Caribbean ports thus opened were Kingston, Savannah la Mar, Montego Bay, Santa Lucia, Port Antonio, Saint Ann, Falmouth, Port Maria, and Morant Bay in Jamaica; St. George, Grenada; Roseau, Dominica; St. John's, Antigua; San Josef, Trinidad; Scarborough, Tobago; Road Harbour, Virgin Islands; Kingston, St. Vincent; Bridgetown, Barbados;

The colonial trade act did not lead to the favorable results which had been anticipated. Exportation to foreign markets was impractical as neither planters nor local merchants had factors in them and the risk and uncertainty attending the sending out of consignments on the chance of making profitable sales were too great to be commonly entertained.

More important, however, was the fact that the proprietors were unable to establish direct relations with foreign buyers even where they were desirous of doing so. By 1822 they, as a class, were all but hopelessly in debt to their British agents. Estates were mortgaged to them and crops were hypothecated; these creditors would brook no agreements which might impair the security of loans whose repayment was already problematical and which would give others the profits of handling shipments from the encumbered estates. They held the whip hand. The West Indians were helpless and found themselves in the position of bailiffs to their representatives on their own estates.[1]

On the other hand, exports from the British Caribbean colonies to the United States rose markedly following the opening of the American trade. Thus, shipments of rum advanced from 53,941 gallons in 1821 to an annual average of 657,102 between 1822 and 1826; exports of molasses, from 11,959 gallons in 1821 to an annual average of 1,330,317 in the five years following.[2] Imports of coffee from the British West Indies into the United States likewise increased from 16,744 pounds in 1821 to an annual average of 1,328,198 in the later

Georgetown, Demerara; New Amsterdam, Berbice; Castries, St. Lucia; Basseterre, St. Kitts; Charlestown, Nevis, and Plymouth, Monserrat. For the negotiations and developments leading to the passage of this bill see Benns, "American Struggle," in *Indiana University Studies*, No. 56, ch. III. See also [Frederick Robinson], *Substance of the Speech . . . on Moving the Resolution to Bring in Two Bills for Regulating the Intercourse Between the West Indies and other Parts of the World* (London, 1822); "Colonial Policy," in *The Quar. Rev.*, Jan., 1822, pp. 522–540, which opposes freeing the Caribbean trade of restrictions, and John P. Musson, *A Letter to Ministers, Suggesting Improvements in the Trade of the West Indies and the Canadas . . .* (London, 1825) opposing the admission of American vessels into British West Indian ports. For a local measure based upon this act, see *An Ordinance Imposing certain Colonial Duties on Articles imported under Authority of an Act of Parliament . . . intitled "An Act to regulate the Trade between His Majesty's Possessions in America and the West Indies and other places in America and the West Indies"* [Castries, St. Lucia, 1822].

[1] "Report from the Select Committee on the Commercial State of the West India Colonies," in *Gt. Br., H. C., Sess. Pap.*, 1831–32, XX (381), p. 674.

[2] "Rum and Molasses Exported from the British West Indies to the United States and to British North America, 1814–1829," in *Gt. Br., H. C., Sess. Pap.*, 1830, XXII (648).

period; entries of cacao from 5,673 to 192,124 pounds respectively; and of muscovado sugar, from 576 to 28,578 hundredweight.[1]

Various difficulties arose which rendered the privilege of entering into direct commercial relations with America of less advantage than had been hoped. The limiting of this intercourse to specified ports worked hardships on planters located at some distance from them. Thus, the proprietors of Trinidad were put to heavy expense in hauling their produce to the lone legal shipping center of the colony. Their request that they be permitted to load consignments on American vessels skirting the coast was denied by the Board of Trade.[2]

Anguilla, singularly enough, had been overlooked in passing the act of 1822; its residents did not, therefore, share in the benefits of the measure and salt-raking, the primary industry, was struck a heavy blow as ships from the United States, having entry elsewhere, no longer resorted to the island.[3]

The demand for rum was far below expectations. This was attributed in part to the Americans having grown accustomed to using corn spirits and also to the high duty charged on its entry into the United States. Many mainland merchants, displeased at the exclusion of their fish and salted provisions, refused to barter and demanded cash or bills of exchange for their cargoes. Few colonists were able to give either.

The government at Washington furthermore failed to meet the requirement that reciprocal privileges be extended British shipping in American ports. A proclamation by President Monroe, issued in August, 1822, and setting forth the conditions under which trade might be carried on with Great Britain's colonial ports, subjected British vessels entering American harbors from there to a discriminatory charge of ninety-four cents a ton and further differential duty of 10 per cent on the value of their cargoes in favor of American bottoms arriving from them and goods they carried.

When, early in the following year, these provisions were embodied in a law which also permitted the exportation of American goods to British colonial ports in British ships only if the latter had come to the United States directly from such points, retaliatory measures were

[1] "Trade With British American Colonies . . . 1815 to . . . 1826 . . .," *United States, 19th Congress, 2d Session, House Document No. 144* (Washington, 1827), pp. 315, 316.

[2] Governor Woodford to Earl Bathurst, Feb. 9, 1825 and memorandum on same, C. O. 295/65.

[3] Governor Maxwell to Earl Bathurst, Aug. 28, 1823, enclosing petition of the Council of Anguilla, C. O. 239/9.

undertaken in London. An order in council of July, 1823, imposed a
duty of 4s. 3d. per ton on American vessels entering colonial North
American and West Indian harbors as well as a discriminatory duty
of 10 per cent on their cargoes.[1]

Two acts of 1825 further relaxed the navigation system by granting not only ships from alien parts of America and the Caribbean
but those from all foreign countries in Europe, Africa, and the
portion of Asia bordering on the Mediterranean as well access to
the free ports in British North America, excepting Newfoundland,
and in the British West Indies. These vessels were permitted to enter
goods of all sorts excepting warlike stores, fish, and salted meats and
to export any articles from thence.

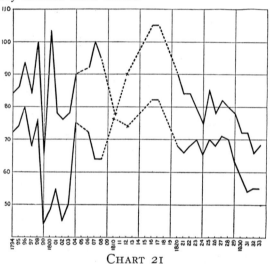

CHART 21

Range in the Wholesale Price of East Indian
Muscovado Sugar Offered English Grocers,
1794–1833, in Shillings per Hundredweight *

* Based on quotations made by Smiths, Nash, and
Kemble and successors of London, in the archives of
Joseph Travers and Sons, Ltd. Upper line = top price
for the year. Lower line = bottom price for the year.

It was provided, however, that these privileges should be extended
only to bottoms of such colonial powers as gave British shipping

[1] Benns, "American Struggle," in *Indiana University Studies*, no. 56, pp.
87–104. For a local measure based upon the same, see *An Ordinance imposing
a Tonnage Duty Upon Vessels of the United States and an additional 10 per
cent upon the duties established upon Articles imported therein* [Castries, St.
Lucia, 1823].

reciprocal rights in their own possessions and to vessels of such other nations as placed British commerce on the footing of the most favored nation, unless otherwise provided by order in council.[1]

These regulations were designed in part to reduce the importance of the United States as a source of supply for the West India planters, in part to force the removal of all discriminations against British shipping arriving in American ports from the colonies, and in part to provide further outlets for British-grown tropical produce. When the objectionable charges in the republic were continued, an order was issued in July, 1826, forbidding vessels registered there to engage in commerce with any of Great Britain's possessions excepting those on the North American mainland. Their unreasonable, grasping attitude in the face of a new, liberal commercial policy adopted in London cost the Americans the highly-prized privilege of dealing directly with the British Caribbean colonies.

A proclamation of President Adams, issued in March, 1827, renewed the prohibitions on intercourse with the British West Indies originally instituted in 1817, 1818, and 1820 [2] and further widened the breach between the two countries.[3]

The renewal of restrictions on the American trade struck a grievous blow at the planters. Interchange of goods had "assumed a regularity that was as advantageous to the Consumer as to the Importer," declared Governor Woodford of Trinidad in expressing his regret at the turn of events.[4] Lumber and provisions from the United States could thereafter be regularly entered only through British North America or the foreign West Indies, in either case at greatly enhanced cost.

Direct relations with the foreign mainland were entered into on but two occasions during this period. In August, 1827, following the worst hurricane of half a century, President Rawlins opened the ports of St. Kitts, Nevis, the Virgin Islands, and Anguilla to vessels of all nations for three months.[5] Shortly after, in order to provide the dis-

---

[1] 6 Geo. IV c. 73, 6 Geo. IV c. 114. See William Huskisson, *Substance of Two Speeches, Delivered in the House of Commons on the 21st and 25th of March, 1825* . . . *Respecting the Colonial Policy and Foreign Commerce of the Country* (London, 1825) and *Parliamentary Debates,* new series, XII, cols. 1097–1127.

[2] See pages 338 ff.

[3] For the course of the controversy see Benns, "American Struggle," in *Indiana University Studies,* no. 56, pp. 105–154.

[4] Despatch to Earl Bathurst, Oct. 3, 1826, C. O. 295/72.

[5] Rawlins to Lord Goderich, Aug. 29, 1827, C. O. 239/16.

tressed salt-rakers of the latter settlement with an outlet for the product of their labor, an order in council authorized American ships arriving in ballast to export salt and fruit, but nothing else.[1]

Loss of the West India trade due to the perverse policy of the Monroe and Adams administrations caused great discontent in American commercial circles. General Jackson was known to favor a recession from the unwarrantable position which had been taken against British vessels in the ports of the United States and his candidacy consequently won the support of the powerful shipping and merchant interests. Promptly following victory at the polls, an attempt was made to regain through diplomacy a valuable concession lost by stupid blundering.

Chances for success were greatly increased by an act of Congress passed in 1830 providing that if the president were assured before the next session that Great Britain would admit American vessels into her Caribbean colonies, the Bahamas, and the Bermudas either temporarily or permanently under the terms set forth in the parliamentary measures of 1825, he was to grant entry to British and American vessels arriving from them and their cargoes upon exactly the same terms, either temporarily or permanently, and should at the same time suspend or repeal the laws of 1817, 1818, 1820, and 1823 as the case might require.

This bid for an understanding was received with good grace and, in October of the same year, President Jackson by proclamation abolished all discriminations and voided the several offensive acts. A month later an order in council gave American ships and the goods they transported access to colonial Caribbean markets on a basis of equality with laden British vessels arriving there from the United States and authorized them to export the produce of those colonies to any part of the world save the British possessions.[2]

[1] President Rawlins to William Huskisson, April 5, 1828, C. O. 239/18.

[2] The various steps by which the "reciprocity of 1830" was arrived at are best related in Benns, "American Struggle," in *Indiana University Studies*, No. 56, ch. VI. For contemporary American points of view on the question see Josiah S. Johnston, *Speech . . . on the Bill to Regulate the Commercial Intercourse Between the United States and the British Colonies: Delivered in the Senate . . . February 23, 1827* (Washington, 1827); Littleton Tazewell, *A Review of the Negotiations Between the United States of America and Great Britain, Respecting the Commerce of the Two Countries, and More Especially Concerning the Trade of the Former With the West Indies* (London, 1829), and Anon., "X. Y.," *Review of the Late Negotiation and Arrangement with the British Government, Respecting the West India Trade . . .* (Philadelphia, 1831). For contemporary British opinion see A. A. Lindo, *The Injurious*

A new schedule of duties, adopted shortly after, increased the rates on foreign pine lumber, staves, and headings entering the British West Indies to afford the North American colonials additional preference, but admitted those products in either alien or British bottoms without discrimination as to carrier and gave entry to foreign grain excepting wheat, to peas, beans, live stock, bread, biscuit, and all varieties of meal or flour excepting wheat free of duty.[1]

From 1830, then, the planters enjoyed regular and continuous free access to the cheapest market for indispensable stores and the additional outlet for their produce afforded by ready intercourse with the United States. Unfortunately, this concession was made only when they had fallen to so low a state that it proved of no avail in stemming the disaster which was overwhelming them.

The opening of the American trade in 1822 not only constituted a hollow victory for the greater part of a decade—it became a veritable boomerang. The chief claim of the Caribbean proprietors for fiscal advantage over East Indian sugar at home had always been that this was a form of compensation for subjecting them to the restrictions of the navigation laws.[2] There had been some logic to this, but, with the latter wholly removed, all ground for preferential treatment disappeared. Therein lies the true significance of the legislation of June, 1822 in imperial history.

Merchants engaged in traffic with the East lost no time in attacking the now unwarranted privileged position of the West Indians. In May, 1822, while relaxation of the old commercial system was still only under discussion, a committee of the Liverpool East India Association, an organization of independent houses which had opened relations with the Orient since the East India Company's exclusive rights had been set aside in 1813,[3] presented that body with a formal statement of existing restrictions on their commerce, largely devoted to a consideration of West Indian preference.[4] Likewise, seven months

Tendency of the Modifying of Our Navigation Laws Made Manifest . . . (London, 1828) ; [Henry Bliss], *On Colonial Intercourse* (London, 1830) ; Bliss, *The Colonial System* (London, 1833) ; "Commerce of the United States and West Indies," in *The Quar. Rev.,* Jan., 1829, pp. 215–248; "Agricola," *pseud.,* "The Colonial Question," in *Blackwood's,* March, 1830, pp. 455–462; "Junius Colonus," *pseud.,* "British America," in *ibid.,* April, 1830, pp. 604–607.

[1] I William IV c. 24.

[2] See for example pages 211 and 213. See also Thomas Fletcher, *Letters in Vindication of the Rights of the British West India Colonies . . .* (London, 1822).

[3] See page 334.

[4] *Report of a Committee of the Liverpool East India Association, Appointed to Take Into Consideration the Restrictions on the East India Trade. Pre-*

later, the East India Company's court of directors drew up and issued an extended account of sugar production in Asia with special reference to British India and the disabilities placed upon shipments from there entering the United Kingdom.[1]

These reports, classics in the literature of the struggle between East and West Indian sugar, were direct attacks on the tropical American monopoly. Elaborate tables and detailed masses of statistics presented damning evidence regarding its cost to the large consuming public for the advantage of a small group of planters.

Sugar, it was declared, could be produced in the Caribbean colonies only at great expense because of the use of slave labor and soil exhaustion. Production costs in India were markedly less since workers there were free wage-earners and endless tracts of virgin land awaited the cultivator. So great was the difference that muscovado from the Orient could be profitably introduced into Great Britain even with the existing discriminatory duty in force, but under those conditions it could be sold at only about the West Indian price.

The preferential rate for the transatlantic article had originated by accident and had only subsequently been regularly set by parliament under influence of the colonial proprietors.[2] If charges were now equalized, East Indian sugar would considerably undersell that from the occident. The protection given the latter therefore actually transferred several million pounds annually from the pockets of consumers in the United Kingdom to those of the estate owners.[3]

"The West Indians claim the exclusive supply of the British market, and are not even content with the fair market price; but the people of England are compelled to submit to a tax to keep it up— *a clear, undisputed and acknowledged tax,* to force up the price of an article to 6½d., which, without any diminution of the revenue, the people could get for 2½d. to 3d." [4]

The Caribbean planters, declared the traders East, had no claim for

<hr />

sented to the Association at a General Meeting, 9th May, 1822, and Ordered to be Printed (Liverpool, 1822).

[1] *East India Sugar. Papers Respecting the Culture and Manufacture of Sugar in British India: Also Notices of the Cultivation of Sugar in Other Parts of Asia. With Miscellaneous Information Respecting Sugar* (London, 1822).

[2] On this point, see pages 210 and 212.

[3] *East India Sugar. Papers Respecting the Culture and Manufacture of Sugar . . . ,* and *Report of a Committee of the Liverpool East India Association . . . , passim.*

[4] *Report of a Committee of the Liverpool East India Association . . . ,* p. 58.

special consideration on the ground that their colonies were peculiarly valuable portions of the empire. The demand for British manufacturers from them was stationary, while that from Hindustan was unlimited. Possession of the West Indies was precarious, and the protection of British interests there made necessary the maintenance of large armies at heavy expense. The territories of the East India Company, on the other hand, were securely held and were defended by native troops at no cost to Great Britain. If, as was alleged, the West India sugar trade was a nursery for seamen, that to the Orient was most certainly a much greater one, since the distance to the East was so much farther.[1]

Early in 1823, at the request of a body of stockholders including David Ricardo, the economist, and Zachary Macaulay of the African trading firm, Macaulay and Babington, and a leader of the emancipation movement,[2] the General Quarterly Court of the East India Company considered the matter of securing uniformity in sugar duties.[3] A petition calling for this adjustment of the tariff, based on the recent revolutionary change in imperial commercial regulations, was presented to the government shortly after. It was met by a counter one of the West Indians praying that the preference accorded them be continued since the Caribbean holdings were colonies of known value to the mother land while the regions controlled by the East India Company were mere dependencies whose real worth to the nation was problematical.[4]

In May, a motion sponsored by the merchants interested in oriental commerce "that a select committee be appointed to inquire into the duties payable on East and West India Sugar," was presented to the House of Commons. A sharp debate followed, with W. Whitmore, who had introduced the measure, Ricardo, and Wilberforce supporting it and Charles Ellis, Keith Douglas, and Joseph Marryat, representing the West India group, leading the opposition. After numerous clashes, the latter triumphed—this attempt to open the question of

---

[1] East India Sugar. Papers Respecting the Culture and Manufacture of Sugar . . . , and Report of a Committee of the Liverpool East India Association . . . , passim.

[2] See Chapters XI and XII.

[3] "Debate at the East-India House on the East-India Sugar Trade," in The Asiatic Journal and Monthly Register for British India and Its Dependencies, April, 1823. Reprinted as Debates at the General Court of Proprietors of East-India Stock, on the 19th and 21st March 1823, on the East-India Sugar Trade (London, n.d.).

[4] Min. W. I. Plant. and Mer., March 12, 1823.

equalization proved unsuccessful through an adverse vote of 34 to 161.[1]

Meanwhile, discussion of the subject in print served to focus public attention on the great issue involved. The attack on preference there was led by Zachary Macaulay and James Cropper, the latter being the founder and head of the independent East India house, Cropper, Benson, and Company of Liverpool. Joseph Marryat became spokesman for the planters; a pamphlet by him, setting forth their views,[2] was given wide circulation as well as distribution among the members of parliament in an attempt to gain favor with them.[3]

Advocates of equalization held thât it would lower the price of sugar [4] and would thus make possible the use of that luxury by large numbers of persons then unable to afford it; [5] that it would be followed by an increase rather than a decrease in revenue from such greater consumption; [6] that it would enlarge the market for British manufactures in the Orient [7] and would in this way improve exchange with the East; [8] that it would not lead to any disuse of docks or warehouses; [9] that it would enable shippers transporting light cargoes of high-priced commodities such as silk and spices to carry sugar as a profitable ballast; [10] that it would benefit the 120,000,000 inhabitants of India as against the less than a million West Indians

---

[1] *Parliamentary Debates*, new series, IX, cols. 444–467. *Substance of a Debate in the House of Commons on the 22nd May, 1823, on the Motion of Mr. W. W. Whitmore. "That a Select Committee be Appointed to Inquire into the Duties Payable on East and West India Sugar"* (London, 1823).

[2] *A Reply to the Arguments Contained in Various Publications, Recommending Equalization of the Duties on East and West India Sugar* (London, 1823).

[3] A thousand copies were purchased for that purpose in March, 1823. *Min. W. I. Plant. and Mer.*, March 1.

[4] Marryat, *A Reply*, pp. 9, 10, (in meeting opponents' arguments).

[5] *Ibid.*, p. 6. James Cropper, *Relief for West-Indian Distress, Showing the Inefficiency of Protecting Duties on East-India Sugar, and Pointing Out Other Modes of Certain Relief* (London, 1823), p. 27.

[6] [Zachary Macaulay], *East and West India Sugar, or a Refutation of the Claims of the West India Colonists to a Protecting Duty on East India Sugar* (London, 1823), p. 4.

[7] Marryat, *A Reply*, p. 12. "East and West India Sugar," in *The Ed. Rev.*, Feb. 1823, pp. 222, 223. [George Larpent], *On Protection to West India Sugar* . . . (London, 1823).

[8] Marryat, *A Reply*, p. 23.

[9] Macaulay, *East and West India Sugar*, p. 3.

[10] Anon., *A Statement of the Claims of the West India Colonies to a Protecting Duty Against East India Sugar* (London, 1823), p. 104. *The Ed. Rev.*, Feb., 1823, pp. 222, 223.

then favored by a preferential rate;[1] and that it would afford compensation to the Hindus for the displacement of their local manufactures through the introduction of cotton and woolen goods from Great Britain.[2]

It was urged, furthermore, that India was in reality far more worthy of special consideration than were the sugar colonies as it paid its entire expenses of government while they were maintained only at heavy cost to Great Britain. Industry in the former should therefore be given this encouragement.[3] The claim of the Caribbean planters to an ancient monopoly was likewise declared to be untenable because the meaning of the geographic term "British West Indies" had changed on several occasions since 1763 and foreigners in the conquered islands had actually been granted privileges identical with those of residents in the old British ones.[4]

Also, tropical American estates were then admittedly of such small value that it would be a matter of little violence to deprive the proprietors of their peculiar, cherished rights.[5] And lastly, the removal of fiscal discriminations would force the West Indians to operate their properties less wastefully;[6] not to adopt equalization would be to prop up decrepit enterprises, "to bribe a parcel of slave-holders to continue in a losing business."[7]

Defenders of colonial Caribbean preference, on the other hand, maintained that the planters held a vested interest in the home-market monopoly; that they, as British subjects, were, in simple justice, as much entitled to protective duties on their products as were the British agriculturists and manufacturers in the home country.[8] Cap-

---

[1] John B. Seely, *A Few Hints to the West-Indians, on Their Present Claims to Exclusive Favour and Protection, at the Expense of the East-India Interests, With Some Observations and Notes on India* (London, 1823), p. 11. Marryat, *A Reply*, p. 45. Larpent, *On Protection.*

[2] Anon., *A Statement of the Claims,* p. 110. Marryat, *A Reply*, p. 25.

[3] [Simon H. Clarke], *Some Considerations on the Present Distressed State of the British West India Colonies, Their Claims on the Government for Relief, and the Advantage to the Nation in Supporting Them, Particularly Against the Competition of East India Sugar* (London, 1823), p. 54 (in replying to arguments of his opponents).

[4] Marryat, *A Reply*, p. 77. Macaulay, *East and West India Sugar*, p. 23.

[5] Clarke, *Some Considerations*, p. 46.

[6] *The Ed. Rev.*, Feb. 1823, p. 219.

[7] *Ibid.*, p. 218.

[8] Anon., *A Statement of the Claims,* p. 5. Clarke, *Some Considerations*, p. 46. Macaulay, *East and West India Sugar*, p. 23. S. P. Hurd, *A Letter to the Right Honourable the Earl of Liverpool, K. G. on the Claims of the West India Proprietors* (London, 1823).

ital estimated at £80,000,000 [1] sterling had been invested in transatlantic properties with full confidence in the British government's
protection. This would now be imperilled or even lost, were equalization to be instituted.[2] Preferential treatment was, after all, but a fair
indemnification for the abolition of the slave trade which made it
impossible for the British-American planters to compete with those
in Cuba and Brazil.[3] If it were ended, Caribbean distress would become ruin [4] and the lot of the slaves would become immeasurably
worse.[5]

The West Indies, argued the colonials, were inhabited by Englishmen; India was a conquered country peopled by Hindus with no valid
claim to the enjoyment of British rights.[6] Unlike the Caribbean proprietors, the owners of sugar estates in the Far East did not spend
their incomes in Great Britain.[7] The sugar islands were a permanent
part of the empire while the hold on India was weak and might be
lost at any time because of Russian ambitions.[8]

As for the commercial and political benefits accruing to the United
Kingdom from ownership of the tropical American colonies, they
were incomparably greater than those arising through Hindustan's
being controlled by a trading corporation [9] and individuals enjoying
free access to the Orient. Sugar would not be sold any cheaper following the removal of preference; [10] the national revenue would be
seriously decreased through the adoption of equalization; [11] owners of

---

[1] This was, of course, an absurd claim. No such sum had been laid out in
the colonies. At best this amount represented a mere capitalization of former
income.

[2] Macaulay, *East and West India Sugar*, p. 33. Anon., *Observations on the
Claims of the West-India Colonists to a Protecting Duty on East India Sugar*
(London, 1823). Anon., *Some Observations Supplementary to the Pamphlets
Recently Published in Support of a Protecting Duty in Favour of the West
Indians on East-India Sugar* (London, 1823).

[3] Macaulay, *East and West India Sugar*, p. 69.

[4] *Ibid.*, p. 56. Marryat, *A Reply*, p. 88.

[5] Macaulay, *East and West India Sugar*, p. 80. John Foster, *To the Editor
of the Globe and Traveller* (Bedford, n.d.).

[6] Clarke, *Some Considerations*, pp. 17–19.

[7] *Ibid.*, pp. 15–20. Macaulay, *East and West India Sugar*, pp. 62, 63.

[8] Marryat, *A Reply*, pp. 101–103. Macaulay, *East and West India Sugar*,
p. 59. Clarke, *Some Considerations*, p. 25.

[9] Anon., *A Statement of the Claims*, p. 5. Macaulay, *East and West India
Sugar*, pp. 62, 63. Anon., *The Inexpediency and Injustice of Equalizing the
Duties on East and West India Sugar, Further Explained* (London, 1823).
Anon., *Memorandum on the Relative Importance of the West and East Indies
to Great Britain* (London, n.d. [1823]).

[10] Anon., *A Statement of the Claims*, p. 6.

[11] Macaulay, *East and West India Sugar*, pp. 2, 3.

warehouses and docks and the shipping interest would suffer heavy losses;[1] there was no ground for believing that exports of British manufactures to Asia would thus be increased[2] and most certainly such encouragement given the East Indians would destroy that ancient training school of the imperial navy, the West Indian sugar trade.[3]

Preferential duties, continued representatives of the colonial group, were being attacked on the ground of monopoly, yet equalization would throw the sugar trade into the hands of the East India Company and a closer control than any the West Indians had ever held would inevitably result.[4] Not the natives of Bengal and adjacent regions, but merely a few merchant princes in England would profit by it.[5]

Hindustan's prosperity did not rest upon its supplying the United Kingdom with sugar as did the welfare of the Caribbean colonies. Sugar cultivation was a mere speculation with eastern land owners, but a matter of existence to the West India planters.[6] As for the lower cost of the oriental article, this was more apparent than real. It was in reality less sweet than that from the occident by a proportion of two to three[7] and much was soft and unfit for refining.[8]

Thus the controversy raged, with selfish interests on both sides painfully apparent, the West Indians on the whole, however, tending to rest their case on sentiment and their rivals on common sense and reason. In reality, the formers' claims for continued preference after 1822 were as preposterous as untenable. Their privileged position could inevitably not be long continued. In the summer of 1825 parliament reduced the duty on muscovado imported from Mauritius from 37s. per hundredweight to 27s., the West Indian rate,[9] equalized the

[1] Macaulay, *East and West India Sugar,* pp. 2, 3. Anon., *The Inexpediency and Injustice of Equalizing the Duties.*

[2] Anon., *A Statement of the Claims,* p. 6.

[3] Macaulay, *East and West India Sugar,* pp. 2, 3. Clarke, *Some Considerations,* p. 25.

[4] Seely, *A Few Hints to the West Indians,* pp. 8, 9.

[5] Seely, *A Few Hints to the West Indians,* pp. 8, 9. Anon., *Some Observations Supplementary to the Pamphlets Recently Published.*

[6] Clarke, *Some Considerations,* p. 21. Anon., *West India Agricultural Distress, and a Remark on Mr. Wilberforce's Appeal* (London, 1823).

[7] Clarke, *Some Considerations,* pp. 13–15.

[8] Marryat, *A Reply,* p. 98. See also a general presentation of West Indian claims in Anon., "A Well-Wisher of the West Indies," *Some Remarks on a Pamphlet Entitled, East and West India Sugar* (London, 1823).

[9] "Rates of Duty Payable on Mauritius Sugar," in *Gt. Br., H. C., Sess. Pap.,* 1826–27, XVIII (346); "Rates of Duty . . . On British Plantation Muscovado

charges on other produce of the island, and extended the privilege of direct trade with foreign Europe to the residents.[1]

These steps were perfectly logical. The conquered Caribbean possessions had been accorded the marketing privileges of the older islands upon their having been added to the empire. Unlike India, which was a dependency, Mauritius was a true colony—the first British sugar-producing one outside the new world. The admission of its products into the home country on equal terms with those from the West Indies did not, therefore, mark a distinct departure in colonial policy—this was, indeed, a measure which might properly have been adopted upon the cession of the island a decade before.

It was violently opposed, nevertheless, by the planter-merchant body which sought to differentiate Mauritius from the new sugar colonies in the Caribbean on the grounds that large amounts of British money had been invested in the latter, even while they had still been under foreign control, and that they were intimately connected with imperial commercial and maritime interests while little or no British capital had been laid out in Mauritius and it was essentialy a mere oriental holding peopled by Frenchmen, a colony in name only. Further justification for the continuance of the discriminatory rates against them was at the same time sought in the charge that the Mauritians were engaged in a large-scale, illicit slave traffic.[2] But these weak arguments proved quite unavailing.

Under the stimulus of such encouragement by the British government, exports of sugar from Mauritius rose from an annual average of 234,577 hundredweight between 1821 and 1825 to 379,369 hundredweight in 1826 and 434,276 two years after.[3] The greater part of the eastern sugar reaching the home market soon came from there. In 1825, shipments of muscovado to England from the Orient, excluding Mauritius, amounted to 145,994 hundredweight and imports into the country from the latter were 93,723 hundredweight. In 1829 the totals were 188,721 and 286,953 hundredweight respectively.[4]

The pressure of Mauritian sugar was soon felt by the West Indians.

Sugar on Entry for Home Consumption . . . , 1776–1826," in *Gt. Br., H. C., Sess. Pap.,* 1826, XXII (328).

[1] 6 Geo. IV c. 76.

[2] *Min. W. I. Plant. and Mer.,* May 24 and 31, 1824. *Min. W. I. Mer.,* July 14, 1824. *Parliamentary Debates,* second series, XIII, cols. 1039–1043.

[3] "Sugar Exported from Mauritius Commencing With the English Conquest," in *Gt. Br., H. C., Sess. Pap.,* 1826–27, XVIII (283).

[4] Customs, 4/20, 24, P. R. O.

Wholesale offerings in London during the fall of 1825 ranged from 65–70s. per hundredweight as against 63–80s. for Caribbean muscovado. In 1826, quotations stood at from 55–65s. and 55–80s. respectively and, in the following year, from 58–70s. as compared with 57–80s. The prices for top qualities of Mauritian sugar were thereafter regularly from six to eighteen shillings per hundredweight below those of similar West Indian grades [1]—the planters' hold on the British market was definitely broken.[2]

Despite the rebuff incurred in 1823, traders to India did not relax their efforts to secure more equitable treatment for sugar entered from British territories there.[3] The legislation regarding Mauritius lent encouragement and they bided their time. An important concession to them was made in 1830, when the duty on West Indian muscovado was lowered from 27s. per hundredweight to 24s. and that on the East Indian product from 37s. to 32s., which decreased the former's preference 20 per cent.[4]

Shortly after, James Cropper proposed that the Caribbean colonists be offered £2,500,000 to voluntarily relinquish their monopoly rights,[5] but such action was quite unnecessary. In 1836, upon solicitation of the independent Liverpool and London mercantile houses with eastern connections, at a time when the planters had already been overwhelmed by their cumulative distress, the charge on East Indian sugar entering the British market was further reduced by 25 per cent, from 32s. per hundredweight to 24s., the West Indian rate.[6] Such justification as seemed necessary for the long-delayed adoption of this equitable and perfectly natural measure was found in the recent voting of compensation to the West Indians upon the adoption

[1] Quotations from the quarterly circulars issued by Smiths, Nash, and Kemble of London and successors.

[2] See Alexander Macdonnell, *Colonial Commerce; Comprising an Inquiry Into the Principles Upon Which Discriminatory Duties Should be Levied on Sugar, the Growth Respectively of the West India British Possessions, of the East Indies, and of Foreign Countries* (London, 1828).

[3] See *Debate at the East-India House, Principally in Reference to Sugars the Production of British India, with the Petition to the House of Commons on the Subject* (London, n.d.), covering a meeting held in December, 1833, and R. Montgomery Martin, *Facts Relative to the East and West-India Sugar Trade* . . . (London, n.d. [1833]).

[4] 11 Geo. IV and 1 Wm. c. 50.

[5] James Cropper, *Another Bonus to the Planters: or, the Advantage Shown of an Equitable Purchase of the Monopoly and Bounty on West India Sugar* (London, 1833).

[6] 6 and 7 William IV c. 26.

of emancipation,[1] to be considered presently.[2] Thus, the long struggle of the Caribbean proprietors and merchants to maintain their
privileged position at length ended in complete defeat.

The rapid spread of cotton culture in virgin parts of the American
South, resulting from the enormously increased British demand after
1814 and the facilities given its entry into the United Kingdom,
spelled ruin for growers in the Caribbean. Land exhaustion in the old
colonies and the difficulty of recruiting a supply of labor in the new
ones resulted in such high costs of production as to make competition
with the mainland impossible.

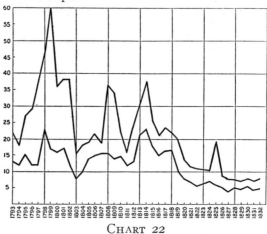

CHART 22

Range in the Wholesale Price of West Indian
Cotton at Liverpool, 1793–1832, in Pence per
Pound *

* Based on *Great Britain, House of Commons, Sessional Papers,* 1847–1848, IX (in 511), 393. Upper
line = top price for the year. Lower line = bottom
price for the year.

At the close of the eighteenth century and early in the nineteenth,
American cotton imported into Great Britain actually enjoyed a favoring duty of more than two shillings per hundredweight over that from
the West Indies.[3] From 1803 to 1819 the rates were equal;[4] there-

---

[1] *Parliamentary Debates,* third series, XXXII, cols. 591, 592, XXXIII, cols.
471, 472.

[2] In Chapter XII.

[3] Thus, from 1798 to 1801, the duty on cotton imported from the British colonies was 8s. 9d. per cwt. and that on imports from the United States but 6s.
6d., and from 1802 to 1803, the rates were 10s. 6d., and 7s. 10d., respectively.
"Duties on Cotton, 1792–1829," in *Gt. Br., H. C., Sess. Pap.,* 1830, XX (466).

[4] From 1803 to 1805, the rate was 16s. 8d. per cwt.; from 1805 to 1809, 16s.

after the colonial article was accorded a preference. For a year, the charge on imports from the colonies was 6s. 3d. per hundredweight and that on shipments from the United States, 8s. 7d.; from 1820 to 1821 the rates were 6s. 3d. and £6 per cent ad valorem respectively; while between 1821 and 1828, the former were entered free and the ad valorem tax against American cotton was continued.[1]

This fiscal encouragement was not, however, sufficient to overcome the disadvantages in production suffered by the West Indians. Their crop never formed more than a fraction of the total amount entered into the home country annually. In 1830, for example, imports from the United States into the United Kingdom were 210,885,358 pounds [2] and those from the British American tropics but a mere 3,429,247.[3] Such foreign sendings consequently regularly set the price.

While the generality of Caribbean planters were experiencing the disastrous rivalry of East Indian sugar and American cotton in the home market, those in the old West Indian islands were, in addition, being more adversely affected each year through the extension of cultivation in the conquered colonies. By 1830, no less than 30 per cent of the British-grown muscovado entering Great Britain from the American tropics was the produce of those possessions, as were 38 per cent of the rum, 23 per cent of the coffee, and 60 per cent each of the cacao and cotton. The sugar industry, in particular, was undergoing rapid development there.[4]

Sales of colonial Caribbean produce on the continent steadily declined. The average annual exportation of British plantation muscovado from Great Britain to foreign Europe between 1822 and 1825 was only 7,940 hundredweight as compared with 56,063 during the four preceding years; from 1830 to 1833, this had sunk to but 1,216 hundredweight. It was steadily undersold in Dutch and German marts not merely by Brazilian and Cuban sugar, but by that from the East Indies and Mauritius and by that from foreign plantations, first warehoused in British ports, as well. Between 1822 and 1825, average

10½d.; from 1809 to 1815, 16s. 11d.; from 1815 to 1819, 8s. 7d. "Duties on Cotton, 1792–1829," in *Gt. Br., H. C., Sess Pap.*, 1830, XX (466).

[1] "Duties on Cotton, 1792–1829," in *Gt. Br., H. C., Sess. Pap.*, 1830, XX (466).

[2] Customs 5/19, P. R. O.

[3] "Quantities of Cotton Imported into the United Kingdom from the West Indies, 1815–1833," in *Gt. Br., H. C., Sess. Pap.*, 1847–48, LVIII (383), p. 325.

[4] Imports from the ceded colonies into Great Britain in 1830 included 1,136,-989 cwt. of British-grown muscovado; 2,537,914 gals. of rum; 6,370,481 lbs. of coffee; 426,846 lbs. of cacao and 1,867,305 lbs. of cotton. Compiled from Customs 5/19, P. R. O.

annual shipments of the East Indian and Mauritian article leaving Great Britain for the adjoining mainland totalled 98,499 hundredweight; by the period 1830 to 1833, they had risen to 111,763. Exports of the foreign-grown article to the same markets averaged 174,751 and 235,119 hundredweight respectively in those years.[1]

Adverse customs duties laid by other colonial powers seeking to encourage tropical agriculture in their own overseas possessions markedly decreased the demand for British produce. Thus, during the 1820's, when the rate on sugar from the French colonies entering France was but forty-five francs per hundred kilograms and that on sendings from abroad was 125 francs, sales of the London and Liverpool houses there reached the vanishing point.

Various countries, once large purchasers of sugar prepared for consumption in Great Britain, now similarly raised bars against it to foster the refining industry within their several boundaries. Holland admitted muscovado at fifty centimes per hundredweight but set the tax on white sugar at thirty-six francs. Russia, which had absorbed half of the latter commodity available for export from the United Kingdom in the period following the Congress of Vienna, forbade the entry of any whatsoever from abroad commencing in 1824. Austria, too, increased the charge on imported refined sugar from sixteen and a half to twenty-one florins per hundred twelve pounds.[2]

The shipping of manufactured British West Indian sugar from homeland ports suffered a further setback in 1828. Foreign muscovado to be worked up for sale on the continent was then granted admission at the West Indian rate of duty whenever its value was no greater than the current average price of raw sugar from the Caribbean colonies.[3] Despite planter opposition,[4] this measure was extended five years later so as to admit both the foreign and British-grown products meant for the export trade into refineries duty free.[5] After decades of wrangling dispute, the British refiners at length triumphed completely over their ancient opponents, the members of the colonial interest.

The outlet for British colonial coffee was severely restricted at this

[1] Customs 11/13–16, 21–24, P. R. O.

[2] "Statements, Calculations, etc.," in *Gt. Br., H. C., Sess. Pap.*, 1830–31, IX (120), pp. 495–497.

[3] 9 Geo. IV c. 93, continued by 10 Geo. IV c. 49 and 11 Geo. IV and I Wm. IV c. 72.

[4] Alexander M'Donnell, *An Examination Into the Expediency of Permitting Foreign Sugar to be Refined in This Country for Exportation* (London, 1831).

[5] 3 and 4 William IV c. 61.

same time, largely in consequence of the competition of foreign, slave-grown consignments reaching the continent. The average annual exportation from the United Kingdom between 1822 and 1826 was 22,769,890 pounds; that from 1828 to 1831, but 7,548,286.[1] Foreign cocoa was offered at so much more favorable terms than the colonial West Indian even in London that 3,713,920 pounds of the former were purchased for use by the British navy between 1824 and 1832, as contrasted with but 134,400 of the other.[2]

With imports into the home market still increasing while sales abroad steadily fell off, the prices of British Caribbean produce continued to decline. Muscovado sold in the capital city between 1822 and 1833 ranged from 22s. 4¼d. per hundredweight exclusive of duty to 43s. 4¾d., with an average value of about 30s.[3] The cost of production and marketing at this time was 24s. 4d.,[4] hence most of that transported across the Atlantic yielded the growers but little profit and sugar was, in many cases, disposed of at an actual loss.

Rum, which should have brought 4s. 3½d per gallon to give the planters a fair return, fell to 1s. 10d. in 1830, 2s. 6d. below the actual cost of production and marketing.[5] By that time, the ordinary British American sugar estate was no longer meeting operating expenses, even disregarding the matter of a return on the investment involved, and the number run at a profit, however small, was negligible.[6]

West Indian coffee sank 50 per cent in value on the average during the same period, falling from 117s.–145s. in 1822 to 75s.–94s. eleven years later and reaching such low levels as 42s.–83s. in the intervening period.[7] Cotton, too, then stood at a uniformly unremunerative price

---

[1] "Imports Into, Exports From and Home Consumption of British West Indian Coffee in the United Kingdom, 1814–1834 . . . ," in *Gt. Br., H. C., Sess. Pap.*, 1831–32, XX (in 381).

[2] "Cocoa Consumed in the British Navy," in *Gt. Br., H. C., Sess. Pap.*, 1830–31, X (380), p. 341; 1831–32, XXXIV (460), p. 281; 1833, XXXIII (322), p. 219.

[3] Prices in 1822 ranged from 28s. 5d.–34s. 10d. per cwt.; from 31s. 7¾d.–37s. in 1823; from 29s. 11¾d.–32s. 4½d. in 1824; from 37s. 2¾d.–43s. 4¾d. in 1825; from 31s. 8½d.–33s. 5½d. in 1826; from 23s. 2d.–30s. 1d. in 1829; from 23s. 4½d.–26s. 3¼d. in 1830; from 22s. 4¼d.–26s. 2d in 1831; from 26s. 9¾d.–30s. 11¾d. in 1832 and from 25s.–34s. 2¼d. in 1833. Weekly returns in *The London Gazette*.

[4] "Statements, Calculations, etc.," in *Gt. Br., H. C., Sess. Pap.*, 1830–31, IX (120), pp. 537, 539.

[5] *Ibid.*, pp. 536, 563.

[6] "Report from Select Committee on the Commercial State of the West India Colonies . . . ," in *Gt. Br., H. C., Sess. Pap.*, 1831–32, XX (381), p. 660.

[7] The prices ranged from 112s.–136s. in 1823; from 73s.–114s. in 1824; from 65s.–103s. in 1825; from 66s.–104s. in 1826; from 58s.–105s. in 1827; from

of from about 5–8d. per pound except during a short period of speculation in 1825.[1] To make a bad situation worse, a financial panic
sweeping Great Britain in that year involved many West India houses
and brought ruin to large numbers of proprietors on whose accounts
consignments had been received.[2]

Such diminishing returns, progressively increasing the Caribbean
residents' distress, plunged them into the depths of despair, and resulted in a general stagnation of life in the colonies. A greater part
of each successive season's crop was engrossed by British mortgage
holders. Commerce in Antigua languished.[3] The clergy of Nevis,
paid 18,000 pounds of sugar per parish annually under an act of
1705, found their money incomes reduced to a fourth of what they
had been in the period of prosperity.[4] Magnificent great houses, falling into ruin the length and breadth of Jamaica and in St. Vincent,
bore mute testimony to the passing of the old-time opulence.[5] Death
by starvation appeared among the miserable salt-rakers of Anguilla.[6]
Entire rows of homes in the port of Roseau stood closed and de-
serted, while grass grew luxuriantly between the cobble-stones of its
once bustling streets.[7]

The population of Road Town, Tortola, dropped from 200 to a
fraction of that number within four years as a result of emigration.
Many estates were thrown out of cultivation because of the shortage
of slaves; thus, the owner of ten properties in the Virgins found it
impossible to cultivate more than half of them.[8] The governor of St.
Lucia, making a tour of the island, found the sugar works and
planters' homes dilapidated and the negroes scantily clad in conse-

48s.–88s. in 1828; from 50s.–88s. in 1829; from 42s.–83s. in 1830; from 46s.–
84s. in 1831; and from 88s.–100s. in 1832. Tooke, *History of Prices*, II, 399.

[1] The price in 1822 was from 5¾d.–11d. per pound; it was from 6¼d.–10¾d.
in 1823; from 7d.–10½d. in 1824; from 6d.–19½d. in 1825; from 5¼d.–8¾d.
in 1826; from 4⅛d.–7¾d. in 1827; from 5d.–7⅜d. in 1828; from 4⅝d.–7d. in
1829; from 5⅜d.–7⅞d. in 1830; from 4¾d.–7¼d. in 1831; and from 5d.–8d.
in 1832. "Prices on Cotton . . . at Liverpool, 1793–1833," in *Gt. Br., H. C.,
Sess. Pap.*, 1847–48, IX (in 511), p. 393.

[2] Reed, *History of Sugar*, p. 151.

[3] Report on the state of the colony, in Sir Patrick Ross to Earl Bathurst,
May 4, 1827, C. O. 7/19.

[4] Memorial of the clergy of Nevis in Governor Nicolay to Viscount Goderich, Feb. 26, 1832, C. O. 239/29.

[5] Wentworth, *West India Sketch Book*, II, 69, 70, 320. Madden, *A Twelvemonth's Residence*, I, 154.

[6] Governor Nickle to Viscount Goderich, Sept. 3, 1832 and enclosures, C. O.
239/30.

[7] Coleridge, *Six Months*, pp. 137, 138.

[8] Wentworth, *West India Sketch Book*, I, 170, 192.

quence of their masters' being unable to provide them with new garments.[1] The far-famed planter banquets with their prodigality of food and drink were but a dim memory of the past.[2]

The problem of procuring sufficient stores for the slaves became a pressing one.[3] While innumerable absentees, finding themselves hopelessly involved, now transferred their estates to their creditors, enough, in desperation, returned to the West Indies intent on saving what they could of their fortunes appreciably to elevate the tone of colonial society.[4] A general spirit of despondency prevailed among all classes of resident whites.[5] Writing about 1830, Charles Shephard, a legal officer of St. Vincent and historian of the colony, declared mournfully "the pressure of the times is severe, the future prospects are gloomy, the days of West Indian prosperity are probably terminated. . . ."[6]

In 1827, the most violent hurricane of half a century wrought terrible destruction in the Leewards [7] and another of August, 1831, one of the greatest in Caribbean history, laid St. Lucia, St. Vincent, and Barbados waste and resulted in a death toll of some 2,500 persons and injuries to twice as many more in the last colony alone.[8] These cataclysms found the planters of the regions affected in such a weakened state that although lumber, fish, and other provisions were given free entry after the second storm and parliament then authorized a loan of £500,000 to the island governments and proprietors,[9] many

[1] Governor Stewart to Sir George Murray, Sept 29, 1829, C. O. 253/26.

[2] Mrs. A. C. Carmichael, *Domestic Manners and Social Condition of the White, Coloured, and Negro Population of the West Indies* (2 vols., London, 1833), I, 41, 42.

[3] *Min. W. I. Plant. and Mer.*, June 9, 1830.

[4] Alexander, *Transatlantic Sketches*, I, 246–248.

[5] *Ibid.*, I, 288.

[6] In his *St. Vincent*, p. 211.

[7] C. O. 239/16.

[8] C. O. 28/107. C. O. 253/29, 30. C. O. 260/48. Anon., "Editor of the West Indian," *Account of the Fatal Hurricane by Which Barbados Suffered in August, 1831* (Bridgetown, 1831). *Recapitulation of the Number of Persons— Killed, Wounded, those who have died of Wounds, and those Missing in consequence of the Hurricane of August, 1831* [Bridgetown, n.d.]. *Dreadful Hurricane at Barbados, on Thursday, August 11, 1831* (St. John's, Antigua, 1831). Mary Browne, ed., "The Hurricane of 1831 in St. Vincent: by an Eyewitness," in *Timehri*, V, 54–78. "Despatches addressed to the Secretary of State by the Governors of Barbados, St. Vincent, and St. Lucia, and Extract Letter from the Bishop of Barbados, relating to the Hurricanes in the West Indies," in *Gt. Br., H. C., Sess. Pap.*, 1831–32, XXXI (197), p. 369.

[9] 1 and 2 William IV c. 46, continued by 2 and 3 William IV c. 36, opened the ports and 2 and 3 William IV c. 125 authorized the loans. By August, 1833, £38,400 had been advanced to 12 St. Vincent proprietors, while 22 ad-

of the latter were obliged to abandon their estates because of being unable to repair the damage done.[1]

Land depreciation continued apace. Thus, a plantation in St. Elizabeth's parish, Jamaica, for which £5,000 currency had been refused in 1824, was sold at a third that figure five years later. Another nearby, worth £64,000 currency in 1817, could not be disposed of at open sale locally or by London auction in 1830. During the latter year, a property near Kingston was purchased for £8,000 currency, one-fifth of its former value. A home in Montego Bay, bought for £2,000 in 1821, realized but £400 upon changing hands a decade later.[2] This general fall in values materially increased the difficulty of securing credit during the periods of great economic pressure following the hurricanes.[3]

Discussion of the West India question—what had occasioned the crisis in the sugar colonies and how it might be met—was widespread throughout the late 1820's and early thirties. Pamphlets galore on the subject appeared and the topic became a favorite one in contemporary reviews.[4] Its culminating features were a careful study of the situation by the Board of Trade in 1830[5] and two parliamentary inquiries undertaken during the sessions of 1831[6] and 1831–1832 respectively.[7]

British Caribbean distress was variously attributed to the extension of cultivation in tropical areas under foreign dominion, above all in Cuba and Brazil, where the soil was rich and the labor supply ample

ditional applications from there for £76,700 as well as 52 from Barbados for £109,250 and 22 from St. Lucia for £20,200 were then under consideration. *Gt. Br., H. C., Sess. Pap.,* 1833, XXVI (736), p. 423. See also William H. Coleridge, *A Letter Addressed to His Excellency Major-General Sir Lionel Smith, K. C. B., &c. &c. &c. Relative to the Distribution of the Parliamentary Grant for the Relief of the Sufferers from the Hurricane of August 11, 1831* (Barbados, 1833).

[1] Governor Hill to Lord Goderich, Sept. 28, 1831, C. O. 260/48.

[2] Anon., "A Retired Military Officer," *Jamaica as it was, as it is, and as it May Be* (London, 1835), pp. 97, 98.

[3] Petition of Council and Assembly of St. Kitts to the King and Parliament, enclosed in President Rawlins to Lord Goderich, Sept. 6, 1827, C. O. 239/16.

[4] See the pamphlets and articles referred to below.

[5] "Statements, Calculations, and Explanations Submitted to the Board of Trade, Relating to the Commercial, Financial, and Political State of the British West India Colonies . . .," in *Gt. Br., H. C., Sess. Pap.,* 1830–31, IX (120), p. 483.

[6] "Report from the Select Committee on the expediency of admitting the use of Molasses in Breweries and Distilleries," in *Gt. Br., H. C., Sess Pap.,* 1831, VII (109, 297).

[7] "Report from the Select Committee on the Commercial State of the West India Colonies," in *Gt. Br., H. C., Sess. Pap.,* 1831–32, XX (381), p. 657.

and cheap because of the slave trade being continued in them;[1] to
overproduction in Great Britain's American possessions;[2] to the
existence of a world surplus;[3] to the admission of alien muscovado
intended for exportation after manufacture into British refineries at
the West Indian rate of duty;[4] to competition of the produce of the
new fresh land colonies acquired in 1802 and 1814;[5] to the admission
of oriental sugar and especially that from Mauritius into the United
Kingdom;[6] to the high charges laid against colonial products entering the home market;[7] to discriminatory duties in countries on the
European mainland;[8] to the lack of free commercial relations with
America;[9] to burdensome trade regulations which increased the
British growers' freight costs as much as 32s. per ton over those
borne by persons of other nationality using their countries' bottoms,
which otherwise raised the cost of marketing, and which effectively
prevented the entry of foreign supplies through the levying of high
impost taxes on them;[10] to restrictions on refining operations in the

[1] [Charles Coles], *Practical Observations on the British West India Sugar
Trade* (London, 1822). Clarke, *Some Considerations*, p. 9. Anon., "A West
Indian Proprietor," *Some Considerations on the Present State of Our West
India Colonies, and on the Regulations Which Influence Their Industry and
Trade* (London, 1830), pp. 7–9. Anon., *A Short Review of Leading and
Operating Causes of the Distress of the British West India Colonies . . .*
(London, 1832), pp. 2, 14–18. "The Colonies," in *Fraser's Mag.*, Nov., 1832,
pp. 437 ff. *Min. W. I. Mer.*, July 4, 1831. "Statements. Calculations, etc.," in
Gt. Br., H. C., Sess. Pap., 1830–31, IX (120), pp. 512, 518–21, 540, 560. "Re-
port from the Select Committee," in *Gt. Br., H. C., Sess. Pap.*, 1831–32, XX
(381), p. 661.

[2] Charles Coles, *To George Hibbert, Esq. Agent for Jamaica, and the other
Agents for the British West India Colonies* (London, 1824).

[3] "East and West India Sugar," in *The Ed. Rev.*, Feb., 1823, pp. 210, 211.
"Colonial Policy—West Indian Distress," in *ibid.*, Dec., 1831, p. 333.

[4] M'Donnell, *An Examination*. Anon., *A Short Review of Leading and
Operating Causes*, p. 3.

[5] [R. Wilmot Horton], *The West India Question Practically Considered*
(London, 1826), p. 3. Anon., *A Short Review of Leading and Operating
Causes*, p. 2. *Min. W. I. Mer.*, July 4, 1831. Clarke, *Some Considerations*, p. 9.

[6] *Min. W. I. Mer.*, July 4, 1831. Clarke, *Some Considerations*, pp. 9, 10.

[7] *Addresses and Memorials to His Majesty, from the House of Assembly
at Jamaica, Voted in the Years 1821 to 1826*, memorials of 1825, 1826, pp.
22–27, 28–39.

[8] "Statements, Calculations, etc.," in *Gt. Br., H. C., Sess. Pap.*, 1830–31, IX
(120), pp. 495–497.

[9] *Ibid.*, pp. 497–506, 542, 543, 548–550. Clarke, *Some Considerations*, p. 10;
"Report from the Select Committee on the Commercial State of the West
India Colonies," in *Gt. Br., H. C., Sess. Pap.*, 1831–32, XX (381), p. 662.

[10] Anon., *Some Considerations on the Present State of Our West India
Colonies*, pp. 14–19. "Statements, Calculations, etc.," in *Gt. Br., H. C., Sess.
Pap.*, 1830–31, IX (120), pp. 553, 554. "Report from the Select Committee on

colonies;[1] to the abolition of the slave trade and the forced adoption of ameliorative measures[2] which materially raised production costs;[3] to contemporary attacks on the existing labor régime[4] which shook confidence in the value of plantation properties;[5] to the decrease in white population in the old sugar colonies;[6] to the mortgage system which bound the planters to marketing through their creditors;[7] and to the tropical American colonists being thrown upon their own resources after two centuries of petting and pampering which had created an artificial state of prosperity.[8]

Proposed relief measures were many and varied according to the causes of prevailing difficulties as seen by different individuals. It was urged that production be severely restricted;[9] that the use of sugar and molasses in distilleries and breweries be made either optional or compulsory;[10] that homeland import duties be lowered and that the rates on West Indian rum and British spirits be equalized;[11]

the Commercial State of the West India Colonies," in *Gt. Br., H. C., Sess. Pap.*, 1831–32, XX (381), p. 662.

[1] "Statements, Calculations, etc.," in *Gt. Br., H. C., Sess. Pap.*, 1830–31, IX (120), p. 553.

[2] See Chapter XII.

[3] "Report from the Select Committee on the Commercial State of the West India Colonies," in *Gt. Br., H. C., Sess. Pap.*, 1831–32, XX (381). pp. 661, 662.

[4] See Chapters XI and XII.

[5] James M'Queen, "The British Colonies. Letters to His Grace the Duke of Wellington, &c. &c. &c.," in *Blackwood's Magazine,* June, 1828, pp. 891 ff.; "Report from the Select Committee on the Commercial State of the West India Colonies," in *Gt. Br., H. C., Sess. Pap.*, 1831–32, XX (381), p. 677.

[6] Governor Ross to Earl Bathurst, Dec. 19, 1826, C. O. 7/15.

[7] "Report from the Select Committee on the Commercial State of the West India Colonies," in *Gt. Br., H. C., Sess. Pap.*, 1831–32, XX (381), p. 674. [James Cropper?], *A Review of the Report of a Select Committee of the House of Commons on the State of the West India Colonies* . . . (Liverpool, 1833).

[8] Anon., *Pauperism on a Great Scale, or the Case of the West India Planters* (London, n.d.).

[9] "East and West India Sugar," in *The Ed. Rev.,* Feb., 1823, pp. 211, 212; Coles, *To George Hibbert.*

[10] *Min. W. I. Mer.,* March 23, 1824; *Min. W. I. Plant. and Mer.,* Oct. 22, 1824, March 12, 1827. "The West India Question," in *The Quar. Rev.,* April, 1831, p. 240. *Application to My Lords Commissioners of His Majesty's Treasury, to Permit the use of Sugar and Molasses in the Breweries and Distilleries, 18th March, 1831* (no imprint, 1831).

[11] Samuel Turner, *A Letter to Charles Ross Ellis, Chairman of the Standing Committee of the West India Planters and Merchants* . . . (London, 1825). Alexander Mundell, *Reasons for a Revision of Our Fiscal Code* (London, 1828). *Addresses and Memorials to His Majesty, from the House of Assembly at Jamaica, Voted in the Years 1821 to 1826 Inclusive,* sessions of 1825 and 1826, pp. 22–39. Anon., *Observations on the Pressure of the Existing*

that a higher discriminatory tax be laid against eastern muscovado;[1] that exportation be stimulated through the granting of a drawback and higher bounties on sugar;[2] that more favorable terms be secured for the admission of colonial Caribbean produce abroad by agreement with other governments;[3] that the ministry seek to secure a general abolition of the slave trade and thus more nearly equalize the laboring conditions in the British and foreign plantations;[4] that the conquered colonies be restored to their old mother countries upon the latter's agreeing to adopt abolition;[5] that provision be made for extensive private or public loans ranging from £5,000,000[6] to £15,000,000[7] on the security of Caribbean plantations; that an understanding be reached with the United States so as to free the American-West Indian trade of restrictions;[8] that the proprietors be given permission to refine sugar on their own estates;[9] and that the cost of production be lowered through discontinuing the use of forced la-

Duties on Sugar & Rum (no imprint, 1830). Anon., ed., *Debate Upon the Sugar Duties; in the House of Commons, on Monday, 14th of June, 1830* (London, 1830). John Innes, *A Letter to the Rt. Hon. Henry Goulburn, M.P. Chancellor of the Exchequer, &c. &c. &c. . . . on the Claims of the West India Distiller to an Equalization of the Duties on Rum and British Spirits* (London, 1830). Alexander M'Donnell, *Rum and British Spirit Duties* (London, 1830). Anon., *Some Considerations on the Present State of Our West India Colonies,* p. 23. "The West India Question," in *The Quar. Rev.,* April, 1831, p. 238. "Colonial Policy—West Indian Distress," in *The Ed. Rev.,* Dec., 1831, pp. 346–348. Anon., *A Short Review of Leading and Operating Causes of the Distress of the British West India Colonies,* pp. 21, 22, 26.

[1] Clarke, *Some Considerations,* p. 12.

[2] Clarke, *Some Considerations,* p. 12. Coles, *Practical Observations.* Anon., *A Short Review of Leading and Operating Causes of the Distress of the British West India Colonies,* pp. 27, 28.

[3] "The West India Question," in *The Quar. Rev.,* April, 1831, p. 241.

[4] Anon., *Some Considerations on the Present State of Our West India Colonies,* p. 27. "The West India Question," in *The Quar. Rev.,* April, 1831, p. 243. "Statements, Calculations, etc.," in *Gt. Br., H. C., Sess. Pap.,* 1830–31, IX (120), p. 568.

[5] Anon., "A West Indian Proprietor," *Brief Observations on the West India Question in the Quarterly Review for April, 1831; With Remarks on the Continuation of the Slave Trade by the Subjects of Other Nations; With the Most Effectual and Just Mode of Inducing Them to Consent to Its Total Abandonment . . .* (London, 1831).

[6] *Min. W. I. Mer.,* June 9 and 27, 1823. *Min. W. I. Plant. and Mer.,* May 24, 1824.

[7] Cropper, *Another Bonus to the Planters.*

[8] *Min. W. I. Mer.,* April 15, 1825. "The West India Question," in *The Quar. Rev.,* April, 1831, p. 242. "Colonial Policy—West Indian Distress," in *The Ed. Rev.,* Dec. 1831, pp. 335–346.

[9] John Galt, "Means of Lessening the West Indian Distress," in *Fraser's Mag.,* April, 1831, pp. 346 ff.

bor and putting an end to absenteeism and antiquated agricultural methods.[1]

A committee of parliament, named to consider the advisability of permitting the use of molasses in the manufacture of beer and whiskey, reporting in 1831, expressed doubt as to whether appreciable assistance would be afforded the West Indians by the adoption of such a measure and opposed it in the interests of British agriculturists, the brewers, the distillers, and the public revenue.[2]

But when a second body, instructed to study the commercial state of the Caribbean colonies and bringing a thorough examination of the planters' position within the scope of its inquiry, presented its findings the following session, it declared the exclusion of this common sugar estate by-product from breweries and distilleries within the United Kingdom to be highly objectionable in principle and recommended a reversal of policy.

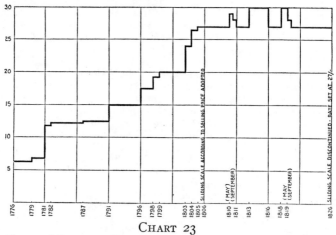

CHART 23

Rates of Duty per Hundredweight on British West Indian Muscovado Sugar Entered into Great Britain for Home Consumption, 1776–1826 *

* Based on *Great Britain, House of Commons, Sessional Papers,* 1826, XXII (328).

[1] "Colonial Policy—West Indian Distress," in *The Ed. Rev.,* Dec., 1831, p. 334. Cropper, *Relief for West Indian Distress.* Cropper, *A Review of the Report of a Select Committee.* Cropper, *The Support of Slavery Investigated* (London, 1824).

[2] "Report from the Select Committee on the Expediency of admitting the use of molasses in breweries and distilleries," in *Gt. Br., H. C., Sess. Pap.,* 1831, VII (109, 297).

At the same time, this group of legislators urged that encouragement be given the refining of sugar beyond the Atlantic and advocated a lowering of duties on tropical American produce, graduation of the sugar tax according to the quality of the product, and a liberal consideration of the question of the discriminating rate against rum in favor of British spirits. It furthermore observed that abolition of the 4½ per cent export duty in force in Barbados and the Leeward Islands [1] would give material relief there, suggested that the foreign office open negotiations with Austria and Russia to secure an adjustment of disadvantageous tariff charges in force there, stressed the fact that allowing a drawback and revising the schedule of bounties would unnaturally stimulate exportation and should not therefore be entertained, and favored the House of Commons giving serious attention to the matter of loaning public money to embarrassed proprietors.[2]

In 1824, the West Indians of London, finding it impossible to secure an advance of £5,000,000 in exchequer bills from the government against Caribbean property,[3] proposed that a corporation with a capital of four million, to make such loans, be established.[4] The ministry declined to sponsor the measure [5] but it was pushed independently. Despite active opposition on the part of the emancipationists who held that such an enterprise would result in the mortgaging of human beings [6] and adversely affect the entire slave population,[7] a bill authorizing the formation of a West India Company along these lines became law in the summer of 1825.[8]

It was immediately organized with a capital of £2,000,000, only half the amount originally intended, 20,000 shares of £100 each being offered to the public at large. William Manning was named chairman, George Hibbert deputy, and prominant members of the planter-merchant group, including Charles Bosanquet and Charles N. Pallmer, became directors.[9] But the concern's resources proved

[1] See pages 104 ff. and 127 ff.

[2] "Report from the Select Committee on the Commercial State of the West India Colonies," in *Gt. Br., H. C., Sess. Pap.,* 1831–32, XX, pp. 667–676.

[3] See page 354.

[4] *Min. W. I. Plant. and Mer.,* May 24, 1824.

[5] *Ibid.,* May 29, 1824.

[6] *Parliamentary Debates,* 2nd series, XII, cols. 1278, 1279.

[7] Anon., *Observations on the West India-Company Bill* . . . (London, 1825).

[8] 6 Geo. IV c. cxcvii (private act). See *Journals of the House of Commons,* LXXX, pp. 419, 623, 627.

[9] [Announcement of the formation of the] West India Company [London, 1825].

wholly inadequate to meet colonial needs and, while individuals here and there profited by its operations, general conditions were in no way improved.

The government did accede to the demand for more favorable duties. The rate on colonial Caribbean coffee entering the United Kingdom was reduced from 1s. per hundredweight to 6d. in 1825.[1] The customs and excise payable on rum, which had amounted to six times its price on entry and to ten times the growers' net return,[2] was lowered from 12s. 7⅕d. to 8s. 6d. the year after.[3] In 1830, the charge on West Indian muscovado was cut from 27s. per hundredweight (a sum about equal to its value upon importation)[4] to 24s.[5]

But this revision of the tariff fell far short of expectations and was not followed by the benefits which had been anticipated. For example, although the home consumption of coffee trebled within a few years, this in no way offset the attending decrease in exports.[6] Furthermore, British spirits continued to enjoy protection against plantation rum and this, with the admission of Mauritian muscovado into the home market at the Caribbean rate[7] and the granting in 1830 of a greater relative reduction on East Indian sugar than West Indian[8] precluded the possibility of material relief being afforded by the adoption of the new schedule.

The substitution of English for French commercial law in St. Lucia, the registration of mortgages and titles there, and passage of a law permitting the seizure and sale of immovable property for the recovery of debt were designed to ease credit locally. These reforms did not, however, become entirely operative until 1833, and the prompt recording of 2000 old real estate loans totalling £1,125,000 sterling[9] gave ample evidence of the hopelessness of the proprietors'

[1] "Rates of Duty on Coffee . . . , 1792–1829," in *Gt. Br., H. C., Sess. Pap.,* 1830, XXV (466).

[2] *Min. W. I. Mer.,* Nov. 27, 1823.

[3] "Rum Admitted Into the United Kingdom for Home Consumption, 1800–1829," in *Gt. Br., H. C., Sess. Pap.,* 1830, XXII (375).

[4] Weekly returns in *The London Gazette.*

[5] 11 Geo. IV and 1 Wm. IV c. 50.

[6] 21,501,966 lbs. of British plantation coffee were retained for home consumption in 1831 as against 7,947,890 lbs. in 1824, but exports were only 2,139,-392 lbs. as compared with 24,824,778 lbs. seven years before. "Imports Into, Exports From and Home Consumption of British West Indian Coffee In the United Kingdom, 1814–1834," in *Gt. Br., H. C., Sess. Pap.,* 1831–32, XX (in 381).

[7] See page 367.

[8] See page 369.

[9] Breen, *St. Lucia,* pp. 281–284. These reforms were instituted by a body of English judges forming a royal court. References to the difficulties they ex-

attempting to secure further advances against estates in that colony.

Although the American trade was finally freed of restrictions in 1830, this was too late to be of marked advantage. With the failure of these several measures to improve the situation of the West Indians, emancipation, adopted when their fortunes were at lowest ebb, struck the final, mortal blow at the old plantation system and completed in spectacular fashion the downfall of the planter class.

perienced will be found in a work by the chief justice of the court, John Jeremie, *Four Essays on Colonial Slavery* (London, 1832); Anon., "An Inhabitant of St. Lucia," *A Reply to Mr. Jeremie's Pamphlet* (London, 1832); and Anon., "An Inhabitant of That Island," *Remarks on Mr. Jeremie's Conduct as President of the Royal Court of St. Lucia* (London, 1832). See also *An Ordinance Defining the Powers and Duties of the First President of the Royal Court or Court of Appeal* [Castries, 1825]; *A Provisional Ordinance Regulating the Sale of Slaves Attached to Estates Under Mortgage* [Castries, 1825]; *An Ordinance by Which all Stock Attached to, or Employed on an Estate are Declared to be Immoveable Property, and Only Seizable with the Plantation* [Castries, 1827] and *Rules and Regulations for the Assessors of the Royal Court of This Island* . . . [Castries, 1833].

CHAPTER XI

THE REGISTRATION CONTROVERSY [1]

Throughout the two-decade-long struggle to end the British slave trade, its supporters had repeatedly charged the abolitionists with secretly aiming to free the Caribbean negroes and with viewing any closing of the traffic in blacks as a mere first step in such a direction.

This had in all sincerity been as often denied, yet, so closely related were the importation of Africans and slavery itself that attacks on the one inevitably led to a challenging of the other. And, since basic arguments adduced against the trade were even more applicable to the prevailing system of forced labor supporting it, nothing was more natural than that the exponents of abolition, becoming thoroughly familiar with the negro problem, should turn their attention to the greater question of emancipation immediately after bringing the initial contest to a successful conclusion.

The African Institution, which was destined to play a leading rôle in the new crusade, was founded in the spring of 1807, only three weeks after the royal assent had been secured for the long-desired act outlawing the trade.[2] Officials of the organization disclaimed any intention of engaging in missionary enterprise or commercial speculations. They announced that, instead, they would concern themselves with watching over the execution of the abolition measures recently enacted in Great Britain, the United States, and Denmark,[3] with endeavoring to prevent their infraction, with suggesting means by which they might be rendered more effectual, with seeking to secure adoption of this reform by other powers, and with promoting the civilization of Africa.

The latter object was to be accomplished by collecting accurate

[1] For a discussion of this subject from the constitutional point of view, see an article by Robert Schuyler, "The Controversy Over the Slave Registry Bill of 1815," in the *Political Science Quarterly*, March, 1925, published after this chapter had been written.

[2] See page 276.

[3] Denmark was the first European power to abolish the slave trade. This was done by a royal order of May 16, 1792, bringing the traffic to an end at the close of 1802. The importation of slaves into the United States after January 1, 1808 was forbidden by act of Congress of March, 1807.

information on the natives as well as on the agricultural and commercial possibilities of the continent and diffusing this in Great Britain, by educating the negroes and cultivating friendly relations with them, by facilitating their entry into legitimate branches of commerce, by introducing such useful arts of Europe as were suited to their condition, by encouraging cultivation of the soil and furnishing the blacks with seeds and tools, by giving them the benefits of recent medical discoveries, and by making a study of their languages and reducing these to writing.[1]

The society enjoyed the Duke of Gloucester's patronage and such substantial personages as the Bishops of London, Durham and Bath and Wells, George Canning, Sir Samuel Romilly,[2] Zachary Macaulay, Henry Brougham, Thomas Clarkson, William Huskisson, Thomas Babington,[3] William Pitt, William Roscoe,[4] Granville Sharp, William Wilberforce, James Stephen, and Thomas Gisborne [5] served on its executive committee. Thus sponsored, it promptly won the support of liberal opinion [6] and was accorded generous financial aid by the foremost families of the day.[7]

Publicity was freely given information on the peoples and resources of Africa which came to the Institution's attention.[8] A noteworthy effort along this line was the publication in 1815 of the long-lost

---

[1] *Report of the Committee of the African Institution Read at the General Meeting on the 15th July, 1807. Together With the Rules and Regulations Which Were Then Adopted for the Government of the Society* (London, 1807).

[2] The well-known law reformer.

[3] Brother-in-law of Zachary Macaulay and uncle of his namesake, Thomas Babington Macaulay.

[4] The Liverpool historian and author of the following abolitionist tracts— *A General View of the African Slave Trade* . . . (London, 1788), *The Wrongs of Africa* (London 1788), and *The Present Age* [Liverpool, n.d.]. See Jean Trepp, "The Liverpool Movement for the Abolition of the English Slave Trade," in *Jour. Negro Hist.*, July, 1928, pp. 265 ff.

[5] The English divine, son-in-law of Thomas Babington and author of *On Slavery and the Slave Trade* (London, 1792), *Remarks on the Late Decision of the House of Commons Respecting the Abolition of the Slave Trade* London, 1792), and The Principles of Moral Philosophy Investigated . . . (London, 1798).

[6] See for example, "Three Reports of the Directors of the African Institution," in *The Ed. Rev.*, Jan., 1810, pp. 485–503; "Fourth Report . . . ," in *ibid.*, Aug., 1810, pp. 430–447; "Fifth Report . . . ," in *ibid.*, Aug., 1811, pp. 305–325; "Sixth Report . . . ," in *ibid.*, July, 1812, pp. 58–79; "Reflections on the Sixth Report of the Directors of the African Institution," in *The Eur. Mag. and Lond. Rev.*, Oct., 1812, pp. 273 ff.

[7] Annual reports, as [*First*] *Report of the Directors of the African Institution* . . . , *July 15, 1807* (London, 1811); *Sixth Report* . . . , *25 March, 1812* (London, 1812); *Fifteenth Report* . . . , *28 March, 1821* (London, 1821), etc.

[8] See the first reports.

journal of Mungo Park's [1] fateful second expedition into the Niger basin which fell into the Colonial Secretary's hands and was offered to this organization by him.[2]

But it was soon found that efforts to civilize the natives were unavailing because of the continuance of the slave trade by foreign nations. With the rapid development of Spain's and Portugal's new world possessions in the post-Napoleonic period,[3] the number of negroes cleared out from Africa rose from an annual average of 85,000 during 1805–1810 to 106,000 between 1815–1819, some 6,000 more than the total number exported in 1788 when British demand had been unabated.[4]

Primary attention was therefore paid to the body's other avowed aims, the suppression of illicit negro traffic in the British Caribbean and propaganda in behalf of international abolition.[5] Though undergoing no formal change of name, the African Institution was in reality transformed into a general anti-slave-trading society.[6] Largely in consequence of agitation carried on by it, a bill declaring any of His Majesty's subjects participating in the slave trade to be guilty of felony, presented to parliament by Henry Brougham,[7] himself an active member, was passed in 1811.[8]

[1] See page 254.

[2] *The Journal of a Mission to the Interior of Africa, in the Year 1805; Eighth Report . . . , 23 March, 1814* (London, 1814), p. 20. By a strange coincidence, a leader of the West India group and former opponents of that body on the question of abolition at different times aided in the publication of Park's travel accounts. That covering the first expedition, *Travels in the Interior Districts of Africa . . . in the Years 1795, 1796, and 1797 . . ., was* brought out by the African Association under the presidency and with the editorial assistance of Bryan Edwards. Macaulay, Wilberforce, and Clarkson were prominent members of the Institution when it undertook the publication of the journal of the 1805 expedition; E. Wishaw, author of the life of Park prefixed to the latter, acknowledges his indebtedness to Macaulay (preface).

[3] See pages 337 ff.

[4] *Gt. Br., H. C., Sess. Pap.,* 1847–48, XXII (623), p. 707.

[5] See for example "Foreign Slave Trade. Abstract of the Information Recently Laid on the Table of the House of Commons on the Subject of the Slave Trade; Being a Report Made by a Committee Specially Appointed for the Purpose, to the Directors of the African Institution," supplement to *Fifteenth Report . . . , 28 March, 1821* (London, 1821).

[6] George Stephen, *Antislavery Recollections* (London, 1854), pp. 4, 5.

[7] See the autobiography, *The Life and Times of Henry Lord Brougham* (3 vols., Edinburgh, 1871). Brougham, ed., *Speeches on Social and Political Subjects, With Historical Introductions* (2 vols., London, 1857). John Campbell, *Lives of Lord Lyndhurst and Lord Brougham . . .* (London, 1869).

[8] 51 Geo. III c. 23. For the first trials under this act, see Anon., *The Trials of the Slave-Traders, Samuel Samo, Joseph Peters, and William Tufft, Tried*

Representatives of the planter interest, while arguing against suppression of the trade, had held that it would be utterly impossible for the British government to prevent the entry of blacks into the West India colonies. A committee of the Jamaican assembly had similarly declared in 1792: "Can there be a doubt that every effort will be made to smuggle slaves? Will not a man face every danger to save himself and his family from ruin? The island abounds with creeks and bays, where small-decked vessels may run in at any time; and, in order to prevent smuggling, a very considerable naval force must be stationed here, at an enormous expense. These ships of war must keep the sea during the hurricane months: But, if this duty is to be left to the custom-house officers, unless they are supported by a military force, not one of them will be able to do their [sic] duty but at the risk of life; and such will be the discontents of the people, from so severe a measure as an abolition of the slave-trade, that the committee have reason to apprehend, that even a military force would prove ineffectual." [1]

In reality, however, the number of cases involving breaches of the abolition law which came to the Caribbean governors' attention in the decade after 1807 was surprisingly small and such violations as did occur were by no means always deliberate. Thus, while four slaves from Martinique and six from St. Vincent reached Trinidad clandestinely in 1814 and were apprehended,[2] as were four from Guadeloupe five years later,[3] mere technical infringements of the act occurred following the outbreak of revolution on the Spanish Main when refugees sought protection in the island and brought their negroes with them. These were forfeited to the Crown on instructions from the home government [4] but such action was clearly based upon a strict construction of the law, dictated by political expediency, rather than on wilful infractions of it.

The case of a Barbadian vessel, the *Monmouth,* seized while becalmed in Chaguaramas Bay, Trinidad, and condemned for having on board two negro boys given the captain and mate by the commander of a Spanish slaver encountered by them some time before,[5]

in April and June, 1812, Before the Hon. Robert Thorpe, LL.D., Chief Justice of Sierra Leone . . . (London, 1813) and "The Trials of the Slave-Traders," in *The Ed. Rev.,* Feb., 1813, pp. 72–93.

[1] *Proceedings of the Hon. House of Assembly of Jamaica, on the Sugar and Slave-Trade, in a Session Which Began the 23d of October, 1792,* p. 13.

[2] Governor Woodford to Earl Bathurst, March 18, 1814, C. O. 295/32.

[3] Governor Woodford to Earl Bathurst, Aug. 31, 1819, C. O. 295/48.

[4] Governor Woodford to Earl Bathurst, July 14, 1814, C. O. 295/33.

[5] Governor Woodford to Earl Bathurst. Feb. 10, 1817, C. O. 295/43.

more clearly fell within the spirit of the reform measure, though here, too, there had apparently been no intention of effecting an illegal landing.

One Brodbelt, a comptroller in Nevis communicating with Wilberforce in the fall of 1814, declared that from forty to fifty blacks had been smuggled into the colony shortly before, that his cousin in the revenue service had a list of forty persons including the local chief justice who had purchased them, that other cases of illicit dealing were rumored, that Mr. Gordon, the customs collector, was a party to such operations and that he uttered dire threats against all who might be inclined to give information on the subject.[1] These sensational allegations appear to have been barren of results.

A year later, when a planter in the same colony was brought to trial on the charge of having purchased a free black, Charles Hamilton, in St. Bartholomew and having introduced him on his own estate, Governor Leith found it well-nigh impossible to secure data on the case and the defendant was acquitted.[2]

In 1818, President Herbert of Montserrat suffered suspension from office because of having placed a thievish slave, Tom Dexter, in the hands of a foreign ship master for sale in St. Croix, a fact reported to Acting-Governor Kerby of Antigua by the customs officer. Herbert defended his action on humanitarian grounds, maintaining that, under the local slave code, this culprit would have suffered the death penalty had he been haled before a court. To substantiate his sincerity of purpose, he demonstrated that the sale of Dexter would have netted him considerably less than the indemnification to which colonial law would have entitled him upon the black's conviction and execution,[3] and so effective was this argument that he was restored to the presidency shortly after.[4]

An actual case of illegal importation did, however, occur in Antigua in the same year. Two Spaniards landed a slave from the schooner *Alexandria* but were promptly arrested while their vessel was taken into custody.[5]

The Duke of Manchester, governor of Jamaica, declared in a despatch written during the summer of 1816 "I . . . express my con-

---

[1] In C. O. 152/104.
[2] Leith to Earl Bathurst, Nov. 10, 1815, C. O. 152/105.
[3] See papers in C. O. 7/4.
[4] See papers in C. O. 7/5.
[5] Acting-Governor Kerby to Earl Bathurst, Dec. 23, 1818 and enclosures, C. O. 7/4.

fident opinion and belief that not only no violation of the abolition Laws has taken place here, but there is no desire on the part of the Planters to increase the number of their Slaves by such means." [1]

Three years later, a vessel suffering from a shortage of water and provisions anchored in Rio Novo Bay and landed twenty-nine Africans who were as quickly seized. This slaver was subsequently condemned and sentences of transportation for seven and three years respectively were meted out to the master and mate. [2] In 1819, also, two former Jamaican bondsmen, one of whom had been deported for crime, arrived in the island from their new home, Cuba, accompanied by two recently imported Spanish blacks who had been persuaded to join them in their daring flight. All were immediately apprehended. [3] Clearly, a deliberate violation of the act of 1807 had occurred in only the first of these cases.

Notwithstanding this marked lack of evidence that illegal importations were being made, the abolitionists of Great Britain became obsessed with the conviction that such were actually taking place on a considerable scale and that they could be prevented only through compulsory registration of all slaves already in the Caribbean colonies. The movement to effect this was inaugurated early in 1812 by James Stephen, a director of the African Institution, who had headed the attack on the neutral American trade following the rupture of the peace of Amiens. [4] It won the hearty support of Wilberforce, Sir Samuel Romilly, and Lord Brougham, [5] and Spencer Perceval, the Prime Minister, was prevailed upon to establish it as an experiment in the crown colony of Trinidad.

This former Spanish possession and St. Lucia, Demerara, and Berbice, conquered from the French and Dutch, [6] had not been ac-

[1] To Earl Bathurst, Aug 17, 1816, C. O. 137/142.

[2] The Duke of Manchester to Earl Bathurst, June 24, July 10, Aug. 6, 1819, C. O. 137/148. See also "Trial for Violation of Abolition Laws," in *The Gent. Mag.*, Dec., 1819, pp. 518–520.

[3] Papers in the case will be found in C. O. 137/148.

[4] See pages 304 ff. His son, James Stephen, Jr., also a member of the African Institution, was named counsel of the colonial department by Lord Brougham in 1813 despite the vigorous opposition of the West India group. Thus began Sir James's remarkable career in that branch of the administration.

[5] See the accounts of a meeting held at Stephen's home on January 6, 1812, attended by them, at which registration was discussed, in Romilly, William, and brothers, editors, *Memoirs of the Life of Sir Samuel Romilly . . .* (3 vols., London, 1840), III, 1, and Wilberforce brothers, *Life of Wilberforce*, IV, 3.

[6] See pages 293 and 332.

corded representative government upon having been incorporated within the British empire because of containing bodies of foreigners sufficiently great to swamp the British element and seize control of local affairs.[1] They were, instead, administered directly in the king's name, which made possible the easy introduction of innovations.

Under an order in council of March 26, 1812, a system of slave registration was instituted for Trinidad with individual owners meeting expenses attending the listing of their hands through paying specified fees. This measure was later extended so as to make impossible the creation of a legal title to blacks unless they had been duly enrolled as prescribed by law.[2]

Census returns for 1811 had showed an official total of 21,288 slaves in the colony; the first registration in 1813, four and a half thousand more—25,717. This increase was seized upon by African Institution officials as proof that extensive smuggling had taken place and became the basis for a four-year-long struggle to establish compulsory registration in all the Caribbean possessions.

The lead was again taken by Stephen. In 1815, he prepared and submitted to the Society a report declaring that there was "abundant reason to conclude" that slaves had been imported into some, if not all, of the Caribbean colonies since the adoption of abolition, that direct information concerning illegal entries had, on several occasions, been received from respectable persons and that this "would suffice to remove all doubts of the existence of such offences, to some extent at least," were the Institution not honor-bound to treat communications confidentially.

He found decisive proof that violations of the act of 1807 were occurring in such condemnations of vessels with slaves on board as had been effected in the transatlantic possessions and in Trinidad's increased servile population. General registration was, according to him, an absolute necessity to give force to the abolition measure.

---

[1] See for example, Gov. Thomas Picton to the Secretary of State, June 28, 1802, C. O. 295/2 and Governor Hislop to Earl Liverpool, Jan. 3, 1811, C. O. 295/26.

[2] *Trinidad. Proclamation. By his Excellency William Monro, Esquire, Major General in His Majesty's Service, and administering the Government of the Island of Trinidad, &c. &c. &c.* [Port of Spain, 1812]. Dated 31 August. See also *Trinidad. By His Excellency Sir Ralph James Woodford, Bart. Governor and Commander in Chief in and over the said Island, and Vice Admiral of the same. A Proclamation* [Port of Spain, 1814]. Dated January 15th.

It would afford owners greater security in their property, facilitate the proving of title to given blacks, and safeguard creditors' interests. The local legislatures would never institute it of their own volition, hence the initiative must be taken by parliament, which, under the British constitution, enjoyed jurisdiction over the colonies and thus possessed full legal right to establish the regulation.[1] The report was promptly acted upon. A bill following the lines of the Trinidad order in council was drafted under the auspices of Institution members, and Mr. Wilberforce presented it to parliament in June of the same year.

Stephen's charges and the proposed foisting of registration upon them brought forth a stiff show of resistance from the West Indians at home and those in the Caribbean alike. The credence given vague allegations that smuggling was rife and the effort being made to secure the enactment of legislation inimical to their proprietary interests stirred them deeply. It was commonly felt that a further Wilberforce victory would but mark the initial step towards emancipation by act of the home government, and all forces were consequently marshalled to stave off catastrophe.

The Society of Planters and Merchants, meeting to consider the situation, held that registration imposed by act of parliament "would be destructive of the constitutional Rights and Interests of the Colonial Legislatures, destructive of the private Right and Interests of Individuals, and aim a deadly Blow at the whole Tenure of West India Property." [2]

The organization called upon the several representative bodies to declare their readiness to enforce abolition and, of their own accord, to devise means whereby illegal trade might be prevented. At the same time it counseled the legislators to consider whether, in deference to the prevailing sentiment in Great Britain, the passage of local registration acts might not be expedient, recommended that they refute the accusations with respect to illicit importations, and, above all, urged that they make vigorous protest against parliamentary interference in colonial affairs.[3]

Similarly, a series of resolutions denouncing the proposed measure was adopted at a general meeting of persons with tropical Amer-

---

[1] [James Stephen], *Reasons for Establishing a Registry of Slaves in the Colonies* . . . (London, 1815), pp. 22, 23, 26–28, 83, 84, 93–107.

[2] *Min. W. I. Plant. and Mer.*, June 13, 1815.

[3] *Ibid,* July 3, 1815.

ican interests held in the capital city.[1] The agents for Barbados [2] and
Grenada [3] sought to turn public opinion against it through the publication of pamphlets; while Charles N. Pallmer, representative for
Surrey in the House of Commons and an active member of the Society of Planters and Merchants, became spokesman of the opposition
in the lower chamber.[4]

Committees of the Tobagan legislature [5] and of the Jamaican assembly [6] denied that unlawful entries had taken place in their respective islands. The former charged the African Institution with
attempting to secure an inquisitorial control over the Caribbean possessions while the latter group, filing a dignified remonstrance, held
that so long as the colonists were unrepresented in parliament they
were entitled to a complete, free system of local government and that
the proposed levying of fees upon registration, as in Trinidad, constituted direct taxation and was therefore unconstitutional under the
act of 1778 [7] granting the inhabitants of overseas possessions exemption from all such charges save those on trade.[8] The Barbadian as-

[1] *Resolutions Passed At a General Meeting of West-India Planters & Merchants, &c., the 19th Day of January, 1816* (London, 1816).

[2] G. W. Jordan, *An Examination of the Principles of the Slave Registry
Bill and of the Means of Emancipation, Proposed by the Author of the Bill*
(London, 1816).

[3] [Joseph Marryat], *Thoughts on the Abolition of the Slave Trade, and
Civilization of Africa; With Remarks on the African Institution, and An
Examination of the Report of Their Committee, Recommending a General
Registry of Slaves in the British West India Islands* (London, 1816). Marryat,
*More Thoughts, Occasioned by Two Publications Which the Authors Call
"An Exposure of Some of the Numerous Misstatements and Misrepresenta-
tions Contained in a Pamphlet, Commonly Known by the Name of Mr.
Marryat's Pamphlet . . ." and "A Defence of the Bill for the Registration of
Slaves"* (London, 1816). Also his *More Thoughts Still on the State of the
West India Colonies, and the Proceedings of the African Institution . . .*
(London, 1818).

[4] See Pallmer, *Substance of the Speech . . . in the House of Commons,
June 19, 1816, on the Motion of Mr. Wilberforce, for Certain Papers,
Relating to the West Indies* (London, 1816) and West India Committee
records.

[5] *Report of the Joint Committee Appointed by the Board of Council, and
the House of General Assembly of Tobago, Upon the Subject of the Registry
Bill; Now pending in the Commons House of Parliament of Great Britain*
[Scarborough, 1816].

[6] *Further Proceedings of the Honourable House of Assembly of Jamaica,
Relative to a Bill Introduced Into the House of Commons, for Effectually
Preventing the Unlawful Importation of Slaves, and Holding Free Persons in
Slavery, in the British Colonies* (London, 1816).

[7] See page 164.

[8] Southey, *Chronological History*, III, 607–608.

sembly adopted this same view.[1] Likewise, the legislatures of St. Vincent,[2] Dominica,[3] Antigua,[4] and Nevis [5] joined in the general protest.

The question was thoroughly discussed during the course of 1816. Advocates of registration followed Mr. Stephen's lead in arguing that the Trinidad census and the condemnations of vessels already reported furnished ample evidence that violations of the abolition act were both frequent and extensive.[6] They declared that the want of more judicial convictions was no proof that the law was not being flagrantly violated, since whites alone could testify in colonial courts and it was obviously to their interest either not to do so or to perjure themselves.[7] Parliament, according to them, had never surrendered the right of legislating for the colonies; as for the measure being forced upon the planters should the bill be adopted, "the gentlemen of the West Indies are far better represented . . . [there] than nine-tenths of the British people." [8]

Its opponents maintained that the charges concerning illicit importations were wholly unfounded, challenged the African Institution to substantiate them with specific cases, explained that the population returns for 1811 had been based upon notoriously slipshod and inaccurate reports of plantation managers while those for 1813 rested upon formal registration, and stoutly maintained that passage of the bill would constitute an illegal interference in a purely local matter.[9]

---

[1] Schomburgk, *Barbados*, p. 394.

[2] Marryat, *Thoughts on the Abolition of the Slave Trade*, pp. 190 ff.

[3] *Journals of the House of Assembly*, Feb. 14, 1816, in C. O. 74/12.

[4] Papers in C. O. 9/47.

[5] *Journals of the House of Assembly*, April 4, 1816, C. O. 186/11.

[6] James Stephen, *A Defence of the Bill for the Registration of Slaves . . . In Letters to William Wilberforce, Esq. M.P. Letter the first* (London, 1816) and *Letter the second* (London, 1816). Anon., *An Exposure of Some of the Numerous Mistatements* [sic] *and Misrepresentations Contained in a Pamphlet Commonly Known by the Name of Mr. Marryat's Pamphlet, Entitled "Thoughts, etc."* (London, 1816). "On the Slave Trade, and the Registry Bill," in *The Gent. Mag.*, Sept., 1816, pp. 226, 227.

[7] Anon., *A Review of the Reasons Given for Establishing a Registry of Slaves in the British Colonies . . .* (London, n.d.).

[8] Anon., *Arguments in Support of the Proposed Bill for the Registration of Slaves in the West India Colonies . . .* (London, 1817).

[9] See Anon., *Brief Remarks on the Slave Registry Bill . . .* (London, 1816); Anon., "A Colonist," *"The Edinburgh Review" and the West Indies, with . . . Remarks on the Slave Registry Bill* (Glasgow, 1816); Anon., "A Zealous Advocate for the Abolition of the Slave Trade," *The Interference of the British Legislature in the Internal Concerns of the British West Islands, Respecting their Slaves, Deprecated* (London, 1816); Anon., "A Colonist," *A Letter to the Members of the Imperial Parliament, Referring to the Evidence Contained in the Proceedings of the House of Assembly of Jamaica, and*

At the height of the controversy, Stephen and his associates published a series of pamphlets containing excerpts from current works which served to illustrate the evils of Caribbean slavery, though this was in no way germane to the project under consideration.[1] The organized West Indians promptly brought out counter numbers showing it in its best light,[2] and the war of ink thus opened soon degenerated into low abuse on both sides and served merely to disgust serious seekers after truth.

Meanwhile, the Institution was attacked by a disgruntled individual, Robert Thorpe, formerly chief justice of Sierra Leone,[3]

shewing the Injurious and Unconstitutional Tendency of the Proposed Slave Registry Bill (London, 1816); Anon., "A British Planter," Negro Emancipation Made Easy; With Reflections on the African Institution, and the Slave Registry Bill (London, 1816); Anon., Observations on the Bill Introduced Last Session, by Mr. Wilberforce, for the More Effectually Preventing the Unlawful Importation of Slaves . . . (London, 1816); Anon., "An Hereditary Planter," Observations Upon the Oligarchy, or Committee of Soi-Disant Saints . . . (London, 1816); Anon., The Penal Enactments of the Slave Registry Bill Examined . . . (London, 1816); George Chalmers, Proofs and Demonstrations How Much the Projected Registry of Colonial Negroes is Unfounded and Uncalled for . . . (London, 1816); "Observations on the Slave Registry Bill," in The Gent. Mag., Aug. 1816, pp. 123–126; "Slave Registry Bill Unnecessary," in ibid., May 1816, pp. 390–392; Thomas Venables, The Reviewer Reviewed, or Some Cursory Observations Upon an Article in "The Christian Observer" for January 1816, Respecting the Slave Registry Bill . . . (London, 1816).

[1] The series bore the general title, West-Indian Sketches, Drawn from Authentic Sources. Typical ones were Anon., ed., Punishment of the Maroons of Demerara. From Pinckard's Notes on the West Indies (London, 1816); Anon., ed., Legal Condition of the Slave Exemplified (London, 1816); Anon., ed., Anecdotes, Tending to Elucidate the Nature of Colonial Bondage . . . (London, 1816); Anon., Remarks on the Antidote to the West-Indian Sketches (London, 1817), and Anon., Further Remarks Occasioned by the Antidote to the West-Indian Sketches (London, 1817).

[2] Known as Antidote to "West Indian Sketches," Drawn from Authentic Sources, and issued in the same form and with the same make-up as the Sketches. Among them may be mentioned Anon., ed., Condition of the Slaves in the British Colonies, from Pinckard's Notes on the West Indies (London, 1816); Anon., A Short Account of the African Institution, and Refutation of the Calumnies of the Directors, by Sir James Leith (London, 1816); Anon., The Actual Condition of the Negroes in the British West India Colonies; and a Further Exposure of the Calumnies of the African Institution (London, 1816); Anon., The Calumnies of the African Institution Further Illustrated by Parliamentary Papers and Other Documents (London, 1816); Anon., An Illustration of the Principles of the African Institution, as they Respect our West India Colonies . . . (London, 1817); Anon., Observations on the Ameliorated Condition of the negroes in the British West India colonies, &c. (London, 1817).

[3] He had tried the first slave trade case under the felony act, 51 Geo. III c. 23. See page 386.

In a number of booklets devoted largely to vitriolic denunciations of the body and to tirades against Zachary Macaulay, sometime the colony's governor [1] and more recently secretary of the Institution, he charged that the latter was identical with the Sierra Leone Company which had been chartered to carry on commercial operations in this African possession, that faith had not been kept with the Jamaican Maroons removed there,[2] that local Institution agents themselves dealt in blacks, and that Macaulay had prostituted his position with the organization by using it to his own financial advantage.[3] The Society of West Indian Planters and Merchants gave wide circulation to these grave accusations by purchasing quantities of the works and anonymously supplying them to libraries and reading clubs.[4]

Thorpe's allegations were, in reality, wholly unfounded and prompt replies by Macaulay [5] and the Institution's directors,[6] exposing their author's personal grievances, bade fair to settle the case with the ex-jurist badly worsted. In the heat of the registration controversy, however, members of the Caribbean interest openly espoused his cause against the common foe, gave further publicity to his assertions [7] and encouraged him to elaborate them.[8]

The good faith of Mr. Stephen and that of the Institution's officials in sponsoring registration cannot be impugned. Yet, to the impartial student, their position appears astonishingly weak. All betrayed a

[1] See page 272.

[2] See page 272.

[3] [Robert Thorpe], *A Letter to William Wilberforce, Esq., Containing Remarks on the Reports of the Sierra Leone Company, and African Institution* (London, 1815) ; Thorpe, *Preface to the Fourth Edition of a Letter to William Wilberforce, Esq., M.P. Containing a Reply to a Letter from Zachary Macaulay, Esq. to the Duke of Gloucester* (London, 1815) ; *A Reply "Point by Point" to the Special Report of the Directors of the African Institution* (London, 1815) ; *Postscript to a Reply "Point by Point"* . . . (London, 1815).

[4] *Min. W. I. Plant. and Mer.,* Mar. 30, 1815.

[5] Macaulay, *A Letter to His Royal Highness the Duke of Gloucester, President of the African Institution* . . . (London, 1815).

[6] *African Institution. Special Report . . . Respecting the Allegations Contained in a Pamphlet Entitled "A Letter to William Wilberforce, Esq., &c. by R. Thorne, Esq., &c."* (London, 1815).

[7] Gilbert Mathison, *A Short Review of the Reports of the African Institution, and of the Controversy With Dr. Thorpe, With Some Reasons Against the Registry of Slaves in the British Colonies* (London, 1816).

[8] Thorpe, *A View of the Present Increase of the Slave Trade, the Cause of That Increase, and Suggesting a Mode for Effecting its Total Annihilation; With Observations on the African Institution and Edinburgh Review* . . . (London, 1817).

strong assumption of guilt in dealing with the West Indians; their charges at best consisted of glittering generalities. However laudable their motives, it cannot but be held that even humanitarian ardor affords no excuse for departure from established canons of legal procedure and that it in no manner warrants appeal to blind partisanship.

Two only of the society's foremost personalities, Macaulay and Stephen, enjoyed personal acquaintance with Caribbean society. The former had been a Jamaican bookkeeper and plantation manager from 1784 to 1792; his colleague had practiced law and had served on the island council in St. Kitts after the close of the American Revolution. Their first-hand knowledge, consequently, embraced only the situation of a generation antedating Mr. Wilberforce's introduction of his bill.

This regrettable ignorance of actual conditions in the West Indies during the second decade of the nineteenth century was matched by the Institution directors' gullibility and by the readiness with which they lent ear to hearsay. Combined, these rendered the organization peculiarly vulnerable to denunciation and ridicule as two instances will illustrate.

Its tenth annual report [1] contained an account of a whipping declared to have been administered to a pregnant Antiguan negress by one of Governor Sir James Leith's aides-de-camp who was unnamed. The affair had not been investigated, the accusation proved to be without basis, and a libel action brought against J. Hatchard, publisher of the volume, by the London commercial-agrarian group in the name of the executive's several staff officers resulted in a judgment of £100 being secured against him. The outcome was loudly broadcast as demonstrating the lack of truth in charges proffered by the body.[2]

During its pamphlet campaign, in portraying "the state of slavery," the Institution made extensive use [3] of a popular travel account of the

---

[1] *Tenth Report of the Directors of the African Institution . . ., 27 March, 1816* (London, 1816).

[2] Anon., *A Short Account of the African Institution, and Refutation of the Calumnies of the Directors by Sir James Leith; A Report of the Trial of the King v. John Hatchard, for a Libel on the Aides-de-Camp of Sir James Leith, Governor and Commander-in-Chief of the Leeward Islands . . .* (London, 1817).

[3] Anon., ed., *Punishment of the Maroons of Demarara.* Anon., ed., *Legal Condition.*

day, George Pinckard's *Notes on the West Indies*.[1] The specific incidents related in it, which were seized upon to attack the plantation labor régime, could doubtless have been duplicated in any one of the British colonies; yet it was singularly unfortunate that fifteen of the sixteen chosen were found upon investigation to have occurred on the Main under Dutch rule preceding the British conquest.[2] No amount of ingenuous explanation [3] could improve the embarrassing position in which the society found itself in consequence of this absurd piece of editorial gaucherie.

The fact that it solicited funds as a body ostensibly undertaking to civilize Africa, but in reality devoted its energies almost exclusively to the Caribbean negro question, likewise exposed the Institution to attack on the ground of securing support under false pretenses and this charge was oft hurled against it in telling fashion.[4]

Unfortunately, this bitter opposition to registration created a false impression in the negro mind. It was rumored among the blacks that Mr. Wilberforce's bill contemplated emancipation but that their masters were determined to withhold this from them.[5] High excitement prevailed and tragic consequences followed in Barbados where the belief that freedom would be proclaimed on New Year's day 1816 became general. This was officially denied and the holiday season passed without untoward incident, but widespread discontent coupled with secret nocturnal assemblies caused growing apprehension. The gravest fears were realized when, on April 14, 1816, Easter Sunday, a reign of carnage opened. Scores of fires broke out simultaneously, bands of slaves sacked the plantations, the canes on one-fifth of the island estates were burned and property valued at £179,000 was destroyed. Martial law was proclaimed and continued in force for three months. During this time, the rebellion was ruthlessly crushed; actual participants were hanged on their owners' properties

---

[1] 3 vols., London, 1806.

[2] Anon., *Condition of the Slaves in the British Colonies*. Anon., *The Actual Condition of the Negroes in the British West India Colonies*. Anon., *An Illustration of the Principles of the African Institution*.

[3] Anon., *Further Remarks Occasioned by the Antidote*.

[4] See for example, Anon., *Observations on the Necessity of a Total Change in the System of Management of the African Institution* (London, 1817) and *Report of the Joint Committee Appointed by the Board of Council, and the House of General Assembly of Tobago, Upon the Subject of the Registry Bill. . . .*

[5] The Duke of Manchester to Earl Bathurst, January 26, 1816, C. O. 137/142. Sir James Leith to Earl Bathurst, April 30, 1816, C. O. 28/85.

with fellow Africans as spectators and 123 found guilty of complicity were transported to the Mosquito shore.[1]

To set the negroes aright, governors throughout the Caribbean were directed to issue proclamations announcing the Prince Regent's displeasure at events in Barbados and denying that emancipation had been ordered by the home government.[2]

Not unnaturally, West Indian opinion held the African Institution responsible for these tragic events. Its supporters denied the charge and in turn attributed them to the Barbadians' failure to revise their servile code and thus ameliorate the lot of their slaves as had been done in neighboring colonies.[3] On the whole, the episode swung popular sympathy to the side of the harassed planters and increased the difficulties confronting humanitarian leaders.

The home government proceeded cautiously when brought face to face with this striking unanimity of sentiment among the colonists and, above all, in light of their raising the question of constitutionality. Immediate action was postponed, which led to Mr. Stephen's retirement from parliament in protest. The governors were informed that emancipation was not contemplated and hope was expressed that the several island legislatures would pass registration measures of their own volition.[4] Thus reassured, the West Indians adopted the latter suggestion and the reform was ultimately introduced by local act in all of the Caribbean possessions enjoying self-government while an order in council of 1814 made it operative in the crown colony of St. Lucia as well.[5]

Not until 1819, when the system was already generally in force, did parliament centralize the formal enrollment of slaves and forbid British subjects in the United Kingdom to purchase unlisted ones or

[1] *The Report from a Select Committee of the House of Assembly, Appointed to Inquire Into the Origin, Causes, and Progress of the Late Insurrection* [Bridgetown, n.d.].

[2] See for example *Barbados. By His Excellency Sir James Leith . . . A Proclamation* [Bridgetown, 1816]; *Dominica. By His Royal Highness the Prince of Wales . . . Proclamation* [Roseau, 1816], dated 20 Aug.; *St. Vincent. A Proclamation by the Honourable Robert Paul . . .* [Kingstown, 1816]; *Trinidad. By His Excellency Sir Ralph James Woodford . . . A Proclamation* [Port of Spain, 1816].

[3] Anon., *Remarks on the Insurrection in Barbados, and the Bill for the Registration of Slaves* (London, 1816).

[4] *Report of the Joint Committee Appointed to Consider the Expediency of Establishing a Registry of Slaves in the British Colonies* (Antigua, n.d.).

[5] Papers in C. O. 7/2; C. O. 28/86; C. O. 71/53; C. O. 239/3; C. O. 260/34.

to make loans with them as security.[1] And even then, despite the African Institution's plea that authorities in the homeland be given complete control,[2] registration continued to rest primarily upon colonial statutes. Its chief value proved to be in increasing the various colonies' revenue through bringing to light negroes not formerly entered on assessment rolls in order to avoid payment of the poll tax on them.[3]

Popular interest in the negro cause was slight during the decade and a half after abolition had become effective. The slave and his woes were all but forgotten in the agonizing last years of the Napoleonic wars and in the period of unrest and depression which followed. Two cases of shocking atrocities committed by masters served, however, to keep the question a live one.

On January 23, 1810, Edward Huggins, Sr., of the island of Nevis, accompanied by his sons Edward and Peter and two expert whippers, led to the public market of Charlestown a gang of twenty blacks who had run away from the Huggins plantation to avoid carrying dung into the fields at night as they had been ordered to do in violation of the local code noir, and had them mercilessly flogged there. Ten men received from forty-seven to 365 lashes each and as many women from forty-nine to 291 a head. So cruel were these punishments that a number of the victims were permanently invalided and one negress subsequently expired. Five magistrates witnessed the affair without seeking to halt proceedings.[4] The existing slave law placed no limitation upon the number of lashes which might be inflicted but did prohibit cruel whipping. Still these public officials entered no protest against what was obviously a gross violation of that section of the statutes.[5]

The island assembly, in a resolution of a week later, held the punishment to have been both barbarous and illegal,[6] and on May first Huggins was brought to trial accused of having administered excessive floggings. He had never been in custody nor had bail been

[1] 59 Geo. III c. 120. See "Acts of Colonial Legislatures for the Registry of Slaves," in *Gt. Br., H. C., Sess. Pap.*, 1823 XVIII (68), 1.

[2] *A Review of the Colonial Slave Registration Acts, in a Report of a Committee of the Board of Directors of the African Institution, Made on the 22nd of February, 1820, and Published by Order of That Board* (London, 1820). *Postscript to "A Review . . ."* [London, 1820].

[3] Stewart, *A View . . . of Jamaica*, pp. 240, 241.

[4] Examination of John Burke, Junior Deputy Secretary of Nevis, in Governor Elliot to the Earl of Liverpool, Nov. 20, 1810, C. O. 152/96.

[5] Elliot to Liverpool, Nov. 21, 1810, C. O. 152/96.

[6] In Elliot to Liverpool, Nov. 20, 1810, C. O. 152/96.

required of him. His trial was a travesty of justice. The prosecutor was one Weekes, lately charged with neglect of duty by a grand jury; among the jurors were the defendant's own overseer and the individual in charge of the estate owned by his son-in-law, President Cottle. Despite clear evidence of guilt, Huggins was promptly acquitted. Weekes was thereupon made chief justice of the island upon Cottle's recommendation and Thomas Howe, printer of the *St. Christopher Gazette* in which the assembly's expression of opinion had been published, was fined £13 sterling for libel.

The female slave's death occurred shortly after Huggins had been freed, but the coroner, in whose presence the floggings had been administered, and his jury, which included two members of the late trial body, declined to hold her master responsible while the local grand jury, on which were found the two Huggins sons and a newcomer residing upon their father's property, wholly ignored the affair.[1]

James Stephen laid these facts before the British government[2] and wide publicity was gained through a pamphlet quarrel between James Webbe Tobin, a planter in the colony who had led the local attack on Huggins,[3] and President Cottle,[4] as well as by the African Institution's later publishing the harrowing details during its campaign against the planting interest.[5] Still no action was taken beyond removing the passive magistrates from office.[6]

[1] Information presented by James W. Tobin, in Elliot to Liverpool, Nov. 20, 1810. C. O. 152/96.

[2] Stephen to the Earl of Liverpool, Aug. 23, 1810, C. O. 152/96.

[3] Son of James Tobin who had carried on the acrimonious dispute over the question of slavery with James Ramsay in the period preceding the opening of the abolition struggle (see page 248), and brother of Rear-Admiral George Tobin and of the dramatist, John Tobin.

[4] T. J. C[ottle], *A Plain Statement of the Motives, which gave rise to the Public Punishment of several Negroes . . . on the 23 January, 1810 . . . With a Sketch of the Characters of Mr. Huggins and Mr. Tobin* (Nevis, 1811). James W. Tobin, *To the Hon'ble Thomas John Cottle, Esq. . . .* (Nevis, n.d.), also issued as *J. W. Tobin's Reply to Mr. Cottle's Pamphlet* (Nevis, 1812).

[5] Anon., *State of the Slave Population Illustrated by a View of Certain Transactions in the Island of Nevis* (London, 1816).

[6] Liverpool to Elliot, May 12, 1811, C. O. 152/96. Several parties to this affair figured in an unenviable light in subsequent but less spectacular cases involving blacks. Edward Huggins, Jr., shot and killed a negro boy in October, 1812, alleging that he had been about to commit a theft. The grand jury threw out a bill for murder and a petty jury subsequently found him guilty of manslaughter, which brought a fine of £250 currency. Weekes had granted Huggins bail. Upon Governor Elliot's questioning this act, Weekes took the execu-

Shocking as were the circumstances attending this case, the Nevis proprietor's crime pales into insignificance when compared with those attributed to Arthur Hodge, a prominent sugar-grower and council member in Tortola, one of the isolated and lawless Virgin group. Reports of his barbarities reached Governor Elliot of the Leewards government early in 1811, while in Nevis personally gathering information on the affair there. He ordered an immediate, thorough-going investigation which revealed a long series of murders on the part of an inhuman monster attended by a brutal ferocity unparalleled in the annals of British Caribbean history. Nearly a hundred of Hodge's negroes had met violent deaths at his hand or under his orders.

To mention but a few instances chosen at random, the slaves Tom, Prosper, and Cuffy had been stretched at length upon the ground and had been flogged continuously for over an hour each, with the result that all had died. Kettles of boiling water had been poured down the throats of Margaret, the plantation cook, and Elsa, a washer-woman, accused by Hodge of trying to poison him, and both had expired. Welcome, sent out to locate runaway slaves, had returned after having been unable to do so and had been whipped to death. A hot iron had been placed in Jupiter's mouth for some misdeed and he had died soon after. A free black, Peter, hired as cooper, had been put at field work and had been clubbed until lifeless when he had protested.

On several occasions, for no apparent reason other than sheer fiendishness, Hodge had taken piccaninnies by the heels, had stuck their heads into tubs of water until they had all but drowned, had then hung them up by both hands and had ended by horsewhipping them. One, aged ten, had been dipped into a kettle of boiling liquid. The colonist had beaten his own bastard daughter, Bella, aged eight,

tive's action as an infringement of the constitutional independence of judges and resigned (Elliot to Bathurst, Nov. 20, 1812, C. O. 152/100; Weekes to Bathurst, Feb. 2, 1813 and enclosures, C. O. 152/103.,

An echo of the cases of 1810 and 1812 was heard two decades later when Governor Nicholay's nomination of Edward Huggins, Jr., for a seat in the island council was not approved by Viscount Goderich on the ground of his "participation in the cruelty practiced by his father." (Nicholay to Goderich, Aug. 24, 1823, with memorandum notes, C. O. 239/29).

In 1817, Huggins, Sr., acting as attorney for Cottle during the latter's absence in England, ordered five negroes whipped in connection with a theft on the estate. Mr. Weekes, a thoroughly despicable figure, had just been refused a £5,000 loan on mortgage by Huggins and, hearing of the punishments, preferred a bill of indictment against the latter. Huggins was, however, acquitted. (See Anon., *Case in Nevis, 1817*, London, 1818.)

so severely as to break in her head and had kicked her with such violence that she had been hurled several feet from him.[1]

Governor Elliot took direct charge of the case. The evidence was largely presented by the defendant's own plantation manager and proved so overwhelming that Hodge was suspended from office, was jailed, was tried on April 29th and 30th, specifically accused of having slain Prosper, and was found guilty. Seven members of the jury recommended mercy but the judges refused to second this. Governor Elliot lent a deaf ear to all pleas and on May 9th, with the island under martial law, Hodge was executed.[2] The strong probability that he would never have been called to account had the executive not taken such prompt action and the jury's attitude furnished strong arguments for those who, both then[3] and later, notably members of the Institution,[4] urged parliamentary action in behalf of the slaves.

Abolition called a halt to the steady introduction of large bodies of savage Africans into West Indian society and was followed by a gradual rise in the level of negro understanding, which offered unparalleled opportunity for understanding spiritual work among them. But the Anglican church was blind to the possibilities which thus opened before it. While the Caribbean clergy of the first quarter of the nineteenth century were of markedly higher quality than those in the past,[5] thanks largely to Beilby Porteus,[6] the Bishop of London, who had introduced university-trained rectors wherever possible, incidents such as the trial of the Reverend William Rawlins, managing a St. Kitts estate, in 1817, on the charge of having caused the death of a runaway, Congo Jack, through flogging, and his sentence to three months' imprisonment plus the payment of a £200 fine,[7] afford ample evidence that the situation still left much to be

[1] Governor Elliot to the Earl of Liverpool, April 1, 1811 and enclosures, C. O. 152/97.

[2] Governor Elliot to the Earl of Liverpool, May 3, 9, 17, and 18, 1811, C. O. 152/97.

[3] Anon., *The Trial of Arthur Hodge, late one of the Members of H. M. Council for the Virgin Islands at the Island of Tortola, for the Murder of his Negro Man Slave, named Prosper* (London, 1811) ; "West Indian Slavery," in *The Ed. Rev.*, Nov. 1811, pp. 129–149.

[4] Anon., *The Nature of West-Indian Slavery Further Illustrated by Certain Occurrences in the Island of Tortola* (London, 1816). Anon., *Further Remarks on the Antidote to The West Indian Sketches, Being a Re-Consideration of the Case of Mr. Hodge* (London, 1817).

[5] Stewart, *A View . . . of Jamaica*, pp. 151, 152.

[6] See pages 244 and 283.

[7] Private letter of Governor Probyn to Earl Bathurst, March 18, 1818; despatch of March 21, 1818, both in C. O. 239/4.

desired. In general, the Established Churchmen of the West Indies continued to ignore the blacks and the Church of England remained essentially a white man's institution.

Nor were its ministers encouraged to serve the negroes. The Reverend Colin Donaldson, rector of St. Mary's, Jamaica, who interested himself in them, found his efforts blocked and, in consequence of his investigations into slave punishments, became involved in a heated dispute with the proprietary class.[1] The rector of Clarendon parish in the same island volunteered to give plantation hands Biblical instruction on their masters' properties, but secured the necessary permission from only two planters.[2]

In Jamaica alone was an attempt made to extend the work of the Anglican organization so as to meet the needs of the blacks. A law of 1816 authorized the appointing of twenty-one curates, one per parish, at salaries of £300 currency a year each, to instruct them in religious truths and ordered the erection of proper meeting places beside the regular parish churches at public expense.

No clergymen could be secured at such a figure and the stipend was consequently raised to £500 currency.[3] Under this attraction, the positions were soon filled, but almost exclusively by altogether unqualified West Indians possessing sufficient influence to secure the appointments. A churchman, suspended for preaching an improper sermon at Kingston, at once secured a curacy in another part of the island where he engaged at the same time in commercial enterprises taking him as far afield as Cuba. Half-pay army and navy officers found comfortable berths in these posts—one of the latter refused to officiate more than every other Sunday, holding the effort entailed by weekly services to be too great for him. Another worthy laid aside his ambition of becoming an iron-monger to accept a charge. Such of those curates who did not disgrace their cloth were little more than assistants to the rectors in the latters' regular duties; the slaves they had been named to serve were not reached. Small wonder, then, that this laudable experiment was viewed as a complete failure.[4]

---

[1] [Rev. Colin Donaldson, ed.], *Copies of the Correspondence Between the Hon. John Shand, the Rev. Colin Donaldson, and D. P. Malony, Esq., on the Subject of the Murder of Caesar, a Slave on Orange-River Estate, in the Parish of St. Mary, in the Island of Jamaica* . . . (London, n.d.).

[2] Phillippo, *Jamaica: Its Past and Present State*, p. 105.

[3] Stewart, *A View . . . of Jamaica*, pp. 291–293.

[4] Rev. R. Bickell, *The West Indies As They Are; or a Real Picture of Slavery; But More Particularly As it Exists in the Island of Jamaica* (London, 1825), pp. 95–101.

The Established Church's rôle in Caribbean missionary activities after 1807, likewise, was not one of great prominence. The Society for the Conversion and Religious Instruction and Education of the Negro Slaves in the British West India Islands, established by Beilby Porteus in 1794,[1] fell into moribundity. In 1823, it still supported two missionaries and a schoolmaster in Antigua, one missionary in St. Kitts, one in Nevis, and four in Jamaica, but their accomplishments were insignificant.[2] As for the body's agent in Barbados, he had turned planter soon after his arrival and no successor had been appointed.[3]

In 1813, the Church Missionary Society for Africa and the East accredited one of its members settling in Antigua as catechist and, three years later, it undertook to support a teacher in the colony.[4] But these laudable beginnings led to no organized enterprise among the Caribbean negroes and are worthy of note more as affording evidence that not all Anglicans were unmindful of the slaves' needs than because of any markedly beneficial results which followed.

Now, as earlier, it was the dissenters, notably the Moravians, Wesleyans, and Baptists, who engaged in extensive missionary labors in the sugar colonies. The Moravians, who had been first in the field,[5] continued quietly to extend their influence, though less rapidly than when they had been alone in their combined humanitarian and spiritual service.

The Methodist missions were reorganized so as to stand upon a more secure foundation. Originally largely under the Reverend Thomes Coke's personal control and maintained by funds raised through his appeals,[6] they were, in 1804, placed under the direction of a committee of the Wesleyan Conference with Coke as superintendent and the Methodist Church as such undertook to finance them.[7]

---

[1] See page 283 and note 2.

[2] Brown, *History of the Propagation of Christianity*, III, 448, 449.

[3] Governor Beckwith to the Earl of Liverpool, Jan. 13, 1812, C. O. 28/81.

[4] *Proceedings of the Church Missionary Society for Africa and the East,* Vol. IV, covering 1812–1815 (London, 1813–1815), on. Also Charles Hole, *The Early History of the Church Missionary Society for Africa and the East* . . . (London, 1896) and Eugene Stock, *The History of the Church Missionary Society—Its Environment, Its Men and Its Work* (4 vols., London, 1899–1917).

[5] See page 28.

[6] See pages 281 and 282.

[7] See for example *The Annual Report of the Spiritual and Financial State of the Missions, Carried on in the West Indies, Nova-Scotia, Newfoundland, Ireland, and Wales, Under the Direction of the Methodist Conference* (London, 1807); *The Annual Report of the State of the Missions, Which Are*

The Wesleyan Methodist Missionary Society was formed ten years later, following the great ecclesiastic's death,[1] and district chapters sprang up in various parts of England, leading to increased interest and greater contributions.[2]

Twelve stations manned by twenty-five missionaries were already operating in the sugar islands at the time this memorable step was taken.[3] A period of rapid expansion followed during which chapels were erected in colonies such as Montserrat, where none had been found in the past.[4] The relative importance of Anglican, Moravian and Methodist activity in Antigua by 1824 may be seen from a report of Governor D'Urban to home authorities stating that 550 slaves were then habitually attending the ten Established churches of the island as against 11,680 at the eight Moravian chapels and 6,650 at the Wesleyan ones.[5]

The third outstanding group of nonconformists, the Baptists, formally inaugurated their work among the West Indian negroes in 1814 when the Baptist Missionary Society sent out a representative to Jamaica under orders to coöperate with leaders of the local native church.[6] Six others followed shortly after.[7] Thenceforth the scope of the organization's undertakings steadily widened.

The Scottish Missionary Society, discouraged by its lack of success at the opening of the century,[8] for the time being turned its attention to other parts of the world. The London Missionary Society[9] maintained but one agent in Berbice and another in Dem-

---

Carried on Both at Home and Abroad by the Society Late in Connexion With the Rev. John Wesley . . . (London, 1808), and other years, 1804–1814.

[1] See *The Report of the Executive Committee for the Management of the Missions . . . Carried on Under the Direction of the Methodist Conference* (London, 1816); *First Report of the General Wesleyan Methodist Missionary Society* (London, 1818) and subsequent annual reports; Findlay and Holdsworth, *History of the Wesleyan Methodist Missionary Society*, Vol. I.

[2] See for example, *A Report of the Formation of a Methodist Missionary Society for the London District, at a Public Meeting Held at the New Chapel City Road, on the First of December, 1814* . . . (London, 1815).

[3] *The Report of the Executive Committee for the Management of the Missions.*

[4] William Moister, *The West Indies, Enslaved and Free* (London, 1883), p. 272.

[5] Enclosure in despatch to Earl Bathurst, March 12, C. O. 7/10.

[6] For this island group of Baptists, see page 29.

[7] Cox, *History of the Baptist Missionary Society*, II, 21 ff. Brown, *History of the Propagation of Christianity*, II, 78 ff.

[8] See page 282.

[9] Founded chiefly by Congregationalists, Episcopalians, and Wesleyans in 1795 and emphasizing no one form of church government, this organization

erara.[1] However, as we shall see,[2] despite that body's modest efforts, momentous consequences ultimately resulted from them.

The British and Foreign Bible Society [3] shipped large quantities of Testaments westward, and branches to supervise their distribution among the negroes were formed in Jamaica and Antigua.[4] An English Romanist, the Reverend James Buckley, was named bishop over the parish priests of Trinidad and the late French islands in 1820,[5] but the Catholic Church disregarded the slaves as completely after that event as it had earlier.

With respect to the Caribbean planters, their attitude toward missionary enterprise of all kinds continued unchanged after 1807. Like a generation earlier,[6] they still looked upon it with most unfriendly eyes, quite irrespective of denominational auspices, holding that it spread pernicious doctrines of equality and independence among the slaves and served to break down their own authority. Representatives of Bishop Porteus's organization and Church Missionary Society agents were given scant encouragement, while the sectarists, and above all the Methodists, were denounced as being "cunning, intriguing, meddling, fanatical, hypocritical, canting knaves, cajoling the poor negroes . . . of all their little savings and every species of property they can amass under the pretence of saving them from the Devil and everlasting damnation," [7] and encountered active opposition at every turn.

The zeal of the sectarist missonaries, the lack of ground for objection to what they taught, and the highly beneficial results of

became in effect a Congregationalist society after the formation of the Church Missionary Society and the Wesleyan Methodist Missionary Society.

[1] Richard Lovett, *The History of the London Missionary Society 1795–1895* (2 vols., London, 1899). John Waddington, *Congregational History, 1700–1800* . . . (London, 1876), Ch. XIX. Waddington, *Congregational Church History. Continuation to 1850* (London, 1878), Ch. III, T[homas] R[ain], "John Wray, Pioneer Missionary," in *The Evangelical Magazine*, Oct., Nov., Dec., 1887, pp. 465–471, 495–500, 544–555. Rain, *The Life and Labours of John Wray, Pioneer Missionary in British Guiana* (London, 1892).

[2] In Chapter XII.

[3] Founded in 1804 under the chairmanship of Granville Sharp to print the Scriptures without note or comment in all languages and to distribute them throughout the world.

[4] John Owen, *The History of the Origin and First Ten Years of the British and Foreign Bible Society* (2 vols., London, 1816), II, 72, 176. William Canton, *A History of the British and Foreign Bible Society* (2 vols., London, 1904), I, 255–258, 386, 387 and II, 318–332.

[5] Governor Woodford to Earl Bathurst, March 20, 1820, C. O. 295/50. Woodford to the Governor of Antigua, Sept. 27, 1820, C. O. 7/8.

[6] See pages 283 ff.

[7] Williams, *Tour,* p. 37.

their attempts to improve negro morals were freely admitted by liberal-minded officials of the day, such as Governor D'Urban,[1] and have been as frankly acknowledged more recently by colonial Established Churchmen.[2] Yet the fact remains that the proprietors as a body viewed all their efforts with open suspicion and barely tolerated them. To the colonists' everlasting shame, this sullen hostility was destined, on occasion, to burst forth in the form of attacks on sectarist chapels accompanied by acts of violence against those officiating in them. In so doing, however, the West Indians were to turn the tide of British public opinion against them and thus make emancipation and the overthrow of the old plantation system inevitable.

[1] Private letter to Earl Bathurst, June 23, 1821, C. O. 7/7.

[2] See for example Ellis, *Diocese of Jamaica,* p. 56. "Indiscreet some [of the sectarist] ministers may have been, and probably were, for indiscretion is no infrequent companion of religious zeal; but the heedless indiscretion of Wesleyan or Baptist compares favourably with the apathetic indifference which characterized many of the ministrations of the Established Church. . . . Honour to whom honour is due. Those who provoked the hostility of the Church and of the planters earned the gratitude of the poor and oppressed. . . . The lion's share of the honours . . . belonged to the Nonconformist churches."

CHAPTER XII

The Overthrow of the Tropical Labor Régime

An organized movement to liberate all blacks within the empire was inaugurated in January, 1823, with the founding in London of the Society for the Mitigation and Gradual Abolition of Slavery Throughout the British Dominions. The majority of its charter members and its officers were closely associated with the African Institution. The latter, because of its nature, had never taken a formal stand for emancipation. This new body, on the contrary, at the outset declared human bondage to be "opposed to the spirit and precepts of Christianity as well as repugnant to every dictate of natural humanity and justice." It at the same time expressed disappointment over the fact that the institution was not dying out in the West Indies following abolition of the trade as had been hoped, and openly avowed its intention of securing immediate amelioration of the negroes' lot as well as their ultimate freedom by any means which might be both prudent and lawful.[1]

The challenge thus hurled at the proprietors, branches were established in all parts of Great Britain[2] and, within a year, 220 had sprung into existence.[3] These served as convenient propaganda agencies[4] and, through their activity, no less than 750 petitions against slavery were drawn up in 1823 and 1824 for presentation to parliament.[5] Emancipationist periodicals, too, were financed and

---

[1] *Prospectus of the Society* . . . (London, 1823). [*First Annual*] *Report of the Committee of the Society* . . . (London, 1824).

[2] See for example, *Declaration of the Objects of the Newcastle Upon Tyne Society for Promoting the Gradual Abolition of Slavery Throughout the British Possessions* (Newcastle Upon Tyne, 1823) and *Declaration of the Objects of the Liverpool Society for Promoting the Abolition of Slavery* . . . (Liverpool, n.d.).

[3] "Abolition of the Slave Trade—and of Slavery," in *The Ed. Rev.,* Oct. 1824, p. 207.

[4] As for example, [Mr. Hill], *An Address on the State of Slavery in the West-India Islands, by the Leicester Auxiliary Anti-Slavery Society* (London, 1824).

[5] *Report of the Committee of the Society* . . . (London, 1823).

widely distributed as a means of gaining popular support for the new crusade after such long lapse of interest in the Africans' woes.[1]

Mr. Wilberforce, grown venerable and bowed with years, now transferred parliamentary leadership of the negro cause to his young disciple-friend, Thomas Fowell Buxton [2] and, in a stirring appeal, called upon the nation to support emancipation.[3] Buxton was fired with the zeal born of devotion and opened the legislative conflict with a celebrated speech delivered in the House of Commons on May 15, 1823, one week to the day before the East India traders began their mass assault on the planters' monopoly rights with respect to supplying home markets in the same body.[4] From the start, there was hearty coöperation between the humanitarians and these merchants and this continued unbroken for upwards of a decade.

The reformers' program was not radical. Their aim, as announced by Buxton, was "the extinction of slavery—nothing less than the extinction of slavery, in nothing less than the whole of the British dominions: not, however, the rapid termination of that state; not the sudden emancipation of the negro; but such preparatory steps, such measures of precaution, as, by slow degrees, and in a course of years, first fitting and qualifying the slaves for freedom, shall gently conduct us to the annihilation of slavery." [5]

As the first definite step in that direction, he laid before the chamber a resolution declaring that bondage was "repugnant to the principles of the British constitution, and of the Christian religion; and that it ought to be gradually abolished . . . with as much ex-

---

[1] *Negro Slavery* was the title given to a series of at least sixteen pamphlets published in London. Typical ones were "Slavery in British Guiana" (No. 1) and "Insurrections of Slaves in the West Indies . . ." (No. 7). *The Anti-Slavery Magazine, and Recorder of the Progress of Christianity in the Countries Connected With Slavery* was published in Derby commencing in January 1824 and *The Humming Bird; or, morsels of invitation on the subject of slavery: with various miscellaneous articles* in Leicester commencing later in the same year.

[2] D. Alcock. W. G. Blaike, E. P. Hood, and S. S. Pugh, *Six Heroic Men* (London, n.d.), pp. 35–64. Thomas Binney, *Sir Thomas Fowell Buxton, Bart. A Study for Young Men* (London, n.d.). Charles Buxton, ed., *Memoirs of Sir Thomas Fowell Buxton, Baronet* (London, 1848). Charles Buxton, *Memoirs of Sir Thomas Fowell Buxton, Bart., With an Inquiry Into the Results of Emancipation* (London, 1860). *Michael, The Slave and His Champions.*

[3] *An Appeal to the Religion, Justice, and Humanity of the Inhabitants of the British Empire, in Behalf of the Negro Slaves in the West Indies* (London, 1823).

[4] See pages 363 and 364.

[5] Buxton, ed., *Memoirs* (1885), p. 113.

pedition as may be found consistent with a due regard to the well-being of the parties concerned."

At the same time he advocated freeing all children born after an unspecified date as well as materially improving the condition of those blacks remaining enslaved.[1] A sharp debate followed, with Charles Ellis and Alexander Baring denouncing the proposals as spokesmen of the West Indians. At length, in the small hours of morning, after a brilliant display of forensic power, Buxton withdrew his measure.[2]

During the course of this notable sitting, Secretary George Canning of the Foreign Office, representing the government, had presented a series of more general substitute declarations, cautiously worded so as to avoid complications which might arise from setting a specific date for emancipation in any form. These were now unanimously adopted. Declaring, "1st. That it is expedient to adopt effectual and decisive measures for ameliorating the condition of the slave population in his majesty's colonies. 2nd. That, through a determined and persevering, but at the same time judicious and temperate, enforcement of such measures, this House looks forward to a progressive improvement in the character of the slave population, such as may prepare them for a participation in those civil rights and privileges which are enjoyed by other classes of his majesty's subjects. 3rd. That this House is anxious for the accomplishment of this purpose, at the earliest period that shall be compatible with the well-being of the slaves themselves, with the safety of the colonies, and with a fair and equitable consideration of the interests of private property," [3] they pledged the popular body to the principle of liberation and thenceforth the triumph of emancipation was but a matter of time.

[1] His proposed measures of amelioration were outlined in a letter of the same day to R. Wilmot Horton, Under-Secretary of State for War and the Colonies, to be perused by the Secretary, Earl Bathurst. They included attaching the slaves to the soil, accepting their testimony under certain conditions, facilitating manumission, allowing slaves to purchase their freedom, giving them religious instruction, enforcing marriage, closing Sunday markets and restricting the masters' right to punish slaves. Buxton, ed., *Memoirs*, p. 112. See also his speech in *Parl. Debates*, 2nd series, IX, col. 273.

[2] *Parl. Debates*, 2nd series IX, cols. 257–360. *Substance of the Debate in the House of Commons, on the 15th May, 1823* . . . (London, 1823). Alexander Baring, *Speech in the House of Commons, on the 15th Day of May, 1823* . . . (London, 1823).

[3] *Parl. Debates*, 2nd series, IX, cols. 285, 286. George Canning, *Speech . . . in the House of Commons, on the Motion of Thomas Fowell Buxton, Esq.* . . . (London, 1823).

Members of the London Caribbean interest had pursued a remarkable line of conduct three weeks earlier when Mr. Buxton's
intention of reopening the negro question had become known. While
maintaining that the colonists had nothing to hide, the Society of
West India Planters and Merchants had expressed apprehension at
rumors of such action reaching slave ears and had determined on
the twenty-second and twenty-fifth of April that the best means
of averting the danger "would be for the Executive Government to
undertake some systematic Plan for the improvement of the Condition of the Negroes in those Colonies which are under their immediate jurisdiction, and to recommend, and enforce with their influence, the adoption of a similar plan by all those Colonies which
are governed by local Legislatures. . . ." A special committee to prepare a list of substantial ameliorative measures and to concert with
the government in carrying them into effect was named at the same
time.[1]

The personnel of this select group, which was easily the most
consequential one named in the four decades of the organization's
existence, is worthy of note. Charles Ellis served as chairman;
Alexander Grant, Henry Bright, Edward Cust, J. H. D. Pennant,
James Blair, John Mitchell, William Manning, John Plummer, J.
W. Ward, Sir Simon Clarke, Sir Edward East, Sir Henry Martin,
William Murray, and John Ellis as members ordinary.[2] All were
prominently connected with plantation affairs and the first ten held
seats in parliament.

Meeting immediately, the committee had formulated a program
of reform so thorough-going that it might well have been drawn up
by a group of the negroes' most ardent champions. This West India body proposed that Sunday markets be abolished throughout
the Caribbean; that the mother country construct and maintain
Episcopalian and Presbyterian churches in sufficient number to afford
all the slaves on all the plantations religious instruction at least once
each Sunday; that the use of the whip in the field as a stimulus to
labor be prohibited and that some other symbol of authority be substituted for it; that floggings be inflicted only in the presence of the
overseer and some other white person attached to the estate; that
punishments be recorded in books presenting the full facts surround-

[1] *Min. W. I. Plant. and Mer.* of those dates.
[2] Nineteen had been named, but only the above fifteen served. Clarke subsequently withdrew on June 5th.

ing each case; that these be sworn to by the overseer and be submitted to local magistrates in vestry for quarterly inspection; that the whipping of females under any circumstances be forbidden; that the power of the justices and vestry as a council of protection for the slaves be enlarged and that all cases of blacks with complaints against their masters be referred to them; that bondsmen be guaranteed possession of their personal property by law and that they be given the right to bequeath it to their legitimate offspring; that the sale of slaves on writs of execution be prohibited; that their evidence be accepted under certain conditions; that manumission be facilitated and made less costly; and that slaves be given the right to purchase their own freedom or that of children born in wedlock at prices determined by competent authority.[1]

Following a conference with this committee, Earl Bathurst, Secretary of State for War and the Colonies on May 28th advised Major-General Murray and Lieutenant-Governor Beard of Demerara that it was His Majesty's desire that the flogging of females be absolutely prohibited but, rather than force the measure upon the settlers, he instructed them to lay the matter before the Court of Policy[2] for action and recommended further that use of the whip by drivers be discontinued.[3]

The governors of Trinidad and St. Lucia, pure crown colonies, were at the same time directed to prepare local planters for an order in council instituting those reforms,[4] while the executives of the West India possessions enjoying self-rule were commanded to present them to the several legislatures and to urge that they be spontaneously adopted in accordance with the spirit of the Canning resolutions.[5]

Most secret and confidential communications accompanying the despatches to the latter authorized them to express it as their opinion to persons of local standing that the state of public opinion in Great Britain was such "that in the unfortunate event of any Colonial Legislature opposing or even intentionally delaying the necessary measures for carrying these Resolutions into Practical Effect, no doubt can be entertained that Parliament would be immediately

---

[1] *Min. W. I. Plant. and Mer.*, April 26 and 29, 1823.

[2] A public body enjoying limited power over local affairs, surviving from the Dutch régime.

[3] C. O. 112/5. The despatch appears in Frank J. Klingberg, *The Anti-Slavery Movement in England* (New Haven, 1926), pp. 336, 337.

[4] C. O. 290/6; C. O. 254/6.

[5] Public circular despatch, May 28, C. O. 29/30.

prepared . . . to supply the Government with necessary powers to enforce them and to require the immediate exercise of those powers by the Government for that purpose." [1]

The Society of Planters and Merchants, in close touch with events, became convinced that the only hope of heading off the anti-slavery drive lay in granting amelioration on a generous scale without delay. Hence, it submitted a detailed account of the situation to the colonial legislatures and most earnestly recommended that they immediately and fully accede to the home government's program.

There was no mincing of words, no attempt to minimize the seriousness of the danger facing the colonists. A general notion that the negroes' lot should be markedly improved prevailed throughout Great Britain, declared the body. It was coupled with a deep impression that the island legislatures had been exceedingly remiss in their duty toward them in the past and that those bodies had no intention of meeting the British public's expectations in the matter. It would be a measure of mere prudence to remove such prejudices; this could be done only through the several local governments anticipating reforms which must otherwise inevitably and speedily be pressed upon them.

Domestic tranquillity demanded that the slaves regard the planters and the island legislatures rather than inhabitants of the homeland and parliament as their protectors. If the colonial governments were dilatory in adopting fundamental changes, angry discussions must inevitably ensue in the House of Commons and their echoes would resound in the negroes' quarters. Meanwhile, no question pertaining to tropical America, even of a purely commercial nature, would be listened to with favor or common justice.

Caribbean estate owners were then in a most perilous position. Parliament might very readily equalize East and West India sugar duties, yet, with the trade at a low state, it was precisely that antagonistic body to which they must appeal for relief. The absentee proprietors and sugar merchants in England had long safeguarded the colonists' welfare but their power was not sufficiently great to meet this new, double attack by the emancipationists and the free traders.

"The various Parties who, from different motives, are hostile to the West India interest, are at least as powerful, and act upon a more extensive system, and with greater means of influence, on the public mind,

[1] In C. O. 29/30.

than the Proprietors and Merchants connected with the Colonies. . . .
We cannot, therefore, beat them by influence—we must trust to reason—
and the only way of getting that weapon into our hands, is by doing
of ourselves, all that is right to be done—and doing it speedily and effectually." [1]

On July 9, 1823, the British government through Earl Bathurst
took the epoch-making step of outlining a series of desired ameliorative measures in a circular despatch to the governors of the self-
governing colonies, directing that these be laid before their respective legislatures at the next sessions with recommendations for
immediate adoption. The close parallelism between them and the Society of Planters and Merchants' urgent representations of some
weeks before affords ample evidence of the close relations which had
developed between that organization and His Majesty's Secretary
of State.

Religious instruction should be afforded the slaves. If a given
colony's revenue were insufficient to maintain an adequate number
of clergymen and teachers under episcopal control, parliament would
be requested to make satisfactory provision. Sunday markets
should be abolished and some other time should be set aside for
trafficking; no colony would be given pecuniary assistance towards
the support of a religious establishment unless this were done.

Laws should be passed enabling a slave to give testimony when
provided with a certificate from his religious instructor vouching for
the fact that he understood the nature of an oath. Marriage should
be given proper encouragement; mothers of a given number of
children born in lawful wedlock should be exempted from further
field labor and all Christian unions should be registered in the
parishes where they occurred.

Restrictions on manumissions, such as taxes and high fees, should
be removed and grants of freedom should be duly recorded. The
removal of blacks from their homes to satisfy masters' debts and the
breaking up of families through sale of the various members to
different owners should be prohibited.

Punishment should not be inflicted until the day after an offence
had been committed and then only in the presence of some free person in addition to the one under whose authority it was being meted
out. Records should be kept of all whippings exceeding three lashes
and quarterly returns covering them should be made under oath

[1] *Min. W. I. Plant. and Mer.*, June 5 and 9, 1823.

to local magistrates by the plantation officials. In addition, savings banks should be established as a means of enabling slaves to accumulate the necessary means for purchasing their freedom.

Far-reaching as these proposals were, Earl Bathurst regarded them as purely tentative ones, merely laying the foundation for farther and more effectual reformation. In a private and confidential despatch accompanying this general one, he advocated instituting a task system whereby slaves would be assigned specific amounts of work and would receive wages for any labor performed over and above this minimum, as well as the emancipation of all female children born after an unnamed date with the provision that their offspring would follow their status, irrespective of sex.[1]

Major-General Murray and Lieutenant-Governor Beard of Demerara were directed to lay these various measures before the Court of Policy, Lord Bathurst adding that the home government would institute them through order in council if they were not voluntarily adopted.[2] In the light of his knowledge of Caribbean affairs, gained through a ten years' residence in the West Indies, Governor Woodford of Trinidad was at the same time invited to draft a plan for introducing these reforms in the crown colonies[3] and readily complied.[4] Eight months later, on March 10, 1824, an order in council inaugurated them in that island. Of the several territories under direct royal control, Trinidad was chosen for the experiment because the Spanish slave law in force there[5] was far milder than either the French code in St. Lucia or the Dutch one in Demerara.[6]

---

[1] In C. O. 29/30. The general despatch is published in Klingberg, *Anti-Slavery Movement*, pp. 338 ff.

[2] Despatches of July 9, 1823 in C. O. 112/5.

[3] Bathurst to Woodford and R. Wilmot Horton to Bathurst, July 9, C. O. 296/6.

[4] Woodford to Bathurst, Aug. 26, 1823, C. O. 295/59.

[5] See pages 273 ff. and 389 ff.

[6] "Papers in Explanation of Measures Adopted by His Majesty for Amelioration of the Condition of the Slave Population in the West Indies," in *Gt. Br., H. C., Sess. Pap.,* 1824 XXIV (427), 1825, XXVI (205) and XXVII (1). *Debate in the House of Commons, on the 16th Day of March, 1824, on the Measures Adopted by His Majesty's Government, for the Amelioration of the Condition of the Slave Population in His Majesty's Dominions in the West Indies* (London, 1824). George Canning, *Speech . . . in the House of Commons on the 16th Day of March, 1824 . . .* (London, 1824). Canning, *Speech . . . on Laying Before the House of Commons the Papers in Explanation of the Measures Adopted by His Majesty's Government with a view of Ameliorating the Condition of the Negro Slaves in the West Indies . . .* (London, 1824). Charles Ellis, *Speech . . . in the Debate in the House of Commons . . .*

Passage of the Canning resolutions and receipt of the Bathurst despatches threw the sugar colonies into a violent uproar. The Dominican assembly, hearing that Mr. Buxton intended to introduce a measure looking toward emancipation, had already adopted a memorial protesting against the enactment of any legislation inimical to colonial interests,[1] and, under the signature of William Anderson, the speaker, on May 30 addressed a circular letter to the other West Indian legislatures calling on them to do likewise in their common danger.

It had been nicely designed to secure unity of action. "Let us . . . combine our Efforts and Energetically mark our firm Determination never to consent to kiss the rod or meekly 'lick the hand Just raised to shed our blood' but with one voice denounce in the face of the World the blind fanaticism of 'the Saints' who would now for a Phantom cast to Perdition these once highly valued and still valuable Colonies, while at the self-same moment they are looking on with cold blooded apathy to the miseries of Ireland, of their own Poor, the Thraldom preparing for the Inhabitants of Greece and Spain, and yea even of Europe at large." [2]

Through a leak in Earl Bathurst's office, exact copies of the confidential despatches of May 28th and July 9th, declaring that parliament would impose its will on the colonies if they did not voluntarily adopt amelioration and suggesting the extinction of slavery through the freeing of female blacks, were soon in ·circulation among the planters, solidifying their opposition and greatly handicapping the governors in seeking favorable action from the legislatures.[3]

---

on the 16th of March, 1824 (London, 1824). *Rules and Regulations for Savings Banks, to be Established in the Island of Trinidad, Under the Royal Order in Council of March 10th, 1824* [Port of Spain, 1824].

[1] *To the Right Honourable the Lords Spiritual and Temporal of the United Kingdoms of Great Britain and Ireland in Parliament Assembled* [Dominica, 1823].

[2] *Circular. Roseau, Dominica, May 30th, 1823. Sir, The House of Assembly of this Island, astonished and appalled at the Enormity of the proposition lately introduced into the House of Commons* [begin] . . . [Roseau, 1823].

[3] Governor Warde to Earl Bathurst, March 22, 1824, C. O. 28/93. Governor Huntingdon to Bathurst, Feb. 8, and April 2, 1824, C. O. 71/61. President Paterson to Bathurst, March 31, 1824, C. O. 101/64. Duke of Manchester to Bathurst, Sept. 6, 1823, C. O. 137/154. Duke of Manchester to Bathurst, May 18, 1824, C. O. 137/156. Governor Maxwell to Bathurst, April 6, 1824, C. O. 239/10. Governor Brisbane to Bathurst, April 12, 1824, C. O. 260/41. Governor Robinson to Bathurst, March 27, 1824, C. O. 285/29. Other leaks occurred in the same office at other times. Thus, several Jamaicans had copies of the Duke of Manchester's instructions (Manchaster to Bathurst, March 17,

The Jamaican assembly held the House of Commons' proceedings and the ministry's conduct to be direct assaults on the island constitutions and advocated adoption of "the most firm, strong, and constitutional measures to resist such attempt, and to preserve to the inhabitants of this Colony those rights which have been transmitted to them from their ancestors." Copies of its protest were distributed among the editors of leading British and American newspapers with the request that this be given the widest possible publicity.[1]

The council of Barbados declared that the proposed reforms could never be adopted as they would sever the bond uniting master and slave,[2] maintained that the emancipationists' portrayals of Caribbean servitude bore "no more resemblance to the actual state of things in this country than a caricature commonly does to the object which it is meant to ridicule" and insisted that no need for amelioration existed.[3]

The Dominican legislature adopted the same attitude [4] and, when unrest appeared among local negroes, a proclamation was issued warning them to place no credence in evil-minded persons who were raising unfounded hopes in their breasts and assuring them that they were not to be freed.[5]

The council and assembly of St. Vincent declared that Earl Bathurst's recommendations excited alarm, astonishment, and indignation in turn, that the colonists had a vested right in their slaves and that it was equally idle and absurd to imagine that they would quietly consent to this being invaded or themselves be instrumental in alien-

1823, C. O. 137/154) and a draft of the Trinidad order in council was published in a local newspaper before the order itself was made public (Governor Woodford to Bathurst, May 7, 1824, C. O. 295/62).

[1] *Proceedings of the Honourable House of Assembly of Jamaica, in Relation to Those Which Took Place in the British House of Commons, on the 15th of May last* . . . (Jamaica, 1823).

[2] *Report of a Debate in Council, on a Despatch from Lord Bathurst* . . . (London, 1823).

[3] *A Report of a Committee of the Council of Barbados, Appointed to Inquire Into the Actual Condition of the Slaves in This Island, With a View to Refute Certain Calumnies Respecting Their Treatment; and Also to Take Into Consideration Certain Measures Affecting the West Indies, Which Have Been Lately Agitated in the House of Commons* (London, 1824).

[4] *Dominica. The Report of the Committee of the Legislature appointed to enquire into and Report on certain Queries relative to the Condition, Treatment, Rights and Privileges of the Negro Population of this Island* [Roseau, 1823].

[5] *Dominica. Proclamation. By His Excellency Hans Francis, Earl of Huntingdon* . . . [Roseau, 1823]. Dated Dec. 20th.

ating it.[1] Indeed, by far the greater number of West Indians both in the new world and in Great Britain raised a cry against the Canning resolutions and the government's program, holding that they constituted an illegal interference in the colonies' affairs.[2]

The urgent plea of the Society of Planters and Merchants, that ameliorative measures be promptly adopted as a means of warding off action by the home government, consequently met with little response. The Antiguan legislature was unwilling to enact them five years after they had been presented to it.[3] In Barbados, a consolidated slave act embracing them failed of passage in 1824 and became law only the next session after considerable modification.[4] The council and assembly of Dominica did not accept a reform bill until 1826, after three years of deliberation.[5] A revised negro code instituted in Grenada was disallowed by the home government on the ground that it did not materially better the slaves' position, but the island legislators rejected suggested changes and the matter hung fire.[6] The Tobagans long refused to fall in line with the Bathurst proposals and not until 1829 were new slave laws put into force.[7] Measures enacted in St.

---

[1] *A Communication from Sir Charles Brisbane, K. C. B. Governor of Saint Vincent, to the House of Assembly of That Colony, Enclosing Lord Bathurst's Dispatch of the 9th of July, With the Joint Reply of the Council and Assembly; and a Letter Depicting the Alarm and Danger Excited by the Insurrection in Demerara* (London, 1823).

[2] Dennis Reid, *An Address to the Right Hon. Geo. Canning, on the Present State of This Island, and Other Matters* (Jamaica, 1823). Sir Henry Martin, *A Counter Appeal in Answer to "An Appeal" from William Wilberforce, Esq. M.P. . . .* (London, 1823). "The West Indian Controversy," in *Blackwood's*, Oct. and Dec. 1823, pp. 437–459, 647–666; Jan. and Dec. 1824, pp. 68–82, 682–698. F. G. Smyth, *An Apology for West Indians, and Reflections on the Policy of Great Britain's Interference in the Internal Concerns of the West India Colonies* (London, 1824). Alexander Barclay, *Effects of the Late Colonial Policy of Great Britain Described . . .* (London, 1830). For a reply to works of this nature, see Anon., *A Review of Some of the Arguments Which are Commonly Advanced Against Parliamentary Interference in Behalf of the Negro Slaves . . .* (London, 1823). See also *To the Honorable the Commons of the United Kingdom of Great Britain and Ireland in Parliament Assembled. The Humble Petition of the Undersigned Planters and Proprietors of Estates in the British West India Islands* [London, 1826].

[3] C. O. 7/22.

[4] C. O. 28/93, 95. See Anon., *Some Remarks in Reference to Recent Proceedings of the Legislature of Barbados &c. &c. &c.* (London, 1826).

[5] C. O. 71/60, 63, 64.

[6] C. O. 101/65, 66.

[7] C. O. 285/29, 36.

Vincent proved unacceptable to British authorities and their objections were not overcome until 1830.[1]

Nowhere was resistance more stubborn than in Jamaica. The lower house in 1823 declined to pass any of the suggested measures save one protecting females from violence against their persons.[2] Three years later, a newly-elected assembly adopted a revised code, but this suffered disallowance as meeting neither the letter nor the spirit of the Bathurst recommendations.[3] It was promptly repassed with no better results[4] and a new one of 1829 met a similar fate.[5] Great bitterness resulted;[6] it was only in 1831 that a bill satisfactory to home officials won the island legislature's sullen approbation.[7]

The British ministry obviously had no desire to force the issue of constitutionality and hence wisely forbore expanding its program, contenting itself with disallowing objectionable measures and with suggesting changes, as already noted.[8] The Trinidad order in council was meanwhile enforced despite protests of the colony's inhabitants.[9]

[1] C. O. 260/47; *A Communication from Sir Charles Brisbane, K.C.B., Governor of Saint Vincent, to the House of Assembly of That Colony. Dated 17th of August, 1826* . . . (London, 1826).

[2] C. O. 137/154.

[3] C. O. 137/163, 165.

[4] C. O. 137/167.

[5] C. O. 137/169.

[6] See Anon., *The Colonial Office versus The Assembly of Jamaica, and the Amelioration of the Negroes* [London, n.d.].

[7] C. O. 139/69.

[8] "Titles of all Acts passed by Colonial Legislatures respecting Slaves, since May, 1823," in *Gt. Br., H. C., Sess., Pap.*, 1826, XXVI (214), p. 395. "Papers Containing Abstract of Acts passed by the Legislatures of the West India Colonies, since 15 May, 1823, for improving the Condition of Slaves," in *Gt. Br., H. C., Sess. Pap.*, 1826, XXIX (607). See Anon., *The Progress of Colonial Reform* . . . (London, 1826) and Anon., *The Further Progress of Colonial Reform* . . . (London, 1827), maintaining that the colonial legislatures were not meeting the central government's recommendations and urging parliamentary action, and Alexander M'Donnell, *The West India Legislatures Vindicated From the Charge of Having Resisted the Call of the Mother Country For the Amelioration of Slavery* (London, 1826), declaring that there had been a progressive softening of the slave régime in the colonies for a quarter of a century and that the government's recommendations had not been fully met because some were based on wrong principles. The contrasting views are nowhere better stated than in these two pamphlets.

[9] See the petition against it in C. O. 295/62; "Laws and Regulations which prescribe the time to be allowed to Slaves in Trinidad for the cultivation of their Provision Grounds; Wages fixed for Sunday Labour; together with the rate of Exchange between Trinidad and England at the time such were fixed," in *Gt. Br., H. C., Sess. Pap.*, 1826–27, XXIII (465), p. 1.

A new slave law embodying the ameliorative measures was put into operation in St. Lucia [1] and, when the Demerara Court of Policy failed to adopt Lord Bathurst's suggestions, the system in force in Trinidad was extended to cover that colony as well.[2]

As concrete evidence of their sincerity in advocating improvement of the blacks' lot, the Planters and Merchants aided in rejuvenating the moribund Incorporated Society for the Conversion and Religious Instruction and Education of the Negro Slaves in the British West India Islands during the summer of 1823. The sum of £1,000 per annum was appropriated towards its support, many members of the Caribbean interest individually became regular contributors and pledges of £100 per year each were secured from the trading associations in Liverpool and Glasgow.[3]

Prominent figures in the London West India group—Sir Henry Martin, C. R. Ellis, George Hibbert, William Manning, C. N. Pallmer, Gilbert Mathison, and James Colquhoun—became members of the missionary body's board of governors. Appeals for funds were issued, absentee proprietors in particular being called upon for assistance,[4] and contributions in the next decade averaged about £3,-

---

[1] C. O. 253/22, 23.

[2] Anon., *The Petition and Memorial of the Planters of Demerara and Berbice, on the Subject of Manumission, Examined* . . . (London, 1827). *Proceedings Before the Privy Council, Against Compulsory Manumission in the Colonies of Demerara and Berbice* (London, 1827). R. Wilmot Horton, *Speech . . . in the House of Commons on the 6th of March, 1828, on Moving for the Production of the Evidence Taken Before the Privy Council, Upon an Appeal Against the Compulsory Manumission of Slaves in Demerara and Berbice* (London, 1828). Anon., "A Gentleman in the Country," *Observations on the Demerara Memorial, and on the False Assumption, That Enslaved British Subjects are Legal Chattels* (London, 1839). "Papers in Explanation of the Measures adopted by His Majesty's Government for the Melioration of the Slave Population in the West India Possessions . . .," in *Gt. Br., H. C., Sess. Pap.*, 1826–27, XXV (53 and 347) and XXVI (1); 1828, XXVII (89); 1829, XXV (333), p. 153. "Minutes of Evidence taken by His Majesty's Privy Council, in the matter of the Berbice and Demerara Manumission in Council on 10, 20, and 21 December, 1827," in *Gt. Br., H. C., Sess. Pap.*, 1828, XXV (261), p. 433. "Orders in Council respecting the Manumission of Slaves in Demerara and Berbice which have been issued since the Examination of Evidence upon that Subject before the Privy Council," in *Gt. Br., H. C., Sess. Pap.*, 1829, XXV (301), p. 29. "Order in Council for Consolidating the Laws for improving the Condition of Slaves in the Colonies of Trinidad, Berbice, Demerara, St. Lucia, Cape of Good Hope, and Mauritius," in *Gt. Br., H. C., Sess. Pap.*, 1830, XXI (676), p. 413; 1830–31, XVI (230), p. 1.

[3] *Min. W. I. Plant. and Mer.*, July 23, 1823 and following.

[4] Circular letter of 1826 accompanying a printed report of the proceedings of a branch society in St. Kitts, in the West India Committee archives.

500 annually. Eight chaplains and three catechists were consequently sent out to the sugar colonies in 1824.[1]

But, unhappily, a fundamental and much needed change in Established Church organization in the West Indies, occurring shortly after, rendered this most laudable effort of little avail. By Royal Letters Patent two colonial dioceses, that of Jamaica and that of Barbados and the Leeward Islands, were created in 1824,[2] and Bishops Christopher Lipscomb and William H. Coleridge,[3] the prelates in control, immediately undertook the arduous task of correcting the manifold abuses which had arisen within their respective jurisdictions through a century of neglect.

Though viewed suspiciously by the planters, who saw in the bishops spies sent out to report on the state of slavery, and with ill-concealed hostility by certain of the island clergy,[4] this measure won the support of leading West Indians in the British capital who hailed it as a step toward bettering social conditions beyond the Atlantic.[5] However, with the formation of these overseas bishoprics, the presence of independent chaplains maintained by the Incorporated Society became incompatible with ecclesiastical discipline and that organization was forced to limit itself to paying the salaries of catechists and school teachers whose activities were directed by the parish clergy. Fifty such lay workers were dependent upon it in 1832. All came to be named by local episcopal authority, the supporting body lost touch with them and the results actually achieved were quite too insignificant to warrant the extensive expenditures entailed.[6]

Adoption of the Canning resolutions and colonial opposition to the

[1] *Address of the Incorporated Society* . . . ([London], 1825). Annual Reports from 1823 (London, 1824 on). J. M. Trew, *An Appeal to the Christian Philanthropy of the People of Great Britain and Ireland, in Behalf of the Religious Instruction and Conversion of Three Hundred Thousand Negro Slaves* (London, 1826).

[2] Financial provision for them was made under 6 Geo. IV c. 88, amended by 7 Geo. IV c. 4. The salaries of the bishops were set at £4,000 sterling each with a retiring pension of £1,000 after ten years' service.

[3] He was accompanied to his see by his nephew, Henry Nelson Coleridge, whose *Six Months in the West Indies*, first published anonymously, became the most popular West Indian travel book of the day. For the bishop's arrival in Barbados, see *Six Months*, pp. 43, 44. Upon Bishop Coleridge's resignation in 1842, his diocese was split and was formed into the Diocese of Barbados and the Diocese of Antigua.

[4] See Bridges, *Annals*, II, 383. Ellis, *Diocese of Jamaica*, pp. 64, 65.

[5] *Min. W. I. Plant. and Mer.*, Oct. 22, 1824.

[6] Brown, *History of the Propagation of Christianity*, III, 449.

Bathurst reform program precipitated a lively discussion of the whole slavery question in Great Britain. This paralleled the abolition controversy of more than three decades before [1] in curious fashion. Both opponents [2] and advocates [3] of the Caribbean labor régime sought to secure support through pamphlets setting forth "the true state of the slave." They were soon in dispute over points of fact and differences between the two groups were brought into high relief by a bitter altercation between the Reverend Thomas Cooper, a Unitarian missionary, and Robert Hibbert, member of a leading Caribbean family in England.

This well-intentioned gentleman had sent Cooper and his wife to Jamaica in 1817 to ascertain the practicability of improving his slaves' condition through giving them religious instruction. The couple had met with little success due to lack of coöperation on the part of their patron's plantation officials and had returned to England much disheartened some years later. Cooper thereupon employed the first-hand knowledge he had gained in advocating emancipation [4] but was soon in difficulties as Hibbert took sharp exception to the published account of conditions on his estate. The resulting war of pens lent spice to the whole question and was eagerly followed by the British public.[5]

[1] See Chapter VIII.

[2] See for example, Bickell, *The West Indies As They Are; or a Real Picture of Slavery;* [Zachary Macaulay, editor], *Negro Slavery; or, a View of Some of the More Prominent Features of That State of Society, as it Exists in . . . the Colonies of the West Indies. Especially in Jamaica* (London, 1823) ; [William Naish], *A Brief Description of the Toil and Sufferings of Slaves in the British Sugar Colonies, at the present time, by several Eye Witnesses* (London, n.d.) ; *James Stephen, The Slavery of the British West India Colonies Delineated* (2 vols., London, 1824, 1830).

[3] Alexander Barclay, *A Practical View of the Present State of Slavery in the West Indies* (London, 1826). Britannicus, pseud., *State of Society and Slavery in Jamaica* (London, 1824). "Condition of the Negroes in Our Colonies," in *The Quar. Rev.,* July 1823, pp. 475–508. Sir Henry T. De la Beche, *Notes on the Present Condition of the Negroes in Jamaica* (London, 1825). John Foster, *Two Letters, On the State of the Negroes in the West Indies* (Bedford, 1824). Gibbs W. Jordan, *A Statement of the Condition and Treatment of Negro Slaves in the Island of Barbados* (London, n.d.). William Sells, *Remarks on the Condition of the Slaves in the Island of Jamaica* (London, 1823). Nathaniel Sotham, *Plain Facts, or Circumstances as They Really Are; Being an Impartial and Unprejudiced Account of the State of the Black Population in the Island of Jamaica* (London, 1824).

[4] In Macaulay, ed., *Negro Slavery; or a View . . .*

[5] Robert Hibbert, *Facts Verified Upon Oath, in Contradiction of the Report of the Rev. Thomas Cooper, Concerning the General Condition of the Slaves in Jamaica* (London, 1824). Thomas Cooper, *Correspondence Between George Hibbert, Esq., and the Rev. T. Cooper, Relative to the Condition of the Negro Slaves in Jamaica . . .* (London, 1824). Cooper, *Facts Illustrative of the*

Scripture was appealed to by both the West Indians and the emancipationists.[1] When the latter called upon the clergy to use their pulpits in diffusing knowledge of slavery's evils, planter spokesmen branded them prostitutors of religion and denounced churchmen preaching anti-slavery sermons as individuals abusing the sacred character of their office.[2]

Reverend John Riland held the Society for the Propagation of the Gospel up to shame because of its owning slaves on estates in Barbados which supported Codrington College [3] and called upon the organization to adopt a genuinely Christian attitude toward them.[4] This phase of the discussion led to renewed interest in West Indian missionary labors.[5]

As in the earlier contest, hot disputes centered around the negroes' position which was regularly contrasted, favorably or unfavorably,

condition of the Negro Slaves in Jamaica (London, 1824). Cooper, A Letter to Robert Hibbert, Jun. Esq., in Reply to His Pamphlet "Facts Verified Upon Oath . . ." (London, 1824). See also Anon., "A West Indian," The Rev. Mr. Cooper and His Calumnies . . . (Jamaica, 1825).

[1] Anon., Is the System of Slavery Sanctioned or Condemned by Scripture? . . . (London, 1824). Anon., Is West Indian Slavery justifiable by the New Testament? (Dublin, n.d.). Rev. B. Bailey, A Dissertation Upon the Nature of Service or Slavery Under the Levitical Law . . . (London, 1824). Edward Eliot, Christianity and Slavery (London, 1833). Robert Lindoe, Observations Upon Slavery; Setting Forth, That to Hold the Principle of Slavery is to Deny Christ (London, 1824). Roberts, The Tocsin, or Slavery the Curse of Christendom (London, 1826). Andrew Thomson, Slavery Not Sanctioned, but Condemned, by Christianity (London, n.d.). Rev. D. Wilson, The Guilt of Forbearing to Deliver Our British Colonial Slaves. A Sermon . . . (London, 1830). Robert Young, A View of Slavery in Connection With Christianity . . . (London, 1825).

[2] Anon., Address to the Clergy of the Established Church, and to Christian Ministers of every Denomination (London, 1826). Replied to in Anon., Negro Slavery. Observations, in Answer to an "Address to the Clergy . . ." (London, 1826) and Alexander McDowell, Christianity and Slavery. An Address to the British Clergy, Showing That the Two are Most Improperly Blended as a Controversial Question (London, 1829).

[3] See page 12.

[4] Two Letters . . . Relative to the Slave-Cultured Estates of the Society for the Propagation of the Gospel (London, 1828). Also his On the Coderington Estates . . . (London, 1830). The slaves on these properties were in no better condition than those on private holdings. Few were married and none were given religious instruction. Their state became a public scandal following Riland's attack and society officials gave in to the extent that negro children under ten were allowed to be taught the catechism, but not reading or arithmetic.

[5] Sir G. H. Rose, A Letter on the Means and Importance of Converting the Slaves in the West Indies to Christianity (London, 1823). Richard Watson, The Religious Instruction of Slaves in the West-India Colonies Advocated and Defended (London, 1824).

with that of the British peasant and factory worker. The rapid industrialization of England since 1800, with its attendant social horrors, gave peculiar force to the colonial contention that the slaves' lot was in reality a relatively happy and carefree one.[1]

The comparative productiveness of free and servile labor was much discussed. Reformers maintained that it was to the planters' own interest to employ hired workmen and advocated the creation of a negro tenantry along the lines adopted by Josiah Steele[2] near the close of the preceding century.[3] In 1829, Seth Driggs of Trinidad proposed to manumit a thousand slaves provided that they would enter into engagements to serve him as apprentices for fourteen years. Great hopes were entertained that a practical demonstration of the superior character of voluntary labor might thus be given,[4] but the project failed to materialize.

Champions of the existing order held that St. Domingo's melancholy state furnished an irrefutable argument against liberation of

[1] See Anon., *The Condition of the West India Slave Contrasted With That of the Infant Slave in Our English Factories* (London, n.d.). Anon., *Anti-Negro Emancipation, An Appeal to Mr. Wilberforce* (London, 1824). John Gladstone, *A Statement of Facts, Connected With the Present State of Slavery in the British Sugar and Coffee Islands . . . Together With a View of the Present Situation of the Lower Classes in the United Kingdom . . .* (London, 1830). "Mackenzie's Haiti and Bayley's Four Years in the West Indies," in *Fraser's Magazine*, Aug. 1830, pp. 61–66. "Sica," *pseud,* "The Slave Trade," in *The Gent. Mag.,* Sept., 1823, p. 222. Nathaniel Sotham, *Plain Facts; or the Question of West India Slavery Seriously Examined by the Test of Truth and Observation* (Cheltenham 1825). For a reply to such reasoning, see Thomas Clarkson, "The Argument,—'That the Colonial Slaves Are Better off Than the British Peasantry,' Answered, From the Royal Jamaica Gazette of June 21, 1823," *Negro Slavery*, No. 11.

[2] See pages 70 and 71. It should be mentioned that a planter whose property lay near to the Steele estate declared at this time that thirty years of negro tenant farming had ruined the latter. See "West India Slavery," in *The Gent. Mag.,* May, 1824, pp. 420, 421.

[3] Anon., *Considerations on the Expediency of an Improved Mode of Treatment of Slaves in the West Indian Colonies . . .* (London, 1820). Josiah Conder, *Wages or the Whip* (London, 1833). Clarkson, *Thoughts on the Necessity of Improving the Condition of the Slaves in the British Colonies.* James Cropper, *A Letter Addressed to the Liverpool Society for Promoting the Abolition of Slavery . . .* (Liverpool, 1823). Adam Hodgson, *A Letter to M. Jean-Baptiste Say, on the Comparative Expense of Free and Slave Labour* (Liverpool, 1823). [William Naish], *The Advantages of Free Labour Over the Labour of Slaves, elucidated in the cultivation of Pimento, Ginger, and Sugar* (London, n.d.).

[4] See papers in C. O. 28/103, 104. *This Indenture of Apprenticeship and Servitude is Voluntarily made and entered into* [begin] . . ., [Bridgetown, 1829].

the slaves.[1] Emancipationists on the other hand declared that the condition of the free blacks there was infinitely superior to that of the bondsmen in the British colonies and added somewhat feebly that, if the island's exports had declined, this must most certainly be because the standard of living had risen and internal consumption had increased.[2]

In general, the emancipation controversy was carried on on a higher plane than the abolition struggle had been. As before, leaders in this new crusade were, on the whole, zealous though somewhat misguided philanthropists, humanitarians without personal stakes in the contest. Their opponents, on the contrary, were defending property and while, for the most part, they readily enough acknowledged the inherent evils of slavery in the abstract, they naturally could not calmly countenance attacks upon an institution affording them their incomes. It is worthy of note that while emancipation would liberate the slaves of South Africa and Mauritius as well as those in the Caribbean colonies, the former regions, recently acquired and almost unknown, were seldom mentioned and efforts were concentrated against bondage as it existed in the closer and more familiar Caribbean.[3]

There was less appeal to blind prejudice than there had been a generation earlier. Tales of atrocities played a much smaller rôle in attacks,[4] doubtless because the islanders themselves now gave full publicity to events which might otherwise have been misinterpreted.[5] Pithy summaries of the question were issued by both parties to provide their supporters with talking points and to win over the busy

[1] Anon., *Deplorable State of Hayti, or St. Domingo,* [London, n.d.]. Anon., *The Rural Code of Haiti* . . . (London, 1827). James Franklin, *The Present State of Hayti* . . . (London, 1828). Charles Mackenzie, *Notes on Haiti* . . . (2 vols., London, 1830).

[2] John Taylor, *Negro Emancipation and West Indian Independence the True Interest of Great Britain* (Liverpool, 1824).

[3] In sharp contrast to the scores of pamphlets defending West Indian slavery, the number of those written in the interest of the planters in other British tropical colonies was negligible. Among them may be mentioned Captain Vicars, *Calumny Exposed* . . . (London, 1831).

[4] One pamphlet savoring of methods of three decades earlier was Anon., *Account of a Shooting Excursion on the Mountains Near Dromilly Estate, in the Parish of Trelawny, and Island of Jamaica, in the Month of October, 1824 ! ! !* (London 1824).

[5] See for example *Report of the Trial of Fourteen Negroes, at the Court-House, Montego-Bay, January 28, 1824, and the Two Following Days, on a Charge of Rebellious Conspiracy; With the Arguments of the Advocates and the Speeches of the Judges* (Montego Bay, Jamaica, 1824).

reader.[1] An interesting feature of the struggle was the fact that while Earl Bathurst urged emancipation, R. Wilmot Horton, Under-Secretary of State for War and the Colonies, supported the planter interest.

Emancipationists tended to question the value of an overseas empire of any kind and to deny the importance of the tropical American colonies in particular: the West India group on the contrary was strongly imperialistic, stressed the economic worth of the sugar islands in the past and held that they were still the most precious of all Great Britain's far-flung possessions.[2] Singularly enough, the two features of the slave régime most shocking to British susceptibilities were the "desecration of the Sabbath" through holding Sunday markets and the lack of marriage relations among the negroes.

The fight on the plantation labor system was increasingly led by the Society for the Mitigation and Gradual Abolition of Slavery Throughout the British Dominions. Virtually every member of the old African Institution joined its ranks and so completely did it absorb the latter that the Institution discontinued its own meetings in 1827 and disbanded some years after.[3] The Society's chief organ became *The Anti-Slavery Monthly Reporter*,[4] founded in 1825 and sold at the exceedingly low price of a half-penny per copy so as to secure extensive circulation. Its editorial supervision was in the hands of Zachary Macaulay, through whose influence the widely-read *Christian Observer* [5] was at the same time turned to propaganda purposes.

Other religious journals, such as *The Wesleyan Methodist Maga-*

---

[1] Anon., *A Brief View of the Nature and Effects of Negro Slavery as it Exists in the Colonies of Great Britain* (London, 1823). Anon., *Cheap Charity; a Dialogue on the Present Condition of the Negroes* . . . (London, 1824). Anon., *Negro Emancipation: A Dialogue Between Mr. Ebenezer Eastlove and Giles Homespun* (London, 1824). Anon., *"An Abolitionist," The Negro's Memorial, or, Abolitionist's Catechism* (London, n.d.). [Alexander McDonnell], *Epitome of the West India Question, in the Form of a Dialogue Between an Abolitionist and a West Indian* (London, 1827).

[2] See for example "Colonial Policy—Value of Colonial Possessions," in *The Ed. Rev.*, Aug. 1825, pp. 271 ff. "Value of the West Indian Colonies to the Mother Country," in *The Gent. Mag.*, March, 1824, pp. 224 ff. "The West India Question," in *Blackwood's*, Feb. 1832, pp. 412 ff. "The West Indies," in *The Ed. Rev.*, Jan. 1825, pp. 464 ff.

[3] It was finally dissolved in 1833. (Annual Reports.)

[4] Later *The Anti-Slavery Reporter*.

[5] Published monthly in London as an organ of the "Clapham Sect." Macaulay had himself served as editor from 1802 to 1816.

zine,[1] *The Evangelical Magazine and Missionary Chronicle,*[2] *The Missionary Herald,*[3] and *Missionary Notices*[4] freely opened their columns to the body and proved of inestimable value in winning public support. Among lay periodicals, the foremost champion of emancipation was *The Edinburgh Review,*[5] while *The Scots Magazine, The Gentleman's Magazine,* and *The Monthly Review* gave the movement qualified support and on occasion sprang stoutly to its defence.[6]

The slavery interest's activities were directed by a "literary committee" of the Society of West India Planters and Merchants. Rejecting a proposal made at the opening of the controversy that *The Sentinel,* edited by one J. Clayton Jennyns, an impecunious, contemnible individual formerly barrister at law in Demerara,[7] be adopted as its official mouthpiece,[8] that body first devoted its energies to the publication or purchase and distribution of pamphlets and periodicals containing articles favorable to the planter cause.

Thus, 1,000 copies of Mr. Baring's speech opposing the Buxton resolutions[9] were ordered printed,[10] as were 2,000 of an appeal for the support of the ordinary citizen of Great Britain,[11] and 30,000 circulars listing pamphlets presenting the Caribbean point of view for binding in current magazines.[12] Mr. Hibbert's reply to the Reverend

---

[1] Founded as *The Arminian Magazine* and continued as such, 1778–1797; then published as *The Methodist Magazine* until 1821, when the new name was adopted.

[2] Founded as *The Evangelical Magazine* in 1793; the later title was adopted in 1812. It was the organ of the new evangelical dissent.

[3] Organ of the Baptist Missionary Society.

[4] Organ of the Wesleyan Missionary Society.

[5] Founded by Henry Brougham, ardent champion of the negro cause, and friends. Brougham was long its foremost contributor.

[6] Notably in reviews of controversial books and pamphlets.

[7] See his *The Substance of a Remonstrance to the Earl Bathurst, on the Abuses in the Administration of Justice, and the Unconstitutional Continuance of Foreign Laws, in the Ceded British Colonies . . .* (London, 1821) and *Appeal to Earl Bathurst . . .* (London, 1828). In 1818, while editor of the British weekly, *The Champion,* he was loaned £500 by the West India interest.

[8] *Min. W. I. Plant. and Mer.,* March 1 and 10, 1823.

[9] For this pamphlet, see note 2, p. 410.

[10] *Min. Lit. Comm., W. I. Plant. and Mer.,* June 30, 1823.

[11] Anon., *Negro Emancipation: A Dialogue Between Mr. Ebenezer Eastlove and Giles Homespun.*

[12] *Min. Lit. Comm., W. I. Plant. and Mer.,* Jan. 5, 1825.

Thomas Cooper's charges [1] was financed,[2] some 2,500 reprints of a favorable essay in *John Bull* were ordered for circulation in provincial towns,[3] and 3,000 copies of a petition to the Crown in defense of plantation interests were published.[4]

Similarly, supplies of Cobbett's *Political Register*,[5] of a pamphlet presenting a sunny view of Jamaican slavery,[6] of *Blackwood's Edinburgh Magazine*,[7] and of reports of the Society for the Conversion and Religious Instruction and Education of the Negro Slaves in the British West India Islands [8] were purchased and given out gratis from time to time, particularly to country booksellers.[9] The paid insertion in newspapers of "communications from readers," setting forth colonial observance of the abolition law and the kind treatment afforded negroes, was authorized.[10] James McQueen, editor of *The Glasgow Courier*, was on two occasions voted one hundred guineas for his exertions in behalf of the planters;[11] Mr. Washborough, in charge of *The Common Sense Book*,[12] was granted £60;[13] Alexander M'Donnell, author of an attack on compulsory manumission,[14] was given £100,[15] and James Franklin, writer of a book depicting the low state to which free St. Domingo had fallen,[16] one hundred guineas.[17]

The patronage thus granted publishers, editors, and authors inevitably drew offers of assistance from individuals of small merit. Mr. Jennyns, debt-ridden and effervescent as ever, proved undaunted by the rebuff accorded him and in 1824 sought aid in establishing a

[1] For this pamphlet, see note 5, page 422.
[2] *Min. Lit. Comm., W. I. Plant. and Mer.*, May 17, 1824.
[3] *Ibid.*, Feb. 21, 1825.
[4] *Ibid.*, Feb. 20, 1826.
[5] *Ibid.*, Dec. 8, 1823.
[6] Sells, *Remarks*.
[7] *Min. Lit. Comm., W. I. Plant. and Mer.*, Jan. 5, 1825, May 24, 1828.
[8] *Ibid.*, May 24, 1828.
[9] *Ibid.*, Dec. 22, 1823.
[10] *Ibid.*, Dec. 1, 1823.
[11] *Ibid.*, Dec. 22, 1823, March 22, 1824. The firm of McQueen, McKay and Co. of Glasgow, with which McQueen was associated, had estates in the Leeward Islands and Trinidad. McQueen also defended colonial interests in *Blackwood's*. His personal collection of Blue Books covering slavery is now in the Colonial Institute, London.
[12] Published in London. Vol. I, no. 1 (undated) was apparently issued in the spring of 1824. But three numbers seem to have appeared.
[13] *Min. Lit. Comm., W. I. Plant. and Mer.*, May 17, 1824.
[14] *Compulsory Manumission; or an Examination of the Actual State of the West India Question* (London, 1827).
[15] *Min. Lit. Comm., W. I. Plant. and Mer.*, March 21, 1827.
[16] *The Present State of Hayti* . . .
[17] *Min. Lit. Comm., W. I. Plant. and Mer.*, April 2, 1828.

pro-colonial newspaper, *Common Sense*,[1] but without success.[2] The former directors of the defunct *Sunday Herald* laid their failure to the support they had given the colonial cause and sought compensation which was, however, refused them.[3] The proprietor of *The Phoenix* likewise requested assistance without result.[4]

Annoyed by such demands, the literary committee in March, 1826, declared that it could not meet the expectations of persons undertaking publications without a specific understanding;[5] but when, a year later, the proprietor of *The New Times* presented a bill for £96.5.0 to cover unauthorized distributions of issues of his paper containing friendly articles, he was allowed £100 lest he turn against the West India interest.[6] At about the same time the request of the proprietor of *The Inspector, Literary Magazine and Review,* that the body take over this periodical, was declined though the editor was allowed £210 to cover his losses in connection with it.[7] In 1826, £500 was voted for "a purpose connected with the objects of this committee requiring the utmost secrecy,"[8] the nature of which can only be conjectured.

The Times, The Chronicle, The British Press, The Herald, The Representative, The Courier, The Globe and Traveler, John Bull, and *The English Gentlemen* opened their columns to the committee in return for monetary consideration.[9] In March, 1827, the Society of Planters and Merchants agreed to bear the expense of publishing *The West India Reporter,* "a very useful publication" founded shortly before.[10] For the next five years it served as official organ [11] of the colonial interest and became *The Anti-Slavery Monthly Reporter's* leading opponent.

News of emancipationist activities, reaching the West Indies by every packet, caused intense excitement among the residents. Feeling ran high, popular opinion turned against the missionaries and dissenting preachers who were generally regarded as local agents of the anti-

---

[1] Not to be confused with *The Common Sense Book.*
[2] *Min. Lit. Comm., W. I. Plant. and Mer.,* June 7th.
[3] *Ibid.,* Feb. 21, 1825.
[4] *Ibid.,* Feb. 20, 1826.
[5] *Ibid.,* March 6th.
[6] *Ibid.,* March 14, 1827.
[7] *Ibid.,* March 21, 1827.
[8] *Ibid.,* March 6th.
[9] *Ibid.,* June 7, 1826.
[10] Vol. I, no. 1 is dated Jan. 1, 1827.
[11] *Min. Lit. Comm., W. I. Plant. and Mer.,* March 21, 1827.

slavery party, and persecutions broke out spontaneously throughout the Caribbean.

The movement in Jamaica was led by the Reverend George Bridges, a bigoted Anglican churchman currying the planters' favor,[1] who also turned his pen to their defense, much to his personal profit.[2] Warrants were served on the missionaries for their failure to perform militia service, a mob damaged the Wesleyan chapel presided over by Mr. Ratcliffe together with the latter's home, slaves were forbidden to attend meetings at the various stations, services were broken up by gangs of rowdies, and laws designed to check nonconformist activities were passed.[3]

When, in August, 1823, a servile revolt of dangerous proportions broke out among the Demerara blacks because of a belief entertained by them that they had been accorded rights by parliamentary action which their masters were withholding, charges of inciting rebellion were preferred against John Smith, a gentle, inoffensive representative of the London Missionary Society in advanced stages of consumption, and he was clapped into prison.[4] Trial by court-martial resulted in a verdict of guilty and Smith was sentenced to

[1] See [Frank Cundall], "The Rev. George Wilson Bridges, Historian," in *Journal of the Inst. of Jam.*, April, 1895, pp. 101 ff., and for the tragedies which shadowed his later years, the autobiographical and privately printed *1834–1862. Outlines and Notes of Twenty-Nine Years* (no imprint, n.d.).

[2] *Bridges, A Voice from Jamaica; in Reply to William Wilberforce, Esq. M.P.* (London, 1823) *and Dreams of Dulocracy; or, the Puritanical Obituary: "An Appeal," Not to the Romantic Sensibility, but to the Good Sense of the British Public* (London, 1824). He was presented with a set of plate by the assembly as well as being voted money for his efforts. See *Outlines and Notes*, pp. 10, 31; Gardner, *Jamaica*, p. 375.

[3] "Despatches from Jamaica relative to Attack on the Wesleyan Meeting House and Dwelling of Mr. Ratcliffe, the Missionary," in *Gt. Br., H. C., Sess. Pap.*, 1826–27, XVIII (554), p. 459. Phillippo, *Jamaica; Past and Present*, p. 66. One of the reasons for disallowing the new slave act of 1826 (see page 419) was because it seriously interfered with missionary work on the part of sectarists. For an attack on the government for supporting religious toleration in the colonies by thus disallowing acts opposed to it, see "Vindex," *pseud., The Conduct of the British Government Towards the Church of England in the West India Colonies* (London, 1831).

[4] David Chamberlin, *Smith of Demerara* (London, 1923). "Wray and Smith Among the Slaves," in *The Chronicle of the London Missionary Society*, August 1823, pp. 175–177. Edwin A. Wallbridge, *The Demerara Martyr* (London, 1848). There is not the slightest doubt regarding Smith's innocence. He was a simple man, sincerely devoted to his duty, and no meddler. His journal, strangely enough still unpublished (the original in the archives of the London Missionary Society; a fair copy in the Public Record office, C. O. 111/46; another in the archives of the West India Committee), filled

death but fell a victim to his disease before this could be carried out.[1]

On October 19, 1823, after having interrupted the services held by the Reverend William Shrewsbury in the Wesleyan chapel in Barbados on the two previous Sundays, an organized band destroyed the structure and the missionary's home and drove him and his wife to St. Vincent, from where they returned to England.[2]

A broadside issued the next day declared: "The inhabitants of this island are respectfully informed that, in consequence of the unmerited and unprovoked attacks which have been repeatedly made upon the community by the Methodist Missionaries (otherwise known as agents to the villanous African Society) a party of respectable Gentlemen formed the resolution of closing the Methodist concern altogether. With this view, they commenced their labours on Sunday evening, and they have the greatest satisfaction in announcing that by twelve o'clock last night, they effected the total destruction of the chapel." All true lovers of religion throughout the Caribbean were called upon to do likewise.[3]

Upon Governor Sir Henry Warde's offering a reward for information leading to the conviction of the rioters, defiant notices were posted

with its record of homely services performed for their black charges by himself and his wife, stands in noble contrast to the pompous laying-down of their duty to the slaves on the part of the Rev. Arch. Browne of Georgetown in his published *Three Discourses . . . Preached in St. Andrew's Church . . . in Consequence of the Insurrection Which Broke Out . . . on the Evening of the 18th August, 1823* (Demerara, 1824).

[1] C. O. 111/53. Anon., ed., *An Authentic Copy of the Minutes of Evidence on the Trial of John Smith . . .* (London, 1824). Anon., *The Case of John Smith, One of the Missionaries in Demerara, as Given by the Directors of the London Missionary Society* (Newcastle, 1824). Anon., ed., *The London Missionary Society's Report of the Proceedings Against the Late Rev. J. Smith . . .* (London, 1824). Anon., *Statement of the Proceedings of the Directors of the London Missionary Society, in the Case of Rev. John Smith . . .* (London, n.d.). *Proceedings of a General Court Martial Held at the Colony House in George Town, on Monday, the 13th Day of October, 1823 . . .* (London, 1824). "Papers respecting the trial of John Smith, a Missionary at Demerara," in *Gt. Br., H. C., Sess. Pap.,* 1824, XXIII (158, 333, 338).

[2] "Demolition of the Methodist Chapel in Barbadoes, and Expulsion of Mr. Shrewsbury, the Methodist Missionary," in *Gt. Br., H. C., Sess. Pap.,* 1825, XXV (113, 127). John V. Shrewsbury, *Memorials of the Rev. William J. Shrewsbury* (London, n.d.). The victim of this attack was accused of having preached incendiary sermons. To clear himself of that charge, he published certain ones to which exception had been taken as *Sermons Preached on Several Occasions in the Island of Barbados* (London, 1825).

[3] *Great and Signal Triumph Over Methodism, and Total Destruction of the Chapel* [Bridgetown, 1823].

threatening anyone coming forward to injure any individual in any shape with "that punishment which their crime will justly deserve," declaring that the persons involved in the late affair were individuals of the first respectability, who had acted from motives of patriotism and with the support of the community and warning all Methodist preachers that they approached the colony's shores at their own peril.[1] So widespread was the feeling against its agents that the Wesleyan Missionary Society felt called upon to make a public declaration of the nature of its operations beyond the Atlantic.[2]

These proceedings had a sharp repercussion in Great Britain. The government, unaware of Smith's tragic end, recalled Governor Murray, while Henry Brougham, in what he later considered his most notable forensic effort,[3] presented a motion to the House of Commons calling for an investigation of the case. This was lost after a debate calling forth the best in parliamentary oratory, during which Mr. Wilberforce made his last speech before the chamber.[4]

A year later, an account of happenings in Barbados was presented to the House by Mr. Buxton and a resolution denouncing "that scandalous and daring violation of the law" and pledging the Commons' concurrence in "every measure which his Majesty may deem necessary for securing ample protection and religious toleration to all his . . . subjects in that part of his . . . dominions" was adopted.[5] While the anti-sectarist demonstration went unpunished, it is interesting to note that, faced with this vigorous condemnation, a

---

[1] *Bridge-Town, Barbados, Thursday, October 23, 1823. Whereas a Proclamation having appeared* |begin] . . . [Bridgetown, 1823].

[2] *Statement of the Plan, Object, and Effects of the Wesleyan Missions in the West Indies* (London, 1824).

[3] Campbell, *Lives of Lord Lyndhurst and Lord Brougham*, p. 344.

[4] Anon., ed., *The Missionary Smith, Substance of the Debate in the House of Commons, on the 1st and . . . 11th of June, 1824* (London, 1824). Anon., ed., *Speeches Delivered in the House of Commons, on June 1st and 11th, 1824, Regarding the Proceedings at Demerara* . . . (Edinburgh, 1824). Anon., ed., *Substance of the Debate in the House of Commons, on Tuesday the 1st, and Friday the 11th, of June 1824, on a Motion of Henry Brougham, Esq.* . . . (London, 1824). *Brougham, Speeches on Social and Political Questions* . . . See also James Bennett, *The History of Dissenters During the Last Thirty Years (from 1808 to 1838)* (London, 1839), pp. 341, 342. The motion was defeated by a vote of 146 to 193.

[5] *Parl. Debates*, 2nd series, XIII, cols. 1285–1347. Anon., ed., *An Authentic Report of the Debate in the House of Commons, June 23d, 1825, on Mr. Buxton's Motion Relative to the Demolition of the Methodist Chapel and Mission House in Barbados* . . . (London, 1825). *Substance of the Debate in the House of Commons, June 23, 1825, on Mr. Buxton's Motion* . . . (London, 1825).

general meeting of the colony's inhabitants, called to petition the Crown for protection against the machinations of their enemies in England, adopted a declaration reprobating destruction of the chapel.[1]

The significance of the Smith and Shrewsbury episodes in the history of the reform movement lies in their influence on public opinion in the motherland. The average Englishman, smug and complacent, had been little moved by appeals made at the opening of this new campaign. Dramatic incidents were needed to arouse him— then his support would be given freely enough. These were afforded by occurrences in Demerara and Barbados. The West Indians could have committed no more fatal blunder than to attack the missionaries. Their hostile actions created a most painful sensation, "Smith" and "Shrewsbury" became rallying cries of all friends of religious freedom and, duly capitalized,[2] the outrages of 1823 cost the planters that general good will and support which had so long been their greatest asset.[3]

Only the outstanding events leading to the triumph of emancipation can be sketched here. Parliamentary legislation of July, 1824 prohibited the removal of slaves other than personal servants in actual attendance upon their masters from one colony to another while reserving the right for His Majesty in council to authorize changes in residence for terms not exceeding three years where it was evident that this was essential for the welfare of the negroes concerned.[4] In actual practice, such permission was not accorded unless female children exported were freed and families were maintained intact.[5]

This stringent regulation closed the possibility of planters on exhausted estates seeking fresh lands in the new colonies and seriously checked the development of Trinidad to which migrations from the old possessions had become increasingly frequent since the opening of the century.[6] In 1828 alone, eleven proprietors with over 2,000 blacks

[1] Anon., *A Declaration of Inhabitants of Barbados, Respecting the Demolition of the Methodist Chapel* (London, 1826).

[2] The press teemed with articles on the question. No matter was before the public more in the winter 1823–1824 than were these cases, and especially that of Mr. Smith. For typical attacks on the West Indians, see "Insurrection in Demerara," in *The Ed. Rev.*, March 1824, pp. 226 ff.; "Spirit of West India Society—Outrage at Barbados," in *ibid.*, August, 1825, pp. 479 ff. For a typical defense, see "Smith, the Missionary," in *Blackwood's*, June, 1824, pp. 679–690.

[3] On this point, see Caldecott, *The Church in the West Indies*, p. 89; Brougham, *Speeches on Social and Political Subjects*, II, 118.

[4] 5 Geo. IV c. 113.

[5] See Governor Woodford to Earl Bathurst, Dec. 22, 1826, C. O. 295/72.

[6] See pages 332 ff.

from seven British islands to the north were prevented from settling there through operation of the law.[1]

Under these circumstances, considerable numbers of field workers were fraudulently entered as servants [2] but local authorities refused to take cognizance of the abuse and vice-admiralty court officials, representing the Crown, were obliged to institute proceedings on their own initiative.[3] Governor Grant urged, in the interests of tranquillity, that offenders be permitted to escape trial and punishment by manumitting the negroes involved, but the home government refused to entertain the proposition and in the subsequent suits, heavy fines were meted out and the slaves were forfeited to the king.[4]

A boycott of Caribbean products was opened by the emancipation party in 1824 and was carried on with great vigor. Arguments adduced against their consumption [5] were identical with those employed thirty years before,[6] but, whereas supporting the movement in the earlier period had frequently deprived one of sugar, such sacrifice was not now necessary as the East Indian supply had become generally available. Advocates of the use of economic pressure consequently recommended purchasing free-grown oriental sugar as an effective means of forcing the planters' hands.[7]

This agitation was carried on principally by the Friends, notably by James Cropper of Liverpool, himself engaged in commerce with Asia.[8] When James Heywood established an East India sugar ware-

---

[1] Acting Governor Farquharson to the Secretary of State, a series of letters from October 12th, C. O. 295/78.

[2] President Laidlow to William Huskisson, March 10, 1828, C. O. 71/66. Governor Nicolay to George Murray, June 27, 1829 and to Mr. Twiss, Aug. 24, 1829, C. O. 71/67. Numerous papers in C. O. 295/80, 81.

[3] Papers covering several cases, C. O. 28/102, 103, 105, 107.

[4] Correspondence in C. O. 295/84.

[5] See for example, Anon., *To the consumers of sugar* [London, ca. 1825]; Anon., *West Indian Slavery Traced to its Actual Source* . . . (London, 1829); "Anthroos," pseud., *The Rights of Man (Not Paine's), But the Rights of Man, in the West Indies* (London, 1824); [Elizabeth Heyrick], *Immediate, Not Gradual Abolition; or, An Inquiry Into the Shortest, Safest, and Most Effectual Means of Getting Rid of West Indian Slavery* (London, 1824).

[6] See Chapter VIII.

[7] "East Indian Sugar Recommended," in *The Gent. Mag.*, March, 1826, pp. 229–231; [William Naish], *Reasons for Using East India Sugar* (London, 1828).

[8] See page 364. Cropper had urged the claims of East India sugar some time before. See his *Letters Addressed to William Wilberforce, M.P. Recommending the Encouragement of the Cultivation of Sugar in Our Dominions in the East Indies, as the Natural and Certain Means of Effecting the General and Total Abolition of the Slave Trade* (Liverpool, 1822).

house in London, such well-known personages as William Allen, Samuel Gurney, and William Crawford urged wholesale and retail buyers to place their orders with him.[1] Ambitious young men with limited means were advised to seek their fortunes as cane cultivators in Bengal.[2] At the same time, a Tropical Free-Labour Sugar Company with a capital of £4,000,000 was formed under authority of parliament[3] to operate plantations in and make importations from Sierra Leone.[4] The movement spread to America where the Quakers instituted a general boycott of produce grown by slaves, a fact which led Jesse Woodward, one of their number in New Brunswick, to propose establishing a sugar estate manned by paid hands in Trinidad.[5]

From the opening of the campaign to break down the Caribbean monopoly in the home market,[6] those championing the equalization of sugar duties made much of the fact that the East Indian article was produced by free labor. Joseph Marryat, agent for Grenada, declared this to be untrue and stoutly insisted that Bengalese estates were tilled by bondsmen, yellow rather than black, it was true, but slaves nevertheless.[7] Although this charge was denied by Zachary Macaulay,[8] it was taken up by other members of the West India group and became their principal defensive argument.[9] The claim was preposterous, stood no investigation, and won little support.

Cropper's dual position as the planters' foe and an East India merchant naturally laid him open to attack, and John Gladstone, also

[1] Lithographed announcement in the author's possession.

[2] Anon., *East India Sugar; or, An Inquiry Respecting the Means of Improving the Quality, and Reducing the Cost of Sugar Raised by Free Labour in the East Indies* (London, 1824).

[3] Journals of the House of Commons, LXXX, p. 474.

[4] *Free Sugar Company. Capital £4,000,000. Application for Shares to John Dougan. Esq., 28, Princes Street, Bank* [London, n.d.]. "Mercator," pseud., *View of Some of the Advantages of the Tropical Free-Labour Company* (London, 1825).

[5] Governor Woodford to Earl Bathurst, June 12, 1825; Bathurst to Woodford, Aug. 25, 1825, C. O. 295/66.

[6] See pages 361 ff.

[7] *A Reply to the Arguments Contained in Various Publications, Recommending Equalization of the Duties on East and West India Sugar.*

[8] "The Author of 'East and West India Sugar,'" *A Letter to William W. Whitmore, Esq. M.P. . . . .* (London, 1823).

[9] James McQueen, *The Colonial Controversy, Containing a Refutation of the Calumnies of the Anti-Colonists . . .* (Glasgow, 1825). George Saintsbury, *East India Slavery* (London, 1829). Williams, *Tour*, pp. 135, 136. For a reply, see B. Henderson, *East India Sugar Basins—East India Sugar Not Made by Slaves* (Camberwell, n.d.).

of Liverpool, a trader both to the Orient and tropical America as well as a Demerara proprietor,[1] made the most of the opportunity.[2] Impugnment of Cropper's motives in denouncing slavery and urging the boycott is perfectly understandable, but this was, in reality, quite unwarranted. His was one of those occasional cases in which conduct is not primarily influenced by self-interest though they may accidentally coincide.

From earliest times, free persons of color in the Caribbean had dwelt under various disabilities, such as not enjoying the right of franchise or of holding office.[3] These restrictions now came prominently to public notice and were largely removed through local enactment in the legislative colonies and by orders in council in those under crown control. Thus, limitations on the rights of free blacks were removed in Grenada in 1824, in Trinidad in 1826, in Barbados in 1829, and in St. Lucia, Jamaica, Dominica, Antigua, and St. Kitts successively in the years which followed.[4] Such action was a direct outcome of the emancipation struggle being carried on in Great Britain.

The outstanding incident connected with this phase of the general West Indian reform movement was the deportation of two native Jamaicans, Louis Lecesne and John Escoffery, persons of color leading the logical agitation against existing disabilities, to St. Domingo on the ground of their being aliens. They hastened to England and there found a supporter in Dr. Lushington who brought their case before parliament and secured redress and pecuniary compensation for them.[5] When the Reverend George Bridges, high church advocate of

---

[1] Father of William Ewart Gladstone.

[2] See *The Correspondence Between John Gladstone, Esq., M.P., and James Cropper, Esq., on the Present State of Slavery in the British West Indies; and on the Importation of Sugar from the British Settlements in India* (Liverpool, 1824).

[3] For the grievances of these people, see the memorials and correspondence in C. O. 7/7; C. O. 28/93; C. O. 71/69; C. O. 239/20; C. O. 253/18, 20; C. O. 295/63.

[4] See the papers in C. O. 7/34; C. O. 28/102; C. O. 71/71; C. O. 101/64; C. O. 137/171; C. O. 239/32; C. O. 253/26; C. O. 295/70.

[5] "Information respecting Lecesne and Escoffery, two free Men of Colour," in *Gt. Br., H. C., Sess. Pap.*, 1825, XXV (74), p. 133. "Estimate required to make good the Losses sustained by Louis Celeste Lescesne and John Escoffery, in consequence of their Removal from Jamaica," in *Gt. Br., H. C., Sess. Pap.*, 1830–31, VI (280) and 1831, XIII (30). *Parliamentary Debates*, 2nd series, XIII, cols. 1173–1205. Papers in C. O. 320/4. Anon., ed., *Report of the Debate in the House of Commons, June 16th, 1825, on Dr. Lushington's Motion Respecting the Deportation of Messrs. L. C. Lecesne and J. Escoffery* (Lon-

colonial rights, took occasion shortly after to cast aspersions upon these individuals in a history designed to present planter grievances,[1] his British publisher was haled into court under accusation of libel and was fined while sale of the offending work was ordered stopped.[2]

Runaway slaves from foreign possessions landing in the British islands had always, heretofore, been held and returned to their owners in accordance with understandings between the several colonial governments. This system had proved mutually advantageous, but in July, 1825 Lord Bathurst directed that the practice cease. His order caused considerable resentment among the proprietors since the French and Spanish immediately retaliated by ceasing to restore fugitive British blacks.[3]

In March, 1826, upon motion of Secretary Bathurst, the House of Lords unanimously concurred in the celebrated Commons resolution of 1823.[4] Two months later, in the popular chamber, Mr. Brougham declared that nothing effective had been done to better the slaves' condition and moved the adoption of a declaration of deep regret that the West India legislatures had so utterly failed to comply with the home government's wishes, coupled with a formal statement that the House of Commons would give serious consideration to such measures as might seem necessary to give them effect at the opening of the next session. His radical proposal was fortunately rejected by a two to one vote.[5]

don, 1825). [Mr. Barret], *A Reply to the Speech of Dr. Lushington, in the House of Commons, on the 12th June 1827, on the Condition of the Free-Coloured People of Jamaica* (London, 1828). William Burge, *A Letter to the Right Honorable Sir George Murray . . . Relative to the Deportation of Lecesne and Escoffery from Jamaica* (London, 1829). Hector Mitchel, *Two Letters to the Colonial Secretary . . . in Answer to the Yellow Book* (no imprint, n.d.).

[1] *Annals of Jamaica.*

[2] Anon., *Report of the Trial of Mr. John Murray . . . on an Endictment for a Libel on Messrs. Lecesne and Escoffery of Jamaica* (London, 1830).

[3] *Governor Woodford to Earl Bathurst*, Sept. 29, 1825, C. O. 295/67.

[4] Anon., ed., *Slavery in the West Indies. The Substance of the Debate in the House of Lords, March 7, 1826, on Lord Bathurst's Motion . . .* (London, 1826). Anon., ed., *The Speeches of the Lord Chancellor, Lord Viscount Dudley and St. Vincent, on Lord Bathurst's Motion* (London, 1826). Anon., ed., *The Substance of the Debate in the House of Lords on Lord Bathurst's Motion . . .* (London, 1826). Lord Viscount Dudley, *Slavery in the West Indies . . . A Speech Delivered in the House of Lords, March 7, 1826, on Lord Bathurst's Motion . . .* (London, 1826).

[5] The vote was 38 to 100. *Parl. Debates*, 2nd series, XV, cols. 1284 ff. Ralph Bernal, *Substance of the Speech . . . in the Debate in the House of Commons, on the 19th May, 1826, Upon Mr. Brougham's Motion For Taking Into Consideration . . . Such Measures as May Appear Necessary for Giving*

Members of the planter interest scored an important victory over their opponents through a memorable judicial decision made shortly after. The emancipationists, arguing from the premise of the Somerset case,[1] maintained that since a slave setting foot upon the free soil of the United Kingdom was automatically liberated, large numbers of negro servants who had accompanied their masters on visits to the mother country and had subsequently returned to the Caribbean were being illegally held in bondage there. Confident of their stand, they forced the issue to definitely determine such individuals' legal status.

Grace Jones, a negress, had been taken to England by her mistress, Mrs. Allen of Antigua, in 1822. A year after, the two had recrossed the Atlantic. In 1825, this female attendant was seized by the waiter of customs at St. Johns on the charge of having been illegally imported in contravention of the abolition law, and when, some months later, she was restored to Mrs. Allen by an island court and her owner was awarded £36 currency damages, the case was appealed to England through the instrumentality of humanitarians interested in the negro cause.

Lord Stowell, revered octogenarian judge of the British Admiralty Court, confirmed the decision of the lower court by an opinion rendered in 1827.[2] The West Indians were jubilant as greater security was thus afforded colonial property and the Society of Planters and Merchants voted £300 to aid in defraying expenses connected with the case.[3]

Three years later, the anti-slavery party again suffered reverses in an affair dear to its members' hearts. Kitty Hylton, a slave owned by the Reverend George Bridges, complained that she had been maltreated by his order. When the local council of protection dismissed the charges as groundless, officers of the Society for the Mitigation and Gradual Abolition of Slavery Throughout the British Domin-

Effect to the Resolution of the House of Commons on the 15th May, 1823 . . . (London, 1826). R. W. Horton, *Speech . . . in the Debate in the House of Commons, On the 19th of May, 1826, Upon Mr. Brougham's Motion . . .* (London, 1826).

[1] See page 246.

[2] "Copy of any Information received respecting the case of a person residing in the Island of Antigua, named Grace Jones, claiming to be Free, but whose Claim has been disputed," in *Gt. Br., H. C., Sess. Pap.,* 1826, XXVI (333), p. 411. Papers in C. O. 7/15, 16. John Haggard, *The Judgment of the Right Hon. Lord Stowell, Respecting the Slavery of the Mongrel Woman, Grace, on an Appeal from the Vice-Admiralty Court of Antigua . . .* (London, 1827).

[3] *Min. W. I. Plant. and Mer.,* Dec. 20, 1827.

ions laid matters before home authorities.[1] An investigation was ordered and the attorney-general of Jamaica found ground for criminal
prosecution,[2] but when an indictment was preferred against Bridges
the grand jury threw out the bill and the matter was dropped.[3] It was
altogether insignificant in itself, but had been pushed with malicious
delight by opponents of the Caribbean labor régime because of their
arch-foe's unfortunate connection with it.

Finally, in 1830, the slavery question entered upon its last phase.
Declaring that the colonists had failed to meet parliament's wishes
with respect to passing the ameliorative measures recommended to
them seven years before [4] and that they clearly could not be relied upon ever to free the negroes of their own volition, advocates
of emancipation now boldly demanded immediate liberation of all
bondmen through act of the central government. This became a
prominent feature of the program of thoroughgoing reform along
all lines then under agitation throughout the United Kingdom, a concerted attempt was made to pledge parliamentary candidates to such
a policy [5] and, in the elections of 1830 and 1831, voters were called
upon to return only those who had taken a positive stand in its favor.[6]
These new anti-colonial tactics were fiercely denounced by the West
Indian body [7] but they brought forth formal statements from numerous aspirants to office including members of the planter interest itself and served to markedly clarify the atmosphere.[8]

[1] Lord Belmore to Sir George Murray, Dec. 16, 1829, C. O. 137/169.

[2] Lord Belmore to Sir George Murray, June 2, 1830 and enclosures, C. O.
137/71.

[3] Lord Belmore to Sir George Murray, Aug. 31, 1830, C. O. 137/172.

[4] For a denial of this charge see [Resolutions Passed at the] Meeting of the
Standing Committee of West India Planters and Merchants, held . . . the
26th April, 1831 (London, n.d.).

[5] This had already been advocated by James Stephen in his England Enslaved by Her Own Slave Colonies (London, 1826). For a reply, see Charles
Thomson, Mr. Stephen's Attempt to Influence Legislation in His Address to
the Electors of Great Britain Considered . . . (London, 1826).

[6] Anon., Address to the Electors and People of the United Kingdom (London, 1830). Anon., Address to the People of Great Britain and Ireland . . .
(London, 1831).

[7] Anon., To the Electors of the United Kingdom (London, 1832). Anon.,
To the People of Great Britain and Ireland [London, n.d.]. [R. W. Horton],
An Address to the Electors of Great Britain on the Condition of the Negroes
in the British West Indies (London, 1831).

[8] R. Wilmot Horton, First Letter to the Freeholders of the County of
York, on Negro Slavery . . . (London, 1830). Horton, Second Letter . . .
(London, 1830). [Rose Price], Pledges on Colonial Slavery, to Candidates for
Seats in Parliament, Rightly Considered (Penzance, 1832).

Events in the Caribbean soon lent emphatic emphasis to the need for strong imperial action. In March, 1831, upon summons of a public meeting of Grenadan proprietors and merchants held two months before,[1] delegates from Barbados, Antigua, Demerara and Essequibo, Dominica, Grenada, St. Kitts, Nevis, St. Vincent, Tobago, and the Virgin Islands, who were members of the several legislatures and who had been named by popular consent,[2] met in Bridgetown, Barbados, to formulate a united expression of colonial sentiment on matters of general concern.

A short session resulted in the adoption of a series of resolutions setting forth the disadvantages under which the tropical American possessions were laboring, with war duties still saddling their produce and foreign growers underselling them in every market because of lower production costs arising from continued enjoyment of the slave trade,[3] as well as protesting vigorously against any contemplated spoliation of their property or interference with it.[4]

News of this West Indian congress, the first assembly of such a nature held in the colonies' history, filled home authorities with apprehension. Fearful lest it have an ominous political significance, Viscount Goderich, the new Secretary of State for War and the Colonies, sent hurried calls for full reports on the gathering of all executives[5] and sharply took to task Governor Lyon of Barbados who, with singular imperspicuity, had not even mentioned it in his official correspondence, holding the matter too insignificant to merit attention.[6]

Vehement protests against the taking of any step which would injure property rights were registered by the leading inhabitants of Grenada[7] and Antigua[8] and by the legislature of St. Vincent as well. The latter gave weight to its action by refusing to make grants of money for any purpose whatsoever other than meeting immediate needs until such time as proprietary interests in the Caribbean should

[1] For the call, see *At a Meeting of the Planters and Merchants, &c., of the Island of Grenada, held at the Court-House, in the Town of St. George, on Thursday, the 6th Day of January, 1831* [begin] . . . [St. George, 1831].

[2] For example see *Public Meeting of Planters, Merchants, &c.* [Kingstown, St. Vincent, 1831].

[3] See Chapter X.

[4] For these resolutions, see Schomburgk, *Barbados*, pp. 433 ff.

[5] For some of these, see President Lockart to Viscount Goderich, July 21, 1831, C. O. 71/72; Governor Campbell to Goderich, April 22, 1831, C. O. 101/71; Governor Hill to Goderich, July 20, 1831, C. O. 260/48; Governor Blackwell to Goderich, July 19, 1831, C. O. 285/38.

[6] See Lyon to Goderich, July 23, 1831, C. O. 28/105.

[7] *Public Meeting of Planters, Merchants, &c.* [St. George, Grenada, 1831].

[8] *Tobago Gezette*, Aug. 26, 1831.

have been secured.[1] At the same time, a gathering of the principal personages of St. Kitts denied parliament's right to legislate for extra-European portions of the empire [2] and Augustus Beaumont, a florid Jamaican journalist, demanded that the West Indies be given representation in the House of Commons or their independence.[3]

These varied demonstrations during the course of 1831 afforded ample evidence of colonial temper. Nevertheless, the British ministry adopted a bold policy late in the same year. An order in council, issued on November 2, laid down a series of carefully-drawn regulations for the care and treatment of slaves in the crown possessions, Trinidad, Berbice, and St. Lucia, specifying in great detail the quarters and allowances of food and clothing which must be provided, restricting punishments, and instituting a nine hour day.

A circular despatch of December 10th, addressed to the governors of all legislative colonies, likewise showed a firm determination to force at length favorable action there despite planter hostility. Charging that not a single effective ameliorative statute had been enacted since 1823 when Lord Bathurst had first urged the adoption of new slave codes harmonizing with the Canning resolutions, Viscount Goderich now called upon the several law-making bodies to pass declaratory acts giving local force to the recent crown colony order in its entirety and threatened to penalize any islands where this might not be done by withholding from them the benefits of a West Indian relief bill then being drawn up for presentation to parliament.[4] A direct bid for prompt compliance was subsequently made on May 13, 1832, when financial aid to the extent of half their respective annual revenues until something of a more permanent nature could be devised, was offered those colonies where the government's program should have been fully carried out.[5]

---

[1] Governor Hill to Lord Goderich, June 29, 1831 (private) and enclosures, C. O. 260/48.

[2] *The St. Christopher Advertiser*, Aug. 2, 1831.

[3] *The Jamaica Petition for Representation in the British House of Commons, or for Independence* [London, 1831].

[4] The order in council will be found in *Gt. Br., H. C., Sess. Pap.*, 1831–32, XLVI (no number; the first paper) pp. 93 ff.; the December despatch in the same volume, (279) pp. 3 ff. The latter also appears in Klingberg, *Anti-Slavery Movement*, pp. 360 ff. For the West Indian view regarding it, see [Frederick J. Robinson], "A Member of the West Indian Body," *Remarks on Lord Viscount Goderich's Dispatch to the Governors of the Colonies, of December 10, 1831* (London, 1832).

[5] See Major-General Grant to Viscount Goderich, Aug. 30, 1832, C. O. 295/93.

The November order was duly promulgated in the crown territories [1] and created an unprecedented sensation. A St. Lucian mass meeting denounced the several measures as being ruinous, charged the ministry with having exceeded its authority in laying them down, and sought parliamentary protection for colonial rights. Merchants in the island held that with such a short working day the proprietors could never meet their obligations and placed business on a cash basis. In January, 1832, all stores were closed in spectacular protest and commerce was at a complete standstill for nine days. [2]

But opposition did not cease there and rapidly assumed a more menacing form. No less than 149 of the colony's estate owners pledged themselves to close their sugar works and to pay no taxes so long as the order stood. [3] Only when the king in council authorized a twelve hour working day during crop time were normal operations resumed. However, as this concession to the West Indians was a qualified one, compensation in the form of increased allowances being required for the additional labor performed, it evoked little gratitude. [4] Nor did a parliamentary grant of £58,000, half the annual revenues of the three regions, to lighten taxes, made in 1832, [5] serve to mollify the residents.

Reports from the self-governing colonies were equally discouraging. The legislatures one and all steadfastly refused to entertain bills making the late order operative within their jurisdictions, while the St. Kitts assembly went so far as to announce its intention of withholding all grants of money and of ignoring all the central government's recommendations on any score until it should be evident that colonial property would be held inviolable. [6] Thus, Lord Goderich's attempt to secure action under strong pressure was no more successful than Earl Bathurst's effort had been to achieve the same end

[1] See for example, *Trinidad. By His Excellency Sir Lewis Grant . . . A Proclamation* [Port of Spain, 1832]. Dated January 5th.

[2] Lieut.-Col. Bozon to Lord Goderich, Jan. 5 and 24, 1832, C. O. 253/37; *Parl. Debates,* 3rd series, XI, cols. 34 ff.

[3] Governor Farquharson to Lord Goderich, April 30, 1832, C. O. 253/38.

[4] Governor Farquharson to Lord Goderich, Jan. 3, and Feb. 23 (confidential), 1833, C. O. 253/43. The colonists at the time declared this modification of the original order to be worse than the latter itself. See *At a General Meeting of the Proprietory Body of St. Lucia, Specially called . . . to take such measures as are rendered necessary by the Proclamation dated 3d of January 1833* [begin]. . . . [Castries, 1833].

[5] Under 2 and 3 William IV c. 125.

[6] See for example the papers in C. O. 28/109, C. O. 101/75. For feeling in St. Kitts, see Governor Nicolay to Viscount Goderich, 25 Feb. 1832 and enclosures in C. O. 239/29.

through plainly stating British desires and relying upon the colonists' better judgment to meet them. The gulf between the mother land and her tropical American possessions was steadily widening and events at this juncture made it all but unbridgeable.

Unrest among the slaves had been painfully evident ever since the spring of 1823. The commotion caused by the demand for early emancipation through parliamentary act served to convince a rapidly increasing number of blacks that their masters were withholding some material advantage afforded them by the home government. So general did the impression become that it was deemed advisable to issue a royal proclamation in certain of the islands assuring them that they had not been liberated. But this announcement, as well as others of a similar nature, had little effect [1] and lamentable consequences followed in Jamaica.

A servile revolt breaking out in St. James parish during the Christmas holiday of 1831 spread to adjoining portions of the island with lightning rapidity and for a time threatened to engulf it entirely in carnage. Estate buildings and canefields were fired, martial law was proclaimed, and both regulars and militiamen were called into action. Following several encounters between these troops and bands of slaves armed with cutlasses in which the latter were relentlessly mowed down by steady gun fire, over a hundred negroes were hanged scores of others were severely flogged, and order was gradually restored, but not until property losses had exceeded £1,150,000 currency.[2]

Through blind perversity, colonial opinion was all but unanimous in attributing the uprising to nonconformist activities which were linked with emancipationist agitation in Great Britain. William Knibb [3] and

[1] *By Authority. Government House, Antigua, August 12, 1831 . . . A Proclamation by the King* (St. John's, 1831). *Grenada; By His Excellency Sir James Campbell . . . A Proclamation* [St. George, 1831], dated 4 April. *Tobago. By His Excellency Major-General Nathanial Blackwell . . . A Proclamation* [Scarborough, 1830].

[2] *Head-Quarters, Montego-Bay, St. James's, Jan. 2, 1832. To the Rebellious Slaves* [Jamaica, 1832]. *A Proclamation. By His Excellency Somerset Lowry, Earl of Belmore, Captain General and Governor-in-Chief of this our Island of Jamaica . . .* [Jamaica, 1832], dated Jan. 3. Two others of Feb. 3 and 5. Papers in C. O. 137/181, 182, 185. "Despatches between the Government and the Colonies relative to the recent Rebellion among the Slaves," in *Gt. Br., H. C., Sess. Pap.,* 1831–32 ,XLVII (285), 259. "Report from House of Assembly, Jamaica, on the Injury sustained during the recent Rebellion," in *Gt. Br., H. C., Sess. Pap.,* 1831–32, XLVII (561), 181.

[3] John H. Hinton, *Memoir of William Knibb, Missionary in Jamaica* (London, 1847). George E. Sargent, *The Jamaica Missionary: A Memoir of*

Thomas Burchell,[1] together with Messrs. Abbot, Gardner, and White-horne, all Baptist agents, were therefore promptly clapped into prison on the charge of having incited rebellion. Never did the Caribbean press betray greater venom. Particularly vitriolic was Mr. Beaumont's scurrilous *Jamaica Courant,* to which the Reverend George Bridges was a frequent contributor. "Shooting is . . . too honourable a death for men whose conduct has occasioned so much bloodshed, and the loss of so much property. There are fine hanging woods in St. James's and Trelawny, and we do sincerely hope, that the bodies of all the Methodist[2] preachers who may be convicted of sedition may diversify the scene," declared this journal in reporting the arrests.[3] Some days later it carried the item "We hear that two of the preachers are to be shot to leeward. We hope this is not the case, as hanging is quite good enough for them."[4]

Terms such as "ruffians," "preaching miscreants," "sturdy beggars," "vagabonding reverends" were freely applied to the missionaries. At the height of disorder, the *Courant* deplored "the supineness of our public authorities [which] allows a single sectarian preacher to be at large, contrary to the general feeling throughout the country. . . . We express a hope that the hypocritical and canting vagabonds should perish amidst the storm, which they have been paid by our enemies at home to raise among us. Can the execution of twenty preachers atone for the lives of thousands, and the destruction of many millions of property?"[5]

These incendiary attacks stirred opposition to a fever-heat of fury. The Colonial Church Union, a body ostensibly designed to resist encroachments of the colonies' enemies by all constitutional means, to spread facts regarding the true state of slavery, and to advance the negroes' temporal and spiritual interests, was founded at St. Ann's Bay by Mr. Hilton of the assembly, aided by the Reverend George Bridges,[6] and became the instrument of nonconformist persecution. Almost from the outset, it cast aside its pacific program and revealed

---

William Knibb (London, n.d.). Mrs. J. J. Smith, *William Knibb, Missionary in Jamaica* (no imprint, n.d.).

[1] William F. Burchell, *Memoir of Thomas Burchell, Twenty-two Years a Missionary in Jamaica* (London, 1849).

[2] A derogatory term applied to all sectarists in the West Indies.

[3] January 5, 1832.

[4] January 14, 1832.

[5] January 16, 1832.

[6] Papers in C. O. 137/182. The best printed account of the activities of the Union, albeit colored by strong prejudice, will be found in Henry Bleby, *Death Struggles of Slavery* (London, 1853).

its true nature by organizing attacks against the Baptists and Wesleyans. Nine of the former's chapels and six belonging to the Methodists as well as the missionaries' homes were destroyed by mobs under its direction, with a total loss of some £25,000.[1]

Knibb, Burchell, and Gardner alone were committed to trial, but after vain attempts on the part of colonial authorities to secure evidence of guilt on their part from ring-leaders in the rebellion, they were at length reluctantly freed.[2] Knibb and Burchell, accompanied by two Wesleyan agents, Duncan and Barry, thereupon hastened to Great Britain to lay their case before the country and became central figures in a conflict raging between the emancipationists, who attributed the revolt to the harsh treatment accorded negroes [3] and the colonial party, which laid it to humanitarian machinations.[4] Shortly after their departure, Mr. Jordan, colored editor of *The Watchman and Jamaica Free Press,* who had supported the sectarists, was tried on the charge of "constructive treason," but was also acquitted.[5]

The Union, meanwhile, was gaining rapidly in strength and developed along radical lines. Members pledged themselves to use every possible exertion to prevent the dissemination of doctrines at variance with those of the Established and Presbyterian churches as well as "to obey, promptly and implicitly, all constitutional orders" of the body. With the formation of branches in every parish, Wesleyan and Baptist activities came to a complete standstill. Feeling rose so high that when a young Englishman, arriving in the colony to assume a position as plantation bookeeper, inquired innocently enough where he might attend Methodist services, he was threatened with

---

[1] C. O. 137/181, 182, 183. "Memorial and Statement of the Baptist Missionaries in Jamaica, April, 1832," in *Gt. Br., H. C., Sess., Pap.,* 1833, XXVI (540). Anon., "The Baptist Missionaries," *A Narrative of Recent Events Connected with the Baptist Mission in this Island* . . . (Kingston, 1833). Thomas F. Abbott, *Narrative of Certain Events Connected With the Late Disturbances in Jamaica* . . . (London, 1832). W. Grinton Berry, *Fox's Book of Martyrs* (New York, n.d.). Brown, *History of the Propagation of Christianity,* II, 78 ff. "Disturbances in Jamaica," in *The Electric Review,* June 1832, p. 544 ff. "Insurrection in Jamaica," in *ibid.,* March 1832, pp. 244 ff. [William Knibb], *Facts and Documents connected with the Late Insurrection in Jamaica* . . . (London, 1832). Edward Underhill, *Life of James Mursell Phillippo, Missionary in Jamaica* (London, 1881).

[2] "Slave Insurrections, and Trials of Missionaries," in *Gt. Br., H. C., Sess. Pap.,* 1831–32, XLVII (482) 227.

[3] See for example, "True Causes of the Late Insurrection of the Slaves in Jamaica," in *Tait's Edinburgh Magazine,* April, 1832, pp. 81 ff.

[4] Anon., *Jamaica Insurrection; or, The Proceedings of the Anti-Slavery Society Exposed and Refuted* (London, 1832).

[5] Bleby, *Death Struggles,* pp. 133, 134.

tarring and feathering and fled precipitately to escape the islanders' wrath.[1]

Formation of the Union with its sweeping oath of allegiance smacked of super-government and occasioned profound uneasiness in official circles in Great Britain. There had long been loose talk among the Jamaicans of freeing themselves from British control and seeking American protection if their interests were not regarded.[2] The desire to break loose from the mother country had been openly expressed by many in parochial meetings held in the late summer of 1831.[3] Augustus Beaumont of the *Courant,* a member of the assembly, was, furthermore, reported to be in treasonable correspondence with the United States and rash acts on his part, such as challenging Great Britain's right to the colony, did not lessen ground for suspicion that a movement to sever existing political bonds was under way.[4]

Thus, firmly convinced that the Union was at the very least a potential revolutionary organization, the home government determined to crush it. Action was somewhat delayed by the recall of the Earl of Belmore as governor shortly after the rebellion,[5] but his successor, Lord Mulgrave, forced the resignation of public officials prominent in Union circles, cancelled the commissions of all militia officers known to be its adherents, and, in January 1833, promulgated a royal proclamation declaring the body to be an illegal association and ordering its dissolution. To the British ministry's intense relief, the entire movement collapsed,[6] affording conclusive evidence of the inherent loyalty of the Jamaicans as a whole. Meanwhile, the offer to advance as much as £500,000 in exchequer bills to the colonial treasury and sufferers in the recent insurrection at low interest [7] had done much to restore good feeling. A parliamentary grant of some

---

[1] Henry Whiteley, *Three Months in Jamaica, in 1832* . . . (London, 1833).

[2] See for example, Williams, *Tour,* p. 138; Coleridge, *Six Months,* p. 131; Anon., *The Voice of the West Indies, and the Cry of England; or, Compensation or Separation Considered* (London, 1832).

[3] Lord Belmore to Viscount Goderich, Sept. 6, 1831, C. O. 137/179.

[4] Lord Belmore to Viscount Goderich, May 2, 1832 (Secret), C. O. 137/182. The Earl of Mulgrave to Goderich, Dec. 16, 1832, C. O. 137/183.

[5] Instructions for his recall had been sent to the colony before news of the rebellion had reached England. *Parl. Debates,* 3rd series, XI, col. 329.

[6] Papers in C. O. 137/183, 188.

[7] Under authority of 2 and 3 William IV c. 125. By August 1833, 16 applicants had been advanced £79,200 in amounts ranging from £2,000 to £10,000, while 23 applications for loans totalling £119,000 were still under consideration. *Gt. Br., H. C., S. P.* 1833, XXVI (736), p. 423.

£12,000, made about the same time, aided in the restoration of the destroyed chapels,[1] which work proceeded without hindrance.

New methods of propaganda were employed by both the organized opposition to Caribbean bondage and the West India interest during the closing year of the emancipation controversy. While *The Anti-Slavery Reporter* was issued in larger editions than ever and new publications of a similar nature [2] won wide support, the "Anti-Slavery Society," as the Society for the Mitigation and Gradual Abolition of Slavery Throughout the British Dominions had come to be popularly known, established a special committee in June, 1831 to disseminate information on the colonial labor system by means of lectures. Six speakers, the best known of whom was George Thompson,[3] were sent on circuit. They delivered scores of addresses and were largely responsible for the demand for definite pledges on the issue from aspirants to seats in the House of Commons.[4]

A new literary committee of the Society of West India Planters and Merchants, formed in December, 1830, secured the use of the recently founded [5] *Fraser's Magazine*,[6] of *The Christian Remembrancer* [7] (through the efforts of the Reverend Isaacson, a canting clergyman who received £100 for his services), of *The Albian* (whose editor "consented to the payment of £50" . . .) [8] of *Bell's Weekly Messenger*, and of *The Observer*.[9]

In April, 1831, however, *The West India Reporter* was changed from a monthly to a quarterly [10] and, a few issues later, it was discontinued.[11] In June 1832, a year after the Anti-Slavery Society had initiated its policy of sponsoring public discourses, the West India

---

[1] "Estimate of Grant to Baptist Missionary Society, on account of Expenses incurred in the Erection of certain Chapels destroyed in the Island of Jamaica," in *Gt. Br., H. C., Sess. Pap.*, 1834, XLII (311) 446. "Estimate of Sum required for Expenses incurred in the Erection of Chapels destroyed in Jamaica," in *ibid.*, 1834, XLII (476) 451.

[2] For example, *The Anti-Slavery Record*, founded in May 1832.

[3] Anon., *The Late George Thompson* (no imprint, n.d.).

[4] *Report of the Agency Committee of the Anti-Slavery Society, Established in June, 1831* . . . (London, 1832). For an attack on this committee, see Joseph Liggins, *A Refutation of the Calumnies Circulated by the Anti-Slavery Agency Committee, Against the West India Planters* (London, 1833).

[5] Vol. I, no. 1 is dated February 1830. Published monthly at London.

[6] *Min. Lit. Comm., W. I. Plant. and Mer.*, Dec. 6, 1830.

[7] *Ibid.*, Jan. 29, 1831.

[8] *Ibid.*, Feb. 26, 1831.

[9] *Ibid.*, June 3, 1831.

[10] *Ibid.*, April 16, 1831.

[11] *Ibid.*, Feb. 25, 1832.

group adopted the same plan, engaging Peter Borthwick and Mr.
Franklin as lecturers at one and a half guineas per day each exclusive of coach hire. They were directed to attend an emancipationist meeting in London for the purpose of studying methods used and
were then sent throughout Great Britain on the anti-slavery orators'
heels.[1]

Borthwick continued this for upwards of nine months [2] and his
forensic clashes during 1832 and 1833 with humanitarian leaders,
notably William Knibb, become one of the foremost reform speakers upon his return from the persecutions in Jamaica,[3] and George
Thompson of the Anti-Slavery Society, marked the high point of
popular interest in the question of liberation. Ordinary lectures [4] by
any of this trio, in which Borthwick replied to Thompson or Knibb
or vice versa, drew large crowds, but their meetings on a common
platform,[5] above all in six debates between Thompson and Borthwick
held in Liverpool,[6] were followed with breathless interest by the
entire country.

[1] *Min. Lit. Comm., W. I. Plant. and Mer.,* June 30, July 21 and 28, 1832.

[2] He was voted an additional hundred guineas in March 1833. *Ibid.,* March
2d. The University of Edinburgh likewise presented him with a loving-cup
"bearing a flattering inscription expressive of a sense of the honour reflected
by his talent upon the university of which he was a member." *Nat. Dic. of
Biography.*

[3] Anon., *Religious Persecution in Jamaica. Report of the Speeches of the
Rev. Peter Duncan, Wesleyan Missionary, and the Rev. W. Knibb, Baptist
Missionary. At a Public Meeting of the Friends of Christian Missions, Held
at Exeter-Hall, August 15, 1832* (London, 1832). F. C. Lusty, *How Wm.
Knibb Fought Slavery and Won Freedom* (London, n.d.).

[4] Peter Borthwick, *The Substance of an Address Delivered . . . at the
Assembly Rooms, Cheltenham, on . . . the 26th of October, 1832* (Cheltenham,
n.d.). Anon., ed., *Colonial Slavery. Mr. Borthwick's Lecture, Delivered at the
Assembly-Rooms, Edinburgh . . . March 23, 1833* (Bath, n.d.). George Thompson, *The Substance of a Speech Delivered in . . . Manchester on . . . August
13th, 1832 . . . Being a Reply to Mr. Borthwick's Statements on the Subject
of British Colonial Slavery* (London, n.d.). Thompson, *The Substance of . . .
[the] Sixth Lecture on Colonial Slavery, Delivered . . . September 20th, 1832,
in . . . Manchester* (Manchester, n.d.). Thompson, *Substance of an Address
to the Ladies of Glasgow and its Vicinity . . . Delivered . . . March 5th,
1833 . . .* (Glasgow, 1833).

[5] Anon., ed., *Colonial Slavery. Defence of the British Missionaries from the
Charge of Inciting the Late Rebellion in Jamaica; in a Discussion Between
the Rev. William Knibb and Mr. P. Borthwick, at . . . Bath, on . . . December 15, 1832* (London, n.d.). Anon., ed., *Full Report of Meetings of Messrs.
Thompson and Borthwick at Dalkeith, 22nd March, 1833* (Glasgow, 1833).

[6] Picton, *Memorials of Liverpool,* I, 445, 446. George Thompson, *Three
Lectures . . . Delivered in . . . Liverpool, on . . . August 28 . . . [and] 30,
and . . . September 6, 1832* (Liverpool, 1832). William L. Garrison, [*Title*

The proprietors and traders, meanwhile, were indulging in a series of last, frantic appeals to all classes.[1] These culminated in a grand meeting of protest attended by 6,000 persons, held at the London Tavern on April 5, 1832, which adopted a series of resolutions affirming the importance of the Caribbean colonies to Great Britain, championing slavery as an institution established under and protected by the laws of the mother country, charging the ministry with illegally seeking to coerce the tropical American possessions through fiscal discrimination, and calling for a parliamentary inquiry into the actual state of slavery as well as immediate relief from the economic distress [2] to which the sugar islands were then subject.[3]

Many and widely different were the proposals of how emancipation might be effected, chiefly made after 1830. These ranged from confiscation by act of the central government to purchase of the slaves, the estates and the owners' vested rights at fancy prices.[4] Typical ones will illustrate this variety.

One planter suggested somewhat facetiously that the negroes' champions contribute £16,500,000, of which sum approximately one tenth should be used immediately to purchase the freedom of such blacks as might be offered for sale, while the balance should be allowed to double under compound interest for fifteen years, at which time it should be employed in liberating those remaining slaves.[5] A "free-

Page of British Museum copy mutilated] of George Thompson, *With a Full Report of the Discussion Between Mr. Thompson and Mr. Borthwick . . . Held at the Royal Amphitheater, Liverpool (Eng.), and Which Continued for Six Evenings with Unabated Interest . . .* (Boston, 1836).

[1] Anon., "An Englishwoman," *An Address to the Females of Great Britain, on the Propriety of Their Petitioning Parliament for the Abolition of Negro Slavery* (London, 1833). Anon., *Address to Manufacturers, Merchants, Traders, and Others, on the Importance of Preserving the Colonies* [London, 1832]. Mr. Barrett and Mr. Burge, *The Speeches [of the above] . . . at a General Meeting of Planters, Merchants, and Others Interested in the West India Colonies; Assembled . . . on the 18th May, 1833* (London, 1833). *Proceedings at a Public Meeting of Persons Interested in the Preservation of the British West India Colonies, Held . . . the 27th May, 1833* [London, 1833]. *Resolutions Adopted At a General Meeting of Noblemen and Gentlemen Interested in the Preservation of the West India Colonies* (London, 1833).

[2] See Chapter X.

[3] *Proceedings at a Public Meeting of Persons Interested in the Preservation of the West India Colonies, Held at the City of London Tavern, the 5th April, 1832* [London, 1832]. *Resolutions of the General Meeting of West India Planters and Merchants, Passed 5 April, 1832* |London, 1832].

[4] For a collection of plans, see C. O. 320/8.

[5] Anon., *Negro Emancipation Made Easy;* the same plan is presented in Anon., "A British Planter," *Brief Remarks, on Scriptural Notices, Respecting*

born Englishman" urged that all bondsmen be converted into hired servants through being paid set wages and being permitted to buy their freedom at specified prices.[1] A member of the Dominican legislature maintained that the reform could be instituted only with the payment of full indemnity, raised by levying an additional annual tax of £3,000,000 for fifteen years on property in the United Kingdom.[2]

An importer of Caribbean produce recommended that the British government purchase all slaves at £100 each, paying for them in colonial annuities and hiring them out to their old masters at rates sufficient to meet interest charges and to extinguish progressively the debt through thirty-seven years.[3] An unknown pamphleteer advocated freeing male children after they had been educated for five years and had served a seven year apprenticeship. They were to purchase their wives. Any other slave should be given conditional freedom upon paying his master two-thirds of his market value. Such as should reach the age of sixty after 1845 without having gained freedom should then be manumitted at the expense of the British Treasury.[4] One John Yates proposed that the blacks be given the right to buy their own freedom or that of others and that all orphans and illegitimate children be liberated through annual grants of parliament.[5]

T. S. Winn set forth a plan to have the home government purchase all hands reaching a certain age so that they might enjoy the balance of their lives in freedom.[6] An anonymous writer would have the present generation of slaves die as such, but would educate the young and would set a distant date at which general emancipation should occur.[7] Fortunatus D'Warris, commissioner of inquiry into the ad-

Bondmen, and a Plan for the Gradual Manumission of Slaves, Without Violation of Public Faith, or Infringement of Vested Rights (London, 1832).

[1] Anon., A Letter to John Bull; to Which is Added the Sketch of a Plan for the Safe, Speedy, and Effectual Abolition of Slavery (London, 1823).

[2] Anon., An Appeal and Caution to the British Nation, with Proposals for the Immediate or Gradual Emancipation of the Slaves (London, 1824).

[3] Anon., An Attempt to Strip Negro Emancipation of its Difficulties as Well as its Terrors . . . (London, 1824).

[4] Anon., Hints on the Propriety of Establishing by Law the Civil Rights of the Free People of Colour . . . As a Preliminary Step to Emancipating the Slaves . . . (Newcastle upon Tyne, 1824).

[5] Letters to the Right Hon. William Huskisson . . . on . . . the Means Best Adapted to Promote the Mitigation and Final Extinction of Slavery in the British Colonies (Liverpool, 1824).

[6] A Speedy End to Slavery in our West India Colonies . . . (London, 1827); Supplement to a Speedy End to Slavery (London, 1827).

[7] Anon., A Plan for the Abolition of Slavery, Consistently with the Interests of all Parties Concerned (London, 1828).

ministration of justice in the West Indies, found a solution of the
problem in voluntary manumission.[1] Colin Macrae urged that the government take over all plantations and negroes, paying for them in
4 per cent bonds and operating the estates through a commercial
company with provision of some sort being made for gradual
emancipation.[2] A member of Cambridge University supported East
and West India sugar duties equalization as a means of forcing the
abandonment of monoculture and thus leading proprietors to free
their workers through self-interest.[3] Another writer advocated
liberating all young and old slaves and permitting the remainder to
work for wages three hours daily five days a week and all day
Saturday. Earnings should be deposited in banks in their names until
their respective purchase prices should have accumulated, at which
time they should be granted their liberty.[4]

A former Jamaican planter favored the purchase of children born
after a certain date with funds appropriated by parliament, these
young Africans to serve as apprentices for a term of years as a
means of guarding against their growing up in idleness.[5] Another
West Indian recommended transferring all or part of the sugar tax to
an ad valorem duty on slaves, their value in every case to be set by
the owners themselves. The latter must thereafter permit the blacks
to purchase their freedom or allow benevolent persons to liberate
them upon payment of those amounts.[6] Anthony Brough suggested
freeing 30,000 negroes triennially beginning December 31, 1834, com-
pensating owners from a special fund raised by a tax of ½d. per
pound on all sugar entering Great Britain irrespective of origin.[7]

John Hancock, long a resident of Guiana, urged granting West
India proprietors land in that colony to the amount of twice their

[1] *The West India Question Plainly Stated* (London, 1828).

[2] *Suggestion of a Plan for the Effectual Abolition of Slavery, in all of the
British West India Colonies* (London, n.d.).

[3] *Suggestions on the Abolition of Slavery in the British Colonies; or, Slavery Gradually Starved to Death Upon a Low Diet* (Cambridge, 1831).

[4] "John Bull," *pseud., A Scheme for a General Taxation on Property, Income, and Trade . . . To which is Added, A Proposal . . . on the Subject of
the Abolition of Negro Slavery* . . . (London, n.d.).

[5] "Plan for the Gradual Abolition of Negro Slavery," in *Blackwood's,* July,
1832, pp. 87 ff.

[6] Anon., *A Letter to the Lord Chancellor on the Abolition of Slavery* (London, 1833).

[7] *The Importance of the British Colonies in the West Indies . . . and a
Sketch of a Plan for a Safe and Gradual Emancipation, on Terms Favourable
to All Parties, and Without any Loan* (London, 1833).

existing holdings as recompense for freeing the negroes who should remain at their service until the new tracts had been opened up.[1] A project put forward by J. F. Barham, M.P., provided for the invoicing of all slaves and estate property and surrending them to the Crown. The plantations were then to be operated under royal control for a period of years during which time a fund sufficient to pay the owners was to be accumulated and the blacks were to be prepared for freedom.[2] On the other hand, Charles Stuart maintained that all hands should be liberated without compensation of any kind.[3]

During the course of this popular agitation, the question of emancipation was increasingly before parliament. On July 13, 1830, Mr. Brougham moved in the House of Commons that the body give it serious consideration early in the next session, but the measure was lost.[4] In April of the following year, Mr. Buxton sought to secure the adoption of a resolution declaring that the local legislatures had taken no steps to carry the Bathurst program of amelioration into effect and that the lower chamber would consequently proceed to a consideration of the best means by which servitude might be ended. Debate on the motion was adjourned and subsequent prorogation of the national legislature rendered this bold effort to precipitate action unavailing.[5]

The liberation of all crown slaves was announced to the new parliament in August [6] and, in May, 1832, with the support of the West India interest,[7] the Commons adopted a motion presented by Mr. Buxton and amended by Lord Althorp, "that a Select Committee be appointed to consider and report upon the measures which it may be expedient to adopt, for the purpose of effecting the extinction of slavery throughout the British dominions, at the earliest period compatible with the safety of all classes in the colonies and in conformity

---

[1] Plan for the Reconciliation of All Interests in the Emancipation of West India Slaves (London, 1833).

[2] Considerations on the Abolition of Negro Slavery, and the Means of Practically Effecting It (London, 1824).

[3] The West India Question . . . An Outline for Immediate Emancipation; and Remarks on Compensation (London, 1832).

[4] Parl. Debates, 2nd series, XXV, cols. 1171 ff. Debate Upon Colonial Slavery; in the House of Commons, on Tuesday, the 13th July, 1830 . . . (London, 1830). The vote was 27 to 55.

[5] Parl. Debates, 3rd series, III, cols. 1408 ff.

[6] Parl. Debates, 3rd series, VI, cols. 100 ff.

[7] Report on the Debate on the Present State of the West India Colonies; in the House of Lords, on Tuesday, the 17th of April, 1832, on the Presentation of a Petition from the Planters, Merchants, Ship-owners, and others, interested in the British West India Colonies (London, 1832).

to the resolutions of this House of the 15th of May, 1823." [1] The report of this body [2] is to-day the most valuable document on the old Caribbean labor system in its last days.

The British government's plan for emancipation, based largely upon the select committee's findings, was brought forward by Mr. Stanley, new Secretary of State for War and the Colonies, in the reform parliament assembling in May, 1833. Children born after passage of the proposed act and those who would then be under six years of age were to be immediately freed. All others were to have prices set upon them by their masters and were to be given the status of apprentice. Under this, they were to receive the customary allowances of garden plots, shelter, food, and clothing together with incidentals and were to serve their former owners for three-fourths of their time per ten hour day or six day working week during twelve years.

The remaining fourth was to be spent in paid employment which would enable them to accumulate means sufficient to purchase their freedom by the close of the apprenticeship period. If the negroes so desired, this time might be spent off the plantation in any form of work that could be secured, wages being regulated by individual contract between employee and employer. Otherwise, the late masters must provide labor for such fraction of a day or week at an annual salary equal to one-twelfth of each worker's declared value.

To compensate owners for the loss of a quarter of their hands' time, it was proposed to make them an interest-bearing loan of £15,000,000, ten times their estimated annual profit on sugar, rum, and coffee. The naming of stipendary magistrates by the Crown was suggested as a means of securing equal justice to black and white, while the opening of negro schools was advocated as an aid to their moral advancement. [3]

Publication of these proposals evoked lively argument as they gave satisfaction to neither the West Indians nor the humanitarians. The planters and merchants, convinced that the extinction of slavery was inevitable, readily enough acceded to emancipation, favoring a long period of apprenticeship with the negroes buying their own freedom. They insisted, however, that £15,000,000 was a wholly in-

---

[1] *Parl. Debates,* 3rd series, XIII, cols. 34 ff. *Report of the Debate on West India Slavery; in the House of Commons, on Thursday, the 24th of May, 1832* . . . (London, 1832).

[2] "Report from the Select Committee on the extinction of Slavery throughout the British Dominions," in *Gt. Br., H. C., Sess. Pap.,* 1831–32, XX (721).

[3] *Parl. Debates,* 3rd series, XVII, cols., 1192 ff.

adequate sum to place at their disposal and clamored for an outright grant in lieu of the proposed advance.[1]

The anti-slavery party, on the contrary, savagely attacked extended apprenticeship and self-liberation through purchase. Payment of any sum to the colonists was looked upon with disfavor, and many showed hostility to even a loan. Debate dragged on for weeks, bringing about a wearisome rehashing of the entire subject of slavery in which the real points at issue were all too often obscured.[2]

The difference of opinion in parliament mirrored that throughout the country. But resting the entire burden of reform upon the West Indians alone was so palpably unjust that Buxton himself became an advocate of compensation, which drew upon him a vote of censure by the more radical emancipation leaders.[3]

Compromise ultimately brought both groups to common ground. A £20,000,000 indemnity grant from the public funds of the United Kingdom was substituted for the original £15,000,000 loan; bond-

[1] Anon., *A Statement of the Objections of the Jamaica Proprietors, Resident in Great Britain, to Certain Enactments in Mr. Secretary Stanley's Bill for the Abolition of Slavery* (London, 1833). Anon., ed., *West India Planters and Merchants. The Proceedings and Resolutions of the West India Body, Including Copies of their Various Communications with His Majesty's Government, Relative to the Measures of the Session, 1833, for the Abolition of Slavery* (no imprint, 1833). *Memorial of the Standing Committee of West India Planters and Merchants . . . to the Right Honorable The Earl Grey, K.G. . . . and to the other Ministers of the Crown* [London, 1833]. *Observations on the Slavery Abolition Bill Communicated to Mr. Secretary Stanley by a Deputation From the General West India Body, July 17th, 1833* (no imprint, 1833). *Petition to Parliament, 18 May, 1833* [*on the part of the planters, proprietors, merchants, and others interested in the British West Indies*] (no imprint, 1833). *To the Right Honorable, The Earl Grey, K.G. . . . and the other Ministers of the Crown. The Memorial of the Standing Committee of West India Planters and Merchants* [London, 1833].

[2] *Parl. Debates*, 3rd. series, XVIII, cols. 204 ff., 308 ff., 458 ff., 515 ff., 573 ff., 1014 ff., 1163 ff.; XIX, cols. 1056 ff., 1184 ff., 1234 ff., 1252 ff.; XX, cols. 60 ff., 95 ff., 129 ff., 196 ff., 290 ff., 336 ff. Anon., ed., *Debate in the House of Lords, on Thursday, June 25, 1833, on Colonial Slavery* (London, 1833). *The Debates in Parliament—Session 1833—on the Resolutions and Bill for the Abolition of Slavery in the British Colonies . . .* (London, 1834). Viscount Howick, *Corrected Report of the Speech . . . in the House of Commons, May 14, 1833, on Colonial Slavery . . .* (London, 1833).

[3] See for example, Anon., *Some Remarks on Mr. Stanley's Proposed Bill for the Abolition of Colonial Slavery* (London, n.d.). James Cropper, *A Vindication of a Loan of £15,000,000 to the West India Planters . . .* (London, 1833). "Legion," pseud., *A Letter . . . to the Right Honourable E. G. Stanley . . . Upon His Scheme for the Abolition of Colonial Slavery* (London, n.d.).

age was forever abolished and all slaves were converted into apprentices subject to civil disabilities; the term of apprenticeship for field hands was lowered to six years and that for all others to four, without possibility of extension; Sunday labor was prohibited; forty-five hours was set as the normal week's work; apprentices were to be left to their own devices at all other times; if they so desired, they might purchase discharges before their indentures expired by paying their former masters the appraised values of their services, but no payment of any kind need be made to secure complete freedom of action with the full rights of freemen at the close of the six or four years as the case might be; customary allowances were to continue; and up to a hundred special justices, appointed and salaried by the king, were to ensure proper execution of the measure.

On August 28, 1833, a year after James Stephen's death and one month before Wilberforce's passing, this project was made into law, becoming effective on August 1, 1834.[1] Thus was the old labor régime of the Caribbean possessions destroyed by act of the home government under stimulus of humanitarian agitation.

To secure greater unity in carrying out the act, Barbados, St. Vincent, Grenada, and Tobago were placed under one governor-general, Sir Lionel Smith, residing in Bridgetown, in 1833. Lieutenant-governors were stationed in the three other colonies. All four executives were granted salaries by the Crown and were strictly forbidden to accept additional emoluments from the several legislatures, thus being kept wholly free from dependence upon the colonies.

Some weeks before news of these events had traversed the Atlantic, the Antiguan proprietors had registered opposititon to apprenticeship in any form and had expressed a preference for immediate, unconditional liberation of all slaves as the lesser of two evils.[2] When the local council and assembly again convened, practical force was given to this desire by the passing of a bill to abolish the intermediary period preceding emancipation and this tiny colony, where early soil exhaustion had made extensive absenteeism impossible and where liberal views regarding the blacks had prevailed for upwards of half a century,[3] won for itself the proud distinction of being the first

[1] 3 and 4 William IV c. 73.
[2] Resolutions passed on Sept. 11, 1833, in Governor Macgregore to Mr. Stanley, Oct. 3, 1833, C. O. 7/37.
[3] See pages 66 and 67.

British colony in which the revolutionary reform became fully operative.[1]

The approach of August 1834 was viewed with intense anxiety in both Great Britain and the Caribbean. The negroes' restlessness under the influence of conflicting rumors from the mother land had been so great during the past two years as to have necessitated the issuing of numerous proclamations to quiet them.[2] The terms of the emancipation law had been promptly made known by official action [3] and, in the wild delirium of excitement which followed, it was widely feared that the slaves would resort to force as a means of obtaining liberty before the appointed time while many predicted that the latter itself would be marked by bloodshed and violence. The situation was tense, but, through laudable self-restraint on the part of the colonials and vigorous efforts of the nonconformist churchmen, the exultant Africans were kept in check—the long-looked-forward-to day came and passed without any unseemly incident to mar the inauguration of a new epoch in British imperial history.

The overthrow of the traditional labor régime marked the final blow at the old-time prosperity of the West India islands. Their decline had first become apparent following the severance of natural trade relations with the Americans at the opening of the Revolution. War profits following the ravaging of St. Domingo had temporarily and artificially checked decay, but the competition of virgin-soil holdings within the empire and of foreign tropical colonies still enjoying the use of forced labor together with the progressive removal of preference enjoyed against East Indian sugar had so weakened them that the shock of emancipation sent that magnificent structure, the old plantation system, tottering to the ground. Nor could it be rebuilt.

While estimates of the value of the transatlantic property concerned vary greatly, the compensation afforded was certainly less than ten

---

[1] This policy was adopted in but one other British possession, the Bermudas.

[2] See for example, *Notice. By His Excellency the Governor* [*E. J. Mac Gregor*]. *Whereas there is the strongest reason to believe that evil-minded Persons* [begin] . . . (Roseau, 1832), dated March 13; *Antigua. By His Excellency Sir Patrick Ross . . . A Proclamation* (St. John's, 1832); *Trinidad. By His Excellency Sir Lewis Grant . . . A Proclamation* |Port of Spain, 1832]; *Saint Christopher. By His Excellency the Lieutenant Governor. A Proclamation* [Basseterre, 1833]; *Jamaica, S. S. A Proclamation. By His Excellency the . . . Earl of Mulgrave . . .* [Jamaica, 1833].

[3] See for example, *By His Excellency Major-General Henry Charles Darling, Lieutenant-Governor of Tobago. To the Slave Population of the Island* [Scarborough, 1833].

shillings in the pound and, with all estate owners deeply involved, no capital remained for them to operate under the new conditions. Emancipation, bringing to an end the old order, completed the downfall of the planter class and brought to a dramatic close the golden era of Caribbean history in which its members had so long played the leading rôles.

BIBLIOGRAPHICAL NOTES

BIBLIOGRAPHICAL NOTES

LIBRARIES

Three comprehensive, specialized collections of Caribbean literature have been formed and are open to students of tropical American affairs—the libraries of the West India Committee and the Colonial Institute in London and that of the Institute of Jamaica in Kingston.

The first of these is the largest as well as the most readily accessible and, in addition to all of the standard histories, contains a nearly complete assortment of travel books and military, medical and legal treatises, together with files of scarce periodicals, handbooks and a superb lot of fifty bound volumes of pamphlets, several of which have been located nowhere else in Great Britain, France, or the United States.

In the second will be found nearly every work appertaining directly to the islands and many choice pamphlets, a number of which are not to be found in the British Museum.

The West Indian Reference Library at Kingston has assumed important proportions through the activity of Mr. Frank C. Cundall, F.S.A., Secretary of the Institute of Jamaica and well-known historian of the colony, and would prove most valuable for investigations carried on in the Caribbean country itself.

The resources of the Library of Congress, the New York Public Library, the British Museum, and the Bibliothèque Nationale are too well known to require more than passing mention. It must be stated, however, that while containing many pamphlets, those institutions' collections are by no means complete. Furthermore, with respect to the last two, the lack of subject catalogues seriously handicaps research work in a field where there has been an immense amount of writing, ephemeral in nature and now quite forgotten, but of great importance in tracing the formation of public opinion on momentous issues.

The *Guide to British West Indian Archive Materials in London and in the Islands, for the History of the United States,* compiled by Herbert C. Bell, David W. Parker and others and published by the Carnegie Institution (Washington, 1926), covers the Caribbean papers in the Public Record Office and the colonial archives to 1815. It is of inestimable value.

The writer's *A Guide to the Official Correspondence of the Governors of the British West India Colonies with the Secretary of State, 1763–1833* (London n.d.) embraces the Public Record Office documents listed in the above and those for the next eighteen years as well and hence supplements it.

The Andrews, the Andrews and Davenport, and the Paullin and Paxson guides published by the Carnegie Institution contain many references to material in the sugar islands, as does the *Handbook of Manuscripts in the Library of Congress* (Washington, 1918).

The *Public Record Office. Lists and Indexes* series catalogues many papers of outstanding importance. See especially No. XVIII (Admiralty), XXVIII (War), XXXVI (Colonial Office) and XLVI (Treasury, etc.).

Seven volumes affording indispensable aid in the use of parliamentary papers are *Catalogue of Papers Printed by Order of the House of Commons, from the Year 1731 to 1800* (1807), *Catalogue of Parliamentary Reports, and a Breviate of Their Contents: Arranged Under Heads According to the Subjects, 1696–1834* (*Gt. Br., H. C., Sess. Pap.,* 1834, L), *General Index to the Accounts and Papers, Reports of Commissioners, Estimates, &c. &c. Printed by Order of the House of Commons, or Presented by Command, 1801–1852* (1853), *General Index to the Bills, Printed by Order of the House of Commons: 1801–1852* (1853), *General Index to the Bills, Reports, Accounts, and Other Papers, Printed by Order of the House of Commons: 1801–1826* (1829); *General Index to the Reports of Select Committes, Printed by Order of the House of Commons: 1801–1852* (1853) and *Indexes to the Subject Matters of the Reports of the House of Commons, 1801–1834* (1834).

The writer's *A Check-List of House of Commons Sessional Papers Relating to the British West Indies and to the West Indian Slave Trade and Slavery, 1763–1834* (London n.d.) will prove a useful time-saver where the particular collection of Blue Books being used is provided with these indexes. This is, however, seldom the case and the list is then essential for any efficient use of the papers.

Of outstanding value are Frank C. Cundall's four bibliographies published by the Institute of Jamaica during a period of nearly fifteen years—*Bibliotheca Jamaicensis* (1895), *Bibliographia Jamaicensis* (n.d.) *Supplement to Bibliographia Jamaicensis* (1908) and *Bibliography of the West Indies (Excluding Jamaica)* (1909). For the sake of economy, many titles in them have been abbreviated. A general catalogue of West Indian literature by this indefatigable worker, incorporating all of the above and containing much else in addition, is now in press.

The "List of Works . . . Relating to the West Indies," in *Bulletin of the New York Public Library*, XVI (1912), nos. 1–8 and reprinted in book form (1912), is the most nearly complete one at present available and is very serviceable.

The most detailed bibliography yet compiled is the writer's specialized *A Guide to the Reference Works, Manuscripts, Documents and Literature for a History of the British West Indies, 1763–1834, Including the Abolition and Emancipation Movements*. A by-product of this study, it is a critical, still unpublished two volume work of more than a thousand typed pages covering all known papers, books, pamphlets, magazine articles, and Caribbean newspapers relating to the period specified. Two copies are available for public use—one in the History Department office of the University of Iowa and the other in the library of the George Washington University.

[Henry Thorpe], "A Bibliography of Sugar," contained in scattered numbers of *The Sugar Cane*, Vols. XVI (1884) and XVII (1885), is almost worthless because numerous titles are so inaccurately given as to make identification impossible and the British Museum call numbers there given have long since been changed. H. L. Roth, *A Guide to the Literature of Sugar* (1890) and H. H. Meyer, *Library of Congress. Select List of References on Sugar* . . . (1910) are of considerable value.

Monroe N. Work's *A Bibliography of the Negro in Africa and America* (New York, 1928), contains incomplete lists of material on the slave trade (pp. 256 ff.) and Caribbean slavery (pp. 267 ff.), without critical comment.

MANUSCRIPTS

Admiralty Records, Public Record Office

For papers relative to naval affairs in the Caribbean 1763–1833, see "West Indies," etc. in *P. R. O. Lists and Indexes, No. XVIII.*

Barrell Papers

William Barrell was a merchant with West Indian connections trading from Portsmouth, N. H. and later from Philadelphia. Twenty-one volumes of ledgers, invoices, etc., covering 1766–1776 are included among the material once belonging to Stephen Collins, his executor, in the Division of Manuscripts of the Library of Congress.

Board of Trade Papers, Public Record Office

These are of slight importance for our period as compared with those of the Secretary of State. The Board's original correspondence on matters pertaining to individual West India islands will be found listed below, colony by colony, with the Colonial Office documents relating to them.

C. O. 323 (B. of T., original correspondence covering the colonies as a whole), vols. 16–30 include duplicates of many Board papers for the separate tropical American possessions. C. O. 326 (indexes of original correspondence), vols. 55–74 contain entries covering West Indian despatches; vols. 75 and 76 list colonial assembly journals and council minutes received, including those from the Caribbean.

Scattered Board material relative to the islands will be found in C. O. 388 (B. of T., commercial, original correspondence), vols. 51–74 and in C. O. 389 (B. of T., commercial, entry books of commissions, instructions, petitions, correspondence, orders in council, etc.), vols. 31–34, 38, 39, 50–53. C. O. 391 (B. of T., commercial, minutes of the Board); vols. 70–89 and 120 include numerous entries relative to the sugar colonies.

B. T. 6, vols. 9–12 contain evidence on West Indian slavery presented before a committee of the privy council in 1788; vol. 17, minutes of the council of Nevis, 1784; vol. 70, data on Chinese immigration; vol. 75, miscellaneous Caribbean documents, 1786–90; vol. 76, papers on the Leeward Islands, 1787–91; vol. 77, others relating to Jamaica, 1787–91; vol. 78, various general West Indian ones, 1800–1815; vols. 80, 81, 83–86 and 88, data on American-Carribean commercial intercourse, 1783–1807; vol. 103, odd papers on the West Indies, 1782–85; vol. 134, lists of exports there, 1789–93; vol. 141, custom house accounts, 1780–1804, including tropical American commercial statistics; vol. 185, tables of trade and navigation, 1697–1802, including the value of imports from and exports to the several sugar islands, for England and Scotland; vol. 186, returns of shipping for Jamaica, 1782; vol. 188, navigation and trade returns from consuls and naval officers stationed in the new world; vol. 235, scattered material relating to Jamaica, 1798–1801.

Bristol West India Club

"There are in the possession of my Society some five or six Minute Books etc. covering the following dates—1782 to 1805, 1805 to 1818, 1822 to 1838, 1839 to 1857." (Letter from W. W. Ward, treasurer, Merchant's Hall, Bristol, under date of October 10, 1923).

This outport body coöperated freely with the Caribbean organizations of London in promoting legislation beneficial to the trade and in opposing abolition and emancipation.

British Museum Manuscripts

Add. Ms. 8, 133 (papers of William Musgrave) includes population and production statistics for Jamaica in 1768 (ff. 95, 96).

Add. Mss. 12, 402–12, 400 (the Edward Long papers) contain material for a proposed new and revised edition of his *History of Jamaica* which did not materialize. In Add. Mss. 12, 431 will be found observations on fortifying the island set down in 1783; data on local agricultural production, particularly of sugar from 1700–1793; an account of the Mosquito Shore expedition, 1779–1782 and letters and papers respecting the slave trade, 1784–1799. In Add. Ms. 12, 432 there are a *Report of the Committee of the Assembly of Jamaica on the Slave Trade, 1792*, communications on the subject, a copy of the consolidated slave act of 1788 with ms. notes by Long and written matter bearing on it.

Add. Ms. 12, 433 contains a speech on the slave trade, delivered before the House of Lords by Edward Law on May 14, 1792. Statistics on the number of estates and negroes in Jamaica from 1700–1792, the amounts of poll tax paid, etc. will be found in Add. Ms. 12, 435. For a manuscript entitled *A Few Conjectural Considerations upon the Creation of the Human Race, occasioned by the present British Quixottical rage of setting the slaves from Africa at liberty,* the work of the Reverend Lindsay of Jamaica and dated 1778, see Add. Ms. 12, 439.

Add. Ms. 13, 975 contains official reports on Martinique and Jamaica for 1788–89 (f. 134). A valuation of negroes, stock and other property on the Wakefield plantation, Jamaica, in 1787 will be found in Add. Ms. 19,049 (f. 9). Papers relative to Jamaica, 1662–1791, presented by C. E. Long, constitute Add. Mss. 22, 676–22, 678. Letters of James Knight, C. Long and various planters and merchants of Jamaica on affairs in the island, 1725–1789, will be found in Add. Ms. 22, 677.

Add. Ms. 23, 608 consists of the manuscript for Lawrence-Archer's *Monumental Inscriptions of the British West Indies* (1875) with numerous notes not included in the printed work. Add. Ms. 27, 969 contains extracts from parish and other public records in Jamaica and Barbados with copies of the inscriptions on all monuments and tombstones in the latter from 1643–1750 as well as on some up to 1800, compiled by Captain J. H. Lawrence-Archer. It duplicates Add. Ms. 23, 608 to some extent, but is not identical with it, entries frequently supplementing the latter. A few pedigrees have also been traced out.

Notes on plantation work in Jamaica, written by Dr. J. H. Archer between 1828 and 1830, will be found in Add. Ms. 27,970. Add. Mss. 32,852 (ff. 200–258) and 33,029 (ff. 182–196) contain miscellaneous papers relative to the island dated 1775. Folio 458 of Add. Ms. 32,902 is a letter from Beeston Long, Sr., chairman of the West India Merchants of London to the Duke of Newcastle written on Feb. 28, 1760, informing the latter that he would be waited upon the following day with a memorial protesting against a proposed additional duty on sugar. The communication is interesting as being the earliest known document connected with that commercial organization whose extant minute books date from only 1769. Add. Ms. 32,975 contains a letter from Newcastle to Long declining an invitation to dine with the West India Merchants because of a previous engagement (folio 416) and Long's reply (folio 430). Both are dated 1766.

Egerton 2,423 consists of Janet Schaw's diary, published under the editorship of Evangeline and Charles Andrews as *Journal of a Lady of Quality . . . 1774 to 1776* (1921). Two copies of the manuscript account of her travels to and experiences in the British West Indies from 1774–1776 are in private hands. (See preface to the published work.)

King's Ms. 214 contains a memoir on Jamaica in 1782 with 7 colored plans, by Major General Archibald Campbell.

George Chalmers Papers

For a list of this West India agent's papers in the Force collection in the Division of Manuscripts of the Library of Congress, see *Handbook of Manuscripts in the Library of Congress.*

Colonial Office Papers, Public Record Office

These constitute the most valuable single source for our purpose. A check list follows. It should be noted that the collections of acts and most of the sessional papers are at this time (1928) provisionally stored in the Cambridge jail. (See the *Cambridge Historical Journal,* October, 1923.)

C. O. 7/1–37, original correspondence of the executives of Antigua and Montserrat with the Secretary of State, 1702–1833.

C. O. 393/1–5, entry books of correspondence of the Secretary of State with the executives of Antigua and Montserrat, 1816–1836.

C. O. 8/13–24, acts of the legislature, 1761–1834.

C. O. 9/25–52, sessional papers of the legislature, 1760–1825.

C. O. 10/1, Antiguan newspapers, 1827–1838; 10/2, shipping and census returns, 1784–1814; 10/4, miscellaneous papers, 1717–1827; 10/5–17, Blue Books of statistics, including Montserrat, 1821–1833.

C. O. 28/32–35, original correspondence of the Board of Trade relative to Barbados, 1760–1782.

C. O. 28/50–112, original correspondence of the executives of Barbados with the Secretary of State, 1761–1833.

C. O. 29/18–33, entry books of commissions, instructions, and of correspondence, largely from the Secretary of State to the executives of Barbados, 1760–1836.

C. O. 30/11–21, acts of the legislature of Barbados, 1761–1834.

C. O. 30/31–51, sessional papers of the legislature of Barbados, 1760–1834.

C. O. 33/1, Barbadian newspapers, 1829–1832; 33/4, ditto 1833–36; 33/17–26, shipping returns etc., 1730–1819; C. O. 33/33–45, Blue Books of statistics on Barbados, 1821–1833.

C. O. 71/1, original correspondence of the Board of Trade relative to Dominica, 1770–1778.

C. O. 71/2–77, original correspondence of the executives of Dominica with the Secretary of State, 1730–1833.

C. O. 72/1–11, entry books of commissions, instructions, and correspondence of the Secretary of State with the executives of Dominica, 1770–1829.

C. O. 73/1–15, acts of the legislature of Dominica, 1768–1835.

C. O. 74/1–21, sessional papers of the legislature of Dominica, 1767–1836.

C. O. 76/4–8, shipping returns, 1763–1819; 76/9, data on land sales in Dominica and St. Vincent, 1765–1772; 76/11–23, Blue Books of statistics on Dominica, 1821–1833.

C. O. 101/1–8, original correspondence of the Board of Trade relative to Grenada, 1763–1812.

C. O. 101/9–77, original correspondence of the executives of Grenada with the Secretary of State, 1762–1833.

C. O. 102/1–20, entry books of commissions, instructions, and correspondence of the Secretary of State with the executives of Grenada, 1763–1834.

C. O. 103/1–13, acts of the legislature of Grenada, 1766–1834.

C. O. 104/1–14, sessional papers of the legislature of Grenada, 1766–1850.

C. O. 106/1–8, shipping returns, 1764–1816; 106/9–12, data on sale of lands in Dominica, Grenada, St. Vincent and Tobago, 1764–1797; 106/15–27; Blue Books of statistics on Grenada, 1821–1833.

C. O. 111/42, 46, 53, papers in the case of the missionary Smith, in Demerara. (A copy of his Journal in Vol. 46.)

C. O. 137/33–40, original correspondence of the Board of Trade relative to Jamaica, 1762–1782.

C. O. 137/61–191, original correspondence of the executives of Jamaica with the Secretary of State, 1761–1833.

C. O. 137/267–271, papers relative to the bishopric of Jamaica, 1824–1834.

C. O. 138/22–56, entry books of commissions, instructions, and correspondence of the Secretary of State with the executives of Jamaica, 1760–1835.

C. O. 139/22–72, acts of the legislature of Jamaica, 1762–1834.

C. O. 140/40–124, sessional papers of the legislature of Jamaica, 1757–1834.

C. O. 141/1–28, files of the *Royal Gazette,* 1794–1833. Also at Cambridge (1928).

C. O. 142/1, 2, Jamaican newspapers, 1830–1836; 142/17–29, shipping returns; 142/32, 33, miscellaneous; 142/34–46, Blue Books of statistics, 1821–1833.

C. O. 152/30–35, original correspondence of the Board of Trade relative to the Leeward Islands, 1760–1782.

C. O. 152/47–106, original correspondence of the executives of the Leeward Islands with the Secretary of State, 1761–1816.

C. O. 153/19–34, entry books of commissions, instructions, and of correspondence of the Secretary of State with the executives of the Leeward Islands, 1761–1816.

C. O. 155/8, sessional papers of the legislature, 1749–1775.

C. O. 157/1, shipping returns, 1683–1787.

C. O. 184/1, original correspondence from Nevis to the Secretary of State, 1703–1787.

C. O. 185/6–10, acts for Nevis, 1789–1839.

C. O. 186/4–14, sessional papers, Nevis, 1762–1833.

C. O. 187/3–7, Blue Books of statistics for Nevis, 1821–1833.

C. O. 239/1–35, original correspondence of the executives of the government of St. Kitts with the Secretary of State, 1702–1833.

C. O. 407/1–3, 5, entry books of correspondence of the Secretary of State with the executives of the government of St. Kitts, 1816–1837.

C. O. 240/4, 10–17, acts, 1711–1833.

C. O. 241/9–28, sessional papers, 1760–1835.

C. O. 243/1, shipping returns for St. Kitts, 1685–1787; 243/11–21, Blue Books of statistics for the colony, 1821–1833.

C. O. 253/1–45, original correspondence of the executives of St. Lucia with the Secretary of State, 1709–1833.

C. O. 254/1–10, entry books of correspondence of the Secretary of State with the executives of St. Lucia, 1794–1837.

C. O. 255/1, 2, acts for the colony, 1818–1835.

C. O. 256/1, 2, sessional papers, 1820–1834.

C. O. 258/5–15, reports of protectors of slaves in St. Lucia, 1826–1834; 258/18–29, Blue Books of statistics, 1821–1833.

C. O. 260/1, 2, original correspondence of the Board of Trade relative to St. Vincent, 1773–1779.

C. O. 260/3–51, original correspondence of the executives of St. Vincent with the Secretary of State, 1668–1833.

C. O. 261/1–13, entry books of commissions, instructions, and correspondence of the Secretary of State with the executives of St. Vincent, 1776–1830.

C. O. 262/1–12, acts for St. Vincent, 1768–1836.

C. O. 263/1–7, sessional papers, 1769–1835.

C. O. 264/1, file of *St. Vincent Gazette,* 1831–1840. Also at Cambridge (1928).

C. O. 265/1, 2, shipping returns for St. Vincent, 1763–1812; 265/4–15, Blue Books of statistics, 1821–1833.

C. O. 285/1, original correspondence of the Board of Trade relative to Tobago, 1778–1781.

C. O. 285/2–40, original correspondence of the executives of Tobago with the Secretary of State, 1700–1833.

C. O. 286/1–6, entry books of the correspondence of the Secretary of State with the executives of Tobago, 1793–1833.

C. O. 287/1–7, acts, 1768–1834.

C. O. 288/1–18, sessional papers, 1768–1835.

C. O. 290/1–3, shipping returns 1766–1815; 290/5–17, Blue Books of statistics on Tobago, 1809–1833.

C. O. 295/1–100, original correspondence of the executives of Trinidad with the Secretary of State, 1783–1833.

C. O. 296/1–11, entry book of correspondence of the Secretary of State with the executives of Trinidad, 1797–1835.

C. O. 297/1, acts, 1832 to 1834.

C. O. 298/1–9, sessional papers, 1803–1834.

C. O. 299/1, file of government gazette, Trinidad, 1833–1835.

C. O. 300/1–4, files of newspapers from Trinidad, 1826–1844; 300/16, shipping returns for the colony, 1804–1811; 300/17, 18, accounts, 1814–1819; 300/19–32, reports of protectors of slaves, 1824–1833; 300/35–47, Blue Books of statistics 1821–1833.

C. O. 314/1, original correspondence of the Board of Trade relative to the Virgin Islands, 1711–1791.

C. O. 315/1–5, acts for the Virgin Islands, 1774–1835.

C. O. 316/1–4, sessional papers, 1773–1841.

C. O. 317/1–4, shipping returns, 1784–1833.

The Bell and Parker guide covers the governors' despatches listed above to 1815; that by the writer, those for the entire period 1763–1833 (see under Guides, Indexes and Bibliographies).

C. O. 318/1, 2 contain original correspondence of the Board of Trade relative to the West Indies as a whole, 1624–1808, but scattering miscellaneous papers only.

C. O. 318/3–117 contain chiefly military despatches from the West Indies to the Secretary of State, 1699–1825; reports of commissioners of legal inquiry and reports of commissioners of enquiry into the state of captured negroes in the islands. See *P. R. O. Lists and Indexes, No. XXXVI*, pp. 310–313 for check list of each volume.

C. O. 319/3–33 contain copies of instructions to various governors and copies of miscellaneous despatches from the Secretary of State, in entry books. For check list, see *P. R. O. Lists and Indexes, No. XXXVI*, p. 314.

C. O. 320/1, 2, 4, 5, 8, 10, are books of memoranda on various subjects. See *P. R. O. Lists and Indexes, No. XXXVI*, p. 314 for check list.

C. O. 323 (Board of Trade, original correspondence) Vols. 16–30 include letters relative to the West Indies frequently duplicating those found under the head of original correspondence for each separate colony.

C. O. 323/34–49 contain reports of law officers on various colonial acts, 1784–1833.

C. O. 323/117–139, contain applications for appointment to divers offices in the West Indies.

C. O. 323/142, 143 contain private letters to Earl Bathurst on West Indian affairs, 1824, 1825; 323/147, 153 contain private letters to Mr. Hay on the West Indies etc., 1825–28.

C. O. 324/17–19, 21, 40–46, 49, 51–54, 58, 60–65, entry books of commissions, instructions, etc., contain scattered West Indian records.

C. O. 324/88, 98 are entry books of private letters written by Mr. Hay and Mr. Horton relative to West Indian affairs, 1825–1836.

C. O. 324/103 contains copies of circular despatches to governors, 1794–1815, including many sent to West Indian executives relative to trade regulations, fish bounties etc.

C. O. 325/2–4, 6, 10–13, 15, 17–19, 32 contain miscellaneous material relative to the West Indies up to 1833. See *P. R. O. Lists and Indexes, No. XXXVI*, p. 321, for check list.

C. O. 326/55–74 consist of indexes to original correspondence of the Board of Trade and include entries covering many letters relative to the West Indies to 1782; 326/75 is a list of journals of assembly, 1778–1787; 326/76 is a list of minutes of council, 1781–1787; 326/77–82 contain records of letters received and sent by the Secretary of State, 1810–1816; 326/84–88, 105, 117, 130, 131, 143, 144, 154, 155, 163, 164, 166, 173, 174, 176, 183, 193, 194 are records of letters relative to the West Indies received by the Secretary of State up to 1833.

C. O. 383/1, 2, 9, 29, 34, 40, 41, 47, 51, 53, 78, 80, 82, 86, 88 are act registers for the several colonies up to 1833.

C. O. 385/1 contains data on settlers allowed to remain in Trinidad, 1814–1822.

C. O. 388 (Board of Trade, commercial, original correspondence) vols. 51–74, include numerous scattered papers dealing with the West Indies. Many miscellaneous entries relative to these colonies will be found in C. O. 389 (Board of Trade, commercial, entry books of commissions, instructions, petitions, correspondence, orders in council etc.) vols. 31–34, 38, 39, 50–53 and in C. O. 391 (Board of Trade, commercial, minutes of the Board, 1763–1782), vols. 70–89.

Custom House Accounts, Public Record Office

Customs 3 (ledgers of imports into and exports from England), vols. 63–80 cover the period 1763–1780; Customs 4 (ledgers of imports under countries), vols. 5–28, 1809–1833, excepting 1813, the records for which were destroyed in the London Custom House fire of 1814. Vols. 5–24 of the latter series contain statistics for England and Scotland in part; vols. 24–28, for the United Kingdom.

Customs 5 (ledgers of imports by articles for Great Britain to

1830, after which for the United Kingdom, specifying the several sections, however), vols. 2–22 provide data for the years 1812–1833, listing as they do shipments of tropical produce colony by colony except for the years 1825, 1826 and 1827, when only totals for the entire British Caribbean are given.

Customs 10 (ledgers of exports of foreign and colonial merchandise, under countries), vols. 1–24 embrace the period 1809–1833. Customs 11 (ledgers of exports of foreign and colonial merchandise, under articles), vols. 1–24, cover 1809–1833; Customs 14 (ledgers of imports and exports, Scotland), vols. 1B–39, 1764–1827; Customs 15 (ledgers of imports and exports, Ireland), vols. 57–140, 1763–1829.

Custom House statistics are so incomplete because many papers were destroyed in the above mentioned conflagration.

N. Darnell Davis Papers

An extensive and as yet (1928) unassorted and uncatalogued lot of notes and more or less completed articles on various phases of West Indian history from earliest to recent times, in the Colonial Institute, London. Unfortunately this well known Caribbean historian seldom indicated the sources of his information and wrote in an almost illegible hand. It is doubtful, therefore, whether his material can ever be profitably employed by anyone.

Lieutenant Howard's Journal

A record of experiences during service with the British army of occupation in St. Domingo beginning in 1793. Three volumes, stressing the invading forces' sufferings. In the Boston Public Library.

Jamaican Agents' Correspondence

Four volumes of letters from the colonial agents in London to the legislative committee of correspondence, 1794–1801, 1814–1834, in the library of the Institute of Jamaica, Kingston.

Records of the Jamaican Committee of Correspondence

Letter book of this group in the colonial legislature covering 1794–1833 and minute book for 1795–1846, both in the library of the Institute of Jamaica.

James McTear's Travel Account

A two volume work, *Journal of a Voyage to and Residence in the Island of Tobago, from the Year 1825 till the Year 1830, with Observations on the State of the Slaves in the British Colonies,* in the Division of Manuscripts of the Library of Congress. One volume is the original journal, the other an expansion of it written some time later.

Diary of John Smith, "the Demerara Martyr"

Bears the title *A Journal Containing various Occurrences at Le Resouvenir, Demerary, Commenced in March 1817* . . . and covers a period of six years. In the London Missionary Society archives.

John Smith, an agent of that organization among the slaves of British Guiana, was accused in August 1823 of having incited them to revolt. He was court-martialled, was found guilty on evidence of the flimsiest nature, was sentenced to death and died in prison before having been executed. The affair created a tremendous stir in England and hastened emancipation.

It is therefore somewhat singular that this primary account has never appeared in print. Fair copies exist in the West India Committee library and among the Colonial Office documents (C. O. 111/46).

Treasury Papers, Public Record Office

4½ per cent duty accounts will be found under T 38; certain West India maps under T 62; papers of the African Company which supplied the sugar colonies with negro hands under T 70; the slavery compensation records under T 71; American loyalist claims under T 79; others arising from the British occupation of St. Domingo beginning in 1793 and ending in 1798 under T 81; records of the West Indian accounts commission named under 41 Geo. III c. 22, under T 94.

War Office Papers, Public Record Office

The chief series of documents relative to military affairs in the West Indies from 1763–1833 will be found listed under W. O. 1, 4,

9, 17, 49, 55, 57, 58, 61, and 62 in *P. R. O. Lists and Indexes, No. XXVIII.*

West India Committee Archives

Several groups of papers are preserved in the Committee's office, 14 Trinity Square, E. C. 3, London.

First Series

A. Minutes of the meetings of the West India Merchants.

Vol. I, April 1769–April 1779.

II, June 1779–August 1783.

III, missing.

IV, March 1794–December 1802.

V, April 1803–July 1804.

VI, Sept. 1804–July 1827.

VII, Jan. 1828–July 1843.

These are the minute books of the Society of West India Merchants, founded ca. 1750 and continuing as a separate organization to 1843.

B. Minutes of the meetings of the Sub-committee of the West India Merchants on loans.

Vol. I. Oct. 1799–July 1800, accompanied by a certification book approving Bank of England advances to specified traders and a register of deposits covering the goods offered as security by borrowers. The latter were discovered in the Bank of England vaults in 1905, a century after having been filed there. (See *W. I. Comm. Circ.*, Dec. 8 and 22, 1905, pp. 489–491, and 514–516.)

This Sub-committee was named in 1799 to arrange loans by the Bank of England to West India houses in distress. Its work was completed in July 1800, when all sums thus borrowed had been repaid.

C. Minutes of the meetings of the Sub-Committee of the West India Merchants for general purposes.

Vol. 1, Jan. 1828–March 1830.

This body was named to consider questions of general importance to the Caribbean interest, such as the emancipation movement, produce duties, etc.

Second Series

A. Minutes of the meetings of the West India Planters and Merchants.

Vol. I, May 1785–December 1792.

II, February 1793–April 1801.

III, December 1801–June 1804.

IV, February 1805–March 1822.

V, March 1822–April 1829.

VI, April 1829–February 1834.

These are the minute books covering the general sessions of the Society of West India Planters and Merchants (founded ca. 1782 and continuing to the present day after its union with the Society of West India Merchants in 1843), of the Standing Committee of that organization and of certain special committees. In April 1829 the Acting Committee, for whose records see below, was created as the working body of the Society of West India Planters and Merchants. The Standing Committee thereafter met but quarterly except as called together specially by the Acting body. Its records and those of the infrequent general meetings are found in Vol. VI, but give way in interest and value to those of the new Acting Committee.

B. Minutes of the meetings of the Sub-committee of the Society of West India Planters and Merchants, appointed by the Standing Committee on Feb. 7, 1788 and enlarged on Jan. 19 and March 19, 1792.

Vol. I, Jan. 1792–June 1804.

This Sub-committee was originally named to keep close watch of anti-slave trade measures before parliament (*Min. W. I. Plant. and Mer.*, Feb. 8, 1788 and March 8, 1791) and twice later had members added to it in an effort to safeguard colonial interests and to actively oppose abolition. Appropriations for its use were voted (*Ibid.*, Jan. 19, 1792, Feb. 20, 1792, Apr. 13, 1792.) On Jan. 19, 1792, the time of the first enlargement, it was desired that the committee "circulate such publications in the Newspapers and otherwise, as shall seem to them useful . . . for the purpose of defending the Cause of the Colonies so far as respects the Colony System in General, and the protection of its Articles of produce and the extension of their consumption" (*Ibid.*, minutes of that day). Two months later, following the addition of other members, full power was given the group "to take such measures as . . . may appear necessary, towards opposing the proposed Abolition of the Slave Trade" (*Ibid.*, March 19, 1792). The few entries after 1794 are of no value.

C. Minutes of the Literary Committee of the Society of West India Planters and Merchants.

Vol. I, June 1823–Dec. 1829.

Vol. II, Dec. 1830–March 1833.

The original "Literary Committee" was created by the Standing

Committee on June 5, 1823, for the purpose of protecting West Indian interests through the press. A drive against the Caribbean planters on the parts of the government (the Canning resolutions), the emancipationists and the East India traders had just begun. The committee functioned as late as July 1828. In November 1829, the Acting Committee (see below) temporarily resolved itself into a Literary Committee and held a number of meetings in that capacity during the following year. In November 1830, it elected a new special Literary Committee as a renewed attack on slavery had opened. That body's records are contained in Vol. II.

D. Minutes of the Acting Committee of the Society of West India Planters and Merchants.

Vol. I, May 1829–July 1833.

Created April 28, 1829 as the working body of the Society. It consisted of twenty members elected from the Standing Committee of that organization plus the colonial agents. The Standing Committee met but quarterly thereafter unless on special call from the Acting one. The latter met weekly from July to November and considered all matters of importance to the colonial interest. All sub-committees were abolished and their duties were transferred to the Acting Committee. It was, however, necessary to re-establish the Literary Committee in 1830 (see above).

E. Society of West India Planters and Merchants—Sugar, Feb. 1825–June 1830.

This volume contains the reports of deputations of the Society which conferred with government officials on the question of sugar duties together with copies of memorials from that body and others interested in the sugar trade (as the Liverpool and Glasgow merchants) to the Commissioners of the Treasury, etc., and some press clippings on these subjects.

F. Society of West India Planters and Merchants—Rum, Feb. 1825–May 1830.

As above, but concerning rum. Many press clippings on the question of corn distillation.

G. Society of West India Planters and Merchants—Documents transmitted to the Board of Trade by W. R. Keith Douglas, Esq. M.P. on the Existing Distress of the British West India Colonies, 1830.

The government held an investigation into the commercial, financial and political state of the Caribbean possessions through the

Board of Trade in that year and the Society was invited to furnish such evidence as it chose on the subject. Thirty-five declarations regarding the then low state of the islands and its causes and twenty-three digests on the cost of production, cost of supplies, etc. were submitted.

Third Series

A. Minutes of the Meetings of the Committee of Demerara and Berbice Planters and Mortgagees.

Vol. I, Nov. 1826–March 1830.

This committee consisted of proprietors of estates in those colonies and their creditors. It was formed to fight compulsory manumission as inaugurated by Lord Bathurst and from the outset co-operated with the Committee of the Society of West India Merchants, the Standing Committee of the Society of West India Planters and Merchants and outport Caribbean bodies. The record of its separate activities closes with the minutes for the meeting of 7 Feb. 1828.

Entries on two meetings of a sub-committee of the Acting Committee of the Society of West India Planters and Merchants, on the affairs of Berbice and Demerara, held in 1830, closes the book. This new sub-committee of the Planter and Merchant body thus appears to have taken over the functions of the original committee of the group of Demerara and Berbice Planters and Mortgagees.

Fourth Series

A. Minutes of the meetings of the Glasgow West India Association, 1802–1809.

This outport body co-operated with the London West India organizations in furthering mutual interests.

Fifth Series

A. Miscellaneous papers.

These include fragments of a London sugar merchant's account book covering sales of tropical American produce 1744–1826, certain legal papers from Antigua (manumitting a slave, ordering the carrying out of a death sentence for felony, and directing the commutation of a death sentence to transportation), a sheaf of correspondence from a Grenada plantation attorney to the absentee owner at the close of the eighteenth century together with certain accounts, an original mortgage on divers properties in Jamaica dated May 1822 and minutes of the meetings of the annuitants of Spring Estate, Jamaica, 1801–1804. In the same bound volume as the latter are found copies of letters from the agent of Richard Boucher, a Jamaican planter, to an individual in Great Britain with whom Boucher had dealings, written from Wickham, England, 1824–31.

B. Authentick Journal of Missionary Smith, Decd. (Copy.)

See "Diary of John Smith," above. Another copy will be found in the Public Record Office (C. O. 111/46).

West India Trade Material

The originals of the papers published under the title "Commerce of Rhode Island, 1726–1800," in *Collections of the Massachusetts Historical Society*, vols. LXIX and LXX (Boston, 1914, 1915) are in the archives of the Newport and the Rhode Island Historical Societies and in the private collections of George P. Wetmore of the Massachusetts Historical Society.

Wilkinson and Gaviller Papers

Letter and account books in the office of Messrs. Wilkinson and Gaviller, 34 Great Tower Street, E. C. 3, London. This company, founded as Lascelles and Maxwell ca. 1743 and since then engaged largely in trade with Barbados, is one of the best known West India houses in Great Britain to-day. The firm's records commence in 1739/40 and are an invaluable source for a study of commerce between the mother country and the Caribbean possessions. They have not yet been thoroughly exploited.

PARLIAMENTARY PAPERS

Many hundred relative to social and economic conditions in the Caribbean after 1790 have been published in the Blue Books, especially among the House of Commons Sessional Papers. For the latter, see the writer's *Check List* referred to under Guides, Indexes, and Bibliographies.

COLONIAL LAWS, ETC.

Collections of acts passed by the legislatures of Antigua (Leeward Islands), Barbados, Dominica, Grenada, Jamaica, Montserrat, Nevis,

St. Kitts, St. Vincent, and Tobago during the period 1763–1833 have been printed. These are, however, very incomplete, giving as they do only the text of such laws as were in actual force at the time of publication.

The original manuscript copies of measures sent to the home country for approval are to be found among the Colonial Office papers, as noted under Manuscripts above. There is great need for a careful study of them and for the publication of all laws ever passed in each colony, with the disallowed and repealed ones properly indicated.

Innumerable acts were printed at the time of their adoption and copies of these are scattered through the governors' correspondence.

Copies of hundreds of proclamations, both in manuscript and in printed form, will be found as enclosures in despatches to the Secretary of State, as will be copies of orders in council, orders of government, and ordinances for the crown colonies St. Lucia (in English and French) and Trinidad (in English and Spanish).

Numerous reports, addresses, and memorials of the legislatures of Antigua, Barbados, Dominica, Jamaica, St. Vincent, and Tobago have been printed. These were frequently published in London by the colonial agents and deal for the most part with slavery, duties on Caribbean produce and economic conditions in the islands. Extensive use has been made of them in the text.

Legislative journals have been published by Grenada and Jamaica. Those for the latter colony are very extensive and of untold value to the student of the island's social and economic history.

GENERAL HISTORIES

There is no work embracing the British West Indies as a whole during the period 1763–1833 which meets the test of modern scholarship. The classic production in this field, Bryan Edwards, *The History, Civil and Commercial, of the British Colonies in the West Indies* (2 vols. 1793), is a veritable gold mine for the social and economic conditions in Jamaica from about 1760–1790 with which the author, long a prominent planter and member of the island legislature, was personally familiar, but is otherwise quite worthless. Abbé Raynal's *Histoire Philosophique et Politique des Etablissemens et du Commerce des Européens dans les deux Indes* (many editions, as 5 vols., 1780), based on hasty reading and on snap judgment, is of interest chiefly as showing what an imaginative Frenchman thought the Caribbean colonies to be. The almost unknown continuation of this unjustly celebrated work, Peuchet's *Etat des Colonies et du Commerce des Européens dans les deux Indes Depuis 1783 Jusqu'en 1821* (2 vols., 1821) is much more sound, but has no particular value for our purpose.

Captain Thomas Southey's *Chronological History of the West Indies* (3 vols., 1827) is the compilation of a naval officer at one time stationed in Caribbean waters and contains a curious hash of information drawn from divers places, including all of the early histories of the colonies. Many interesting items relative to social and economic conditions will be found by the reader able to wade through endless pages, but the sources of many of these are not indicated. There is no index and little order was employed in presenting material. Everything has, however, been faithfully adapted and documents have proven to be accurately reproduced wherever it has been possible to check up on them.

Thomas Coke, "father of West Indian missions," borrowed extensively from other works for his *A History of the West Indies* (3 vols., 1808–1811), hence it is for the most part of little value. A genuine contribution is, however, made in his account of the labors of the Methodist missionaries which were carried on in the several colonies under his direction. Adrien Dessalles, *Histoire Générale des Antilles* (5 vols., 1847–48) and Elias Regnault, *Histoire des Antilles* (1849) have all the defects of the English histories of the islands with none of the virtue arising from personal knowledge of the contemporary state of affairs in them.

Algernon Aspinall's *The British West Indies* (1912), his *West Indian Tales of Old* (1912) and Amos Fiske's *The West Indies* (1899) are good popular accounts.

R. Montgomery Martin's *History of the West Indies* (2 vols., 1836, 1837) was for half a century the standard historical geography of the colonies and contains a large amount of accurately reproduced statistical data excerpted from parliamentary papers. Charles P. Lucas's *Historical Geography of the West Indies . . .* (2nd. ed., 1905), an excellent work, is the latest in the field.

Lillian M. Penson's *The Colonial Agents of the British West*

Indies (1924) is a scholarly study thoroughly covering an interesting phase of general island history falling in part within the years 1763–1833.

Two treatises on constitutional developments in the British Caribbean have appeared in recent times. The first of these, Eugène Sicé's *Comment Gouverner les Colonies Tropicales. Étude sur le Gouvernement Local et l'Organisation Législative des Antilles Anglaises* (1913), is an elaboration of his *Étude sur les Colonies de la Couronne Britannique; les Antilles Anglaises, le Gouvernement Local et L'Organisation Legislative,* a University of Paris doctoral dissertation of the same year. The other, Hume Wrong's *Government of the West Indies,* was published a decade later (1923). Unfortunately both are very superficial, being based only upon readily accessible printed matter and ignoring the mass of documents on this subject in the Colonial Office papers.

LOCAL HISTORIES

Such works have been published for all of the West India colonies with the exception of Grenada and St. Kitts-Nevis. Only two, however, are the result of scholarly research. Still unsurpassed in this respect after three quarters of a century is Sir Robert Schomburgk's *The History of Barbados* (1848), resting largely upon an exhaustive study of records in the island and in Great Britain. The author was a celebrated scientist and colonial administrator.

William J. Gardner's *A History of Jamaica* (1873), based to a considerable extent on papers in local archives, holds a position second only to Schomburgk's classic. Gardner was a sectarist clergyman and an active figure in island society. It is to be regretted that no other books of a similar high quality have appeared.

Most local writers have been uncritical and have mixed facts drawn from earlier volumes with fancy to such an extent that their accounts have no value to-day save for those portions recording contemporary events and describing conditions which the authors themselves knew at first hand. For such information, the importance of these colonial histories cannot be overestimated.

The outstanding production of this kind is [Edward Long], *History of Jamaica* (3 vols., 1774), an almost inexhaustible treasure house for the state of the colony immediately preceding the disruption of the old British empire. The author was for many years secretary to the lieutenant-governor and later served as judge in the local vice-admiralty court. Bridges's *Annals of Jamaica* (2 vols., 1828) was written by a bigoted Established Churchman as a defense of the planter interest against the attacks of the emancipationists and is of value chiefly as presenting the views of the pro-colonial group. Frank Cundall, *Historic Jamaica* (1915) contains useful reference lists of colonial officials.

Vere L. Oliver, *The History of the Island of Antigua* (3 vols., 1894–99) is primarily a monumental genealogical work. John Poyer's *The History of Barbados* (1808) was written by a well-informed native who held the welfare of the colony to be indissolubly bound up with slavery. George Hirst's *Notes on the History of the Cayman Islands* [1910] is a chronological work. Thomas Atwood, *History of Dominica* (1791) is worthy of attention chiefly for its account of the French occupation of a decade before. The author was chief judge of the colony.

The economic data contained in Henry Breen's *St. Lucia: Historical, Statistical, and Descriptive* (1844), gives it high rank. The author resided in the island for thirteen years. Charles Shephard's *Historical Account of the Island of Saint Vincent* (1831), written by a law officer of the colony, deals largely with the Carib war of 1795. Henry Woodcock's *History of Tobago* (1868) contains a considerable amount of material on local plantations and production statistics for an earlier time.

Anon., "A Gentleman of the Island," *A Political Account of the Island of Trinidad . . .* (1807) is essentially an address to the public of Great Britain on the part of resident Englishmen, calling for the replacement of the then current Spanish law by that of the home country. Pierre Borde, in his *Histoire de l'Ile de la Trinidad . . .* (2 vols., 1876, 1882), was interested chiefly in the colonization of the island by Frenchmen under the Spanish régime. Lionel M. Fraser's *History of Trinidad* (2 vols., n. d. and 1893) is a compilation but is valuable because it contains an immense number of excerpts from official correspondence and some entire documents. Edward L. Joseph, for twenty years a resident of the colony, wrote a *History of Trinidad* [1836], of inestimable value to-day because a considerable part of it was based upon Cabildo records which have since been destroyed.

George Suckling's *An Historical Account of the Virgin Islands*

. . . (1780) is the work of an aggrieved chief justice, designed to call attention to the lawless state of the colony.

Various narratives covering spectacular incidents in the history of the several islands, such as civil disturbances and natural disasters, have appeared and are fairly reliable.

DESCRIPTION AND TRAVEL

The number of works portraying British Caribbean society as it existed in the three quarters of a century after the Peace of Paris is considerable, due to interest in the subject having been aroused by the agitation for abolition and emancipation. These range from sketchy impressions gained through a few months' stay to two or three volume treatises based upon many years' residence and came chiefly from the pens of estate owners, military men, and feminine relatives of colonial officials.

Tourists were struck by bizarre features of the novel life they encountered and tended to stress these; the writings of actual dwellers in the tropical colonies, on the other hand, show an understanding of forces in operation there, though they are often thinly-veiled defenses of the slave régime. Both are of immense value when used with caution. Only the outstanding ones are given here.

Capt. J. E. Alexander's *Transatlantic Sketches* . . . (2 vols., 1833) is the work of a keen observer, an unattached army officer who visited the islands in 1831. Evangeline and Charles Andrews, ed., *Journal of a Lady of Quality* [*Janet Schaw*]; *Being a Narrative of a Journey from Scotland to the West Indies, North Carolina, and Portugal, in the Years 1774 to 1776* (1921), is one of the most charming West Indian travel accounts in existence. Anon., *Letters from the Virgin Islands: Illustrated Life and Manners in the West Indies* (1843) was written by an English official in the colony during the third decade of the nineteenth century and gives a vivid account of the low state of life in that isolated group together with indications of the extensive smuggling operations then being carried on there.

Four Years' Residence in the West Indies, During the Years 1826, 7, 8, and 9 (1833), by Frederic Bayley, the son of a British officer, is a rather dull and stupid book but contains useful currency tables. William Beckford's *A Descriptive Account of the Island of Jamaica* . . . (2 vols., 1790) was written by a one-time wealthy resident while languishing in Fleet prison where he had been incarcerated because of debts incurred through a hurricane and through having gone security for a friend. While excellent, it does not merit the characterization "standard work on the earlier state of the colony" (*Lit. of Am. His.,* A. L. A. 1902, p. 458.).

[Henry] Capadose's *Sixteen Years in the West Indies* (2 vols., 1845) is the account of a lieutenant-colonel in Caribbean service who was thoroughly familiar with all of the sugar islands, but unfortunately it contains a hodge-podge of historical data and excerpts from earlier writers mixed with a personal narrative and thus lacks continuity. Mrs. A. C. Carmichael, author of *Domestic Manners and Social Conditions of the White, Coloured, and Negro Population of the West Indies* (2 vols., 1833), was the wife of a planter and resided in St. Vincent and Trinidad for five and a half years. Her rather sprightly book is extremely pro-colonial and whitewashes the islanders of all charges against them on the negro question.

Six Months in the West Indies in 1825 (1826), by Henry Coleridge, was perhaps the most popular Caribbean travel work. It is interesting for our purpose chiefly because the author, nephew and son-in-law of Samuel Coleridge, the poet, made the transatlantic trip in company with another uncle, William H. Coleridge, first bishop of Barbados. *Antigua and the Antiguans* (2 vols., 1844), by "Mrs. Flannigan," an English lady for many years in the colony, is an invaluable mirror of contemporary island society.

James Hakewill, *A Picturesque Tour of the Island of Jamaica . . . in the Years 1820 and 1821* (1825) and J. Johnson, *Views in the West Indies* . . . [1827] contain large-sized color prints of a high order. An excessively rare work, William Clark's *Ten Views in the Island of Antigua* . . . (1823) illustrates the method of making sugar in superbly executed color plates.

Mathew Lewis's *Journal of a West India Proprietor* . . . (1834) is the record of two visits to estates inherited by this well-known novelist, made in 1815–1817, and is one of the best in this field. "Monk" Lewis sought to overcome the evils of absenteeism and instituted many reforms among the negroes on his properties. The *Brief Account of the Island of Antigua* . . . (1789), by John Luffman, in the form of a series of forty letters dated 1786, 1787, and 1788, gives one of the best pictures of plantation colony life in existence. Unfortunately, the book itself is so scarce as to be almost inaccessible.

Richard Madden's *A Twelvemonth's Residence in the West Indies* . . . (2 vols., 1835) is an important work as it covers the year 1834, during the transition from slavery to apprenticeship. The author was a newspaper correspondent. [Peter Marsden's] *An Account of the Island of Jamaica. . . .* (Newcastle, 1788), a modest recital of one resident in the colony for a year, presents an excellent view of contemporary social conditions. *Notices Respecting Jamaica in 1808–1809–1810* (1811) was written by Gilbert Mathison, a proprietor returning to the island after an absence of thirteen years. He was exceedingly optimistic as to the future; his accounts of the inefficiency of tropical agriculture are especially valuable.

Daniel McKinnen's *A Tour Through the British West Indies, in the Years 1802 and 1803* . . . (1804), while devoted largely to the Bahamas, gives some attention to the prevalence of absenteeism in Jamaica. J. B. Moreton, author of *Manners and Customs of the West India Islands* (1790), had been a Jamaican bookkeeper for five years. His work is rather poorly written and coarse but is well worth reading.

Maria, Lady Nugent's *A Journal of a Voyage to and Residence in the Island of Jamaica from 1801 to 1805* (2 vols., 1839. Also issued as *Lady Nugent's Journal. Jamaica One Hundred Years Ago* under the editorship of Frank C. Cundall in 1907) has but one rival, the diary of Janet Schaw, already mentioned. The keeper of this purely personal record was the wife of Sir George Nugent, the colony's lieutenant-governor from 1801 to 1806. She here presents an utterly inimitable and imperishable picture of planter society as seen through the eyes of English gentility.

George Pinckard, author of *Notes on the West Indies* (3 vols., 1806), was a deputy inspector-general of hospitals in the British army who accompanied General Sir Ralph Abercromby to the Caribbean and when not in active service became well acquainted with the regions where he was stationed. *An Account of Jamaica, and its Inhabitants* (1808) and *A View of the Past and Present State of the Island of Jamaica* (1823) were written by John Stewart, who resided in the colony for twenty-one years. Their value for the student of social and economic conditions cannot be overestimated. His accounts are rather uncomplimentary to the planters and to the Established Church.

The West India Sketch Book (2 vols., 1834) by Trelawny Wentworth, is a racy account of a several years' stay and much travel in the sugar islands without any other apparent object than to pass the time. Cynric Williams, author of *A Tour Through the Island of Jamaica from the Western to the Eastern End in the Year 1823* (1826), visited the Caribbean to receive settlement for a property left him and spent about three months there. His work is that of a cock-sure young smart aleck, contains wild exaggerations and misstatements from cover to cover, and is of interest only because of the hatred for sectarist activities and the support of slavery shown throughout.

Sir William Young's "History of the West Indies &c. A Tour Through the Several Islands of Barbados, St. Vincent, Antigua, Tobago, and Grenada, in the years 1791, and 1792," in Bryan Edwards's *An Historical Survey of the Island of St. Domingo . . .* (1801) is the narrative of a trip made to visit his scattered estates. The writer was later named governor of Tobago. Of particular value for the state of the slaves.

THE RELIGIOUS SITUATION

The Established Church played a rôle of minor importance in the West Indies up to 1833. Most of the active Christian work carried on there was sponsored by the sectarists who organized special missionary bodies to provide for the blacks' spiritual welfare. The Wesleyans proved particularly enterprising. Many pamphlets by the Rev. Thomas Coke, listed in the footnote references, and his West Indian history are source accounts for their early operations, while the annual reports of the Wesleyan Missionary Society from 1818 on serve a similar purpose for the later period. Popular accounts of the Methodists' great achievements are given in the various books by the Rev. William Moister.

The numerous narratives setting forth Moravian and Baptist accomplishments and those covering the activities of such organizations as the London Missionary Society, listed in the footnotes, are usually based upon personal knowledge or contemporary papers and, while strongly biased, contain much valuable information not to be found elsewhere. Annual and other reports of the rejuvenated Incorporated Society for the Conversion and Religious Instruction and Education of the Negro Slaves in the British West India Islands are important for the work done under Anglican auspices with the Caribbean interest's support after the late date of 1823.

ECONOMIC LITERATURE

There is no lack of material of this nature. Several hundred contemporary pamphlets and articles give excellent accounts of plantation management, of the estate owners' problems, and of the difficulties they experienced from increased costs of production and marketing and from the competition of the ceded and foreign colonies' produce and of East India sugar. These are of the utmost importance for our purpose and extensive use has been made of them.

Minute books of the Society of West India Merchants and of the Society of West India Planters and Merchants show many such writings to have been issued for propaganda purposes. A careful study of those records makes possible the proper evaluation of much of this ephemeral output.

Wholesale quotations for the chief articles of Caribbean produce from 1777 on will be found in quarterly circulars preserved in the archives of Messrs. Joseph Travers and Sons, Ltd. of London. *The London Gazette,* by act of parliament, regularly published current trade prices on sugar commencing in 1792.

The House of Commons Sessional Papers contain several extended reports on the state of the colonies as well as numerous import, export, duty and other tables and are of prime importance. The author's *Statistics for the Study of British Caribbean Economic History, 1763–1833* (London, 1928) contains a mass of figures from many sources, largely unpublished hitherto. Frank W. Pitman's *The Old Plantation System in the British West Indies,* to be published shortly, holds great promise.

THE SLAVE TRADE, SLAVERY, ABOLITION, AND EMANCIPATION

Singularly enough, no study of the African slave trade in its hey-day, from the Peace of Paris to 1808, has yet been made. Miss

Elizabeth Donnan's forthcoming three volume work containing a collection of documents illustrating the methods and sources of supply from the beginning of this form of British commerce to its close will fill a long felt need and should stimulate research in a most fascinating field.

The best account of Caribbean bondage is Frank W. Pitman's "Slavery on the British West India Plantations in the Eighteenth Century," published in *The Journal of Negro History* for October 1926, pp. 584 ff. Ample descriptions of the tropical labor régime will also be found in standard histories such as Edwards's work and in the various travel works, q. v.

No treatise on humanitarian activities in behalf of the negroes within the British Empire as a whole has yet appeared. Frank J. Klingberg's *The Anti-Slavery Movement in England* (New Haven, 1926), and William L. Mathieson's *British Slavery and its Abolition 1823–1838*, are noteworthy first steps in that direction.

Much exceedingly important matter is to be found in Clarkson's *History of the Rise, Progress and Accomplishment of the Abolition of the African Slave Trade by the British Parliament* (2 vols., 1808), in the several works on Granville Sharp, William Wilberforce, James Stephen, Zachary Macaulay, and Thomas Fowell Buxton referred to in the footnotes, in the annual and other reports of the Society for Effecting the Abolition of the Slave Trade, of the African Institution and of the Society for the Mitigation and Gradual Abolition of Slavery Throughout the British Dominions, in the host of parliamentary papers dealing with those subjects and in the minute books of the Society of West India Planters and Merchants which record the efforts made by members of the colonial interest to combat movements so inimical to their welfare.

Robert Bissett's *History of the Negro Slave Trade and its Connection with the Commerce and Prosperity of the West Indies* (2 vols., 1805), the work of a rabid supporter of the trade, is an uncritical tirade against and vilification of the abolitionists. Franz Hochstetter, in his *Die wirtschaftlichen und politischen Motive für die Abschaffung des britischen Sklavenhandels . . .* (1905), holds abolition to have been adopted by the British because the traffic in blacks had ceased to be profitable for them, but does not support his argument with documentary evidence. *Anglo-Saxon Abolition of Negro Slavery* (1889), by F. W. Newman, presents nothing not already known, but is a thoughtful consideration of the subject.

The number of pamphlets on the negro question is legion, those attacking the trade and slavery being about twice as numerous as those written in their defense. The records of the bodies organized to effect abolition and emancipation and of the trader-proprietor societies in England are an indispensable aid in weighing them since the former reveal the intimate details of propaganda campaigns and the latter show how these were met by the West India interest.

NEWSPAPERS AND PERIODICALS

Most colonies boasted two newspapers which were bitter rivals, one supporting the administration and the other serving as the opposition organ. Their news columns were ordinarily filled with reprinted foreign items and are consequently of less value for our purpose than are the notices, proclamations, and advertisements. Valuable accounts of local gatherings are, however, to be found occasionally. Only broken files, widely scattered about Great Britain, the United States and the islands themselves, have survived.

The periodical press of the home country admirably reflected the conflicting views on fundamental questions of West Indian policy. The stands taken by leading organs of opinion have been made clear in the text. The minute books of the Society of West India Planters and Merchants, showing which articles were published as paid insertions of that body, are a necessary aid to the proper use of a considerable amount of this material.

APPENDICES

Appendix I

Comparative Table of Imports from the Thirteen Colonies and Other British North American Possessions into the British West Indies in 1771, 1772, and 1773

(From *Considerations on the Present State of the Intercourse Between His Majesty's Sugar Colonies and the Dominions of the United States of America* [London, 1784], published by the Society of West India Planters and Merchants of London in the interest of freeing the American-Caribbean trade of restrictions.)

Based on Custom House Records

Product	From the 13 colonies	From Canada and Nova Scotia	From Newfoundland
Boards and timber, ft.	76,767,695	232,040	2,000
Shingles, no.	59,586,194	185,000	——
Staves, no.	57,998,661	27,350	——
Hoops, no.	4,712,005	16,250	9,000
Corn, bu.	1,204,389	24	——
Peas, beans, bu.	64,006	1,017	——
Bread, flour, bbls.	396,329	991	——
Ditto, kegs	13,099	——	——
Rice, bbls.	39,912	——	——
Ditto, tierces	21,777	——	——
Fish, hhd.	51,344	449	2,307
Ditto, bbls.	47,686	646	202
Ditto, quintals	21,500	2,958	11,764
Ditto, kegs	3,304	609	——
Beef and pork, bbls.	44,782	170	24
Poultry, dozen	2,739	10	——
Horses, no.	7,130	28	——
Oxen, no.	3,647	——	——
Sheep and hogs, no.	13,815	——	——
Oil, barrels	3,189	139	118
Tar, pitch, turpentine, bbls.	17,024	——	——
Masts, no.	157	——	——

Product	From the 13 colonies	From Canada and Nova Scotia	From Newfoundland
Spars, no.	3,074	30	——
Shook casks, no.	53,857	40	141
Soap and Candles, boxes	20,475	——	——
Ox Bows and Yoakers, no.	1,540	——	——
House Frames, no.	620	——	——
Iron, tons	399 ¼	——	——

APPENDIX II

SALES ACCOUNT OF A LONDON MERCHANT
WITH A WEST INDIA PLANTER, 1795–1796

(From a fragmentary account book, 1744–1826, in the West India
Committee archives.)

(folio 110.)

William Stimpson Jamaica on account of J. Nightingale Estate Cr.

1796 By Messrs. Gaviller & Co. for 10 Casks d'd 25 Feby.

	[Cask]	[Weight]		[Cask]	[Weight]
Feby. 23	1.	14–1–23		13.	13–3–14
	7.	14–2–16		10.	14–0–23
	3.	15–0–19		20.	14–1–7
	8.	14–0–19		16.	14–0–19
N	2.	14–3–14		9.	13–3–2
				[Cd. fwd.]	73–1–7
E L		73–1– 7			
[cask					143–2–16
mark]			[Tare, breakage]		16–0–14

127–2–2 at 88/–561   1 6

25 By Messrs. Waikerbarth & Co. for 10 Casks d'd 1 April

[Cask]	[Weight]		[Cask]	[Weight]
5.	13–2–19		17.	13–1–23
19.	15–0–19		18.	13–2–0
4.	13–0–4		6.	13–2–5
12.	13–3–0		15.	14–0–21
11.	13–3–16		14.	12–3–12
			[Cd. fwd.]	69–2–2
	69–2–2			
				137–0–7
		[Tare, breakage]		15–1–13

121–2–22 at 87/–529   7 6

£ 1090   9 0

Dr.   Sales of 20 Casks of Sugar imported in the Phoenix

1795   To Custom of 259–2–21 at 15/ 194 15 6
8th Oct. Bills & Billmoney & Landw^{rs} Fees 12 4

	Wharf^a. Light^a. Landg. and housing	2	7	3
	Cooperage & Weighing		18	4
N	To Freight of 259–2–21 at 9/–per cwt. & trade			
E L	2d per hhd.	117		6
[Cask	Primage Dover Pier, & Ramsgate Harbour		17	6
mark]	Warehouse Room and insurance from fire 2/–per			
	hhd.	7	17	11
	Brokerage 1/2 per cent	5	9	
		329	18	4
	To Commission £2 1/2%	27	5	2
		357	3	6
	To the Acc^t. Curr^t. for Nett Proceed	733	5	6

Ent^d. fo. 222   London the 25th of April 1796   £1090 9 0

Errors Excepted

INDEX

INDEX

A

Abolition bill passed (1807), 276

Abolition law: breaches of, 387 ff.

Abolition movement, 239 ff.; opens in 1787, 250; triumph of in 1807, 276

Absentee landords: additional taxes laid on, in Jamaica, 50; in Tobago, 50; both laws disallowed, 50; communities of, in England, 50; their luxurious life, 50; Geo. III displeased at ostentation of one, 50; organization of, 51; close watch kept of legislation bearing on colonies, 52 ff.; oppose development of ceded islands, 115

Absenteeism: causes of, 42 ff.; great prevalence of, after first quarter of eighteenth century, 44 ff.; lamentable consequences of, 44 ff.; lack of, in Antigua, 67; the explanation, 67 ff.

Act for the prevention of excessive exportation of sugar to the detriment of British consumers (1792), 207

Adams, John, on importance of free commericial intercourse with the British Caribbean (1782), 174

Adams, President, proclamation by, 1827, governing American-West Indian trade, 359

African Institution founded in 1807, 384; its program, 384 ff.; support given, 385; work carried out by, 385 ff.; sponsors slave registration, 389 ff.; gives publicity to the Huggins case, 400; no formal stand taken on emancipation, 408; passing of the, 426

Agrarian system, characteristics of the Caribbean, 37 ff.

Agricultural Association (Barbados), 68

Agricultural clubs: St. Vincent, 69; St. Kitts, 70; Antigua, 70; Grenada, 70

Agricultural societies in the British West Indies, 68 ff.

Agriculture, Board of, aids in introduction of economic plants, 75

Alien tropical produce fraudulently entered into British markets, 102; attempts to curb the evil, 102 ff.

Allen, James, secretary of Society of West India Merchants and Society of West India Planters and Merchants, 95

American carrying trade during French Revolution and Napoleonic wars, 287; attack on, by British shipping-mercantile interests and colonial group, 303 ff.; checked by decisions in *Essex* and *William* cases, 304; extent of, in 1805, 310; necessity for ending, 313 ff.; seizure of American vessels begun, 315 ff.

American-West Indian commerce: controversy with respect to laying restrictions on, after American Revolution, 173 ff.; restrictions imposed, 179 ff.; stimulation afforded British North American fisheries and lumbering industry by new policy, 184; breakdown of restriction on, during French war, 229 ff.; opening of, during French Revolution and Napoleonic wars, 297; renewal of restrictions on, 299; negotiations to effect permanent opening of, 300; regulated by act of 1806, 301; consequent distress, 302 ff.; renewal of restrictions on, after close of Napoleonic wars, 338

Amiens, Treaty of (1802), 229; pleasing to West India interest, 292; broken, 293

Amusements of island residents, 23 ff.

Angola negroes as slaves, 85

Anguilla: distress in, following laying of restrictions on American-West Indian commerce, 192; ports of, opened (1821), 343; overlooked in passing of West Indian and American trade bill (1822), 357; suffering in, 374

Antigua: advanced state of agriculture in, 66; high level of life in, 66; superior status of negro in, 66 ff.; distress in (1805), 306; proprietors of, prefer outright emancipation without apprenticeship, 455 ff.

Antiguan legislature opposes institution of slave registration by act of parliament, 393; establishes it by local act, 398; refuses to adopt new slave code, 418